United States Civil War Revenue Stamp Taxes

United States Civil War Revenue Stamp Taxes

A Compendium of Statutes, Decisions, Rulings and Correspondence Pertaining to the Documentary and Proprietary Taxes

by

Michael Mahler

Castenholz and Sons
Publishers
1055 Hartzell Street
Pacific Palisades, California 90272

Castenholz and Sons
1055 Hartzell Street
Pacific Palisades, CA 90272

Current printing (last digit):

5 4 3 2 1

ISBN: 0-9603498-3-9

Library of Congress Catalog Card Number: 88-72215

Typesetting: Scientific Composition, W.L.A., California

Printed in the United States of America

TABLE OF CONTENTS

PUBLISHER'S PREFACE

Nine years ago Castenholz and Sons published *The Revenue Stamps of the United States* by Christopher West (Elliot Perry). Since that time we have published two further volumes by West, *United States Match and Medicine Stamps* and *Private Die Match Stamps.* However, it is this fourth volume in our Revenue Series that brings to mind a statement in the Publisher's Preface of our first West book: "Yet the First Issue (Civil War) revenues are as fertile a field for research as any in all of philately. The surface has not been scratched." Now we bring to you an in-depth "compendium of statutes, decisions, rulings and correspondence pertaining to documentary and proprietary taxes." It will undoubtedly become *the* classic background reference book for students of U.S. revenues. It is the revenue equivalent of all postal history works dealing with rates, classifications, and usages!

With the surge of interest in the 1980's in collecting revenue stamped documents, a more welcome addition to the body of revenue literature can hardly be imagined.

The production of this volume has taken over two years. Its size has nearly doubled from the original expectations, and yet the original intent, that of offering a very useful, well-organized single-volume reference work embodying all significant government determinations relating to the stamp tax laws, has been very sucessfully achieved.

I hope you enjoy using this book.

Bill J. Castenholz

P.S. To a greater extent than in any of our previous publications I must thank my wife Jeanette for her encouragement and wise counsel which has brought this work to a successful conclusion.

INTRODUCTION

On July 1, 1862, as part of a broad program of taxation designed to offset the costs of the Civil War, the United States Congress enacted an extensive schedule of stamp taxes on documents, patent medicines, perfumery and cosmetics, and playing cards, the duties to be paid by adhesive stamps affixed to the articles taxed, or by stamps imprinted directly on certain documents. Later this schedule was expanded to tax matches, photographs, and preserved foods as well. By the standards of the era, the revenue generated by these levies was impressive: at the time of their final repeal in 1883, Americans had paid over $210 million in stamp taxes, using an estimated eight billion stamps in the process.

A delightful profusion of stamps was printed, 157 different for use on documents and 584 more for proprietary articles (Scott, 1988). These are avidly sought by collectors, and have been the subject of a substantial literature (American Revenue Association Directory, 1984; Riley, 1985). However, in contrast to this considerable attention paid to the stamps themselves, until recently little had been written about their usage, and of this, the most detailed treatments had apparently been all but forgotten. I found this incomprehensible, for the usage of these stamps is no pale, academic concern. It is best revealed by surviving stamped documents and proprietary articles, which after well over a century can still be found in surprising abundance. Because the taxes were so broadly based, these stamped artifacts reveal a veritable slice of life as it was in those days. From checks for a few dollars to million-dollar mortgages on railroads and mines; from personal transactions like agreements, deeds, and receipts, and official documents such as a customs entry or court summons, through the record of American business in all its vigor, shown by bankers' checks, certificates of deposit, and bills of foreign exchange, brokers' contracts and the stocks and bonds they traded, receipts of the express companies, policies of insurance, the gaudy panoply of patent medicines, shipping bills of lading, charters, manifests and passage tickets, telegraph despatches, and more; records as ephemeral as a lottery ticket or pawner's check, and as enduring as a hundred-year mortgage; from the cities of the Northeast to the ravaged post-war South, the rural Midwest and the remotest territories of the West, almost every piece of paper that changed hands was taxed. Much of this material is prized by collectors of paper Americana for a variety of reasons quite apart from the presence of revenue stamps, and when these already varied and appealing pieces are viewed within the extremely detailed context established by the stamp taxes, an area for collecting and study emerges that is exquisitely rich and complicated.

In addition to its obvious importance within classic United States philately, this field may well furnish useful research material for economic and legal historians. With reference to the latter, for example, I note that the stamp tax on legal documents initiating court suits was rescinded in 1867 after being widely challenged on the grounds that it violated the Constitutional prohibition against federal taxation of the state governments. Similarly, by U.S. statute any document liable to stamp tax, but not stamped, was inadmissible as evidence in any court; however, state courts in Massachusetts and Illinois ruled this an infringement of their rights, and interpreted the statute as applying only to federal courts.

The literature of this field can be reviewed quickly. The economic historian Smith (1914) summarized the tax schedules in tabular form, stated the penalties established by statute for various violations, and also included material that went beyond the letter of the law, such as rulings of the Commissioner of Internal Revenue on controversial points, and Congressional debate preceding certain Acts. In the philatelic literature, West (1918, reprinted 1979) gave a slightly abbreviated summary of the tax schedules. Bopeley (1937) reviewed the documentary tax rates, citing many of the Commissioner's supplementary decisions, and gave examples of several hundred surviving documents. Shellabear (1964, 1965 a, b) discussed the taxes on documents used in the railroad and shipping industries, describing existing examples where possible. Finally, various specialized studies of stamp cancellations shed some indirect light on stamp usage. As valuable as these pioneering efforts have been, for me their most provocative aspect was not the admittedly very useful information they conveyed, but the desire they kindled to see for myself the sources of information they relied on, as well as any that these authors may have overlooked. My goal in the present volume has been to present, insofar as practicable, all primary sources dealing with the usage of documentary and proprietary stamps, with an emphasis on material relevant to the study of surviving stamped documents and proprietary articles.

Assembling the relevant U.S. statutes was straightforward, but the material that went beyond the letter of the law proved more elusive. The key element of my search for it was the realization that after January 1865, virtually every official pronouncement on documentary and proprietary stamp taxes (and indeed on all aspects of internal revenue), other than the statutes themselves, had been published in *The Internal Revenue Record,* a New York weekly newspaper (see Mahler, 1987). I found that this included a wealth of information not cited by previous authors, and began the fascinating but arduous task of locating the thousand or so issues of the *Record* published between 1865 and 1883, extracting from them every reference I could find to documentary and proprietary stamps, and rearranging these by subject. This is the information that forms the bulk of this book. Most of it consists of rulings on questions raised by the public or on various infractions, and the number of these entries shows that correct compliance with the stamp taxes was not always a straightforward and simple matter.

For material of this sort dated prior to 1865, I relied on the Decisions, Rulings, and Correspondence published in the 1863 *Manual* and 1865 *Tax-Payer's Manual* of George S. Boutwell, who served in 1862-1863 as the first Commissioner of Internal Revenue, and later as Secretary of the Treasury. Incidentally, I have yet to learn the difference between a Decision and a Ruling. The distinction was not Boutwell's alone, for there exists an 1871 government pamphlet entitled *Decisions Published by the Office of Internal Revenue to 1871* which gives 176 such Decisions, of which the first 119 are noted to have been reprinted from Boutwell (1863). As the present work shows, by 1871 there had been many hundreds of pronouncements dealing with stamp taxes alone, and the total on all internal revenue matters ran well into the thousands. For some reason just 176 of these constituted "Decisions." It might be guessed that this is a matter of origins, with Decisions emanating from judicial processes; however, the title page of Boutwell (1863) refers specifically to "the Decisions and Rulings of the Commissioner," and Decision No. 97 is in fact signed by the Commissioner. Probably the distinction lies in the more important subject matter of the Decisions, and the greater weight attached to them. Boutwell (1863) states that "The Rulings are based upon the correspondence of the office, and, in some cases, the language used in the letters of the Commissioner has been retained. Generally, however, the language has been changed, and in several instances the opinion given has been modified or reversed by the experience of the office. Consequently, the Rulings should not be regarded as binding upon the Office of Internal Revenue, but rather as the opinions of the editor of this volume. . . . " Evidently the Rulings and Correspondence listed by Boutwell are similar in nature, the latter being those which it was judged useful to give verbatim. The *Internal Revenue Record* did not use the terms "Ruling" or "Correspondence," but the few Decisions it printed were always identified as such.

This question of terminology is complicated by the 1906 government publication, *Digest of Decisions and Regulations Made by the Commissioner of Internal Revenue . . . from December 24, 1865 to June 13, 1898,* which contains several thousand synopsized entries and refers to all of them as "Treasury Decisions." I mention this work only in passing, as it adds nothing to the material in Boutwell (1865) and the *Internal Revenue Record,* and in fact omits much that is in the latter, but does provide useful corroboration.

Two other sources that provided selected material for this book are the *Collection of Circulars and Specials to January 1, 1871,* which are regulations and instructions issued to internal revenue employees, and the annual *Report of the Commissioner of Internal Revenue,* first made in 1863. Because of space limitations, much of the material referring to stamps in these two sources could not be included here. In the case of the Circulars and Specials, the omitted portions are essentially duplicated by material already included from other sources, notably the 1866 Schedule of Stamp Duties (see Appendix). As for the Commissioner's Reports, I have selected only a few passages most directly relevant to the taxes on specific documents. There is much here of general interest, including the yearly totals of stamp sales, that unfortunately could not be included, and I recommend these reports to specialists. The *Report of the United States Revenue Commission* (1866) and the *Report of the Special Commissioner of Revenue* for 1867 and 1868 may also be useful for specialists. Interesting debate that helped shape the form of the tax laws can be found in the *Congressional Globe* and *Congressional Record* (see references by Smith, 1914). Finally, there were a number of contemporary manuals similar to those of Boutwell (1863, 1865), including those of Bump, Emerson, Estee, and Redfield, but I have not consulted these.

REFERENCES

The American Revenue Association 1984 Biennial Directory. Supplement to *The American Revenuer* 38(10), November-December, 1984.

Bopeley, Joe L. "Revenue Stamped Documents of the Civil War Period," *The American Philatelist* 50:358-362 (I); 473-476 (II); 556-562 (III); 690-694 (IV); 51:63-67 (V); 347-352 (VI); 944-951 (VII), 1937-1938.

Boutwell, George S. *A Manual of the Direct and Excise Tax System of the United States.* Little, Brown and Company, Boston, 1863.

Boutwell, George S. *The Tax-Payer's Manual.* Little, Brown and Company, Boston, 1865.

Collection of Circulars and Specials Issued by the Office of Internal Revenue, to January 1, 1871. Government Printing Office, Washington, 1871.

The Congressional Globe: Containing the Debates and Proceedings of the [United States] Congress. 37th Congress, 1862, to 42nd Congress, 1873 (Continued by *The Congressional Record*). Congressional Globe Office, Washington, 1862-1873.

The Congressional Record: Containing the Proceedings and Debates of the [United States] Congress. 43rd Congress, 1873, to 47th Congress, 1883. Government Printing Office, Washington, 1873-1883.

Decisions Published by the Office of Internal Revenue to January 1, 1871. Government Printing Office, Washington, 1871.

Digest of Decisions and Regulations Made by the Commissioner of Internal Revenue Under Various Acts of Congress Relating to Internal Revenue, and Abstracts of Judicial Decisions, and Opinions of Attorneys-General, as to Internal-Revenue Cases. From December 24, 1864 to June 13, 1898. Treasury Department document 2438. Government Printing Office, Washington, 1906.

The Internal Revenue Record and Customs Journal. Weekly newspaper published by P. Vr. Van Wyck and Company, New York. vv. 1-29, 1865-1883.

Mahler, Michael. "*The Internal Revenue Record,* an Unmatched Information Source," *The American Revenuer* 41:148-156, September, 1987.

Riley, Richard F. *An Indexed Bibliography to Published Pamphlets, Monographs and Catalogues Devoted Wholly or in Part to the Revenue Stamps of the World.* Supplement to *The American Revenuer* 39(4), April, 1985.

Report of the Commissioner of Internal Revenue on the Operations of the Internal Revenue System. Annual reports for fiscal years 1863 through 1883. Government Printing Office, Washington, 1863-1883.

Report of the United States Revenue Commission. (39th Cong. 1st Sess., Ex. Doc. 34, Serial no. 1255), Government Printing Office, Washington, 1866.

Report of the Special Commissioner of the Revenue. Reports of 1867 (39th Cong. 2d Sess., Ex. Doc. 2, Serial no. 1276) and 1868 (40th Cong. 2d Sess., Ex. Doc. 81, Serial no. 1332), Government Printing Office, Washington, 1867.

Scott Specialized Catalogue of United States Stamps, 1988. Scott Publishing Co., Sidney, Ohio.

Shellabear, H.P. "Straight Line Steamship Cancels, Which Stamp Tax Paid?" *The American Revenuer* 18:17-19, March, 1964.

Shellabear, H.P. "Stamp Tax Usage Schedule B. Civil War Revenues as Found on Railroad Documents," *The American Revenuer* 19:21-24, 30-31, February and March, 1965.

Shellabear, H.P. "Stamp Tax Usage Schedule B. Civil War Revenues as Found on Ship Documents," *The American Revenuer* 19:33-37, April, 1965.

Smith, Harry Edwin. *The United States Federal Internal Tax History from 1861 to 1871.* The Riverside Press, Cambridge (Houghton Mifflin Company, Boston and New York), 1914.

The Statutes at Large, Treaties, and Proclamations of the United States of America, vv. 12-22 (encompassing statutes of 37th Congress, 1862, through 47th Congress, 1883), George P. Sanger, ed., Little, Brown and Company, Boston (vv. 12-17, 1863-1873), and Government Printing Office, Washington (vv. 18-22, 1875-1883).

West, Christopher. *The Revenue Stamps of the United States.* Castenholz and Sons, Pacific Palisades, California, 1979 (Based on original 1918 edition).

WASHINGTON No 401 PENN AVE.
PROVIDENCE 36 DORRANCE ST
BOSTON 98 WASHINGTON ST
BALTIMORE 209 BALTIMORE ST
ANNAPOLIS
PHILADELPHIA 207 CHESTNUT ST
FORT'S MONROE

Office of HARNDEN'S EXPRESS.

Boston, Dec 9 1862

Received from One Box

Marked Sam'l T. Putnam Co. K 14 Reg. Mass

Quartermaster or other officer of the Regiment to which the Consignee is attached.

Freight, $3.75

Insurance,

For the Proprietors.

74 BROADWAY NEW YORK

Plate 1A — Receipt of Harnden's Express of Boston, printed in red, for one box sent to a soldier in the 14th Massachusetts Regt. at Washington, at a cost of $3.75. Executed December 9, 1862, and correctly stamped with a 5¢ Express, imperforate.

Organized under the General Laws of the State of New York

SCHREIBER CORNET MANUFACTURING CO.

CAPITAL No. 66 $300,000.

SHARES 25 SHARES. $100 EACH.

This is to certify, that Wm. H. Brown is entitled to Twenty Five Shares of ONE HUNDRED DOLLARS each in the Capital Stock of the Schreiber Cornet Manufacturing Company, (not liable to assessment), transferable only on the Books of the Company in the City of New York in Person or by Attorney, upon surrender of this Certificate.

NEW YORK, Nov 3 1866

A. E. Juillerat Secretary Louis Schreiber President

Plate 1B — 1866 stock certificate of the Schreiber Cornet Manufacturing Co. of New York, with exquisite custom lithographed vignette, correctly taxed at 25¢.

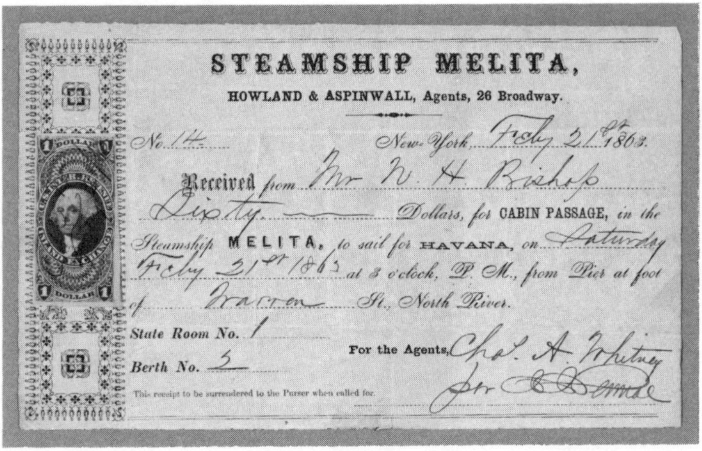

STEAMSHIP MELITA,

HOWLAND & ASPINWALL, Agents, 26 Broadway.

No. 14 New-York, Feby 21st 1863.

Received from Mr W. H. Bishop

Sixty Dollars, for CABIN PASSAGE, in the Steamship MELITA, to sail for HAVANA, on Saturday Feby 21st 1863 at 3 o'clock, P. M., from Pier at foot of Warren St., North River.

State Room No. 1

Berth No. 3

For the Agents, Chas. A. Whitney

This receipt to be surrendered to the Purser when called for.

Plate 2A — Receipt for $60 paid for Cabin Passage from New York to Havana on the steamer "Melita," February 21, 1863, bearing a $1 Inland Exchange imperforate. This is the only recorded example of a passage ticket taxed at the 1862 rates.

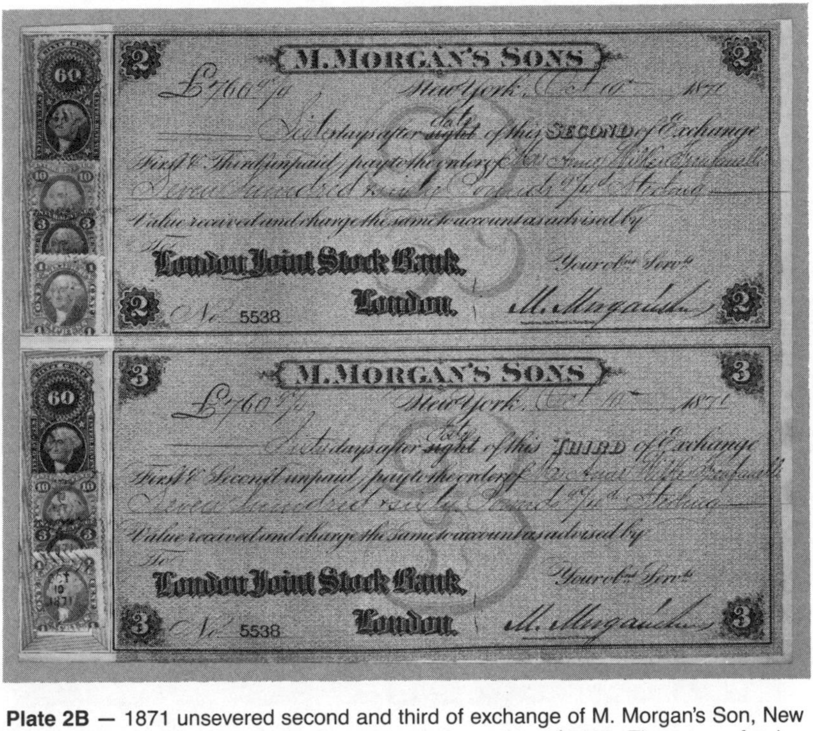

M. MORGAN'S SONS

£760 00/00 New York, Oct 10th 1871

Sixty days after date of this SECOND of Exchange First & Third unpaid, pay to the order of [illegible] Seven Hundred & sixty Pounds 00/00 Sterling

Value received and charge the same to account as advised by

To London Joint Stock Bank. London.

Your obt Servt M. Morgan's Sons

No. 5538

M. MORGAN'S SONS

£760 00/00 New York, Oct 10th 1871

Sixty days after date of this THIRD of Exchange First & Second unpaid, pay to the order of [illegible] Seven Hundred & sixty Pounds 00/00 Sterling

Value received and charge the same to account as advised by

To London Joint Stock Bank. London.

Your obt Servt M. Morgan's Sons

No. 5538

Plate 2B — 1871 unsevered second and third of exchange of M. Morgan's Son, New York, to the London Joint Stock Bank for £760, or about $3680. The tax on foreign exchange of 2¢ per $100 called for a payment of 74¢, correctly made with stamps of 60¢, 10¢, 3¢ & 1¢.

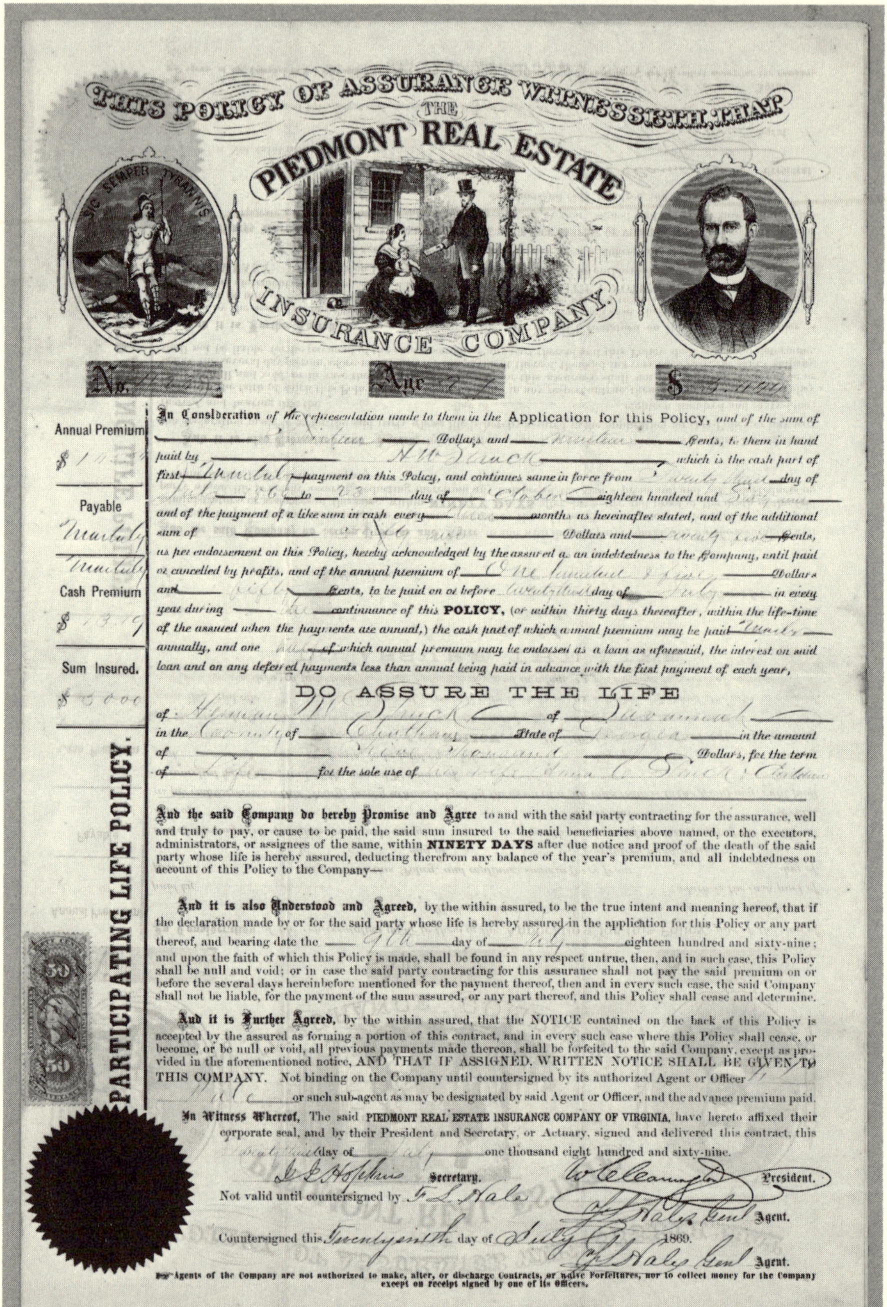

Plate 3 — 1869 $5000 Participating Life Policy of the Piedmont Real Estate Insurance Company of Virginia, on the life of a man in Savannah, Georgia, correctly taxed at 50¢. Life insurance was uncommon in the 1860's.

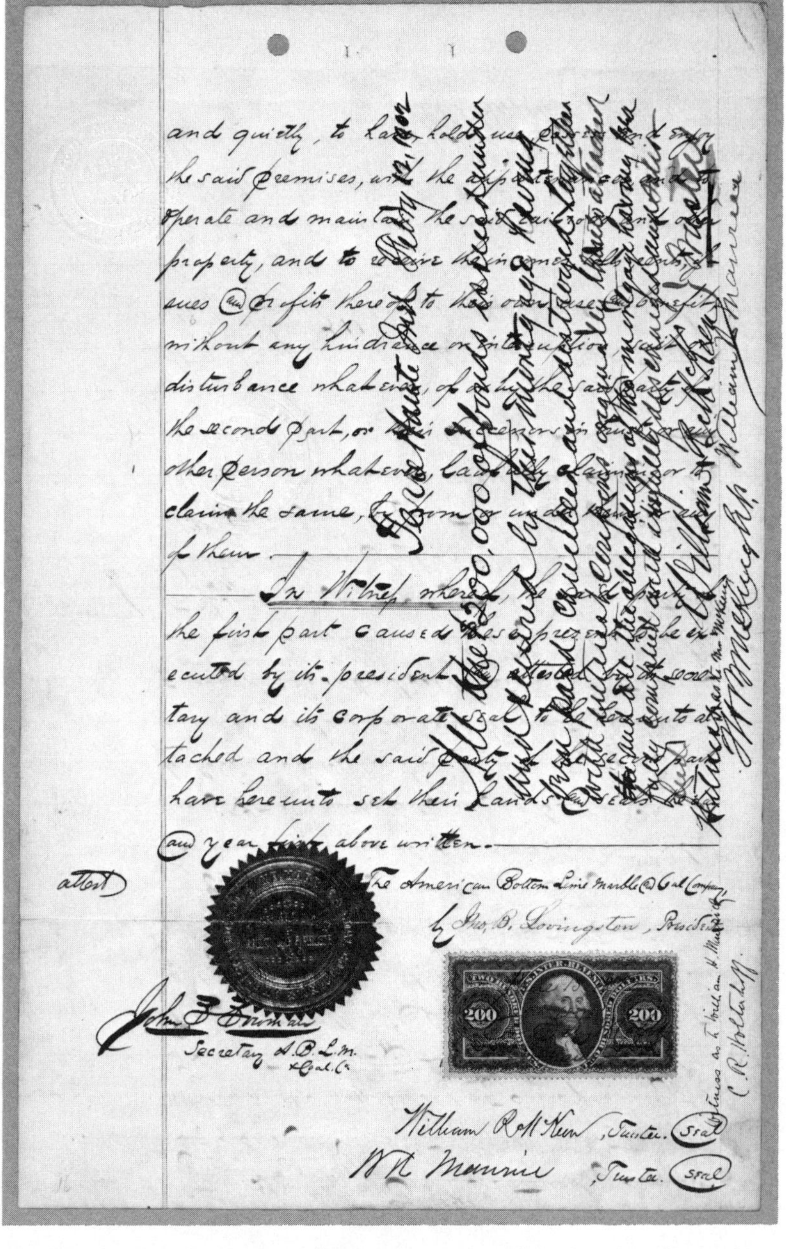

Plate 4 — Final page of an 1872 $200,000 mortgage of the American Bottom Lime Marble and Coal Company of East St. Louis, Illinois, to support a bond issue of like amount for the construction of a railroad on the company's land, with silver metallic seal and the beautiful $200 U.S.I.R. stamp in yellow green & scarlet.

Plate 5 — 1868 ornate pictorial marriage certificate attesting to the union of a Fairfield, Michigan couple by Rev. A. M. Swain, "Bap. Minister," correctly taxed at the general certificate rate of 5¢.

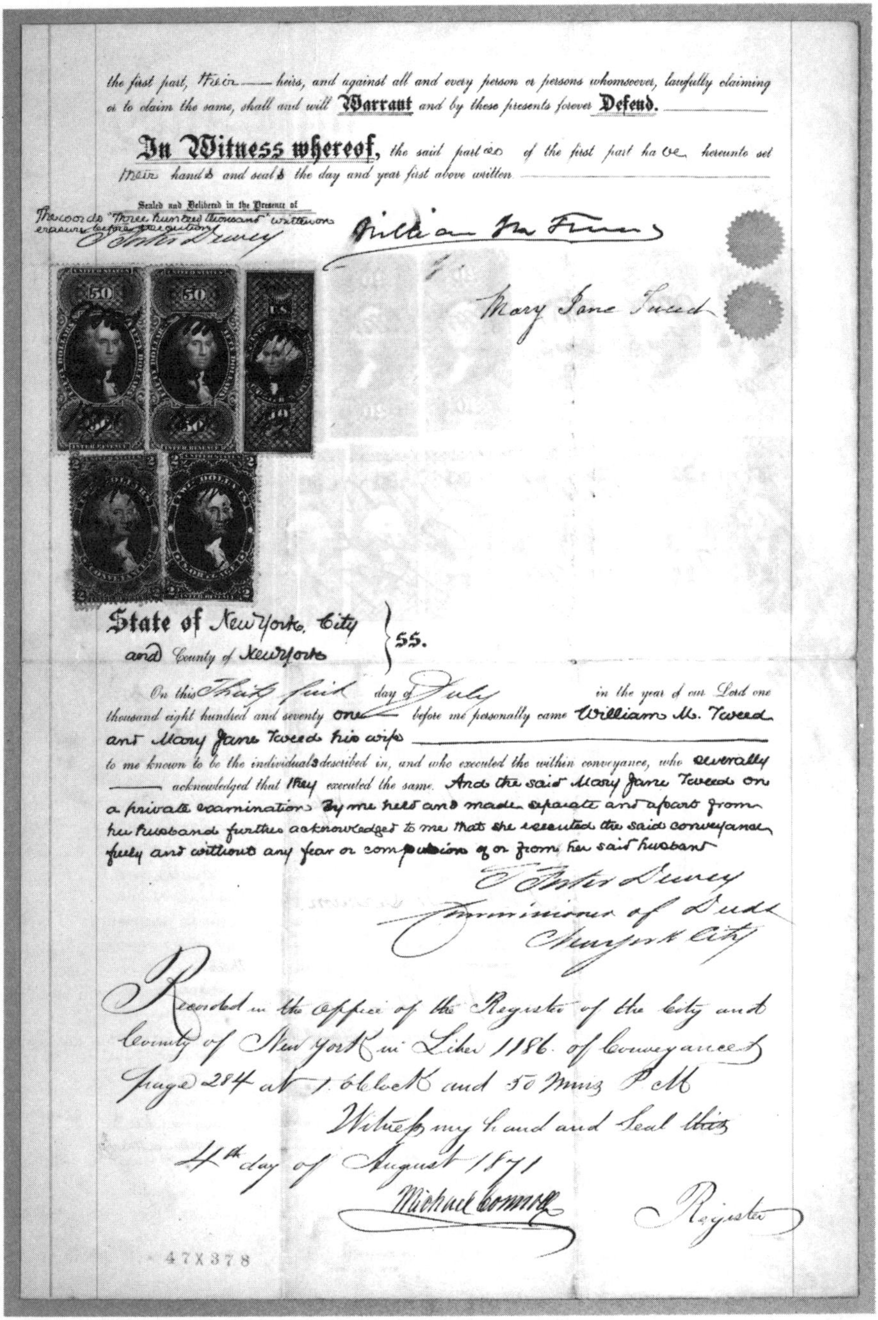

the first part, their —— heirs, and against all and every person or persons whomsoever, lawfully claiming or to claim the same, shall and will **Warrant** and by these presents forever **Defend.**

In Witness whereof, the said parties of the first part have hereunto set their hands and seals the day and year first above written.

Sealed and Delivered in the Presence of

The words "Three hundred thousand" written on erasure before execution

T. Foster Dewey

William M. Tweed

Mary Jane Tweed

State of New York, City and County of New York } ss.

On this Thirty first day of July in the year of our Lord one thousand eight hundred and seventy one before me personally came William M. Tweed and Mary Jane Tweed his wife to me known to be the individuals described in, and who executed the within conveyance, who severally acknowledged that they executed the same. And the said Mary Jane Tweed on a private examination by me held and made separate and apart from her husband further acknowledged to me that she executed the said conveyance freely and without any fear or compulsion of or from her said husband

T. Foster Dewey
Commissioner of Deeds
New York City

Recorded in the Office of the Register of the City and County of New York in Liber 1186 of Conveyances page 284 at 1 o'clock and 50 mins P.M.

Witness my hand and seal this 4th day of August 1871

Michael Connolly Register

47X378

Plate 6 — A page from a deed for the sale of property at 57th St. and Ninth Ave. in New York by William M. Tweed and his wife for $300,000, the $300 tax paid by 23 stamps of various denominations including the $20, $25 and $50. William Marcy Tweed was the infamous political swindler "Boss" Tweed of Tammany Hall. This deed was executed July 31, 1871, just months before Tweed's "Ring" was toppled from power and he was jailed.

ADDENDA

Act of December 25, 1862

Commissioner to furnish adhesive stamps, &c., to collector at San Francisco and Portland.

No greater commission to be allowed.

Sec. 94. *And be it further enacted,* That the Commissioner of Internal Revenue shall be authorized and empowered, and hereby is authorized and empowered, to furnish and supply the assistant treasurers or collectors of the United States at San Francisco, State of California, and Portland, State of Oregon, with adhesive stamps, or stamped paper, vellum, or parchment, according to the provisions of the internal revenue laws referred to in the preceding section, under such regulations and conditions as he may from time to time prescribe, and without requiring payment in advance therefor, anything in existing laws to the contrary notwithstanding: *Provided,* That no greater commission shall be allowed than is now provided by law.

GENERAL DOCUMENTARY

Cancellation of adhesive revenue stamps.
[Circular No. 39.]

Office of Internal Revenue,
Washington, Jan. 16, 1866.

In the 156th section of the act of June 30th, 1864, it is enacted that, in any and all cases where an adhesive stamp shall be used for denoting any duty imposed by said act, except as thereinafter provided, the person using or affixing the same *shall write thereupon the initials of his name and the date upon which the same is attached or used, so that the same may not again be used;* and that if any person shall fraudulently make use of an adhesive stamp, to denote any duty imposed by said act, without so effectually cancelling and obliterating the same, except as thereinafter provided, he, she, or they *shall forfeit the sum of fifty dollars.*

In a subsequent part of the same section it is provided that the proprietor or proprietors of any proprietary article or articles, subject to stamp duty under schedule C, may, in a certain designated manner, furnish his or their own dies or designs for stamps, and that in all cases where *such* stamps are used, instead of his or their writing the date thereon the said stamps shall be so affixed on the boxes, bottles, or packages that in opening the same or using the contents thereof the stamps shall be effectually destroyed; *and that in default thereof such proprietor or proprietors shall forfeit the sum of fifty dollars.*

In section 169 it is enacted that any person who shall offer or expose for sale any of the articles mentioned in schedule C, shall be deemed the manufacturer thereof and subject to the *same penalties and liabilities.*

In section 157 the Commissioner of Internal Revenue is authorized to prescribe such method for the cancellation of stamps as he may deem expedient and effectual.

Under the power thus conferred authority has been given to *imprint* the initials and date upon stamps *in ink* instead of writing them. The imprint must be *distinct* and *legible.*

If proprietary stamps cannot be so affixed to the boxes, bottles, or packages, that in opening the same, or in using the contents thereof, they shall and must be unavoidably and effectually destroyed, they should be cancelled in the ordinary manner, by writing or imprinting thereon the initials and date.

Cancellation by writing or imprinting the initials and date, in ink, whereby the stamp is made to correspond in those particulars with the instrument to which it is affixed, is not only the legal but also the most effectual method against fraud, *and must be adopted,* except in the case of proprietary articles, where it is otherwise specially provided.

Frequent reports have reached this office showing that the law upon this subject is very often disregarded. In some instances stamps are used without being obliterated or destroyed in any manner whatever; in others a cross simply, generally with ink, but sometimes even a pencil is used, or a hole is punched through the stamp.

These and similar methods of cancellation afford little or no protection against the use of stamps a second time. Great frauds may be, and as investigation shows, have been, practised upon the public revenue in this manner.

Collectors, assessors, inspectors, and all other officers of this bureau are therefore instructed to give this subject their special attention; to bring it to the notice of persons using stamps, and to require strict conformity to the law.

If persons, after having been fully notified of the requirements of the statute respecting the cancellation of stamps, and of their liabilities for non-compliance therewith, wilfully persist in their fraudulent use, without effectually cancelling and obliterating them *in the manner required by law,* legal proceedings should be instituted for the recovery of the prescribed penalties.

E. A. Rollins,
Commissioner.

IRR v.III, January 20, 1866, p. 23

Supplement No. 3 to Circular No. 82.

Treasury Department,
Office of Internal Revenue,
Washington, April 19, 1870.

In accordance with the terms of Circular No. 82, issued from this office February 10, 1870, reference to which is hereby made, I do hereby, in addition to the machine named in said Circular, designate and prescribe "Thomson's National Revenue Stamp Canceller," as a machine which may be used, on and after May 1, 1870, for the purpose of cancelling adhesive stamps, used upon instruments, documents, writings, and papers, mentioned and described in Schedule B, Internal Revenue Laws.

C. Delano,
Commissioner.

[Ed. Note. Using identical wording, Supplement 1 of April 1, 1870, approved "E.D. Chamberlain's Cutting and Dating Stamp," and Supplement 2, of April 5, 1870, approved "Holt's Self-inking Canceller," of the Secombe Manufacturing Co., and "Hill's Patent Revenue Cancelling Machine."]

SECTION I.

United States Statutes Pertaining to Documentary and Proprietary Stamp Taxes.

Act of July 1, 1862

CHAP. CXIX.—*An Act to provide Internal Revenue to support the Government and to pay Interest on the Public Debt.*

Be it enacted by the Senate and House of Representatives of the United States of America in Congress assembled, That, for the purpose of superintending the collection of internal duties, stamp duties, licenses, or taxes imposed by this act, or which may be hereafter imposed, and of assessing the same, an office is hereby created in the Treasury Department to be called the office of the Commissioner of Internal Revenue; and the President of the United States is hereby authorized to nominate, and, with the advice and consent of the Senate, to appoint, a Commissioner of Internal Revenue, with an annual salary of four thousand dollars, who shall be charged, and hereby is charged, under the direction of the Secretary of the Treasury, with preparing all the instructions, regulations, directions, forms, blanks, stamps, and licenses, and distributing the same or any part thereof, and all other matters pertaining to the assessment and collection of the duties, stamp duties, licenses, and taxes, which may be necessary to carry this act into effect, and with the general superintendence of his office, as aforesaid, and shall have authority, and hereby is authorized and required, to provide proper and sufficient stamps or dies for expressing and denoting the several stamp duties, or the amount thereof in the case of percentage duties, imposed by this act, and to alter and renew or replace such stamps from time to time, as occasion shall require; and the Secretary of the Treasury may assign to the office of the Commissioner of Internal Revenue such number of clerks as he may deem necessary, or the exigencies of the public service may require, and the privilege of franking all letters and documents pertaining to the duties of his office, and of receiving free of postage all such letters and documents, is hereby extended to said commissioner.

Office of Commissioner of Internal Revenue, created.

Commissioner, appointment, salary, duty, &c.,

to prepare rules, forms, blanks, &c.,

to provide stamps and dies,

to have clerks.

Franking privilege.

STAMP DUTIES

Sec. 94. *And be it further enacted,* That on and after the first day of October, eighteen hundred and sixty-two, there shall be levied, collected, and paid, for and in respect of the several instruments, matters, and things mentioned, and described in the schedule (marked B) hereunto annexed, or for or in respect of the vellum, parchment, or paper upon which such instruments, matters, or things, or any of them, shall be written or printed, by any person or persons, or party who shall make, sign, or issue the same, or for whose use or benefit the same shall be made, signed, or issued, the several duties or sums of money set down in figures against the same, respectively, or otherwise specified or set forth in the said schedule.

Stamp duties on articles in schedule B.

Post, p. 11.

Sec. 95. *And be it further enacted,* That if any person or persons shall make, sign, or issue, or cause to be made, signed, or issued, any instrument, document, or paper of any kind, or description whatsoever, without the same being duly stamped for denoting the duty hereby imposed thereon, or without having thereupon an adhesive stamp to denote said duty, such person or persons shall incur a penalty of fifty dollars, and such instrument, document, or paper, as aforesaid, shall be deemed invalid and of no effect.

Penalty for making, &c., instrument without using stamp.

Post, pp. 10-11, 15.

Sec. 96. *And be it further enacted,* That no stamp appropriated to denote the duty charged on any particular instrument, and bearing the name of such instrument on the face thereof, shall be used for denoting any other duty of the same amount, or if so used the same shall be of no avail.

Stamps to be used only for designated duty.

Sec. 97. *And be it further enacted,* That no vellum, parchment, or paper, bearing a stamp appropriated by name to any particular instrument, shall be used for any other purpose, or if so used the same shall be of no avail.

Stamped paper, &c., to be so used.

Sec. 98. *And be it further enacted,* That if any person shall forge or counterfeit, or cause or procure to be forged or counterfeited, any stamp or die, or any part of any stamp or die, which shall have been provided, made, or used in pursuance of this act, or shall forge, counterfeit, or resemble, or cause or procure to be forged, counterfeited, or resembled, the impression, or any part of the impression, of any such

Forging or counterfeiting stamps, or dies, &c., how punished.

stamp or die, as aforesaid, upon any vellum, parchment, or paper, or shall stamp or mark, or cause or procure to be stamped or marked, any vellum, parchment, or paper, with any such forged or counterfeited stamp or die, or part of any stamp or die, as aforesaid, with intent to defraud the United States of any of the duties hereby imposed, or any part thereof, or if any person shall utter, or sell, or expose to sale, any vellum, parchment, or paper, article or thing, having thereupon the impression of any such counterfeited stamp or die, or any part of any stamp or die, or any such forged, counterfeited, or resembled impression, or part of impression, as aforesaid, knowing the same respectively to be forged, counterfeited, or resembled; or if any

Using a forged stamp, &c.

person shall knowingly use any stamp or die which shall have been so provided, made or used, as aforesaid, with intent to defraud the United States; or if any person shall fraudulently cut, tear, or get off, or cause or procure to be cut, torn, or got off, the impression of any stamp or die which shall have been provided, made, or used in pursuance of this act, from any vellum, parchment, or paper, or any instrument or writing charged or chargeable with any of the duties hereby imposed, then, and in every such case, every person so offending, and every person knowingly and wilfully aiding, abetting, or assisting in committing any such offence as aforesaid, shall be deemed guilty of felony, and shall, on conviction thereof, forfeit the said counterfeit stamps and the articles upon which they are placed, and be punished by fine not exceeding one thousand dollars, and by imprisonment and confinement to hard labor not exceeding five years.

Persons using certain stamps to mark them.

Post, p. 15.

Penalty for neglect.

Certain persons may furnish their own stamps, &c.

Sec. 99. *And be it further enacted,* That in any and all cases where an adhesive stamp shall be used for denoting any duty imposed by this act, except as hereinafter provided, the person using or affixing the same shall write thereupon the initials of his name, and the date upon which the same shall be attached or used, so that the same may not again be used. And if any person shall fraudulently make use of an adhesive stamp to denote any duty imposed by this act without so effectually cancelling and obliterating such stamp, except as before mentioned, he, she, or they shall forfeit the sum of fifty dollars: *Provided, nevertheless,* That any proprietor or proprietors of proprietary articles, or articles subject to stamp duty under schedule C of this act, shall have the privilege of furnishing, without expense to the United States, in suitable form, to be approved by the Commissioner of Internal Revenue, his or their own dies or designs for stamps to be used thereon, to be retained in the possession of the Commissioner of Internal Revenue, for his or their separate use, which shall not be duplicated to any other person. That in all cases where such stamp is used, instead of his or their writing, his or their initials and the date thereon, the

Stamp, how destroyed.

said stamp shall be so affixed on the box, bottle, or package, that in opening the same, or using the contents thereof, the said stamp shall be effectually destroyed; and in default thereof shall be liable to the same penalty imposed for neglect to affix

Private stamps. Penalty for forging, &c.

said stamp as hereinbefore prescribed in this act. Any person who shall fraudulently obtain or use any of the aforesaid stamps or designs therefor, and any person forging, or counterfeiting, or causing or procuring the forging or counterfeiting any representation, likeness, similitude or colorable imitation of the said last-mentioned stamp, or any engraver or printer who shall sell or give away said stamps, or selling the same, or, being a merchant, broker, peddler, or person dealing, in whole or in part, in similar goods, wares, merchandise, manufactures, preparations, or articles, or those designed for similar objects or purposes, shall have knowingly or fraudulently in his, her, or their possession any such forged, counterfeited likeness, similitude, or colorable imitation of the said last-mentioned stamp, shall be deemed guilty of a misdemeanor, and, upon conviction thereof, shall be subject to all the

Post, p. 12.

penalties, fines, and forfeitures prescribed in section ninety-*three* [eight] of this act.

Penalty for making, &c., bills of exchange, &c., without stamps, &c.

Sec. 100. *And be it further enacted,* That if any person or persons shall make, sign, or issue, or cause to be made, signed, or issued, or shall accept or pay, or cause to be accepted or paid, with design to evade the payment of any stamp duty, any bill of exchange, draft or order, or promissory note for the payment of money, liable to any of the duties imposed by this act, without the same being duly stamped, or having thereupon an adhesive stamp for denoting the duty hereby charged thereon, he, she, or they shall, for every such bill, draft, order, or note, forfeit the sum of two hundred dollars.

Sec. 101. *And be it further enacted,* That the acceptor or acceptors of any bill of exchange or order for the payment of any sum of money drawn, or purporting to be drawn, in any foreign country, but payable in the United States, shall, before paying or accepting the same, place thereupon a stamp indicating the duty upon the same, as the law requires for inland bills of exchange, or promissory notes; and no bill of exchange shall be paid or negotiated without such stamp; and if any person shall pay or negotiate, or offer in payment, or receive or take in payment, any such draft or order, the person or persons so offending shall forfeit the sum of one hundred dollars.

Acceptors of bills of exchange to place stamps thereon.

Penalty for paying, &c., without stamp.

Sec. 102. *And be it further enacted,* That the Commissioner of Internal Revenue, be, and is hereby, authorized to sell to and supply collectors, deputy collectors, postmasters, stationers, or any other persons, at his discretion, with adhesive stamps or stamped paper, vellum, or parchment, as herein provided for, upon the payment, at the time of delivery, of the amount of duties said stamps, stamped paper, vellum, or parchment, so sold or supplied, represent, and may thereupon allow and deduct from the aggregate amount of such stamps, as aforesaid, the sum of not exceeding five per centum as commission to the collectors, postmasters, stationers, or other purchasers; but the cost of any paper, vellum, or parchment shall be added to the amount, after deducting the allowance of per centum, as aforesaid: *Provided,* That no commission shall be allowed on any sum or sums so sold or supplied of less amount than fifty dollars. *And provided, further,* That any proprietor or proprietors of articles named in schedule C, who shall furnish his or their own die or design for stamps, to be used especially for his or their own proprietary articles, shall be allowed the following discount, namely: on amounts purchased at one time of not less than fifty nor more than five hundred dollars, five per centum; on amounts over five hundred dollars, ten per centum. The Commissioner of Internal Revenue may from time to time make regulations for the allowance of such of the stamps issued under the provisions of this act as may have been spoiled or rendered useless or unfit for the purpose intended, or for which the owner may have no use, or which through mistake may have been improperly or unnecessarily used, or where the rates or duties represented thereby have been paid in error or remitted; and such allowance shall be made either by giving other stamps in lieu of the stamps so allowed for, or by repaying the amount or value, after deducting therefrom, in case of repayment, the sum of five per centum to the owner thereof.

Commissioner to sell stamps to certain officials and other persons.

Post, p. 12.

Commission.

Post, p. 12.

Proviso.

Discount to persons furnishing their own stamps.

Post, p. 12.

Allowance to be made for stamps rendered useless, &c.

Sec. 103. *And be it further enacted,* That it shall be lawful for any person to present to the Commissioner of Internal Revenue any instrument, and require his opinion whether or not the same is chargeable with any duty; and if the said commissioner shall be of opinion that such instrument is not chargeable with any stamp duty, it shall be lawful for him, and he is hereby required, to impress thereon a particular stamp, to be provided for that purpose, with such word or words or device thereon as he shall judge proper, which shall signify and denote that such instrument is not chargeable with any stamp duty; and every such instrument upon which the said stamp shall be impressed shall be deemed to be not so chargeable, and shall be received in evidence in all courts of law or equity, notwithstanding any objections made to the same, as being chargeable with stamp duty, and not stamped to denote the same.

Commissioner may decide whether any instrument is liable to stamp duty.

Special stamp in such case.

Sec. 104. *And be it further enacted,* That on and after the date on which this act shall take effect, no telegraph company or its agent or employee shall receive from any person, or transmit to any person, any despatch or message without an adhesive stamp denoting the duty imposed by this act being affixed to a copy thereof, or having the same stamped thereupon, and in default thereof shall incur a penalty of ten dollars: *Provided,* That only one stamp shall be required, whether sent through one or more companies.

Telegraph companies not to send, &c., messages, unless, &c.

Sec. 105. *And be it further enacted,* That on and after the date on which this act shall take effect, no express company or its agent or employee shall receive for

Express companies not to receive articles for transportation without stamp.

transportation from any person any bale, bundle, box, article, or package of any description, without either delivering to the consignor thereof a printed receipt, having stamped or affixed thereon a stamp denoting the duty imposed by this act, or without affixing thereto an adhesive stamp or stamps denoting such duty, and in default thereof shall incur a penalty of ten dollars: *Provided,* That but one stamped receipt or stamp shall be required for each shipment from one party to another party at the same time, whether such shipment consists of one or more packages: *And provided, also,* That no stamped receipts or stamp shall be required for any bale, bundle, box, article, or package transported for the government, nor for such bales, bundles, boxes, or packages as are transported by such companies without charge thereon.

Articles in schedule C subject to provisions of this act.

Sec. 106. *And be it further enacted,* That all the provisions of this act relating to dies, stamps, adhesive stamps, and stamp duties, shall extend to and include (except where manifestly inapplicable) all the articles or objects enumerated in schedule marked C, subject to stamp duties, and apply to the provisions in relation thereto.

Drugs, cosmetics, &c., not to be sold, &c., without stamp.
Post, p. 16.

Sec. 107. *And be it further enacted,* That on and after the first day of August, eighteen hundred and sixty-two, no person or persons, firms, companies, or corporations, shall make, prepare, and sell, or remove for consumption or sale, drugs, medicines, preparations, compositions, articles, or things, including perfumery, cosmetics, and playing-cards, upon which a duty is imposed by this act, as enumerated and mentioned in schedule C, without affixing thereto an adhesive stamp or label denoting the duty before mentioned, and in default thereof shall incur a penalty of ten dollars: *Provided,* That nothing in this act contained shall apply to any uncompounded medicinal drug or chemical, nor to any medicine compounded according to the United States or other national pharmacopoeia, nor of which the full and proper formula is published in either of the dispensatories, formularies, or text-books in common use among physicians and apothecaries, including homoeopathic and eclectic, or in any pharmaceutical journal now used by any incorporated college of pharmacy, and not sold or offered for sale, or advertised under any other name, form, or guise, than that under which they may be severally denominated and laid down in said pharmacopoeias, dispensatories, text-books, or journals, as aforesaid, nor to medicines sold to or for the use of any person, which may be mixed and compounded specially for said persons, according to the written recipe or prescription of any physician or surgeon.

Proviso.

Penalty on makers of drugs, &c., for removing, &c., stamp;
Post, p. 16.

Sec. 108. *And be it further enacted,* That every manufacturer or maker of any of the articles for sale mentioned in schedule C, after the same shall have been so made, and the particulars hereinbefore required as to stamps have been complied with, who shall take off, remove, or detach, or cause or permit, or suffer to be taken off, or removed or detached, any stamp, or who shall use any stamp, or any wrapper or cover to which any stamp is affixed, to cover any other article or commodity than that originally contained in such wrapper or cover, with such stamp when first used, with the intent to evade the stamp duties, shall for every such article, respectively, in respect of which any such offence shall be committed, be subject to a penalty of fifty dollars, to be recovered, together with the costs thereupon accruing, and every such article or commodity as aforesaid shall also be forfeited.

for selling without stamp.

Sec. 109. *And be it further enacted,* That every maker or manufacturer of any of the articles or commodities mentioned in schedule C, as aforesaid, who shall sell, send out, remove, or deliver any article or commodity, manufactured as aforesaid, before the duty thereon shall have been fully paid, by affixing thereon the proper stamp, as in this act provided, or who shall hide or conceal, or cause to be hidden or concealed, or who shall remove or convey away, or deposit, or cause to be removed or conveyed away from or deposited in any place, any such article or commodity, to evade the duty chargeable thereon, or any part thereof, shall be subject to a penalty of one hundred dollars, together with the forfeiture of any such article or commodity: *Provided,* That medicines, preparations, compositions, perfumery, and cosmetics, upon which stamp duties are required by this act, may, when intended for exportation, be manufactured and sold, or removed without having stamps affixed

In cases of exportation.

thereto, and without being charged with duty, as aforesaid; and every manufacturer or maker of any article, as aforesaid, intended for exportation, shall give such bonds and be subject to such rules and regulations to protect the revenue against fraud as may be from time to time prescribed by the Secretary of the Treasury.

Monthly statement in writing.

Sec. 110. *And be it further enacted,* That every manufacturer or maker of any of the articles or commodities, as aforesaid, or his chief workman, agent, or superintendent, shall at the end of each and every month make and sign a declaration in writing that no such article or commodity, as aforesaid, has, during such preceding month, or time when the last declaration was made, been removed, carried, or sent, or caused, or suffered, or known to have been removed, carried, or sent from the premises of such manufacturer or maker, other than such as have been duly taken account of and charged with the stamp duty, on pain of such manufacturer or maker forfeiting for every refusal or neglect to make such declaration one hundred dollars; and if any such manufacturer or maker, or his chief workman, agent, or superintendent, shall make any false or untrue declaration, such manufacturer or maker, or chief workman, agent, or superintendent, making the same, shall forfeit five hundred dollars.

SCHEDULE B.

STAMP DUTIES.

Stamp duties.

	Duty. Dolls. cts.	
Agreement or contract, other than those specified in this schedule; any appraisement of value or damage, or for any other purpose; for every sheet or piece of paper upon which either of the same shall be written, five cents	5	Agreements.
Bank check, draft, or order for the payment of any sum of money exceeding twenty dollars, drawn upon any bank, trust company, or any person or persons, companies, or corporations at sight or on demand, two cents	2	Bank checks.
Bill of exchange, (inland,) draft, or order for the payment of any sum of money exceeding twenty and not exceeding one hundred dollars, otherwise than at sight or on demand, or any promissory note except bank notes issued for circulation, for a sum exceeding twenty and not exceeding one hundred dollars, five cents	5	Bills of exchange, inland. *Post,* p. 13.
Exceeding one hundred dollars and not exceeding two hundred dollars, ten cents	10	
Exceeding two hundred dollars and not exceeding three hundred and fifty dollars, fifteen cents	15	
Exceeding three hundred and fifty dollars and not exceeding five hundred dollars, twenty cents	20	
Exceeding five hundred dollars and not exceeding seven hundred and fifty dollars, thirty cents	30	
Exceeding seven hundred and fifty dollars and not exceeding one thousand dollars, forty cents	40	
Exceeding one thousand dollars and not exceeding fifteen hundred dollars, sixty cents	60	
Exceeding fifteen hundred dollars and not exceeding twenty-five hundred dollars, one dollar	1 00	
Exceeding twenty-five hundred dollars and not exceeding five thousand dollars, one dollar and fifty cents	1 50	
And for every twenty-five hundred dollars, or part of twenty-five hundred dollars in excess of five thousand dollars, one dollar	1 00	
Bill of exchange (foreign) or letter of credit, drawn in but payable out of the United States, if drawn singly, or otherwise than in a set of three		Bills of exchange, foreign.

		Duty. Dolls. cts.
	or more, according to the custom of merchants and bankers, shall pay the same rates of duty as inland bills of exchange or promissory notes.	
	If drawn in sets of three or more: For every bill of each set, where the sum made payable shall not exceed one hundred and fifty dollars, or the equivalent thereof, in any foreign currency in which such bills may be expressed, according to the standard of value fixed by the United States, three cents	3
	Above one hundred and fifty dollars and not above two hundred and fifty dollars, five cents	5
	Above two hundred and fifty dollars and not above five hundred dollars, ten cents	10
	Above five hundred dollars and not above one thousand dollars, fifteen cents	15
	Above one thousand dollars and not above one thousand five hundred dollars, twenty cents	20
	Above one thousand five hundred dollars and not above two thousand two hundred and fifty dollars, thirty cents	30
	Above two thousand two hundred and fifty dollars and not above three thousand five hundred dollars, fifty cents	50
	Above three thousand five hundred dollars and not above five thousand dollars, seventy cents	70
	Above five thousand dollars and not above seven thousand five hundred dollars, one dollar	1 00
	And for every two thousand five hundred dollars, or part thereof, in excess of seven thousand five hundred dollars, thirty cents	30
Bills of lading.	Bill of lading or receipt, (other than charter-party,) for any goods, merchandise, or effects, to be exported from a port or place in the United States to any foreign port or place, ten cents	10
Expresses. *Post*, pp. 14, 15.	Express.—For every receipt or stamp issued, or issued by any express company, or carrier, or person whose occupation it is to act as such, for all boxes, bales, packages, articles, or bundles, for the transportation of which such company, carrier, or person, shall receive a compensation of not over twenty-five cents, one cent	1
	When such compensation exceeds the sum of twenty-five cents, and not over one dollar, two cents	2
	When one or more packages are sent to the same address at the same time, and the compensation therefor exceeds one dollar, five cents	5
Bond.	Bond.—For indemnifying any person who shall have become bound or engaged as surety for the payment of any sum of money, or for the due execution or performance of the duties of any office, and to account for money received by virtue thereof, fifty cents	50
	Bond of any description other than such as may be required in legal proceedings and such as are not otherwise charged in this schedule, twenty-five cents	25
Certificates.	Certificate of stock in any incorporated company, twenty-five cents	25
	Certificate of profits, or any certificate or memorandum showing an interest in the property or accumulations of any incorporated company, if for a sum not less than ten dollars and not exceeding fifty dollars, ten cents	10
	For a sum exceeding fifty dollars, twenty-five cents	25
	Certificate.—Any certificate of damage, or otherwise, and all other certificates or documents issued by any port warden, marine surveyor, or other person acting as such, twenty-five cents	25
	Certificate of deposit of any sum of money in any bank or trust company,	

	Duty. Dolls. cts.	
or with any banker or person acting as such —		
If for a sum not exceeding one hundred dollars, two cents	2	
For a sum exceeding one hundred dollars, five cents	5	*Post,* pp. 13, 14.
Certificate of any other description than those specified, ten cents	10	
Charter-party.—Contract or agreement for the charter of any ship or vessel, or steamer, or any letter, memorandum, or other writing between the captain, master, or owner, or person acting as agent of any ship or vessel, or steamer, and any other person or persons for or relating to the charter of such ship or vessel or steamer, if the registered tonnage of such ship or vessel, or steamer, does not exceed three hundred tons, three dollars	3 00	Charter-party. *Post,* pp. 14, 15.
Exceeding three hundred tons, and not exceeding six hundred tons, five dollars	5 00	
Exceeding six hundred tons, ten dollars	10 00	
Contract.—Broker's note, or memorandum of sale of any goods or merchandise, stocks, bonds, exchange, notes of hand, real estate, or property of any kind or description issued by brokers or persons acting as such, ten cents	10	Contract.
Conveyance.—Deed, instrument, or writing, whereby any lands, tenements, or other realty sold shall be granted, assigned, transferred, or otherwise conveyed to, or vested in, the purchaser or purchasers, or any other person or persons by his, her, or their direction, when the consideration or value exceeds one hundred dollars and does not exceed five hundred dollars, fifty cents	50	Conveyance.
When the consideration exceeds five hundred dollars and does not exceed one thousand dollars, one dollar	1 00	
Exceeding one thousand dollars and not exceeding two thousand five hundred dollars, two dollars	2 00	
Exceeding two thousand five *thousand* [hundred] dollars and not exceeding five thousand dollars, five dollars	5 00	
Exceeding five thousand dollars and not exceeding ten thousand dollars, ten dollars	10 00	
Exceeding ten thousand dollars and not exceeding twenty thousand dollars, twenty dollars	20 00	
And for every additional ten thousand dollars, or fractional part thereof, in excess of twenty thousand dollars, twenty dollars	20 00	
Despatch, telegraphic.—Any despatch or message, the charge for which for the first ten words does not exceed twenty cents, one cent	1	Despatch, telegraphic.
When the charge for the first ten words exceeds twenty cents, three cents	3	
Entry of any goods, wares, or merchandise at any custom-house, either for consumption or warehousing, not exceeding one hundred dollars in value, twenty-five cents	25	Entry.
Exceeding one hundred dollars and not exceeding five hundred dollars in value, fifty cents	50	
Exceeding five hundred dollars in value, one dollar	1 00	
Entry for the withdrawal of any goods or merchandise from bonded warehouse, fifty cents	50	
Insurance (life).—Policy of insurance, or other instrument by whatever name the same shall be called, whereby any insurance shall be made upon any life or lives—		Insurance, life; *Post,* p. 12.
When the amount insured shall not exceed one thousand dollars, twenty-five cents	25	
Exceeding one thousand and not exceeding five thousand dollars, fifty cents	50	
Exceeding five thousand dollars, one dollar	1 00	

		Duty. Dolls. cts.
marine and inland.	Insurance, (marine and inland)—Each policy of insurance or other instrument, by whatever name the same shall be called, by which insurance shall be made or renewed, upon property of any description, whether against perils by the sea or by fire, or other peril of any	
Post, p. 14.	kind, made by any insurance company, or its agents, or by any other company or person, twenty-five cents	25
Lease, &c.	Lease, agreement, memorandum, or contract for the hire, use, or rent of any land, tenement, or portion thereof—	
	If for a period of time not exceeding three years, fifty cents	50
	If for a period exceeding three years, one dollar	1 00
Manifest.	Manifest for custom-house entry or clearance of the cargo of any ship, vessel, or steamer, for a foreign port—	
	If the registered tonnage of such ship, vessel, or steamer does not exceed three hundred tons, one dollar	1 00
	Exceeding three hundred tons, and not exceeding six hundred tons, three dollars	3 00
	Exceeding six hundred tons, five dollars	5 00
Mortgage.	Mortgage of lands, estate, or property, real or personal, heritable or	
Post, p. 14.	movable whatsoever, where the same shall be made as a security for the payment of any definite and certain sum of money lent at the time, or previously due and owing or forborne to be paid, being payable; also any conveyance of any lands, estate, or property whatsoever, in trust to be sold or otherwise converted into money, which shall be intended only as security, and shall be redeemable before the sale or other disposal thereof, either by express stipulation or otherwise; or any personal bond given as security for the payment of any definite or certain sum of money exceeding one hundred dollars, and not exceeding five hundred dollars, fifty cents	50
	Exceeding five hundred dollars, and not exceeding one thousand dollars, one dollar	1 00
	Exceeding one thousand dollars, and not exceeding two thousand five hundred dollars, two dollars	2 00
	Exceeding two thousand five hundred dollars, and not exceeding five thousand dollars, five dollars	5 00
	Exceeding five thousand dollars, and not exceeding ten thousand dollars, ten dollars	10 00
	Exceeding ten thousand dollars, and not exceeding twenty thousand dollars, fifteen dollars	15 00
	And for every additional ten thousand dollars, or fractional part thereof, in excess of twenty thousand dollars, ten dollars	10 00
Passage ticket. *Post,* p. 14.	Passage ticket, by any vessel from a port in the United States to a foreign port, if less than thirty dollars, fifty cents	50
	Exceeding thirty dollars, one dollar	1 00
Power of attorney.	Power of attorney for the sale or transfer of any stock, bonds, or scrip, or for the collection of any dividends or interest thereon, twenty-five	
Post, p. 14.	cents	25
	Power of attorney or proxy for voting at any election for officers of any incorporated company or society except religious, charitable, or literary societies, or public cemeteries, ten cents	10
	Power of attorney to receive or collect rent, twenty-five cents	25
	Power of attorney to sell and convey real estate, or to rent or lease the same, or to perform any and all other acts not hereinbefore specified, one dollar	1 00
Probate of will.	Probate of will, or letters of administration: Where the estate and effects for or in respect of which such probate or letters of administration	

	Duty. Dolls. cts.	
applied for shall be sworn or declared not to exceed the value of two thousand five hundred dollars, fifty cents	50	
To exceed two thousand five hundred dollars and not exceeding five thousand dollars, one dollar	1 00	
To exceed five thousand dollars and not exceeding twenty thousand dollars, two dollars	2 00	
To exceed twenty thousand dollars and not exceeding fifty thousand dollars, five dollars	5 00	
To exceed fifty thousand dollars and not exceeding one hundred thousand dollars, ten dollars	10 00	
Exceeding one hundred thousand dollars and not exceeding one hundred and fifty thousand dollars, twenty dollars	20 00	
And for every additional fifty thousand dollars, or fractional part thereof, ten dollars	10 00	
Protest.—Upon the protest of every note, bill of exchange, acceptance, check or draft, or any marine protest, whether protested by a notary public or by any other officer who may be authorized by the law of any State or States to make such protest, twenty-five cents	25	Protest.
Warehouse receipt for any goods, merchandise, or property of any kind held on storage in any public or private warehouse or yard, twenty-five cents	25	Warehouse receipt.
Legal documents:		Legal documents.
Writ, or other original process by which any suit is commenced in any court of record, either law or equity, fifty cents	50	Writ.

Provided, That no writ, summons, or other process issued by a justice of the peace, or issued in any criminal or other suits commenced by the United States or any State, shall be subject to the payment of stamp duties: *And provided, further,* That the stamp duties imposed by the foregoing schedule B on manifests, bills of lading, and passage tickets, shall not apply to steamboats or other vessels plying between ports of the United States and ports in British North America. Suits by States, &c., and criminal process exempt.

SCHEDULE C.

Schedule C.

	Duty.	
Medicines or preparations.—For and upon every packet, box, bottle, pot, phial, or other enclosure, containing any pills, powders, tinctures, troches or lozenges, syrups, cordials, bitters, anodynes, tonics, plasters, liniments, salves, ointments, pastes, drops, waters, essences, spirits, oils, or other preparations or compositions whatsoever, made and sold, or removed for consumption and sale, by any person or persons whatever, wherein the person making or preparing the same has, or claims to have, any private formula or occult secret or art for the making or preparing the same, or has, or claims to have, any exclusive right or title to the making or preparing the same, or which are prepared, uttered, vended, or exposed for sale under any letters-patent, or held out or recommended to the public by the makers, venders, or proprietors thereof as proprietary medicines, or as remedies or specifics for any disease, diseases, or affections whatever affecting the human or animal body, as follows: where such packet, box, bottle, pot, phial, or other enclosure, with its contents, shall not exceed, at the retail price or value, the sum of twenty-five cents, one cent	1	Medicines or preparations.
Where such packet, box, bottle, pot, phial, or other enclosure, with its contents, shall exceed the retail price or value of twenty-five cents, and not exceed the retail price or value of fifty cents, two cents	2	

	Duty. Dolls. cts.
Where such packet, box, bottle, pot, phial, or other enclosure, with its contents, shall exceed the retail price or value of fifty cents, and shall not exceed the retail price or value of seventy-five cents, three cents	3
When such packet, box, bottle, pot, phial, or other enclosure, with its contents, shall exceed the retail price or value of seventy-five cents, and shall not exceed the retail price or value of one dollar, four cents .	4
When such packet, box, bottle, pot, phial, or other enclosure, with its contents, shall exceed the retail price or value of one dollar, for each and every fifty cents or fractional part thereof over and above one dollar, as before mentioned, an additional two cents	2
Perfumery and cosmetics. Perfumery and cosmetics.—For and upon every packet, box, bottle, pot, phial, or other enclosure, containing any essence, extract, toilet water, cosmetic, hair oil, pomade, hairdressing, hair restorative, hair dye, toothwash, dentifrice, tooth paste, aromatic cachous, or any similar articles, by whatsoever name the same heretofore have been, now are, or may hereafter be called, known, or distinguished, used or applied, or to be used or applied as perfumes or applications to the hair, mouth, or skin, made, prepared, and sold or removed for consumption and sale in the United States, where such packet, box, bottle, pot, phial, or other enclosure, with its contents, shall not exceed at the retail price or value the sum of twenty-five cents, one cent	1
Where such packet, box, bottle, pot, phial, or other enclosure, with its contents, shall exceed the retail or value of twenty-five cents, and shall not exceed the retail price or value of fifty cents, two cents	2
Where such packet, box, bottle, pot, phial, or other enclosure, with its contents, shall exceed the retail price or value of fifty cents, and shall not exceed the retail price or value of seventy-five cents, three cents	3
Where such packet, box, bottle, pot, phial, or other enclosure, with its contents, shall exceed the retail price or value of seventy-five cents, and shall not exceed the retail price or value of one dollar, four cents .	4
Where such packet, box, bottle, pot, phial, or other enclosure, with its contents, shall exceed the retail price or value of one dollar, for each and every fifty cents or fractional part thereof over and above the one dollar, as before mentioned, an additional two cents	2
Playing cards. Playing cards.—For and upon every pack of whatever number, when the price per pack does not exceed eighteen cents, one cent	1
Over eighteen cents and not exceeding twenty-five cents per pack, two cents	2
Over twenty-five and not exceeding thirty cents per pack, three cents	3
Over thirty and not exceeding thirty-six cents per pack, four cents . .	4
Over thirty-six cents per pack, five cents	5

Approved July 1, 1862.

Act of 1862, ch. 119, Sec. 95, amended. *Ante,* p. 1.

[Repealed, 1863, ch. 4, Sec. 5. *Post,* p. 11.]

Instruments not to be invalid without stamp prior to Jan. 1, 1863. *Post,* pp. 15, 16.

Act of July 14, 1862

CHAP. CLXIII.—*An Act increasing, temporarily, the Duties on Imports, and for other Purposes.*

Sec. 24. *And be it further enacted,* That *in* the ninety-fifth section of the act entitled "An act to provide internal revenue to support the government and [to] pay interest on the public debt," approved July first, eighteen hundred and sixty-two, be so amended that no instrument, document, or paper, made, signed, or issued prior to the first day of January, eighteen hundred and sixty-three, without being duly stamped, or having thereon an adhesive stamp to denote the duty imposed thereon, shall for that cause be deemed invalid and of no effect: *Provided, however,* That no such instrument, document, or paper shall be admitted or used as evidence in any court until the same shall have been duly stamped, nor until the holder thereof shall be proved to the satisfaction of the court that he has paid to the collector or deputy collector of the district within which such court may be held the sum of five dollars, for the use of the United States.

Must be stamped, &c., before they are used in evidence.

Sec. 25. *And be it further enacted,* That no part of the act aforesaid, in relation to stamp duties, shall be held to take effect before the first day of September, eighteen hundred and sixty-two. And so much of said act as relates to the appointment of collectors and assessors shall be held to take effect on the twenty-first day of July, eighteen hundred and sixty-two, instead of from and after its approval by the President.

When parts of act 1862, ch. 119 take effect.

Ante, p. 1.

Approved, July 14, 1862.

Act of December 25, 1862

CHAP. IV.—*An Act to amend an Act entitled "An Act to provide Internal Revenue to support the Government and to pay Interest on the Public Debt," approved July first, eighteen hundred and sixty-two.*

1862, ch. 119. *Ante,* p. 1.

Sec. 3. *And be it further enacted,* That no instrument, document, writing, or paper of any description, required by law to be stamped, shall be deemed or held invalid and of no effect for the want of the particular kind or description of stamp designated for and denoting the duty charged on any such instrument, document, writing, or paper, provided a legal stamp, or stamps, denoting a duty of equal amount, shall have been duly affixed and used thereon: *Provided,* That the provisions of this section shall not apply to any stamp appropriated to denote the duty charged on proprietary articles.

No instrument to be void for want of particular stamp, if a legal stamp of equal value be used thereon.

Proprietary articles excepted.

Sec. 4. *And be it further enacted,* That all official instruments, documents, and papers, issued or used by the officers of the United States Government shall be, and hereby are, exempt from duty.

Official documents, &c., of United States exempt from duty.

Sec. 5. *And be it further enacted,* That the ninety-fifth section of an act entitled "An act to provide internal revenue to support the Government and to pay interest on the public debt," approved July first, eighteen hundred and sixty-two, be so amended that no instrument, document, or paper made, signed, or issued prior to the first day of March, Anno Domini, eighteen hundred and sixty-three, without being duly stamped, or having thereon an adhesive stamp to denote the duty imposed thereon shall, for that cause, be deemed invalid and of no effect: *Provided,* That no instrument, document, writing, or paper, required by law to be stamped, signed, or issued, without being duly stamped prior to the day aforesaid, or any copy thereof, shall be admitted or used as evidence in any court until a legal stamp or stamps, denoting the amount of duty charged thereon, shall have been affixed thereto, or used thereon, and the initials of the person using or affixing the same, together with the date when the same is so used or affixed, shall have been placed thereon by such person. And the person desiring to use any such instrument, document, writing, or paper, as evidence, or his agent or attorney, is authorized in the presence of the court to stamp the same as hereinbefore provided. And section twenty-four of an act entitled "An act increasing, temporarily, the duties on imports, and for other purposes," approved July fourteen, Anno Domini, eighteen hundred and sixty-two, is hereby repealed.

Instruments required to be stamped, issued prior to March 1, 1863, without a stamp, not for that reason to be void.

Instruments, &c., not to be used in evidence until stamped.

Who may affix stamp.

Repeal of act of 1862, ch. 163, Sec. 24.

Ante, p. 10.

Approved, December 25, 1862.

Act of March 3, 1863

CHAP. LXXIV.—*An Act to amend an Act entitled "An Act to provide Internal Revenue to support the Government and pay Interest on the Public Debt," approved July first, eighteen hundred and sixty-two, and for other Purposes.*

1862, ch. 119. *Ante,* p. 1.

Be it enacted by the Senate and House of Representatives of the United States of America in Congress assembled, That "An Act to provide internal revenue to

Amendments.

support the Government and pay interest on the public debt,'' approved July first, eighteen hundred and sixty-two, be, and the same hereby is, amend[ed] as hereinafter set forth, namely:—

Section 99. *Ante,* p. 2. Section 102. *Ante,* p. 3.

That action ninety-nine be amended by striking out the words "ninety-three" preceding the words "of this act," and inserting "ninety-eight."

That section one hundred and two be, and hereby is, amended, by striking out the words "thereupon allow and deduct from," and inserting in lieu thereof the words "allow upon;" by striking out the words "added to the amount, after deducting the allowance of per centum, as aforesaid," and inserting in lieu thereof the words, "paid by the purchaser of such stamped paper, vellum, or parchment;" and by striking out the word "discount" and inserting in lieu thereof the word "commission."

Penalty for making, selling, &c., lottery ticket without adhesive stamp.

Sec. 2. *And be it further enacted,* That on and after the first day of May, eighteen hundred and sixty-three, no person or persons, association, firm, or corporation, shall make, sell, or offer for sale, or dispose of any lottery ticket, or fractional part thereof, or any policy of numbers in any lottery, or any token, certificate, or device representing or intended to represent the holder, or any other person or person[s], as entitled or to be entitled, in any lottery, lottery scheme or game of hazard or chance to be drawn, to any prize or share or part of a prize, or any sum or part or share of any sum of money, or other article of value, or any fractional part thereof, without affixing thereto an adhesive stamp or stamps denoting the duty imposed by this act, and in default thereof shall incur a penalty of fifty dollars for each and every such offence; and no prize or part of a prize drawn to or by any ticket, or fractional part thereof, token, certificate, or device as aforesaid, and no sum of money or thing of value made payable or deliverable upon any stake or investment or risk in, or upon any policy of numbers, shall be demanded or recovered by any legal proceedings or otherwise without the ticket or fractional part thereof, or policy of numbers, token, certificate, or device, shall have been duly stamped at the time of the making sale or delivery or disposal thereof: *Provided,* That, in addition to all other penalties and forfeitures now imposed by law for the evasion of stamp duties, any person who shall purchase, obtain, or receive any lottery ticket, or fractional part thereof, or any token, certificate, or device representing or intended to represent a lottery ticket, or fractional part thereof, or any policy or numbers, without first having thereon the stamp imposed by this act, may recover from the person of whom the same was purchased, obtained, or received, at any time within three years, thereafter, before any court of competent jurisdiction, a sum equal to twice the amount paid for such ticket or fractional part thereof, token, certificate, or device, or staked or invested in or upon any policy of numbers as aforesaid, with just and legal costs: *Provided, further,* That the stamp duty herein provided for shall be classed in the act to which this act is an amendment under Schedule B, as follows, to wit:

Prizes not recoverable.

Additonal penalties.

Lottery tickets.

''Lottery tickets, fractional parts of lottery tickets, policies of numbers in lotteries, tokens, certificates, or devices in any form, representing the holder, or any person or persons, as entitled, or to be entitled, in any lottery, scheme, or game of hazard or chance, hereafter to be drawn, to any prize or portion of a prize or sum of money, or share thereof, or other article of value, or any portion or share thereof, when such ticket, fractional part of a ticket, policy of numbers, token, certificate, or device, shall not exceed one dollar in the amount risked, or in the retail price thereof, fifty cents, (50;) when such ticket, fractional part of a ticket, policy, token, certificate, or device, shall exceed one dollar in the amount risked, or in the retail price thereof, then for each and every dollar, or fractional part thereof, over and above one dollar, as before mentioned, an additional fifty cents, (50:) *Provided, however,* That no stamp duty herein provided for shall be construed to authorize any lottery, or the sale of any lottery tickets, tokens, or certificates, representing shares or fractional parts of shares therein, within any state or territory of the United States in which lotteries or the sale of lottery tickets is or shall be specially prohibited by the laws thereof, or in violation of the laws of any state or territory; and nothing in this act shall be held or construed so as to prevent the several states, within the limits

Stamp duty not to authorize lotteries.

thereof, from placing a duty, tax, or license, for state purposes, on any sale of lottery tickets on which a duty is required to be paid by this act."

Sec. 3. *And be it further enacted,* That any person or persons, firm, company, or corporation, who shall issue tickets or contracts of insurance against fatal or non-fatal injury to persons while travelling by land or water, shall pay a duty of one per centum on the gross amount of all the receipts for such insurance, and shall be subject to all the provisions and regulations of existing law applicable thereto, in relation to insurance companies: *Provided,* That no stamp duty shall be required upon tickets or contracts of insurance as aforesaid, when limited to fatal or non-fatal injury to persons while traveling.

Insurance against injury by travelling.

Ante, p. 7.

Sec. 4. *And be it further enacted,* That all contracts for the purchase or sale of gold or silver coin, or bullion, and all contracts for the loan of money or currency secured by pledge or deposit, or other disposition of gold or silver coin of the United States, if to be performed after a period exceeding three days, shall be in writing or printed, and signed by the parties or their agents or attorneys, and shall have one or more adhesive stamps, as provided in the act to which this is an amendment, equal in amount to one half of one per centum and interest at the rate of six per centum per annum on the amount so loaned, pledged, or deposited. And if any such loan, pledge, or deposit, made for a period not exceeding three days, shall be renewed or in any way extended for any time whatever, said loan, pledge, or deposit, shall be subject to the duty imposed on loans exceeding three days. And no loan of currency or money on the security of gold or silver coin of the United States, as aforesaid, or of any certificate or other evidence of deposit payable in gold or silver coin, shall be made exceeding in amount the par value of the coin pledged or deposited as security; and any such loan so made, or attempted to be made, shall be utterly void: *Provided,* That if gold or silver coin be loaned at its par value it shall be subject only to the duty imposed on other loans: *Provided however,* That nothing herein contained shall apply to any transaction by or with the government of the United States.

Contracts for purchase of coin or bullion.

Stamp duty.

Loans on pledge of coin not to exceed par value of coin.

Sec. 5. *And be it further enacted,* That all contracts, loans, or sales of gold and silver coin and bullion, not made in accordance with this act, shall be wholly and absolutely void; and in addition to the penalties provided in the act to which this is an amendment, any party to said contract may, at any time within one year from the date of the contract, bring suit before any court of competent jurisdiction to recover back, for his own use and benefit, the money paid on any contract not made in accordance with this act.

Certain contracts, loans, and sales of coin and bullion void.

The money paid may be recovered back.

Sec. 6. *And be it further enacted,* That section one hundred and ten be, and hereby is, amended as follows: "Any memorandum, check, receipt, or other written or printed evidence of an amount of money to be paid on demand, or at a time designated, shall be considered as a promissory note within the meaning of that section, and shall be stamped accordingly; and that Schedule B, following said section be, and is hereby amended, so that any inland bill of exchange, draft, or order for the payment of any sum of money exceeding twenty dollars, otherwise than at sight or on demand, and any promissory note shall (in lieu of the duties prescribed in Schedule B) have a stamp or stamps affixed thereon denoting a duty, upon every sum of two hundred dollars or any fractional part thereof, if payable on demand or at any time not exceeding thirty-three days including the grace from the date or sight, of one cent, (01.)

Promissory notes.

Section 110. *Ante,* p. 5.

Schedule B amended.

Duties upon bills of exchange, drafts, &c.

Ante, p. 5.

If payable at any time not less than thirty-three days as aforesaid, and not exceeding sixty-three days, including the grace, from date or sight, of two cents, (02.)

If payable at any time not less than sixty-three days, as aforesaid, and not exceeding ninety-three days, including the grace, from date or sight, of three cents, (03.)

If payable at any time not less than ninety-three days, as aforesaid, and not exceeding four months from date or sight and grace, of four cents, (04.)

If payable at any time not less than four months, as aforesaid, and not exceeding six months from date or sight, or grace, of six cents, (06.)

If payable at any time exceeding six months from date or sight and grace, of ten cents, (10.)

On certificates other than those specified. *Ante,* p. 7.

And that Schedule B, following section one hundred and ten be, and is hereby further amended, so that the stamp duty on certificates of any other description than those specified in said schedule, in lieu of ten cents as therein prescribed, shall be five cents, (05.)

Passage-tickets. *Ante,* p. 8.

On passage tickets by any vessel from a port of the United States to a foreign port, costing thirty dollars or less, fifty cents, (50.)

Power of attorney. *Ante,* p. 8.

On any power of attorney for the sale or transfer of any scrip or certificate of profits or memorandum showing an interest in the profits or accumulations of any corporation or association, if for a sum not exceeding fifty dollars, ten cents, (10.)

Policies of insurance. *Ante,* p. 8.

On any policy of insurance or other instrument, by whatever name the same shall be called, by which insurance shall be made or renewed upon property of any description whether against perils by sea, or by fire, or other peril of any kind, made by any insurance company or its agents, or by any other company or person in which the premium or assessment shall not exceed ten dollars, ten cents, (10.)

Bill of sale of vessel.

On any bill of sale by which any ship or vessel or any part thereof shall be conveyed to or vested in any other person or persons when the consideration shall not exceed five hundred dollars, there shall be affixed a stamp or stamps denoting a duty of twenty-five cents, (25.)

If the consideration exceeds five hundred and does not exceed one thousand dollars, the duty shall be fifty cents, (50.)

If the consideration exceeds one thousand dollars, for each and every additional amount of one thousand dollars, or any fractional part thereof, in excess of one thousand dollars, the duty in addition shall be fifty cents, (50.)

Assignment of mortgage, lease, policy of insurance.

On each and every assignment or transfer of a mortgage, lease, or policy of insurance, a stamp duty shall be paid equal to that imposed on the original instrument.

Documents made in a foreign country for use here, to pay same duty as though made here. Who to affix stamp.

Any power of attorney, conveyance, or document of any kind made, or purporting to be made, in any foreign country to be used in the United States shall pay the same duty as is required by law on similar instruments or documents when made or issued in the United States; and the party to whom the same is issued or by whom it is to be used, shall, before using the same, affix thereon the stamp or stamps indicating the duty required.

Personal mortgages as security for money. *Ante,* p. 8.

Any mortgage or personal bond for the payment of money, or as security for the payment of any definite or certain sum of money, in lieu of the duties imposed as prescribed in Schedule B following the one hundred and tenth section, shall have a stamp or stamps affixed thereon denoting a duty upon every sum of two hundred dollars, or any fractional part thereof, of ten cents, (10.)

Any conveyance, &c., not to pay a stamp duty of over $1000.

No conveyance, deed, mortgage, or writing, whereby any lands, tenements, realty, or other property shall be sold, granted, assigned or otherwise conveyed, or shall be made as security for the payment of any sum of money, shall be required to pay a stamp duty of more than the sum of one thousand dollars, anything to the contrary notwithstanding.

Stamp duty not required on papers relating to bounties, &c. One stamp on bond and mortgage. To be of highest rate. Certificates of measurement, &c. Deposit notes. Certificates of record, &c., of deeds.

No stamp duty shall be required on powers of attorney or any other paper relating to applications for bounties, arrearages of pay, or pensions, or to the receipt thereof from time to time; or indemnity awarded for depredations and injuries by certain bands of Sioux Indians; nor on any warrant of attorney accompanying a bond or note, when such bond or note shall have affixed thereto the stamp or stamps denoting the duty required; and whenever any bond or note shall be secured by a mortgage but one stamp duty shall be required to be placed on such papers: *Provided,* That the stamp duty placed thereon is the highest rate required for said instruments, or either of them; nor on certificates of the measurement or weight of animals, wood, coal, or other articles; nor on deposit notes to mutual insurance companies for insurance upon which policies subject to stamp duties have been, or are to be, issued; nor on any certificate of the record of a deed or other instrument in writing, or of the acknowledgment or proof thereof by attesting witnesses.

The duty or stamp required for transportation by express companies and others is hereby repealed, and such transportation shall be exempt from stamp duty.

Transportation by express exempt from stamp duty.

Charter-parties.

That the stamp duty on a contract or agreement for the charter of any ship, or vessel, or steamer, as now provided for in Schedule B, or any letter, memorandum, or other writing between the captain, master, or owner, or person acting as agent of any ship, or vessel, or steamer, and any other person or persons for or relating to the charter of such ship, or vessel, or steamer, if the registered tonnage of such ship, or vessel, or steamer, does not exceed one hundred and fifty tons, shall be one dollar, ($1.)

Ante, p. 7.

Exceeding one hundred and fifty tons and not exceeding three hundred tons, three dollars, ($3.)

Exceeding six hundred tons, ten dollars, ($10.)

Sec. 7. *And be it further enacted*, That the commissioner of internal revenue be, and he is hereby, authorized to prescribe such method for the cancellation of stamps as a substitute for or in addition to the method now prescribed by law, as he may deem expedient and effectual. And he is further authorized in his discretion to make the application of such method imperative upon the manufacturers of proprietary articles, and upon stamps of a nominal value exceeding twenty-five cents each.

Cancellation of stamps.

Ante, p. 2.

Sec. 10. *And be it further enacted*, That on and after the first day of April, eighteen hundred and sixty-three, any person or persons, firms, companies, or corporation carrying on or doing an express business shall, in lieu of the tax and stamp duties imposed by existing laws, be subject to and pay a duty of two per centum on the gross amount of all the receipts of such express business, and shall be subject to the same provisions, rules, and penalties as are prescribed in section eighty of the act to which this is an amendment, for the persons, firms, companies, or corporations owning or possessing or having the management of railroads, steamboats, and ferry-boats; and all acts or part[s] of acts inconsistent herewith are hereby repealed.

Express companies.

Ante, p. 6.

Sec. 16. *And be it further enacted*, That in any collection district where, in the judgment of the commissioner of internal revenue, the facilities for the procurement and distribution of stamped vellum, parchment or paper, and adhesive stamps are or shall be insufficient, the commissioner, as aforesaid, is authorized to furnish, supply, and deliver to the collector of any such district a suitable quantity or amount of stamped vellum, parchment, or paper, and adhesive stamps, without prepayment therefor, and shall allow the highest rate of commissions to the collector allowed by law to any other parties purchasing the same, and may, in advance, require of any such collector a bond, with sufficient sureties to an amount equal to the value of any stamped vellum, parchment or paper, and adhesive stamps which may be placed in his hands and remain unaccounted for, conditioned for the faithful return, whenever so required, of all quantities or amounts undisposed of, and for the payment, monthly, of all quantities or amounts, sold or not, remaining on hand. And it shall be the duty of such collector to supply his deputies with, or sell to other parties within his district who may make applications therefor, stamped vellum, parchment or paper, and adhesive stamps, upon the same terms allowed by law, or under the regulations of the commissioner of internal revenue, who is hereby authorized to make such other regulations, not inconsistent herewith, for the security of the United States and the better accommodation of the public in relation to the matters hereinbefore mentioned, as he may judge necessary and expedient: *Provided*, that no instrument, document, or paper made, signed, or issued prior to the first day of June, Anno Domini eighteen hundred and sixty-three, without being duly stamped, or having thereon an adhesive stamp to denote the duty imposed thereon, shall, for that cause, be deemed invalid and of no effect: *And provided*, That no instrument, document, writing, or paper, required by law to be stamped, signed, or issued, without being duly stamped prior to the day aforesaid, or any copy thereof, shall be admitted or used as evidence in any court until a legal stamp, or stamps, denoting the

In certain collection districts Commissioner may deliver stamps without prepayment.

Commissions.

Bond.

Collector to supply deputies.

No instrument issued prior to June 1st, 1863, without a stamp, to be invalid for that cause.

Ante, pp. 1, 11.

Not to be admitted in evidence without a stamp.

Stamp may be affixed in court.

amount of duty charged thereon, shall have been affixed thereto or used thereon, and the initials of the persons using or affixing the same, together with the date when the same is so used or affixed, shall have been placed thereon by such person. And the person desiring to use any such instrument, document, writing, or paper as evidence, or his agent or attorney, is authorized in the presence of the court to stamp the same as heretofore provided by law.

Who to be deemed manufacturer of articles in Schedule C. *Ante*, p. 4.

Sec. 27. *And be it further enacted,* That any person who shall offer for sale, after the thirtieth of September, eighteen hundred and sixty-three, any of the articles named in Schedule C of the act to which this act is an amendment, whether the articles so offered are imported, or are of foreign or domestic manufacture, shall be deemed the manufacturer thereof, and subject to all the duties, liabilities, and penalties in said act imposed in regard to the sale of such articles without the use of the proper stamp or stamps, as in said act is required.

Medicines, &c., intended for exportation may be manufactured where.

Sec. 28. *And be it further enacted,* That all medicines, preparations, compositions, perfumery, and cosmetics, intended for exportation, as provided for in section one hundred and nine of the act to which this act is an amendment, in order to be manufactured and sold or removed, without being charged with duty, and without having a stamp affixed thereto, may, under such rules and regulations as the Secretary of the Treasury may prescribe, be made and manufactured in warehouses known and designated in treasury regulations as bonded warehouses, class two: *Provided,* such manufacturer shall first give satisfactory bonds to the collector of internal revenue for the faithful observance of the rules and regulations of the Secretary of the Treasury from persons allowed bonded warehouses, class two. Such goods, when manufactured in such warehouses, may be removed for exportation, under the direction of the revenue officer having charge thereof, without being charged with duty, and without having a stamp affixed thereto. Any manufacturer of the articles aforesaid, or of any of them, having such bonded warehouse as aforesaid, shall be at liberty, under such rules and regulations as the Secretary of the Treasury may prescribe, to convey therein any materials to be used in such manufacture which are allowed by the provisions of the said act to be exported free from tax or duty, as well as the necessary materials, implements, packages, vessels, brands, and labels for the preparation, putting up, and export of the said manufactured articles, and every article so used shall be exempt from stamp and excise duty. Articles and materials so to be used may be transferred from any bonded warehouse in which the same may be, under such regulations as the Secretary of the Treasury may prescribe, into any bonded warehouse, class two, in which such manufacture may be conducted, and may be used in such manufacture, and, when so used, shall be exempt from stamp and excise duty; and the receipt of the officer of the revenue in charge shall be received as a voucher for the manufacture of such articles. Any materials imported into the United States may, under such rules as the Secretary of the Treasury may prescribe, and under the direction of the proper officer of the customs, be removed in original packages from on ship-board, or from the bonded warehouses in which the same may be, into the bonded warehouse, class two, in which such manufacture may be carried on, for the purpose of being used in such manufacture, without payment of duties thereon, and may there be used in such manufacture. No article so removed, nor any article manufactured in said bonded warehouse, class two, shall be taken therefrom except for exportation, under the direction of the proper officer of the customs having charge thereof, whose certificate, describing the articles by their marks, or otherwise, the quantity, the date of importation, and name of vessel, with such additional particulars as may from time to time be required, shall be received by the collector of customs in cancellation of the bonds, or return of the amount of foreign import duties. All labor performed and services rendered under these regulations shall be under the supervision of an officer of the customs, and at the expense of the manufacturer.

Proviso.

How removed.

What may be carried to warehouse free of duty,

or transferred.

Imports, in original packages, may be removed thither.

Nothing to be removed but for exportation.

Labor to be under supervision of officer, &c.

SEC. 37. *And be it further enacted,* That this act, except where otherwise indicated, shall take effect from and after its passage, and all acts and parts of acts repugnant to the provisions of this act be, and the same are hereby, repealed: *Provided,* That the existing laws shall extend to and be in force, as modified, for the collection of the duties imposed by this act, for the prosecution and punishment of all offences, and for the recovery, collection, distribution and remission of all fines, penalties, and forfeitures, as fully and effectually as if every regulation, penalty, forfeiture, provision, clause, matter, and thing to that effect, in the existing laws contained, had been inserted in, and reenacted by, this act.

This act to take effect on its passage.

Saving of existing laws.

Approved March 3, 1863.

Act of June 17, 1864

CHAP. CXXVII.—*An Act to prohibit Sales of Gold and Foreign Exchange.*

Be it enacted by the Senate and House of Representatives of the United States of America in Congress assembled, That it shall be unlawful to make any contract for the purchase or sale and delivery of any gold coin or bullion to be delivered on any day subsequent to the day of making such contract, or for the payment of any sum, either fixed or contingent, in default of the delivery of any gold coin or bullion, or to make such contract upon any other terms than the actual delivery of such gold coin or bullion, and the payment in full of the agreed price thereof, on the day on which such contract is made, in United States notes or national currency, and not otherwise; or to make any contract for the purchase or sale and delivery of any foreign exchange to be delivered at any time beyond ten days subsequent to the making of such contract; or for the payment of any sum, either fixed or contingent, in default of the delivery of any foreign exchange, or upon any other terms than the actual delivery of such foreign exchange within ten days from the making of such contract, and the immediate payment in full of the agreed price thereof on the day of delivery in United States notes or national currency; or to make any contract whatever for the sale and delivery of any gold coin or bullion of which the person making such contract shall not, at the time of making the same, be in actual possession. And it shall be unlawful to make any loan of money or currency not being in coin to be repaid in coin or bullion, or to make any loan of coin or bullion to be repaid in money or currency other than coin.

Certain contracts for the purchase, &c., of gold coin and bullion and foreign exchange made unlawful.

[Repealed, 1864, ch. 209. *Post,* p. 31.]

Certain loans made unlawful.

SEC. 2. *And be it further enacted,* That it shall be further unlawful for any banker, broker, or other person, to make any purchase or sale of any gold coin or bullion, or of any foreign exchange, or any contract for any such purchase or sale, at any other place than the ordinary place of business of either the seller or purchaser, owned or hired, and occupied by him individually, or by a partnership of which he is a member.

Contracts for purchase of gold, &c., to be made only at the ordinary place of business, &c.

SEC. 3. *And be it further enacted,* That all contracts made in violation of this act shall be absolutely void.

Void contracts.

SEC. 4. *And be it further enacted,* That any person who shall violate any provisions of this act shall be held guilty of a misdemeanor, and, on conviction thereof, be fined in any sum not less than one thousand dollars, nor more than ten thousand dollars, or be imprisoned for a period not less than three months, nor longer than one year, or both, at the discretion of the court, and shall likewise be subject to a penalty of one thousand dollars for each offence.

Penalty for violations of this act to be fine or imprisonment.

SEC. 5. *And be it further enacted,* That the penalties imposed by the fourth section of this act may be recovered in an action at law in any court of record of the United States, or any court of competent jurisdiction, which action may be brought in the name of the United States by any person who will sue for said penalty, one half for the use of the United States, and the other half for the use of the person bringing such action. And the recovery and satisfaction of a judgment in any such action shall be a bar to the imposition of any fine for the same offence in any prosecution instituted

Penalties. How may be recovered.

Half of money to go to person bringing the suit.

Judgment, &c., not to be bar of imprisonment.

subsequent to the recovery of such judgment, but shall not be a bar to the infliction of punishment by imprisonment, as provided by said fourth section.

Repealing clause.

Sec. 6. *And be it further enacted,* That all acts and parts of acts inconsistent with the provisions of this act are hereby repealed.

Approved, June 17, 1864.

[Ed. note: Secs. 4 and 5 of the Act of March 3, 1863 established a stamp tax on contracts for the sale of gold coin or bullion if for a period exceeding three days. By making such contracts illegal, the present act implicitly rescinded this stamp tax. Note that coin or bullion contracts were not mentioned (and therefore not taxed) by the Act of June 30, 1864. However, on July 2, 1864, the Act of June 17, 1864 was repealed, and the legal restrictions on coin and bullion contracts thereby removed. A stamp tax on these documents was re-established by the Act of July 13, 1866.]

Act of June 30, 1864

CHAP. CLXXIII.—*An Act to provide Internal Revenue to support the Government, to pay Interest on the Public Debt, and for other Purposes.*

Sec. 94. . . . there shall be levied, collected, and paid the following duties, to be paid by the producer or manufacturer thereof, that is to say:— . . .

Photographs.

Post, p. 31.

On photographs, or any other sun picture, being copies of engravings or works of art, or used for the illustration of books, and on photographs so small in size that stamps cannot be affixed, a duty of five per centum ad valorem.

Brokers, &c.

BROKERS.

Duty on sales.

Sec. 99. *And be it further enacted,* That all brokers, and bankers doing business as brokers, shall be subject to pay the following duties and rates of duty upon the sales of merchandise, produce, gold and silver bullion, foreign exchange, uncurrent money, promissory notes, stocks, bonds, or other securities as hereinafter mentioned, and shall be subject to all the provisions, where not applicable thereto, for the returns, assessment, collection of the duties, and liens and penalties as are prescribed for the persons, firms, companies, or corporations, owning or possessing, or having the management of railroads, steamboats, and ferry-boats, that is to say: Upon all sales of merchandise, produce, or other goods, one eighth of one per centum; upon all sales and contracts for sales of stocks and bonds, one twentieth of one per centum on the par value thereof; and of gold and silver bullion and coin, foreign exchange, promissory notes, or other securities, one twentieth of one per centum on the amount of such sales, and of all contracts for such sales: *Provided,* That any person, firm, or comapny not being licensed as a broker, or banker, or wholesale or retail dealer, who shall sell, or offer to sell, any merchandise, produce, or gold and silver bullion, foreign exchange, uncurrent money, promissory notes, stocks, bonds, or other securities, not bona fide at the time his own property, and actually on hand, shall be liable, in addition to all other penalties provided in such cases, to pay fifty per centum in addition to the foregoing duties and rates of duty. [Ed. note: This section referred to by the Act of July 13, 1866, which established a stamp tax on brokers' contracts or memos for sale of stocks, bonds, bullion, etc. (See pp. 33, 37).]

Telegraph companies.

TELEGRAPH COMPANIES.

Sec. 107. *And be it further enacted,* That any person, firm, company, or corporation owning or possessing or having the care or management of any telegraphic line by which telegraphic despatches or messages are received or transmitted, shall be subject to, and pay a duty of, five per centum on the gross amount of all receipts of such person, firm, company, or corporation. [Ed. note: This duty replaced the previous stamp tax.]

LOTTERIES.

Lotteries.

Sec. 111. *And be it further enacted,* That every individual partnership, firm, and association, being proprietors, managers, or agents of lotteries, shall pay a tax of five per centum on the gross amount of the receipts from the said business; . . .[Ed. note: This tax replaced the previous stamp tax.]

STAMP DUTIES.

Stamp duties.

Sec. 151. *And be it further enacted,* That all laws in force at the time of the passage of this act in relation to stamp duties shall continue in force until the first day of August, eighteen hundred and sixty-four, and on and after the first day of August, eighteen hundred and sixty-four, there shall be levied, collected, and paid, for and in respect of the several instruments, matters, and things mentioned and described in the schedule (marked B) hereunto annexed, or for or in respect of the vel[l]um, parchment, or paper upon which such instruments, matters, or things, or any of them shall be written or printed, by any person or persons, or party who shall make, sign, or issue the same, or for whose use or benefit the same shall be made, signed, or issued, the several duties or sums of money set down in figures against the same, respectively, or otherwise specified or set forth in the said schedule.

Stamp duties to be paid by party signing instrument, &c.

Sec. 152. *And be it further enacted,* That it shall not be lawful to record any instrument, document, or paper required by law to be stamped, unless a stamp or stamps of the proper amount shall have been affixed; and the record of any such instrument, upon which the proper stamp or stamps aforesaid shall not have been affixed, shall be utterly void, and shall not be used in evidence.

Instruments not to be recorded without a stamp.

Sec. 153. *And be it further enacted,* That no intrument, document, writing, or paper of any description, required by law to be stamped, shall be deemed or held invalid and of no effect for the want of the particular kind or description of stamp designated for and denoting the duty charged on any such instrument, document, writing, or paper, provided a legal stamp, or stamps, denoting a duty of equal amount, shall have been duly affixed and used thereon: *Provided,* That the provisions of this section shall not apply to any stamp appropriated to denote the duty charged on proprietary articles, or articles enumerated in schedule C.

What stamp may be used.

Proviso.

Sec. 154. *And be it further enacted,* That all official instruments, documents, and papers, issued or used by the officers of the United States government, shall be, and hereby are, exempt from duty.

Official United State documents exempt, &c.

Sec. 155. *And be it further enacted,* That if any person shall forge or counterfeit, or cause or procure to be forged or counterfeited, any stamp or die, or any part of any stamp or die, which shall have been provided, made, or used in pursuance of this act, or shall forge, counterfeit, or resemble, or cause or procure to be forged, counterfeited, or resembled, the impression, or any part of the impression, of any such stamp or die, as aforesaid, upon any vellum, parchment, or paper, or shall stamp or mark, or cause or procure to be stamped or marked, any vellum, parchment, or paper, with any such forged or counterfeited stamp or die, or part of any stamp or die, as aforesaid, with intent to defraud the United States of any of the duties hereby imposed, or any part thereof; or if any person shall utter or sell, or expose to sale, any vellum, parchment, or paper, article, or thing, having thereupon the impression of any such counterfeited stamp or die, or any part of any stamp or die, or any such forged, counterfeited, or resembled impression, or part of impression, as aforesaid, knowing the same respectively to be forged, counterfeited, or resembled; or if any person shall knowingly use any stamp or die which shall have been so provided, made, or used as aforesaid, with intent to defraud the United States; or if any person shall fraudulently cut, tear, or remove, or cause or procure to be cut, torn, or removed, the impression of any stamp or die which shall have been provided, made, or used in pursuance of this act, from any vellum, parchment, or paper, or any instrument or writing charged or chargeable with any of the duties hereby imposed;

Penalty for forging, &c., stamps, &c.

or the impression of stamps, &c.;

for stamping with forged stamps;

for selling paper, &c., with forged stamp, &c., thereon;

for using forged stamps;

for fraudulently, &c., removing impression of dies, &c.;

for selling washed or restored stamps, &c.

or if any person shall wilfully remove, or cause to be removed, from any stamped envelope the cancelling or defacing marks thereon, with intent to use the same, or cause the use of the same, the second time, or shall knowingly or wilfully sell or buy such washed or restored stamps, or offer the same for sale, or give or expose the same to any person for use, or knowingly use the same, or prepare the same with intent for the second use thereof, then, and in every such case, every person so offending, and every person knowingly and wilfully aiding, abetting, or assisting in committing any such offence as aforesaid, shall be deemed guilty of felony, and shall, on conviction thereof, forfeit the said counterfeit stamps and the articles upon which they are placed, and be punished by fine not exceeding one thousand dollars, or by imprisonment and confinement to hard labor, not exceeding five years, or both, at the discretion of the court.

Cancellation of stamps.

Penalty.

Proprietary articles.

Dies, &c., for stamps.

Stamps to be so affixed as to be destroyed.

Fraudulently using or forging.

Sec. 156. *And be it further enacted,* That in any and all cases where an adhesive stamp shall be used for denoting any duty imposed by this act, except as hereinafter provided, the person using or affixing the same shall write thereupon the initials of his name and the date upon which the same shall be attached or used, so that the same may not again be used. And if any person shall fraudulently make use of an adhesive stamp to denote any duty imposed by this act without so effectually cancelling and obliterating such stamp, except as before mentioned, he, she, or they shall forfeit the sum of fifty dollars: *Provided,* That any proprietor or proprietors of proprietary articles, or articles subject to stamp duty under schedule C of this act, shall have the privilege of furnishing, without expense to the United States, in suitable form, to be approved by the commissioner of internal revenue, his or their own dies or designs for stamps to be used thereon, to be made under the direction, and to be retained in the possession of, the commissioner of internal revenue for his or their separate use, which shall not be duplicated to any other person. That in all cases where such stamp is used, instead of his or their writing the date thereon, the said stamp shall be so affixed on the box, bottle, or package, that in opening the same, or using the contents thereof, the said stamp shall be effectively destroyed; and in default thereof, shall be liable to the same penalty imposed for neglect to affix said stamp as hereinbefore prescribed in this act. Any person who shall fraudulently obtain or use any of the aforesaid stamps, or designs therefor, and any person forging, or counterfeiting, or causing or procuring the forging or counterfeiting any representation, likeness, similitude, or colorable imitation of the said last-mentioned stamp, or any engraver or printer who shall sell or give away said stamps, or selling the same, or, being a merchant, broker, peddler, or person dealing, in whole or in part, in similar goods, wares, merchandise, manufactures, preparations, or articles, or those designed for similar objects or purposes, shall have knowingly or fraudulently in his, her, or their possession, any such forged, counterfeited likeness, similitude, or colorable imitation of the said last-mentioned stamp, shall be deemed guilty of a felony, and, upon conviction thereof, shall be subject to all the penalties, fines, and forfeitures prescribed in the preceding section of this act.

Mode of cancellation.

Sec. 157. *And be it further enacted,* That the commissioner of internal revenue be, and he is hereby, authorized to prescribe such method for the cancellation of stamps, as substitute for, or in addition to, the method now prescribed by law, as he may deem expedient and effectual. And he is further authorized in his discretion to make the application of such method imperative upon the manufacturers of proprietary articles, or articles included in schedule C, and upon stamps of a nominal value exceeding twenty-five cents each.

Penalty for making, paying, &c., unstamped instruments, &c.

[Amended, *Post,* p. 31.]

Sec. 158. *And be it further enacted,* That any person or persons who shall make, sign, or issue, or who shall cause to be made, signed, or issued, any instrument, document, or paper of any kind or description whatsoever, or shall accept or pay, or cause to be accepted or paid, any bill of exchange, draft, or order or promissory note, for the payment of money, without the same being duly stamped, or having thereupon an adhesive stamp for denoting the duty chargeable thereon, with intent to evade the provisions of this act, shall, for every such offence, forfeit the sum of two hundred dollars, and such instrument, document, or paper, bill, draft, order, or note shall be deemed invalid and of no effect: *Provided,* That the title of a purchaser of land by a deed duly stamped, shall not be defeated or *effected* [affected] by the want of a proper stamp on any deed conveying said land by any person from, through, or under whom his grantor claims or holds title.

Sec. 159. *And be it further enacted,* That the acceptor or acceptors of any bill of exchange or order for the payment of any sum of money drawn, or purporting to be drawn, in any foreign country, but payable in the United States, shall, before paying or accepting the same, place thereupon a stamp, indicating the duty upon the same, as the law requires for inland bills of exchange, or promissory notes, and no bill of exchange shall be paid or negotiated without such stamp; and if any person shall pay or negotiate, or offer in payment, or receive or take in payment, any such draft or order, the person or persons so offending shall forfeit the sum of two hundred dollars.

Foreign bills of exchange to be stamped before payment.

Sec. 160. *And be it further enacted,* That no stamp duty shall be required on powers of attorney or any other paper relating to applications for bounties, arrearages of pay, or pensions, or to the receipt thereof from time to time, or upon tickets or contracts of insurance when limited to injury to persons while travelling; nor on certificates *or* [of] the measurement or weight of animals, wood, coal, or other articles; nor on deposit notes to mutual insurance companies for insurance upon which policies subject to stamp duties have been, or are to be issued; nor on any certificate of the record of a deed or other instrument in writing, or of the acknowledgment or proof thereof by attesting witnesses; nor to any indorsement of a negotiable instrument, or on any warrant of attorney, accompanying a bond or note, when such bond or note shall have affixed thereto the stamp or stamps denoting the duty required; and whenever any bond or note shall be secured by a mortgage, but one stamp shall be required to be placed on such papers: *Provided,* That the stamp duty placed thereon shall be the highest rate required for said instruments, or either of them.

Stamp duty not required on, &c.

Post, p. 32.

Mortgages.

Sec. 161. *And be it further enacted,* That the commissioner of internal revenue be, and is hereby, authorized to sell to and supply collectors, deputy collectors, postmasters, stationers, or any other persons, at his discretion, with adhesive stamps, or stamped paper, vellum, or parchment, as herein provided for, in amounts of not less than fifty dollars, upon the payment, at the time of delivery, of the amount of duties said stamps, stamped paper, vellum, or parchment, so sold or supplied, represent, and may allow, upon the aggregate amount of such stamps, as aforesaid, the sum of not exceeding five per centum as commission to the collectors, postmasters, stationers, or other purchasers; but the cost of any paper, vellum, or parchment shall be paid by the purchaser of such stamped paper, vellum, or parchment, as aforesaid: *Provided,* That any proprietor or proprietors of articles named in schedule C, who shall furnish his or their own die or design for stamps, to be used especially for his or their own proprietary articles, shall be allowed the following commission, namely: On amounts purchased at one time, of not less than fifty nor more than five hundred dollars, five per centum; on amounts over five hundred dollars, ten per centum. The commissioner of internal revenue may, from time to time, make regulations, upon proper evidence of the facts, for the allowance of such of the stamps issued under the provisions of this act as may have been spoiled, destroyed, or rendered useless or unfit for the purpose intended, or for which the owner may have no use, or which through mistake may have been improperly or unnecessarily used, or where the rates or duties represented thereby have been paid in error, or remitted; and such allowance shall be made either by giving other stamps in lieu of the stamps so allowed for, or by repaying the amount or value, after deducting therefrom, in case of repayment, the sum of five per centum to the owner thereof; but no allowance shall be made in any case until the stamps so spoiled or rendered useless shall have been returned to the commissioner of internal revenue, or until satisfactory proof has been made showing the reason why said stamps cannot be so returned: *Provided,* That the commissioner of internal revenue may, from time to time, furnish, supply, and deliver to any manufacturer of friction or other matches,

Stamps, stamped papers, &c., may be sold to collectors, &c.

Commission.

Commission on stamps for proprietary articles, when, &c.

Allowance for spoiled, &c., stamps.

Certain stamps may be delivered on credit, by giving security.

cigar-lights, or wax tapers, a suitable quantity of adhesive or other stamps, such as may be prescribed for use in such cases, without prepayment therefor, on a credit not exceeding sixty days, requiring, in advance, such security as he may judge necessary to secure payment therefor to the treasurer of the United States, within the time prescribed for such payment. And upon all bonds or other securities taken by said commissioner, under the provisions of this act, suits may be maintained by said treasurer in the circuit or district court of the United States, in the several districts where any of the persons giving said bonds or other securities reside, or may be found, in any appropriate form of action.

Instruments not used may be presented to commissioner to determine the duty.

Sec. 162. *And be it further enacted,* That it shall be lawful for any person to present to the collector of the district, subject to the rules and regulations of the commissioner of internal revenue, any instrument not previously issued or used, and require his opinion whether or not the same is chargeable with any stamp duty; and if the said collector shall be of opinion that such instrument is chargeable with any stamp duty, he shall, upon the payment therefor, affix and cancel the proper stamp; and if of the opinion that such instrument is not chargeable with any stamp duty, or is chargeable only with the duty by him designated, he is hereby required to impress thereon a particular stamp, to be provided for that purpose, with such words or device thereon as he shall judge proper, which shall denote that such instrument is not chargeable with any stamp duty, or is chargeable only with the duty denoted by the stamp affixed; and every such instrument, upon which the said stamp shall be impressed, shall be deemed to be not chargeable, or to be chargeable only with the duty denoted by the stamp so affixed, and shall be received in evidence in all courts of law or equity, notwithstanding any objections made to the same by reason of it being unstamped, or of it being insufficiently stamped.

Instruments required to be stamped not to be used without;

or recorded.

Stamps may be subsequently affixed to certain deeds, &c.

Provisos.

Sec. 163. *And be it further enacted,* That no deed, instrument, document, writing, or paper, required by law to be stamped, which has been heretofore signed or issued without being duly stamped, or with a deficient stamp, nor any copy thereof, shall be recorded, or admitted, or used as evidence in any court until a legal stamp or stamps, denoting the amount of duty, shall have been affixed thereto, and the date when the same is so used or affixed, with his initials, shall have been placed thereon by the person using or affixing the same; and the person desiring to use or record any such deed, instrument, document, writing, or paper as evidence, his agent or attorney, is authorized in the presence of the court, register, or recorder, respectively, to affix the stamp or stamps thereon required: *Provided,* That no instrument, document, or paper made, signed, or issued, prior to the passage of this act, without being duly stamped, or having thereon an adhesive stamp or stamps, to denote the duty imposed thereon, shall, for that cause, if the stamp or stamps required shall be subsequently affixed, be deemed invalid and of no effect: *Provided, further,* That any power of attorney, conveyance, or document of any kind, made, or purporting to be made, in any foreign country to be used in the United States, shall pay the same duty as is required by law on similar instruments or documents when made or issued in the United States; and the party to whom the same is issued, or by whom it is to be used, shall, before using the same, affix thereon the stamp or stamps indicating the duty required.

Provisions as to dies, to include what.

Sec. 164. *And be it further enacted,* That all the provisions of this act relating to dies, stamps, adhesive stamps, and stamp duties shall extend to and include (except where manifestly impracticable) all the articles or objects enumerated in schedule marked C, subject to stamp duties, and apply to the provisions in relation thereto.

Penalty for making, selling, &c., certain articles without affixing stamps.

Sec. 165. *And be it further enacted,* That if any person, firm, company, or corporation shall make, prepare, and sell, or remove for consumption or sale, drugs, medicines, preparations, compositions, articles, or things, including perfumery, cosmetics, lucifer or friction matches, cigar-lights, or wax tapers, photographs, ambrotypes, daguerreotypes, or other sun-pictures of any description, and playing-cards, upon which a duty is imposed by law, as enumerated and mentioned in schedule C, without affixing thereto an adhesive stamp or label denoting the duty before mentioned, he or they shall incur a penalty of ten dollars for every omission to affix such stamp: *Provided,* That nothing in this act contained shall apply to any uncompounded medicinal drug or chemical, nor to any medicine compounded according to the United States or other national pharmacopoeia, nor of which the full and proper formula is published in either of the dispensatories, formularies, or text-books in common use among physicians and apothecaries, including homoeopathic and eclectic, or in any pharmaceutical journal now used by any incorporated college of pharmacy, and not sold or offered for sale, or advertised under any other name, form, or guise, than that under which they may be severally denominated and laid down in said pharmacopoeias, dispensatories, text-books, or journals, as aforesaid, nor to medicines sold to, or for the use of, any person, which may be mixed and compounded specially for said persons, according to the written recipe or prescription of any physician or surgeon.

Proviso.

Post, p. 32.

Sec. 166. *And be it further enacted,* That every manufacturer or maker of any of the articles for sale mentioned in schedule C, after the same shall have been so made, and the particulars hereinbefore required as to stamps have been complied with, who shall take off, remove, or detach, or cause, or permit, or suffer to be taken off, or removed, or detached, any stamp, or who shall use any stamp, or any wrapper or cover to which any stamp is affixed, to cover any other article or commodity than that originally contained in such wrapper or cover, with such stamp when first used, with the intent to evade the stamp duties, shall for every such article, respectively, in respect of which any such offence shall be committed, be subject to a penalty of fifty dollars, to be recovered together with the costs thereupon accruing; and every such article or commodity as aforesaid shall also be forfeited.

Penalty for removing stamps once affixed to evade duty;

Sec. 167. *And be it further enacted,* That on and after the passage of this act every maker or manufacturer of any of the articles or *or* commodities mentioned in schedule C, as aforesaid, who shall sell, send out, remove, or deliver any article or commodity, manufactured as aforesaid, before the duty thereon shall have been fully paid, by affixing thereon the proper stamp, as provided by law, or who shall hide or conceal, or cause to be hidden or concealed, or who shall remove or convey away, or deposit, or cause to be removed or conveyed away from or deposited in any place, any such article or commodity, to evade the duty chargeable thereon, or any part thereof, shall be subject to a penalty of one hundred dollars, together with the forfeiture of any such article or commodity.

for selling, &c., certain articles without stamps.

Post, p. 32.

Sec. 168. *And be it further enacted,* That all medicines, preparations, compositions, perfumery, cosmetics, lucifer or friction matches, and cigar-lights, or wax tapers, cordials, and other liquors manufactured wholly or in part of domestic spirits, intended for exportation, as provided for by law, in order to be manufactured and sold or removed, without being charged with duty, and without having a stamp affixed thereto, shall, under such rules and regulations as the Secretary of the Treasury may prescribe, be made and manufactured in warehouses similarly constructed to those known and designated in treasury regulations as bonded warehouses, class two: *Provided,* That such manufacturer shall first give satisfactory bonds to the collector of internal revenue for the faithful observance of all the provisions of law and the rules and regulations as aforesaid, in amount not less than half of that required by the regulations of the Secretary of the Treasury from persons allowed bonded warehouses. Such goods, when manufactured in such warehouses, may be removed for exportation, under the direction of the proper officer having charge thereof, who shall be designated by the Secretary of the Treasury, without being charged with duty, and without having a stamp affixed thereto. Any manufacturer of the articles aforesaid, or of any of them, having such bonded warehouse, as aforesaid, shall be at liberty, under such rules and regulations as the Secretary of the Treasury may prescribe, to convey therein any materials to be used in such manufacture which are allowed by the provisions of law to be exported free from tax or duty, as well as the necessary materials, implements, packages, vessels, brands, and labels for the preparation, putting up, and export of the said manufactured articles;

Medicines, &c., to be made, &c., without duty, to be manufactured in warehouses.

Post, p. 32.

Manufacturers to give bonds, &c.

Manufactured goods may be removed for exportation.

Warehouses may be used for what.

and every article so used shall be exempt from the payment of stamp and excise duty by such manufacturer. Articles and materials so to be used may be transferred from any bonded warehouse in which the same may be, under such regulations as the Secretary of the Treasury may prescribe, into any bonded warehouse in which such manufacture may be conducted, and may be used in such manufacture, and, when so used, shall be exempt from stamp and excise duty; and the receipt of the officer in charge, as aforesaid, shall be received as a voucher for the manufacture of such articles. Any materials imported into the United States may, under such rules as the Secretary of the Treasury may prescribe, and under the direction of the proper officer, be removed in original packages from on shipboard, or from the bonded warehouse in which the same may be, into the bonded warehouse in which such manufacture may be carried on, for the purpose of being used in such manufacture, without payment of duties thereon, and may there be used in such manufacture. No article so removed, nor any article manufactured in said bonded warehouse, shall be taken therefrom, except for exportation, under the direction of the proper officer having charge thereof, as aforesaid, whose certificate, describing the articles by their marks, or otherwise, the quantity, the date of importation, the name of vessel, with such additional particulars as may from time to time be required, shall be received by the collector of customs in cancellation of the bonds, or return of the amount of foreign import duties. All labor performed and services rendered under these regulations shall be under the supervision of an officer of the customs, and at the expense of the manufacturer.

Materials used in the manufacture.

Labor.

Who to be deemed manufacturers of certain articles.

Post, p. 32.

Proviso.

Post, p. 32.

Sec. 169. *And be it further enacted,* That any person who shall offer for sale any of the articles named in schedule C, whether the articles so offered are imported, or are of foreign or domestic manufacture, shall be deemed the manufacturer thereof, and subject to all the duties, liabilities, and penalties imposed by law in regard to the sale of domestic articles without the use of the proper stamp or stamps denoting the duty paid thereon: *Provided,* That when any such imported articles shall be sold in the original and unbroken package in which the bottles or other enclosures were packed by the manufacturer, the person so selling said articles shall not be subject to any penalty on account of the want of the proper stamp.

In certain districts, stamps, &c., may be delivered to collector without prepayment.

Bond to be given.

Deputy collectors to be supplied with stamps.

Regulations.

Sec. 170. *And be it further enacted,* That in any collection district where, in the judgment of the commissioner of internal revenue, the facilities for the procurement and distribution of stamped vellum, parchment, or paper, and adhesive stamps, are or shall be insufficient, the commissioner, as aforesaid, is authorized to furnish, supply, and deliver to the collector and to the assessor of any such district, and to any assistant treasurer of the United States, or designated depositary thereof, or any postmaster, a suitable quantity or amount of stamped vellum, parchment or paper, and adhesive stamps, without prepayment therefor, and shall allow the highest rate of commissions allowed by law to any other parties purchasing the same, and may in advance require of any such collector, assessor, assistant treasurer of the United States, or postmaster, a bond, with sufficient sureties, to an amount equal to the value of any stamped vellum, parchment, or paper, and adhesive stamps which may be placed in his hands and remain unaccounted for, conditioned for the faithful return, whenever so required, of all quantities or amounts undisposed of, and for the payment, monthly, of all quantities or amounts, sold or not, remaining on hand. And it shall be the duty of such collector to supply his deputies with, or sell to other parties within his district who may make application therefor, stamped vellum, parchment, or paper, and adhesive stamps, upon the same terms allowed by law, or under the regulations of the commissioner of internal revenue, who is hereby authorized to make such other regulations, not inconsistent herewith, for the security of the United States and the better accommodation of the public, in relation to the matters hereinbefore mentioned, as he may judge necessary and expedient. And the Secretary of the Treasury may, from time to time, make such regulations as he may find necessary to insure the safe-keeping or prevent the illegal use of all such stamped vellum, parchment, paper, and adhesive stamps.

SCHEDULE B.

Schedule B.

STAMP DUTIES.

Stamp duties.

	Duty. Dolls. cts.
Agreement or contract, other than those specified in this schedule; any appraisement of value or damage, or for any other purpose; for every sheet or piece of paper upon which either of the same shall be written, five cents	5
Provided, That if more than one appraisement, agreement, or contract shall be written upon one sheet or piece of paper, five cents for each and every additional appraisement, agreement, or contract.	
Bank check, draft, or order for the payment of any sum of money whatsoever, drawn upon any bank, banker, or trust company, or for any sum exceeding ten dollars drawn upon any other person or persons, companies, or corporations, at sight or on demand, two cents	2
Bill of exchange, (inland,) draft, or order for the payment of any sum of money not exceeding one hundred dollars, otherwise than at sight or on demand, or any promissory note (except bank-note issued for circulation, and checks made and intended to be forthwith presented, and which shall be presented to a bank or banker for payment,) or any memorandum, check, receipt, or other written or printed evidence of an amount of money to be paid on demand, or at a time designated, for a sum not exceeding one hundred dollars, five cents	5
And for every additional hundred dollars, or fractional part thereof in excess of one hundred dollars, five cents	5
Bill of exchange, (foreign,) or letter of credit, drawn in but payable out of the United States, if drawn singly, or otherwise than in a set of three or more, according to the custom of merchants and bankers, shall pay the same rates of duty as inland bills of exchange or promissory notes.	
If drawn in sets of three or more: For every bill of each set, where the sum made payable shall not exceed one hundred dollars, or the equivalent thereof, in any foreign currency in which such bills may be expressed, according to the standard of value fixed by the United States, two cents	2
And for every additional hundred dollars or fractional part thereof in excess of one hundred dollars, two cents	2
Bill of lading or receipt, (other than charter-party,) for any goods, merchandise, or effects, to be exported from a port or place in the United States to any foreign port or place, ten cents	10
Bill of sale by which any ship or vessel, or any part thereof, shall be conveyed to or vested in any other person or persons, when the consideration shall not exceed five hundred dollars, fifty cents	50
Exceeding five hundred dollars and not exceeding one thousand dollars, one dollar	1 00
Exceeding one thousand dollars for every additional amount of five hundred dollars, or fractional part thereof, fifty cents	50
Bond for indemnifying any person for the payment of any sum of money, where the money ultimately recoverable thereupon is one thousand dollars or less, fifty cents	50
Where the money ultimately recoverable thereupon exceeds one thousand dollars, for every additional one thousand dollars or fractional part thereof in excess of one thousand dollars, fifty cents	50

Stamp duties.

	Duty. Dolls. cts.
Bond for the due execution or performance of the duties of any office, one dollar	1 00
Bond of any description, other than such as may be required in legal proceedings, or used in connection with mortgage deeds, and not otherwise charged in this schedule, twenty-five cents	25
Certificate of stock in any incorporated company, twenty-five cents	25
Certificate of profits, or any certificate or memorandum showing an interest in the property or accumulations of any incorporated company, if for a sum not less than ten dollars and not exceeding fifty dollars, ten cents	10
Exceeding fifty dollars and not exceeding one thousand dollars, twenty-five cents	25
Exceeding one thousand dollars, for every additional one thousand dollars, or fractional part thereof, twenty-five cents	25
Certificate.—Any certificate of damage, or otherwise, and all other certificates or documents issued by any port warden, marine surveyor, or other person acting as such, twenty-five cents	25
Certificate of deposit of any sum of money in any bank or trust company, or with any banker or person acting as such—	
If for a sum not exceeding one hundred dollars, two cents	2
For a sum exceeding one hundred dollars, five cents	5
Certificate of any other description than those specified, five cents	5
Charter-Party.—Contract or agreement for the charter of any ship or vessel, or steamer, or any letter, memorandum, or other writing between the captain, master, or owner, or person acting as agent of any ship or vessel, or steamer, and any other person or persons for, or relating, to the charter of such ship or vessel, or steamer, or any renewal or transfer thereof, if the registered tonnage of such ship or vessel, or steamer, does not exceed one hundred and fifty tons, one dollar	1 00
Exceeding one hundred and fifty tons, and not exceeding three hundred tons, three dollars	3 00
Exceeding three hundred tons, and not exceeding six hundred tons, five dollars	5 00
Exceeding six hundred tons, ten dollars	10 00
Contract.—Broker's note, or memorandum of sale of any goods or merchandise, stocks, bonds, exchange, notes of hand, real estate, or property of any kind or description issued by brokers or persons acting as such, for each note or memorandum of sale, ten cents	10
Conveyance.—Deed, instrument, or writing, whereby any lands, tenements, or other realty sold shall be granted, assigned, transferred, or otherwise conveyed to, or vested in, the purchaser or purchasers, or any other person or persons by his, her, or their direction, when the consideration or value does not exceed five hundred dollars, fifty cents	50
When the consideration exceeds five hundred dollars, and does not exceed one thousand dollars, one dollar	1 00
And for every additional five hundred dollars, or fractional part thereof, in excess of one thousand dollars, fifty cents	50
Entry of any goods, wares, or merchandise at any custom-house, either for consumption or warehousing, not exceeding one hundred dollars in value, twenty-five cents	25
Exceeding one hundred dollars, and not exceeding five hundred dollars in value, fifty cents	50
Exceeding five hundred dollars in value, one dollar	1 00

	Duty. Dolls. cts.	
Entry for the withdrawal of any goods or merchandise from bonded warehouse, fifty cents	50	Stamp duties.
Gaugers' returns, if for a quantity not exceeding five hundred gallons gross, ten cents	10	
Exceeding five hundred gallons gross, twenty-five cents	25	
Insurance, (Life.)—Policy of insurance, or other instrument, by whatever name the same shall be called, whereby any insurance shall be made upon any life or lives—		
When the amount insured shall not exceed one thousand dollars, twenty-five cents	25	
Exceeding one thousand dollars and not exceeding five thousand dollars, fifty cents	50	
Exceeding five thousand dollars, one dollar	1 00	
Insurance, (Marine, Inland, and Fire.)—Each policy of insurance or other instrument, by whatever name the same shall be called, by which insurance shall be made or renewed upon property of any description, whether against perils by the sea or by fire, or other peril of any kind, made by any insurance company, or its agents, or by any other company or person, the premium upon which does not exceed ten dollars, ten cents	10	
Exceeding ten and not exceeding fifty dollars, twenty-five cents	25	
Exceeding fifty dollars, fifty cents	50	
Lease, agreement, memorandum, or contract for the hire, use, or rent of any land, tenement, or portion thereof, where the rent or rental value is three hundred dollars per annum or less, fifty cents	50	*Post,* p. 32.
Where the rent or rental value exceeds the sum of three hundred dollars per annum, for each additional two hundred dollars, or fractional part thereof in excess of three hundred dollars, fifty cents	50	
Manifest for custom-house entry or clearance of the cargo of any ship, vessel, or steamer for a foreign port—		
If the registered tonnage of such ship, vessel, or steamer does not exceed three hundred tons, one dollar	1 00	
Exceeding three hundred tons, and not exceeding six hundred tons, three dollars	3 00	
Exceeding six hundred tons, five dollars	5 00	
Measurers' returns, if for a quantity not exceeding one thousand bushels, ten cents	10	
Exceeding one thousand bushels, twenty-five cents	25	
Mortgage of lands, estate, or property, real or personal, heritable or movable, whatsoever, where the same shall be made as security for the payment of any definite and certain sum of money lent at the time or previously due and owing or forborne to be paid, being payable; also any conveyance of any lands, estate, or property whatsoever, in trust, to be sold or otherwise converted into money, which shall be intended only as security, and shall be redeemable before the sale or other disposal thereof, either by express stipulation or otherwise; or any personal bond given as security for the payment of any definite or certain sum of money exceeding one hundred dollars, and not exceeding five hundred dollars, fifty cents	50	
Exceeding five hundred dollars, and not exceeding one thousand dollars, one dollar	1 00	
And for every additional five hundred dollars, or fractional part thereof, in excess of one thousand dollars, fifty cents	50	
Provided, That upon each and every assignment or transfer of a mortgage, lease, or policy of insurance, or the renewal or continuance of		*Post,* p. 32.

		Duty. Dolls. cts.
Stamp duties.	any agreement, contract, or charter, by letter or otherwise, a stamp duty shall be required and paid equal to that imposed on the original instrument.	
	Passage ticket, by any vessel from a port in the United States to a foreign port, not exceeding thirty-five dollars, fifty cents	50
	Exceeding thirty-five dollars and not exceeding fifty dollars, one dollar	1 00
	And for every additional fifty dollars, or fractional part thereof, in excess of fifty dollars, one dollar	1 00
	Power of attorney for the sale or transfer of any stock, bonds, or scrip, or for the collection of any dividends or interest thereon, twenty-five cents	25
	Power of attorney or proxy for voting at any election for officers of any incorporated company or society, except religious, charitable, or literary societies, or public cemeteries, ten cents	10
	Power of attorney to receive or collect rent, twenty-five cents	25
	Power of attorney to sell and convey real estate, or to rent or lease the same, one dollar	1 00
	Power of attorney for any other purpose, fifty cents	50
	Probate of will, or letters of administration: Where the estate and effects for or in respect of which such probate or letters of administration applied for shall be sworn or declared not to exceed the value of two thousand dollars, one dollar	1 00
	Exceeding two thousand dollars, for every additional thousand dollars, or fractional part thereof, in excess of two thousand dollars, fifty cents	50
	Protest.—Upon the protest of every note, bill of exchange, acceptance, check or draft, or any marine protest, whether protested by a notary public or by any other officer who may be authorized by the law of any state or states to make such protest, twenty-five cents	25
Post, p. 32.	Receipts for the payment of any sum of money, or for the payment of any debt due, exceeding twenty dollars, not being for the satisfaction of any mortgage or judgment or decree of any court, and a receipt for the delivery of any property, two cents	2
	Warehouse receipt for property, goods, wares, or merchandise, not otherwise provided for, in any public or private warehouse, when the property or goods so deposited or stored shall not exceed in value five hundred dollars, ten cents	10
	Exceeding in value five hundred dollars and not exceeding one thousand dollars, twenty cents	20
	Exceeding in value one thousand dollars, for every additional one thousand dollars, ten cents	10
	Warehouse receipt for any goods, merchandise, or property of any kind, not otherwise provided for, held on storage in any public or private warehouse or yard, twenty-five cents	25
	Weighers' returns, if for a weight not exceeding five thousand pounds, ten cents	10
	Exceeding five thousand pounds, twenty-five cents	25
	Legal Documents:	
	Writ, or other original process by which any suit is commenced in any court of record, either of law or equity, fifty cents	50
	Where the amount claimed in a writ, issued by a court not of record, is one hundred dollars or over, fifty cents	50
	Upon every confession of judgment, or cognovit, for one hundred dollars or over, (except in those cases where the tax for the writ of a commencement of suit has been paid,) fifty cents	50

	Duty. Dolls. cts.	
Writs or other process on appeals from justices' courts or other courts of inferior jurisdiction to a court of record, fifty cents	50	Stamp duties.
Warrant of distress, when the amount of rent claimed does not exceed one hundred dollars, twenty-five cents	25	
When the amount claimed exceeds one hundred dollars, fifty cents . .	50	

Provided, That no writ, summons, or other process issued by, and returnable to, a justice of the peace, except as hereinbefore provided, or by any police or municipal court having no larger jurisdiction as to the amount of damages it may render than a justice of the *piece* [peace] in the same state, or issued in any criminal or other suits commenced by the United States, or any state, shall be subject to the payment of stamp duties: *And provided, further,* That the stamp duties imposed by the foregoing schedule B on manifests, bills of lading, and passage-tickets, shall not apply to steamboats or other vessels plying between ports of the United States and ports in British North America.

Affidavits in suits or legal proceedings shall be exempt from stamp duty.

SCHEDULE C

Schedule C.

Medicines or Preparations.

Medicines or preparations.

For and upon every packet, box, bottle, pot, phial, or other enclosure, containing any pills, powders, tinctures, troches, lozenges, sirups, cordials, bitters, anodynes, tonics, plasters, liniments, salves, ointments, pastes, drops, waters, essences, spirits, oils, or other medicinal preparations or compositions whatsoever, made and sold, or removed for consumption and sale, by any person or persons whatever, wherein the person making or preparing the same has, or claims to have, any private formula or occult secret or art for the making or preparing the same, or has, or claims to have, any exclusive right or title to the making or preparing the same, or which are prepared, uttered, vended, or exposed for sale under any letters-patent, or held out or recommended to the public by the makers, venders, or proprietors thereof as proprietary medicines, or as remedies or specifics for any disease, diseases, or affections whatever affecting the human or animal body, as follows: where such packet, box, bottle, pot, phial, or other enclosure, with its contents, shall not exceed, at retail price, or value, the sum of twenty-five cents, one cent	1	
Where such packet, box, bottle, pot, phial, or other enclosure, with its contents, shall exceed the retail price or value of twenty-five cents, and not exceed the retail price or value of fifty cents, two cents .	2	
Where such packet, box, bottle, pot, phial, or other enclosure, with its contents, shall exceed the retail price or value of fifty cents, and shall not exceed the retail price or value of seventy-five cents, three cents	3	
Where such packet, box, bottle, pot, phial, or other enclosure, with its contents, shall exceed the retail price or value of seventy-five cents, and shall not exceed the retail price or value of one dollar, four cents .	4	
Where such packet, box, bottle, pot, phial, or other enclosure, with its contents, shall exceed the retail price or value of one dollar, for each and every fifty cents or fractional part thereof over and above the one dollar, as before mentioned, an additional two cents	2	

Perfumery, Cosmetics, Photographs, Matches, and Cards.

Perfumery, &c.

For and upon every packet, box, bottle, pot, phial, or other enclosure, containing any essence, extract, toilet water, cosmetic, hair oil,

Duty.
Dolls. cts.

Stamp duties.

pomade, hair-dressing, hair restorative, hair dye, tooth-wash, dentifrice, toothpaste, aromatic cachous, or any similar articles, by whatsoever name the same heretofore have been, now are, or may hereafter be called, known or distinguished, used or applied, or to be used or applied as perfumes or applications to the hair, mouth, or skin, made, prepared, and sold or removed for consumption and sale in the United States, where such packet, box, bottle, pot, phial, or other enclosure, with its contents, shall not exceed, at the retail price or value, the sum of twenty-five cents, one cent 1

Where such packet, box, bottle, pot, phial, or other enclosure, with its contents, shall exceed the retail price or value of twenty-five cents, and shall not exceed the retail price or value of fifty cents, two cents 2

Where such packet, box, bottle, pot, phial, or other enclosure, with its contents, shall exceed the retail price or value of fifty cents, and shall not exceed the retail price or value of seventy-five cents, three cents 3

Where such packet, box, bottle, pot, phial, or other enclosure, with its contents, shall exceed the retail price or value of seventy-five cents, and shall not exceed the retail price or value of one dollar, four cents . 4

Where such packet, box, bottle, pot, phial, or other enclosure, with its contents, shall exceed the retail price or value of one dollar, for each and every fifty cents or fractional part thereof over and above the one dollar, as before mentioned, an additional two cents 2

Friction matches, or lucifer matches, or other articles made in part of wood, and used for like purposes, in parcels or packages containing one hundred matches or less, for each parcel or package, one cent 1

When in parcels or packages containing more than one hundred and not more than two hundred matches, for each parcel or package, two cents 2

And for every additional one hundred matches or fractional part thereof, one cent 1

For all cigar-lights and wax tapers, double the rates herein upon friction or lucifer matches: *Provided,* That the stamp duties herein provided for on friction or lucifer matches made in part of wood, or cigar-lights or wax tapers, shall not be imposed until the first day of September, eighteen hundred and sixty-four; but until that time the tax shall be assessed and collected as heretofore, and on and after said first day of September, every package or parcel sold by any person, firm, company, or corporation, shall be stamped as herein required.

Photographs, ambrotypes, daguerreotypes, or any sun-pictures, except as hereinbefore provided, upon each and every picture of which the retail price shall not exceed twenty-five cents, two cents 2

Exceeding the retail price of twenty-five cents, and not exceeding the sum of fifty cents, three cents 3

Exceeding the retail price of fifty cents, and not exceeding one dollar, five cents 5

Exceeding the retail price of one dollar, for every additional dollar or fractional part thereof, five cents 5

Playing-cards.—For and upon every pack of whatever number, when the retail price per pack does not exceed eighteen cents, two cents .. 2

Post, p. 32.

Exceeding the retail price of eighteen cents, and not exceeding twenty-five cents per pack, four cents 4

Exceeding the retail price of twenty-five cents, and not exceeding fifty cents per pack, ten cents 10

Exceeding the retail price of fifty cents, and not exceeding one dollar per

	Duty. Dolls. cts.
pack, fifteen cents	15
Exceeding the retail price of one dollar, for every additional fifty cents, or fractional part thereof, in excess of one dollar, five cents	5

Approved, June 30, 1864.

Act of July 2, 1864

CHAP. CCIX.—*An Act to repeal the Act of the seventeenth of June, eighteen hundred and sixty-four, prohibiting the Sales of Gold and Foreign Exchange.*

Be it enacted by the Senate and House of Representatives of the United States of America, in Congress assembled, That the act entitled "An act to prohibit certain sales of gold and foreign exchange," approved June seventeen, eighteen hundred and sixty-four, be, and the same is hereby, repealed.

Repeal of act prohibiting certain sales of gold. 1864, ch. 127. *Ante,* p. 17.

Approved, July 2, 1864.

Act of March 3, 1865

CHAP. LXXVIII.—*An Act to amend an Act entitled "An Act to provide Internal Revenue to support the Government, to pay Interest on the Public Debt, and for other Purposes," approved June thirtieth, eighteen hundred and sixty-four.*

1864, ch. 173. *Ante,* p. 18.

Be it enacted by the Senate and House of Representatives of the United States of America in Congress assembled, That the act entitled "An act to provide internal revenue to support the government, to pay interest on the public debt, and for other purposes," approved June thirtieth, eighteen hundred and sixty-four, be, and the same is hereby, amended as hereinafter set forth, namely:—

Photographs.

. . .by inserting in the paragraph relating to photographs, after the words "being copies of engravings or works of art," the words "when the same are sold by the producer at wholesale at a price not exceeding ten cents each, or are;" . . .

Ante, p. 20.

Penalty for making, paying, &c., unstamped instruments, &c.

That section one hundred and fifty-eight be amended by striking out all after the enacting clause, and inserting in lieu thereof the following, to wit: "That any person or persons who shall make, sign, or issue, or who shall cause to be made, signed, or issued, any instrument, document, or paper of any kind or description whatsoever, or shall accept, negotiate, or pay, or cause to be accepted, negotiated, or paid, any bill of exchange, draft, or order, or promissory note, for the payment of money, without the same being duly stamped or having thereupon an adhesive stamp for denoting the duty chargeable thereon, with intent to evade the provisions of this act, shall for every such offence forfeit the sum of fifty dollars, and such instrument, document, or paper, bill, draft, order, or note shall be deemed invalid and of no effect: *Provided,* That the title of a purchaser of land, by deed duly stamped, shall not be defeated or affected by the want of a proper stamp on any deed conveying said land by any person from, through, or under whom his grantor claims or holds title: *And provided, further,* That hereafter, in all cases where the party has not affixed to any instrument [as] required by the one hundred and fifty-first section of the act of June thirtieth, eighteen hundred and sixty-four, or the schedule marked B thereunto annexed, *and* the stamp thereby required to be thereunto affixed, at the time of making or issuing the said instrument, and he or they or any party having an interest therein shall be subsequently desirous of affixing such stamp to said instrument, he or they shall appear before the collector of the revenue of the proper district, who shall, upon the payment of the price of the proper stamp required by law, and of a penalty of fifty dollars, and, where the whole amount of the duty denoted by the stamp required shall exceed the sum of fifty dollars, on payment also of interest at the rate of six per cent, on said duty from the day on which such stamp ought to have been affixed, affix the proper stamp to such instrument and note upon the margin of said instrument the date of his so doing, and the fact that such penalty has been paid, and such instrument shall thereupon be deemed and held to be as valid to all intents

Title to real estate.

When and how unstamped instruments may be stamped.

Ante, p. 19.

Penalty may be remitted when, &c.

and purposes as if stamped when made or issued: *And provided, further,* That where it shall appear to said collector, upon oath or otherwise, to his satisfaction that any such instrument has not been duly stamped at the time of making or issuing the same by reason of accident, mistake, inadvertence, or urgent necessity, and without any wilful design to defraud the United States of the stamp duty, or to evade or delay the payment thereof, then and in such case, if such instrument shall, within twelve calendar months after the making or issuing thereof, be brought to the said collector of revenue to be stamped and the stamp duty chargeable thereon shall be paid, it shall be lawful for the said collector to remit the penalty aforesaid and to cause such instrument to be duly stamped."

Stamp duty not required on, &c.

Ante, p. 21.

That section one hundred and sixty be amended by inserting before the word "injury" the word "accidental," and by striking out the words "while travelling;" also by striking out after the words "nor on certificates" the word "or," and inserting in lieu thereof the word "of;" and by striking out the words "other articles," and inserting in lieu thereof the word "hay."

That section one hundred and sixty-five be amended by striking out in the proviso the words "act contained," and inserting in lieu thereof the word "section."

Ante, p. 23.

That section one hundred and sixty-seven be amended by striking out the word "or" where it occurs the second time, and inserting after the word "sell" the words "expose for sale."

Matches, &c., not to be made in bonded warehouse.

That section one hundred and sixty-eight be amended by striking out the words "lucifer or friction matches and cigar-lights or wax tapers."

Ante, p. 24.

That section one hundred and sixty-nine be amended by inserting after the words "who shall offer," the words "or expose;" and by inserting after the words "so offered," the words "or exposed;" and by inserting in the proviso, after the words "imported articles," the words "except lucifer or friction matches, cigar-lights, and wax tapers."

Receipts of express companies.

Ante, p. 28.

Playing cards.

Ante, pp. 30-31.

Ante, p. 28.

That "Schedule B," preceding section one hundred and seventy-one, be amended in the paragraph marked "receipts," by inserting, after the word "property," the words "except receipts issued by any persons, firms, or companies doing business as an express or express company on the delivery of any property for transportation," and that "Schedule C," preceding section one hundred and seventy-one, be amended in all the paragraphs concerning "playing-cards" by striking out, wherever it occurs, the word "retail." Add at the end of the paragraph marked "receipts," the following: "*Provided,* That when two or more persons shall sign the same receipt, one or more stamps, equal in value to the several stamps required by this act, may be affixed to said receipt in lieu of said several stamps."

Assignment of lease.

That "Schedule B," preceding section one hundred and seventy-one, be further amended by striking out the word "lease" in the proviso in the clause taxing "mortgages," &c.; and also by adding to said proviso the following: "*And provided further,* That upon each and every asignment of any lease a stamp duty shall be required and paid equal to that imposed on the original instrument, increased by a stamp duty on the consideration or value of the assignment equal to that imposed upon the conveyance of land for similar consideration or value."

Ante, p. 24.

Matches, lights, and tapers.

Sec. 2. *And be it further enacted,* That from and after the passage of this act the proviso to section one hundred and sixty-nine of the act to which this act is an amendment shall not be held to apply to lucifer matches, friction matches, or other articles made in part of wood and used for like purposes, nor to cigar-lights and wax tapers.

When act takes effect.

Sec. 18. *And be it further enacted,* That this act shall be in force and effect on and after the first day of April, in the year eighteen hundred and sixty-five, unless otherwise provided by this act.

Approved, March 3, 1865.

Act of July 13, 1866

CHAP. CLXXXIV.—*An Act to reduce Internal Taxation and to amend an Act entitled "An Act to provide Internal Revenue to support the Government, to pay Interest on the Public Debt, and for other Purposes," approved June thirtieth, eighteen hundred and sixty-four, and Acts amendatory thereof.*

1864, ch. 173. *Ante,* p. 18. 1865, ch. 78. *Ante,* p. 31. 1867, ch. 169. *Post,* p. 38.

Sec. 9. . . .That section ninety-nine be amended by striking out all after the enacting clause, and inserting in lieu thereof the following: That there shall be paid on all sales made by brokers, banks or bankers, whether made for the benefit of others or on their own account, the following taxes, that is to say: Upon all sales and contracts for the sale of stocks, bonds, gold and silver bullion and coin, promissory notes or other securities, a tax at the rate of one cent for every hundred dollars of the amount of such sales or contracts; and on all sales and contracts for sale negotiated and made by any person, firm or company not paying a special tax as a broker, bank or banker, of any gold or silver bullion, coin, promissory notes, stocks, bonds, or other securities, not his or their own property, there shall be paid a tax at the rate of five cents for every hundred dollars of the amount of such sales or contracts; and on every sale and contract for sale, as aforesaid, there shall be made and delivered by the seller to the buyer a bill or memorandum of such sale or contract, on which there shall be affixed a lawful stamp or stamps in value equal to the amount of tax on such sale, to be determined by the rates of tax before mentioned; and in computing the amount of stamp tax in any case herein provided for; any fractional part of one hundred dollars of value or amount on which tax is computed shall be accounted at one hundred dollars. And every bill or memorandum of sale, or contract of sale, before mentioned, shall show the date thereof, the name of the seller, the amount of the sale or contract, and the matter or thing to which it refers. And any person or persons liable to pay the tax as herein provided, or any one who acts in the matter as agent or broker for such person or persons, who shall make any such sale or contract, or who shall, in pursuance of any sale or contract, deliver or receive any stocks, bonds, bullion, coin, promissory notes, or other securities, without a bill or memorandum thereof as herein required, or who shall deliver or receive such bill or memorandum without having the proper stamps affixed thereto, shall forfeit and pay to the United States a penalty of five hundred dollars for each and every offence where the tax so evaded, or attempted to be evaded, does not exceed one hundred dollars, and a penalty of one thousand dollars when such tax shall exceed one hundred dollars, which may be recovered with costs in any court of the United States of competent jurisdiction, at any time within one year after the liability to such penalty shall have been incurred; and the penalty recovered shall be awarded and distributed by the court between the United States and the informer, if there be any, as provided by law, who, in the judgment of the court, shall have first given the information of the violation of the law for which recovery is had: *Provided,* That where it shall appear that the omission to affix the proper stamp was not with intent to evade the provisions of this section, said penalty shall not be incurred. And the provisions of law in relation to stamp duties in schedule B of this act shall apply to the stamp taxes herein imposed upon sales and contracts of sales made by brokers, banks or bankers, and others as aforesaid. And there shall be paid monthly on all sales by commercial brokers of any goods, wares, or merchandise, a tax of one twentieth of one per centum upon the amount of such sales; and on or before the tenth day of each month, every commercial broker shall make a list or return to the assistant assessor of the district of the gross amount of such sales as aforesaid for the preceding month, in form and manner as may be prescribed by the commissioner of internal revenue: *Provided,* That in estimating sales of goods, wares, and merchandise for the purposes of this section, any sales made by or through another broker upon which a tax has been paid shall not be estimated and included as sold by the broker for whom the sale was made.

Section 99.
Sales and contracts for sale by brokers, banks, or bankers.
Rate of tax.
Rate for sales by those not paying a special tax.
Memorandum of sales, &c., to be given, and proper stamps placed thereon.
Fractional part of $100 to be accounted $100.
Memorandum to show what.
Penalty for selling, &c., or delivering, or receiving stocks, &c., without a memorandum;
for delivering or receiving memorandum without stamps;
how to be recovered.
Suit to be brought within one year.
Penalty recovered, how distributed.
Penalty not to be incurred where there was no intent to evade the law.
Law in relation to stamp duties to apply hereto.
Monthly tax on sales by commercial brokers.
Monthly returns to be made to assessor.
In estimating sales, those made by or through another broker not to be included.

Section 152.

No instrument, &c., required to be stamped, to be recorded unless stamped.

Record void.

That section one hundred and fifty-two be amended by striking out all after the enacting clause and inserting in lieu thereof the following: That it shall not be lawful to record any instrument, document, or paper required by law to be stamped, unless a stamp or stamps of the proper amount shall have been affixed, and cancelled in the manner required by law; and the record of any such instrument, upon which the proper stamp or stamps aforesaid shall not have been affixed and cancelled as aforesaid, shall be utterly void, and shall not be used in evidence.

Section 154.

Official instruments, &c., issued by officers of the United States, or of any State, county, town, &c. to be exempt from tax.

That section one hundred and fifty-four be amended by striking out all after the enacting clause and inserting in lieu thereof the following: That all official instruments, documents, and papers issued by the officers of the United States government, or by the officers of any State, county, town, or other municipal corporation, shall be, and hereby are, exempt from taxation: *Provided,* That it is the intent hereby to exempt from liability to taxation such State, county, town, or other municipal corporation, in the exercise only of functions strictly belonging to them in their ordinary governmental and municipal capacity.

Section 155.

Penalty for forging or counterfeiting any stamp, die, &c.

Penalty for forging any stamp upon any paper, &c., or stamping, &c., with intent to defraud;

for knowingly uttering or selling paper, &c., with forged stamp;

for knowingly using or permitting the use of forged stamp;

for fraudulently removing stamp, or impression of stamp, from paper, &c.;

for fraudulently using, &c., stamp, cut, &c., from any other paper required to be stamped;

for wilfully removing or altering the cancelling of a stamp, &c.;

for knowingly buying or selling, or having in possession washed, &c., stamps.

That section one hundred and fifty-five be amended by striking out all after the enacting clause and inserting in lieu thereof the following: That if any person shall forge or counterfeit, or cause or procure to be forged or counterfeited, any stamp, die, plate, or other instrument, or any part of any stamp, die, plate, or other instrument, which shall have be[en] provided, or may hereafter be provided, made, or used in pursuance of this act, or shall forge, counterfeit, or resemble, or cause or procure to be forged, counterfeited, or resembled, the impression, or any part of the impression, of any such stamp, die, plate, or other instrument, as aforesaid, upon any vellum, parchment, or paper, or shall stamp or mark, or cause or procure to be stamped or marked, any vellum, parchment, or paper, with any such forged or counterfeited stamp, die, plate, or other instrument, or part of any stamp, die, plate, or other instrument, as aforesaid, with intent to defraud the United States of any of the taxes hereby imposed, or any part thereof; or if any person shall utter, or sell, or expose to sale, any vellum, parchment, paper, article, or thing, having thereupon the impression of any such counterfeited stamp, die, plate, or other instrument, or any part of any stamp, die, plate, or other instrument, or any such forged, counterfeited, or resembled impression, or part of impression, as aforesaid, knowing the same to be forged, counterfeited, or resembled; or if any person shall knowingly use or permit the use of any stamp, die, plate, or other instrument, which shall have been so provided, made, or used, as aforesaid, with intent to defraud the United States; or if any person shall fraudulently cut, tear, or remove, or cause or procure to be cut, torn, or removed, the impression of any stamp, die, plate, or other instrument, which shall have been provided, made, or used, in pursuance of this act, from any vellum, parchment, or paper, or any instrument or writing charged or chargeable with any of the taxes imposed by law; or if any person shall fraudulently use, join, fix, or place, or cause to be used, joined, fixed, or placed, to, with, or upon any vellum, parchment, paper, or any instrument or writing charged or chargeable with any of the taxes hereby imposed, any adhesive stamp, or the impression of any stamp, die, plate, or other instrument, which shall have been provided, made, or used in pursuance of law, and which shall have been cut, torn, or removed from any other vellum, parchment, or paper, or any instrument or writing charged or chargeable with any of the taxes imposed by law; or if any person shall wilfully remove or cause to be removed, alter or cause to be altered, the cancelling or defacing marks on any adhesive stamp, with intent to use the same, or to cause the use of the same after it shall have been once used, or shall knowingly or wilfully sell or buy such washed or restored stamps, or offer the same for sale, or give or expose the same to any person for use, or knowingly use the same, or prepare the same with intent for the further use thereof; or if any person shall knowingly and without lawful excuse (the proof whereof shall lie on the person accused) have in his possession any washed, restored, or altered stamps, which have been removed from any vellum, parchment, paper, instrument, or writing, then, and in every such case, every person so offending, and every person knowingly and wilfully aiding, abetting, or assisting in committing any such offence as aforesaid, shall, on conviction thereof, forfeit the said counterfeit stamps and the articles upon which they are placed, and be punished by fine not exceeding one thousand dollars, or by imprisonment and confinement to hard labor not exceeding five years, or both, at the discretion of the court.

Forfeiture.

Fine or imprisonment, or both.

That section one hundred and fifty-eight be amended by striking out all after the enacting clause and inserting in lieu thereof the following: That any person or persons who shall make, sign, or issue, or who shall cause to be made, signed, or issued, any instrument, document, or paper of any kind or description whatsoever, or shall accept, negotiate, or pay, or cause to be accepted, negotiated, or paid, any bill of exchange, draft, or order, or promissory note for the payment of money, without the same being duly stamped, or having thereupon an adhesive stamp for denoting the tax chargeable thereon, and cancelled in the manner required by law, with intent to evade the provisions of this act, shall, for every such offence, forfeit the sum of fifty dollars, and such instrument, document, or paper, bill, draft, order, or note, not being stamped according to law, shall be deemed invalid and of no effect: *Provided,* That the title of a purchaser of land by deed duly stamped shall not be defeated or affected by the want of a proper stamp on any deed conveying said land by any person from, through, or under whom his grantor claims or holds title: *And provided further,* That hereafter, in all cases where the party has not affixed to any instrument the stamp required by law thereon, at the time of making or issuing the said instrument, and he or they, or any party having an interest therein, shall be subsequently desirous of affixing such stamp to said instrument, or if said instrument be lost, to a copy thereof, he or they shall appear before the collector of the revenue of the proper district, who shall, upon the payment of the price of the proper stamp required by law, and of a penalty of fifty dollars, and where the whole amount of the tax denoted by the stamp required shall exceed the sum of fifty dollars, on payment also of interest, at the rate of six per centum on said tax from the day on which such stamp ought to have been affixed, affix the proper stamp to such instrument or copy, and note upon the margin thereof the date of his so doing, and the fact that such penalty has been paid; and the same shall thereupon be deemed and held to be as valid, to all intents and purposes, as if stamped when made or issued: *And provided further,* That where it shall appear to said collector, upon oath or otherwise, to his satisfaction that any such instrument has not been duly stamped at the time of making or issuing the same, by reason of accident, mistake, inadvertence, or urgent necessity, and without any wilful design to defraud the United States of the stamp, or to evade or delay the payment thereof, then and in such case, if such instrument, or, if the original be lost, a copy thereof duly certified by the officer having charge of any records in which such original is required to be recorded, or otherwise duly proven to the satisfaction of the collector, shall, within twelve calendar months after the first day of August, eighteen hundred and sixty-six, or within twelve calendar months after the making or issuing thereof, be brought to the said collector of revenue to be stamped, and the stamp tax chargeable thereon shall be paid, it shall be lawful for the said collector to remit the penalty aforesaid, and to cause such instrument to be duly stamped. And when the original instrument, or a certified or duly proved copy thereof, as aforesaid, duly stamped so as to entitle the same to be recorded, shall be presented to the clerk, register, recorder, or other officer having charge of the original record, it shall be lawful for such officer, upon the payment of the fee legally chargeable for the recording thereof, to make a new record thereof, or to note upon the original record the fact that the error or omission in the stamping of said original instrument has been corrected pursuant to law; and the original instrument or such certified copy or the record thereof may be used in all courts and places in the same manner and with like effect as if the instrument had been originally stamped: *And provided further,* That in all cases where the party has not affixed the stamp required by law upon any instrument made, signed, or issued, at a time when and at a place where no collection district was established, it shall be

Section 158.

Person making, issuing, receiving, or paying, &c., any instrument, note, &c., required to be stamped, without having thereon a stamp cancelled, with intent to evade the law, to forfeit $50, and instrument, &c., to be void.

Title to land not affected, if, &c.

If stamp is not put on instrument when made, how it may be placed thereon afterward, or upon a copy, if original is lost.

Proceedings where instrument was not duly stamped by accident, &c.

May be recorded.

If instrument not having stamp was made when and where there was no collection district, stamp may be affixed before January 1, 1867.

lawful for him or them, or any party having an interest therein, to affix the proper stamp thereto, or if the original be lost, to a copy thereof; and the instrument or copy to which the proper stamp has been thus affixed prior to the first day of January, one thousand eight hundred and sixty-seven, and the record thereof, shall be as valid, to all intents and purposes, as if stamped by the collector in the manner hereinbefore provided. But no right acquired in good faith before the stamping of such instrument or copy thereof, and the recording thereof, as herein provided, if such record be required by law, shall in any manner be affected by such stamping as aforesaid.

Intervening bona fide rights not affected.

Section 163.

No deed, &c., required to be stamped, to be hereafter admitted in evidence, until proper stamps are affixed.

Documents made in a foreign country for use here, to pay same tax as though made here.

Who to affix stamp.

That section one hundred and sixty-three be amended by striking out all after the enacting clause and inserting in lieu thereof the following: That hereafter no deed, instrument, document, writing, or paper, required by law to be stamped, which has been signed or issued without being duly stamped, or with a deficient stamp, nor any copy thereof, shall be recorded, or admitted, or used as evidence in any court until a legal stamp or stamps, denoting the amount of tax, shall have been affixed thereto, as prescribed by law: *Provided,* That any power of attorney conveyance, or document of any kind, made or purporting to be made in any foreign country to be used in the United States, shall pay the same tax as is required by law on similar instruments or documents when made or issued in the United States; and the party to whom the same is issued, or by whom it is to be used, shall, before using the same, affix thereon the stamp or stamps indicating the tax required.

Section 165.

Penalty for making, selling, or removing for sale, &c., drugs, preparations, matches, &c., without affixing proper stamp.

That section one hundred and sixty-five be amended by striking out all after the enacting clause and inserting in lieu thereof the following: That if any person, firm, company, or corporation shall make, prepare, and sell, or remove for consumption or sale, drugs, medicines, preparations, compositions, articles, or things, including perfumery, cosmetics, lucifer or friction matches, cigar lights, or wax tapers, and playing cards, and also including prepared mustards, preserved meats, fish, shell-fish, fruits, vegetables, sauces, sirups, jams, and jellies, when packed or sealed in cans, bottles, or other single packages, whether of domestic manufacture or imported, upon which a duty or tax is imposed by law, as enumerated and mentioned in schedule C, without affixing thereto an adhesive stamp or label denoting the tax before mentioned, he or they shall incur a penalty of fifty dollars for every omission to affix such stamp.

Section 169.

Persons offering for sale any article named in schedule C, to be deemed the manufacturers.

Such articles, if imported, to pay stamp tax.

Proviso.

That section one hundred and sixty-nine be amended by striking out all after the enacting clause and inserting in lieu thereof the following: That any person who shall offer or expose for sale any of the articles named in schedule C, or in any amendments thereto, whether the articles so offered or exposed are imported or are of foreign or domestic manufacture, shall be deemed the manufacturer thereof, and subject to all the duties, liabilities, and penalties imposed by law in regard to the sale of domestic articles without the use of the proper stamp or stamps denoting the tax paid thereon, and all such articles imported, or of foreign manufacture, shall, in addition to the import duties imposed on the same, be subject to the stamp tax, respectively, prescribed in schedule C, as aforesaid: *Provided,* That when such imported articles, except playing cards, lucifer or friction matches, cigar lights, and wax tapers, shall be sold in the original and unbroken package in which the bottles or other enclosures were packed by the manufacturer, the person so sėlling said articles shall not be subject to any penalty on account of the want of the proper stamp.

Schedule B, amended.

Post, p. 38.

Receipts, stamp upon.

That schedule B, preceding section one hundred and seventy-one, be amended by striking out all after the paragraphs relating to "gauger's returns" and "measurer's returns;" and by striking out all from "receipts for the payment of any sum of money," down to "weigher's returns, if of weight not exceeding five thousand pounds, ten cents; exceeding five thousand pounds, twenty-five cents," inclusive, and inserting in lieu thereof the following: Receipts for any sum of money, or for the payment of any debt, exceeding twenty dollars in amount, not being for the satisfaction of any mortgage or judgment or decree of any court, or by indorsement on any stamped obligation in acknowledgment of its fulfilment, for each receipt two cents: *Provided,* That when more than one signature is affixed to the same paper, one or more stamps may be affixed thereto representing the whole amount of the stamp required for such signatures; and that the term money, as herein used, shall be held to include drafts and other instruments given for the payment of money.

Where there are several signatures to the same paper.

"Money" to include drafts.

That schedule B, preceding section one hundred and seventy-one, be amended by inserting, immediately preceding the proviso relating to stamps on mortgages, the following: Upon every assignment or transfer of a mortgage the same stamp tax upon the amount remaining unpaid thereon as is herein imposed upon a mortgage for the same amount. Also by striking out the words "mortgage or" in said proviso. Also by inserting the words "domestic and inland bills of lading and" after "than" and before "those" in the first line of said schedule.

Assignments and transfers of mortgages.

Domestic and inland bills of lading.

That schedule B be amended, under the head of contract, by striking out the words following: "Stocks, bonds," and "notes of hand." Also, by inserting under the head of contract, after the words "for each note or memorandum of sale, ten cents," the words following: Bill or memorandum of the sale or contract for the sale of stocks, bonds, gold or silver bullion, coin, promissory notes, or other securities, shall pay a stamp tax at the rate provided in section ninety-nine.

Bill or memorandum of sale or contract for sale of stocks, &c.

That schedule C be amended by striking out the paragraph in relation to photographs.

Schedule C amended.

Photographs.

That schedule C be further amended by striking out the paragraph relating to cigar lights and wax tapers, and inserting in lieu thereof the following: For wax tapers, double the rates herein imposed upon friction or lucifer matches; on cigar lights, made in part of wood, wax, glass, paper, or other materials, in parcels or packages containing twenty-five lights or less in each parcel or package, one cent; when in parcels or packages containing more than twenty-five and not more than fifty lights, two cents; for every additional twenty-five lights or fractional part of that number, one cent additional; and by striking out all after the words "playing cards," and inserting in lieu thereof the following:—

Cigar lights, wax tapers.

For and upon every pack, not exceeding fifty-two cards in number, irrespective of price or value, five cents;

Playing cards.

For and upon every can, bottle, or other single package, containing meats, fish, shell-fish, fruits, vegetables, sauces, sirups, prepared mustard, jams or jellies contained therein and packed or sealed, made, prepared, and sold, or offered for sale, or removed for consumption in the United States, on and after the first day of October, eighteen hundred and sixty-six, when such can, bottle, or single package, with its contents shall not exceed two pounds in weight, the sum of one cent ($0.01).

Preserved meats, fish, vegetables, &c.

When such can, bottle, or other single package, with its contents, shall exceed two pounds in weight, for every additional pound or fractional part thereof, one cent ($0.01).

Sec. 13. *And be it further enacted,* That no stamp tax shall be imposed upon any uncompounded medicinal drug or chemical, nor upon any medicine compounded according to the United States or other national pharmacopoeia, or of which the full and proper formula is published in any of the dispensatories now or hitherto in common use among physicians or apothecaries, or in any pharmaceutical journal now issued by any incorporated college of pharmacy, when not sold or offered for sale, or advertised under any other name, form, or guise than that under which they may be severally denominated and laid down in said pharmacopoeias, dispensatories, or journals as aforesaid; nor upon medicines sold to or for the use of any person, which may be mixed and compounded for said person according to the written receipt or prescription of any physician or surgeon. But nothing in this section shall be construed to exempt from stamp tax any medicinal articles, whether simple or compounded by any rule, authority, or formula, published or unpublished, which are put up in a style or manner similar to that of patent or proprietary medicines in general, or advertised in newspapers or by public handbills for popular

Stamp tax not to be imposed upon certain drugs, medicines, or chemicals.

No patent or proprietary medicine exempted from tax.

sale and use, as having any special proprietary claim to merit, or to any peculiar advantage in mode of preparation, quality, use, or effect, whether such claim be real or pretended.

General bonded warehouses for storage, &c., may be established.

Storekeepers and their pay.

Removal of articles manufactured in a bonded warehouse in the Atlantic States to a customs bonded warehouse on Pacific coast.

Ante, pp. 23-4.

Sec. 28. *And be it further enacted,* That general bonded warehouses, for the storage of spirits or other merchandise allowed by law to be placed in bond to secure the payment of the internal revenue tax thereon, or the exportation thereof, may be established under such rules and regulations and upon the execution of such bonds as the Secretary of the Treasury may prescribe, and shall be in the immediate custody of storekeepers who shall be appointed for that purpose, whose compensation shall be paid monthly to the collector of the district by the owners, or proprietors of such warehouse, and shall not exceed the rates which may be allowed to storekeepers of bonded warehouses established under the laws and regulations relating to customs: *Provided,* That any article manufactured in a bonded warehouse established under the one hundred and sixty-eighth section of the internal revenue act of June thirtieth, eighteen hundred and sixty-four, and located in any of the Atlantic States, may be removed therefrom for transportation to a customs bonded warehouse at any port on the Pacific coast of the United States, for the purpose only of being exported therefrom, under such rules and regulations and upon the execution of such bonds or other security as the Secretary of the Treasury may prescribe.

When this act shall take effect.
Repeal of inconsistent laws.

Sec. 70. *And be it further enacted,* That this act shall take effect, where not otherwise provided, on the first day of August, eighteen hundred and sixty-six, and all provisions of any former act inconsistent with the provisions of this act are hereby repealed.

Approved, July 13, 1866.

Act of March 2, 1867

CHAP. CLXIX.—*An Act to amend existing Laws relating to Internal Revenue, and for other Purposes.*

Additional penalty upon manufacturers for selling, &c., without a stamp articles required to be stamped.

Proceedings in such cases.

Sec. 5. *And be it further enacted,* That if the manufacturer of any article upon which a tax is required to be paid by means of a stamp shall have sold or removed for sale any such articles without the use of the proper stamp, in addition to the penalties now imposed by law for such sale or removal, it shall be the duty of the proper assessor or assistant assessor, within a period of not more than two years after such removal or sale, upon such information as he can obtain, to estimate the amount of the tax which has been omitted to be paid, and to make an assessment therefor, and certify the same to the collector; and the subsequent proceedings for collection shall be in all respects like those for the collection of taxes upon manufactures and productions.

Schedule B.
Legal documents.

Tax on manifests, not to apply, &c.

Affidavits exempt from stamp duty.
No stamp for probate of wills, &c., unless value of estate exceeds $1,000;

[Sec 9.] That schedule B, in relation to stamp duties, named in section one hundred and fifty-one, be amended by striking out of said schedule the words "legal documents," and all thereafter, and inserting in lieu thereof the following: "*Provided,* That the stamp duties imposed by the foregoing schedule (B) on manifests, bills of lading, and passage tickets, shall not apply to steamboats or vessels plying between ports of the United States and ports of British North America: *And provided further,* That all affidavits shall be exempt from stamp duty."

Also by inserting at the end of the last paragraph relating to "probate of will," the following words: "*Provided,* That no stamp either for probate of wills, or letters testamentary, or of administration, or on administrator or guardian bond, shall be required when the value of the estate and effects, real and personal, does not exceed one thousand dollars: *Provided further,* That no stamp tax shall be required upon any papers necessary to be used for the collection from the government of claims by soldiers or their legal representatives of the United States, for pensions, back pay, bounty, or for property lost in the service. The reduction of taxes provided in this section shall take effect on and after March one, eighteen hundred and sixty-seven."

none upon papers for collecting soldiers' claims on government for pay, pensions, &c.

When this takes effect.

Sec. 11. *And be it further enacted,* That on and after March first, eighteen hundred and sixty-seven, in addition to the articles now exempt by law, the articles and products hereinafter enumerated shall be exempt from internal tax, namely:—. . .

Additional articles and products exempt from internal tax.

Canned and preserved meats, and shell-fish; . . .

Canned and preserved vegetables and fruits; . . .

Approved, March 2, 1867.

Act of April 10, 1869

CHAP. XVIII.—*An Act to amend an Act entitled "An Act imposing Taxes on distilled Spirits and Tobacco, and for other Purposes," approved July twentieth, eighteen hundred and sixty-eight.*

Sec. 2. *And be it further enacted,* That section one hundred and fifty-five of the act entitled "An act to provide internal revenue to support the government, to pay interest on the public debt, and for other purposes," approved June thirtieth, eighteen hundred and sixty-four, as amended by the ninth section of the act of July thirteenth, eighteen hundred and sixty-six, be further amended by adding thereto the following: And the fact that any adhesive stamp so bought, sold, offered for sale, used, or had in possession as aforesaid, has been washed or restored by removing or altering the cancelling or defacing marks thereon, shall be prima facie proof that such stamp has been once used and removed by the possessor thereof from some vellum, parchment, paper, instrument, or writing, charged with taxes imposed by law, in violation of the provisions of this section.

The fact that a stamp sold, &c., has been washed, &c., to be prima facie proof that the possessor thereof has once used and removed it from, &c. 1864, ch. 173, *Ante,* pp. 19-20. 1866, ch. 184, *Ante,* pp. 34-5.

Approved, April 10, 1869.

Act of July 14, 1870

CHAP. CCLV.—*An Act to reduce internal Taxes, and for other Purposes.*

Sec. 4. *And be it further enacted,* That on and after the first day of October, eighteen hundred and seventy, the stamp tax imposed in schedule B on promissory notes for a less sum than one hundred dollars, and on receipts for any sum of money, or for the payment of any debt, and the stamp tax imposed in schedule C on canned and preserved fish, be, and the same are hereby, repealed. And no stamp shall be required upon the transfer or assignment of a mortgage, where it or the instrument it secures has been once duly stamped. And the proprietor or proprietors of articles named in said schedule C, who shall furnish his or their own die or design for stamps to be used especially for his or their own proprietary articles, shall be allowed the following commissions, namely: On amounts purchased at one time of not less than fifty dollars nor more than five hundred dollars, five per centum; and on amounts over five hundred dollars, ten per centum on the whole amount purchased: *Provided,* That lucifer or friction matches, and cigar lights, and wax tapers, may be removed from the place of manufacture for export to a foreign country without payment of tax, or affixing stamps thereto, under such rules and regulations as the commissioner of internal revenue may prescribe; and all provisions of existing laws inconsistent herewith are hereby repealed.

Certain stamp taxes to cease October 1, 1870 *Post,* p. 40.

Mortgages.

Commissions to certain proprietors of articles in schedule C.

Matches, cigar lights, and wax tapers may be removed from, &c., for export, without, &c.

Sec. 5. *And be it further enacted,* That section one hundred and fifty-eight of the act entitled "An act to provide internal revenue to support the government, to pay interest on the public debt, and for other purposes," approved June thirty, eighteen hundred and sixty-four, as amended by section nine of the internal revenue act, approved July thirteen, eighteen hundred and sixty-six, be, and is hereby, amended

Penalty for making, issuing, receiving, &c., any unstamped instrument

which the law requires to be stamped, modified.
1866, ch. 184, *Ante,* p. 35.

Time for affixing stamp omitted by accident, &c., extended.

by striking out the words "fifty dollars" in the second proviso, and inserting in lieu thereof the following: "double the amount of tax remaining unpaid, but in no case less than five dollars"; also, by striking out the words "sixty-six" in the third proviso, and inserting in lieu thereof the words "seventy-one"; also, by striking out the words "sixty-seven" in the last proviso, and inserting in lieu thereof the words "seventy-two."

Approved, July 14, 1870.

(Second) Act of July 14, 1870

CHAP. CCLIX.—*An Act to amend existing Laws relating to internal Revenue.*

Certain articles exempt from internal tax. *Ante,* p. 39.

Be it enacted by the Senate and House of Representatives of the United States of America in Congress assembled, That on and after the passage of this act, in addition to the articles now exempt by law, the articles and products hereinafter enumerated shall be exempt from internal tax, namely: Canned and preserved fish, shell-fish, meats, fruits, and vegetables.

Approved, July 14, 1870.

Act of March 5, 1872

CHAP. XXXIII.—*An Act to repeal the Paragraphs of Schedule C of the internal Revenue Acts imposing Taxes on canned Meats, Fish, and certain other Articles.*

Internal revenue tax on canned meats, &c., repealed. 1866, ch. 184, *Ante,* p. 37.

Be it enacted by the Senate and House of Representatives of the United States of America in Congress assembled, That from and after the passage of this act so much of Schedule C of the internal revenue acts as imposes a tax on any "can, bottle, or other single package containing meats, fish, shell-fish, fruits, vegetables, sauces, sirups, prepared mustard, jams, or jellies," be, and the same is hereby, repealed.

Approved, March 5, 1872.

Act of June 6, 1872

CHAP. CCCXV.—*An Act to reduce Duties on Imports, and to reduce Internal Taxes, and for other Purposes.*

Section 169.

Sec. 34. That section one hundred and sixty-nine of the act of June thirtieth, eighteen hundred and sixty-four, as amended by the act of July thirteenth, eighteen hundred and sixty-six, be amended by striking out the proviso at the end thereof.

All stamp taxes under schedule B of act 1864, ch. 178, sec. 170, &c., repealed, except on bank checks, &c. *Ante,* p. 25.

[Section 151 of ch. 173 of the acts of 1864 imposes the taxes by stamps upon the several things mentioned in under Schedule B.]

Certain mortgages.

Instruments without any stamp, or with deficient stamp.

Sec. 36. That on and after the first day of October, eighteen hundred and seventy-two, all the taxes imposed by stamps under and by virtue of Schedule B of section one hundred and seventy of the act approved June thirtieth, eighteen hundred and sixty-four, and the several acts amendatory thereof, be, and the same are hereby repealed, excepting only the tax of two cents on bank checks, drafts, or orders: *Provided,* That where any mortgage has been executed and recorded, or may be executed and recorded, before the first day of October, anno Domini eighteen hundred and seventy-two, to secure the payment of bonds or obligations that may be made and issued from time to time, and such mortgage not being stamped, all such bonds or obligations so made and issued on or after the said first day of October, anno Domini eighteen hundred and seventy-two, shall not be subject to any stamp duty, but only such of their bonds or obligations as may have been made and issued before the day last aforesaid: *And provided further,* That in the mean time the holder of any instrument of writing of whatever kind and description which has been made or issued without being duly stamped, or with a *defunct* [deficient] stamp, may make application to any collector of internal revenue, and that upon such application such collector shall thereupon affix the stamp provided by such holder upon such instrument of writing as [is] required by law to be put upon the same, and subject to the provisions of section one hundred and fifty-eight of the internal-revenue laws.

Sec. 41. That section one hundred and sixty-one of the act entitled "An act to provide internal-revenue to support the government, to pay interest on the public debt, and for other purposes," approved June thirtieth, eighteen hundred and sixty-four, be amended by striking out the words "this act," occurring after the words "stamps issued under the provisions of," and inserting in lieu thereof the words "any internal-revenue act."

Allowance for spoiled, &c., revenue stamps.

1864, ch. 173, sec. 161. *Ante*, p. 22.

Approved, June 6, 1872.

Revised Statutes of the United States. . .in force on the first day of December, one thousand eight hundred and Seventy-three. . .

TITLE XXXV.
INTERNAL REVENUE

[Ed. note: These Revised Statutes merely re-state material from preceding acts, but are included here because they are referred to specifically by subsequent acts.]

Ch. 9. STAMP-TAXES ON SPECIFIC OBJECTS.

Sec. 3418. There shall be levied, collected, and paid for and in respect of every bank-check, draft, or order for the payment of money, drawn upon any bank, banker, or trust company, at sight or on demand, by any person who makes, signs, or issues the same, or for whose use or benefit the same is made, signed, or issued, two cents.

Tax on bank-checks.

30 June, 1864, c. 173, ss. 151, 170, pp. 19, 25.

6 June, 1872, c. 315, s. 36, p. 40.

Sec. 3419. There shall be levied, collected, and paid on the articles mentioned in Schedule A, and in the manner hereinafter provided, the taxes mentioned in said schedule; and all the provisions of this chapter relating to dies, stamps, adhesive stamps, and stamped duties, shall extend to and include (except where otherwise provided for, or manifestly impracticable) all the articles or objects enumerated in

Tax on medicines or preparations, perfumery, cosmetics, &c.

30 June, 1864, c. 173, s. 164, p. 22.

schedule marked A, subject to stamp duties, and shall apply to the provisions in relation thereto.

Official checks exempt.

30 June, 1864, c. 173, s. 154, p. 19.
13 July, 1866, c. 184, s. 9, p. 34.

Sec. 3420. All bank-checks, drafts, or orders, as aforesaid, issued by the officers of the United States Government, or by officers of any State, county, town, or other municipal corporation, are exempt from taxation: *Provided,* That it is the intent hereby to exempt from liability to taxation such State, county, town, or other municipal corporations in the exercise only of functions strictly belonging to them in their ordinary governmental and municipal capacity.

Unstamped checks not admitted in evidence.

30 June, 1864, c. 173, s. 163, p. 22.
13 July, 1866, c. 184, s. 9, p. 36.

Sec. 3421. No bank-check, draft, or order, required by law to be stamped, which is issued without being duly stamped, nor any copy thereof, shall be admitted or used in evidence in any court until a legal stamp, denoting the amount of tax, is affixed thereto, as prescribed by law. And it shall not be lawful to record any instrument, document, or paper required by law at the time of its issue to be stamped, unless a stamp or stamps of the proper amount shall have been affixed, and canceled in the manner required by law; and the record of any such instrument, upon which the proper stamp or stamps aforesaid shall not have been duly affixed and canceled, shall be utterly void and shall not be used in evidence.

Omission to stamp bank-checks, &c.; penalties and remedies.

30 June, 1864, c. 173, s. 158, p. 20.
13 July, 1866, c. 184, s. 9, p. 35
14 July, 1870, c. 255, s. 5, pp. 39-40

Sec. 3422. Any person or persons who shall make, sign, or issue, or who shall cause to be made, signed, or issued, any instrument, document, or paper of any kind or description whatsoever, or shall accept, negotiate, or pay, or cause to be accepted, negotiated, or paid, any draft, or order, for the payment of money, without the same being duly stamped, or having thereupon an adhesive stamp for denoting the tax chargeable thereon, and canceled in the manner required by law, with intent to evade the provisions of this Title, shall, for every such offense, forfeit the sum of fifty dollars, and such instrument, document, or paper, draft, order, not being stamped according to law, shall be deemed invalid and of no effect: *Provided,* That hereafter, in all cases where the party has not affixed to any instrument the stamp required by law thereon, at the time of making or issuing the said instrument, and he or they, or any party having an interest therein, shall be subsequently desirous of affixing such stamp to said instrument, or if said instrument be lost, to a copy thereof, he or they shall appear before the collector of the revenue of the proper district, who shall, upon the payment of the price of the proper stamp required by law, and of a penalty of double the amount of tax remaining unpaid, but in no case less than five dollars, and where the whole amount of the tax denoted by the stamp required shall exceed the sum of fifty dollars, on payment also of interest, at the rate of six per centum on said tax from the day on which such stamp ought to have been affixed, affix the proper stamp to such instrument or copy, and note upon the margin thereof the date of his so doing, and the fact that such penalty has been paid; and the same shall thereupon be deemed and held to be as valid, to all intents and purposes, as if stamped when made or issued. And when the original instrument, or a certified or duly proved copy thereof, as aforesaid, duly stamped so as to entitle the same to be recorded, shall be presented to the clerk, register, recorder, or other officer having charge of the original record, it shall be lawful for such officer, upon the payment of the fee legally chargeable for the recording thereof, to make a new record thereof, or to note upon the original record the fact that the error or omission in the stamping of said original instrument, has been corrected pursuant to law; and the original instrument, or such certified copy of the record thereof may be used in all courts and places in the same manner and with like effect as if the instrument had been originally stamped. But no right acquired in good faith before the stamping of such instrument or copy thereof, and the recording thereof, as herein provided, if such record be required by law, shall in any manner be affected by such stamping as aforesaid.

Stamps to be canceled; proprietary stamps; penalty for their fraudulent use.

Sec. 3423. In all cases where an adhesive stamp is used for denoting any tax imposed under this chapter, except as hereinafter provided, the person using or affixing the same shall write thereon the initials of his name and the date on which such stamp is attached or used, so that it may not again be used. And every person who fraudulently makes use of an adhesive stamp to denote any tax imposed by this chapter without so effectually canceling and obliterating such stamp, except as before mentioned, shall forfeit the sum of fifty dollars: *Provided,* That any proprietor of proprietary articles, or articles subject to stamp-tax under Schedule A, shall have the privilege of furnishing, without expense to the United States, in suitable form, to be approved by the Commissioner of Internal Revenue, his own dies or designs for stamps to be used thereon, which shall be made under the direction and retained in the possession of the said Commissioner, for the separate use of such proprietor, and shall not be duplicated to any other person; and that in all cases where such stamp is used, instead of said proprietor writing the date thereon, the said stamp shall be so affixed on the box, bottle, or package, that in opening the same, or using the contents thereof, the said stamp will be effectually destroyed; and, in default thereof, such proprietor shall be liable to a penalty of fifty dollars. And every person who fraudulently obtains or uses any of the aforesaid stamps, or designs therefor, or who forges or counterfeits, or causes or procures to be forged or counterfeited, any representation or similitude, or colorable imitation of the said last-mentioned stamp, or any engraver or printer who sells or gives away said stamps, or selling the same, or, being a merchant, broker, peddler, or person dealing, in whole or in part, in similar goods, wares, merchandise, manufactures, preparations, or articles, or those designed for similar objects or purposes, has knowingly or fraudulently in his possession any such forged, counterfeited likeness, similitude, or colorable imitation of the said last-mentioned stamp, shall forfeit the said stamps and the articles upon which they are placed, shall be deemed guilty of felony, and be punished by a fine not exceeding one thousand dollars, or by imprisonment and confinement to hard labor not exceeding five years, or both, at the discretion of the court.

30 June, 1864, c. 173, ss. 155, 156, pp. 19-20.

Sec. 3424. The Commissioner of Internal Revenue is authorized to prescribe such method for the cancellation of stamps as substitute for, or in addition to the method prescribed in this chapter, as he may deem expedient and effectual. And he is authorized, in his discretion, to make the application of such method imperative upon the manufacturers of proprietary articles, or articles included in Schedule A.

Method of cancellation.

30 June, 1864, c. 173, s. 157, p. 20.

Sec. 3425. The Commissioner of Internal Revenue is authorized to sell and supply to collectors, deputy-collectors, postmasters, stationers, or any other persons, at his discretion, adhesive stamps, or stamped paper, as herein provided for, in amounts of not less than fifty dollars, upon the payment, at the time of delivery, of the amount of duties said stamps or stamped paper, so sold or supplied, represent, and may allow, upon the aggregate amount of such stamps, the sum of not exceeding five per centum as commission to such purchasers; but the cost of any paper shall be paid by the purchaser of such stamped paper. The proprietor of articles named in Schedule A, who furnishes his own die or design for stamps to be used especially for his own proprietary articles, shall be allowed the following commissions: On amounts purchased at one time of not less than fifty dollars nor more than five hundred dollars, five per centum; and on amounts over five hundred dollars, ten per centum on the whole amount purchased: *Provided,* That the Commissioner may, from time to time, deliver to any manufacturer of friction or other matches, cigar-lights, or wax-tapers, a suitable quantity of adhesive or other stamps, such as may be prescribed for use in such cases, without prepayment therefor, on a credit not exceeding sixty days, requiring, in advance, such security as he may judge necessary to secure payment therefor to the Treasurer of the United States, within the time prescribed for such payment. And upon all bonds or other securities taken by said Commissioner, under the provisions of this chapter, suits may be maintained by said Treasurer in the circuit or district court of the United States, in the several districts where any of the persons giving said bonds or other securities reside or may be found, in any appropriate form of action.

Stamps, how supplied.

30 June, 1864, c. 173, s. 161, pp. 21-22.
14 July, 1870, c. 255, s. 4, p. 39.

Sec. 3426. The Commissioner of Internal Revenue may, from time to time, make regulations, upon proper evidence of the facts, for the allowance of such of the stamps issued under the provisions of this chapter, or any internal revenue act, as may have been spoiled, destroyed, or rendered useless or unfit for the purpose intended, or for which the owner may have no use, or which through mistake may

Replacement of spoiled stamps, &c.

30 June, 1864, c. 173, s. 161, p. 21.

have been improperly or unnecessarily used, or where the rates or duties represented thereby have been paid in error, or remitted; and such allowance shall be made either by giving other stamps in lieu of the stamps so allowed for, or by repaying the amount or value, after deducting therefrom, in case of repayment, the sum of five per centum to the owner thereof; but no allowance shall be made in any case until the stamps so spoiled or rendered useless shall have been returned to the Commissioner of Internal Revenue, or until satisfactory proof has been made showing the reason why said stamps cannot be so returned.

Stamps furnished to certain officers for sale.

30 June, 1864, c. 173, s. 170, p. 24.

Sec. 3427. In any collection-district where, in the judgment of the Commissioner of Internal Revenue, the facilities for the procurement and distribution of stamped paper and adhesive stamps, as provided in this chapter, are insufficient, the Commissioner is authorized to supply to collectors, assistant treasurers of the United States, designated depositaries, and postmasters, without prepayment therefor, suitable quantities of stamped paper, as aforesaid, and of adhesive stamps, as required by this chapter; and he may in advance require of any such person a bond, with sufficient sureties, in an amount equal to the value of any such stamped paper or stamps which may be placed in his hands and remain unaccounted for, conditioned for the faithful return of all quantities or amounts undisposed of, and for the payment, monthly, of all quantities or amounts sold or not remaining on hand. And he shall allow to such persons the highest rates of commissions allowed to any other parties purchasing such stamped paper or stamps. It shall be the duty of such collector to supply his deputies with, or to sell to other parties within his district who may apply therefor, such stamped paper and adhesive stamps, upon the same terms allowed by law, or under the regulations of the said Commissioner.

Regulations as to disposal and safe-keeping of stamps.

30 June, 1864, c. 173, s. 170, p. 24.

Sec. 3428. The Commissioner of Internal Revenue is authorized to make such regulations, not inconsistent herewith, for the security of the United States and the better accommodation of the public, in relation to the matters provided in the preceding section, as he may deem necessary and expedient. And the Secretary of the Treasury may, from time to time, make such regulations as he may find necessary to insure the safe-keeping or to prevent the illegal use of all such stamped paper and adhesive stamps.

Forging, counterfeiting, &c., or fraudulently using or selling stamps, &c.

30 June, 1864, c. 173, s. 155, pp. 19-20.
13 July, 1866, c. 184, s. 9, pp. 34-35.
10 April, 1869, c. 18, s. 2, p. 39.

Sec. 3429. If any person shall forge or counterfeit, or cause or procure to be forged or counterfeited, any stamp, die, plate, or other instrument, or any part of any stamp, die, plate, or other instrument, which shall have been provided, or may hereafter be provided, made, or used in pursuance of the provisions of this chapter, or of any previous provisions of law on the same subjects, or shall forge, counterfeit, or resemble, or cause or procure to be forged, counterfeited, or resembled, the impression, or any part of the impression, of any such stamp, die, plate, or other instrument as aforesaid, upon any paper, or shall stamp or mark, or cause or procure to be stamped or marked, any paper, with any such forged or counterfeited stamp, die, plate, or other instrument, or part of any stamp, die, plate or other instrument, as aforesaid, with intent to defraud the United States of any of the taxes hereby imposed, or any part thereof; or if any person shall utter, or sell, or expose to sale, any paper, article, or thing, having thereupon the impression of any such counterfeited stamp, die, plate, or other instrument, or any such forged, counterfeited, or resembled impression, or part of impression, as aforesaid, knowing the same to be forged, counterfeited, or resembled; or if any person shall knowingly use or permit the use of any stamp, die, plate, or other instrument which shall have been so provided, made, or used, as aforesaid, with intent to defraud the United States; or if any person shall fraudulently cut, tear, or remove, or cause or procure to be cut, torn, or removed, the impression of any stamp, die, plate, or other instrument, which shall have been provided, made, or used, in pursuance of this chapter, or of any previous provisions of law on the same subjects, from any paper, or any instrument or writing charged or chargeable with any of the taxes imposed by law; or if any person shall fraudulently use, join, fix or place, or cause to be used, joined, fixed, or placed to, with, or upon any paper, or any instrument or writing charged or chargeable with any of the taxes hereby imposed, any adhesive stamp, or the impression of any stamp, die, plate, or other instrument, which shall have been provided, made, or used in pursuance of law, and which shall have been cut, torn, or removed from any other paper, or any instrument or writing charged or chargeable with any of the taxes imposed by law; or if any person shall willfully remove or cause to be removed, alter or cause to be altered, the canceling or defacing marks on any adhesive stamp, with intent to use the same, or to cause the use of the same, after it shall have been once used, or shall knowingly or willfully sell or buy such washed or restored stamps, or offer the same for sale, or give or expose the same to any person for use, or knowingly use the same, or prepare the same with intent for the further use thereof; or if any person shall knowingly and without lawful excuse (the proof whereof shall lie on the person accused) have in his possession any washed, restored, or altered stamps, which have been removed from any paper, instrument, or writing, then, and in every such case, every person so offending, and every person knowingly and willfully aiding, abetting, or assisting in committing any such offense as aforesaid, shall, on conviction thereof, forfeit the said counterfeit stamps and the articles upon which they are placed, and be punished by fine not exceeding one thousand dollars, or by imprisonment and confinement to hard labor not exceeding five years, or both, at the discretion of the court. And the fact that any adhesive stamp so bought, sold, offered for sale, used, or had in possession as aforesaid, has been washed or restored by removing or altering the canceling or defacing marks thereon, shall be prima-facie proof that such stamp has been once used and removed by the possessor thereof from some paper, instrument, or writing, charged with taxes imposed by law, in violation of the provisions of this section.

Selling or removing articles for sale without affixing stamps; penalty.

30 June, 1864, c. 173, s. 165, pp. 22-23.
13 July, 1866, c. 184, s. 9, p. 36.
14 July, 1870, c. 255, s. 4, p. 39.

[5 March, 1872, c. 33, p. 40.]

Sec. 3430. Whenever any person makes, prepares, and sells, or removes for consumption or sale, drugs, medicines, preparations, compositions, articles, or things, including perfumery, cosmetics, lucifer or friction-matches, cigar-lights, wax-tapers, and playing cards, whether of domestic manufacture or imported, upon which a tax is imposed by law, as enumerated and mentioned in Schedule A, without affixing thereto an adhesive stamp or label denoting the tax before mentioned, he shall incur a penalty of fifty dollars for every omission to affix such stamp: *Provided,* That lucifer or friction matches and cigar-lights and wax-tapers may be removed from the place of manufacture for export to a foreign country, without payment of tax or affixing stamps thereto, under such regulations as the Commissioner of Internal Revenue may prescribe.

Removing stamps from articles in schedule; penalty.

30 June, 1864, c. 173, s. 166, p. 23.

Sec. 3431. Every manufacturer or maker of any of the articles for sale mentioned in Schedule A, who, after the same are so made, and the particulars hereinbefore required as to stamps have been complied with, takes off, removes, or detaches, or causes, or permits, or suffers to be taken off, or removed, or detached, any stamp, or who uses any stamp, or any wrapper or cover to which any stamp is affixed, to cover any other article or commodity than that originally contained in such wrapper or cover, with such stamp when first used, with the intent to evade the stamp-duties, shall, for every such article, respectively, in respect of which any such offense is committed, be subject to a penalty of fifty dollars, to be recovered together with the costs thereupon accruing; and every such article or commodity aforesaid shall also be forfeited.

Selling articles in Schedule A without affixing stamp; penalty.

30 June, 1864, c. 173, s. 167, p. 23.
3 March, 1865, c. 78, s. 1, p. 32.

Sec. 3432. Every maker or manufacturer of any of the articles or commodities mentioned in Schedule A, who, to evade the duty chargeable thereon, or any part thereof, sells, exposes for sale, sends out, removes, or delivers any article or commodity, manufactured as aforesaid, before the duty thereon has been fully paid, by affixing thereon the proper stamp, as provided by law, or who to evade as aforesaid hides or conceals, or causes to be hidden or concealed, or removes or conveys away, or deposits, or causes to be removed or conveyed away from or deposited in any place, any such article or commodity, shall be subject to a penalty of one hundred dollars, together with the forfeiture of any such article or commodity.

Articles in schedule, intended for exportation, to be manufactured in bonded warehouses.

30 June, 1864, c. 173, s. 168, pp. 23-24.
3 March, 1865, c. 78, s. 1, p. 32.

Sec. 3433. All medicines, preparations, compositions, perfumery, cosmetics, cordials, and other liquors manufactured wholly or in part of domestic spirits, intended for exportation, as provided by law, in order to be manufactured and sold or removed, without being charged with duty, and without having a stamp affixed thereto, shall, under such regulations as the Secretary of the Treasury may prescribe, be made and manufactured in warehouses similarly constructed to those known and designated in Treasury regulations as bonded warehouses, class two: *Provided,* That such manufacturer shall first give satisfactory bonds to the collector of internal revenue for the faithful observance of all the provisions of law and the regulations as aforesaid, in amount not less than half of that required by the regulations of the Secretary of the Treasury from persons allowed bonded warehouses. Such goods, when manufactured in such warehouses, may be removed for exportation, under the direction of the proper officer having charge thereof, who shall be designated by the Secretary of the Treasury, without being charged with duty, and without having a stamp affixed thereto. Any manufacturer of the articles aforesaid, or of any of them, having such bonded warehouse as aforesaid, shall be at liberty, under such regulations as the Secretary of the Treasury may prescribe, to convey therein any materials to be used in such manufacture which are allowed by the provisions of law to be exported free from tax or duty, as well as the necessary materials, implements, packages, vessels, brands, and labels for the preparation, putting up, and export of the said manufactured articles; and every article so used shall be exempt from the payment of stamp and excise duty by such manufacturer. Articles and materials so to be used may be transferred from any bonded warehouse in which the same may be, under such regulations as the Secretary of the Treasury may prescribe, into any bonded warehouse in which such manufacture may be conducted, and may be used in such manufacture, and when so used shall be exempt from stamp and excise duty; and the receipt of the officer in charge, as aforesaid, shall be received as a voucher for the manufacture of said articles. Any materials imported into the United States may, under such rules as the Secretary of the Treasury may prescribe, and under the direction of the proper officer, be removed in original packages from on shipboard, or from the bonded warehouse in which the same may be, into the bonded warehouse in which such manufacture may be carried on, for the purpose of being used in such manufacture, without payment of duties thereon, and may there be used in such manufacture. No article so removed, nor any article manufactured in said bonded warehouse, shall be taken therefrom except for exportation, under the direction of the proper officer having charge thereof, as aforesaid, whose certificate, describing the articles by their marks, or otherwise, the quantity, the date of importation, and name of vessel, with such additional particulars as may from time to time be required, shall be received by the collector of customs in cancellation of the bonds, or return of the amount of foreign import duties. All labor performed and services rendered under these regulations shall be under the supervision of an officer of the customs, and at the expense of the manufacturer.

Removal in bond to Pacific coast for exportation.

13 July, 1866, c. 184, s. 28, p. 38.

Sec. 3434. Any article manufactured in a bonded warehouse established under the preceding section, and situated in any of the Atlantic States, may be removed therefrom for transportation to a customs bonded warehouse at any port on the Pacific coast of the United States, for the purpose only of being exported therefrom, under such regulations and upon the execution of such bonds or other security as the Secretary of the Treasury may prescribe.

Persons offering for sale articles in schedule deemed manufacturers.

30 June, 1864, c. 173, s. 169, p. 24.
13 July, 1866, c. 184, s. 9, p. 36.
6 June, 1872, c. 315, s. 34, p. xxx.

Sec. 3435. Every person who offers or exposes for sale any of the articles named in Schedule A, whether the articles so offered or exposed are of foreign manufacture and imported or are of domestic manufacture, shall be deemed the manufacturer thereof, and subject to all the duties, liabilities, and penalties imposed by law in regard to the sale of domestic articles without the use of the proper stamps denoting the tax paid thereon, and all such articles of foreign manufacture shall, in addition to the import duties imposed on the same, be subject to the stamp-tax, respectively, prescribed in said schedule.

Sec. 3436. No stamp-tax shall be imposed upon any uncompounded medicinal drug or chemical, nor upon any medicine compounded according to the United States or other national pharmacopoeia, or of which the full and proper formula is published in any of the dispensatories now or hitherto in common use among physicians or apothecaries, or in any pharmaceutical journal now issued by any incorporated college of pharmacy, when not sold or offered for sale, or advertised under any other name, form, or guise than that under which they may be severally denominated and laid down in said pharmacopoeias, dispensatories, or journals as aforesaid; nor upon medicines sold to or for the use of any person, which may be mixed and compounded for said person according to the written receipt or prescription of any physician or surgeon. But nothing in this section shall be construed to exempt from stamp-tax any medicinal articles, whether simple or compounded by any rule, authority, or formula, published or unpublished, which are put up in a style or manner similar to that of patent or proprietary medicines in general, or advertised in newspapers or by public handbills for popular sale and use, as having any special proprietary claim to merit, or to any peculiar advantage in mode of preparation, quality, use, or effect, whether such claim be real or pretended.

Medicines compounded according to pharmacopoeias exempt.

13 July, 1866, c. 184, s. 13, pp. 37-38.

Sec. 3437. Whenever any article upon which a tax is required to be paid by means of a stamp is sold or removed for sale by the manufacturer thereof, without the use of the proper stamp, in addition to the penalties imposed by law for such sale or removal, it shall be the duty of the Commissioner of Internal Revenue, within a period of not more than two years after such removal or sale, upon such information as he can obtain, to estimate the amount of the tax which has been omitted to be paid, and to make an assessment therefor upon the manufacturer or producer of such article. He shall certify such assessment to the collector, who shall immediately demand payment of such tax, and, upon the neglect or refusal of payment by such manufacturer or producer, shall proceed to collect the same in the manner provided for the collection of other assessed taxes.

Assessment of unpaid taxes payable by stamps.

2 March, 1867, c. 169, s. 5, p. 38.

24 Dec. 1872, c. 13 [not included in this volume].

SCHEDULE A.

Schedule A.

Medicines or Preparations.

Medicines or preparations.

For and upon every packet, box, bottle, pot, phial, or other inclosure, containing any pills, powders, tinctures, troches, lozenges, sirups, cordials, bitters, anodynes, tonics, plasters, liniments, salves, ointments, pastes, drops, waters, essences, spirits, oils, or other medicinal preparations or compositions whatsoever, made and sold, or removed for consumption and sale, by any person or persons whatever, wherein the person making or preparing the same has or claims to have any private formula, or occult secret, or art for the making or preparing the same, or has or claims to have any exclusive right or title to the making or preparing the same, or which are prepared, uttered, vended, or exposed for sale under any letters patent, or held out or recommended to the public by the makers, venders, or proprietors thereof as proprietary medicines, or as remedies or specifics for any disease, diseases, or affections whatever affecting the human or animal body, as follows:

30 June, 1864, c. 173, s. 170, pp. 29-31.

13 July, 1866, c. 184, s. 9, p. 37.

[5 March, 1872, c. 33, p. 40.]

Where such packet, box, bottle, pot, phial, or other inclosure, with its contents, shall not exceed, at retail price or value, the sum of twenty-five cents, one cent.

Where such packet, box, bottle, pot, phial, or other inclosure, with its contents, shall exceed the retail price or value of twenty-five cents, and not exceed the retail price or value of fifty cents, two cents.

Where such packet, box, bottle, pot, phial, or other inclosure, with its contents, shall exceed the retail price or value of fifty cents, and shall not exceed the retail price or value of seventy-five cents, three cents.

Where such packet, box, bottle, pot, phial, or other inclosure, with its contents, shall exceed the retail price or value of seventy-five cents, and shall not exceed the retail price or value of one dollar, four cents.

Where such packet, box, bottle, pot, phial, or other inclosure, with its contents, shall exceed the retail price or value of one dollar, for each and every fifty cents or fractional part thereof over and above the one dollar, as before mentioned, an additional two cents.

Perfumery, cosmetics, &c.

Perfumery and Cosmetics, etc.

For and upon every packet, box, bottle, pot, phial, or other inclosure, containing any essence, extract, toilet-water, cosmetic, hair-oil, pomade, hair-dressing, hair-restorative, hair-dye, tooth-wash, dentifrice, toothpaste, aromatic cachous, or any similar articles, by whatsoever name the same heretofore have been, now are, or may hereafter be called, known or distinguished, used or applied, or to be used or applied as perfumes or applications to the hair, mouth, or skin, made, prepared, and sold or removed for consumption and sale in the United States, where such packet, box, bottle, pot, phial, or other inclosure, with its contents, shall not exceed, at the retail price or value, the sum of twenty-five cents, one cent.

Where such packet, box, bottle, pot, phial, or other inclosure, with its contents, shall exceed the retail price or value of twenty-five cents, and shall not exceed the retail price or value of fifty cents, two cents.

Where such packet, box, bottle, pot, phial, or other inclosure, with its contents, shall exceed the retail price or value of fifty cents, and shall not exceed the retail price or value of seventy-five cents, three cents.

Where such packet, box, bottle, pot, phial, or other inclosure, with its contents, shall exceed the retail price or value of seventy-five cents, and shall not exceed the retail price or value of one dollar, four cents.

Where such packet, box, bottle, pot, phial, or oher inclosure, with its contents, shall exceed the retail price or value of one dollar, for each and every fifty cents or fractional part thereof over and above the one dollar, as before mentioned, an additional two cents.

Friction-matches, or lucifer-matches, or other articles made in part of wood, and used for like purposes, in parcels or packages containing one hundred matches or less, for each parcel or package, one cent.

When in parcels or packages containing more than one hundred and not more than two hundred matches, for each parcel or package, two cents.

And for every additional one hundred matches or fractional part thereof, one cent.

For wax-tapers, double the rates herein imposed upon friction or lucifer-matches; on cigar-lights, made in part of wood, wax, glass, paper, or other materials, in parcels or packages containing twenty-five lights or less in each parcel or package, one cent.

When in parcels or packages containing more than twenty-five and not more than fifty lights, two cents.

For every additional twenty-five lights or fractional part of that number, one cent additional.

Playing-cards.

Playing-Cards.

For and upon every pack not exceeding fifty-two cards in number, irrespective of price or value, five cents.

[Ed. note: Enacted June 22, 1874 and published February, 1875.]

Act of June 23, 1874

CHAP. 462.—An act to provide for the stamping of unstamped instruments, documents or papers.

Stamps may be affixed to unstamped instruments, &c., when.

Be it enacted by the Senate and House of Representatives of the United States of America in Congress assembled, That all instruments, documents, and papers heretofore made, signed or issued, and subject to a stamp-duty or tax under any law heretofore existing and remaining unstamped, may be stamped by any person having an interest therein, or, where the original is lost, a copy thereof, at any time prior to the first of January, eighteen hundred and seventy-six. And said instruments, documents, and papers and any record thereof, shall be as valid, to all intents and purposes as if stamped when made, signed or issued, but no right acquired in good faith shall in any manner be affected by such stamping as aforesaid. *Provided,* That to render such stamping valid, the person desiring to stamp the same shall appear with the instrument, document, or paper, or copy thereof, before some judge or clerk of a court of record, and before him affix the proper stamp; and the said judge or clerk shall indorse on such writing or copy a certificate, under his hand, when made by said judge, and under his hand and seal, when made by said clerk, setting forth the date at which, and the place where, the stamp was so affixed, the name of the person presenting said writing or copy, the fact that it was thus affixed, and that the stamp was duly cancelled in his presence.

Validity of instruments.

Stamps, how to be affixed.

Certificate of judge or clerk.

Sec. 2. That all laws or parts of laws in conflict with the above, are hereby repealed.

Repealing clause.

Approved, June 23, 1874.

Act of February 8, 1875

CHAP. 36.—An act to amend existing customs and internal-revenue laws, and for other purposes.

Sec. 14. That the existing provisions of law for the redemption of, or allowance for, internal-revenue documentary stamps, the use of which has been rendered unnecessary by the repeal of the taxes for the payment of which such stamps were provided, shall apply only to such of said stamps as shall be presented to the Commissioner of Internal Revenue for allowance or redemption before the first day of October, eighteen hundred and seventy-five; and no allowance, redemption, or refunding on account of such of the aforesaid stamps as shall not be so presented to the said Commissioner prior to the date last mentioned shall be thereafter made.

Allowance for unused stamps for repealed taxes.

Post, p. 50.

Bank-check, draft, &c.

1864, c. 173, *Ante,* p. 25.
R.S., 3418, *Ante,* p. 41.

Sec. 15. That the words "bank-check, draft, or order for the payment of any sum of money whatsoever, drawn upon any bank, banker, or trust-company, at sight or on demand, two cents," in Schedule B of the act of June thirtieth, eighteen hundred and sixty-four, be, and the same is hereby, stricken out, and the following paragraph inserted in lieu thereof:

"Bank-check, draft, order, or voucher for the payment of any sum of money whatsoever, drawn upon any bank, banker, or trust-company, two cents."

Sec. 22. That hereafter nothing contained in the internal revenue laws shall be construed so as to authorize the imposition of any stamp tax upon any medicinal articles prepared by any manufacturing chemist, pharmaceutist, or druggist, in accordance with a formula published in any standard dispensatory or pharmacopoeia in common use by physicians and apothecaries, or in any pharmaceutical journal issued by any incorporated college of pharmacy, when such formula and where found shall be distinctly referred to on the printed label attached to such article, and no proprietary interest therein is claimed. Neither shall any stamp be required when the formula of any medicinal preparation shall be printed on the label attached to such article where no proprietorship in such preparation shall be claimed.

Exemption of medicines prepared according to dispensatory, &c.

Approved, February 8, 1875.

Act of February 18, 1875

CHAP. 80.—An act to correct errors and to supply omissions in the Revised Statutes of the United States.

Amendment of Revised Statutes.

Be it enacted by the Senate and House of Representatives of the United States of America in Congress assembled, That for the purpose of correcting errors and supplying omissions in the act entitled "An act to revise and consolidate the statutes of the United States in force on the first day of December, anno Domini one thousand eight hundred and seventy-three," so as to make the same truly express such laws, the following amendments are hereby made therein:

R. S., 3422, *Ante*, p. 42.

Section three thousand four hundred and twenty-two is amended by inserting, after the word "issued," in the twenty-seventh line, the following: "*And provided further,* That where it shall appear to said collector, upon oath or otherwise, to his satisfaction, that any such instrument has not been duly stamped at the time of making or issuing the same, by reason of accident, mistake, inadvertence, or urgent necessity, and without any willful design to defraud the United States of the stamps, or to evade or delay the payment thereof, then, and in such case, if such instrument, or, if the original be lost, a copy thereof, duly certified by the officer having charge of any records in which such original is required to be recorded, or otherwise duly proven to the satisfaction of the collector, shall, within twelve calendar months after the making or issuing thereof, be brought to the said collector of revenue to be stamped, and the stamp tax chargeable thereon shall be paid, it shall be lawful for the said collector to remit the penalty aforesaid, and to cause such instrument to be duly stamped."

Approved, February 18, 1875.

Act of March 3, 1875

CHAP. 127.—An act to further protect the sinking-fund and provide for the exigencies of the Government.

No stamp on receipt in receipt-book of savings-bank. 1875, c. 36, *Ante*, p. 49.

Sec. 6. That nothing contained in the act entitled "An act to amend existing customs and internal-revenue laws, and for other purposes," approved February eighth, eighteen hundred and seventy-five, shall be construed to impose any duty on bolting-cloths theretofore admitted free of duty; nor to require the use of a stamp upon the receipt in the receipt-book of a savings-bank or institution for savings having no capital stock, and doing no other business than receiving deposits to be loaned or invested for the sole benefit of the parties making such deposits without profit or compensation to the association or company, when money is paid to a depositor on his pass-book.

Approved, March 3, 1875.

Act of February 25, 1876

CHAP. 13.—An act to extend the time for stamping unstamped instruments.

1874, ch. 462. *Ante*, p. 48.

Time for stamping unstamped instruments extended.

Be it enacted by the Senate and House of Representatives of the United States of America in Congress assembled, That the provisions of the act entitled "An act to provide for the stamping of unstamped instruments, documents, or papers," approved the twenty-third day of June, in the year eighteen hundred and seventy-four, be, and the same are hereby, extended to the first day of January, in the year eighteen hundred and seventy-seven.

Approved, February 25, 1876.

Act of July 12, 1876

CHAP. 181.—An act relative to the redemption of unused stamps.

1875, ch. 36, sec. 14, repealed. *Ante*, p. 49.

Be it enacted by the Senate and House of Representatives of the United States of America in Congress assembled, That the fourteenth section of the act passed February eighth, eighteen hundred and seventy-five, entitled "An act to amend existing customs and internal-revenue laws, and for other purposes," be, and the same is hereby, repealed; and all unused stamps shall be redeemed when properly presented, as was done prior to the passage of the aforesaid act: *Provided,* That from and after the passage of this act no allowance shall be made for documentary stamps, except those of the denomination of two cents, which when presented to the Commissioner of Internal Revenue are not found to be in the same condition as when issued by the Internal Revenue Department, or, if so required by the said Commissioner, when the person presenting the same can not satisfactorily trace the history thereof from their issue to their presentation as aforesaid. Redemption of unused stamps. Allowance for documentary stamps.

Approved, July 12, 1876.

Act of March 1, 1879

CHAP. 125.—An act to amend the laws relating to internal revenue.

STAMPS.

Sec. 17. That the Revised Statutes be amended as follows, namely: R. S. 3426, Amended.

That section thirty-four hundred and twenty-six be amended by striking out all after the said number, and substituting therefor the following:

"The Commissioner of Internal Revenue may, upon receipt of satisfactory evidence of the facts, make allowance for or redeem such of the stamps issued under the provisions of this title, or of any internal-revenue act, as may have been spoiled, destroyed, or rendered useless or unfit for the purpose intended, or for which the owner may have no use, or which, through mistake, may have been improperly or unnecessarily used, or where the rates or duties represented thereby have been excessive in amount, paid in error, or in any manner wrongfully collected; and such allowance or redemption shall be made either by giving other stamps in lieu of the stamps so allowed for or redeemed, or by refunding the amount or value to the owner thereof, deducting therefrom, in case of repayment, the percentage, if any, allowed to the purchaser thereof; but no allowance or redemption shall be made in any case until the stamps so spoiled or rendered useless shall have been returned to the Commissioner of Internal Revenue, or until satisfactory proof has been made showing the reason why the same cannot be so returned: *Provided,* That nothing herein shall be held as authorizing redemption of, or allowance for, any of the stamps allowance for which is prohibited by the provisions of 'An act relative to the redemption of unused stamps', approved July twelfth, eighteen hundred and seventy-six." Redemption of spoiled stamps. *Proviso.* 1876, ch. 181, *Ante,* pp. 50-51.

"That claims for allowance on account of stamps arising under section thirty-four hundred and twenty-six of the Revised Statutes as restricted by an act relative to the redemption of unused stamps, approved July twelfth, eighteen hundred and seventy-six, may be allowed, if presented within three years after the purchase of said stamps from the government, or a government agent for the sale of stamps, and not otherwise: *Provided,* That no existing claim for the redemption of or allowance for any internal-revenue stamps other than the two-cent documentary stamps shall be allowed, unless presented within one year from the date of the passage of this act: *Provided further,* That from and after June thirtieth, eighteen hundred and seventy-nine, no allowance shall be made, in any manner, for documentary stamps other than those of the denomination of two cents." R. S. 3426. 1876, ch. 181, *Ante,* pp. 50-51. *Proviso.* *Proviso.*

That section thirty-four hundred and twenty-nine be amended by striking out all after the said number, and substituting therefor the following: R. S. 3429, Amended.

"If any person shall forge or counterfeit, or cause or procure to be forged or counterfeited, any stamp, die, plate, or other instrument, or any part of any stamp, die, plate, or other instrument, which shall have been provided, or may hereafter be provided, made, or used in pursuance of the provisions of this chapter, or of any previous provisions of law on the same subjects, or shall forge, counterfeit, or resemble, the impression, or any part of the impression, of any such stamp, die, plate, or other instrument as aforesaid, upon any paper, or shall stamp or mark, or cause or procure to be stamped or marked, any paper, with any such forged or Counterfeiting, etc. Stamps, etc.

counterfeited stamp, die, plate, or other instrument, or part of any stamp, die, plate, or other instrument, as aforesaid, with intent to defraud the United States of any of Selling, etc. the taxes hereby imposed, or any part thereof; or if any person shall utter, or sell, or expose to sale, any paper, article, or thing, having thereupon the impression of any such counterfeited stamp, die, plate, or other instrument, or any part of any stamp, die, plate, or other instrument, or any such forged, counterfeited or resembled impression, or part of impression, as aforesaid, knowing the same to be forged, Using, etc. counterfeited, or resembled; or if any person shall knowingly use or permit the use of any stamp, die, plate, or other instrument which shall have been so provided, made, or used, as aforesaid, with intent to defraud the United States; or if any person shall Mutilating, etc. fraudulently cut, tear, or remove, or cause or procure to be cut, torn, or removed, the impression of any stamp, die, plate, or other instrument, which shall have been provided, made, or used in pursuance of this chapter, or of any previous provisions of law on the same subjects, from any paper, or any instrument or writing charged or chargeable with any of the taxes imposed by law; or if any person shall fraudulently use, join, fix, or place, or cause to be used, joined, fixed, or placed, to, with, or upon any paper, or any instrument or writing charged or chargeable with any of the taxes hereby imposed, any adhesive stamp, or the impression of any stamp, die, plate, or other instrument, which shall have been provided, made, or used in pursuance of law, and which shall have been cut, torn, or removed from any other paper, or any instrument or writing charged or chargeable with any of the taxes Washing, etc. imposed by law; or if any person shall willfully remove or cause to be removed, alter or cause to be altered, the canceling or defacing marks on any adhesive stamp, with intent to use the same, or to cause the use of the same, after it shall have been once used, or shall knowingly or willfully sell or buy such washed or restored stamps, or offer the same for sale, or give or expose the same to any person for use, or knowingly use the same, or prepare the same with intent for the further use thereof; or if any person shall knowingly and without lawful excuse (the proof whereof shall lie on the person accused) have in his possession any washed, restored, or altered stamps, which have been removed from any article, paper, instrument, or writing, Penalty. then, and in every such case, every person so offending, and every person knowingly and willfully aiding, abetting, or assisting in committing any such offense as aforesaid, shall, on conviction thereof, forfeit the said counterfeit, washed, restored, or altered stamps, and the articles upon which they are placed, and be punished by fine not exceeding one thousand dollars, or by imprisonment and confinement to hard labor not exceeding five years, or both, at the discretion of the Evidence of washing, etc. court. And the fact that any adhesive stamp so bought, sold, offered for sale, used, or had in possession as aforesaid, has been washed or restored by removing or altering the canceling or defacing marks thereon, shall be prima-facie proof that such stamp has been once used and removed by the possessor thereof from some paper, instrument, or writing, charged with taxes imposed by law, in violation of the provisions of this section."

R. S. 3441, Amended. That section thirty-four hundred and forty-one be amended by striking out all after the said number, and substituting therefor the following:

Export drawback. "There shall be an allowance of drawback on fermented liquors and on all articles mentioned in Schedule A, on which any internal tax shall have been paid, except lucifer or friction matches, cigar-lights, and wax-tapers, equal in amount to the tax Payment. paid thereon, and no more, when exported, to be paid by the warrant of the Secretary of the Treasury on the Treasurer of the United States, out of any money arising from *Proviso.* internal duties not otherwise appropriated: *Provided,* That no allowance of drawback shall be made for any such articles exported prior to March thirty-first, eighteen Evidence. hundred and sixty-eight. The evidence that any such tax has been paid as aforesaid shall be furnished to the satisfaction of the Commissioner of Internal Revenue by the person claiming the allowance of drawback, and the amount shall be ascertained under such regulations as shall be prescribed from time to time by the Commissioner, under the direction of the Secretary of the Treasury. And the said Secretary may make such regulations with regard to the form of certificates of drawback, and the issuing thereof, as he may deem necessary."

Sec. 18. That section thirty-four hundred and forty-six of the Revised Statutes of the United States be, and the same is hereby, amended so as to read as follows: R. S. 3446, Amended.

"Sec. 3446. The Commissioner of Internal Revenue, with the approval of the Secretary of the Treasury, may establish and, from time to time, alter or change the form, style, character, material, and device of any stamp, mark, or label used under any provision of the laws relating to internal revenue. Such stamps shall be attached, protected, removed, canceled, obliterated, and destroyed, in such manner and by such instruments or other means as he, with the approval of the Secretary of the Treasury, may prescribe; and he is hereby authorized and empowered to make, with the approval of the Secretary of the Treasury, all needful regulations relating thereto; and all pains, penalties, fines, and forfeitures now provided by law relating to internal-revenue stamps shall apply to and have full force and effect in relation to any and all stamps which may or shall be so established by the Commissioner of Internal Revenue": *Provided,* Such stamps or device or instrument or means of removal or obliteration, shall entail no additional expense upon the persons required to affix or use the same. Change of stamps. Canceling, etc. Penalties, etc., applied to new stamps. *Proviso.*

Sec. 19. That the proviso to section thirty-four hundred and thirty of the Revised Statutes is hereby amended to read as follows: R. S. 3430, Amended.

"*Provided,* That lucifer or friction matches, and cigar-lights, and wax-tapers, and all articles upon which a tax is imposed by law, as enumerated and mentioned in Schedule A following section thirty-four hundred and thirty-seven of the Revised Statutes, may be removed from the place of manufacture for export to a foreign country, without payment of tax, or affixing stamps thereto, under such regulations as the Commissioner of Internal Revenue may prescribe." Export of matches, etc.

Sec. 20. That under such regulations and requirements as to stamps, bonds, and other security as shall be prescribed by the Commissioner of Internal Revenue, any manufacturer of perfumery, medicines, or preparations for export, manufacturing the same in a duly constituted manufacturing warehouse, shall be authorized to withdraw, in original packages from any distillery-warehouse, so much alcohol as he may required for the said purpose, without the payment of the internal-revenue tax thereon. Alcohol for perfumery, etc., for export.

Approved, March 1, 1879.

Act of March 3, 1883

CHAP. 121.—An act to reduce internal-revenue taxation, and for other purposes.

Be it enacted by the Senate and House of Representatives of the United States of America in Congress assembled, That the taxes herein specified imposed by the laws now in force be, and the same are hereby, repealed, as hereinafter provided, namely: On capital and deposits of banks, bankers, and national banking associations, except such taxes as are now due and payable; and on and after the first day of July, eighteen hundred and eighty-three, the stamp tax on bank checks, drafts, orders, and vouchers, and the tax on matches, perfumery, medicinal preparations, and other articles imposed by Schedule A following section thirty-four hundred and thirty-seven of the Revised Statutes: *Provided,* That no drawback shall be allowed upon articles embraced in said schedule that shall be exported on and after the first day of July, eighteen hundred and eighty-three: *Provided further,* That on and after May fifteenth, eighteen hundred and eighty-three, matches may be removed by manufacturers thereof from the place of manufacture to warehouses within the United States without attaching thereto the stamps required by law, under such regulations as may be prescribed by the Commissioner of Internal Revenue. Internal-revenue taxes repealed, on: Banks, etc. Stamp tax on bank checks, etc., matches, medicinal preparations, etc., Schedule A, R. S., *Ante,* pp. 47-48. *Proviso.* *Proviso.*

Approved, March 3, 1883.

SECTION II.

Decisions, Rulings, Correspondence, and other pronouncements pertaining to documentary and proprietary stamp taxes.

AGREEMENT

If the indorsement upon a writ required in an action brought by a citizen of another State is under seal, it is a bond, and will require a twenty-five cent revenue stamp.

If not under seal, it is liable to stamp duty as an agreement.

Boutwell (1863), Rulings (No. 238)

The tax of five cents per sheet on "agreements" applies to agreements, appraisements, &c., and not to deeds and mortgages.

Boutwell (1863), Rulings (No. 257)

Executory agreements, for purchase of real estate, should be stamped as "agreements."

Boutwell (1863), Rulings (No. 258)

An appraisement of property made by freeholders selected by the sheriff of a county, in accordance with the law providing for the sale of real estate, under executions issued by a court, as well as appraisements of personal property taken in actions of replevin, are in each case subject to a stamp duty of five cents for each sheet.

Boutwell (1863), Rulings (No. 288)

If the duplicate copy of a contract is required as evidence, it must be stamped as well as the original.

Boutwell (1863), Rulings (No. 299)

If a subscription list for the payment of a clergyman's salary, or for the building of a church, or for any benevolent purpose, is in the form of an agreement, it is subject to a stamp duty of five cents per sheet.

If it be in the form of a promissory note, it is subject to stamp duty under the head of "inland bills of exchange."

Any agreement of trustees or others with regard to the disposition of the funds raised on such subscription is subject to a further stamp duty of five cents.

Boutwell (1863), Rulings (No. 307)

Sir: I have received your letter, together with a copy of a letter from the Quartermaster General, and of a charter-party, and of a contract. It is stated that the army regulations, approved June 2, 1862, require all contracts with the government to be made in quintuplicate.

Upon this state of facts the question arises whether each part of the contract is subject to stamp duty under the provisions of Schedule B, of the act of July 1, 1862.

It has been held by this office, in the case of papers which are usually prepared in several parts, but which would be valid under the law if executed in one part only, that the parties interested might exercise a discretion, and affix a stamp to each part when several were made, or to one part only. It has been a custom, however, to inform parties that the enforcement of their legal rights must depend entirely upon the stamped instrument.

The case presented differs from those which have been considered heretofore by the Commissioner of Internal Revenue, in the circumstance that the regulations of the War Department, which have, as I suppose, the force of law, require each contract to be executed in five parts. It may reasonably be assumed that it is the purpose of the regulation to make each part of full legal value. It therefore follows that the proper stamps should be affixed to each part of every contract.

To Wm. Whiting, Esq.,
Solicitor of the War Department,
Washington, D.C.

Boutwell (1863), Correspondence (No. 9)

The assignment of a government land-warrant requires a five-cent stamp as an agreement.

Boutwell (1865), Rulings (No. 200)

Where commutation tickets are issued by a railroad company, and the persons receiving them indorse their names on the back, binding themselves to fulfill certain conditions, such instruments require stamp as contracts.

Boutwell (1865), Rulings (No. 253)

A pew-deed is merely a conveyance of personal property, and is subject to a stamp-duty of five cents as an agreement.

Boutwell (1865), Rulings (No. 269)

It is a principle of the English stamp-law that instruments are to be stamped according to their legal effect, and I have always adhered to the same principle in expounding our own stamp-act. If a written contract operates as a conveyance, it must therefore be stamped as such; if as an agreement before the conveyance of land, an agreement stamp only is necessary when another instrument is required in order to carry the agreement into effect.

Boutwell (1865), Rulings (from No. 275)

Under the construction given to the statute by the courts of Massachusetts, a sale of standing wood is not a sale of an interest in real estate, and such bill of sale would therefore be subject to a stamp-duty of five cents, as an agreement or contract, being a transfer of personal property.

Boutwell (1865), Rulings (No. 280)

Where a party executes a note to a bank for a sum of money, and assigns a warehouse receipt for property in store, as collateral security for the payment of the money when it shall become due, both the note and the assignment of the warehouse receipt are subject to stamp-duty—the latter as an agreement.

Boutwell (1865), Rulings (No. 291)

Stamp on New Certificate of Stock on Transfer thereof.

Washington, June 29, 1865.

Sir: Your letter of the 26th inst., in relation to stamp duty required on certificates of stock, transfers of the same, &c., and inclosing forms for my consideration, is received.

In reply, I have to say that the certificate of stock required a stamp duty of twenty-five cents, and the power of attorney on the back of the certificate is chargeable with the same amount, twenty-five cents, as specially provided by Schedule B. The transfer is subject to a stamp duty of five cents as an agreement or contract.

Sometimes this transfer is made on the back of the certificate, and when that is the case, and it is duly stamped, the record of the transfer made in the books of the company does not require to be stamped. But if the actual transfer is made—as in the present case—in the transfer book of the company, and no such instrument is executed on the back of the certificate, then the instrument in the transfer book becomes more than a record of transfer; it is a regular transfer of stock, and as such, is chargeable with a stamp duty of five cents as an agreement or contract, as above stated.

Very respectfully,
E. A. Rollins,
Dep. Commissioner.

IRR v.II, July 8, 1865, p.5

Check and Contract Stamp on Subscription List.

In the case of a subscription list where the heading involves a promise to pay the sums annexed, the party signing is liable to the stamp-duty required on promissory notes *unless* he pay the amount annexed his name at the time of signature; in which case the signing of his name should be regarded as a mere part of a memorandum. Where the heading of the list involves a condition on which the subscribers will pay the sums annexed their names, then each signature is held to create an agreement subject to a duty of five cents.

IRR v.II, July 22, 1865, p.21

Assignment of Judgment.

The assignment or transfer of a judgment should be stamped as an agreement or contract.

IRR v.II, August 12, 1865, p.44

Pawners' checks or tickets given for pledged articles should be stamped with a five cent stamp, instead of a two cent stamp as has recently been the practice. Pawnbrokers will be required by the Department to make good the amount of tax for which they have fallen in arrears by the non-use of proper stamps.

IRR v.II, October 7, 1865, p.105

Stamping of Pawners' Checks.

Treasury Department,
Washington, Sept. 26, 1865.

Sir: I reply to your letter of the 23d inst., that Pawners' checks such as are enclosed by you, are subject to a stamp duty of five cents each when duly signed and issued.

Very respectfully,
(Signed) E. A. Rollins,
Acting Commissioner.

Horace Dresser, Esq., *Revenue Inspector, New York City.*

The following is the form of Pawners' checks upon which the above ruling was made:

E. Koon, 384 Seventh Avenue.

186 Dlls. Cts.

Not accountable for loss, damage, fire, robbery, moth or broken.
Loans at twenty-five per cent.

IRR v.II, October 7, 1865, p.108

Stamping of Domestic Bills of Lading as Receipts and Agreements.

Office of Internal Revenue,
Washington, Jan. 24, 1866.

Sir: The letter of Mr. Henry Lincoln, addressed to you, and by you referred to me, has been received. Mr. Lincoln asks if domestic bills of lading are subject to stamp duty, and if so, how much: also if each and every bill of lading should bear a stamp?

He encloses a copy of a ruling from this Office, by which inland and domestic bills of lading are held subject to stamp duties as receipts or agreements, according to their form, and says, "as we understand the law, bills of lading of vessels for ports of the United States or British North America are exempt." [Ed note: No other record of this ruling has been found.]

An examination of Schedule B, following Section 170 of the Act of June 30, 1864, will show that a stamp duty is specifically imposed upon one class of bills of lading only, viz: upon bills of lading for any goods, merchandise, or effects to be exported from a port or place of the United States to any foreign port or place. To this even, there is an exception. In the last part of said schedule, it is provided that the stamp duties therein imposed upon bills of lading, "shall not apply to steamboats, or other vessels, plying between ports in the United States and ports in British North America."

The Act of Congress then, imposes a stamp duty of ten cents upon each foreign bill of lading, except those for goods, &c., transported upon steamboats, or other vessels, plying between the ports of the United States and ports in British North America—but it is silent respecting inland and domestic bills of lading, *as such*.

A stamp duty of two cents, however, is imposed upon each receipt for the delivery of property; a duty of five cents is imposed upon each sheet or piece of paper upon which an agreement or contract is written.

It is admitted by Mr. Lincoln that all bills of lading contain an agreement or contract. Domestic and inland bills of lading, being neither otherwise charged, nor expressly exempted from all stamp duty, fall under the general provisions of the law, and are to be taxed not "as bills of lading," with ten cents each, but with two cents or five cents, according to whether they are receipts simply or agreements.

If they are executed in sets of two or three or more, each one should be stamped. Each has the same legal effect as the other, and the holder of either of them *may* find it necessary to use his copy in evidence.

I see no good reason for making any change in the ruling in question.

Very respectfully,
(Signed) E. A. Rollins,
Commissioner.

Hon. A. H. Rice,
House of Representatives,
Washington, D.C.

IRR v.III, February 3, 1866, pp.36-7

Stamping of Insurance Receipts.

Assessor's Office, 10th Dist., Indiana,
Goshen, April 26th, 1866.

Hon. E. A. Rollins, Com. of Internal Revenue:

Sir: Ought the enclosed receipt or memorandum to be stamped as a receipt or a contract?

Respectfully yours,
(Signed,) Geo. D. Copland
Assessor.

(Receipt.)

Received of ____ ____, an application for Insurance by the Protection Insurance Company, of Goshen, Ind., on property to the amount of $____, for the term of ____ years; also, a Note or Notes for the payment of Premium as represented on the back of this Receipt; also, $____ Policy and Survey Fee, and $____ Lightning Premium, all of which are to be returned if Policy be not issued.

Dated at ____, this ____ day of ____, 186_.

____ ____, Agent.

(Endorsement.)

You have given Note amounting to $____ for first installment upon your Premium, and for payment of Policy and Survey Fee and Lightning Premium, which will fall due on the first day of ____ ____ 1866; also a note for four installments, due as follows:

$ _____ due on the first day of _____ 1867.
$ _____ due on the first day of _____ 1868.
$ _____ due on the first day of _____ 1869.
$ _____ due on the first day of _____ 1870.

You will receive a printed Notice before each installment falls due, and will be furnished with a blank Envelope, duly directed in which you can remit the amount at the risk of the Company. Do not fail to be prompt in remitting each installment.

[Answer.]

Treasury Department,
Office of Internal Revenue,
Washington, May 2, 1866.

Sir: I reply to your letter of the 26th ultimo, that the instrument therewith enclosed should, before being issued or used, be stamped with a five cent revenue stamp as an agreement or contract.

Very respectfully,
(Signed,) D. C. Whitman
Deputy Commissioner.

Geo. D. Copland.
Assessor, Goshen, Indiana.

IRR v.III, May 19, 1866, pp. 156-7

Stamp Duty on Canal Towing Permits.

Office of Internal Revenue,
Washington, June 19, 1866.

Sir: I reply to your letter of the 16th inst., that the form of instrument enclosed by you designated as a permit "of a towing company on the canal," is regarded by this office as an agreement or contract, and subject to a stamp duty of five cents.

Very respectfully,
D. C. Whitman,
Deputy Commissioner.

Otis F. Presbrey,
Buffalo, N.Y.

IRR v.III, June 30, 1866, p.204

Stamping of Promissory notes on Renewal Thereof by Endorsement, and when Protest is waived.

Office, St. Louis Insurance Company,
St. Louis, June 7, 1866.

To the Commissioner of Internal Revenue, Washington City:

Sir: I desire to know whether the usual stamp be necessary under the law upon the renewal of an endorsed note when protest has been waived, and the receipt of interest on the extended time acknowledged on the note.

Very respectfully, your obedient servant,
George K. McGunnefle,
President

[Answer.]

Office of Internal Revenue,
Washington, July 6, 1866.

Sir: Your letters of the 7th and 22d ultimo, relative to the extension of the time of payment for promissory notes, have been received.

The endorsement of a partial payment on the back of a note is regarded as a new memorandum, not subject to stamp duty, and the fact that by an implication of law it operates as an extension of the time of payment, does not effect the case.

The agreement to waive protest, and notice of protest, signed by the party making it, is subject to stamp duty as a contract or agreement.

Very respectfully,
E. A. Rollins,
Commissioner.

IRR v.IV, August 18, 1866, p.55

City Railroad Tickets–Stamp Tax.

No. 330 Henry Street,
New York City, Aug. 7, 1866.

Hon. E. A. Rollins,
Commissioner of Internal Revenue, Washington, D.C.

Sir: As a matter of importance to the travelling community of this City, will you kindly oblige me by saying whether or not an agreement, of which the inclosed is a copy, should have a five cent revenue stamp thereon? It is evidently a compact between vendor and vendee.

The company using these "agreements" also charges the purchaser two cents extra on these contracts for the printing thereof. It is humbly submitted that each of these acts is a violation of the Internal Revenue act.

Yours, with much respect,
John Butcher,
Notary Public.

[Answer.]

Office of Internal Revenue,
Washington, Aug. 14, 1866.

Sir: In reply to your communication of August 7, concerning the tickets issued by the East Broadway and Battery Railroad Company, I have to say that it is held by this office that the first of such tickets is an agreement which requires a stamp denoting the duty of five cents, and it is believed that the additional charge of two cents gives evidence of an intent on the part of the Company to defraud the public.

A letter has been addressed to Collector Putnam, giving him the proper instructions in regard to the matter.

Very respectfully,
Thomas Harland,
Acting Commissioner.

John Butcher, *Esq., No. 330 Henry St., New York City.*

Office of Dry Dock, East Broadway
and Broadway, Railroad Co.,
New York, Aug. 17, 1866.

Hon. Thomas Harland, Acting Commissioner, Internal Revenue Department:—

Sir: I have just received from George P. Putnam, Collector of this district, a copy of your letter to him of the 14th instant, in reference to the issue and sale of tickets by this company.

And, first, I wish to remove from your mind the impression caused by the statement of Mr. B[u]tcher (honestly, but erroneously made), that this company has attempted the petty larceny of charging two cents additional to the legal rate for the issue of each two tickets.

. . . I understand your decision to be that, in its present form, the ticket is an agreement, and as such is liable to a five cent revenue stamp.

We desire to give the public every accommodation in the matter of the issue and sale of tickets, so far as it can be done with safety to the company; but it is necessary for us to guard against the danger of forgery on the one hand, and on the other to insure that each ticket issued shall be used but once for the transportation of a passenger. We propose to change the form of the tickets so that the signed one shall read as follows:

"One Passenger."

"Each of the tickets on this sheet entitles the holder hereof to one ride for a passenger in a car of this company. The conductor alone is authorized to tear off the small tickets."

This we propose shall be numbered, dated and signed by the President and the receiver who sells it.

Each of the small tickets we propose shall read:

"One ride due the holder of the signed ticket. Not good unless torn off by the conductor."

Will you please inform me if in the form above proposed the ticket would be liable to the addition of a stamp, as we wish, if possible, to avoid the necessity which would in that case exist of increasing the "revenue tax" which we are authorized by law to collect from the purchaser of tickets from two and a half to seven and a half per cent?

Very respectfully, your obedient servant,
William Richardson, President.

[Reply.]

Office of Internal Revenue,
Washington, August 18, 1866.

Sir:—Your letter of the 17th inst., has been received in relation to the tax upon railway tickets. You say, "We propose to change the form of the tickets so that the signed one shall read as follows:—'One passenger. Each of the tickets on this sheet entitles the holder thereof to one ride for a passenger in a car of this company. The conductor is alone authorized to tear off the small tickets.'

And the 'coupon' tickets entitle the holder to 'one ride,' but are not to be 'good' unless torn off by the conductor.'' In reply to your inquiry I have to say that, with the above change, the ''signed ticket'' is not liable to stamp duty, as an agreement. And I have to say, further, that the evidence furnished by you in the matter of the alleged extortion from purchasers of tickets, of a larger percentage, as tax, than is allowed by law, shows very conclusively that the officers of the company should be exonerated from such charge; and that, in the instance alleged, they are free from blame.

Very respectfully,
Thomas Harland,
Acting Commissioner.

IRR v.IV, September 1, 1866, p.70

Assignments for Benefit of Creditors Liable to Stamp Duty.

An assignment of real or personal property or of both for the benefit of creditors, should be stamped as an agreement or contract.

IRR v.V, February 9, 1867, p.45

Assignment of Lease–Assignment of Rents, &c.

An assignment of a lease within the meaning and intent of Schedule B, is an assignment of the *leasehold* or of some portion thereof by the *lessee*, or by some person claiming by, from, or under him, such an assignment as subrogates the assignee to the rights, or some portion of the rights, of the *lessee*, or of the person standing in his place. A transfer by the *lessor* of his part of a lease, neither giving nor purporting to give a claim to the leasehold, or to any part thereof, but simply a right to the rents, &c., is subject to stamp tax as a contract or agreement only.

IRR v.V, February 23, 1867, p.59

Subscription Lists, Contracts, Promissory Notes.

When a subscription is for a purpose in which there is a community of interest among the subscribers, the list should be stamped as a contract, or agreement, at the rate of five cents for each sheet or piece of paper upon which it is written.

When there is no community of interest, and the subscription is conditional, each signer executes a separate contract, requiring its appropriate amount of stamps; this amount depends upon the number of sheets or pieces of paper upon which the contract is written.

When each of the subscribers contracts to pay a certain and definite sum of money on demand, or at a time designated, the separate contract of each should be stamped at the same rate as a promissory note.

IRR v.V, February 23, 1867, p.59

Bills of Sale of Vessels–Contract for Transfer of Property.

The stamp tax upon a bill of sale, by which any ship or vessel, or any part thereof, is conveyed to, or vested in, any other person or persons, is at the same rate as that imposed upon conveyances of realty sold; a bill of sale of any other personal property should be stamped as a contract or agreement.

IRR v.V, February 23, 1867, p.59

Insurance Permits changing terms of Policies.

A permit issued by a life insurance company changing the terms of a policy as to travel, residence, occupation, &c., should be stamped as a contract or agreement.

IRR v.V, February 23, 1867, p.60

Mortgage, when Taxable as Contract.

A mortgage given to secure a surety from loss, or given for any purpose whatever, other than as security or the payment of a definite and certain sum of money, is taxable only as an agreement or contract.

IRR v.V, February 23, 1867, p.60

Collector.—The following decision will answer your question, and save you the trouble of refering the matter to Washington:—"When for the purpose of transferring property from husband to wife, or from wife to husband, or from one of them to both jointly, deeds are made to a third party and then back from him to either or both, such instruments need not to be stamped as conveyances, as there is no sale, but only as agreements; but if they contain Powers of Attorney, these should have their appropriate stamps.—Ed.

IRR v.V, March 30, 1867, p.99

Waiver of Protest, or Demand, on Negotiable Paper.

A waiver of protest, or of demand, and notice written upon negotiable paper and signed by the endorser, is an agreement, and requires a five cent stamp.

IRR v.V, March 30, 1867, p.100

Contract for Sale of Land, or to make Title-Deed

A contract for the sale of land, or to make a title-deed to the purchaser on the payment of the purchase money, requires a five cent stamp as an agreement for each sheet or piece of paper upon which it is written.

IRR v.V, May 11, 1867, p.148

Executors, Administrators Receipts, Inventories and Appraisements.

Receipts taken by executors and administrators should be stamped as in other cases. Inventories of the property of deceased persons, returned for record, or otherwise, should be stamped as "Appraisements of value," at the same rate as agreements.

IRR v.VI, September 28, 1867, p.105

Guaranty Endorsed on Note, Bond, Mortgage or Contract.

A guaranty endorsed upon a note, bond, mortgage or contract, whether made at the time of the execution of the note, &c., or subsequently, should be stamped as an agreement.

IRR v.VI, November 9, 1867, p.162

Wife's Conveyance to Trustee for Benefit of Husband without Valuable Consideration–Agreement.

When a wife conveys real property, without valuable consideration to her husband, through the intervention of a trustee, neither her deed to the trustee, nor the trustee's to the husband, need be stamped as a conveyance of "*realty sold*," but each should be stamped as a contract or agreement.

IRR v.VI, December 21, 1867, p.210

Agreement to convey Real Estate—Containing promise to pay money.

A written agreement to sell and convey real estate, upon the fulfilment of specified conditions, such as the payment of a certain sum of money, should be stamped at the rate of five cents for each sheet, or piece of paper, upon which it is written, but if the instrument contains the promise of one of the parties signing it to pay a certain amount of money on demand, or at a time designated, it should also be stamped at the same rate as a promissory note.

IRR v.VII, January 11, 1868, p.11

Stamp Duty on Promises to Pay Money on a Contingency.

A. H. B., Buffalo.—The following is the substance of the letter to which you refer. It was addressed by the Department to Assessor Neher, and is reliable:

"A written agreement to sell and convey real estate upon the fulfilment of specified conditions, such as the payment of a certain sum of money, should be stamped at the rate of five cents for each sheet or piece of paper, upon which it is written, but if the instrument contains the promise of one of the parties signing it to pay a certain amount of money on demand, or at a time designated, it should also be stamped at the same rate as a promissory note."

You say, "It is urged in objection to the ruling that the promise is contingent, is not for value received, is not negotiable, therefore is in no sense a 'bill of exchange' or 'promissory note,' or 'evidence of an amount of money to be received,' as designated by law, as the designated sum cannot be collected by law, the damage being only for non-fulfilment of the agreement."

The instrument described in the ruling is not claimed to be either a bill of exchange or a promissory note. The law taxes any ''memorandum, check, receipt, or other written or printed evidence of an amount of money to be paid upon demand or at a time designated,'' at the same rate as a promissory note.

I am unable to perceive that the ruling in question is outside of the plain terms of the statute. If any particular agreement does not contain ''the promise of one of the parties signing it to pay a certain amount of money on demand, or at a time designated,'' it does not fall within the ruling; if it does contain such a promise, then it certainly falls within the terms of the act.

The unqualified written promise to pay a *certain* sum of money *upon demand, or at a time designated,* can hardly be called *contingent*. An agreement such as is contemplated in the ruling in question, contains the promise of one party to pay a sum of money on demand, or at a time designated, and the agreement of the other to convey certain real estate, mentioned and described, upon the payment of the *designated* sum at the *designated* time. The promise to pay the money is absolutely, upon the face of the paper, like that in a promissory note, not negotiable; the agreement to convey the land is contingent. The written agreement to convey real estate is believed to be a legal consideration for the promise to pay money; and the liability of a promissory note or of a memorandum, check, receipt or other written or printed evidence of an amount of money to be paid upon demand, or at a time designated, to a stamp tax, depends in no degree upon its negotiability.

It has never been claimed by this office that the written promise to pay money which is contingent upon the face of the paper should be stamped as anything but an agreement, but in this case, the promise is absolute upon the face of the instrument.—Ed.

IRR v.VII, February 29, 1868, pp.66-7

Stamp Duty on ''Consents'' of Property Holders and Subscriptions to Railroad Stock.

Assistant Assessor—A similar question to that presented by you, was submitted to the Commissioner by Assessor Follett of the 19th New York, and as the information is generally interesting, it is herewith given. The law and the decision are applicable to your case. The Assessor said:

''Under the statutes of this State, Cities and Towns are allowed to issue bonds to aid in the construction of certain Railways, upon obtaining the written consent of a majority of the tax-payers of the town to be bonded, representing a majority of the taxable property of the town. I enclose a copy of the consent which is circulated and signed by the tax-payers—marked No. 1. Is it subject to stamp duty? and if so, how should it be stamped? There are already several towns within this State, bonded upon such consents, without the consents being stamped in any manner, and at least fifty towns are in the process of being bonded. It is a mooted question whether the bonds are legal.

''How should the enclosed stock subscription (marked No. 2) be stamped?—five cents for each sheet—five cents for each name, or is it exempt?''

No. 1.

We, The Undersigned, tax-payers, inhabitants of the town of Norwich, in the County of Chenango, and State of New York, being a majority of the tax-payers of such town, representing a majority of the taxable property of such town, do hereby assent to and fix upon the sum of Three hundred thousand dollars, being thirty per cent, of the assessed valuation of the real and personal property of such town as shown by the assessment roll for the year eighteen hundred and sixty-five of such town, for the construction of the New York and Oswego Midland Railroad and we do hereby authorize and require the commissioners of such town, duly appointed in accordance with the provisions of the act entitled ''An Act to Facilitate the Construction of the New York and Oswego Midland Railroad, and to authorize towns to subscribe to the capital stock thereof," passed April 5th, 1866, three-fifths being present, to carry into effect the purposes of said Act; to borrow on the faith or credit of such town, the said sum of Three hundred thousand dollars; to execute bonds therefor, and to do and perform all other acts required of them by said Act, to carry into effect the purposes of said Act.

Done and subscribed at the town of Norwich, in the County of Chenango, on the 10th day of September, 186 .

Assessed Valuation of Property

J. K. Buel $50,000.00

C. C. Wait	25,000.00
R. A. Stanton	40,000.00

No. 2.

New York & Oswego Midland Railroad Stock Subscription

Witnesseth, That we, the undersigned, have severally subscribed and by these presents do severally subscribe to the Capital Stock of the New York & Oswego Midland Railroad Company the sums set opposite our respective names hereunto subscribed, and in consideration of the great benefits to result from the construction of said Road, and of the Certificates of Stock, to be issued to each of us on payment of the amount of said subscription and in order to induce and ensure its construction, we do hereby severally promise, and agree to and with the said Company, to pay to the said Company the amount of said subscription in such sum or sums, at such time or times, and in such manner as the Directors of said Road from time to time shall call for the same; each of us having severally paid down at the time of subscribing, ten per cent of the amount of such subscription according to the form of the statute in such case made and provided.

Dated, ______________________ 186___

Names.	Residences.	No. Shares.	Amount Sub.
Thomas Johnson,	Norwich, Chenango co., N.Y.	100.	$10,000.
Charles Parker,	Norwich, Chenango co., N.Y.	200.	$20,000.

The Commissioner of Internal Revenue replied:

"That a 'consent' of the form enclosed authorizing the town Commissioners to issue bonds and do certain other acts in accordance with the provisions of a State law, requires a five-cent stamp as an agreement for every sheet or piece of paper upon which it is written.

"As in a subscription list of the form enclosed, each of the subscribers for stock, contracts to pay a certain and definite sum of money on demand, or at a time designated. The separate contract of each should be stamped at the same rate as a promissory note. Whether bonds issued under the circumstances are legal, is a question for the Courts."—Ed.

IRR v.VIII, July 11, 1868, p.11

Stamp Tax on Shipping Articles.

A question under the stamp act was recently raised before Commissioner Wilkins. Three seamen libelled the steamer *Susan Ward* for wages. In defence the captain of the steamer claimed that the men were acting under shipping articles, and that the time for which they were hired not having expired the men were not legally entitled to their wages. The articles were produced in court, and showed the signatures of the men. Assistant District Attorney Finney, for the seamen, claimed that the articles were invalid, for the reason that they were not properly stamped. They showed a single five cent stamp, but it was claimed by the Assistant District Attorney that the agreement being between the captain and each man individually, was to be regarded as so many separate specific contracts, and that therefore a stamp was required for each seaman bound by it. The case was very fully argued, *pro* and *con*, and after mature deliberation the commissioner decided in favor of the ground taken by the Assistant District Attorney, that a stamp was required for each signature. The instrument in court was, therefore, held invalid, and a decision was rendered in favor of the libellants. The case is different with stevedores, who work under a foreman, who makes the contract himself for the gang. The contract is with the foreman, and hence but a single stamp is required. But in the case of seamen each man is regarded as making the contract for himself.—*Detroit Post*.

IRR v.X, October 9, 1869, p.116

Liability to Special Tax as Brokers of Persons Buying or Discounting Notes with their own Capital.

Office of Internal Revenue,
Washington, January 15, 1870.

W. E. Barber, *Esq., Assessor, Seventh District, West Chester, Pa.*

Sir: Yours of the 31st ult. is received, and I reply at this time to so much of same as relates to brokers' liability and the question of stamping the assignments of bonds. . . . Assignments of bonds should be stamped as agreements.

J. W. Douglass,
Acting Commissioner.
IRR v.XI, April 9, 1870, p.114

Agreement Clauses in Notes–Additional Stamp Required.

R. Hill, Esq.—An agreement stamp is required for stipulations waiving relief, promising to pay fees, &c., in promissory notes, in addition to the stamps appropriate to the note itself. A warrant of attorney, however, or power to confess judgment, is specially exempt by section 160 of act of June 30, 1864, amended March 3, 1865.

IRR v.XI, April 30, 1870, p.138

U.S. District Court—E. D. of Michigan.

United States v. C. G. Learned and F. S. Ayres, impleaded with W. Wisnall.

(Before Judge Longyear.)

On a motion by the defendant's counsel (Mr. G.V.N. Lothrop) to set aside a verdict of guilty rendered by a jury in this court in March, and for a new trial on account of errors and omissions in the charge to the jury. The facts in the matter are as follows: The defendants did business at Port Austin, and from a time anterior to the passage of the first internal revenue law were in the habit of issuing due bills to the men, of which the one upon which this case is founded read as follows:

Port Austin, Mich. No. 1,550.
October 28, 1868.

Due the bearer, or J. L. Coy, Seven Dollars, in merchandise out of our store.

(Signed) Ayers, Learned & Wisnall,
Van Wart.

These due bills were not stamped, and the firm were, therefore prosecuted for a violation of the revenue law, the Government taking the ground that they were contracts and should be stamped accordingly. In the testimony, it was shown that large numbers of these were issued by the firm, of which about one-fourth were used merely as vouchers in the store while three-fourths went into actual circulation and were frequently traded off by the men to third parties. The defendants admitted that they were intentionally issued unstamped, and while counsel in the course of the argument stated that the firm did not believe that they came within the scope of the law, yet in the evidence no explanation of the omission of the stamps was given. The opinion of Judge Longyear was elaborate and lengthy. The following is the portion in which the legal points bearing upon the case are summed up:

Is the instrument mentioned in the indictment such an one as was required by the internal revenue law to be stamped?

If covered by the law at all, it is covered by the first clause of schedule B, under the head of "Agreement or Contract" (3 Stat., 208). The question then resolves itself simply into this: Is it an agreement or contract? The answer to this question seems too apparent to admit of argument. But as the question is presented, I shall proceed to consider it:

First. Upon the face of the instrument, the word "due" imports a consideration, an indebtedness; it is between parties capable of contracting named in the instrument; the amount of the indebtedness or consideration is fixed and definite; the manner and place of payment is clearly defined; a promise to pay is clearly implied; and it was signed by the defendants and delivered. Here are all the elements of a contract, and is pronounced to be such by the laws of the land. An action could be maintained upon it without any other proof than that of demand and refusal.

Second. Upon matters outside of the instrument: The defendants owed Coy the amount in money, for work and labor; the due bill was charged to Coy as so much money and thereby cancelled the indebtedness in that form; there was an actual consideration. It was due on open account, in money; it became due on written contract, in merchandise. Here was a new undertaking on both sides, as to the manner of payment. It is true, it was testified by one of the book-keepers, that if any of these due bills should have been brought back and delivered up by the man to whom it was payable, he would, if requested, cancel it and credit it back to the man in his account, and so change the obligation back to a cash obligation; but there was no pretence that there was any such agreement or understanding with the men, and even if there had been it could not change the character of the instrument so long as it was out, as it was not expressed upon its face. Neither could any such verbal understanding be relied on to change the written agreement.

Therefore, by the law relating to contracts the instrument was an agreement, and by the internal revenue law it was required to be stamped. . . . [Ed. note: There follows a long discussion of the legal consequences of the failure to stamp the documents; for text, see General section.]

IRR v.XI, May 7, 1870, pp.149-50

A Five Cent Stamp is Required for each Signature to a Book Agent's Subscription Paper–The Person Delivering Subscription Books is a Peddler.

Assessor's Office, 16th District, N.Y.,
Plattsburgh, September 19, 1870.

Hon. C. Delano, Commissioner of Internal Revenue.

Sir: Messrs. W. J. Holland & Co., publishers, etc., of Springfield, Mass., and who have a branch office at Chicago, Ill., have large numbers of agents travelling about the country selling their books, or books published by them. The agents have a small hand-book with a printed prospectus, giving the name of the book (the one before me is entitled "The Laws of Health in Relation to the Human Frame," etc.), the price and style of binding, etc.; then comes the following: "We whose names are herein annexed, agree to take of (here follows the name of the agent or canvasser), or bearer, the number of copies of the above work set opposite our names respectively, and pay the specified price on delivery of the same.

"Names. | Residence. | No. of Copies."

What I desire to know is, whether the above agreement is liable to a stamp duty of five cents, under Schedule B, or is it such an order as requires no stamp at all? If it requires a stamp as an agreement, should there be one for each page on which names are added, besides the page on which the agreement appears, or should there be a stamp of five cents attached to each name signed?

Is the agent who sells and delivers at a subsequent time the books under such an agreement liable as a peddler or as a commercial broker, he having his compensation for his labor by having the books at a certain discount from the publisher's price?

George L. Clark,
Assessor.

Office of Internal Revenue
Washington, September 22, 1870.

G. L. Clark, Esq., Assessor, Sixteenth District, Plattsburgh, N.Y.

Sir: In yours of the 19th instant you state that there are agents travelling and selling books; that one class of these agents carry hand-books with a printed prospectus giving the name, price, and style of binding, etc., of the books to be sold, and with the terms of agreement by which purchasers bind themselves to pay for the book, on delivery of the same; and what you desire to know is, "whether the above agreement is liable to a stamp duty of 5 cents?" I reply by referring you to "Series 5, No. 10," page 17. As there is no community of interest in the above agreement, and the subscription is conditional, each signer requires a separate stamp.

You ask also "if the person selling and delivering the book agreed for, is a commercial broker or a peddler?" I reply again by referring you to a letter addressed to Assessor Easton on page 81, Vol. X. of the Record. He is a peddler.

J. W. Douglass,
Acting Commissioner.

IRR v.XII, October 1, 1870, p.109

Assignments of Certificates of Sales of Public Lands should be Stamped as Agreements–A Governor's Patents and Certificates of Land Commissioner are considered Exempt.

State Department, Michigan, Secretary's Office,
Lansing, March 4, 1872.

To the Hon. Commissioner of Internal Revenue, Washington, D.C.

Dear Sir: For the purpose of obtaining your decision on a point of considerable interest to the people of this State, allow me to call your attention to the following statement of facts:

Certain lands belonging to this State are sold on part payment, and a certificate of purchase issued by the Commissioner of the State Land Office in the form shown by the inclosed blank marked "A." These certificates are frequently held for a long term of years, and transferred from one occupant of the land to another in the manner indicated by the inclosed blank marked "B," the law requiring the execution to be the same as for a deed. When any owner of such certificate desires to obtain a patent for his land, he pays the amount of the principal, interest, taxes, etc., due the State to the Commissioner of the State Land Office, who attaches to the aforesaid certificate another certificate in the form shown by the inclosed blank marked "C," to the effect that such payment has been made in full, and that the holder thereof is entitled to a patent therefor on presentation at the office of the Secretary of State, such presentation *usually* taking place *immediately*, but sometimes transfers are made as above *after full payment*.

Under the provision in the "Stamp Duties" law requiring every "conveyance, deed, instrument or writing, whereby lands, tenements, or other realty sold, shall be granted, assigned, or otherwise conveyed or vested in the purchaser," to be stamped to the amount of fifty cents for each and every $500 (or part thereof) of the consideration received therefor, backed up (as I am credibly informed by the gentleman who was Deputy Secretary of State of this State at the time aforesaid "Stamp Duties" law took effect) by the decision of the then Acting Commissioner of Internal Revenue, it has been the practice of this Department to require that each and every assignment of certificate aforesaid be stamped as required by the provision aforesaid before issuing a patent for the lands described therein. Occasionally the application of the aforesaid provision of the "Stamp Duties" law to the case under consideration has been questioned by different attorneys in the State, but not until recently has any great objection been made to stamping the papers as required. We are now, however, confronted by a formidable document from an old practitioner, denying its application, a copy of which I also inclose.

For your information as to our laws relating to the sale of lands by the State, I forward to you by mail, to-day, one copy first vol. Com. Laws of Mich., 1871 (the second is not yet in print). I also inclose herewith a blank form of patent, which is issued by the Governor through this office on the surrender of the certificates aforesaid.

You will greatly oblige by giving this matter your immediate attention, and state in your letter to me:

1. Whether in your opinion the aforesaid provision of the Stamp Duties law applies to the aforesaid assignments which bear date prior to the date of the full payment of the purchase price of the land.

2. Whether such provision applies to such assignments which bear date subsequent to the date of full payment.

3. Whether the provision of the Stamp Duties law relating to the stamping of contracts applies to such assignments either before or after the date of full payment, or both.

You will see by section 3,825 of the Compiled Laws aforesaid, where the title to the land is vested previous to the issue of patent, or date of full payment, and by section 3,834, what are the rights of the holder of such certificates of purchase.

Very respectfully,
Daniel Striker,
Secretary of State.

By G. M. Hasty, Deputy.

Treasury Department,
Office of Internal Revenue,
Washington, March 13, 1872.

The Hon. Daniel Striker, Secretary of State, Lansing, Mich.

Sir: Your letter of March 4, 1872, respecting stamp duty on assignments of certificates of sale of public lands in Michigan has been received. C. H. Miller, Esq., Collector of Internal Revenue, Ann Arbor, has this day been specially instructed in the case, and you are respectfully referred to him.

Very respectfully,
B. J. Sweet,
Acting Commissioner.

U.S. Internal Revenue, Collector's Office,
Third District, Mich.,
Ann Arbor, March 27, 1872.

The Hon. Daniel Striker, Secretary of State, Lansing, Mich.

Sir: Your letter addressed to the Commissioner of Internal Revenue, respecting stamp duty on assignments of certificates of sale of public lands has been referred to this office with instructions to reply that certificates of sale of the form inclosed by you should be stamped as agreements; this applies both before and after payment for the land. The patents of the Governor and certificates of the Land Commissions are considered exempt, under section 154, of the act of June 30, 1864, as amended.

Very respectfully,
B. F. Granger,
Collector of Third District, Michigan.

State Department,
Michigan, Secretary's Office,
Lansing, March 29, 1872.

The Hon. B. F. Granger, Collector, Third District, Michigan, Ann Arbor.

Dear Sir: Your favor of the 27th inst. is at hand. You say, "Certificates of sale of the form inclosed by you should be stamped as agreements." Do you mean by this that *assignments* of certificates of sale, of form inclosed by me, should be stamped as agreements?

Very respectfully,
Daniel Striker,
Secretary of State.

By G. M. Hasty, Deputy.

U.S. Internal Revenue, Collector's Office,
Third District Mich.,
Ann Arbor, March 30, 1872.

The Hon. Daniel Striker, Secretary of State, Lansing, Mich.

Sir: I mean *assignments* of certificates of the form inclosed require stamps as agreements.

Respectfully,
B. F. Granger,
Collector.

IRR v.XV, April 13, 1872, pp.109-110

BANK CHECK

Checks drawn on a bank by one of its proprietors for his daily expenses, or by its employees for their wages, must be stamped.

The check of a correspondent, on money to his credit, to transfer an amount of money collected for him, is also subject to stamp duty.

Boutwell (1863), Rulings (No. 266)

Demand loans made on checks stamped as such, are an evasion of the law, if made with an understanding that the check is not to be presented, or not to be presented till a day future.

Notes, whether on demand or on time, are subject to stamp duty as "inland bills of exchange."

Boutwell (1863), Rulings (No. 275)

When a note is made payable at a certain bank, and a check is drawn upon the same bank for the amount of it, a check stamp is required for the check.

When the note is charged at the bank to the account of the promisor, and a check is not used, then a stamp is not required.

Boutwell (1863), Rulings (No. 282)

If your check or draft on your bookkeeper is used merely as a memorandum to show your liability to the firm of which you are a member, it is exempt from stamp duty; but if used for any other purpose, and especially if paid out, or transferred, or negotiated to a third party without being duly stamped, you will be liable to the penalty provided in section 95 of the excise law.

Boutwell (1863), Rulings (No. 294)

In reply to your queries respecting the additional liability of promissory notes payable at bank, to stamp duty as bank checks, I have to state, that although the words "promise to pay at bank" may be accepted by the bank as sufficient authority to pay the note at maturity, and to charge the amount thereof to the account of the maker, they nevertheless do not constitute or convey any pledge, or guarantee on the part of the maker that he has the money in bank to meet the note when it falls due.

A check, on the other hand, is always supposed to be drawn against funds, and is to be regarded as an absolute appropriation of so much money as it calls for, in the hands of the banker, to the holder thereof, and, in ordinary practice, is payable on presentation.

I therefore hold that said form of note does not come within the meaning of the stamp act pertaining to bank checks, but is only liable to tax as a promissory note.

Boutwell (1863), Rulings (No. 303)

Memorandum checks, drawn by a cashier on the institution of which he is an officer, require no stamp.

Boutwell (1865), Rulings (No. 211)

Cancellation of Check-stamp by Drawer's Agent or Attorney.

The attorney or agent of the drawer of a check may affix a stamp thereto, and cancel the same if duly authorized so to do, such drawer being absent. But the initials of the drawer should be used. If a check is used before the stamp is affixed and cancelled, the user is liable to penalty, consequently the attorney or agent should affix and cancel the stamp before use thereof.

IRR v.II, July 22, 1865, p.23

Foreign and Inland Bills of Exchange–Duplicates.

A foreign bill of exchange or letter of credit drawn in but payable out of the United States, if drawn singly, or otherwise than in sets of three or more, according to the custom of merchants and bankers, is liable to the same stamp tax as an inland bill of exchange, i.e., if drawn at sight or on demand, it is liable to a tax of two cents; if drawn otherwise than at sight or on demand, it should be stamped at the rate of five cents for each hundred dollars or fractional part thereof. Duplicates require the same amount of stamps as their original.

IRR v.V, June 15, 1867, p.188

Checks Drawn upon a Bank by its Cashier, and Check Drawn by Individual upon Himself.

A check drawn by an individual upon himself, or drawn upon a bank by its cashier, in his official capacity, and in the discharge of his official duty, is in its legal effect "written or printed evidence of an amount of money to be paid on demand or at a time designated," and should be stamped like a promissory note, at the rate of five cents for each hundred dollars or fractional part thereof.

IRR v.V, June 22, 1867, p.196

Checks Drawn by an Individual upon Himself, or upon a Bank by its Cashier in his Official Capacity–How Stamped.

Office of Internal Revenue,
Washington, June 9, 1870.

F. M. Patrick, Esq., Stamp Agent, 24 Vesey Street, New York City.

Sir: It was ruled by my predecessor in this office, June 22, 1867, that "a check drawn by an individual upon himself, or drawn upon a bank by its cashier in his official capacity, and in the discharge of his official duties, is in its legal effect 'written or printed evidence of an amount of money to be paid upon demand or at a time designated,' and should be stamped at the rate of a promissory note, five cents for each $100, or fractional part thereof" (Internal Revenue Record, Vol. V., p. 196, Series 5, No. 10, page 15); and you have heretofore been directed not to imprint a two-cent stamp upon instruments of this character.

You are instructed hereafter to treat such checks, except when designed to be used for circulation, like checks drawn by one party upon another. Except when designed to be so used, a two-cent stamp only is to be required upon each one when drawn for any sum whatsoever at sight or on demand upon a bank, banker, or trust company. A like stamp is to be required upon each for a sum exceeding ten dollars when drawn at sight or on demand upon any other person or persons, companies or corporations than those above named. When such checks, drafts, etc., are drawn otherwise than at sight or on demand, they are liable to tax at the same rate as promissory notes, five cents for each hundred dollars or fractional part thereof. Inasmuch as the amount of tax varies upon time drafts, stamps cannot be *imprinted* upon them, but the tax must be paid by adhesive ones.

C. Delano,
Commissioner.

IRR v.XI, June 18, 1870, pp.193-194

We learn that some careless readers of the act of July 14, 1870, "to reduce internal taxes and for other purposes," have received the impression that the act abolishes the stamp tax on bank checks. A reference to the act, as published officially in the Internal Revenue Record of August 6, will show that section 4 abolishes, "on and after October 1, 1870," "the stamp tax imposed in schedule B on promissory notes for a less sum than one hundred dollars, and on receipts for any sum of money, or for the payment of any debt," etc., but not the stamp tax on bank checks. As will be seen by the notice from Acting Commissioner Douglass, which we publish this week, all unofficial tables of taxes based upon the new law need to be followed with caution, and it is at all times to be borne in mind that the internal revenue taxes abolished by the act continue in force until October 1, 1870, and some of them until May 1, 1871. The income tax is continued by section 6 of the act "for the years 1870 and 1871."

IRR v.XII, August 18, 1870, p.69

Receipts used Instead of Bank Checks Exempt from Tax.

Office of Internal Revenue,
Washington, Feb. 25, 1871.

Thomas E. Grisell, Esq., Collector of Internal Revenue,
Fifth District, Upper Sandusky, Ohio.

Sir: I reply to your letter relative to stamp duty on receipts used instead of bank checks, that these seem to come under the general exemption of receipts by section 4 of the act of July 14, 1870.

If banks and their depositors choose to substitute receipts for checks, they must of course incur any legal risk which may arise from the use of such vouchers.

A. Pleasonton,
Commissioner.

IRR v.XIII, March 4, 1871, p.66

A Paper Purporting to be a Receipt, but Containing Additions from which it Appears upon its Face to be in the Nature of a Check, should be Stamped as a Check.

Office of Internal Revenue,
Washington, November 17, 1871.

Francis Springer, Esq., Collector of Internal Revenue,
Burlington, First District, Iowa.

Sir: Your letter of the 9th instant, relative to stamp duty on a receipt used as a substitute for a bank check, has been received.

With regard to more receipts thus substituted, see Internal Revenue Record, Vol. XIII., page 66. But when, as in the form enclosed by you, a paper which purports to be a receipt, contains the name of a third party as payee, negotiable words, or other additions, from which it appears upon its face to be of the nature of a check, it should be stamped as such.

Very respectfully,
J. A. Douglass,
Commissioner.

IRR v.XIV, November 25, 1871, p.170

No Stamp Tax required on Checks, Drafts, or Orders, except when Drawn at Sight or on Demand upon a Bank, Banker, or Trust Company.

Treasury Department,
Offices of Internal Revenue,
Washington, Sept. 30, 1872.

S. B. Dutcher, Esq., Supervisor Internal Revenue, New York, N.Y.

Sir: That portion of Schedule B of the internal revenue laws which relates to the stamp-tax upon checks, drafts and orders, is as follows:

''Bank-check, draft, order for the payment of any sum of money whatsoever, drawn upon any bank, banker, or trust company, or for any sum exceeding ten dollars drawn upon any other person or persons, companies or corporations, at sight or on demand, two cents.''

The amendment of the act of June 6, 1872, is as follows:

''That on and after the first day of October, eighteen hundred and seventy-two, all the taxes imposed by stamps under and by virtue of Schedule B of section one hundred and seventy of the act approved June thirtieth, eighteen hundred and sixty-four, and the several acts amendatory thereof, be, and the same are hereby repealed, excepting only the tax of two cents on bank-checks, drafts, or orders.''

It will seem that there is room for doubt whether the words ''bank-checks, drafts, or orders,'' as used in the act of 1872, were designed to include everything included under the same words as used in said schedule, and thus to retain the stamp-tax upon drafts and orders drawn at sight or on demand for sums exceeding ten dollars upon persons, companies, or corporations other than banks, bankers, and trust companies or whether it was the design to exempt all checks, drafts, and orders, except such as are drawn at sight or on demand upon banks, bankers, and trust companies.

I have decided to give the tax-payers the benefit of the doubt. On and after October 1, 1872, no stamp-tax will be required upon checks, drafts, or orders, except such as shall be drawn at sight or on demand upon a bank, banker, or trust company.

Foreign bills of exchange, whether drawn at sight or otherwise, will be exempt on and after October 1, 1872.

Very respectfully,
B. J. Sweet,
Acting Commissioner.

IRR v.XVI, October 5, 1872, p.105

Checks Payable One Day after Date without Grace.

Treasury Department,
Office of Internal Revenue,
Washington, July 7, 1873.

D. W. Munn, Esq., Supervisor Internal Revenue, Cairo, Ill.

Sir: Your letter of the 26th ultimo, respecting stamp duty upon checks on banks, etc., drawn payable one day after *date*, without grace, is acknowledged.

If such checks are really not payable until one day after they are given, *issued*, or delivered, they come under the general exemption of time checks. But if actually payable when they are given, at sight or on demand, it does not render them exempt to have them dated back one day or more, for the purpose of giving them the false appearance of time checks.

Any party who with intent to evade the law, issues, accepts, negotiates, or pays a check, draft, or order, without due stamping and cancellation, incurs a liability to a penalty of fifty dollars in each case. (Act June 30, 1864, section 158, amended.)

When there is sufficient evidence of such violation of the law, a prosecution should be instituted.

Very respectfully,
J. W. Douglass,
Commissioner.

IRR v.XVIII, July 12, 1873, p.9

Proceedings in U.S. Courts.

U.S. Supreme Court–Washington, D.C., October 23

A Stamp Act Prosecution – Drafts by a Corporation on its own Treasury – No. 45 – United States v. Isham – Certificate of Division between Judges of the Circuit Court for the Eastern District of Michigan.

This is a criminal information for issuing without a stamp, and with intent to evade the provisions of the internal revenue laws, a paper in the form of a draft drawn on Charles J. Canda, treasurer of the Iron Cliffs Company, by the defendant as superintendent. The paper was as follows:

[5] Iron Cliffs Company [Five.]
[1,190] Negannee, Mich., January 3, 1870.
To Charles J. Canda, Esq., New York.
Pay to the order of E. B. Isham, Superintendent, or bearer, five dollars, value received, and charge to the account of E. B. Isham.
(Countersigned) E. S. Green, Clerk.

On the trial the court were divided on the questions—first, whether this paper, on its face, required a stamp; second, whether evidence to show that Isham was superintendent of the company and drew the paper in that capacity, or that Canda was treasurer of the company and the instrument was drawn on him in that capacity, or was drawn in the course of the company's business, was admissible; third, whether, if the paper was made and issued with the design that it should be used as a local circulating medium, and was actually used by the holders as such, it thereby became subject to be stamped, and whether evidence given by the Government tending to show these facts was admissible; fourth, whether assuming all the facts which the evidence offered tended to prove, the defendant was guilty of the offence charged; and fifth, whether the information sufficiently charges any offence under the laws of the United States. These questions were certified to this court for answer, and were now argued.

The U.S. Supreme Court at its last term made the following amendment to the 8th rule:

That hereafter, in all cases brought into this court by writ of error or appeal, to review any judgment or decree, the clerk of the court by which such judgment or decree was rendered shall annex to and transmit with the record a copy of the opinion or opinions filed in the case.

IRR v.XVIII, October 25, 1873, pp.134-5

[Ed. note: for the resolution of this case, see General section, *IRR* v.XIX, March 14, 1874.]

Straws show the way the wind blows, and the pitiful attempts made by some of the banks to evade the petty tax on checks show the drift of their inclination. Their ingenuity is exhausted in inventing various forms and substitutes for regular checks and drafts in order to escape this trifling tax. Such efforts are meaner and no more honest than the devices of some tobacco and whiskey men to avoid taxation, which are punished by fine and imprisonment.

IRR v.XX, August 17, 1874, p.50

Liability to Stamp duty on Checks or Drafts Payable one Day After Sight.

Treasury Department
Office of Internal Revenue
Washington, Sept. 2, 1874.

Levi T. Hull, Esq., Collector of Internal Revenue Second District, Constantine, Mich:

Sir: C. D. Randall, Esq., of Coldwater, President of the Southern Michigan National Bank, has written to this office respecting the liability to stamp duty of checks or drafts payable "one day after date without grace," and also of receipts used as a substitute for bank checks.

Please advise him that bank checks, drafts, or orders payable at sight or on demand, drawn by any party, for any amount, upon a bank, banker, or trust company, are subject to a stamp tax of two cents. All other papers issued on or after October 1, 1872, are exempt.

It is not to be expected that this office will aid in inventing Forms for the evasion of the tax on bank checks.

Very respectfully,
H. C. Rogers,
Deputy Commissioner.

IRR v.XX, September 7, 1874, p.69

Stamp Duty on Receipts used as Substitute for Bank Checks.

Treasury Department,
Office of Internal Revenue,
Washington, September 11, 1874.

J. M. Johnson, Esq., Collector Twelfth District, Hudson, N.Y.:

Sir: In reply to your letter of the 31st ult. respecting stamp duty on receipts used as a substitute for bank checks, you are referred to office letters on the subject. *Int. Rev. Record,* Vol. XIII., page 66, and Vol. XIV., page 170. See also Vol. XX., page 69, No. for September 7, 1874.

It is not, however, considered advisable to commence suits at present on such papers.

When the stamps are improperly omitted on regular bank checks there is no occasion for delaying the prosecutions.

Very respectfully,
Jas. M. Ray,
Deputy Commissioner.

IRR v.XX, September 21, 1874, p.85

Liability to Stamp Tax of Receipts Used as a Substitute for Bank Checks.

Treasury Department,
Office of Internal Revenue
Washington, February 9, 1875.

Sir: S. H. Morgan, Esq., of Cuba, Alleghany county, Cashier of the "Cuba Banking Company," has written to this Office respecting the liability to stamp tax of receipts used as a substitute for bank checks, and of checks payable "one day after date without grace." He has been referred to you.

Section 15, of the Act of February 8, 1875, provides: That a Bank-check, draft, or voucher for the payment of any sum whatsoever, drawn upon any bank, banker, or trust company, shall be subject to a stamp tax of two cents.

By this enactment checks, drafts, etc., drawn on time, are liable to the stamp tax as well as those payable at sight, or on demand, as are also receipts or other vouchers taken by banks, etc., for the payment of money.

Very respectfully,
J. W. Douglass,
Commissioner.

IRR v.XXI, February 15, 1875, p.50

1875.—Department No. 16.—Internal Revenue.—Circular No. 124.—Concerning the Stamp Tax on Bank Checks, Drafts, Orders, and Vouchers.

Treasury Department,
Office of Internal Revenue,
Washington, Feb. 12, 1875.

Section 15 of the act of February 8, 1875, provides: That a bank check, draft, order, or voucher for the payment of any sum of money whatsoever, drawn upon any bank, banker, or trust company, shall be subject to a stamp tax of two cents.

By this enactment, checks, etc., drawn on time, are liable to the stamp tax, as well as those payable at sight or on demand; so also are *receipts* and all *other vouchers,* taken by banks, bankers, or trust companies for the payment of money by them.

Collectors are hereby instructed to cause a copy of this Circular to be delivered to all banks, bankers, and trust companies in their respective districts, and to note upon their lists of such banks, etc., the date of delivery.

J. W. Douglass,
Commissioner.

IRR v.XXI, March 1, 1875, p.65

Liability to Stamp Tax of Notes and Drafts Made Payable at a Bank, etc.

Treasury Department,
Office of Internal Revenue,
Washington, April 2, 1875.

Lucian Hawley, Esq., Supervisor Int. Rev., New York, N.Y.

Sir: Numerous letters have been received at this Office, making inquiry as to the liability to stamp tax of notes and drafts made payable at a bank, etc.

It is not believed to have been the meaning and intent of Congress, to require stamps upon promissory notes made in the usual commercial form and payable at a bank, when such notes are given in good faith and in the ordinary course of business. Under a strict interpretation of the law, they might perhaps be held liable as "vouchers." It is well known, however, that the leading purpose of the recent enactment, with regard to stamping bank checks, vouchers, etc., (Section 15, Act of February 8, 1875,) was to cut off the frequent evasions of the stamp tax on checks, as, for instance, by the use of receipts, checks payable nominally one day after date without grace, etc., etc.

Unless the notes referred to are used simply as a substitute for checks, as evasions of the stamp tax on checks, this Office will not insist upon their being stamped.

The above remarks will also apply to drafts upon private parties not bankers, etc., accepted payable at a bank.

A receipt which performs the work of a bank check, as for instance, where a person who has money on deposit with a bank, draws out a portion of it, but instead of drawing it out upon a check, gives the bank his receipt therefor, which is taken by the bank and held as a voucher, is considered liable to the tax.

If a dividend due a stockholder has been credited to his deposit account, upon the books of a bank, it has become a deposit, and a receipt given for it or for any portion of it, would, in my opinion, be liable to stamp tax.

But while a receipt given for a dividend which has not lost its identity by taking the form of a deposit, might perhaps under a strict construction of the statute be liable to the stamp tax, it would not in my opinion fall within its intent and meaning, and this Office will not insist upon its being stamped.

Section 6, of the Act of March 3, 1875, exempts from the tax "the receipts in the receipt book of a savings bank or institution for savings, having no capital stock and doing no other business than receiving deposits, to be loaned or invested for the sole benefit of the parties making such deposits without profit or compensation to the association or company, when money is paid to a depositor on his pass book."

The Banks referred to in the above exemption, are those which properly make returns on "Form 106 *a,*" and Collectors should require stamps on the receipts of depositors in receipt books kept by any other banks. Some banks whose returns should properly be made on "Form 106 *b,*" are in fact erroneously making them on "Form 106 *a.*" This error should be corrected. Receipt books of such banks should of course be stamped.

A certificate of deposit, which is such on its face, and represents money actually deposited in a bank by the person to whom it is issued, is not considered liable to stamp tax. The money represented by such certificates should be returned and taxed as deposits.

Checks drawn on their bank, by bank officers or clerks for their salaries, should be stamped. "Cashiers' checks" in general, issued or delivered to outside parties for payments, etc., require stamps.

Checks drawn by bank officers merely for the purpose of charging an account with items, as an inside transaction of a bank, but not *issued,* are held to be exempt.

Inland Bills of Exchange upon a bank, etc., and bills drawn in a foreign country upon a bank, banker, or trust company in the United States, should be stamped before being accepted, negotiated or paid.

Drafts or bills drawn in the United States upon a foreign country, need not be stamped, not being "vouchers" in the meaning of the law while in this country. Interest coupons are exempt. Duplicates of bills, orders, etc., are liable the same as originals. Receipts not relating to bank business, for instance for rent, are exempt.

Checks drawn by a bank upon itself, for the purpose of paying its own dividends, and the dividends, coupons, or interest of other corporations, and *issued,* should be stamped.

Checks drawn by State, county or city officers, in their official capacity, upon public funds deposited in a bank, are exempt if said funds are kept separate from private accounts.

Section 15 of the act of February 8, 1875, imposes a stamp tax of two cents upon a "bank check, draft, order or *voucher* for the payment of any sum of money whatsoever, drawn upon any bank, banker, or trust company." This is the only stamp tax upon written instruments issued on or after October 1, 1872, now in force.

It imposes the tax upon checks, orders, etc., drawn on time, as well as those payable at sight or on demand, so also on receipts or other vouchers *substituted for checks, etc., as commonly used according to the custom of banks and merchants.*

Very respectfully,
J. W. Douglass,
Commissioner.

IRR v.XXI, April 5, 1875, p.105

Liability to Stamp Tax of Notes Payable at a Bank.

Treasury Department,
Office of Internal Revenue,
Washington, March 29, 1875.

Hon. Jas. S. Biery, M. C., Allentown, PA:

Sir: I reply to your letter respecting the liability to stamp tax of notes payable at a Bank: That it is understood that Section 15, of the Act of February 8, 1875, which is quoted by you, was enacted mainly to meet evasions of the stamp tax on checks by the substitution of *receipts, "orders payable one day after date,"* and other subterfuges.

Accordingly it is held by this Office that if there is any understanding between a bank, (as shown by its practice, etc.,) and the maker of notes, or drawer or acceptor of checks, drafts, or orders payable at the bank, that all such notes and acceptances shall be paid by the bank and charged in the account of the maker, drawer or acceptor, in the same manner as ordinary checks would be, *and to avoid the use of bank checks,* such notes and acceptances are liable to the two cent stamp tax as "vouchers," for the payment of money by the bank.

The law in its widest sense and taken literally, includes in the tax all bank "vouchers" for the payment of money. But out of respect to the supposed object of the enactment as above referred to, it has been the endeavor of this Office to confine its operation as far as a practicable line can be drawn, to such vouchers as are used *as a substitute for checks, etc.,* as commonly employed according to the custom of Banks. To include all instruments which under strict interpretation are vouchers would be to tax a large variety of papers hitherto exempt and which it is believed Congress had no design of taxing.

Very respectfully,
J. W. Douglass,
Commissioner.

IRR v.XXI, April 5, 1875, pp. 105-6

Some country banks have been endeavoring to raise a clamor respecting the stamp tax on checks, etc. The construction of the recent law on the subject, by the Commissioner of Internal Revenue, is as liberal as is consistent with the duty of collecting the tax. Under a strict interpretation of the act taxing bank checks, drafts, orders and *vouchers,* he might insist upon the stamping of a variety of papers hitherto exempt. But as it is understood that the chief object of the recent enactment was to cut off the frequent evasions of the stamp tax on checks by substituting therefor receipts, orders payable nominally "one day after date without grace," and other subterfuges, it has been the endeavor of the Commissioner, as far as a practicable line could be drawn, to limit the stamp tax on "vouchers" to such vouchers as are substituted for checks, drafts, and orders, as these have been commonly used according to the custom of banks and merchants. Any existing trouble or difficulty in the matter has been caused directly, or indirectly, by the numerous petty devices to evade this little tax.

IRR v.XXI, April 26, 1875, p. 129

1875.—Department No. 44.—Internal Revenue.—Decision No.177.—Concerning the Stamp Tax upon Bank Checks, Drafts, Orders, or Vouchers, and as to Stamping Instruments Issued Unstamped.

Treasury Department,
Office of Internal Revenue,
Washington, April 12, 1875.

Section 15 of the act of February 8, 1875, imposes a stamp tax of two cents upon a "bank check, draft, order, or *voucher* for the payment of any sum of money whatsoever, drawn upon any bank, banker, or trust company." This is the only stamp tax upon written instruments issued on or after October 1, 1872, now in force.

It imposes the tax upon checks, orders, etc., drawn on time as well as those payable at sight or on demand; so also on receipts or other vouchers *substituted for checks, drafts, or orders, as commonly used according to the custom of banks and merchants.*

Numerous letters have been received at this office making inquiry as to the liability to stamp tax of notes and drafts made payable at a bank, etc.

It is not believed to have been the meaning and intent of Congress to require stamps upon promissory notes made in the usual commercial form and payable at a bank, when such notes are given in good faith and in the ordinary course of business. Under a strict interpretation of the law, they might perhaps be held liable as "vouchers." It is well known, however, that the leading purpose of the recent enactment with regard to stamping bank checks, vouchers, etc. (section 15, act of February 8, 1875), was to cut off the frequent evasions of the stamp tax on checks, as, for instance, by the use of receipts, checks payable nominally one day after date without grace, and other subterfuges.

Accordingly it is held by this office that if there is any understanding between a bank (as shown by its practice, etc.), and the maker of notes, or drawer or acceptor of checks, drafts, or orders payable at the bank, that all such notes and acceptances shall be paid by the bank and charged in the account of the maker, drawer, or acceptor, in the same manner as ordinary checks would be, *and to avoid the use of bank checks,* such notes and acceptances are liable to the two cent stamp tax as "vouchers," for the payment of money by the bank.

But unless the notes referred to are used as substitutes for checks, etc., as evasions of the stamp tax on checks, this office will not insist upon their being stamped.

The law in its widest sense, and taken literally, includes in the tax all bank "vouchers" for the payment of money. But in view of the well-known object of the enactment above referred to, it has been the endeavor of this office to confine its operation, as far as a practicable line can be drawn, to such vouchers as are used *as a substitute for checks, etc.,* as commonly employed, according to the custom of banks.

The above observations will also supply to drafts upon private parties not bankers, etc., accepted payable at a bank.

A receipt which performs the work of a bank check, as, for instance, where a person who has money on deposit with a bank draws out a portion of it, but instead of drawing it out upon a check, gives the bank his receipt therefor, which is taken by the bank and held as a voucher, is considered liable to the tax.

If a dividend due a stockholder has been credited to his deposit account upon the books of a bank, it has become a deposit, and a receipt given for it, or for any portion of it, would, in my opinion, be liable to stamp tax.

But while a receipt given for a dividend which has not lost its identity by taking the form of a deposit, might perhaps under a strict construction of the statute be liable to the stamp tax, it would not in my opinion fall within its intent and meaning, and this office will not insist upon its being stamped.

Section 6 of the act of March 3, 1875, exempts from the tax the receipts "in the receipt book of a savings bank or institution for savings, having no capital stock and doing no other business than receiving deposits, to be loaned or invested for the sole benefit of the parties making such deposits, without profit or compensation to the association or company, when money is paid to a depositor on his pass book."

The banks referred to in the above exemption are those which properly make returns on "Form 106 *a,*" and collectors should require stamps on the receipts of depositors in receipt books kept by any other banks. Some banks whose returns should properly be made on "Form 106 *b*" are in fact erroneously making them on "Form 106 *a.*" This error should be corrected. Receipts in receipt books of such banks should of course be stamped.

A certificate of deposit, which is such on its face, and represents money actually deposited in a bank by the person to whom it is issued, is not considered liable to stamp tax, as commonly used. The money represented by such certificates should be returned and taxed as deposits.

Checks drawn on their own bank by bank officers or clerks, for their salaries, should be stamped. "Cashiers' checks," in general, issued or delivered to outside parties for payments, etc., require stamps.

Checks drawn by a bank upon itself, for the purpose of paying its own dividends, and the dividends, coupons, or interest of other corporations, and *issued,* should be stamped.

Checks drawn by bank officers merely for the purpose of charging an account with items, as an inside transaction of a bank, but not *issued,* are held to be exempt.

Checks drawn by State, county, or city officers, in their official capacity, upon public funds deposited in a bank, are exempt if said funds are kept separate from private accounts.

Inland bills of exchange upon a bank, etc., and bills drawn in a foreign country upon a bank, banker, or trust company in the United States, should be stamped before being accepted, negotiated, or paid.

Drafts or bills drawn in the United States upon a foreign country need not be stamped, not being "vouchers" in the meaning of the law while in this country. Interest coupons are exempt. Duplicates of bills, orders, etc., are liable the same as originals. Receipts not relating to bank business, for instance for rent, are exempt.

• • •

J. W. Douglass,
Commissioner

IRR v.XXI, April 26, 1875, pp.129-30

[Ed. note: A portion of this Decision, regarding the stamping of unstamped instruments, appears in the General section.]

Supplement to Decision No. 177.—Concerning the Stamp Tax upon Drafts, Bills, Checks or Orders, drawn in the United States, upon a Bank, Banker or Trust Company, in a foreign country.

Treasury Department,
Office of Internal Revenue,
Washington, June 30, 1875.

In Decision No. 177, dated April 12, 1875, "concerning the stamp tax upon bank checks, drafts, orders or vouchers," etc., it was held that "Drafts or bills drawn in the United States upon a foreign country need not be stamped, not being 'vouchers' in the meaning of the law, while in this country." This ruling is, from and after this date, reversed.

The statute in question, section 15 of the act of February 8, 1875, imposes the stamp tax of two cents upon every "bank check, draft, order or voucher for the payment of any sum of money whatsoever, drawn upon any bank, banker, or trust company."

Drafts, bills, checks or orders drawn in the United States on a bank, banker or trust company in a foreign country, although perhaps not "vouchers" while in this country, appear to me to be clearly taxable under the terms of the statute. They are drafts, checks, or orders, drawn upon a bank, banker or trust company, and there is nothing in the law limiting to this country the locality of the bank, etc., upon which the paper is drawn.

Collectors will at once notify the banks, bankers and trust companies in their several districts, of this change of ruling, and will require the payment of the stamp tax, on the instruments referred to, from and after this date.

D. D. Pratt,
Commissioner.

IRR v.XXI, July 5, 1875, p.209

BILL OF LADING

Stamping of Foreign Bills of Lading.

Office of Internal Revenue,
Washington, Nov. 27, 1865.

Sir: I reply to your letter of the 21st inst., enclosing a letter addressed to you by the agent of the Grand Trunk Railway Company, that the forms of instruments given by the New York Central Railroad Company to the Grand Trunk Railroad Company on the delivery of property by the latter to the former road, as follows:

N.Y.C.R.R., Ohio St., Buffalo, N.Y.
November 17th, 1865.

Pro. No. 47, Car. No. 170. From Batavia.

Received from the Grand Trunk Railway Company, in good order and condition, the following goods, subject to charges as under:

Port Calbourn, C.W.

4 Boxes Clocks .... 470 lbs.

R. R. charges $10.00

are subject to a stamp duty of ten cents each, as Foreign Bills of Lading, and if duplicates or triplicates are issued, they are subject to the same amount of duty as the original.

Very respectfully,
D. C. Whitman,
Acting Commissioner.

Otis F. Presbrey, *Assessor,*
30th District, Buffalo, N.Y.

IRR v.II, December 23, 1865, p.196

[Ed. note: For domestic bills of lading, see the several references under Agreement and Receipt.]

BILL OF SALE OF SHIP

When "bills of sale," or deeds of vessels, are given as security for money, they must be treated as conveyances in trust, and stamped under head of Mortgage.

Boutwell (1863), Rulings (No. 281)

Bills of Sale of Vessels–Contract for Transfer of Property.

The stamp tax upon a bill of sale, by which any ship or vessel, or any part thereof, is conveyed to, or vested in, any other person or persons, is at the same rate as that imposed upon conveyances of realty sold; a bill of sale of any other personal property should be stamped as a contract or agreement.

IRR v.V, February 23, 1867, p.59

BOND, SURETY

Concerning Administrator's and Executor's Bonds.
April, 1863.

A bond of an executor or administrator, taken by a judge of probate, register, or other officer taking probates of wills, or granting letters of administration, requires a fifty cent stamp.

Whether such a bond is conditioned for the faithful performance of the general duties of the office of executor, or administrator, or for the payment of collateral inheritance tax, or for the performance of any special duty required of such executor or administrator by a law of the State, makes no difference as to the necessity of a stamp. It is the duty of collectors to inquire of, and report to this office, cases in which there shall have been any neglect or omission, by executors or administrators, to place the proper stamps on their bonds, and it is made by law obligatory on judges of probate and registers of wills to exhibit to the collector, assistant collector, or other law officer of the United States, all such papers belonging to their offices as he may need to examine, concerning personal property or estate of which decedent may die possessed, and to which legatees or distributees may be entitled. The facilities for obtaining information as to the proper use of stamps by executors or administrators are ample, and neglect of duty in this particular, on the part of collectors, is not excusable on the ground of the want of means for obtaining information.

Boutwell (1863), Decisions (No. 105)

The official bonds of sheriffs, constables, executors, administrators, trustees, guardians, &c., come within the meaning of the first clause of Schedule B, title "bond," and are each subject to stamp duty of fifty (50) cents.

Letters of guardianship are exempt from stamp.

Boutwell (1863), Rulings (No. 239)

The bond, on an appeal from a lower to a higher court, is exempt from stamp duty, as a bond "required in legal proceedings."

Boutwell (1863), Rulings (from No. 249)

Bonds of administrators, executors, and guardians should *each* have a fifty cent stamp affixed.

Boutwell (1863), Rulings (No. 265)

The bond of a guardian, being for the due execution or performance of the duties of his office, is subject to a stamp-duty of $1.00. The letters of a guardian are a certificate of appointment, and require a stamp-duty of five cents.

Boutwell (1865), Rulings (No. 215)

The stamping of letters of administration covers all orders, notices, certificates, and affidavits issued in the settlement of the estate. The bond of administrator requires an additional stamp of one dollar. Guardian's bond requires a stamp of one dollar.

Boutwell (1865), Rulings (No. 252)

A *bond* given to procure an appeal is exempt from stamp-duty *as a bond,* it being given in a legal proceeding. Where, however, such bond is the process by which the case is transferred from an inferior to a superior court, it is subject to a stamp-duty of fifty cents *as an appeal*.

Boutwell (1865), Rulings (from No. 270)

Where a party executes a bond to a bank for a sum of money, and assigns a mortgage to the bank as security for the payment of the bond at its maturity, both the bond and the assignment of the mortgage are subject to stamp-duty. The fact that stamped collateral security is given does not exempt the principal instrument from stamp-duty. Neither would the stamp upon the principal instrument relieve the collateral from stamp-duty.

Boutwell (1865), Rulings (No. 282)

Stamp Duty on Bonds.

Office of Internal Revenue,
Washington, Jan. 30, 1866.

Sir: . . . I reply that the law requiring stamps upon conveyances, bonds, notes, &c., took effect October 1st, 1862 and that no stamps are necessary upon instruments issued prior to that date.

A bond for the *payment* of money, is subject to stamp duty at the rate of five cents for each one hundred dollars, or each fractional part thereof, as "written or printed evidence of an amount of money to be paid on demand or at a time designated"; a personal bond, given *as security* for the payment of any definite or certain sum of money, exceeding one hundred dollars, and not exceeding five hundred dollars, is subject to a stamp duty of fifty cents, and to fifty cents additional for each additional five hundred dollars or fractional part thereof.

An instrument subject to stamp duty, but issued and used, unstamped, prior to August 1st, 1864, may be made valid by stamping it as required by section 163 of the act of June 30, 1864; if issued since that date, the case falls under section 158 of said act as amended by the act of March 3, 1865.

Very respectfully,
D. C. Whitman,
Deputy Commissioner.

H. Powers, Esq.
Berryville, Clarke Co., Va.

IRR v.III, February 10, 1866, p.45

Administrators, Executors, and Guardians Bonds.

The official bonds of administrators, executors, and guardians, are subject to a stamp tax of one dollar each, as bonds for the due execution, or performance of the duties of an office.

IRR v.V, Feb. 23, 1867, p.60

Stamp Duty on Bonds of County Officers.

Treasury Department,
Office of Internal Revenue,
Washington, March 26, 1867.

Sir: —I reply to your letter of the 20th instant, that the official bonds of Town and County officers require a one dollar stamp in all cases, as a bond for the due execution or performance of the duties of an office.

It is not lawful to record any instrument or paper required by law to be stamped, unless a stamp or stamps of the proper amount shall have been duly affixed and cancelled, and the record of such instrument is utterly void and cannot be used in evidence. The files of an office constitute a part of the records, and the filing of a paper required only to be filed, is the record of it.

Very respectfully,
Thomas Harland,
Deputy Commissioner.

Thomas Cunningham, Esq.,
Acting Collector, 16th District, N.Y.
[Ed. note: But cf. *IRR* v.X, Dec. 18, 1869, p. 198, below.]

IRR v.V, April 27, 1867, p.130

Bond of State Officers not Void for Want of U.S. Revenue Stamp.

An opinion was rendered in the Supreme Court of Indiana on the 24th ultimo, on a case from Wells county, where suit was brought upon the bond of a county officer. One of the grounds of defence was that the bond was not stamped as required by law, and was therefore void.

The Court, in an opinion pronounced by Judge Ray, after arguing the question at great length, decided that the General Government has no power to impose such a tax upon officers of a State Government, and that the bond of a county officer cannot be rendered void and of no effect by a failure to stamp it. The case of *Dobbins* v. *The Commissioners of Erie County* (16 Peters, 435) is cited, in which the argument against the right of a State to tax the salary of an officer of the United States, is that under the Constitution the General Government has the right to employ its officers and agents to execute its laws and fix its compensation for the discharge of those services, and that this being a sovereign power, it can not be controlled by the State. So the State has, under the same Constitution, the right to perpetuate itself, to employ its officers to execute its laws and fix their compensation. Again, it is said the taxation of the office or its salary is in effect a tax upon the United States Government. If so, a tax upon the State officers is to that extent a tax upon the State, and Congress can only impose such a tax by apportionment directly. True, the amount exacted is small. So it was in the case of the Government officer whose office was appraised for taxation. But the power to exact one dollar involves the power to levy one thousand. The power to tax involves the power to destroy.

IRR v.X, December 18, 1869, p.198

Stamp Duty on Bonds of Town and County Officers—Receipts of Town Collectors Exempt.

Office of Internal Revenue,
Washington, February 25, 1870.

R. R. Crowley, Esq., Collector Internal Revenue, Dunkirk, N.Y.

Sir: Mr. E. Denton, postmaster, Mayville, Chautauqua county, has written to this office respecting stamp duty on the bonds of town and county officers, and the receipts of town collectors and has been referred to you.

At the time of giving official bonds the obligors are not yet public officers, having not already qualified. The bonds require therefore a $1 stamp.

But the receipts of town collectors, given for the payment of taxes, are exempt under section 154, Revenue Law Compilation.

C. Delano,
Commissioner.

Bond given by a Town Supervisor for the Proper Disbursement of School Money Exempt from Stamp Duty.

Office of Internal Revenue,
Washington, April 5, 1870.

Rodney R. Crowley, Collector Internal Revenue, Randolph, N.Y.

Sir: I reply to your letter of the 31st ult., that a bond given by a town supervisor for the proper disbursement of school money, after he has given his official bond and qualified as a public officer, is exempt by section 154 from stamp duty, as you suggest, if such bond is required of him in discharge of his official duty.

J. W. Douglass,
Deputy Commissioner.

IRR v.XI, April 16, 1870, p.123

BOND, GENERAL

If the indorsement upon a writ required in an action brought by a citizen of another State is under seal, it is a bond, and will require a twenty-five cent revenue stamp.

If not under seal, it is liable to stamp duty as an agreement.

Boutwell (1863), Rulings (No. 238)

All bonds required in legal proceedings are exempt from stamp tax; but this does *not* exempt bonds of guardians, administrators, assignees, trustees, &c.

Boutwell (1863), Rulings (No. 250)

Every bond issued by a city must bear a stamp as inland bills of exchange, whether issued in redemption of an old bond or for a new debt.

Boutwell (1863), Rulings (No. 306)

After due consideration of the article referred to, and of the several papers submitted by you, I hold that they are respectively subject to stamp duty as follows, viz:

. . .

I am also of the opinion that three several bonds, numbered and named, respectively, 11, warehouse bond; 12, enrolment bond; 13, license bond (and all other penal bonds of a similar character required in the transaction of the business of the custom-house), come within the meaning of the second clause of Schedule B, relating to ''bond,'' and are therefore subject to stamp duty of 25 cents. . . .

To Edwin Palmer, Esq., *Collector of Customs, Milwaukee, Wis.*

Boutwell (1863), Correspondence (from No. 32)

Interest coupons, attached to city or county bonds, require no stamp, even if detached and passed from one person to another. The stamps of the bond cover the coupon.

Boutwell (1865), Rulings (No. 214)

Bonds or other official papers, issued by public municipal corporations, are held to be exempt from stamp-duty.

Boutwell (1865), Rulings (No. 217)

Where parties are arrested by military authority, and released upon taking the oath of allegiance and giving bond for good conduct, such bond is subject to stamp-duty as a bond not otherwise specified.

Boutwell (1865), Rulings (No. 228)

Bond to Convey Real Estate.

A bond to convey real estate, requires stamps to the amount of twenty-five cents.

IRR v.V, February 23, 1867, p.60

The decision respecting the stamp duty on bonds and mortgages is of great moment in its bearings on the issue of bonds by railroad and other corporations. Much uneasiness has been caused by the diversity of practice which has prevailed in the stamping of such instruments. (Editor's "Review")

IRR v.V, May 4, 1867, p.137

Bonds and Mortgage.

Whenever a bond or note is secured by a mortgage, but one stamp is necessary upon such papers, "provided that the stamp duty placed thereon shall be the highest required for said instruments or either of them." (Section 160.) A mortgage given to secure bonds which are to be issued from time to time as sales of them can be made, is valid so far as stamp taxes are concerned, though no stamps are affixed thereto if the bonds are properly stamped as provided in the section above mentioned, *as they are issued*.

IRR v.V, May 4, 1867, p.138

Notes and Bonds given in Purchase of Realty.

A note or bond given for a part of the consideration for realty sold and conveyed, is not relieved from stamp tax by the fact that a lien to secure the payment thereof is retained in the conveyance.

IRR v.V, May 18, 1867, p.163

Municipal Coupon Bonds.

Bonds issued by Cities or towns to aid in the construction of Rail Roads, and to purchase stock therein, are not considered as issued by municipal officers "in the exercise only of functions *strictly* belonging to them in their *ordinary* govermental and municipal capacity." They are held liable, therefore, to stamp tax at the same rate as promissory notes, being 5 cents for every $100, or fractional part thereof. The coupons are a part of the bond, and do not require additional stamps.

IRR v.VI, September 28, 1867, p.105

Bond of Treasurer of Odd Fellows' or Free Masons' Association.

The position of Treasurer in the organization of "Odd Fellows" or "Free Masons," or in any other similar organization, is not an office within the meaning of the statute. Bonds given by the persons holding such positions are not therefore subject to a dollar stamp each as bonds "for the due execution or performance of the duties" of an office, but to a twenty-five cent stamp only as bonds "not otherwise charged" in Schedule B.

IRR v.VI, December 14, 1867, p.202

Bond of Executors, Administrators, Guardians, &c.

A bond for the faithful disposition of the proceeds of sale, &c., required by the Court of an executor, administrator, guardian or trustee, upon his application for license to sell property, is exempt from stamp tax as a bond "required in legal proceedings."

IRR v.VI, December 21, 1867, p.210

Insolvent Bond–Omission of Stamp.–An insolvent's bond is a bond made necessary by legal proceedings and does not require a stamp: *McGovern* v *Hosback*, 53 Penna.

IRR v.VI, December 21, 1867, p.212

Circular Instructions Concerning Duplicate Bounty Checks.

Treasury Department,
May 15, 1868.

In compliance with the third section of the Act entitled "An Act to facilitate the payment of soldiers' bounties," approved March 19, 1868, the following regulations are established in regard to the payment of duplicate checks of Paymasters, for bounties under the Act aforesaid, by the Assistant Treasurers of the United States in the cities of New York and San Francisco.

Immediately upon the loss of a check, the owner, to protect his interests, must, in writing, notify the Assistant Treasurer upon whom it was drawn, of the fact of such loss, describing the check, and requesting that payment of the same be stopped. In order to procure the issue of a duplicate of the check, an affidavit in duplicate will be required by the Paymaster General, or the Paymaster acting under him who issued the original check, from the party in interest, showing his interest, describing the check, setting forth the circumstances attending its loss, and that it was not endorsed in blank, or to bearer, either by the payee or any other person entitled to receive pay therefor. The bond hereinafter referred to, and the original affidavit, are to be countersigned by the Paymaster as having been submitted to him and being the proof and security upon which he has acted, and are then to be delivered to the party to whom the duplicate check is issued, and by said party forwarded to the Second Comptroller of the Treasury. The duplicate of the affidavit will be retained by the Paymaster as his evidence upon which he has issued the check. In executing the affidavit, the 1st, 2d, and 5th of the instructions appended to the bond must be observed.

No duplicate check shall be issued prior to the execution of a bond in the form and according to the instructions as shown and embraced in printed forms, which will be delivered to the Paymaster General for distribution to the Paymaster authorized to issue checks in payment of bounties, nor shall such duplicate check be issued unless it is an exact transcript of the original check, especial pains being taken that the number and date correspond with the original check.

The original affidavit, the bond and the duplicate check, having been received by the Second Comptroller, he will advise the Assistant Treasurer that an application for a certain duplicate check is pending, on receipt of which advice the Assistant Treasurer will inform the Second Comptroller whether a request has been made to stop payment of the original thereof, and whether the said original has been paid or not. If the reply of the Assistant Treasurer is satisfactory, the Second Comptroller will then decide on the sufficiency of the reason and the proof for the issue of the duplicate check; and if he approves of the same and of the accompanying bond, he will certify such approval in writing on the papers, also certifying upon the duplicate check the fact of such approval, filing the affidavit and bond in his office, and returning the check to the person from whom it was received. All duplicate checks issued in pursuance of these instructions, bearing such certificate of the Second Comptroller, may, if properly endorsed, be paid on presentation at either of the two officers named, but only at the one on which the original check was drawn, if sufficient funds to pay the duplicate shall, on its presentation, remain standing to the credit of the officer who made the check; but no such duplicate check shall be paid if the original shall already have been paid.

As these regulations, and the law under which they are promulgated, apply only to checks given for a specific purpose exclusively, it is indispensable that all Paymasters who give such duplicate checks should certify, either on the face or back of such check, that it is a "duplicate for bounty under the Act of June 30, 1867," and in no event will duplicate checks be paid without such endorsements.

H. McCulloch,
Secretary of the Treasury.

Form of Indemnity Bond.

Know all men by these presents, That we, of in the , as principal, and of in the of in the , as sureties, are held and firmly bound unto the United States of America in the sum of lawful money, to be paid to the United States of America, or their assigns; to which payment, well and truly to be made, we bind ourselves, our heirs, executors, and administrators jointly and severally, firmly by these presents.

Sealed with our seals, and dated this day of , in the year of our Lord one thousand eight hundred and

Whereas Check No. , drawn by Paymaster, U.S. Army, on the U.S. Assistant Treasurer in the city of on the day of , Anno Domini one thousand eight hundred and , payable to the order of for the sum of dollars, in payment of a bounty under the Act of Congress approved June 30th, 1867, has not been paid by the United States, but has been lost and a duplicate requested to be issued;

And Whereas the regulations of the Treasury Department of the United States require the party thus situated to give bond to the United States, with two sureties, to indemnify the United States, before a duplicate will be issued or any payment be made on account thereof; and the Second Comptroller of the Treasury will certify that a duplicate of the aforesaid Check should be paid in consideration of the premises and of the execution of this bond:

Now, the condition of this obligation is such, That if the above-bounden obligors, their heirs, executors, administrators, or any of them, shall and do well and truly pay, or cause to be paid, unto any person who shall estabish a valid adverse claim to the above described original check, the full value thereof, on demand, with interest until paid, or shall pay to the United States of America or their assigns, in lawful money, any sum which shall be erroneously paid, or which shall be ascertained to have been erroneously paid, to the order of said original payee in consequence of the application for a duplicate of said original Check, together with all legal costs, and interest on said sum until paid, without any defalcation or delay; then this obligation to be void, or else to be and remain in full force and virtue.

SIGNED, SEALED, AND DELIVERED IN PRESENCE OF—

{ 25 cent revenue stamp. } Two witnesses.

____
____
____

Put a wax or wafer seal to each name.

Affidavit Required for Each Surety to the Foregoing Bond.

____________________ *ss:*
____

I, , one of the sureties on the annexed bond, being duly sworn, depose and say that I am worth, after paying my just debts, the sum of dollars, over and above property exempt from execution.

Subscribed and sworn to before me, this day of ,A.D., 186

____________________ *ss:*
____

I, , one of the sureties on the annexed bond, being duly sworn, depose and say that I am worth, after paying my just debts, the sum of dollars, over and above property exempt from execution.

Subscribed and sworn to before me, this day of ,A.D., 186

Certificate Required in Case the Magistrate who Administered the Oaths to the Foregoing Affidavits is not a Judge or Clerk of a Court of Record.

I, , do hereby certify that , who administered the above , was at the time of doing so, duly authorized to administer the same; and that full faith and credit are due to his official attestations; and that his signature is genuine.

In Testimony Whereof, I have hereto set my hand and affixed the seal of this day of A.D., 186

{ 5 cent stamp. }

Certificate of Responsibility of Sureties.

I certify that the sureties in the foregoing bond are sufficient for the penalty thereof.

{ 5 cent revenue stamp. } Govern- ment officer.

Note.—The 1st, 2d, and 5th of the following Instructions must be observed in the execution of the AFFIDAVITS as to the loss of the original check.

The following instructions must be particularly observed and complied with in the execution of the Bond, viz:

1st. The Christian names must be written in the body of the Bond in full, and so signed to the Bond.

2d. Each signature must be made in the presence of two persons, who must sign their names as witnesses.

3d. Each surety must make and sign an affidavit that he is worth the amount of the Bond after paying his just debts.

4th. Either a United States judge, commissioner, district attorney, marshal, assessor or collector of Internal Revenue, collector, naval officer, or surveyor of the Customs, assistant treasurer or designated depositary of the United States, president or cashier of a national bank that is a depository of the United States, under his proper official designation and seal, or a clerk of a court of record under the seal and designation of the court, county, and State, must certify that the sureties are sufficient to pay the penalty of the Bond.

5th. The affidavits of the sureties must be taken and signed before an officer authorized to administer oaths generally. The officer must certify that he administered the oaths. If the magistrate is not a judge or clerk of a court of record, his authority to administer oaths must be certified by the clerk of a court of record having official knowledge of that fact, according to the forms on the opposite page.

6th. Bond to be dated and stamped (a twenty-five cent stamp being required).

7th. Each certificate must have a five-cent stamp attached.

8th. A seal of wax or wafer to be attached to each signature.

9th. The residence and Post Office address, giving number and street, if possible, of the principal and of each surety and witness, must be given below.

Endorsement.

No. ______

BOND OF INDEMNITY.

and sureties, to the United States. Check No. drawn by , Paymaster, U.S. Army, on the U.S. Assistant Treasurer in the city of , on the day of , 18 , payable the order of for the sum of $. Duplicate issued on the within Bond and affidavit hereto ATTACHED 18

__________________ Paymaster, U.S.A.

Approved, and duplicate check certified , 18 .

__________________ Comptroller.

IRR v.VII, May 23, 1868, pp.165-166

Internal Revenue Stamps should be Affixed to Certain Bonds.

Bonds given previous to the enrollment and licensing of vessels should be executed, and have proper internal revenue stamps affixed thereto, in accordance with the laws and regulations. (Letter to Surveyor of Customs, Albany, N.Y., July 12, 1871.)

IRR v.XIV, December 30, 1871, p.213

CERTIFICATE OF DAMAGE (ETC.)

January 7, 1863.

Sir: Your letter of the 2d instant was duly received.

In reply thereto I have to state that, in my opinion, the certificates and other papers signed and issued by custom-house collectors cannot be regarded as coming within the meaning of the third clause of the excise law, pertaining to "certificate" of damages and all other certificates or documents issued by any port warden, marine surveyor, or other person acting as such, except when such certificates are signed and issued by the collector at a port to which no warden or surveyor is appointed, or in the absence of, and under authority from, said warden or surveyor.

Boutwell (1863), Correspondence (No. 28)

I cannot hold with you that the term "port warden," as used in the clause of Schedule B under consideration, is synonymous with that of "collector of customs."

Had Congress, in framing the law, intended to have included, under this head, such certificates and other documents as are ordinarily issued by custom-house collectors, it would scarcely have been left a matter for conjecture.

Section 1, article 567, of the revenue regulations (1857), sets forth in full the general duties of collectors or surveyors.

After due consideration of the article referred to, and of the several papers submitted by you, I hold that they are respectively subject to stamp duty as follows, viz:

1st, certificate of enrollment; 2d, certificate of license; 3d, transit certificate; 4th, certificate to cancel transportation bond; each requires the general (five cent) certificate stamp. Nos. 5, 6, being certificates of clearance, and partial discharge of cargo of vessels bound for inland (American) ports, are exempt from tax.

No. 7, certificate of clearance for a Canadian port, is also exempt under the last clause of Schedule B, which provides that the stamp duties imposed upon manifests, bills of lading, and passage tickets *shall not apply to vessels plying between United States ports and ports in British North America*.

No. 8, oath to an invoice, is exempt.

No. 9, the certificate of the master builder, requires the general (five-cent) certificate stamp.

No. 10, certificate of admeasurement. This paper, as I understand, is issued by the surveyor in his official capacity, and, as such, is subject to the twenty-five-cent stamp.

I am also of the opinion that three several bonds, numbered and named, respectively, 11, warehouse bond; 12, enrollment bond; 13, license bond (and all other penal bonds of a similar character required in the transaction of the business of the custom-house), come within the meaning of the second clause of Schedule B, relating to "bond," and are therefore subject to stamp duty of 25 cents.

In reply to your queries respecting certificates issued in duplicate and triplicate, I refer you to the enclosed copy of official regulations.

If these or any of these papers are signed by the collector, or surveyor, or warden, they will require the twenty-five-cent stamp, as provided in clause No. 3.

To Edwin Palmer, *Esq., Collector of Customs, Milwaukee, Wis.*

Boutwell (1863), Correspondence (No. 32)

Revenue Stamps not Required on Certificates of Damage, Official Fees, etc.

Internal revenue stamps are not required on warrants for damage, or on certificates of damage, those papers being exempt from taxation under section 154, act of June 30, 1864, as amended by act of July 13, 1866, which declares that no official certificate or document signed by an officer of the Government shall be taxed.

The charge of twenty cents for permit to send goods, without invoice, from vessel to public store for appraisement is correct, as is also the collection for the order to appraise, including oath. An official certificate issued by a collector, showing the payment of tonnage tax, being for the benefit of the party to whom it is issued, a fee of twenty cents should be collected therefor. (Letter to Collector at Baltimore, April 15, 1872. Navigation Division.)

IRR v.XV, May 25, 1872, p.158

CERTIFICATE OF DEPOSIT

Certificate of deposit is subject to stamp-duty, but not as a receipt.

Boutwell (1865), Rulings (No. 230)

Bank Memoranda of Money Borrowed to be Stamped as Promissory Notes–Such Memoranda Distinguished from Certificates of Deposit.

Office of Internal Revenue,
Washington, January 29, 1870.

Hon. H. R. Hurlburd, Comptroller of Currency, Washington, D.C.

Sir: Your letter of October 12th was duly received. The reply has been unavoidably delayed.

In answer I have to say that the letter addressed to you September 29, 1869, requires explanation or modification.

When a bank *borrows* money, and instead of giving its note gives a memorandum containing "evidence of an amount of money to be paid on demand or at a time designated," such memorandum should be stamped at the rate of a promissory note, even though it is *in the form* of a certificate of deposit.

When, however, the money is received as a *bona fide* deposit, taxable under section 110 of the act of June 30, 1864, as amended, and against which the depositor may draw, the certificate issued therefor need be stamped only with a two-cent stamp or a five-cent one, according to whether the amount of the deposit exceeds one hundred dollars or not, even though the deposit draws interest for a part or for all the time it remains in the bank.

The fact that a deposit draws interest does not relieve it from taxation under said section 110.

Very respectfully,
J. W. Douglass,
Acting Commissioner.

IRR v.XI, February 5, 1870, p.43

Certificate of General and Special Deposits Subject to the same Tax.

Office of Internal Revenue,
Washington, April 12, 1870.

John R. Breitenbach, Esq., Collector of Internal Revenue,
Sixth District Pennsylvania, Norristown, Pa.

Sir: Mr. William L. Williamson, of Pottstown, in your district, has written to this office asking whether there is any difference between the stamp duty on "certificates" of general and special deposits, and has been referred to you.

When *bona fide* deposits are made with a bank, bankers, etc., it makes no difference as to the stamp duty on certificates of deposit whether they are general or special, that is, subject to recall or check on sight, or redeemable at a future time designated.

Both are equally subject to the monthly tax of one twenty-fourth of one per cent on their amount.

J. W. Douglass,
Deputy Commissioner.

IRR v.XI, April 30, 1870, p.137

CERTIFICATE OF STOCK

Relative to stamps required upon certificates of stocks in corporations.

February, 1863.

Whenever the officers of a corporation receive satisfactory evidence that any person, persons, or party have become stockholders in such corporation, and shall make in the books thereof the requisite entries, showing that such person, persons, or party have become stockholders, and shall make and sign a certificate or certificates thereof, it shall be the duty of such officers to affix to every such certificate the appropriate revenue stamp; the expense thereof to be paid by the person, persons, or party for whose use or benefit such certificate or certificates are made and signed.

Boutwell (1863), Decisions (No. 70)

This office has no power to decide whether corporations or stockholders shall pay the cost of the stamp used upon certificates. The law subjects a party issuing an instrument without a stamp to a penalty.

Boutwell (1863), Rulings (No. 300)

Stamp on New Certificate of Stock on Transfer Thereof.

Washington, June 29, 1865.

Sir: Your letter of the 26th inst., in relation to stamp duty required on certificates of stock, transfers of the same, &c., and inclosing forms for my consideration, is received.

In reply, I have to say that the certificate of stock required a stamp duty of twenty-five cents, and the power of attorney on the back of the certificate is chargeable with the same amount, twenty-five cents, as specially provided by Schedule B. The transfer is subject to a stamp duty of five cents as an agreement or contract.

Sometimes this transfer is made on the back of the certificate, and when that is the case, and it is duly stamped, the record of the transfer made in the book of the company does not require to be stamped. But if the actual transfer is made—as in the present case—in the transfer book of the company, and no such instrument is executed on the back of the certificate, then the instrument in the transfer book becomes more than a record of transfer; it is a regular transfer of stock, and as such, is chargeable with a stamp duty of five cents as an agreement or contract, as above stated.

Very respectfully,
E. A. Rollins,
Dep. Commissioner.

IRR v.II, July 8, 1865, p.5

CERTIFICATE, GENERAL

A stamp will be required upon every certificate which has, or may have, a legal value in any court of law or equity.

Boutwell (1863), Decisions (from No. 30)

Concerning affidavits and certificates.

June, 1863.

Affidavits made before officers of internal revenue, or certificates issued by such officers, when required by law or by regulations of this office, are not subject to stamp duty.

Boutwell (1863), Decisions (No. 111)

A certificate of ownership of a burial lot in a cemetery is subject to stamp duty.

Boutwell (1863), Rulings (No. 240)

The certificate of a master in chancery, in the case of a debtor, that the plaintiff has good cause of action, &c., and the certificate of the master in chancery that he has administered the oath to a poor debtor, are both subject to stamp as certificates.

Certificates of sheriffs upon processes, that such processes have been duly served, are exempt from stamp tax.

Boutwell (1863), Rulings (No. 255)

Papers filed in court, on which there is an indorsement made by the clerk or register that they were filed at a certain time, do not require a certificate or other stamp.

If copies of paper which have been filed in court are issued with certificate, a certificate stamp will be required on such copies.

Boutwell (1863), Rulings (No. 256)

Certificates of dismission and recommendation of church members are *not* subject to stamp tax.

Boutwell (1863), Rulings (No. 278)

If possession of real estate is taken by the mortgagee, or surrendered by the mortgagor, the certificate of the witnesses will require a general certificate stamp.

Boutwell (1863), Rulings (No. 285)

This office has no power to decide whether corporations or stockholders shall pay the cost of the stamp used upon certificates. The law subjects a party issuing an instrument without a stamp to a penalty.

Boutwell (1863), Rulings (No. 300)

The jurat of an affidavit taken before a justice of the peace, notary public, or other officer duly authorized to take affidavits, is held to be a certificate, and as such a stamp denoting a duty of five cents must be affixed by the party before whom the affidavit is made.

Boutwell (1863), Rulings (No. 317)

Washington, April 28, 1863.

Yours of the 27th instant just received. The ordinary acknowledgment by the grantor of a deed before a justice of the peace, notary public, or other officer, was, in my opinion, under the act of July 1, 1862, subject to tax as a certificate; but, by the 6th section of the act of March 3, 1863, it is provided that no certificate of the record of a deed or other instrument in writing, or of the acknowledgment or proof thereof, shall be subject to stamp duties.

The ordinary form of an affidavit before a justice of the peace, or other officer authorized to administer oaths and affirmations, when certified, comes, in my opinion, under the provision of the law, and I do not propose to adhere to my predecessor's construction upon that subject. It appears to me that the jurat affixed by the officer is a certificate, if anything, and as such is subject to the duty provided for such a paper.

Very respectfully,
Joseph J. Lewis,
Commissioner.

Hon. G. Adams, *Sixth Auditor of the Treasury, Washington, D.C.*

Boutwell (1863), Correspondence (No. 40)

The certificate of the qualification of a school-teacher requires a five-cent stamp.

Boutwell (1865), Rulings (No. 206)

Jurat to the oaths of judges and clerks of elections, &c., requires a five-cent stamp.

Boutwell (1865), Rulings (No. 213)

The bond of a guardian, being for the due execution or performance of the duties of his office, is subject to a stamp-duty of $1.00. The letters of a guardian are a certificate of appointment, and require a stamp-duty of five cents.

Boutwell (1865), Rulings (No. 215)

An "antenuptial declaration," although drawn as a deed of trust, can be considered merely as a certificate, and requires a five-cent stamp.

Boutwell (1865), Rulings (No. 218)

A physician's certificate of vaccination, though containing several names, is but one certificate, and subject to a duty of five cents.

Boutwell (1865), Rulings (No. 251)

Affidavits of disability do not come within terms of section 154, and are not exempt from stamp-duty.

Boutwell (1865), Rulings (No. 257)

Marriage certificates are subject to stamp-duty; marriage licenses are exempt.

Boutwell (1865), Rulings (from No. 275.)

Certificates of Loan, in which there shall appear any written or printed evidence of an amount of money to be paid on demand, or at a time designated, are subject to stamp duty as "Promissory Notes."

IRR v.I, January 7, 1865, p.7

Affidavit to Chattel Mortgage Exempt from Stamp-Duty.

Where by State laws a chattel mortgage requires an affidavit of the parties that the debt is secured as a just one, &c., such affidavit is a part of the mortgage, and is covered by the stamp placed upon the mortgage. If the mortgage, being for less than $100, is exempt, the affidavit is also exempt.

IRR v.I, April 1, 1865, p.100

Excise Bonds and Jurats require Stamps.

Treasury Department,
Office of Internal Revenue,
Washington, May 20, 1865.

Sir: I reply to your letter of the 18th inst., that the several jurats contained in the inclosed petition for "an innkeeper's license," and the "bond," are subject to a stamp duty of five cents each as certificates.

Very respectfully,
E. A. Rollins,
Acting Commissioner.

W. Jay Haskett, Esq., No. 15 Centre Street, N.Y.

IRR v.I, May 27, 1865, p.164

Burial-lot Certificates.

Certificates of burial-lots being in the nature of conveyances, are subject to stamp-duty as such.

IRR v.II, August 12, 1865, p.45

Jurat to an Affidavit Exempt from Stamp Duty in Certain Cases.

The jurat to an affidavit of the correctness of a return of property for taxation when made before an assessor of State, County, Town, or other municipal taxes, is exempt from tax duty if the administration of the oath is part of the Assessor's official duties.

IRR v.V, February 9, 1867, p.45

Jurats Administered by Revenue Officers.

The words "or used" were stricken out of Section 154, by the Act of July 13th, 1866. When a Notary Pubiic or Justice of the Peace administers the oath to an assistant assessor, upon his monthly account for services, a five cent stamp should be affixed to the jurat. No stamp will be required when the oath is administered, and the jurat issued by an assessor, assistant assessor, collector, deputy collector, revenue agent, or inspector.

IRR v.V, February 23, 1867, p.59

Marriage Certificates, when, and when not, Liable.

A marriage certificate issued by the officiating clergyman or magistrate, to be returned to any officer of a state, county, city, town, or other municipal corporation to constitute part of a public record, requires no stamp; but if it is to be retained by the parties, a five cent stamp should be affixed.

IRR v.V, February 23, 1867, p.60

Certificate to Capacity of persons administering Oaths.

The Act of March 2nd, 1867, relieves all affidavits from stamp taxes, but the certificate of the Clerk of a Court or of any other person concerning the official character of the person who signs the jurat, the genuineness of the signature and the authority of that person to administer oaths, is still like every other certificate, subject to a stamp tax of five cents.

IRR v.V, June 29, 1867, p.204

Protest–Certificate of Notice.

The certificate of notice to parties, usually appended to a Notary's certificate of protest, forms no part of the protest and requires additional stamps to the amount of five cents.

IRR v.VI, October 12, 1867, p.130

County Clerk's Certificate to Powers of Notary or Commissioner.

A County Clerk's certificate respecting the authority of a person to administer oaths, &c., issued to be used by a private party for his own benefit, is not regarded as within Section 154, which exempts instrument issued by the County, "in the exercise of functions *strictly* belonging to it, in its *ordinary* Governmental capacity."

IRR v.VI, November 9, 1867, p.162

The certificate of the officer taking a deposition is not subject to stamp duty, under the act of Congress "to provide internal revenue," &c., approved June 30, 1864.—*Prather* v. *Pritchard*, 26 Ind, 65.

IRR v.VI, November 23, 1867, p.181

A Notary's Certificate to his Notice of Protest is not relieved from the Stamp Tax by the fact that it is printed in Blank on the same sheet of paper with the Certificate of Protest.

Office of Internal Revenue,
Washington, October 21, 1871.

R. N. McRaren, Esq., Assessor, St. Paul, Minnesota.

Sir: Yours of the 6th instant, enclosing copies of notaries' certificates of protest, is acknowledged.

You say, "It is claimed by parties using these forms that the notice is incorporated with the protest and *does form* part of the same, and therefore does not require additional stamp."

It is not perceived that the certificate of notice in the forms which you enclose, is otherwise than "appended" to the certificate of protest. The fact that the said certificate of notice is printed in blank on the same sheet of paper with the certificate of protest does not "incorporate" the former with the latter in any manner to relieve the same from stamp duty.

It will be observed that the tax in question is not a tax *upon* the *notice*, but *is* upon the certificate of the service of notice. The notary sends out his notice of protest, and then certifies that he has done so. This certificate is evidently of *service*, and is designed for use as such. Being legal evidence of an essential act, it is liable to stamp tax, and none the less so, simply because it is made upon the same piece of paper with the certificate of protest.

Enclosed I send you copy of a letter to J. H. Fay, Esq., dated August 28, 1867.

Respectfully,
G. B. Williams,
Deputy Commissioner.

Office of Internal Revenue,
Washington, August 28, 1867.

James H. Fay, Esq., No. 9 Nassau Street, New York City.

Sir: I reply to your letter of the 18th ultimo, that the certificate of notice to parties usually appended to a notary's certificate of protest forms no part of the certificate last named, and requires additional stamps to the amount of five cents.

The stamp tax in the case of a protest is not imposed strictly upon the notarial certificate, although as a matter of practice that is the appropriate place for it; but it is imposed upon the "protest of any note, bill of exchange, check, or draft," and upon every marine protest. It has accordingly been held by this office, that if several notes, bills of exchange, etc., are protested at the same time, and are all attached to one and the same certificate, stamps should be affixed to the amount of twenty-five cents for each and every note, bill, draft, etc., thus protested. Not only is the certificate of notice to parties no part of the protest, but it is no part of the official duty of a notary by the law (Merchant) to give notice of the dishonor of a promissory note, unless required by some State law or general usage. (Burke v. McRay, 2 Howard, 66.)

In the form submitted by you the certificate of notice is as follows:

"And I, the said notary, do hereby certify that on the day of in the year aforesaid, I deposited in the Post-office of the United States, in the said city of New York, fully prepaying the postage thereon, notice of the foregoing protest," etc.

The blank itself treats the *protest* as something distinct from the *certificate of notice*, when it speaks of the *foregoing protest*. The certificate in question is a distinct instrument and requires a five cent stamp, and same as if made upon a separate piece of paper.

Very respectfully,
Thomas Harland,
Deputy Commissioner.

IRR v.XIV, November 4, 1871, p.145

CHARTER PARTY

See Boutwell (1863), Correspondence (No. 9), under Agreement.

CONTRACT, BROKER'S

Relative to the purchase and sale of gold and silver coins, or bullion, and loans thereon.

June 9, 1863.

First. All contracts for the purchase and sale of gold and silver coin, or bullion, and all contracts for the loan of money or currency secured by the pledge or deposit or other disposition of gold or silver coin of the United States, if to be performed after a period exceeding three days, must be in writing, or printed, and signed by the parties, their agents, or attorneys.

Second. Such contracts must bear adhesive stamps equal in amount to one-half of one per cent of the price to be paid, or of the amount of money or currency loaned; and in addition thereto, stamps, equal to the amount of interest, at the rate of six per cent per annum, upon the contract for the longest time named therein.

Third. A renewal of the contract would be subject to the same conditions; and if a contract originally made for a period not exceeding three days, be renewed or in any way extended, such contract must be duly stamped, when so renewed or extended.

Fourth. No loan of currency or money on the security of gold or silver coin of the United States, or of any certificate or other evidence of deposit payable in gold or silver coin, can be made for an amount exceeding the par value of the coin pledged or deposited.

Fifth. Gold and silver coin, loaned at the par value thereof, is subject only to the duty imposed on loans.

Sixth. Contracts, loans, or sales of gold or silver coin, or bullion, not made in accordance with this decision, are void; and in addition to existing penalties for violation of the excise law, any party to said contract may, within one year from the date thereof, bring suit to recover back, for his own use and benefit, the money paid on any such contract.

Seventh. Nothing in this decision shall apply to any transactions by or with the government of the United States.

Boutwell (1863), Decisions (No. 115)

Memorandums of purchase and sale must be regarded as within the meaning of the clause pertaining to contracts or brokers' notes (Schedule B, excise law), and therefore subject to a stamp tax of ten cents.

Boutwell (1863), Rulings (No. 264)

The clause of Schedule B, imposing a stamp duty upon brokers' contracts, is construed to include both the original and the duplicate—the one issued to the seller as well as that given to the buyer.

Boutwell (1863), Rulings (No. 274)

---

1. Contracts for the loan of money secured by deposit of gold, if to be performed after a period exceeding three days, must be in writing, and the writing must have a stamp affixed equal in value to

one-half of one per cent on the whole sum loaned, and interest at the rate of six per cent for the time the loan is to continue.

The design of the act was to discourage the traffic in gold, silver coin, and bullion, as marketable commodities, and to prevent speculations on their rise and fall. This was effected by making all contracts for the sale or loan of those metals in coin or bullion, on time exceeding three days, void, unless reduced to writing, and subject to a burdensome stamp duty.

Provisions against the purchase and sale of gold and silver, without being extended to loans on a pledge or deposit as security, would not have answered the purposes of the act, for a loan of money secured collaterally by a pledge or deposit of coin or bullion is a mode of use as objectionable as the purchase and sale, and is as much within the mischief intended to be remedied.

All contracts, loans, or sales of gold and silver coin and bullion not made in accordance with the act of Congress are absolutely void. A contract for the loan of money payable on demand, secured by a pledge or deposit of gold, which, by its terms, may run for an indefinite period, and, of course, longer than three days, cannot be legally made unless in writing, and, as a stamp must be affixed to the writing, I am unable to see how the value of the stamp is to be ascertained. The time being indefinite, the interest on the sum loaned, which determines in part the value of the stamp, cannot be calculated. It follows, therefore, that the act of Congress, by omitting to provide a stamp for such contracts, and by making all contracts void not in accordance with the act, has put loans payable on demand, and secured by a deposit of gold, outside of the pale of legitimate business transactions.

When the contract requiring the stamp is changed, under agreement with the parties, by increasing the amount of the purchases or loan, or extending the time, a new stamp is required. So, also, where the amount of the coin or bullion pledged as collateral is altered.

Boutwell (1863), Rulings (No. 351)

March 21, 1863.

Gentlemen: I have considered your communication of the 14th instant, and have the honor to say, in reply, that a deposit of gold dust made with you by your correpondents in Colorado, on which you make advances to them, or to other persons on their account, is not such a transaction as requires a written and stamped contract.

When, however, gold dust so deposited is converted into coin of the United States, and upon a deposit of that coin you make advances, which, by the terms of the agreement, are not to be repaid within three days, there must be a written contract stamped agreeably to the provisions of the amendment to the excise law contained in the sixth section.

It must, however, be observed, that any advance of currency or money upon a pledge or deposit of coin of the United States, exceeding in amount the par value of the coin, will render the transaction utterly void.

Boutwell (1863), Correspondence (No. 25)

Stamp-Tax on Broker's Sales–each Note requires Stamp.

Office of Internal Revenue,
Washington, August 10, 1866.

Sir: I reply to yours of the 7th inst., that the Act of July 13, 1866 allows, and requires, the sales of commercial brokers to be returned monthly; but there is no such provision relating to the sales of banks, bankers, and money or stock brokers. The law distinctly requires a memorandum or bill of sale to be given in respect of each and every sale or contract for sale of stocks, bonds, gold, &c., &c., and if any assessor is permitting brokers to stamp their books, instead of giving stamped memorandums, you will save the brokers considerable expense, and this office some trouble, by furnishing the name of such assessor.

The law provides, that "any person or persons liable to pay the tax as herein provided, or any one who acts in the matter as agent or broker for such person or persons, who shall make any such sale or contract, or who shall, in pursuance of any sale or contract, deliver or receive any stocks, bonds, bullion, coin, promissory notes, or other securities, without a bill or memorandum thereof as herein required, or who shall deliver or receive such bill or memorandum without having the proper stamp affixed thereto, shall forfeit and pay to the United States a penalty," &c., &c.

A bill of sale by a bank, banker or broker of a less amount than $100, requires a one cent stamp, by express provision of the law.

Very respectfully,
Thomas Harland,
Dep. Commissioner.

IRR v.IV, August 25, 1866, p.62

Tax on Brokers' Sales.

One of the most successful modifications effected by the Act of July 13, 1866, has been that which substituted in place of a general tax on the sales of stockbrokers of one-twentieth of one per cent, payable monthly, a tax of one one-hundredth of one per cent, payable by means of stamps affixed to the bill or memorandum of each sale; a heavy penalty being provided for the delivery or reception of any bill or memorandum of such sale without the necessary stamps affixed. The law, as it formerly stood, was a source of constant trouble, vexation, and litigation between the Government and the brokers, while the tax in itself was so oppressive as to induce a very general evasion of it, and consequent loss to the revenue. The Commissioner is now happy to report that the operation of the present law is most satisfactory; that its provisions are all but universally complied with; while the indications are that, although the tax has been reduced from one-twentieth to one one-hundredth of one per cent, the revenue from this souce, so far from being diminished, is likely to be considerably increased.—*Com. Wells' [Special] Report.*

IRR v.V, February 23, 1867, p.58

Brokers' and Bankers' Sales.

The tax upon brokers' and bankers' sales of stocks, bonds, gold and silver bullion, coin, promissory notes and other securities, was reduced, in 1866, to the rate of one cent for every one hundred dollars of the amount of such sales, and the tax was made payable by the attachment of the requisite stamp upon every bill or memoraundum of sale.

The purchaser of real estate naturally insists upon the delivery of a deed of conveyance, and the attachment of the appropriate stamp; otherwise he has no legal evidence of ownership. But in this case the bill or memorandum unnecessary for the passage of title is of little or no value to the receiver. The revenue, therefore, is deprived of its greatest security, for the monetary penalties for non-compliance with the law, applying with equal force to the purchaser and seller, do not furnish great protection; as both are alike, neither will complain against the other. The representations, therefore, to this office that in many places the statute is disregarded, sustained as they are by the failure of expected increase from stamp duties, seem to me reasonable. The bills of sale when received duly stamped are not always preserved as valuable papers are, but are often thrown away, and the stamps removed by those who do not hesitate by the use of chemicals to destroy their marks of cancellation and dispose of them to innocent purchasers.

I believe the return of sales to assessors, and the payment of the tax to collectors, are less inconvenient to the public than the use of stamps, while they furnish better opportunities for testing the observance of the laws.

Report of the Commissioner of Internal Revenue [E. A. Rollins] for the year ending June 30, 1867, p.XXXVIII.

Tax on Contracts for Future Delivery of Bond and Stocks.

Mr. Abrams, the assessor detailed in charge of banks, bankers, and brokers in the Wall Street district, informs us that the Department has ruled that *contracts* for the future delivery of stocks, bonds, or other securities are taxable, precisely the same as bills accompanying the delivery; but when deliveries ensue under said contract, no additional tax is required. This ruling is in consequence of the cancelling of contracts before maturity, by the payment of differences, by which course the Government is deprived of lawful revenue as provided in the amended law of July 13, 1866.

IRR v.VI, October 5, 1867, p.122

Stamps– Broker's Sale.

Assistant Assessor.—We entertain no doubt that the law is correctly stated, and you are in duty bound to see that the practice of brokers doing business in your division conforms to it. You are entitled to a moiety of fines or penalties imposed for violation of the law in question. In order to protect your interest you should file information in writing with your assessor, and serve copy on the collector, and retain copy for your own use. The Revenue Board has nothing to do with the matter. The letter in question is reprinted correctly.

Washington, Jan. 14, 1868.

Sir: Your letter of the 11th inst., inclosing one from— —, addressed to — —, under the date of the 9th inst., has been received. Their letter is as follows:

"The Government agent, in refusing to stamp our contracts, confounds them probably with the sales tickets which we give on delivery of stocks, and which have to be stamped on the amount of the transaction. The contract itself only requires a ten cent stamp, and we are constantly receiving contracts from other brokers with stamps affixed by the Government agent. We prefer to have them in that way."

You yourself write as follows: "The enclosed form of brokers' contract is precisely similar, except in names, to one submitted for approval some two weeks since, and returned with the endorsement that the amount of tax varies with the value of stocks, &c., and that hence no stamp should be imprinted. It seems to be the general custom of the brokers to stamp all their contracts ten cents, and the ticket of sale, when the stock is delivered, one-tenth of one per cent."

"The contracts referred to as bearing the imprinted ten cent stamp, are a few which were presented prior to the amendment of the law and the adoption of existing regulations, and which the owners continue to use."

Prior to the Act of July 13, 1866, brokers were required to make monthly returns of their sales of merchandise, produce, gold and silver bullion, foreign exchange, uncurrent money, promissory notes, stocks, bonds and other securities, and to pay the tax assessed thereon to the Collector (Act of June 30, 1864, Section 99); and a stamp tax of ten cents was imposed upon each broker's note or memorandum of sale of any goods or merchandise, stocks, bonds, exchange, notes of hand, real estate or property of any kind or description issued by brokers or by persons acting as such (Act of June 30, 1864, Schedule B, Contract). By the Act of July 13, 1866, a tax was imposed upon all broker's sales, and contracts for the sale of stocks, bonds, gold and silver bullion, and coin, promissory notes and other securities, and the law declares that "on every sale or contract for sale as aforesaid, there shall be made and delivered by the seller to the buyer a bill or memorandum of such sale or contract on which there shall be affixed a lawful stamp or stamps in value equal to the amount of tax on such sale," and that every such bill or memorandum of sale, or contract of sale, shall show the date thereof, the name of the seller, the amount of the sale or contract, and the matter or thing to which it refers. By the same act Schedule B was "amended under the head of contract, by striking out the words following: 'Stocks, bonds and notes of hand'." Also, by inserting under the head of contract, after the words "for each note or memorandum of sale, ten cents"; the words following: "Bill or memorandum of the sale or contract for the sale of stocks, bonds, gold or silver bullion, coin, promissory notes or other securities, shall pay a stamp tax at the rate provided in section ninety-nine."

It is plain, then, that the form presented by — —, which relates to the sale of shares of stock, does not fall within that portion of the amended Schedule B by which a tax of ten cents is imposed upon each "broker's note or memorandum of sale of any goods or merchandise, or property of any kind or description issued by brokers or by persons acting as such"; for Congress relieved it from that tax by striking out the words "stocks, bonds," and "notes of hand." For this reason the office has declined to authorize the imprinting of ten cent stamps upon blanks of this character.

At the same time that the stamp tax of ten cents was removed from the broker's note or memorandum of the sale of stocks, another tax was imposed upon bills or memoranda not only of sales but of contracts of sales (Section 99). The delivery of the stocks is not necessary to create liability to the tax under Section 99; it is sufficient if there be a contract of sale.

The instrument enclosed by you contains all that is required in a bill or memorandum of the sale of the contract for the sale of stocks, &c.; the date, name of the seller, amount of sale or contract, and the matter or thing to which it refers. It is admitted by these gentlemen that the instrument is given upon the contract for a sale of stocks; it is required by law upon such a contract, and should be stamped as prescribed in Section 99. They are in error in supposing they incur liability to tax under that section only when a sale is completed by delivery, and if they have been acting upon that understanding they have failed to comply with the requirements of the law.

You say "it seems to be the general custom of brokers to stamp all their contracts ten cents, and the ticket of sale when the stock is delivered one-tenth of one per cent." I shall take early steps to have this practice brought to the notice of the proper officers.—Ed.

IRR v.VII, February 1, 1868, p.36

Bankers' and Brokers' Sales.

I have heretofore in my annual reports expressed the opinion that the attempt to collect taxes by means of stamps upon instruments having no permanent value for purposes of evidence would prove a failure. Certainty rather than severity of punishment must be relied on to support the sanction of penal statues. When both the maker and receiver of an instrument believe that the paper will never come under the eye of a revenue officer, it matters little what penalty is denounced for the omission to affix a stamp. If the writing is of such a character that its invalidity as an instrument of evidence is of slight consequence, evasions of the tax will naturally result. To no one of the various stamp taxes now imposed do these considerations apply with greater force than to the memoranda required of brokers when making sales of coin and securities. These memoranda are in no sense evidences of title. In fact, they are only passed in obedience to the statute requirement, and are soon thrown aside, and destroyed. If stamps have been affixed they can easily be removed, and it is hardly necessary to make an attempt to efface the cancellation marks before placing them upon another memoranda. So little scrutiny is bestowed upon these papers as they pass from brokers, that specimens have been presented of stamps which had been issued by gentlemen of the highest respectability while bearing plainly the marks of two and even three successive cancellations. During the fiscal year 1866, when the tax upon sales of this description was paid monthly to the collectors, the receipts from this source were in excess of $2,500,000. In August, 1866, the tax was reduced from one-twentieth to one-hundredth of one per cent, and made payable by stamps; but at the same time such changes were made in the terms of the statute as to render subject many sales which had before escaped taxation, and thus to some extent to counteract the effect of the reduction in rate. Since that time the sales of stamps have been scarcely larger than before, and I am satisfied that a return to the former method would secure a more thorough enforcement of the law and yield much richer results.

Report of the Commissioner of Internal Revenue [E. A. Rollins] for the year ending June 30, 1868, pp.XXIV-XXV.

The Stamp Tax on Bankers' and Brokers' Sales Repealed by Act of June 6, 1872.

Treasury Department,
Office of Internal Revenue,
Washington, August 23, 1872.

M. B. Blake, Esq., Collector of Internal Revenue, New York City.

Sir: Yours of the 5th instant, enclosing a letter addressed to yourself by John T. Denny, Esq., Chairman of the Law Committee of the New York Stock Exchange, has been received.

You inquire whether the act of June 6, 1872, repeals the stamp tax on bankers and brokers sales.

In reply I have to say that, in my opinion it does.

The tax in question, as originally imposed by Section 99, of the Act of June 30, 1864, was regularly assessed and collected as therein prescribed. That section, however, was subsequently so amended by Section 9, of the Act of July 13, 1866, as to change the tax from an assessed tax to a stamp tax, and require brokers, banks, and bankers, on every sale and contract for the sale of stocks, bonds, gold or silver bullion, coin, promissory notes or other securities made by them, to make and deliver to the purchaser of such sale or contract, a bill or memorandum, and to affix thereto a lawful stamp or stamps in value equal to the amount of tax due upon such sale.

By the same section of the same act, Schedule B, preceding one hundred and seventy-one of the Act of June 30, 1864, as amended, was still further amended "by inserting under the head of contract after the words for each note or memorandum of sale, ten cents," the words following: "Bill or memorandum of the sale or contract for the sale of stocks, bonds, gold or silver bullion, promissory notes or other securities, shall pay a stamp tax at the rate provided in section ninety-nine."

Section 99 was at the same time so amended as to declare that the provisions of law in relation to stamp duties in Schedule B of the Act of June 30, 1864, as amended should apply to the stamp taxes imposed by Section 99; and it was enacted in Section 131, of the Act of June 30, 1864, that "there shall be levied, collected and paid for, and in respect of the several instruments, matters and things mentioned in the schedule (marked B) . . . the several duties or sums of money set down in figures against the same respectively, or otherwise specified or set forth in said schedule."

The statute upon this subject as amended by the Act of July 13, 1866, remained unchanged until June 6, 1872.

It is enacted in Section 36 of the Act of June 6, 1872, as follows: "That on and after the first day of October, eighteen hundred and seventy-two, all taxes imposed by stamps under and by virtue of Schedule B of section one hundred and seventy of the act approved June thirtieth, eighteen hundred and sixty-four, and the several acts amendatory thereof, be and the same are hereby repealed, excepting only the tax of two cents on bank checks, drafts, or orders."

You will notice that this repeal is not simply a striking out of the schedule or of some portion thereof, but is a repeal of the tax itself, without regard to whether it is imposed by two distinct provisions of the law or not.

Though, strictly, Schedule B is not a schedule of Section 170, but of Section 151, and the stamp duties mentioned in Schedule B are imposed not by the schedule itself, but by Section 151, the purpose and intent of Congress is too clear from the context, and from the other parts of the statute, to admit of a doubt that the several duties set down in figures against the several instruments, matters, and things mentioned and described in Schedule B, or otherwise specified or set forth therein, are repealed on and after the first day of October next.

A bill or memorandum of the sale of stocks, bonds, etc., is one of the instruments, matters, or things mentioned and described in Schedule B. The duty thereon is not "set down in figures against the same," but it is "otherwise specified or set forth in the said schedule." "That is certain which may be made certain"; and the reference to Section 99 is a clear specification and setting forth within the meaning of the words of the statute.

In his letter to you, Mr. Denny calls attention to certain newspaper correspondence in which it is stated to have been the intention of Congress to retain this tax.

A statute should be so construed as to effect the intention of the Legislature; but this intention is to be searched for in the words which the Legislature has employed to convey it; and where the words of a statute are plain and unambiguous, the Legislature must be understood to mean what they have plainly expressed, and consequently no room is left for construction.

In my opinion there is no such ambiguity in the language of the statute upon the point under consideration as to warrant me in supposing that Congress intended anything different from what that language imparts.

Very respectfully,
B. J. Sweet,
Acting Commissioner.

IRR v.XVI, August 24, 1872, p.57

CONVEYANCE

In all cases of conveyance of real estate by deed, the stamps used must answer to the value of the estate conveyed.

When the consideration is nominal, the value of the property conveyed is the measure of the stamp duty.

When an estate that is encumbered by mortgage or deed of trust is conveyed, subject to the encumbrance, the stamp must answer to the value of the equity, unless the payment of the mortgage debt is assumed by the grantor; in which case the stamp must answer to the value of the whole estate.

Note—Where land is sold subject to a mortgage without a covenant by the grantee to pay the mortgage debt, the stamp must be appropriate to the consideration of the grant, of which consideration the mortgage will not form a part. Where the grantee assumes to pay the mortgage debt, that debt is properly estimated as a part of the consideration, and the stamp will be such as is appropriate to the whole value of the land.—(Com'r Lewis.)

Boutwell (1863), Decisions (from No. 75)

Deeds of land made under the decree of a master in chancery are subject to stamp duty as conveyances.

Boutwell (1863), Rulings (No. 233)

The conveyance of property to heirs, by an executor, administrator, or trustee, should be stamped, according to the full value of the property.

Boutwell (1863), Rulings (No. 249)

In all conveyances of real estate by deed, the law provides that the stamp or stamps affixed must answer to the *value* of the estate conveyed. If the *consideration* specified does not correspond with the *value,* the grantee and all holders under him will accept the title with all its perils. If the consideration named in a deed be "natural love and affection," and the grantor neglect to affix stamps corresponding in amount to the value of the estate, it is not easy to see how the title could be sustained, when it appears from the deed itself that there was a sale of the estate, although the consideration named is not such as to require a stamp under the excise law.

Boutwell (1863), Rulings (No. 261)

Although the writ or original process in a suit may have been properly stamped, a sheriff's deed under an execution issued upon the judgment will require to be stamped under the head of "conveyance."

The date of the deed must determine its liability to stamp duty, independently of the date of the original process.

Boutwell (1863), Rulings (No. 271)

Every conveyance, whether by quit-claim or warranty-deed, must bear a stamp, or stamps, corresponding to the value of the estate conveyed, whether the conveyance be made by quit-claim or warranty-deed. In several States it is the custom to discharge a mortgage or deed of trust by a quit-claim deed from the mortgagee to the mortgagor. A quit-claim deed, in such a case, does not operate to convey the estate; it is merely in substance a release of the mortgage under it. Being, therefore, equivalent to a discharge of the mortgage, it has been held that such a quit-claim deed is exempt from stamp duty.

Boutwell (1863), Rulings (No. 280)

Deeds of real estate sold by a sheriff under process of law are subject to stamp duty.

Boutwell (1863), Rulings (No. 284)

If A, as the grantee of the widow and heirs of B, conveys the interest granted to him by their deed, together with his own interest, to another party, the stamp duty upon his deed must answer to the entire value of his estate.

A quitclaim deed, made to A by the widow and heirs of B, must be stamped, according to the value of the interest conveyed by them.

Boutwell (1863), Rulings (No. 291)

The *actual value* of an estate conveyed is the measure of the stamp duty required upon a deed conveying it.—(See "conveyance" in Schedule B, in the act of July 1, 1862.)

A stamp should be affixed to an instrument subject to stamp duty, by the party executing the instrument, at the time of its execution; and the stamp should be cancelled by the party affixing it, by writing his initials and the date thereof upon the stamp.

A party executing an instrument, and failing to stamp it, is liable to a penalty of $50, which penalty should be enforced by the local collector of internal revenue.

On and after June 1, 1863, any instrument executed without the requisite stamp will for that cause be invalid, and the record thereof will likewise be of no effect.

Boutwell (1863), Rulings (No. 302)

In the case of conveyance of property subject to a ground rent, the rent is to be regarded as a separate and distinct estate in the land from that held by the owner of the property.

Boutwell (1863), Rulings (No. 309)

When an estate is conveyed subject to widow's dower, actually assigned, the following rules should be observed in ascertaining the amount of stamp duty imposed by law upon the deed:

The present value of the portion of the estate covered by the dower should be ascertained by appropriate tables; that sum deducted from the value of the estate, estimated free of all encumbrances, and the stamp duty upon the deed measured by the remainder.

In most cases the consideration named in a conveyance of an estate subject to dower, as above, would indicate the value of the required stamps.

Boutwell (1863), Rulings (No. 312)

In all cases of deeds given for real estate, they should be stamped under head of "Conveyance," in "Schedule B," act of July 1, 1862, except in case of "trust deed" for security for the payment of money. In the latter case the deed, or the note or bond secured thereby, must be stamped as a "mortgage."

Boutwell (1863), Rulings (No. 313)

May 5, 1863.

Sir: Your letter of February 5 was duly received, but as a decision upon the stamp duty required upon "coal land leases," or upon assignments thereof, has been withheld for careful consideration, yours, with other letters upon the same subject, has not been answered ere this.

In reply thereto I have the honor to state that those leases are construed to be "conveyances," and as such to be stamped under head of "conveyance," as per "Schedule B," in the act of July 1, 1862. The assignment of such a lease should also be stamped under the head of "conveyance," as above, the consideration paid being the measure of stamp duty. If the consideration in such an assignment is $33,000, the stamp duty required is $60.

In the case presented of a price per ton of coal mined, there being nothing in the contract to indicate more accurately its probable value, the practical difficulty of ascertaining the value will be met, should it arise, by the resident revenue officers.

Very respectfully,
Edward McPherson,
Deputy Commissioner.

To J. Brisbin, Esq., *Superintendent, &c.*

Boutwell (1863), Correspondence (No. 2)

January 31, 1863.

Sir: Your letter of the 29th instant has been received, giving the statement of Charles Remelin, esq., deceased, on which you ask an opinion.

Said Jacob Lohweigsehop died about ten years since, leaving a widow and four daughters. He left his property to the former, during her life, and then it was to revert to the heirs, as aforesaid. He further states that these heirs have now agreed to a partition among themselves, and have made quitclaim deeds to each other, in each of which the consideration is one dollar. Mr. Remelin desires to know whether these deeds are subject to stamp duty, and if so, to what stamp.

In reply, I would say that if, as I presume from your letter, the heirs are tenants in common, and are making an equal division of the property among themselves, each deed will be a conveyance of three-fourths of the estate described in the deed, and must be stamped to answer to three-fourths of the value of the property so described.

In all cases, whether a conveyance is a "quitclaim," or a "warranty deed," if the consideration named in the deed, or the value of the property conveyed exceeds $100, stamps, as prescribed under the head of conveyance, are required.

To R. M. W. Taylor, Esq., *Cincinnati, Ohio.*

Boutwell (1863), Correspondence (No. 6)

I have received your letter, with form of lease of land for ninety-nine years, with right of renewal forever, and assignment of the same by the lessee or his representatives, enclosed.

I am of opinion that the assignment, or deed as it more properly is, must be stamped as a conveyance. The lease must also be regarded as a conveyance, and when made, it must bear stamps proportionate to its value. This valuation may be fixed by the market price, or by converting the annual rent into a capital sum at the legal rate of interest at which money may be obtained upon such security.

The assignment of a lease is subject to the same stamp as the original.

George E. Sangston, Esq.,
Clerk of the Superior Court, Baltimore, Md.

Boutwell (1863), Correspondence (No. 10)

Deeds of partition, or releases between tenants in common, are not deeds or conveyances by which title to real estate is conveyed, nor does consideration pass between the parties, but the object of such release is simply to limit and define the right of the respective parties, and are not subject to stamp.

Boutwell (1865), Rulings (No. 199)

A "antenuptial declaration," although drawn as a deed of trust, can be considered merely as a certificate, and requires a five-cent stamp.

Boutwell (1865), Rulings (No. 218)

Where parties owning lands as tenants in common become a corporation, the conveyance of lands by the individuals to the corporation changes the title and is subject to stamp-duty.

Boutwell (1865), Rulings (No. 222)

Stamp-duty on deed of conveyance must be appropriate to the full value of the estate conveyed. . . . . If the conveyance is a deed of gift or other assurance of title made without valuable and adequate consideration, it is not subject to stamp-duty, but confers a succession and is subject to tax.

Boutwell (1865), Rulings (No. 224)

If a company hold land in their associate name, and convey to an individual, whether a member of the company or not, in exchange for the stock, or for money, such conveyance requires a stamp, and the amount is determined by the value of the estate conveyed.

Boutwell (1865), Rulings (No. 225)

Where two tenants in common, for the purpose of making partition, convey the land to a third party who conveys to each his share, such conveyances are not subject to stamp-duty as conveyances, because there was no sale. If the three conveyances are but a part of one transaction and made at the same time, although deeds of gift, they do not confer a succession and become liable to the ad valorem tax.

Boutwell (1865), Rulings (No. 232)

A release or discharge of a mortgage is not subject to stamp-duty; neither would a quitclaim deed given by a mortgagee not in possession to the party holding the equity of redemption, be subject to stamp-duty as a conveyance, as there is no sale, and the payment of the mortgage-debt discharges the mortgage.

Boutwell (1865), Rulings (No. 239)

Where an instrument is not a conveyance of land sold, but merely a confirmation of a preexisting title, it is not subject to stamp-duty.

Boutwell (1865), Rulings (No. 260)

An instrument conveying a life-estate, in consideration of pay, is liable to stamp, which is determined by the amount paid. If a life-estate is conveyed without valuable and adequate consideration, it is a succession, not liable to stamp-duty.

Boutwell (1865), Rulings (No. 261)

A pew-deed is merely a conveyance of personal property, and is subject to a stamp-duty of five cents as an agreement.

Boutwell (1865), Rulings (No. 269)

It is a principle of the English stamp-law that instruments are to be stamped according to their legal effect, and I have always adhered to the same principle in expounding our own stamp-act. If a written contract operates as a conveyance, it must therefore be stamped as such; if as an agreement before the conveyance of land, an agreement stamp only is necessary when another instrument is required in order to carry the agreement into effect.

Boutwell (1865), Rulings (from No. 275)

Under the construction given to the statute by the courts of Massachusetts, a sale of standing wood is not a sale of an interest in real estate, and such bill of sale would therefore be subject to a stamp-duty of five cents, as an agreement or contract, being a transfer of personal property.

Boutwell (1865), Rulings (No. 280)

Stamp On Quit Claim Deeds.

Quit claim deeds, as conveying the same property as warrantee deeds, are exempt from stamp duty.

IRR v.I, February 4, 1865, p. 34

Stamping of Perpetual Leases, Conveyances, &c.

Office of Internal Revenue
Washington, May 4, 1865.

Gentlemen: Your letters of April 15 and 21, and also your letter of February 3, an answer to which has been delayed for the purpose of affording a better opportunity to examine the questions raised, have been received.

The decisions holding perpetual leases to be conveyances, and subject to stamp duty as such, were made in conformity with the local State law within the jurisdiction of which the cases arose.

The stamp duty on an instrument is to be determined by its legal effect, rather than its particular form, and as the United States court in questions affecting real estate follow the local laws, this office will of course adopt the same construction in determining the liability of particular instrument to stamp duty. In the absence of information as to how the leases in question are held and treated under the local laws of your State, I can only lay down the following rule for your guidance:—

If, under the local law of your State, such instruments are held to be in legal effect conveyances of a fee simple estate, they must be held subject to stamp duty as conveyances of such a title, and the stamp duty will be measured by resolving the annual rental into a capital sum. If, on the other hand, it is held to be a conveyance of a leasehold estate merely, the instrument is subject to stamp duty as a lease.

If the lessee assigns his interest, such assignment will be subject to the same duty as the original lease, and if any consideration is to be paid for such assignment beyond the yearly rent, it will be subject to an additional stamp duty as a conveyance on the consideration or value of the assignment.

Your practice, as stated by you, in regard to stamping assignment of leases, is correct.

The determination of the question as to what under your State law is held to be the legal effect of such an instrument as the lease referred to, will, under the foregoing rule, enable you to determine readily all the questions raised by you.

Very respectfully,
Joseph J. Lewis,
Commissioner.

IRR v.I, June 24, 1865, p.196

[Ed. note: cf. *IRR* v.II, August 12, 1865, p.45, under Inland Exchange.]

Deeds of Joint Tenants and Tenants in Common.

Where a partition of real estate between joint tenants or tenants in common cannot be made without being detrimental to the parties concerned, and the Court orders the referees to sell the land at public auction, and a deed of the same is made to the purchaser, such deed must be stamped as other deeds. There is an actual sale and a valuable consideration passed. The stamp on the original process does not cover the deed.

IRR v.II, August 12, 1865, p.45

Foreclosure of Mortgage and Sheriffs' Deed.

Where a mortgage is foreclosed and special execution issues, and the land is sold the same as on general execution, the deed made by the sheriff must be stamped as other deeds.

IRR v.II, August 12, 1865, p.45

Burial-lot Certificates.

Certificates of burial-lots being in the nature of conveyances, are subject to stamp-duty as such.

IRR v.II, August 12, 1865, p.45

Deed to Child—Succession.

The deed which you enclose may be regarded as a deed of gift from parent to child.

As there is no sale, no stamp is required. But the Act of Congress of June 20, 1864, section 133, imposes upon the property thus conveyed to children, a succession duty of one per cent. upon the value of the interest of the succession.

Though the above deed is dated April 1st, 1864, yet there are no indications upon the face of it, that the deed became *effective* until after the passage of the above act.

"The interest of the grantee, therefore, in the property conveyed, is taxable at the above rate of duty."

To Assessor Presbrey, Buffalo, N.Y.

IRR v.III, January 13, 1866, p.13

Stamping of Deeds.

Office of Internal Revenue,
Washington, Feb. 10, 1866.

Sir: Your letter of the 31st ult., enclosing one from Messrs. Rutledge & Young, has been received. They write that, during the existence of slavery, manumission was impossible, and gifts to slaves were impossible. At the same time there were a large number of slaves held in nominal servitude only, who were allowed to enjoy their own earnings, and because they could not hold their property in their own names, they were accustomed to select some white persons in whom they reposed confidence, and such persons took the title absolutely in their own names, without any declaration of trust. Now that slavery has ceased to exist, and the freedmen have become capable of taking, holding, and granting title to lands, they propose to have their property conveyed and confirmed to them by deed. No consideration passes, and a nominal one only is expressed in the deeds. You inquire if such conveyances are subject to stamp duty.

In reply I have to say that a stamp duty is imposed only upon conveyances of *realty sold*. In the case stated there is no *sale;* the purpose and effect of such deeds is merely to place the *legal* title where the *equitable* one is. No stamp, therefore, is necessary, unless the deed contain covenants, in which case it should be stamped as any agreement. Neither in such cases is there any succession tax. The grantee acquires no additional property by such a transfer; the deed simply confirms the preexisting equitable title.

Very respectfully,
D. C. Whitman,
Deputy Commissioner.

IRR v.III, March 10, 1866, p.78

Stamping of Partition Deeds.

Treasury Department
Office of Internal Revenue
Washington, March 19, 1866.

Sir: In reply to your letter I have to state that when land is held by parties as tenants in common, and an equal partition is made, the deeds are not subject to stamp duty, since there is no *sale,* but a mere marking or defining the boundaries of the portion which each party owns, and after the partition is made the estate which was owned by each is the same that was before. But if any money is paid by one party to the other because the share taken by him is worth more than the other, then the deed from his grantor should be stamped appropriate to the amount of such consideration.

The case stated by you comes under this rule, and the deed executed by B should bear a stamp duty appropriate to $1,000, if that is the consideration paid by A. The same rule prevails in the case of deeds of partition made by order of the court and executed by the sheriff.

Very respectfully,
D. C. Whitman,
Deputy Commissioner.

IRR v.III, April 14, 1866, p.118

Deeds to a Trustee for Wife, Without Consideration, Not Liable to Stamp.

Office of Internal Revenue,
Washington, April 24th, 1866.

Sir: I reply to your letter of the 20th inst., that, where real estate is conveyed from a husband to the wife through a third person, without any consideration passing, the deeds from the husband to the trustee, and from the trustee to the wife, are not regarded as conveyances within the meaning of the law subject to stamp duty.

Very respectfully,
D. C. Whitman,
Deputy Commissioner.

Alfred Wells, Esq.,
Assessor, Ithaca, N.Y.

IRR v.III, May 12, 1866, p.151

Conveyances of Property for Account of Wives–Income Succession.

Office of Internal Revenue,
Washington, March 7, 1865.

Sir: I reply to yours of the 9th inst., that a conveyance of real property by husband to wife through a third party is considered for all purposes of the law a conveyance directly to the wife or equitable grantee. Such a conveyance, without consideration, constitutes a succession—but the wife is not liable to succession tax.

No stamp is required on a conveyance of property without valuable or adequate consideration. Such a conveyance cannot, however, be allowed to affect the liability of the grantor to the same income tax which he would have otherwise been subject to. In other words, no deduction can be made from income on account of such conveyance.

Respectfully,
D. C. Whitman,
Deputy Commissioner

R. Savage, Esq.,
Assessor, San Jose, Cal.

IRR v.III, June 2, 1866, p.172

Stamp Tax on Conveyance and Succession Tax on Gift to a Son.

Treasury Department,
Office of Internal Revenue,
Washington, June 7, 1866.

Sir: Your letter of the 2d inst. has been received, and is as follows: "A. is the owner of a tract of land valued at $19,000, which he desires to convey to his son B. A. also desires to give his son $15,000, therefore requires B. to pay only $4,000 for the land. B. returns $15,000 as a succession. The consideration named in the deed is its full value, $19,000. What stamp duty is required?" I reply that the stamp duty upon the deed is four dollars.

In section 132 it is provided that a conveyance of real estate "without valuable and adequate consideration" shall be held and taken to confer upon the grantee a succession. To prevent liability to a succession tax the consideration must be not only valuable but also adequate; and when the consideration is manifestly inadequate, a succession tax should be paid upon the value of the *entire* estate conveyed, in addition to any stamp tax that may be imposed upon the conveyance.

In the case stated by you there is a stamp tax of four dollars, and a succession tax of one hundred and ninety dollars.

Very respectfully,
D. C. Whitman,
Deputy Commissioner.

J. M. Barrett, Esq.,
Assessor, Spring Valley, Green Co., O.

IRR v.III, June 23, 1866, p.197

Stamps Duty on Re-Conveyances.

Office of Internal Revenue
Washington, Oct. 19, 1866.

Sir: In your letter of the 16th instant you state a case, in substance as follows:

''A conveyed certain real estate to B by a deed, which were recorded in March, 1866. The consideration for the deed was $2,900, and stamps were affixed to it to the amount of three dollars. B fails to pay for the land, and upon the payment of one hundred dollars by A, and the cancellation of the debt, reconveys it. You inquire how the conveyance should be stamped.''

I reply that the consideration for the reconveyance is three thousand dollars; if interest has accrued upon the $2,900 it is more. The second deed should bear stamps appropriate to the consideration, which is not less that $3,000, and may be more; the stamp duty is three dollars, and MAY be three dollars and fifty cents.

Very respectfully,
Thomas Harland,
Deputy Commissioner.

To A. H. Brown, Esq., *Collector, Indianapolis*

IRR, v.IV, November 3, 1866, p. 142

Conveyance from Municipal Corporations, &c., of Lands Sold for Taxes Exempt from Stamp Duty.

A conveyance of lands sold for unpaid taxes issued since August 1st, 1866, by the officers of any county, town, or other municipal corporation in the discharge of their strictly official duties, is exempt from stamp tax.

IRR v.V, February 9, 1867, p.45

Collector.—The following decision will answer your question, and save you the trouble of referring the matter to Washington:—''When for the purpose of transferring property from husband to wife, or from wife to husband, or from one of them to both jointly, deeds are made to a third party and then back from him to either or both, such instruments need not to be stamped as conveyances, as there is no sale, but only as agreements; but if they contain Powers of Attorney, these should have their appropriate stamps.''

Ed.

IRR v.V, March 30, 1867, p.99

Revenue Stamps on Bankrupt Documents.

The attention of Registers in Bankruptcy is directed to the ruling of the office of Internal Revenue respecting the revenue stamps to which certain papers in bankruptcy are held to be liable. The communication was addressed to Register Finnell, of Covington, Kentucky, under date of the 6th inst., and states:

A register's deed to the assignee should be stamped as a general contract or agreement, and if it contains powers these should have their appropriate stamps.

The bond of the assignee for the faithful discharge of duty requires a $1 stamp.

A letter of attorney to represent creditors, requires a fifty-cent stamp, as a power for a purpose not particularly specified in schedule B.

The deed of assignee to purchasers should be stamped at the usual rate of deeds.

It is understood that the professions are not united in their opinion as to the correctness of the ruling which requires Register's deed to assignee to be stamped, inasmuch as the deed is regarded as issued by an officer of the United States, and therefore exempt. The question will probably soon be presented for judicial opinion. The expense of stamps would curtail the Register's fees.

IRR v.VI, August 31, 1867, p.68

Ground-Rent Deeds.

Ground-rent deeds should be stamped at the same rate as other conveyances of realty sold; fifty cents for each five hundred dollars, or fractional part of five hundred dollars, of the *consideration or value.*

IRR v.VI, November 9, 1867, p.162

Partition Deeds between Tenants in Common and Joint Tenants.

Partition deeds between *tenants in common* need be stamped only as agreements, unless money or other valuable consideration is paid for equality of partition: (Series 3, No. 10, p.11, also Internal Revenue RECORD, vol. V., p. 173,) but deeds between *joint tenants* should be stamped as conveyances of realty sold. In the first case, each tenant owns the *the whole of a part,* and there is no sale, but merely a marking out or defining of the part belonging to each; in the latter case, each owns *a part of the whole,* and in what is usually denominated a *division* in such case, there is an *exchange* of lands. An exchange does not differ materially from bargain and sale.

IRR v.VI, November 9, 1867, p.162

Basis of Stamp Duty on Deed for Inadequate Valuable Consideration.

When a conveyance of realty is made upon an actual valuable consideration which is *manifestly inadequate,* the deed should be stamped according to the amount of valuable consideration, and a succession tax (unless the successor be the wife of the predecessor,) should be assessed upon the value of the land conveyed, *less* such consideration.

IRR v.VI, November 23, 1867, p.179

Instruments for Transfer Land under Decree of Court.

When the property of a deceased person is sold under a decree of Court for the purpose of dividing the proceeds among the heirs, the deed, *proces verbal,* or other instrument whereby the transfer is made, should be stamped at the usual rate of conveyances of realty sold.

IRR v.VI, November 23, 1867, p.179

Release to Remainder-Man for Valuable Consideration.

A release of his estate, by a tenant for life to the owner of the remainder, for a valuable consideration, should be stamped at the usual rate of conveyances of realty sold.

IRR v.VI, November 30, 1867, p.186

Wife's Conveyance to Trustee for Benefit of Husband Without Valuable Consideration—Agreement.

When a wife conveys real property, without valuable consideration to her husband, through the intervention of a trustee, neither her deed to the trustee, nor the trustee's to the husband, need be stamped as a conveyance of "*realty sold,*" but each should be stamped as a contract or agreement.

IRR v. VI, December 21, 1867, p. 210

Stamp on Deed given after Property Improved by Purchaser.

Editor of Record:–

In 1865, A purchased a piece of land on contract for $500; at the end of three years he pays for it and receives his deed. He had improved it to such an extent that it is now worth $5,000. What stamp does the deed require?

Asst. Assr.

The deed is subject to 50c. stamp duty. That is the consideration agreed upon and is not questioned as being adequate at the time when the contract was made. The increased value accruing to the land as improved by the purchaser and equitable owner belongs to him by right of his acts and his ownership, and does not come to him by the conveyance of the legal title. The consideration was $500 only and the appropriate stamp duty is fifty cents.—Ed.

IRR v.VIII, December 19, 1868, p.198

Stamp Duty on Ground Rent Deeds.

This question was not long since presented to the department by a law firm in Philadelphia. They wrote:

"In a deed conveying property of the value of $1,000, by which a ground rent of $60 per annum is reserved as the actual payment therefore, an additional nominal consideration of $1 is perhaps invariably inserted, though never paid. Custom affixes $1 stamp.

"It has been recently suggested, however, that owing to the insertion of the one dollar clause, an additional stamp charge of fifty cents is incurred.

"Should not the stamp duty be regulated by the actual consideration or value rather than by the merely nominal amount expressed? A negative decision would render defective nearly all the ground rent deeds executed in Philadelphia since the passage of the first stamp act."

In reply, instructions were communicated through Mr. Wm. R. Leeds, Collector of Internal Revenue, to the effect that in the opinion of the Department a *one dollar stamp* would suffice—the merely nominal consideration being entirely disregarded.—Ed.

IRR v.X, October 23, 1869, p.124

Assignments of Certificates of Sales of Public Lands should be Stamped as Agreements.—
A Governor's Patents and Certificates of Land Commissioner are considered Exempt.

State Department, Michigan,
Secretary's Office,
Lansing, March 4, 1872.

To the Hon. Commissioner of Internal Revenue, Washington, D.C.

Dear Sir: For the purpose of obtaining your decision on a point of considerable interest to the people of this State, allow me to call your attention to the following statement of facts:

Certain lands belonging to this State are sold on part payment, and a certificate of purchase issued by the Commissioner of the State Land Office in the form shown by the inclosed blank marked "A." These certificates are frequently held for a long term of years, and transferred from one occupant of the land to another in the manner indicated by the inclosed blank marked "B," the law requiring the execution to be the same as for a deed. When any owner of such certificate desires to obtain a patent for his land, he pays the amount of the principal, interest, taxes, etc., due the State to the Commissioner of the State Land Office, who attaches to the aforesaid certificate another certificate in the form shown by the inclosed blank marked "C," to the effect that such payment has been made in full, and that the holder thereof is entitled to a patent therefore on presentation at the office of the Secretary of State, such presentation *usually* taking place *immediately,* but sometimes transfers are made as above *after full payment*.

Under the provision in the "Stamp Duties" law requiring every "conveyance, deed, instrument or writing, whereby lands, tenements, or other realty sold, shall be granted, assigned, or otherwise conveyed or vested in the purchaser," to be stamped to the amount of fifty cents for each and every $500 (or part thereof) of the consideration received therefore, backed up (as I am credibly informed by the gentleman who was Deputy Secretary of State of this State at the time aforesaid "Stamp Duties" law took effect) by the decision of the then Acting Commissioner of Internal Revenue, it has been the practice of this Department to require that each and every assignment of certificate aforesaid be stamped as required by the provision aforesaid before issuing a patent for the lands described therein. Occasionally the application of the aforesaid provision of the "Stamp Duties" law to the case under consideration has been questioned by different attorneys in the State, but not until recently has any great objection been made to stamping the papers as required. We are now, however, confronted by a formidable document from an old practitioner, denying its application, a copy of which I also inclose.

For your information as to our laws relating to the sale of lands by the State, I forward to you by mail, to-day, one copy first vol. Com. Laws of Mich., 1871 (the second is not yet in print). I also inclose herewith a blank form of patent, which is issued by the Governor through this office on the surrender of the certificates aforesaid.

You will greatly oblige by giving this matter your immediate attention, and state in your letter to me:

1. Whether in your opinion the aforesaid provision of the Stamp Duties law applies to the aforesaid assignments which bear date prior to the date of the full payment of the purchase price of the land.

2. Whether such provision applies to such assignments which bear date subsequent to the date of full payment.

3. Whether the provision of the Stamp Duties law relating to the stamping of contracts applies to such assignments either before or after the date of full payment, or both.

You will see by section 3,825 of the Compiled Laws aforesaid, where the title to the land is vested previous to the issue of patent, or date of full payment, and by section 3,834, what are the rights of the holders of such certificates of purchase.

Very respectfully,
Daniel Striker,
Secretary of State.

By G. M. Hasty, Deputy.

Treasury Department,
Office of Internal Revenue,
Washington, March 13, 1872.

The Hon. Daniel Striker, Secretary of State, Lansing, Mich.

Sir: Your letter of March 4, 1872, respecting stamp duty on assignments of certificates of sale of public lands in Michigan has been received. C. H. Miller, Esq., Collector of Internal Revenue, Ann Arbor, has this day been specially instructed in the case, and you are respectfully referred to him.

Very respectfully,
B. J. Sweet,
Acting Commissioner.

U.S. Internal Revenue, Collector's Office,
Third District, Mich.,
Ann Arbor, March 27, 1872.

The Hon. Daniel Striker, Secretary of State, Lansing, Mich.

Sir: Your letter addressed to the Commissioner of Internal Revenue, respecting stamp duty on assignments of certificates of sale of public lands, has been referred to this office with instructions to reply that certificates of sale of the form inclosed by you should be stamped as agreements; this applies both before and after payment for the land. The patents of the Governor and certificates of the Land Commissioners are considered exempt, under section 154, of the act of June 30, 1864, as amended.

Very respectfully,
B. F. Granger,
Collector of Third District, Michigan.

State Department, Michigan,
Secretary's Office,
Lansing, March 29, 1872.

The Hon. B. F. Granger, Collector, Third District, Michigan, Ann Arbor.

Dear Sir: Your favor of the 27th inst. is at hand. You say, "Certificates of sale of the form inclosed by you should be stamped as agreements." Do you mean by this that *assignments* of certificates of sale, of form inclosed by me, should be stamped as agreements?

Very respectfully,
Daniel Striker,
Secretary of State.

By G. M. Hasty, Deputy.

U.S. Internal Revenue, Collector's Office,
Third District Mich.,
Ann Arbor, March 30, 1872.

The Hon. Daniel Striker, Secretary of State, Lansing, Mich.

Sir: I mean *assignments* of certificates of the form inclosed require stamps as agreements.

Respectfully,
B. F. Granger,
Collector.

IRR v.XV, April 13, 1872, pp.109-10

ENTRY OF GOODS

Concerning stamp duty on entries of free goods coming from Canada.

June, 1863.

By Schedule B of the excise law, one of the subjects of stamp duty is an entry of any goods, wares, or merchandise at any custom-house, either for consumption or warehousing, not exceeding $100 in value, in which case the stamp duty is 25 cents; when the goods exceed $100, and do not exceed $500 in value, the duty is 50 cents; when the value exceeds $500, the duty is $1.

In the treaty with Great Britain, made June 5, 1854, called the reciprocity treaty, it is stipulated that certain articles, principally agricultural products, shall not be subject to impost. The language of the treaty in this particular is: "The articles enumerated in the schedule herewith annexed, being the growth and produce of the aforesaid British colonies or of the United States, shall be admitted into each country, respectively, free of duty." One of the last clauses in the schedule provides that the stamp duties imposed by the foregoing Schedule B, on manifests, bills of lading, and passage tickets, shall not apply to steamboats or other vessels plying between ports of the United States and ports in British North America.

This proviso shows that the subject of the trade between ports of the United States and ports of the British provinces was considered by Congress in passing the law, and there was no room to doubt that it was also considered by the committees of the two houses in preparing and maturing the bill, which it is well known was long in preparation, and thoroughly discussed in every point. It cannot be supposed to be, in any important provision, the product of hasty legislation. The existence of the reciprocity treaty could not have escaped the attention of the committee which had the bill in charge, nor of the members of either branch of the legislature, whose immediate constituents were interested in maintaining the faith of the treaty.

I am warranted, therefore, in assuming that Congress deliberately imposed this duty on entries with the treaty full in view, and that if there is any conflict between the provisions of the act and the stipulations of the treaty, that conflict was seriously purposed, and was not inadvertent or accidental. If there is a conflict, then a question of unusual gravity arises. That question is, whether an act of Congress that requires the levy of a duty, which an existing treaty declares shall not be levied, shall be carried into effect by the executive officers of the government, or whether, holding themselves bound by the conditions of the treaty as constituting a rule of municipal law of superior obligation, they will refuse to obey the statute, as being without authority.

As to that question, I do not propose to enter upon its consideration precipitately, or to go out of the way to meet it. I must first be convinced that there is an obvious, unquestionable, certain conflict between the stipulations of the treaty and the *requisitions* of the statute before I shall deem myself warranted in giving instructions to the collectors of the internal revenue as to which of two laws, each emanating from constitutional sources, shall be deemed paramount in the execution of their duties. I have deliberately considered the subject, and I am not prepared to say that there is any conflict between the treaty and the statute.

The duties contemplated by the treaty are clearly frontier duties or customs. Those imposed by the statute are stamp duties. The subjects of the customs are foreign products entering the ports of the country. The subjects of the stamp duties are, for the most part, written or printed instruments used in the ordinary business of the country. A stamp on a port entry is no more a duty on the goods described in the paper than a stamp on a conveyance is a tax on the lands granted by the deed. The instrument used is but a vehicle of the law used in the transportation or transfer of property, or in carrying out the contracts of the parties concerned, that may bear an appropriate burden of duty, without the subject of commercial transactions or contract being touched by it.

The tax ordered must be paid by the buyer or the seller, or both, and the necessity of such payment may enter into the consideration of the parties in making their bargain, but that is a consequence necessarily attendant on all taxes. The stamp duty on entries of grain from Canada may affect its price slightly in the market, but only incidentally, and not directly. An inconsiderable increase in the cost of transportation or of tolls on the New York canals would affect it much more seriously.

An agreement with Great Britain that Canadian breadstuffs shall be admitted into ports of the United States free of duty does not import that they shall be exempt from inland regulations relating to their receipts and transit, or to the expenses to which those regulations may subject them. It is true, indeed, that regulations might be made that would seriously embarrass the trade with the British provinces, and interfere with the objects of the treaty, and if such should appear to be the deliberate purpose of Congress in an act passed ostensibly as a tax law, Great Britain might have reason to complain; but even in such cases—in the silence of any complaint, officially, and of the recognition of its reasonableness by the executive head of our government—it would be assuming more authority than I see any title for, if this office were to take upon itself to interfere between the high contracting parties, and to release the agents of the government from their obligations to collect a tax imposed by act of Congress.

But there is nothing tending to show that Congress contemplated a restriction on the importation of free goods from Canada in the form of a stamp tax. Whatever may be the effect of the tax, it is but an incident, and, as such, the way it may happen to operate is not a subject of legitimate objection. If the two species of tax are different, it is certain that the imposition of one cannot be considered a violation of an agreement not to levy the other, when no such violation was designed. The one was clearly within the terms of the treaty. The other had no existence in this country as a national regulation at the date of the treaty, and there was certainly at that time no anticipation of its being brought into use during the ten years the treaty had to run.

The imposition of such a tax is not expressly forbidden by the conditions of the contract, and I do not see that any prohibition is implied.

The officers of the internal revenue are, therefore, instructed that the act of Congress requiring stamp entries must be enforced in relation to entries of free goods coming from Canada, as well as of goods coming from other foreign places.

Boutwell (1863), Decisions (No. 116)

The entry by the captain should include the manifest of the cargo, and the entry is therefore exempt from stamp duty, under the proviso of Schedule B of the excise law, when the vessel plies between ports of the United States and ports of British North America. If the owners enter the goods owned by them, respectively, the "entry" stamp will be required.

Boutwell (1863), Rulings (No. 293)

The withdrawal or entry of any goods from bonded warehouse, requires a fifty-cent stamp. Duplicates and triplicates the same stamp as original. Affidavit to withdrawal, being part of the same document, requires no stamp.

Boutwell (1865), Rulings (No. 210)

Duplicate Entries—Stamps on, not required.

The effect of the recent decision of the Commissioner of Internal Revenue, that stamps are not requisite upon duplicates of entries, is simply to discontinue the use of stamps upon such papers and not to make any other change in them, or dispense with any other formalities heretofore necessary in their preparation.—

Letter to Naval Officer, Charleston, S.C., May 7, 1868.

IRR v.VIII, August 22, 1868, p.62

Stamp Duty on Constructive Warehouse and Withdrawal Entries.

Office of Internal Revenue
Washington, June 30th, 1869.

Sir: I reply to your letter of the 26th instant, respecting stamp duty on "Warehouse and Withdrawal Entries."

That a constructive entry for warehousing, is considered the same as an actual one, as far as the stamp tax is concerned. This kind of entry is made for benefit of the parties, and not of the Government. When the entries for warehousing and withdrawal are simultaneous, stamp tax should be paid for both; 50 cents for the withdrawal entry, and from 25 cents to $1.00 for the warehouse entry, according to the value of the merchandise, making from 75 cts to $1.50 in all.

Very respectfully,
J. W. Douglass,
Deputy Commissioner.

Hon. T. Feran, *Act. Com. of Customs,*
Treasury Department.

IRR v.X, July 10, 1869, p.11

Revenue Stamps on Custom House Papers.
Treasury Department.
Oct. 5th, 1869.

It appearing that there exists a want of uniformity in practice at the several ports in affixing to Custom-house entries the stamps requisite under the Internal Revenue laws, the following instructions are hereby issued for the guidance of Collectors and other officers of customs.

Whenever entries are made for warehousing, or re-warehousing and withdrawal combined, according to the following forms of "Revised Warehouse Regulations of October 30th, 1868," viz:

Form 24. "Re-warehouse and withdrawal entry for consumption." (9 Record, 94.)

Form 26. "Re-warehouse entry for immediate exportation." (9 Record, 94.)

Form 31. "Entry for warehouse and immediate transportation in the United States." (9 Record, 95.)

Form 39. "Warehouse and exportation entry." (9 Record, 102.)

Form 45. "Entry for immediate transportation and exportation in bond to Canada,"– the stamps affixed thereto must be of sufficient amount to cover the separate entries of which they are composed. (9 Record, 103.)

The requisite stamps are of the denomination of 25 cents to $1 for the warehouse entry, according to the value of the merchandise, and 50 cents for the withdrawal entry, making from 75 cents to $1.50 in all.

To all official papers, the stamps required by law, and the official seal of office required, must be affixed at the time of completion.

Geo. S. Boutwell,
Secretary of the Treasury.

IRR v.X, October 16, 1869, p.122

Entries for Immediate Transportation not Subject to Internal Revenue Stamp Duty.

Entries for immediate transportation, which are prescribed by section 29, act of July 14, 1870, (Form A, in article of the regulations for the transportation of merchandise without appraisement, dated October 1, 1870,) are, in the opinion of the Commissioner of Internal Revenue, not subject to internal revenue stamp duty, for the reason that such entries are not made for any of the purposes specified in Schedule B, act of June 30, 1864. In this view the Department concurs. (Letter to Collector at New York, June 3, 1871.)

IRR v.XIV, December 30, 1871, p.211

EXPRESS

Concerning stamp tax on express receipts.
October, 1862.

The item marked "Express," schedule B of the excise law, was not intended to embrace the freight business of railroads and ordinary wagoners, but is limited to persons who are express carriers, and not merely common carriers, under the law. The distinction is well known in practical business. The express carrier is usually expected to take the parcel, box, or bundle, from the house or place of business of the consignor to the house or place of business of the consignee, while a railway company receives and delivers goods only at its own stations.

In the absence of specific language in the statutes, authorizing the broader construction, persons and companies engaged in transporting goods over the country, as such business is usually performed by railway corporations, are not liable to the payment of a stamp tax upon the receipt given for such goods. The first item in schedule B does not include such receipts for freight as are usually given by railway companies.

A receipt is, no doubt, in a technical sense, an agreement or contract, but in the ordinary use of language this close construction does not hold. Had Congress intended to include receipts, it would have been easy to have so provided in plain language.

Note.–By statute of March 3, 1863, section 10, express companies are subject to a duty of two per cent. on their gross receipts, and by the sixth section of the same act the stamp duty on express packages and receipts is repealed; but the foregoing decision still has practical value.

Boutwell (1863), Decisions (No. 28)

FOREIGN EXCHANGE

The act of March 3, 1863, does not change the stamp tax upon inland [Ed. note: should read "foreign"] bills of exchange when drawn singly, in duplicate, or in sets of three or more.

Boutwell (1863), Rulings (No. 230)

The phrase "Letter of Credit," as used in the excise law, Schedule B, is construed to refer to such letters as are equivalent to a "Bill of Exchange," the payment of which is not contingent upon any other transaction.

Boutwell (1863), Rulings (No. 308)

Foreign and Inland Bills of Exchange–Duplicates.

A foreign bill of exchange or letter of credit drawn in but payable out of the United States, if drawn singly, or otherwise than in sets of three or more, according to the custom of merchants and bankers, is liable to the same stamp tax as an inland bill of exchange, *i.e.* if drawn at sight or on demand, it is liable to a tax of two cents; if drawn otherwise than at sight or on demand, it should be stamped at the rate of five cents for each hundred dollars or fractional part thereof. Duplicates require the same amount of stamps as their original.

IRR v.V, June 15, 1867, p.188

Negotiable Foreign Promissory Note Endorsed in U.S.

A negotiable promissory note made, signed and issued in a foreign country, and made payable there, may be negotiated by endorsement in this country without liability to any United States stamp tax.

IRR v.VI, November 9, 1867, p.162

INLAND EXCHANGE

A renewal of a promissory note subjects it to the same amount of stamp as an original note.

Boutwell (1863), Rulings (No. 232)

Every foreign bill of exchange must be stamped by the party accepting it in this country, if the acceptor be not a fiscal agent or other public officer of the United States acting in his official capacity in accepting the bill. If the bill be drawn abroad and be negotiated before acceptance, it must be stamped at the time of its negotiation. If it be drawn at sight and paid on presentation, it must be stamped by the party paying it at the time of payment.

Boutwell (1863), Rulings (No. 243)

"Are sterling bills drawn in a foreign country, and sent to the United States for sale, and sold here, liable to the tax law requiring stamps?"

The law is not clear upon this point; but I am of opinion that any person who should issue such a bill in this country unstamped would be subject to the penalty prescribed in section 100 of the excise law of July 1, 1862.

It is also provided in section 100 that no bill of exchange shall be paid or negotiated without such stamp; and by the same section any person who shall pay or negotiate, or offer in payment any such draft or order without stamp, shall forfeit the sum of $100.

The provisions seem to be sufficient for the case suggested, and, I think, it will be a violation of the law for any person to negotiate in this country bills of exchange drawn in England, and payable there, unless they are stamped as required in Schedule B, under the head of "inland bills of exchange."

Boutwell (1863), Rulings (No. 245)

A note payable in corn is subject to stamp duty.

The party making the note, and the party receiving the same, must estimate the value of the corn at the date of the note, and affix a stamp thereto proportionate to the value thereof, agreeably to Schedule B.

The party receiving the note, without an adequate stamp, will do so at his peril, and the party making and issuing it, without an adequate stamp, will be subject to the penalties of section 95 of the excise law.

Boutwell (1863), Rulings (No. 251)

The sixth section of the act of March 3, 1863, in amendment of the excise law, is undoubtedly inconsistent with itself. It would seem to be a reasonable construction, to permit the use of the lowest denomination of stamp which the law allows. Under this construction, a note payable at any time not exceeding thirty-three days, including the grace days, would be subject to stamp duty at the rate of one cent for every two hundred dollars, or any fractional part thereof; it follows, of course, that a note payable at any time exceeding thirty-three days, and not exceeding sixty-three days, including the grace days, would be subject to a tax of two cents on every $200 or any fractional part thereof. The same rule should be applied to notes which fall into the other classes enumerated in said section.

Boutwell (1863), Rulings (No. 268)

Demand loans made on checks stamped as such, are an evasion of the law, if made with an understanding that the check is not to be presented, or not to be presented till a day future.

Notes, whether on demand or on time, are subject to stamp duty as "inland bills of exchange."

Boutwell (1863), Rulings (No. 275)

A promissory note which was executed prior to the passage of the excise law, and the payment of which has been, subsequently to the passage of that law, extended by agreement, is subject to stamp duty, under the head of "inland bills of exchange."

Boutwell (1863), Rulings (No. 297)

A promissory note, given for payment of twenty dollars, or less, is, by the act of March 3, 1863, subject to stamp duty, under head of "inland bills of exchange."

Boutwell (1863), Rulings (No. 298)

In reply to your queries respecting the additional liability of promissory notes payable at bank, to stamp duty as bank checks, I have to state, although the words "promise to pay at bank" may be accepted by the bank as sufficient authority to pay the note at maturity, and to charge the amount thereof to the account of the maker, they nevertheless do not constitute or convey any pledge, or guarantee on the part of the maker that he has the money in bank to meet the note when it falls due.

A check, on the other hand, is always supposed to be drawn against funds, and is to be regarded as an absolute appropriation of so much money as it calls for, in the hands of the banker, to the holder thereof, and, in ordinary practice, is payable on presentation.

I therefore hold that said form of note does not come within the meaning of the stamp act pertaining to bank checks, but is only liable to tax as a promissory note.

Boutwell (1863), Rulings (No. 303)

Every bond issued by a city must bear a stamp as inland bills of exchange, whether issued in redemption of an old bond or for a new debt.

Boutwell (1863), Rulings (from No. 306)

If a subscription list for the payment of a clergyman's salary, or for the building of a church, or for any benevolent purpose, is in the form of an agreement, it is subject to a stamp duty of five cents per sheet.

If it be in the form of a promissory note, it is subject to stamp duty under the head of "inland bills of exchange."

Any agreement of trustees or others with regard to the disposition of the funds raised on such subscription is subject to a further stamp duty of five cents.

Boutwell (1863), Rulings (No. 307)

The stamp duty required upon a demand note is the same as upon a note for thirty-three days.

Boutwell (1863), Rulings (No. 315)

Promissory notes made payable nominally on demand, and stamped as demand notes, (at the rate of one cent for every $200, or any fractional part thereof,) but given and received with an understanding between the parties that demand of payment will not be made within 33 days from date, are in fraud of the law, are not appropriately stamped, and when issued on or after the 1st of June, 1863, and not paid within 33 days from date, will be invalid and of no effect.

In addition to the stamp duty required upon notes drawn according to the forms you enclose, (as notes,) the power of attorney *to sell* stock, which is incorporated in each of them, is subject to a stamp duty of twenty-five cents, and the power of attorney to *transfer* stock, which is appended to one of them, is also subject to a stamp duty of twenty-five cents.

Boutwell (1863), Rulings (No. 316)

An instrument reading "Fourteen Dollars: R. Porter, Ferguson & Co., January 30, 1865," if given to Porter by Ferguson & Co., as an authority to draw or receive the sum mentioned, is substituted for a more formal instrument and used as a written evidence for an amount of money to be paid, and is subject to a stamp-duty of five cents on each hundred dollars or fractional part thereof, the same as a promissory note.

Boutwell (1865), Rulings (No. 287)

Certificates of Loan, in which there shall appear any written or printed evidence of an amount of money to be paid on demand, or at a time designated, are subject to stamp duty as "Promissory Notes."

IRR v.I, January 7, 1865, p.7

Check and Contract Stamp on Subscription List.

In the case of a subscription list where the heading involves a promise to pay the sums annexed, the party signing is liable to the stamp-duty required on promissory notes *unless* he pay the amount annexed his name at the time of signature; in which case the signing of his name should be regarded as a mere part of a memorandum. Where the heading of the list involves a condition on which the subscribers will pay the sums annexed their names, then each signature is held to create an agreement subject to a duty of five cents.

IRR v.II, July 22, 1865, p.21

Stamping of notes given to secure Deferred Payments on purchase of Real Estate.

Under the statute of Kentucky, a lien is retained upon the land conveyed for the payment of the purchase sum, if in any way the amount remaining unpaid appears in the deed. If notes for such unpaid sums are also given, such notes are liable to stamp duty. The fact that the notes are taken merely for convenience, and are in one sense a repetition of the liability expressed in the deed, in no manner releases them from stamp duty, for it is a well-established ruling of this Office that duplicates must be stamped the same as originals. If a person sees fit to bind himself by two different or distinct instruments, both should be stamped. The stamp upon the deed in the present case is necessary to validate the conveyance, and the fact that under the statute of Kentucky certain recitals in a deed create a lien upon the land, does not relieve the notes from stamp duty. If this were not so both the evidence of debt and the instrument securing it would escape all taxation, for the stamp affixed to the deed would be the same even if the whole purchase sum were paid at the time of the conveyance. But the obligation under the deed and upon the notes is not the same in character and intent. The deed simply creates a lien upon that particular tract of land. Payments of the notes may be enforced by the attachment of other property belonging to the maker or indorser of them, and collectable in the hands of the holder. They may have been negotiated, and have passed through the hands of, and been indorsed by, a dozen different persons, and the payment of them may be enforced against either of the indorsers, regardless of the lien upon the land.

IRR v.II, August 12, 1865, p.45

A custom prevails among some sharp financiers by which the government tax on notes is evaded. The Internal Revenue law requires stamps to be placed on all notes, at the rate of fifty cents per thousand dollars. In order to evade this tax a borrower of say one hundred thousand dollars, instead of giving his note for the amount, with a fifty dollar stamp upon it, draws a check, dated ahead, which calls only for a two cent stamp, and passes the check with the collaterals to the banker, thus evading the lawful tax of fifty dollars, less the two cent stamp.

IRR v.II, October 7, 1865, p.105

Stamp Duty on Bonds.

Office of Internal Revenue,
Washington, Jan. 30, 1866.

Sir: * * * I reply that the law requiring stamps upon conveyances, bonds, notes, &c., took effect October 1st, 1862, and that no stamps are necessary upon instruments issued prior to the date.

A bond for the *payment* of money, is subject to stamp duty at the rate of five cents for each one hundred dollars, or each fractional part thereof, as "written or printed evidence of an amount of money to be paid on demand or at a time designated;" a personal bond, given *as security* for the payment of any definite or certain sum of money, exceeding one hundred dollars, and not exceeding five hundred dollars, is subject to a stamp duty of fifty cents, and to fifty cents additional for each additional five hundred dollars or fractional part thereof.

An instrument subject to stamp duty, but issued and used, unstamped, prior to August 1st, 1864, may be made valid by stamping it as required by section 163 of the act of June 30, 1864; if issued since that date, the case falls under section 158 of said act as amended by the act of March 3, 1865.

Very respectfully,
D. C. Whitman,
Deputy Commissioner.

H. Powers, Esq.
Berryville, Clarke Co. VA

IRR v.III, February 10, 1866, p.45

Stamping of Promissory Notes on renewal thereof by Endorsement, and when Protest is waived.

Office, St. Louis Insurance Company,
St. Louis, June 7, 1866.

"*To the Commissioner of Internal Revenue, Washington City:*

"Sir: I desire to know whether the usual stamp be necessary under the law upon the renewal of an endorsed note when protest has been waived, and the receipt of interest on the extended time acknowledged on the note.

"Very respectfully, your obedient servant,
"George K. McGunnefle
President."

[Answer.]

Office of Internal Revenue,
Washington, July 6, 1866.

"Sir: Your letters of the 7th and 22d ultimo, relative to the extension of the time of payment for promissory notes, have been received.

The endorsement of a partial payment on the back of a note is regarded as a new memorandum, not subject to stamp duty, and the fact that by an implication of law it operates as an extension of the time of payment, does not effect the case.

The agreement to waive protest and notice of protest, signed by the party making it, is subject to stamp duty as a contract or agreement.

"Very respectfully,
"E. A. Rollins,
Commissioner."

IRR v.IV, August 18, 1866, p.55

Stamping of promissory notes, new notes, and notes given in lieu of those accidentally destroyed.

Office of Internal Revenue,
Washington, November 28, 1866.

Sir: I reply to your letter of the 21st inst., that new promissory notes substituted for others that had been destroyed after having been properly stamped and which are evidence of the same debt, and not renewals of the notes payable at a different date, do not require to be stamped. But a memorandum of the circumstances should be made on the new notes.

If, however, notes are taken up, and new notes given in lieu thereof payable at a different date or otherwise changed, the new notes are subject to stamp duty.

Very Respectfully,
Thomas Harland,
Dept. Commissioner.

Lewis Hall Esq.
Assessor Int. Rev., Jamestown, N.Y.

IRR v.IV, December 8, 1866, p.182

Stamp Duty on bills, single or obligatory.

A bill single or a bill obligatory, *i.e.*, an instrument in the form of a promissory note, *under seal,* is subject to stamp duty as written or printed evidence of an amount of money to be paid on demand or at a time designated, at the rate of five cents for each one hundred dollars or fractional part thereof.

IRR v.V, February 9, 1867, p.45

Subscription lists, Contracts, Promissory notes.

When a subscription is for a purpose in which there is a community of interest among the subscribers, the list should be stamped as a contract, or agreement, at the rate of five cents for each sheet or piece of paper upon which it is written.

When there is no community of interest, and the subscription is conditional, each signer executes a separate contract, requiring its appropriate amount of stamps; this amount depends upon the number of sheets or pieces of paper upon which the contract is written.

When each of the subscribers contracts to pay a certain and definite sum of money on demand, or at a time designated, the separate contract of each should be stamped at the same rate as a promissory note.

IRR v.V, February 23, 1867, p.59

Promissory Notes and their Substitutes.–

It has been the practice with certain banks to take instruments in the form of a receipt instead of promissory notes. A. B. applies for a loan of $10,000, which he procures upon lodging United States bonds, &c., as collateral security. Instead of giving the bank his promissory note, he gives an instrument in substance as follows:

Received of ____ Bank ten thousand dollars advance on $10,000 United States bonds.

To this he affixes a two cent stamp only. The Commissioner of Internal Revenue has decided that such an instrument is evidence of an amount of money to be paid, and as such, is liable to stamp tax at the same rate as a promissory note, and the Comptroller of the currency has directed all bank examiners not to recognize such an instrument with a two cent stamp only affixed, as valid and legal. [Editor's "Review"]

IRR v.V, May 18, 1867, p.153

Receipts, Checks, Memorandums, &c., Money to be Paid.

Every "memorandum, check, receipt or other written or printed evidence of an amount of money to be paid upon demand or at a time designated," is subject to stamp tax at the same rate as a promissory note. When a loan is obtained upon collateral security, and an instrument substantially as follows is given:___ Received of ___ Bank, Ten Thousand Dollars advance on $10,000 U.S. Bonds, it should be stamped at the rate of five cents for each one hundred dollars or fractional part thereof.

IRR v.V, May 18, 1867, p.163

Notes and Bonds given in Purchase of Realty.

A note or bond given for a part of the consideration for realty sold and conveyed, is not relieved from stamp tax by the fact that a lien to secure the payment thereof is retained in the conveyance.

IRR v.V, May 18, 1867, p.163

Foreign and Inland Bills of Exchange–Duplicates.

A foreign bill of exchange or letter of credit drawn in but payable out of the United States, if drawn singly, or otherwise than in sets of three or more, according to the custom of merchants and bankers, is liable to the same stamp tax as an inland bill of exchange, i.e. if drawn at sight or on demand, it is liable to a tax of two cents; if drawn otherwise than at sight or on demand, it should be stamped at the rate of five cents for each hundred dollars or fractional part thereof. Duplicates require the same amount of stamps as their original.

IRR v.V, June 15, 1867, p.188

Checks drawn upon a Bank by its Cashier, and Check drawn by individual upon himself.

A check drawn by an individual upon himself, or drawn upon a bank by its cashier, in his official capacity, and in the discharge of his official duty, is in its legal effect "written or printed evidence of an amount of money to be paid on demand or at a time designated," and should be stamped like a promissory note, at the rate of five cents for each hundred dollars or fractional part thereof.

IRR v.V, June 22, 1867, p.196

Municipal Coupon Bonds.

Bonds issued by Cities or towns to aid in the construction of Rail Roads, and to purchase stock therein, are not considered as issued by municipal officers "in the exercise only of functions *strictly* belonging to them in their *ordinary* governmental and municipal capacity." They are held liable, therefore, to stamp tax at the same rate as promissory notes, being 5 cents for every $100, or fractional part thereof. The coupons are a part of the bond, and do not require additional stamps.

IRR v.VI, September 28, 1867, p.105

Negotiable Foreign Promissory Note Endorsed in U.S.

A negotiable promissory note made, signed and issued in a foreign country, and made payable there, may be negotiated by endorsement in this country without liability to any United States stamp tax.

IRR v.VI, November 9, 1867, p.162

Use and Cancellation of Stamp on Promissory Note.

There is no stamp tax upon a promissory note until it is issued. A stamp is to be canceled *when* it is "attached, or *used*," and although a stamp may be affixed when a note is signed, it cannot be said to be *used* until the note is issued.

IRR v.VI, November 23, 1867, p.179

Stamp Duty on Checks, Drafts Orders, not on Sight or Demand.

A check, draft or order for the payment of a sum of money, *drawn otherwise than at sight, or on demand,* is liable to stamp tax at the rate of five cents for each one hundred dollars, or fractional part thereof.

IRR v.VI, November 23, 1867, p.179

Stamp Duty on Judgment Notes.

Assistant Assessor:– The ruling you refer to found its way into the papers without the instrument, on which the same was founded. Assessor Welsh, of the 15th Pennsylvania District, wrote to the

Commissioner, that there was "some diversity of opinion as to the kind of stamp required on judgment notes" of which a copy was submitted, running as follows:

$5,000 January 5, 1869.

One day after I promise to pay ___ ___, the sum of $5,000, with legal interest on the same without defalcation, for value received; and further, I do hereby empower any attorney of any court of record in this State or elsewhere to appear for me and confess judgment for the same in favor of the above named ___ ___, his executors, administrators, or assigns, together with cost of suit and release of errors.

Witness my hand and seal, the day and year above written.

___ ___, [Seal]

The Commissioner, replied:

"That by section 100 of the Revenue Act of June 30, 1864, amended March 3, 1866, (section 160 of Revenue law compilation), no stamp duty shall be charged up on any warrant of attorney accompanying a bond or note duly stamped.

A judgment note, therefore, of the form you enclosed should be stamped at the usual rate of promissory notes, being five cents for every one hundred dollars or fractional part thereof, with five cents additional on account of the clause relating to defalcation."

The penalty for failure to affix and cancel proper stamp is $50 for each offence, and half goes to the informer. We do not hold it derogatory in an officer to inform of violations of law. On the contrary it is his duty, and we do not see how he can observe his official oath as binding if he permits parties to break and disregard a plain provision of law.–.

IRR v.IX, February 20, 1869, p.62

Stamp Duty on "Consents" of Property Holders and Subscriptions to Railroad Stock.

Assistant Assessor– A similar question to that presented by you, was submitted to the Commissioner by Assessor Follett of the 19th New York, and as the information is generally interesting, it is herewith given. The law and the decision are applicable to your case. The Assessor said:

"Under the statutes of this State, Cities and Towns are allowed to issue bonds to aid in the construction of certain Railways, upon obtaining the written consent of a majority of the tax-payers of the town to be bonded, representing a majority of the taxable property of the town. I enclose a copy of the consent which is circulated and signed by the tax-payers– marked No. 1. Is it subject to stamp duty? and if so, how should it be stamped? There are already several towns with this State, bonded upon such consents, without the consents being stamped in any manner, and at least fifty towns are in the process of being bonded. It is a mooted question whether the bonds are legal.

"How should the enclosed stock subscription (marked No. 2) be stamped?– five cents for each sheet– five cents for each name, or is it exempt?"

No. 1.

We, The Undersigned, tax-payers, inhabitants of the town of Norwich, in the County of Chenango, and State of New York, being a majority of the tax-payers of such town, representing a majority of the taxable property of such town, do hereby assent to and fix upon the sum of Three hundred thousand dollars, being thirty per cent, of the assessed valuation of the real and personal property of such town as shown by the assessment roll for the year eighteen hundred and sixty-five of such town, for the construction of the New York and Oswego Midland Railroad, and we do hereby authorize and require the commissioners of such town, duly appointed in accordance with the provisions of the act entitled "An Act to Facilitate the Construction of the New York and Oswego Midland Railroad, and to authorize towns to subscribe to the capital stock thereof," passed April 5th, 1866, three-fifths being present, to carry into effect the purposes of said Act; to borrow on the faith or credit of such town the said sum of Three hundred thousand dollars; to execute bonds therefor, and to do and perform all other acts required of them by said Act, to carry into effect the purposes of said Act.

Done and subscribed at the town of Norwich, in the County of Chenango, on the 10th day of September, 186 .

	Assessed Valuation of Property.
J. K. Buel.	$50,000.00
C. C. Wait.	25,000.00
R. A. Stanton.	40,000.00

No. 2.

New York & Oswego Midland Railroad Stock Subscription.

Witnesseth, That we, the undersigned, have severally subscribed and by these presents do severally subscribe to the Capital Stock of the New York & Oswego Midland Railroad Company the sums set opposite our respective names hereunto subscribed, and in consideration of the great benefits to result from the construction of said Road, and of the Certificates of Stock, to be issued to each of us on payment of the amount of said subscription and in order to induce and ensure its construction, we do hereby severally promise, and agree to and with the said Company, to pay to the said Company the amount of said subscription in such sum or sums, at such time or times, and in such manner as the Directors of said Road from time to time shall call for the same; each of us having severally paid down at the time of subscribing, ten per cent. of the amount of such subscription according to the form of the statute in such case made and provided.

Dated,. 186

Names.	Residences.	No. Shares.	Amount Sub.
Thomas Johnson,	Norwich, Chenango co., N.Y.	100.	$10,000.
Charles Parker,	Norwich, Chenango co., N.Y.	200.	$20,000.

The Commissioner of Internal Revenue replied:

"That a 'consent' of the form enclosed authorizing the town Commissioners to issue bonds and do certain other acts in accordance with the provisions of a State law, requires a five-cent stamp as an agreement for every sheet or piece of paper upon which it is written.

"As in a subscription list of the form enclosed, each of the subscribers for stock, contracts to pay a certain and definite sum of money on demand, or at a time designated. The separate contract of each should be stamped at the same rate as a promissory note. Whether bonds issued under the circumstances are legal, is a question for the Courts."–.

IRR v.VIII, July 11, 1868, p.11

Stamp Duty on Deed Securing Vendor's Lien and Notes for Deferred Payments Purchase Money.

In relation to stamp duty on notes given for the purchase money of an estate secured by a vendor's lien in the deed of conveyance, it is held that such a lien should be stamped at the rate of mortgages, in addition to the conveyance stamps. In that case the notes need not be stamped, which are secured by it. But in general, notes given for purchase money are liable.

IRR v.X, August 21, 1869, p.57

Bank Memoranda of Money Borrowed to be Stamped as Promissory Notes–Such Memoranda Distinguished from Certificates of Deposit.

Office of Internal Revenue,
Washington, January 29, 1870.

Hon. H. R. Hurlburd, Comptroller of Currency, Washington, D.C.

Sir: Your letter of October 12th was duly received. The reply has been unavoidably delayed.

In answer I have to say that the letter addressed to you September 29, 1869, requires explanation or modification.

When a bank *borrows* money, and instead of giving its note gives a memorandum containing "evidence of an amount of money to be paid on demand or at a time designated," such memorandum should be stamped at the rate of a promissory note, even though it is *in the form* of a certificate of deposit.

When, however, the money is received as a *bona fide* deposit, taxable under section 110 of the act of June 30, 1864, as amended, and against which the depositor may draw, the certificate issued therefor need be stamped only with a two-cent stamp or a five-cent one, according to whether the amount of the deposit exceeds one hundred dollars or not, even though the deposit draws interest for a part or for all the time it remains in the bank.

The fact that a deposit draws interest does not relieve it from taxation under said section 110.

Very respectfully,
J. W. Douglass,
Acting Commissioner.

IRR v.XI, February 5, 1870, p.43

Bonds issued by Counties and Towns, in aid of the Construction of Railways, Require Stamps.

Office of Internal Revenue,
Washington, April 18, 1870.

John T. Harper, Esq., Collector, Eighth District, Springfield, Ill.

Sir: C. E. Lippincott, Esq., of Springfield, in your district, has addressed a letter to this office respecting the necessity of stamps upon bonds issued by counties and towns in aid of the construction of railroads. He claims that such bonds are exempted from stamp duty by Section 154 of the act of June 30, 1864, as amended by Section 9 of the act of July 13, 1866.

Section 154 of the act of June 30, 1864, is as follows:

And be it further enacted, That all *official instruments,* documents, and papers issued or used by the officers of the United States Government, shall be and hereby are exempt from duty."

Prior to the passage of the amendatory act of July 13, 1866, no special mention was made in the statute of instruments issued by States, counties, towns, etc. It was, however, ruled by this office, under the act of 1864, that no stamps should be required upon instruments, documents, and papers issued by States, counties, towns, or other municipal corporations in cases where the expenses, if they were used, would fall upon the State, county, etc., on the ground that it could not have been the intention of Congress to tax public treasuries.

With a full knowledge of this ruling, and to make special provision for papers of this kind, Congress, in the act of July 13, 1866, amended said Section 154 by striking out all after the enacting clause and inserting in lieu thereof the following: "That all *official instruments, documents, and papers* issued by the officers of the United States Government, or by the officers of any State, county, town, or other municipal corporation, shall be and hereby are exempt from taxation: *Provided,* That it is the intent hereby to exempt from liability to taxation such State, county, town, or other municpal corporation in the exercise only of functions *strictly belonging to them* in their *ordinary* governmental and municipal capacity."

It seems quite clear that Congress designed to place a limit upon the exemption of papers issued by States, etc. The exemption of such papers under the present law is of those issued "in the exercise of functions *strictly* belonging to them in their *ordinary* governmental and municipal capacity." It is not only restricted to the exercise of functions in the "*ordinary* governmental and municipal capacity," but it is enacted that the exempting clause shall be "*strictly*" construed.

In all cases of this character hitherto presented, this office has ruled that such bonds issued by a State, county, or town must be stamped at the rate of five cents for each hundred dollars or fractional part of a hundred dollars, as "evidence of an amount of money to be paid upon demand, or at a time designated;" that the issuing of bonds to aid in the construction of a railroad is not, under a strict construction, one of the *ordinary governmental* acts of a State. If it is, it would not be easy to specify one that is not; and if every thing which a State or town does under authority of law is to be construed as done in the discharge of one of its *ordinary* governmental duties, the proviso to section 154 is entirely without force or meaning, for Congress did not, of course, assume that States, counties, and towns would issue papers *contrary* to law, or without legal authority.

The ruling holding such bonds to be liable to stamp taxes is nearly as old as the act of July 13, 1866, and was published in the Internal Revenue Record, vol. VI, page 105, as early as September, 1867. The ruling as therein published is as follows:

"Bonds issued by cities or towns to aid in the construction of railroads, and to purchase stock therein, are not considered as issued by municipal officers 'in the exercise only of functions *strictly* belonging to them in their *ordinary* governmental and municipal capacity.' They are held liable, therefore, to stamp tax at the same rate as promissory notes, being five cents for every $100, or fractional part thereof. The coupons are a part of the bond, and do not require additional stamps."

I have examined the statute with considerable care, and while I am free to admit that the exemption of such bonds, issued as they are to encourage and advance internal improvements, should, perhaps, be granted by Congress, I feel strong in the opinion that it has not been done.

The distinction Mr. Lippincott seeks to draw between the officer and the county seems to me more ingenious than sound. Besides, it is based simply upon the wording of the *regulation,* and not upon the *law*. The proviso to section 154 is as follows: "*Provided,* That it is the intent hereby to exempt from liability to taxation such State, county, town, or other municipal corporation in the exercise only of functions belonging to them in their ordinary governmental and municipal capacity." The word *them* plainly refers to State, county, town, etc.

A State, county, or town can act only through officers, and the only possible way to exempt the State, county, etc., from stamp tax upon instruments used by them "in the exercise of functions strictly belonging to them in their ordinary governmental and municipal capacity" is *not to require the officers* representing them to use stamps upon papers executed by them in their official capacity and in the discharge of such functions. The act of the officer is the act of the State, and there seems to me no ground for a distinction.

It cannot, of course, escape the notice of Mr. Lippincott, and of all others interested in the bonds in question, that it is a matter of far greater importance to them that they should be stamped, if stamps are necessary, than it is to the Government. To the Government it is simply a question of a few hundred dollars of tax, but to the bond-holders it is a question of the validity of their securities.

I am not only willing but desirous that the courts shall correct my error, if I am wrong in my opinion of the law upon this point; and if the parties interested so elect, will consent to have the question submitted at once to the United States Court upon an agreed case, and will do what I can to insure an early decision.

I have referred Mr. Lippincott to you. You will furnish him with a copy of this letter, if he desires it.

C. Delano,
Commissioner.

IRR v.XI, May 28, 1870, pp.169-70

All the Instruments Mentioned under the Head of Bill of Exchange (Inland), Schedule B, Act of June 30, 1864, Exempt from Tax on and after October 1, when Issued for Less than $100.

Office of Internal Revenue,
Washington, Oct. 5, 1870.

A. Pleasonton, Esq., Collector, 32d District, New York city.

Sir: Schedule B of the act of June 30, 1864, under the head of "Bill of Exchange (Inland)," is as follows: "Bill of exchange (inland), draft, or order, for the payment of any sum of money not exceeding one hundred dollars, otherwise than at sight or on demand, or any promissory note (except bank notes issued for circulation and checks made and intended to be forthwith presented, and which shall be presented to a bank or banker for payment), or any memorandum, check, receipt, or other written or printed evidence of an amount of money to be paid on demand, or at a time designated, for a sum not exceeding one hundred dollars, five cents.

"And for every additional hundred dollars, or fractional part thereof, in excess of one hundred dollars, five cents."

Section 4 of the act of July 14, 1870, relieves "promissory notes for a less sum than one hundred dollars," on and after the 1st day of October, 1870.

I am of the opinion that by the spirit of the statute all the instruments mentioned under the head of "bills of exchange (inland)," as above quoted, are exempted when issued for a sum less than one hundred dollars, on and after the 1st inst.

This is not to be understood as applying to checks, drafts, or orders drawn at sight or on demand. The tax upon them remains unchanged, viz.: two cents when drawn for any sum whatever upon any bank, banker, or trust company, and a like amount when drawn "for any sum exceeding ten dollars upon any other person or persons, companies, or corporations."

The word *check*, as used in the last part of the paragraph relating to "bills of exchange (inland)," must not be understood to refer to the bank and other checks above mentioned as liable to two-cent stamps. The words "memorandum, check, receipt," as employed in said paragraph, refer to acknowledgments and evidences of debt, such as "I.O.U. $100," "Due you $100," etc., often given instead of formal promissory notes.

J. W. Douglass,
Acting Commissioner.

IRR v.XII, October 8, 1870, p.117

Checks Payable One Day after Date without Grace.

Treasury Department,
Office of Internal Revenue,
Washington, July 7, 1873.

D. W. Munn, Esq., Supervisor Internal Revenue, Cairo, Ill.:

Sir: Your letter of the 26th ultimo, respecting stamp duty upon checks on banks, etc., drawn payable one day after *date,* without grace, is acknowledged.

If such checks are really not payable until one day after they are given, *issued,* or delivered, they come under the general exemption of time checks. But if actually payable when they are given, at sight or on demand, it does not render them exempt to have them dated back one day or more, for the purpose of giving them the false appearance of time checks.

Any party who with intent to evade the law, issues, accepts, negotiates, or pays a check, draft, or order, without due stamping and cancellation, incurs a liability to a penalty of fifty dollars in each case. (Act June 30, 1864, section 158, amended.)

When there is sufficient evidence of such violation of the law, a prosecution would be instituted.

Very respectfully,
J. W. Douglass,
Commissioner.

IRR v.XVIII, July 12, 1873, p.9

Proceedings in U.S. Courts.

U.S. Supreme Court—Washington, D.C., October 23.

A Stamp Act Prosecution—Drafts by a Corporation on its own Treasury.—No. 45—United States v. Isham—Certificate of Division between Judges of the Circuit court for the Eastern District of Michigan.

This is a criminal information for issuing without a stamp, and with intent to evade the provisions of the internal revenue laws, a paper in the form of a draft drawn on Charles J. Canda, treasurer of the Iron Cliffs Company, by the defendant as superintendent. The paper was as follows:

[5] Iron Cliffs Company [Five.]
[1,190] Negannee, Mich., January 3, 1870.
To Charles J. Canda, Esq., New York.
Pay to the order of E. B. Isham, Superintendent, or bearer, five dollars, value received, and charge to the account of E. B. Isham.
(Countersigned) E. S. Green, Clerk.

On the trial the court were divided on the questions—first, whether this paper, on its face, required a stamp; second, whether evidence to show that Isham was superintendent of the company and drew the paper in that capacity, or that Canda was treasurer of the company and the instrument was drawn on him in that capacity, or was drawn in the course of the company's business, was admissible; third, whether, if the paper was made and issued with the design that it should be used as a local circulating medium, and was actually used by the holders as such, it thereby became subject to be stamped, and whether evidence given by the Government tending to show these facts was admissible; fourth, whether, assuming all the facts which the evidence offered tended to prove, the defendant was guilty of the offence charged; and fifth, whether the information sufficiently charges any offence under the laws of the United States. These questions were certified to this court for answer, and were now argued.

The U.S. Supreme Court at its last term made the following amendment to the 8th rule:

That hereafter, in all cases brought into this court by writ of error or appeal, to review any judgement or decree, the clerk of the court by which such judgment or decree was rendered shall annex to and transmit with the record a copy of the opinion or opinions filed in the case.

[Ed. note: for the resolution of this case, see General section, *IRR* v.XIX, March 14, 1874.]

IRR v.XVIII, October 25, 1873, pp.134-5

INSURANCE

In regard to insurance companies.

October, 1862.

1. Each insurance policy, whether fire or marine, must be stamped.
2. An open policy will require but one stamp, where the risks, entered under such policy, are all upon property shipped by, or consigned or belonging to, the policy holder.

3. Whenever certificates, or other evidences of insurance, are issued by the holder of an open policy, every such paper must bear an appropriate insurance stamp.

4. Whenever an insurance company refunds to the holder of an open policy any part of the premium, for the reason that the policy has not been used in full, the amount so refunded may be deducted from the premium received during the quarter, and the tax to the government may be paid upon the remainder. *Provided,* that this regulation shall not apply to money so refunded, on which the tax to the government shall not have been previously paid.

5. Dividends by mutual insurance companies, when paid to the insured, in scrip or money, upon expired or expiring policies, are subject to the tax of three per cent., under section 82 of the excise law.

6. The agents of insurance companies, located within the United States, are not, in consequence of such agency, commercial brokers, nor do they appear to be taxable under the law. Foreign agents are taxable under section 85 of the same act.

Note.–Paragraph 6 is annulled in part by the act of March 3, 1863, section 1, paragraph 38, which provides that insurance agents of a certain class must take license.–See decision 86. Edwards on the Stamp Act, making a proper distinction, divides open policies into two classes.–pp. 154, 160. I agree with him that a memorandum of insurance under an open policy which requires the concurrent assent of the insurer and the policy-holder to every risk entered, will need a stamp as a new policy. I do not agree, however, with Mr. Edwards, that the policy when issued is exempt from stamp duty. The holder of the policy has acquired certain rights thereby, of which he cannot be deprived by the mere unreasonable will or caprice of the party issuing the policy. The validity of the policy, which has a value independent of the fact that a risk may or may not have been made under it, depends upon the use of a stamp at the time the policy is issued.

Boutwell (1863), Decisions (No. 29)

In regard to insurance companies.
Insurance, (Marine, Inland, and Fire.)
June 1, 1863.

Each policy of insurance or other instrument, by whatever name the same shall be called, by which insurance shall be made or renewed upon property of any description, whether against perils by the sea, or by fire, or other peril of any kind, made by any insurance company, or its agents, or by any other company or person, (act July 1, 1862) 25
(This also includes policies of insurance upon live stock.)

On any policy of insurance or other instrument, by whatever name the same shall be called, by which insurance shall be made or renewed upon property of any description, whether against perils by sea, or by fire, or other peril of any kind, made by any insurance company or its agents, or by any other company or person, in which the premium or assessment shall not exceed ten dollars, (act March 3, 1863) 10

The phrase "premium or assessment," here used, is construed to include all payments for insurance, whether in money or in a premium or deposit note.

1. Each insurance, re-insurance, and duplicate policy, whether fire, marine, or stock, and each assignment or transfer of the same, must be stamped according to the above rates.

2. An open policy will require but one stamp where the risks entered under such policy are all upon property shipped by, or consigned, or belonging to the policy holder.

3. Indorsements upon open policies of insurance, made at the pleasure of the insured, and for definite and specific sums, do not require separate stamps; but all renewals, renewal receipts, extensions, additional insurance, certificates of continuance, and indorsements upon other than open policies, must be regarded as fresh policies, and stamped accordingly; whenever an entry under an open policy requires the assent of the company, such entry will require a stamp, as a new policy.

4. Whenever certificates or other evidences of insurance are issued, either by the insurance company or by the holder of an open policy, every such paper must bear its appropriate insurance stamp.

5. Permits or agreements, by which the terms of a policy are varied or changed in any respect, are subject to stamp duty of five cents, as "agreements."

6. Deposit notes to mutual insurance companies for insurance, upon which policies subject to stamp duties have been or are to be issued, are exempt from stamp duty.

The term ''deposit notes'' is construed to include all notes given to mutual insurance companies, whether under the name of ''deposit'' or ''premium'' notes, the payment of which is not absolute, but contingent upon the losses of the company, and which are held for purposes of assessment and not otherwise used.

7. Commissions or letters of appointment to insurance agents, containing powers of attorney to accept service in legal proceedings &c., are subject to general power of attorney stamp—$1 00.

8. Notification by the assured to mutual companies that he has changed tenants, &c., approved by the company, is not subject to stamp; but the certificate by the president or secretary that the statement has been received and approved by the company, and that the policy is confirmed, requires general certificate stamp of five cents.

9. An application for a policy is held to form part of the policy, and therefore is not subject to separate stamp.

Boutwell (1863), Decisions (No. 100)

The act of March 3, 1863, has changed the stamp required from twenty-five to ten cents, only in those cases in which the premium or assessment upon a policy of insurance shall not exceed ten dollars.

The words ''premium or assessment'' are held to include as well cash payments as the amount of premium or deposit notes upon which assessments are actually made.

The section does not appear to apply to the case of an interest or annual payment, which must necessarily be contingent and variable.

Boutwell (1863), Rulings (No. 270)

The annual payment of interest on a premium note is not a renewal of the policy. If payment be delayed beyond the day when due, its acceptance afterwards would be a renewal and subject the party to a stamp on the policy.

Boutwell (1863), Rulings (No. 279)

In fire and marine insurance policies, the stamp-duty is determined by the amount of the premium paid,—and the simple question to be determined is, ''What is the amount paid on issuing the policy?'' This amount is sometimes paid in money, or in part by note. If an unconditional note is given for a fixed and definite sum, that note is to be recorded as a part of the premium, whether payable on demand or on time, even though there may be an agreement outside of the note that it shall not be called for except in case of loss. If the note upon its face is merely an agreement to pay the assessments which *may* be made, and the note shows that it is a mere security for such payments, it should not be recorded as premium.

Boutwell (1865), Rulings (No. 281)

Renewal of Insurance Policies—Definition.

An instrument which operates as the renewal of a policy of insurance, is subject to the same stamp tax as the policy itself; but such a receipt as is usually given for the payment of the monthly, quarterly, or annual premium, is not a renewal within the meaning of the statute. The payment simply prevents the policy from expiring, by reason of non-performance of its conditions: a receipt given for such a payment requires a two cent stamp, if the amount received exceeds twenty dollars, and a two cent stamp only.

But when the time of payment has passed, and a tender of the premium is not sufficient to bind the Company, but a new policy or a new contract in some form, with the mutuality essential to every contract, becomes necessary between the insurer and the insured, the same amount of stamps should be used as that required upon the original policy.

IRR v.V, February 23, 1867, p.60

Duplicate Policies of Insurance.

When a policy of insurance properly stamped has been issued and lost, no stamp is necessary upon another issued by the same company to the same party, covering the same property, time, &c., and designed simply to supply the loss. The second policy should recite the loss of the first.

IRR v.V, March 30, 1867, p.100

Continuation or Renewal of Policies of Insurance.

When a policy of insurance is issued for a certain time, whether it be for one year only or for a term of years, a receipt for premium or any other instrument which has the legal effect to continue the contract and extend its operation beyond that time, requires the same amount of revenue stamps as the policy itself.

IRR v.V, March 30, 1867, p.100

Mutual Fire Insurance Policies–Deposit Notes.

The stamp tax upon a fire insurance policy is based upon the *premium*.

Deposit notes taken by a Mutual Fire Insurance Company, not as payment of premium nor as evidence of indebtedness therefor, but to be used simply as a basis upon which to make rateable assessments to meet the losses incurred by the company should not be reckoned as premium in determining the amount of stamp taxes upon the policies.

IRR v.V, April 20, 1867, p. 123

Insurance Policies and Contracts.

When the contract of insurance is entered in a Register, instead of issuing a policy, whether it is a new insurance or a re-insurance, or renewal of a policy, each entry requires a stamp at the usual rate, based on the premium. It would not be legal, or sufficient to estimate the tax on the sum total of the premiums entered at one date, as if it were a single policy.

IRR v.VI, September 28, 1867, p.105

Surrender of Imperfect and Issue of Correct Insurance Policy.

When a policy of insurance has been issued, properly stamped, but incorrectly written, and it is afterwards surrendered, and another substituted, solely to cure the defect in the first, the new policy requires no stamp. In such case the second policy should contain a recital of the facts, and show the reasons for its execution.

IRR v.VI, September 28, 1867, p.105

Policies of Health Insurance Companies.

The law imposes no stamp tax upon the policies of Health Insurance Companies, nor is there a tax upon the gross receipts of such Companies.

IRR v.VI, December 7, 1867, p.195

Alteration of Policy–New Stamp.

When a material change, such as a change of the property insured, or in the amount of insurance, is made in an insurance policy by erasures, interlining, or otherwise, after it has been issued, the changed policy is a new contract of insurance, and requires a new stamp.

IRR v.VI, December 21, 1867, p.210

Irregularities in Stamping Insurance Policies, Transfers, &c.

Asst. Assessor.–The ruling in question is believed to be authentic, and you may act upon that belief without apprehension. It is correctly printed below.–Ed.

"When officers of insurance companies issue or transfer policies, without the proper stamps or cancellation thereof, with intent to evade the Revenue law, they are liable to a penalty of $50 for each offence. Instruments should be stamped when issued; a collector of Internal Revenue alone can stamp them at a subsequent period.

"Any written agreement, which has the effect of assigning a policy, should have the same stamp as the policy.

"There is nothing in the Revenue Law to prevent the depositing or loan of United States Bonds without writing, and in that case there is nothing to stamp. If any persons fraudulently use stamps a second time, or remove those which have been used for that purpose, they are liable to a fine not exceeding $1,000, and imprisonment not exceeding five years.

"If parties deposit, as a collateral security of loan, United States Bonds by mere delivery, they of course must run the risk of any loss which may arise from the want of written evidence, but as before stated, they do not violate the Revenue Law.

"Any wilful violations should be reported to the Collector or United States District Attorney for prosecution. In case of conviction, the informer is entitled to a moiety of the penalty.–February 22, 1869.

IRR v.IX, April 3, 1869, p.111

The Insurance Companies and the Revenue Department.

Paying taxes for the support of the Government is not a duty in which unregenerate human nature can be expected to engage with entire satisfaction. This is doubtless the explanation of such complaints as the following, which we take from the *Spectator,* an insurance journal. Its conclusion that the United States Government should be "blotted out of the list of nations" is alarming; but after living through the war of the Rebellion we may hope that the United States may survive the wrath of the *Spectator:*

The present period seems opportune for remark upon the relation of the insurance companies to the Revenue Department of the United States.

We premise by stating that during the war no institutions more loyal were to be found than the insurance companies of the country. In aid afforded to raise and encourage new regiments they often exercised doubtful powers in their liberal donations. When the income law was enacted they cheerfully complied with its requirements, and so with the stamp act. Anxious to sustain the Government, they liberally subscribed to its treasury notes and bonds, and freely paid all that was honestly due under the revenue laws.

It would seem, however, that while distillers and other large operators capable of practising bribery went nearly free from taxation, the insurance companies (and perhaps others), incapable of purchasing exemption, became the subjects of most unjust exactions by the Revenue Department. Each succeeding half year saw some new decisions of the department in violation at once of the plain reading of the law and the still plainer dictates of common honesty and common sense, until the measure has become not only full but overflowing, and at the recent meeting of the New York Board of Underwriters it was, after a free and earnest discussion and denunciation of the extreme injustice of the decisions of the Revenue Department, determined not only to resist, to the full extent of their legal ability, all future encroachments, but to secure all practical redress and indemnity for past extortions.

We take occasion to state a few instances only of the manifold and perverse (we hope not tricky) decisions of the Revenue Department.

The law requires a stamp to be attached to each policy, to which nobody objects; but it is a common thing to endorse upon policies a change of firm, or change of location, or change of hazard, or privilege for mechanics to put up shelves or other fixtures, for which no charge is made by the companies; and a year or two after the passsage of the law the Commissioner decided that each note upon a policy should have a stamp attached, of the same value as that originally put upon the policy. Thus fifty cent stamp upon fifty cent stamp is compelled to be expended when not one cent of profit has accrued to either the company or its customer, and often the real value of the policy, on account to the nearness of its termination, is not worth the amount of the required stamp.

Again, the companies find it inevitable, at times, that risks assumed by them be re-insured with other companies. In marine business this is the case to a large extent, and, of course, the company which takes the risk and receives the premium pays the one and a half per cent. tax upon it; but the wisdom and honesty of the Revenue Department permits its head (after having first promulgated the contrary decision and acted upon it) to decide that the company which pays the re-insurance shall also pay a tax of one and a half per cent. upon the amount! This sounds incredible, but is notoriously true; and company after company has paid this exaction under the influence of threats of distraint upon its effects.

Again, by the plain terms of the income law, and in accordance with the blanks prepared by the Department, individuals deduct from their taxable income such part thereof as is from investments in corporations which have already paid the income tax upon it. The insurance companies, during all the years of the tax, have justly made the same deduction; but here was an opportunity for a new exaction, and a recent decision is fulminated that a second five per cent. shall be paid where the Government has already received the first and only percentage it can honestly receive. If this be not swindling, it puzzles us to know what is! The revenue officials, by such performances, prove themselves apt pupils of the distillery operator.

• • •

Again, not long since, a company had a considerable amount of defaced but unused stamps, and such as, by the provisions of the law, it was entitled to have replaced by new stamps, on surrender and proper proof concerning those defaced. The stamps were carried to the nearest Assessor's office. The proofs were completed. The order came from Washington that they should be forwarded to the Revenue Department. They were mailed by the Assessor, and were by the Government post office somewhere lost. Proof of the mailing by the Government officer was forwarded, and the cool reply is made that the Government is not responsible either for its own officer or its own post office, and the company must lose the amount! It would seem that a government which tolerates such action on the part of its officials, deserves to be blotted out of the list of nations.

These are specimen bricks; others equally gross abound, and it is not a cause for surprise that the companies at last rebel. Their power is great, and especially when to the host of stockholders, officers, agents, and employees is added the immense constituency of the scrip companies. By tens of thousands these constituents are numbered, and many a doubtful Congressional district can be turned in a direction which would tend to honesty instead of roguery.

IRR v.XI, February 26, 1870, p.70

Each and Every Assignment or Transfer of a Policy of Insurance Subject to a Stamp Duty Equal to that Imposed upon Original Investment.

Office of Internal Revenue,
Washington, July 14, 1870.

Thomas L. Tullock, Esq., Collector Internal Revenue, Washington, D.C.

Sir: Joshua Whitney & Co., real estate, stock, and insurance brokers, 416 Seventh street, in this city, have written to this office respecting stamp duty on certain transfers of policies of insurance, and have been referred to you. The case they state is as follows:

"An insurance company issues a policy to A, insuring him against a loss of property by fire. After the policy has been issued, A procures a loan of B, to secure which he gives a deed of trust, in the nature of a mortgage of the property described on said policy. For further security, he proposes to assign said policy to B; but, instead of making a formal assignment thereof, the company, by his direction, enter upon the policy, and also in their books, substantially the following: 'Loss payable as interest may appear to J.D., Trustee.' J.D. is the trustee in the deed of trust before mentioned. Is there any stamp tax upon the entry thus made upon the policy?"

You are instructed that in the case presented a stamp is required equal to that imposed on the policy. The law declares, "That upon each and every assignment or transfer of a policy of insurance * * * a stamp duty shall be required and paid equal to that imposed upon the original instrument." (Schedule B.) An entry like the one above mentioned, made at the time the policy is drawn, and before it has been issued and become binding upon the company, forms a part of the original instrument, and requires no additional stamp. Such an entry, however, made after the policy has been issued and become a binding contract between the company and A, has the effect to transfer the rights of A thereunder to J.D., B's trustee. Such a transfer is the very purpose for which the entry is made.

It has been claimed that no stamp is required in a case like the foregoing, for the reason that it is not a regular assigment. It will be noticed, however, that the tax is not restricted to *assignments*. It is imposed on "each and every *assignment or transfer*.". It is quite apparent that Congress was aware the word assignment might not cover all cases falling within the spirit of the provision, and therefore imposed the tax not only upon what are generally known as assignments, but also upon all transfers of which, as in this case, there is written or printed evidence.

You will inquire into the practice of the different insurance companies and agencies in your district in matters of this kind, and will report the result of your investigation to this office.

I shall cause this letter to be published in the Internal Revenue Record, for the purpose of calling the attention of revenue officers to the point in question.

Very respectfully,
C. Delano,
Commissioner.

IRR v.XII, July 16, 1870, p.21

Any Writing Containing a Contract Renewing an Insurance Policy should be Stamped the same as Original Policy.

Office of Internal Revenue,
Washington, Feb. 15, 1871.

Willard Bullard, Esq., Acting Collector Internal Revenue, Thirty-second District, New York.

Sir: In your letter of the 7th instant, you enclose a fire policy of the Merchants' Insurance Company of New York, with a renewal receipt attached, and submit the question whether the latter should be stamped.

By the terms of the policy, it expires by limitation in one year. The "renewal receipt" contains a new contract, renewing or continuing the policy for another year, and it should have stamps to the same amount as the original policy. (Internal Revenue Record, Vol. V., p.60.)

Some misapprehension on this subject has been occasioned by the exemption of receipts from stamp duty, under section 4 of the act of July 14, 1870. Previous to that amendment, receipts for premiums, which simply prevented a policy from expiring by reason of non-performance of its conditions, as in the case of a common form of life policies of indefinite duration, were held to require only a two-cent receipt stamp.

Accordingly, they are now considered as coming under the general exemption of receipts. There is no other change in the stamp tax affecting insurance.

Any writing, whether called a "receipt" or otherwise, which contains a contract renewing a policy that has expired from any cause, or is about to expire by limitation, should be stamped the same as an original policy. (Schedule B, 1st proviso under the head of Mortgage.)

A. Pleasonton,
Commissioner.

IRR v.XIII, March 4, 1871, p.65

[Ed. note: See the following two entries]

Renewal Receipts of Insurance Companies not Liable to Stamp Duty–Former Decision Reconsidered.

Office of Internal Revenue,
Washington, March 16, 1871.

S. B. Dutcher, Esq., Supervisor Internal Revenue, New York.

Sir: I have reconsidered the question of the liability of "renewal receipts" of insurance companies to stamp duty, and I now hold that any writing, whether called a receipt or otherwise, which contains a contract to continue in force any policy of insurance which has not expired, is exempt from stamp duty.

A receipt or other writing given after the expiration of the term for which premium has been paid is a "renewal" and requires stamps to the same amount as the original policy. All former rulings inconsistent herewith are hereby reversed.

A. Pleasonton,
Commissioner.

IRR v.XIII, March 25, 1871, p.89

[Ed. note: See following entry]

Renewal Receipts on Insurance Policies Require the same Stamp as Original Policy–Commissioner Pleasonton's Decision Overruled, and Original Ruling Reaffirmed.

Treasury Department,
Office of Internal Revenue,
Washington, August 16, 1871.

Wm. Ames, Esq., Collector Internal Revenue, First District, Providence, R.I.

Sir: Walter Paine, Esq., President of the "Merchants' Insurance Company" of Providence, has written to this office respecting stamp duty on receipts renewing policies of insurance, when said receipts are made previous to the expiration of the policies. He has been referred to you.

The common form of renewal receipt contains a contract or agreement *continuing* or renewing a policy. The law imposes upon the renewal or *continuance* of any agreement or contract a stamp duty equal to that required on the original instrument. (Schedule B, of Stamp Duties, first proviso under Mortgage.)

Any written contract, therefore, made in the form of a receipt or otherwise, which renews or *continues* a policy, requires the same stamp as the original policy. It makes no difference whether such "renewal receipt" is given before or after the expiration of the policy.

A different construction would almost nullify the tax upon the renewal of policies, one of the most important items in Schedule B, as renewal receipts are nearly always given before the expiration of a policy.

This overrules the decision of Commissioner Pleasonton, in a letter to Supervisor S. B. Dutcher, published in the Internal Revenue Record, No. 325, for March 25, 1871, and restores the previous holding of this office as given in the Record, No. 322, for March 4, 1871.

This is an important matter for parties insured, as the renewal receipts would be invalid unless duly stamped, and it should be brought to the notice of policy-holders in your district.

Very respectfully,
J. W. Douglass,
Commissioner.

IRR v.XIV, August 19, 1871, p.57

Cancelling a Stamp Exhausts its Efficiency; it cannot be Removed from one paper to another. Cancellation with a Ribbon Stamp is Insufficient.

Office of Internal Revenue,
Washington, November 27, 1871.

S. B. Dutcher, Supervisor Internal Revenue, 83 Cedar Street, New York:

Sir: In your letter of the 18th inst. you state that the ___ Fire Insurance Company of New York have the practice of removing *cancelled* stamps from policies which have not been taken, and affixing them to other policies, cancelling them again with a common ribbon stamp and a new date.

This is considered entirely improper and illegal, and opening the way for fraud. There is no objection to removing an *uncancelled* stamp from an instrument which has not been used and attaching it to another paper. But after a stamp has been cancelled its efficacy is exhausted and it should not be reused, but if used unnecessarily or inadvertently will be redeemed (Ser. 6, No. 10).

Any parties continuing the practice referred to after being notified of its illegality should be prosecuted. Cancellation with a ribbon stamp is insufficient.

Very respectfully,
J. W. Douglass,
Commissioner.

IRR v.XIV, November 25, 1871, p.170

LEASE

Both agreements, that held by the tenant as well as that held by the landlord, are subject to stamp duty, under the head of "Lease."

Boutwell (1863), Rulings (No. 248)

May 5, 1863.

Sir: Your letter of February 5 was duly received, but as a decision upon the stamp duty required upon "coal land leases," or upon assignments thereof, has been withheld for careful consideration, yours, with other letters upon the same subject, has not been answered ere this.

In reply thereto I have the honor to state that those leases are construed to be "conveyances," and as such to be stamped under head of "conveyance," as per "Schedule B," in the act of July 1, 1862. The assignment of such a lease should also be stamped under the head of "conveyance," as above, the consideration paid being the measure of stamp duty. If the consideration in such an assignment is $33,000, the stamp duty required is $60.

In the case presented of a price per ton of coal mined, there being nothing in the contract to indicate more accurately its probable value, the practical difficulty of ascertaining the value will be met, should it arise, by the resident revenue officers.

Very respectfully,
Edward McPherson,
Deputy Commissioner.

To J. Brisbin, Esq., *Superintendent, &c.*

Boutwell (1863), Correspondence (No. 2)

I have received your letter, with form of lease of land for ninety-nine years, with right of renewal forever, and assignment of the same by the lessee or his representatives, enclosed.

I am of opinion that the assignment, or deed as it more properly is must be stamped as a conveyance. The lease must also be regarded as a conveyance, and when made, it must bear stamps proportionate to its value. This valuation may be fixed by the market price, or by converting the annual rent into a capital sum at the legal rate of interest at which money may be obtained upon such security.

The assignment of a lease is subject to the same stamp as the original.

George E. Sangston, Esq.,
Clerk of the Superior Court, Baltimore, Md.

Boutwell (1863), Correspondence (No. 10)

Stamp-duty on a lease, where the value is not ascertained, must cover the largest amount stipulated in the lease, as in lease for the delivery of wood.

Boutwell (1865), Rulings (No. 212)

As each copy of a lease has a legal value, each requires stamp.

Boutwell (1865), Rulings (No. 221)

The stamp-duty on lease for a fractional part of a year should be appropriate to the rental value of the property per annum.

Boutwell (1865), Rulings (No. 231)

Notice from landlords to tenants to quit possession of premises is not subject to stamp-duty.

Boutwell (1865), Rulings (No. 234)

Leases and other indentures, executed by the United States through its authorized officers on the one part, are not subject to stamp-duty from either party.

Boutwell (1865), Rulings (No. 238)

The stamp-duty on a lease is to be determined by the annual rent, or rental value, and when a rent is stipulated to be a certain proportion of the annual product of the land, it must be estimated, and the party must fix it sufficiently high to prevent imputation of fraud.

Boutwell (1865), Rulings (No. 242)

The *period* covered by a lease does not affect the denomination of the stamp, where the annual rental value is fixed.

Boutwell (1865), Rulings (No. 254)

The stamp-duty on a lease of land, where the consideration is partly a fixed money rental and partly a proportionate share in the prospective profits of the use of the land, &c., must depend on the *estimated* rental, &c., &c.

Boutwell (1865), Rulings (No. 258)

Each lease of duplicates or triplicates is liable to the stamp-duty. If, however, but one lease is made, and certified copies thereof, the certificates of the copies only are liable to stamp appropriate to certificates.

Boutwell (1865), Rulings (No. 259)

An ordinary notice of a landlord to a tenant, to vacate at the expiration of his term, is not subject to stamp-duty.

Boutwell (1865), Rulings (No. 283)

Important Revenue Decision Respecting Stamp On "Oil Leases."

Sir: Your letter of Dec. 7, in relation to the stamp duty on an "oil lease," so called, has been received.

The law makes the "rent or rental value" the test which determines the amount of the stamp duty, and of course where the rent is fixed at a specified sum in money the stamp duty is easily determined.

In the case of these oil leases there is, however, very rarely a fixed rental value in money agreed upon. In some cases the lessee contracts to erect valuable machinery or sink shafts as well as to pay a certain rate per gallon or barrel, for the oil produced, or deliver a certain portion of the oil instead of cash payments, and in others the rent is to be a certain portion of the oil or its value in money—the machinery, as in the first case, to become the property of the lessor at the end of the term.

In such cases, the annual rent or rental value can only be determined by estimation. If the lease is of new and untried lands, there is, of course, a possibility that it may turn out to be worthless, so far as the production of oil is concerned; but it would not be safe to assume that it would always, or perhaps ever be so. If the lessee has erected valuable machinery upon the premises, or made valuable improvements, which, upon the termination or surrender of the lease became the property of the lessor, it is evident that he has received a portion of the *rent,* or compensation for the use of his land agreed upon, although no oil is produced.

The rental value cannot in such cases be accurately determined, and, of course, the stamp duty can no more be accurately calculated; and therefore, parties in such cases are advised to apply to the collector, under Section 162 of the act of June 30, to have the stamp duty determined, which, of course, involves the calculation, of the annual rental value.

If the land has been worked before the lease is made, or if the original lessee in such case underlets or assigns his lease, or a portion, or undivided interest in it, the collector will, in such case, have some reliable data to start upon, but in all cases he should estimate, from the best information he can get, the probable average rental value, and, of course, in doing this, he will have regard to his own knowledge of the premises—the information derived from the parties and others, and the stipulations of the lease, and if the rent is payable in oil, the average market value of the oil is an element in the calculation, and in cases where he is in doubt, he will, of course, receive such instructions as may be derived from this office.

Such leases, whether of oil, coal or mineral lands, are held to be subject to stamp duty as leases, and a stamp, as an agreement or contract, is of course insufficient.

There are thousands of farms in the country which are leased "upon shares," as it is termed, and as it is of course impossible to determine at a given date what the farm will produce for the ensuing year, the rental value must be estimated, and the quantity as well as value of the several products must become elements in the calculation, and yet no difficulty seems to have arisen in such cases. The calculation in the case of a coal or oil lease may be more complicated, but the principle is the same.

Very respectfully,
Joseph J. Lewis
Commissioner.

IRR v.I, January 7, 1865, p.2

Stamping of Perpetual Leases, Conveyances, &c.

Office of Internal Revenue,
Washington, May 4, 1865.

Gentlemen: Your letters of April 15 and 21, and also your letter of February 3, an answer to which has been delayed for the purpose of affording a better opportunity to examine the questions raised, have been received.

The decisions holding perpetual leases to be conveyances, and subject to stamp duty as such, were made in conformity with the local State law within the jurisdiction of which the cases arose.

The stamp duty on an instrument is to be determined by its legal effect, rather than its particular form, and as the United States court in questions affecting real estate follow the local laws, this office will of course adopt the same construction in determining the liability of a particular instrument to stamp duty. In the absence of information as to how the leases in question are held and treated under the local laws of your State, I can only lay down the following rule for your guidance:—

If, under the local law of your State, such instruments are held to be in legal effect conveyances of a fee simple estate, they must be held subject to stamp duty as conveyances of such a title, and the stamp duty will be measured by resolving the annual rental into a capital sum. If, on the other hand, it is held to be a conveyance of a leasehold estate merely, the instrument is subject to stamp duty as a lease.

If the lessee assigns his interest, such assignment will be subject to the same duty as the original lease, and if any consideration is to be paid for such assignment beyond the yearly rent, it will be subject to an additional stamp duty as a conveyance on the consideration or value of the assignment.

Your practice, as stated by you, in regard to stamping assignment of leases, is correct.

The determination of the question as to what under your State law is held to be the legal effect of such an instrument as the lease referred to, will, under the foregoing rule, enable you to determine readily all the questions raised by you.

Very respectfully,
Joseph J. Lewis,
Commissioner.

IRR v.I, June 24, 1865, p.196

Stamping Of Oil Leases.

Treasury Department,
Office of Internal Revenue,
Washington, Oct. 9, 1865.

Sir: Your letter of the 10th instant, inclosing an assignment of four leases of oil lands in Kentucky, and inquiring the amount of stamp duty thereon, is received.

It appears that no fixed and definite sum of money is paid for the assignments, but that a certain proportion of the oil is to be paid as a royalty, and in addition thereto a ''bonus'' of $72,000 is to be paid out of the money first realized from the sale of stocks, or upon ''bonuses'' upon sub-leases. Under the head of Mortgages in Schedule B of the amended Act of June 30, 1864, it is provided that ''upon each and every assignment of any lease a stamp duty shall be required and paid equal to that imposed upon the original instrument, increased by a stamp duty upon the consideration or value of the assignment equal to that imposed upon the conveyance of land for a similar consideration."

The amount of stamp duty upon leases such as those mentioned by you must depend upon the estimated annual rent or rental value.

The actual value of the bonus of $72,000 in the case presented by you must also be estimated. These estimates, if made by any other person than the Collector, are made at the risk of the parties. For this reason parties are recommended to apply to the Collector, who will affix stamps under the provisions of section 162, and thus give them titles which will be quiet upon the stamp question. In addition to the stamp upon the original lease, there should be affixed stamps equal to fifty cents for each five hundred dollars of the estimated value of the $72,000 bonus.

You say that these leases are each stamped with a fifty cent stamp. It would seem that the original leases are insufficiently stamped, and unless the stamp was affixed by a *Collector,* in compliance with the law, the parties are recommended now to have the rent or rental value of the property leased estimated by the Collector, and stamps affixed by him.

Very respectfully,
E. A. Rollins,
Deputy Commissioner.

O. F. Presbrey, Esq.,
Assessor 30th Dist., Buffalo N.Y.

IRR v.II, October 28, 1865, p.132

Stamp Duty on Leases, or Contracts For Rent or Use of Real Estate Based on Annual Value.

The stamp duty upon a lease, agreement, memorandum or contract for the hire, use, or rent of any land, tenement or portion thereof, is based upon the *annual* rent or retail value of the property leased, and the duty is the same whether the lease be for one year, for a term of years, or for the fractional part of a year only.

IRR v.V, February 9, 1867, p.45

Assignment of Lease—Assignment of Rents, &c.

An assignment of a lease within the meaning and intent of Schedule B, is an assignment of the *leasehold* or of some portion thereof by the *lessee,* or by some person claiming by, from, or under him, such an assignment as subrogates the assignee to the rights, or some portion of the rights, of the *lessee,* or of the person standing in his place. A transfer by the *lessor* of his part of a lease, neither giving nor purporting to give a claim to the leasehold, or to any part thereof, but simply a right to the rents, &c., is subject to stamp tax as a contract or agreement only.

IRR v.V, February 23, 1867, p.59

Receipts by Endorsement on Leases, or Stamped Instruments.

A receipt by endorsement upon a stamped obligation in acknowledgment of its fulfilment, is exempt from stamp tax. Fulfilment as used in this connection in Schedule B, is understood to mean completion, accomplishment, *entire* fulfilment. No receipt is subject to a stamp tax *unless it is issued*. When a receipt for an *installment* of rent is written upon that part of a lease held by the tenant and issued to him, a two cent stamp should be affixed to it, if the amount received exceeds twenty dollars.

IRR v.V, June 15, 1867, p.188

LEGAL DOCUMENTS

A citation from the surrogate's court is not an original process, (a surrogate's court not being a court of record,) and is not subject to stamp duty.

Boutwell (1863), Rulings (No. 235)

A *''dedimus potestatem''* or commission issued out of any court in one State to take the deposition of a witness in any other State, or in the same State, to be used on a trial of a cause pending, is not subject to stamp duty.

Boutwell (1863), Rulings (No. 236)

If the indorsement upon a writ required in an action brought by a citizen of another State is under seal, it is a bond, and will require a twenty-five cent revenue stamp.

If not under seal, it is liable to stamp duty as an agreement.

Boutwell (1863), Rulings (No. 238)

The bond, on an appeal from a lower to a higher court, is exempt from stamp duty, as a bond ''required in legal proceedings.''

Boutwell (1863), Rulings (from No. 249)

All bonds required in legal proceedings are exempt from stamp tax; but this does *not* exempt bonds of guardians, administrators, assignees, trustees, &c.

Boutwell (1863), Rulings (No. 250)

Papers filed in court, on which there is an indorsement made by the clerk or register that they were filed at a certain time, do not require a certificate or other stamp.

If copies of papers which have been filed in court are issued with certificate, a certificate stamp will be required on such copies.

Boutwell (1863), Rulings (No. 256)

Although the writ or original process in a suit may have been properly stamped, a sheriff's deed under an execution issued upon the judgment will require to be stamped under the head of ''conveyance.''

The date of the deed must determine its liability to stamp duty, independently of the date of the original process.

Boutwell (1863), Rulings (No. 271)

Bonds required in legal proceedings, are not subject to stamp duty; if, however, a bond is not absolutely indispensable, as a part of such proceedings, but only incidental or voluntary, it is subject to stamp duty.

A certificate of a justice of the peace certifying a transcript to the district court is subject to a stamp duty of five cents.

Boutwell (1863), Rulings (from No. 288)

Suits are commenced in many States by other process than writ, viz: summons, warrant, petition, &c.; in which cases, these as the original processes, severally, require stamps.

Boutwell (1863), Rulings (No. 292)

An appeal or instrument by which a suit is transferred from a justice of the peace to a superior court is an original process, and subject to stamp duty as such.

If, by the laws of a State, a suit is commenced against a non-resident defendant, by an order or application under authority of the court, such order or application is subject to stamp duty as an original process.

A writ of "habeas corpus," of "error," or of "certiorari," not being an "original process," is not subject to stamp duty.

Alias and pluries writs, and counterpart, are not original processes, and are, therefore, exempt from stamp duty.

Writs of scire facias, in either civil or criminal causes, are original processes, and subject to stamp duty.

Certificates issued to grand and petit jurors should be stamped as certificates.

Boutwell (1863), Rulings (No. 311)

A claim, filed in a county court, is considered an original summons, and requires a stamp.

Boutwell (1865), Rulings (from No. 213)

The law imposes a stamp-duty of fifty cents upon writs issued by a court not of record, where the amount claimed in such writ is $100 or over, without regard to the amount ultimately recovered, and it is not exempt, even with the addition of the words "or under."

Boutwell (1865), Rulings (No. 216)

An indictment is not subject to stamp-duty, nor is any criminal process commenced in the name of the United States or any state.

Boutwell (1865), Rulings (No. 236)

Petitions for naturalization are not original processes, and are not subject to stamp-duty.

Boutwell (1865), Rulings (No. 265)

A *bond* given to procure an appeal is exempt from stamp-duty *as a bond,* it being given in a legal proceeding. Where, however, such bond is the process by which the case is transferred from an inferior to a superior court, it is subject to a stamp-duty of fifty cents *as an appeal*. An *alias* summons is not an original process, but an interlocutory one, issued in a suit which has been commenced, and is standing upon the docket of the court, and in such case, the original summons having been duly stamped, such *alias* summons would be exempt from stamp-duty.

Boutwell (1865), Rulings (No. 270)

An original summons requires a stamp. If several summonses are issued in one action, and there is nothing to indicate that either one is the original compared with the others, each is subject to stamp-duty. Copies of an original summons served upon defendants are not subject to stamp-duty.

Boutwell (1865), Rulings (No. 271)

Whenever a confession of judgment is entered up, such confession becomes subject to stamp-duty; and upon the execution of an agreement that no appeal shall be taken, that also will be subject to stamp-duty as an agreement.

Boutwell (1865), Rulings (No. 272)

The process stamp on the original writ covers all orders, notices, certificates, and papers issued in the prosecution of a suit. If, therefore, "the exemplifications of record taken from one court to be filed in and proceeded on in another," are issued in the due prosecution of a pending suit, they are not subject to stamp-duty.

Boutwell (1865), Rulings (No. 273)

In actions on contracts the amount actually claimed in the declaration or complaint of the plaintiff determines the liability to stamp-duty, and not the allegation of damages set forth in the summons. In actions in tort, sounding altogether in damages, the allegation of damages defines the amount claimed, and determines the liability to stamp-duty. If the amount claimed is one hundred dollars or over, the process is subject to stamp-duty.

Boutwell (1865), Rulings (No. 276)

The stamp-duty is not imposed upon judgment, but upon the confession of judgment, and if that is not stamped it is invalid, and the court cannot enter up the judgment.

Boutwell (1865), Rulings (No. 285)

Appointments of Guardians and Commissioners for Lunatics Do Not Require Stamps—Administrators' Bonds Subject To Stamp.

Office of Internal Revenue,
Washington, April 23, 1866.

Sir: I reply to your letter of the 14th instant, That *ex parte* applications to Surrogate Courts or Courts of Probate for the admission of wills to proof, for the appointment of guardians, the sale of an infant's real estate, or the appointment of commissioners for lunatics, and the like, are not regarded as writs or other original processes by which suits are commenced in any court of law or equity within the meaning of the Internal Revenue law; and, hence, no stamp is required in such cases. Administrators' bonds and the like are official, and should be stamped with a $1 stamp.

Very respectfully,
D. C. Whitman,
Deputy Commissioner.

Alfred Wells,
Assessor, Ithaca, Tompkins Co., N. Y.

IRR v.III, May 12, 1866, p.151

Stamp Duty on Writ or Other Process on Appeal to Court of Record.

A fifty cent stamp is required upon a writ or other process on appeal from a Justice's court or other court of inferior jurisdiction to a court of record; and this stamp covers all the papers necessary to the taking of the appeal and to the entry of the action in the court of appellate jurisdiction.

IRR v.V, February 9, 1867, p.45

Registry of a Judgment Exempt From Stamp Duty.

No stamp is necessary upon the registry of a judgment, even though the registry is such in its legal effect as to create a lien which operates as a mortgage upon the property of the judgment debtor.

IRR v.V, February 9, 1867, p.45

Internal Revenue Law Decisions—Stamp.

We are indebted for the following notes to the "American Law Review," a periodical that has taken a formost rank among American law publications. This quarterly is edited with judgment and dignity, and richly merits the favor with which it has been received by the profession.

United States Revenue Stamp.

The words "writs or other process on appeals," in the amended Revenue Law of August, 1864, comprehend any instrument on paper whatever, which in effect transfers a cause from an inferior to a superior court.—*Musselman* v. *Mauk,* 18, Iowa, 239.

In this State, appeals from a justices' court are effected by a notice of appeal, an appeal bond, and a certified transcript of the proceedings. *Held,* that the affixing the stamp required by the Internal Revenue Act to be affixed to the writ or other process, on appeals from a justices' court, to either of these papers, would be a virtual compliance with the provisions of that act.—*May* v. *Wilson,* 20 Iowa, 117.

But if, in such an appeal, the appellant does not affix the Revenue stamp to any paper connected therewith, his appeal will be dismissed.—*Bitkins* v. *Spurgeon,* 20 Iowa, 598.

Plaintiff, in an appeal from a justice of the peace, ommitted to affix to any paper connected therewith the stamp required by the Revenue Act of June 30, 1864; and, pending a motion by the defendant to dismiss said appeal on account of such omission, plaintiff offered to affix the proper stamp. *Held,* that, while the intent to defraud the government is essential to a liability for a penalty for omitting to place a stamp on any instrument, required by said act, yet, when the stamp is omitted the instrument is invalid, whether such omission is from accident or design. The courts have no power to supply such a defect when it exists: it can be done only in the manner provided by the statute.—*Hugus* v. *Strickler,* 19 Iowa, 413.

"..."

In Indiana, the filing of an appeal bond operates to transfer a cause from a justices' court to a court of appeal. *Held,* that such bond is neither a "writ" nor "process" within the meaning of the Internal Revenue Act, approved June 30, 1864, and requires no revenue stamp.—*Smith* v. *Waters,* 25 Ind. 397.

...

IRR v.VI, November 23, 1867, p.181

[We give below abstract of decisions of State Courts upon questions of stamp duty under the United States laws, taken from the *American Law Review* of January, 1868. We cannot commend in terms too high or just the merits of this publication. Every lawyer who subscribes will greet each issue as the appearance of an old and valued friend.]

Petition to Set Aside Probate Will not Subject to Stamp Duty.

A petition to set aside the probate of a will, is not "process by which a suit is commenced" within the United States Revenue Laws, and does not require a stamp.—*Sowell* v. *Sowell,* 40 Ala. 243.

Stamp Duty on Process from State Courts Unconstitutional.

The Act of Congress, approved June 30, 1864, so far as it requires a stamp to be affixed to legal process issuing from the State Courts, is unconstitutional.

By Byrd, J.—Said act does not apply to process issuing from State Courts.—*Smith* v. *Short,* 40 Ala. 385.

IRR v.IX, January 16, 1869, p.21

LIFE INSURANCE

In reference to life insurance policies.

November, 1862.

All life insurance policies are subject to stamp duty when the policy is conditional that the assured is to pay, as premium, a certain sum annually, or at any other stated period. Receipts for such payments are not subject to stamp duty.

If the policy has expired by limitation, or by non-fulfilment of the conditions by the assured, a renewal or revival of the policy, in whatever form made, will be subject to stamp tax.

Permits or agreements, by which the terms of a policy are varied or changed in any respect, are subject to stamp duty as agreements.

Boutwell (1863), Decisions (No. 35)

Insurance, (Life.)

Policy of insurance, or other instrument, by whatever name the same shall be called, whereby any insurance shall be made upon any life or lives—

When the amount insured shall not exceed $1,000	$0 25
Exceeding $1,000, and not exceeding $5,000	50
Exceeding $5,000	1 00

1. All life insurance policies, and assignments or transfers of the same, are subject to stamp duty when the policy is conditional that the assured is to pay a certain sum annually, or at any other stated period.

2. All receipts for such payments are exempt from tax.

3. If the policy has expired by limitation, or by non-fulfilment of the conditions of the assured, a renewal or revival of the policy, in whatever form made, will be subject to the above rates.

On and after this date, no policy of insurance, or other instrument issued in lieu thereof, will be valid without stamp: *Provided,* That no stamp duty shall be required upon tickets or contracts of insurance, when limited to fatal or non-fatal injury to persons while traveling. (act March 3, 1863.)

Boutwell (1863), Decisions (from No. 100)

Insurance Permits changing terms of Policies.

A permit issued by a life insurance company changing the terms of a policy as to travel, residence, occupation, &c., should be stamped as a contract or agreement.

IRR v.V, February 23, 1867, p.60

Life Insurance Policy.

The word *life,* as used under the head Insurance, in Schedule B, is to be construed as relating to *human* life only.

IRR v.VI, December 21, 1867, p.210

LOTTERY TICKET

March 28, 1863.

Sir: In reply to your letter of the 26th instant, I respectfully call your attention to the first section of the act of March 3, a copy of which is enclosed, wherein lottery tickets are described, and a stamp duty imposed thereon; and also to item thirty-seven of said act, wherein it is provided that lottery ticket dealers shall pay $1,000 for each license.

By the same act it is declared that every person, association, firm, or corporation, who shall make, sell, or offer to sell lottery tickets, or fractional parts thereof, or any token, certificate, or device representing or intending to represent a lottery ticket, or any fractional part thereof, or any policy of numbers in any lottery, or prepare schemes of lotteries, or superintend the drawing of any lottery, shall be deemed a lottery ticket dealer under this act.

In attempting to apply this legislation to the facts of the case presented by you, I have only to inquire whether the gift concert which you have advertised, and for which you purpose to sell tickets, is, in its essential features, a lottery.

You purpose to sell a thousand tickets at $1 each, and to distribute by lot or hazard one hundred prizes among the holders of the thousand tickets. There are, of course, nine blanks for every prize. This proceeding answers to a definition given to lotteries, viz: ''A distribution of prizes and blanks by chance, a game of hazard, in which small sums are ventured for the chance of obtaining a larger value, either in money or other articles.''

This definition conforms to the letter and spirit of the law of Congress, and describes with exactness the character of the gift concert to which your letter, handbills, and tickets enclosed, refer.

You will readily understand that it is not possible for this office to make distinction growing out of any actual or supposed difference in the objects to which the proceeds of the enterprise are to be devoted.

It is the peculiar characteristic of the lottery system in all countries, that it has had its origin in real or pretended purposes to give aid to philanthropic or benevolent movements.

To Hon. S. P. Chase,
Secretary of the Treasury.

Boutwell (1863), Correspondence (No. 19)

By the act of March 3 a license tax of $1,000 is imposed upon lottery ticket dealers. A particular description of such dealers is contained in the same clause. Does this description embrace persons appointed by authority of a State to superintend the drawing of a lottery? Such persons are usually appointed to protect the purchasers of tickets from fraud, and to secure the revenue usually accruing to the State from the grant of a lottery. They are State functionaries assigned to administer a public office, and to require such officers to take out licenses would be to impose a tax upon the performance of a public duty, or to compel a State to forego the exercise of a wholesome supervision of lottery drawings. That, in my opinion, was not the intention of the statute.

It is further provided in the same act that no person shall make, sell, or offer to sell any lottery ticket without affixing a stamp, which is not less than fifty per cent. of the retail value of the ticket. Not forty per cent. of the tickets embraced in a scheme are ever actually sold, and if those remaining undisposed of at the time of drawing are to be taxed 50 per cent. upon the price at which they were held for retail, it is clear that a few drawings must exhaust the whole capital. The privileges derived from State grant must become of no value, the business cease to exist, and the government fail to derive any revenue from this source. A law of Congress directly prohibiting the sale of lottery tickets in the States would be void. But had it been the declared purpose, in this act, to exercise a moral censorship and to crush out the business by means of a tax, I should leave its validity to be determined by the courts. But Congress certainly did not legislate with a view to moral results. Money was needed for the support of public credit, and the question was, not how were the morals of the people to be reformed, but how were the resources of the nation to be made available.

This, then, being a revenue law, its parts are to be construed in harmony with the whole, and no interpretation is to be admitted, except upon the strictest reading, which will render the law inoperative as a means of revenue.

The provision is, "that no person shall *make,* sell, or offer for sale, or dispose of, any lottery ticket" without a stamp. Does the word "make" mean merely printing and signing a paper, which, without delivery, would confer no right and devolve no obligation? In the hands of the proprietors it is useless, either before or after the drawing. When in the hands of a purchaser it becomes evidence of a contract, or, like a promissory note, derives all its efficacy from delivery. After that process the holder becomes owner of that on which he may recover judgment against the managers in a court of law. It is not "*made*" as an instrument till delivered, but at that moment it becomes complete for all the purposes for which it was intended. The word "make" in this sense has a sensible application. The stamp is to be affixed at the moment the ticket acquires legal efficacy, or begins to exist as an article of value.

In the 100th section of the original act, the same word "*make*" is used in the sense we have attributed to it. The same observation applies to "make," in the 94th and 95th sections, and to "made," in the proviso of the 16th section of the act of March 3. In no part of the act do we find the word used in such a way as to indicate that a stamp is required to be affixed before the instrument becomes complete, and there is no reason for holding a lottery ticket an exception to the general rule.

The literal requirement of the act is that no person shall make any lottery ticket without affixing a stamp. When is the penalty incurred if the ticket be found without a stamp? To hold that the ticket is "made," so as to render the maker liable for the penalty the instant it is printed, or that it receives the signature of the manager, would render an escape from such liability impossible.

But it may be said that we have the words "offer for sale," which necessarily require the affixing a stamp as a condition precedent to an attempt to sell. I consider that the meaning of these words is equivalent to this: that no person shall attempt to *sell;* that is to say, to perfect a sale. He may offer to make a contract of sale; he may even make a contract of sale without incurring the penalty, if the contract contemplate that the stamp be affixed at the instant the contract is executed. The offer to sell without a stamp does not occur, if the offer to sell is accompanied by an offer to affix a stamp.

If a ticket in the hands of a lottery manager were a representative of capital, it would not be reasonable to hold it taxable while it remains there, for the taxing of capital is not consistent with the policy of the law. It aims at an excise of annual gains, such as is least severely felt and most easily paid. Had it been intended to tax the mere possession of lottery tickets in the manager's hands, it would have been easy to select apt phraseology; but in the absence of such language, it is but respectful to the legislature to hold that in assuming to provide revenue for the support of the government, it was not intended, by a side blow, to strike down any interest which constituted a fair and fruitful subject of taxation.

Though I should rejoice in the suppression of lotteries, I do not feel at liberty to wrest a law made to raise revenue for the support of the government by a forced interpretation from its avowed and legitimate purpose, and to convert it into an instrument of moral reform, however desirable on the score of humanity.

Joseph J. Lewis,
Commissioner.
Boutwell (1863), Correspondence (No. 41)

MANIFEST

The masters' inward and outward manifests of the whole cargo are subject to stamp duty under the provisions of the internal revenue excise law, except in the case of vessels plying between the United States and British North America.

Boutwell (1863), Rulings (No. 276)

The entry by the captain should include the manifest of the cargo, and the entry is therefore exempt from stamp duty, under the proviso of Schedule B of the excise law, when the vessel plies between ports of the United States and ports of British North America. If the owners enter the goods owned by them, respectively, the "entry" stamp will be required.

Boutwell (1863), Rulings (No. 293)

Manifests—Clearance of Vessels in Ballast.

A stamp tax is imposed upon every "manifest for custom-house entry or clearance of the *cargo* of any ship, vessel, or steamer for a foreign port." The amount of this tax in each case, depends upon the registered tonnage of the vessel.

If a vessel clears in ballast and has no cargo whatever, no stamp is necessary; but if she has any—however small the amount—a stamp should be used.

IRR v.V, March 7, 1867, p.74

MORTGAGE

A mortgage or trust deed being duly stamped as "mortgage" is not subject to further stamp duty by virtue of a power of attorney or power of sale contained therein.

The stamp duty required upon assignment of mortgage is 10 cents for each $200, or fractional part thereof, of the "equity" secured thereby.

Boutwell (1863), Rulings (No. 237)

A chattel mortgage, made prior to 1st October, 1862, is valid without stamp; and the renewal thereof, by notice entered upon the record, as provided by laws of several States, does not render the use of a stamp necessary. Upon the same principle, it must be held that when a mortgage has been stamped, agreeably to the act of July 1, 1862, its revival or renewal, in the same manner, does not render the use of the stamp necessary.

Boutwell (1863), Rulings (No. 259)

When "bills of sale," or deeds of vessels, are given as security for money, they must be treated as conveyances in trust, and stamped under head of Mortgage.

Boutwell (1863), Rulings (No. 281)

A "general indemnity mortgage," or a mortgage made to secure indorsements, past and future, must be stamped at the time of delivery; and the mortgage cannot be enforced for any sum greater than the amount covered by the stamps so affixed and cancelled at the time of the execution and delivery of the mortgage.

Boutwell (1863), Rulings (No. 295)

In all cases of deeds given for real estate, they should be stamped under head of "Conveyance," in "Schedule B," act of July 1, 1862, except in case of "trust deed" for security for the payment of money. In the latter case the deed, or the note or bond secured thereby, must be stamped as a "mortgage."

Boutwell (1863), Rulings (No. 313)

An assignment or transfer of property bonds or mortgages requires stamp as an original bond, &c.

Boutwell (1865), Rulings (No. 226)

Mortgages for property, less than one hundred dollars in value, are exempt, as is the affidavit required in some states, to make them valid; but the note for which the mortgage is security requires a stamp.

Boutwell (1865), Rulings (No. 229)

An acknowledgment of a mortgage or other written instrument is exempt from stamp-duty.

Boutwell (1865), Rulings (No. 235)

A release or discharge of a mortgage is not subject to stamp-duty; neither would a quitclaim deed given by a mortgagee not in possession to the party holding the equity of redemption, be subject to stamp-duty as a conveyance, as there is no sale, and the payment of the mortgage-debt discharges the mortgage.

Boutwell (1865), Rulings (No. 239)

In estimating stamp-duty on an assignment of a mortgage, a part of which has been paid, it must be computed on that portion of the original sum which remains unpaid at time of assignment.

Boutwell (1865), Rulings (No. 240)

Where a party executes a bond to a bank for a sum of money, and assigns a mortgage to the bank as security for the payment of the bond at its maturity, both the bond and the assignment of the mortgage are subject to stamp-duty. The fact that stamped collateral security is given does not exempt the principal instrument from stamp-duty. Neither would the stamp upon the principal instrument relieve the collateral from stamp-duty.

Boutwell (1865), Rulings (No. 282)

Stamp Duty in the Case of Two Mortgages to Secure One Bond.

Where a bond is secured by two mortgages, the stamp-duty required to validate all the instruments will be double, (if governed by the mortgages,) what it would have been in the case of one mortgage. If, however, the stamp appropriate to a bond be affixed to the same, then the bond will be valid, though the mortgages might not be.

IRR v.II, July 15, 1865, p.11

Stamp Duty on Assignment of Mortgages.

If a mortgage executed years ago is assigned at the present time, the assignment must be governed by the law now in force. If the mortgage has been reduced by payments, the amount of stamps to be affixed to the assignment depends upon the amount actually due on the mortgage when the assignment is made, not on the sum secured by the mortgagor, without regard to deductions made by subsequent payments.

IRR v.II, July 29, 1865, p.29

Mortgage and Power of Attorney.

Where a mortgage contains a power of attorney to sell, it is subject to stamp duty as a power of attorney, in addition to the duty required upon it as a mortgage.

IRR v.II, August 12, 1865, p.45

Stamp Mortgage to Secure an Annuity.

A mortgage to secure an annuity of $500 per annum during the life of an annuitant, the present value of the annuity being specified in the condition of the mortgage at $6,000 is subject to a stamp duty of six dollars.

Aug. 3, 1865.

IRR v.II, August 12, 1865, p.45

Stamps on Mortgages.

Office of Internal Revenue,
Washington, Nov. 15, 1866.

Sir: In reply to your letter of the 12th inst., that a Power of Sale in a mortgage of the form inclosed, being an essential part of such a mortgage, does not require an additional stamp.

Extraordinary Powers, Special Covenants, &c., sometimes inserted in Deeds of various kinds, but not contained in their common forms, are liable to the same tax as if they were issued separately.

Very respectfully,
Thomas Harland,
Deputy Commissioner.

Geo. W. Parker, Esq., *Jamestown, N.Y.*

The "form inclosed" was the following:

"And in case default shall be made in the payment of the principal sum hereby intended to be secured, or in the payment of the interest thereof, or any part of such principal or interest, as above provided, it shall be lawful for the party of the second part______________ Executors, Administrators, or Assigns, at any time thereafter, to sell the premises hereby granted, or any part thereof, in the manner prescribed by law."

IRR v.IV, December 1, 1866, p.171

Assignment or Transfer of Mortgage on Insurance Policy, Liable to Stamp Duty.

The assignment or transfer of a mortgage of a policy of insurance is subject to stamp tax, whether there be a sale or not; such for instance as a transfer from the legal owner to the equitable one.

IRR v.V, February 9, 1867, p.45

Registry of a Judgment Exempt From Stamp Duty.

No stamp is necessary upon the registry of a judgment, even though the registry is such in its legal effect as to create a lien which operates as a mortgage upon the property of the judgment debtor.

IRR v.V, February 9, 1867, p.45

Mortgage, when Taxable as Contract.

A mortgage given to secure a surety from loss, or given for any purpose whatever, other than as security for the payment of a definite and certain sum of money, is taxable only as an agreement or contract.

IRR v.V, February 23, 1867, p.60

Transfer of Mortgages—Endorsement on Negotiable Instruments.

Upon every assignment or transfer of a mortgage, a stamp tax is required equal to that imposed upon a mortgage for the amount remaining unpaid; this tax is required upon every such transfer in writing, whether there is a *sale* of the mortgage or not; but no stamp is necessary upon the endorsement of a negotiable instrument, even though the legal effect of such endorsement is to transfer a mortgage by which the instrument is secured.

IRR v.V, February 23, 1867, p.60

L. C., Baltimore, Md.–The stamp tax on a mortgage is 50c. for each $1,000, or fractional part of $1,000. You will see by the renewal in the following case that under the law in force, the renewal of a mortgage, is subject to tax. A bond for a certain sum secured by mortgage, falls due. The obligor desires an extension of three years; the obligee is willing to grant it. Question—Does the agreement or consent for such extension require a stamp equal to that on the bond, or is the stamp for an agreement simply sufficient, the agreement or consent to extend being in writing?

On this it is held that the renewal of a bond, or extension of the time of its payment, requires the same stamp as the original instrument.

IRR v.V, April 13, 1867, p.114

Two Mortgages to Secure the Payment of one Sum.

The stamp tax upon a mortgage is based upon the amount it is given to secure. The fact that the value of the property mortgaged is less than that amount, and that consequently the security is only partial, does not change the liability of the instrument. When, therefore, a second mortgage is given to secure the payment of a sum of money partially secured by a prior mortgage upon other property, or when two mortgages upon separate property are given at the same time to secure the payment of the same sum, each should be stamped as though it were the only one.

IRR v.V, April 13, 1867, p.115

The decision respecting the stamp duty on bonds and mortgages is of great moment in its bearings on the issue of bonds by railroad and other corporations. Much uneasiness has been caused by the diversity of practice which has prevailed in the stamping of such instruments. [Editor's Review]

IRR v.V, May 4, 1867, p.137

Bonds and Mortgage.

Whenever a bond or note is secured by a mortgage, but one stamp is necessary upon such papers, "provided that the stamp duty placed thereon shall be the highest required for said instruments or either of them." (Section 160.) A mortgage given to secure bonds which are to be issued from time to time as sales of them can be made, is valid so far as stamp taxes are concerned, though no stamps are affixed thereto if the bonds are properly stamped as provided in the section above mentioned, *as they are issued.*

IRR v.V, May 4, 1867, p.138

Power of Sale and other Powers Inserted in Mortgages or Deeds.

The ordinary power of sale commonly inserted in a mortgage or in a trust deed given as security for the payment of money, is regarded as part of the mortgage or deed, and requires no additional stamps. Extraordinary powers and agreements should be separately stamped.

IRR v.VI, October 12, 1867, p.130

Basis Stamp Duty on Mortgage or Trust Deeds.

The stamp tax on a mortgage, or trust deed, is based upon the definite or certain sum of money originally secured thereby, without including any interest which may accrue after the date of the instrument.

IRR v.VI, December 7, 1867, p.195

Mortgage for less than $100—Bond—Affixing Stamp.

A mortgage securing $100 or less is not subject to stamp duty, but the liability of the bond or note which is evidence of the amount secured is the same as though there were no mortgage; the necessary stamp may, however, be affixed either to the bond or note or to the mortgage, Sec. 160.

IRR v.VI, December 14, 1867, p.202

Assignment of Mortgage.

Assistant Assessor.—The following ruling answers your enquiry.

"The assignment of a mortgage requires, in every case, the same stamp as a new mortgage, for the sum still secured. The tax does not depend as in the case of a conveyance upon a valuable consideration."—Ed.

IRR v.VIII, November 14, 1868, p.158

Stamp Duty on Deed Securing Vendor's Lien and Notes for Deferred Payments Purchase Money.

In relation to stamp duty on notes given for the purchase money of an estate secured by a vendor's lien in the deed of conveyance, it is held that such a lien should be stamped at the rate of mortgages, in addition to the conveyance stamps. In that case the notes need not be stamped, which are secured by it. But in general, notes given for purchase money are liable.

IRR v.X, August 21, 1869, p.57

Assignment of Mortgages by Order of Court.

Office of Internal Revenue,
Washington, August 19, 1869.

Sir: I reply to your letter of the 14th inst., that upon every assignment of a mortgage a stamp tax is required equal to that imposed upon a mortgage for the amount remaining unpaid. The tax is required upon every such transfer in writing, whether there is a sale of the mortgage or not. (Series 5, No. 10, last paragraph, page 15.) 9 Record, 166.

The fact that the transfer is made by order of Court does not relieve it, any more than in the case of a deed made under a judgment.

It would be proper to stamp it, either in the district where the property is situated, or where the holder resides.

Very respectfully,
J. W. Douglass,
Deputy Commissioner.

G. L. Ford, Esq.,
Collector Internal Revenue,
Brooklyn, N.Y.

IRR v.X, September 11, 1869, p.85

Mortgages to be Stamped according to the Amount expressly Secured. Agreement Stamp required on Mortgages securing other Matters besides a Definite Sum.

Second District, Ala.,
Montgomery, January 20, 1870.

Hon. Columbus Delano, Commissioner Internal Revenue, Washington, D.C.

Sir: I have the honor to transmit herewith form of mortgage taken by the Montgomery Mutual Building and Loan Association for the security on certain sums advanced to stockholders who may purchase the funds subscribed from time to time; also letter of the Secretary of the Association, asking as to amount of stamps to be placed on such mortgages, whether on the actual amount advanced, or on the nominal amount as appearing on the face of the mortgage.

The matter having been submitted to me, I decided that such mortgages should be stamped for their face value, as the revenue law does not contemplate the recognition of any arrangements looking toward an enhancement of the value of stocks or shares issued by associations of this nature, coupled with the fact that the mortgager gives his note for the same amount secured by mortgage.

It is understood that "the stamp tax on a mortgage or trust deed" (Series 5, No. 10, par. 7, page 15) "is based upon the definite or certain sum of money originally secured, etc."

The Constitution of the Association is partly embodied in the language of the mortgage, but it is held by me that there should be something more definite in the mortgage as to the amount actually advanced.

Your decision in the matter will settle the question of stamp duty, and will relieve the officers of these associations, who are anxious to comply with law.

Francis Widmer,
Collector, Second District, Ala.

Office of Internal Revenue
Washington, February 3, 1870.

Francis Widmer, Esq., Collector Internal Revenue, Montgomery, Ala.

Sir: I reply to your letter of the 20th ult., relative to stamp duty on mortgages of the Montgomery Mutual Building and Loan Association, of the form enclosed, that your opinion is considered correct, that they should be stamped according to the amount *expressly* secured by them. It would be impossible to carry out the stamp laws if it were necessary to go behind the instruments themselves, and investigate the business affairs of the parties, to ascertain if something different was not intended from what was expressed. It might require a committee of examination and a long course of operations before a single paper could be stamped. Such a mortgage required also an agreement stamp as securing other matters besides a definite and certain sum.

J. W. Douglass,
Acting Commissioner.

IRR v.XI, February 26, 1870, pp.65-6

PASSAGE TICKET

Basic Stamp Tax on Foreign Passenger Tickets.

Stamps placed upon the passage tickets of passengers leaving for foreign ports, should be based upon the currency value of the tickets, and not upon the gold value.

IRR v.VI, September 28, 1867, p.105

Passage Tickets Sold for Paper or Gold Dollars.

The amount of stamp tax upon a foreign passage ticket, sold for gold coin, is controlled, not by the *relative value,* but by the *number* of gold dollars received for it; for the purpose of this tax the difference between the market value of a gold dollar, and that of a paper one, is to be disregarded. If, however, such a ticket is sold for paper currency, it must be stamped according to the number of paper dollars received therefor.

IRR v.VI, November 30, 1867, p.185

POWER OF ATTORNEY, SALE OF REAL ESTATE

Mortgage and Power of Attorney.

Where a mortgage contains a power of attorney to sell, it is subject to stamp duty as a power of attorney, in addition to the duty required upon it as a mortgage.

IRR v.II, August 12, 1865, p.45

Stamping of Powers of Attorney.

Office of Internal Revenue,
Washington, Sept. 24, 1866.

Sir: I reply to your letter of the 18th inst.: That a power of Attorney to sell and convey real estate, contained in a mortgage is subject to a stamp duty of one dollar, in addition to the mortgage stamp, the same as if it were made and issued as a separate instrument.

If an instrument is not properly stamped at the time it is issued, it should be presented to the Collector to have the appropriate stamps affixed. After being stamped by him, it will be valid and legal except as against rights acquired in good faith before it is so stamped, and recorded if a record is necessary.

E. A. Rollins,
Commissioner.

Mr. Luther Webster,
Fredonia, N.Y.

IRR v.IV, November 3, 1866, p.142

Stamps on Mortgages.

Office of Internal Revenue
Washington, Nov. 15, 1866.

Sir: In reply to your letter of the 12th inst., that a Power of Sale in a mortgage of the form inclosed, being an essential part of such a mortgage, does not require an additional stamp.

Extraordinary Powers, Special Covenants, &c., sometimes inserted in Deeds of various kinds, but not contained in their common forms, are liable to the same tax as if they were issued separately.

Very respectfully,
Thomas Harland,
Deputy Commissioner.

Geo. W. Parker, Esq.,
Jamestown, N.Y.

The "form inclosed" was the following:

"And in case default shall be made in the payment of the principal sum hereby intended to be secured, or in the payment of the interest thereof, or any part of such principal or interest, as above provided, it shall be lawful for the party of the second part__________ Executors, Administrators, or Assigns, at any time thereafter, to sell the premises hereby granted, or any part thereof, in the manner prescribed by law."

IRR v.IV, December 1, 1866, p.171

Powers of Sale and other Powers Inserted in Mortgage or Deeds.

The ordinary power of sale commonly inserted in a mortgage or in a trust deed given as security for the payment of money, is regarded as part of the mortgage or deed, and requires no additional stamps. Extraordinary powers and agreements should be separately stamped.

IRR v.VI, October 12, 1867, p.130

POWER OF ATTORNEY, SALE OF STOCK

In relation to transfers of shares by stockholders.

January, 1863.

Any written authority, in whatever form drawn, made by a stockholder in a corporation for the transfer of shares in such corporation, is regarded as a power of attorney; and as such is subject, under Schedule B, to a stamp duty of twenty-five cents.

Boutwell (1863), Decisions (No. 63)

Powers of attorney to sell and transfer stock executed prior to October 1, 1862, are exempt from stamp duty; but if such powers of attorney were executed subsequently to that date, they are liable to stamp duty.

Boutwell (1863), Rulings (No. 286)

In addition to the stamp duty required upon notes drawn according to the forms you enclose, (as notes,) the power of attorney *to sell* stock, which is incorporated in each of them, is subject to a stamp duty of twenty-five cents, and the power of attorney to *transfer* stock, which is appended to one of them, is also subject to a stamp duty of twenty-five cents.

Boutwell (1863), Rulings (from No. 316)

POWER OF ATTORNEY, VOTING

Power of Attorney to vote by proxy for Officers for any Incorporated Company.

When a "power of attorney or proxy for voting at any election for officers of any incorporated company or society, except religious, charitable, or literary societies or public cemeteries," is signed by several stockholders, owning separate and distinct shares, it is, in its legal effect, the separate instrument of each, and requires stamps to the amount of ten cents for each and every signature; one or more stamps may be used representing the whole amount required.

IRR v. V, March 30, 1867, p. 100

Powers of Attorney, Proxy, &c.

A "Power of Attorney, or proxy, for voting at any election for officers in any incorporated company or society, except religious, charitable, or literary societies, or public Cemeteries," is subject to a stamp tax of ten cents. When several stockholders, who are the owners of distinct shares, sign a power of attorney, each authorizing a person to act for him, the instrument is to be regarded as the separate power of each, and should be stamped accordingly.

If the power relates to general business and not merely to the election of officers, it should be stamped at the rate of fifty cents for each signer, whether it is to be used at the elections of the societies, &c., above named, or not.

IRR v.VI, December 28, 1867, p.218

POWER OF ATTORNEY, GENERAL

Concerning stamps on powers of attorney to draw pay, bounty, &c.

May, 1863.

The following words in section 6, (page 11,) of the act of March 3, 1863: "No stamp duty shall be required on powers of attorney, or any other paper relating to applications for bounties, arrearages of pay, or pensions, or to the receipt thereof from time to time," are held to exempt only those applications which are made in pursuance of law, for or on behalf of the special classes of discharged, disabled, or deceased officers, soldiers, sailors, or marines entitled thereto.

Boutwell (1863), Decisions (No. 106)

Do powers of attorney for foreign countries for the collection of moneys abroad, or the sale of property there, require stamps?

If such powers of attorney are so prepared and authenticated as to conform to the laws of the country in which moneys are to be collected or property sold by virtue thereof, I am of opinion that the transaction would be valid as between the principal and attorney, and that the rights of third parties could not be questioned, upon the ground that such powers were not stamped according to the laws of the United States.

The law provides that bills of exchange drawn in, but payable out of, the United States shall be stamped. No such provision exists with regard to powers of attorney; nor is there reason to suppose, from the language employed, that stamps are required upon such instruments when made in this country, but which could be operative and of value only in another country.

Boutwell (1863), Rulings (No. 262)

The act of March 3, 1863, and decision No. 106, cannot be construed to exempt from stamp duty applications or claims for prize-money or papers relating to such applications or claims.

Boutwell (1863), Rulings (No. 310)

March 9, 1863.

Sir: The communication from the honorable Secretary of State, under date of January 14, and the letter of C. F. Hagedorn, esq., consul of Baden, dated Philadelphia, January 10, have been considered, and I respectfully submit the following reply:

Mr. Hagedorn inquires, first, "whether powers of attorney for foreign countries for the collection of moneys abroad, or the sale of property there, require stamps?" If such powers of attorney are so prepared and authenticated as to conform to the laws of the country in which moneys are to be collected or property sold by virtue thereof, I am of opinion that the transaction would be valid as between the principal and attorney, and that the rights of third parties could not be questioned, upon the ground that such powers were not stamped according to the laws of the United States.

The law provides that "bills of exchange," drawn in but payable out of the United States, shall be stamped. No such provision exists with regard to powers of attorney, nor is there reason to suppose, from the language employed, that stamps are required upon such instruments when made in this country, but which could be made operative and of value only in another country.

Mr. Hagedorn next inquires, "whether the certificates of notaries public attached to such powers require stamps, and to what amount?"

In all cases the certificate of the notary, that the party appeared and duly executed the power, &c., is exempt from duty.

To Hon. S. P. Chase,
Secretary of the Treasury.

Boutwell (1863), Correspondence (No. 3)

Sir: In your letter you call my attention to the following provision of the amendments to the excise law approved 3d March, 1863: "No stamp duty shall be required on powers of attorney or any other paper relating to applications for bounties, arrearages of pay, or pensions, or to the receipt thereof from time to time."

I am of opinion that this provision exempts from stamp duty all papers relating to applications for bounties, arrearages of pay, or pensions, made by or on behalf of officers or privates of the army, or officers, marines, or sailors of the navy, who are, or at the time of such application may have been, in the service of the United States; but it cannot be construed to exempt from stamp duty applications or claims for prize-money or papers relating to such applications or claims.

Boutwell (1863), Correspondence (No. 11)

Powers of attorney, and all other papers connected with arrearages of pay, &c., are exempt from stamp-duty.

Boutwell (1865), Rulings (No. 244)

Claims on government, for an allowance for property lost in war, are not applications for arrearages of pay, nor official accounts exempted by the terms of sections 154 and 160 [Ed. note: of the Act of June 30, 1864]. *This* application contains a distinct power of attorney.

Boutwell (1865), Rulings (No. 256)

Where an *auditor* of the United States adjudicates that such an amount has been found due, the power of attorney to collect the amount would be exempt under section 160 [Ed. note: of the Act of June 30, 1864]. If, however, the amount of pay had been determined and a certificate of indebtedness, bond, or other obligation had been received in payment, a power of attorney to collect such certificate, &c., &c., would require stamp.

Boutwell (1865), Rulings (No. 268)

Letters of attorney made in the United States, and sent to the attorney residing abroad, where the powers conferred are to be executed, do not require a stamp.

The mere execution of an instrument does not impose any duty in relation to the stamp. If it is stamped, and delivered according to the law of the country where the delivery takes place, it is enough. At all events no stamp is required by law. If, however, a letter of attorney is made and delivered to the attorney in the United States, though the power conferred by it is to be executed in a foreign land, it should be stamped when delivered.

Boutwell (1865), Rulings (No. 278)

Stamping of Warrant of Attorney Accompanying Bonds or Notes Secured By Mortgage.

No stamp is required on any warrant of attorney accompanying a bond or note when such bond or note has affixed thereto the stamp or stamps denoting the duty required; and whenever any bond or note is secured by mortgage, but one stamp duty is required on such papers, such stamp duty being the highest rate required for such instruments, or either of them. In such case a note or memorandum of the value or denomination of the stamp affixed should be made upon the margin or in the acknowledgment of the instrument which is not stamped. Jan. 30, 1866.

IRR v.III, February 10, 1866, p.45

Stamping of Power of Attorney.

The following instrument, viz.:

"G______, Feb. 8, 1866.

"To the R. Mntg. Co.:

"Please pay P. M_______, whatever may become my due for labor until further order, and his receipt shall be sufficient for the same.

(Signed,) J.F_______."

is a power of attorney for another purpose than those specially named in Schedule B, and subject to a stamp duty of fifty cents. February, 1866.

IRR v.III, February 24, 1866, p.60

Powers of Appointment and Attorney—National Banks.

Section 25 of the act commonly known as the National Currency Act, is as follows:—

"*And be it further enacted,* That it shall be the duty of every banking association having bonds deposited in the office of the Treasurer of the United States, once or oftener in each fiscal year, and at such time or times during the ordinary business hours as said officer or officers may select, to examine and compare the bonds so pledged, with the books of the Comptroller and the accounts of the Association, and, if found correct, to execute to the said Treasurer a certificate, setting forth the different kinds and the amounts thereof, and that the same are in the possession and custody of the Treasurer at the date of such certificate. Such examination may be made by an officer or agent of such Association, duly appointed in writing for that purpose, whose certificate before mentioned shall be of like force and validity as if executed by such president or cashier; and a duplicate signed by the Treasurer shall be retained by the Association.''

The written appointment mentioned in said section is a power of attorney for a purpose not particularly mentioned in Section B, and is subject to a stamp tax of fifty cents.

IRR v.V, June 29, 1867, p.204

PROBATE OF WILL

The value of all the property of the testator, whether real or personal, which, under the law or by virtue of the terms of the will, can be administered upon, and is within the jurisdiction of the court wherein the will is approved, is the measure of the stamp duty chargeable upon the will when proved.

Should the will be approved in another jurisdiction, it will then be necessary to affix an additional stamp proportionate to the value of the property within such jurisdiction, and subject to the law and terms of the will.

Boutwell (1863), Rulings (No. 246)

Probate of Will stamps are the proper stamps to be affixed to letters of administration on intestate estates.

Boutwell (1863), Rulings (No. 253)

''Probate of Will'' is subject to stamp tax, but letters testamentary issued thereupon are exempt.

Boutwell (1863), Rulings (from No. 265)

The stamp used upon letters of administration upon the estates of intestates must answer to the value of the real and personal estate within the jurisdiction of the court.

Boutwell (1863), Rulings (No. 283)

March 6, 1863.

Sir: In your letter of the 17th ultimo you make the following inquiries:

''In the probate of wills, under the national tax law, is the duty chargeable upon the value of the real estate devised, as well as upon the personalty?''

I am of opinion that the value of all the property of the testator, whether real or personal, which, under the law, or by virtue of the terms of the will, can be administered upon, and which is within the jurisdiction of the court wherein the will is approved, is the measure of the stamp duty chargeable upon the will when approved.

Should the will be approved in another jurisdiction, it will then be necessary to affix an additional stamp, proportionate to the value of the property within such jurisdiction, and subject to the law, and terms of the will.

This latter remark is in reply to your second inquiry, in which you say:

''If the real estate is embraced in the law requiring a stamp duty, and there are pieces of real property lying in different counties and in different States, in each of which the will must be admitted to probate, is the stamp duty to be affixed for the whole value on the first probate, or must the stamp be affixed for the portion of the estate within the jurisdiction of each particular court of probate?''

To L. Anderson, Esq., *Cincinnati, Ohio.*

Boutwell (1863), Correspondence (No. 7)

The stamp-duty, paid on letters of administration and the administrator's bond, covers all papers that are necessary in the settlement of an estate; therefore petition for sale of real estate is exempt.

Boutwell (1865), Rulings (No. 203)

Administrator's bond is liable to stamp-duty of one dollar. . . . One stamp-duty only is required on a probate of will with letters of administration, and should be placed on the probate.

Boutwell (1865), Rulings (No. 207)

The stamp-duty on probate of will and letters of administration must correspond to the value of the estate, in respect of which such letters are taken.

When the will devises the real estate to the executors in trust for specific purposes, or directs its sale, or subjects it to the payment of debts, the value of that estate must be taken as a basis for estimating stamp-duty.

Boutwell (1865), Rulings (No. 233)

Where a will is proved and stamped in one state, and sent into another for probate, in order to reach property in the latter state, the stamp-duty must be appropriate to the value of the property sought to be affected by such probate.

Boutwell (1865), Rulings (No. 237)

The stamping of letters of administration covers all orders, notices, certificates, and affidavits issued in the settlement of the estate. The bond of administrator requires an additional stamp of one dollar. Guardian's bond requires a stamp of one dollar.

Boutwell (1865), Rulings (No. 252)

Letters of administration *de bonis non* are subject to stamp-duty. The amount of stamp-duty required upon such instruments is determined by the value of the estate to be administered upon by the administrator *de bonis non*.

Boutwell (1865), Rulings (No. 279)

The presentation of a will for probate, applications for the appointment of administrators and guardians do not require stamps. The probate of will, letters of administration, and bond of executors, administrators, guardians, and trustees are subject to stamp-duty, as is also the appraisal or inventory of the estate, being an appraisal of value. But all other proceedings, such as petitions, orders, notices, certificates, and affidavits used in the settlement of the estate, are exempt.

Boutwell (1865), Rulings (No. 286)

The stamp-duty upon "letters of administration" must be appropriate to the value of the estate administered upon. If the administrator has no authority or control over the real estate vested in him, the stamp-duty must be determined by the value of the personal estate. When under the laws of a state, the administrator taking letters has an office or duty to perform in respect to the real estate, the value of that estate must be included as a basis for the estimate of stamp-duty.

Boutwell (1865), Rulings (No. 289)

Letters of administration, taken out for the purpose of obtaining soldiers' or sailors' bounty-money, back pay, and pensions, are not papers relating to application for bounties, arrearages of pay or pensions within the meaning of the exemption-clause of section 160 of the act of June 30, 1864, and are therefore subject to stamp-duty.

Boutwell (1865), Rulings (No. 290)

Stamp Duty On Wills.

When the will devises the real estate to the executors in trust for specific purposes, or directs its sale, or subjects it to the payment of the debts, the value of that estate must be included as a basis for the estimate of stamp duty.

When under the laws of the State the administrator taking letters has an office or duty to perform in respect to the real estate, the same rule obtains. It is otherwise when the personal estate only does or can come under the authority or cognizance of the administrator of such.

IRR v.I, March 11, 1865, p.75

Stamping of Letters of Administration.

Office of Internal Revenue
Washington, March 15, 1866.

Sir: In reply to your letter of the 8th inst. that where an administrator dies, before the estate is settled, and it becomes necessary to appoint another person to administer the balance of the estate, the new letters of administration are subject to a stamp duty appropriate to the value of the estate remaining unadministered.

Very respectfully,
D. C. Whitman,
Acting Commissioner.

S. P. Allen, Esq.,
Collector, Rochester, N.Y.

IRR v.III, March 31, 1866, p.101

Appointments of Guardians and Commissioners for Lunatics Do Not Require Stamps— Administrators' Bonds Subject To Stamp.

Office of Internal Revenue,
Washington, April 23, 1866.

Sir: I reply to your letter of the 14th instant, That *ex parte* applications to Surrogate Courts or Courts of Probate for the admission of wills to proof, for the appointment of guardians, the sale of an infant's real estate, or the appointment of commissioners for lunatics, and the like, are not regarded as writs or other original processes by which suits are commenced in any court of law or equity within the meaning of the Internal Revenue law; and, hence, no stamp is required in such cases. Administrators' bonds and the like are official, and should be stamped with a $1 stamp.

Very respectfully,
D. C. Whitman,
Deputy Commissioner.

Alfred Wells,
Assessor, Ithaca, Tompkins Co., N.Y.

IRR v.III, May 12, 1866, p.151

PROTEST

Stamp Duties On Protests Accrue For Each and Every Note, Bills of Exchange, Drafts, &c.

A stamp duty of twenty-five cents is imposed upon the "protest of every note, bill of exchange, check or draft," and upon every marine protest. If several notes, bills of exchange, drafts, &c., are protested at the same time and all attached to one and the same certificate, stamps should be affixed to the amount of twenty-five cents for each note, bill, draft, &c., thus protested.

IRR v.V, February 9, 1867, p.45

Waiver of Protest, or Demand, on Negotiable Paper.

A waiver of protest, or of demand, and notice written upon negotiable paper and signed by the endorser, is an agreement, and requires a five cent stamp.

IRR v.V, March 30, 1867, p.100

Protest—Certificate of Notice.

The certificate of notice to parties, usually appended to a Notary's certificate of protest, forms no part of the protest and requires additional stamps to the amount of five cents.

IRR v.VI, October 12, 1867, p.130

A Notary's Certificate to his Notice of Protest is not relieved from the Stamp Tax by the fact that it is printed in Blank on the same sheet of paper with the Certificate of Protest.

Office of Internal Revenue,
Washington, October 21, 1871.

R. N. McRaren, Esq., Assessor, St. Paul, Minnesota.

Sir: Yours of the 6th instant, enclosing copies of notaries' certificates of protest, is acknowledged.

You say, "It is claimed by parties using these forms that the notice is incorporated with the protest and *does form* part of the same, and therefore does not require additional stamp."

It is not perceived that the certificate of notice in the forms which you enclose, is otherwise than "appended" to the certificate of protest. The fact that the said certificate of notice is printed in blank on the same sheet of paper with the certificate of protest does not "incorporate" the former with the latter in any manner to relieve the same from stamp duty.

It will be observed that the tax in question is not a tax *upon* the *notice*, but *is* upon the certificate of the service of notice. The notary sends out his notice of protest, and then certifies that he has done so. This certificate is evidently of *service*, and is designed for use as such. Being legal evidence of an essential act, it is liable to stamp tax, and none the less so, simply because it is made upon the same piece of paper with the certificate of protest.

Enclosed I send you copy of a letter to J. H. Fay, Esq., dated August 28, 1867. Respectfully,

G. B. Williams,
Deputy Commissioner.

Office of Internal Revenue,
Washington, August 28, 1867.

James H. Fay, Esq., No. 9 Nassau street, New York city.

Sir: I reply to your letter of the 18th ultimo, that the certificate of notice to parties usually appended to a notary's certificate of protest forms no part of the certificate last named, and requires additional stamps to the amount of five cents.

The stamp tax in the case of a protest is not imposed strictly upon the notarial certificate, although as a matter of practice that is the appropriate place for it; but it is imposed upon the "protest of any note, bill of exchange, check, or draft," and upon every marine protest. It has accordingly been held by this office, that if several notes, bills of exchange, etc., are protested at the same time, and are all attached to one and the same certificate, stamps should be affixed to the amount of twenty-five cents for each and every note, bill, draft, etc., thus protested. Not only is the certificate of notice to parties no part of the protest, but it is no part of the official duty of a notary by the law (Merchant) to give notice of the dishonor of a promissory note, unless required by some State law or general usage. (Burke v. McRay, 2 Howard, 66.)

In the form submitted by you the certificate of notice is as follows:

"And I, the said notary, do hereby certify that on the day of in the year aforesaid, I deposited in the Post-office of the United States, in the said city of New York, fully prepaying the postage thereon, notice of the foregoing protest," etc.

The blank itself treats the *protest* as something distinct from the *certificate of notice*, when it speaks of the *foregoing protest*. The certificate in question is a distinct instrument and requires a five cent stamp, the same as if made upon a separate piece of paper. Very respectfully,

Thomas Harland,
Deputy Commissioner.

IRR v.XIV, November 4, 1871, p. 145

RECEIPT

In reply to inquiry if the following form—"I have to acknowledge your favor with enclosures, &c."—is liable to duty as a receipt,—such an acknowledgment contains in itself no evidence that any sum of money or any debt has been paid, or that any property has been received for delivery, and is therefore not taxable.

Boutwell (1865), Rulings (No. 198)

The indorsement of the payment of interest on a bond or mortgage requires no stamp, although in the form of a receipt, because delivery is necessary to subject to duty any instrument of writing requiring a stamp.

Boutwell (1865), Rulings (No. 201)

There is no provision in the law requiring railroad and express companies to give receipts for the delivery of goods, but whenever such are given, they require stamp.

Boutwell (1865), Rulings (No. 202)

A receipt for money, given to any charitable institution, does not require a stamp, as it is not a payment of money for a debt due; neither does a receipt for goods delivered to such society require stamp, as no rights would be acquired by any party through such receipt.

Boutwell (1865), Rulings (No. 205)

Bills of lading or receipts for the transportation of goods from one port or place in the United States to another, require a two-cent stamp. Duplicates require the same as originals.

Boutwell (1865), Rulings (No. 209)

Any person acknowledging the receipt of money, and naming the amount received, and duly signed by the person receiving it, would require a stamp. But a written acknowledgment of the receipt requires no stamp, the draft itself having been stamped.

Boutwell (1865), Rulings (from No. 211)

An unstamped receipt is invalid, and the person who signs and issues the receipt is subject to penalty.

Boutwell (1865), Rulings (No. 223)

A receipt for telegram is not subject to stamp-duty.

Boutwell (1865), Rulings (No. 245)

A receipted bill for labor, when the amount exceeds $20, is subject to stamp-duty, as a receipt for the payment of money, or a debt due.

Boutwell (1865), Rulings (No. 246)

A credit of money on the books of a party on account, or the indorsement of part-payment on the back of a note or bond, is not considered a receipt.

Boutwell (1865), Rulings (No. 248)

If a check, draft, or note is received in payment of a debt due, and the receipt is so expressed, such receipt would require a stamp. But a check is not ordinarily considered money, but merely the evidence of a certain amount to be paid, and in such a case is exempt.

Boutwell (1865), Rulings (No. 249)

''Dray tickets,'' given for each load of coal or other article delivered, are subject to stamp-duty as receipts.

Boutwell (1865), Rulings (No. 255)

Where indorsement is made on an insurance policy, and is signed by the company or its agent, it is subject to stamp-duty as a receipt; but if it is merely a memorandum or indorsement without a signature attached, it is not a receipt, and is therefore exempt.

Boutwell (1865), Rulings (No. 274)

A receipt like the following: ''Chicago, Jan. 9, 1865. J. H. Rodamiul & Co. Yours of the 6th received: All right. $500. Yours truly, W. C. M'Cormick,''—is subject to stamp-duty. From the evidence on the face of the instrument it is undoubtedly given as a receipt for money, and therefore subject.

Boutwell (1865), Rulings (No. 277)

The receipt given to a sheriff by a plaintiff or his attorney, for money collected upon a judgment, is subject to stamp-duty where the amount of such receipt is for a sum exceeding twenty dollars. Such receipt cannot be held to be exempt under the provisions of the statute exempting receipts given for the satisfaction of any mortgage or judgment, or decree of court; but a receipt given by the sheriff to the defendant, upon payment or satisfaction of the judgment on the return of the sheriff upon the order of execution, can be regarded as exempt from stamp-duty.

Boutwell (1865), Rulings (No. 284)

Of Receipts, and the Stamping of the Same.

Perhaps there is no more generally accepted fallacy among laymen than the belief that a written receipt is conclusive evidence of the statements embodied in it. Men resolutely infer that all the testimony that is required to establish the payment of any sum of money or to sustain a claim for goods entrusted to the guardianship of another, is to walk into a court of law and exhibit a written receipt. This delusion requires to be dispelled in order that it may not mislead.

This belief most probably has its origin in the faith which men naturally place in written evidence, and this faith is well founded, for written evidence is truly the highest order of testimony that can be adduced, and in no case can the terms of a written agreement be varied or explained by oral testimony. But the truth of the whole contents, or any part of a written receipt, may be disproved by oral testimony. The legitimacy of the signature attached to any written instrument, or of the instrument itself is always a proper subject for judicial inquiry, where such an issue is raised, and in which case it must be duly and satisfactorily proved.

An ordinary writing, not being an agreement, is regarded by common law as prima facie evidence only, and liable to be controverted and rebutted; and where it takes rank as a higher order of evidence it is by virtue of the express provisions of statute law.

The Internal Revenue law does not vary the character of a receipt from that given to it by common law. Within the scope of its provisions such an instrument is still prima facie evidence of the facts set forth in it, *provided* that where it purports to be an acknowledgment for the payment of any sum of money exceeding $20, or for the delivery of any property, it shall not be accepted as evidence unless it is duly stamped in accordance with the requirements of the Revenue law.

The Internal Revenue law does not prescribe that a receipt shall be given in any case by a party receiving money or property, but where such a receipt is voluntarily given for an amount exceeding $20, it must be duly stamped, and any failure so to stamp it is a penal offence, for which the offender must answer.

A tender of money due is not legal if based upon any condition precedent; such as requiring a receipt from the party to whom the money is tendered, as a condition of its payment. And the party receiving is not required by any law to give a receipt, although it is the almost universal practice among business men to sign receipts for money received.

Receipts are constantly passing between business men without a stamp affixed, in open violation of law, and any time these paper witnesses are liable to become living accusers in the hands of public informers or private enemies.

The signing or issuing any instrument or writing, subject to stamp duty, without the same being duly stamped, subjects the party so issuing or signing the same, to a penalty of two hundred dollars, and renders the instrument invalid.

The failure to cancel any stamp duly affixed as aforesaid, renders the person so failing liable to a penalty of fifty dollars.

The stamp must be cancelled by the party affixing or using the same, and the mode of cancelling prescribed by law is by writing upon the stamp the initials of the name, and also the date on which the stamp is attached or used.

IRR v.I, January 21, 1865, p.18

Stamp On Receipts.

The affixing of a stamp (in relation to receipts on dividend), sufficient to cover the number of receipts on a dividend sheet, upon the same, will necessarily negative any prosecution on the part of this office for not affixing the stamps exactly in accordance with the law; for the presence of such a comprehensive stamp is evidence of no intent to defraud the Government.

But such validity might be questioned if brought into court, and individuals must assume the responsibility if such stamp is affixed.

IRR v.I, January 28, 1865, p.26

Treasury Department,
Office of Internal Revenue,
Washington, April 23, 1866.

The law requires all receipts for the payment of any sum of money or for the payment of any debt due exceeding twenty dollars, or for the delivery of any property, to be stamped, excepting receipts for the satisfaction of any mortgage or judgment or decree of any court, which are exempt.

Receipts for the payment of money, or of a debt due, require to be stamped only when the amount exceeds twenty dollars. This includes receipts for salaries or pay on the pay rolls of companies or corporations or individuals, or for dividends or interest on the books of banks or other trust companies, or any receipt for the payment of an amount exceeding twenty dollars, signed by the party receiving it or by his authority. Such signature may be the full name—christian or surname—initials, or any mark or character adopted for that purpose, and may be written with ink or pencil, or printed or stamped upon the instrument.

A credit on an account or pass-book, or on a bill, without a signature, is not a receipt, and is not subject to stamp duty. A letter acknowledging the payment of a debt due is to all intents and purposes a receipt, and subject to stamp duty as such, but the acknowledgment of a note, check or draft is not a receipt for money, nor yet of property, in the ordinary acceptation of that term, and is not subject to stamp duty, unless specified to have been received in payment of a debt due exceeding $20.

Receipts for the delivery of any property are subject to stamp duty without regard to the amount or value of such property, and this covers every receipt or acknowledgment of the delivery of any property. If several receipts are given which are afterward taken up and a new one given for the whole, each receipt must be stamped. Where a number of receipts are taken on one sheet or page, such as dividend books, pay rolls, receipt books of savings banks, express companies, or the like, the party paying out the money or delivering the property may affix one or more stamps to each page covering the aggregate amount of stamp duty required on the several receipts upon that page, and the claim of the government would be thereby satisfied; but the question as to the validity of any one of the receipts so stamped, is one which such party must settle for himself.

Section 151 of the law imposes the stamp duty upon the party making, signing, or issuing the instrument, or upon the party for whose use the instrument is made; and section 156 provides that the party using or affixing the stamp shall cancel the same with his initials and the date upon which the same shall be attached or used, thus clearly contemplating that the stamp may be affixed and cancelled by either the maker or the party for whose use it was made.

Under the provisions of section 151, the payment of the stamp duty is imposed upon the party for whose use the instrument is made—in just as strong terms as it is upon the party making the instrument, and it is not in the power of the commissioner to say, or prescribe that it means one any more than the other.

If the instrument is made and issued, it must be stamped as required by law. It might have been better that Congress should have made this matter certain by imposing the payment of the stamp duty upon the maker in all cases, but it was not so done. They have, to be sure, imposed a penalty upon the party making, signing or issuing an instrument required by law to be stamped, with intent to evade the law, but if there is no intent to evade the law no penalty attaches to the maker.

Where a party is bound by law, or contract, to execute and deliver an instrument, he would be bound to deliver a valid and legal instrument, and of course stamp it, if a stamp is required by the law; but where he is not bound to deliver such instrument, he may well enough decline to execute it unless the party for whose use it is made furnish the stamp.

As the law stands, the Commissioner cannot require one party to pay the stamp duty any more than the other, but if any instrument is made and issued upon which a stamp is imposed, the law requires that it should have the proper stamp for denoting that stamp duty affixed and cancelled.

Very respectfully,
Joseph J. Lewis,
Commissioner.

IRR v.I, February 11, 1865, p.45

———

Stamps on Express Receipts.

Treasury Department,
Office of Internal Revenue,
Washington, March 16, 1865.

Sir:—Your letter of March 13th, stating that Express Companies have discontinued the use of stamps, under directions received from the home office, and asking what course you shall take in the matter, has been received. In reply, I have to say, that by provision of the act of March 3, 1865, Express Companies are not required to stamp receipts on or after the first day of April, 1865, but there is nothing in the act releasing them from the necessity of stamping such receipts before that time. You will therefore report each and every case of violation of law by Express Companies in failing to stamp receipts to the Collector for prosecution, on the fact coming to your knowledge.

Very respectfully yours,
Joseph J. Lewis,
Commissioner.

P. H. Neher, Esq.
Assessor 15th District, Granville, N.Y.

IRR v.I, March 25, 1865, p.90

Stamps On Receipts Of Express Companies.

Treasury Department,
Office of Internal Revenue,
Washington, April 11, 1865.

Sir: Your letter of the 6th inst., stating that "the General Superintendent of the United States Express Company, New York, had instructed its agents to discontinue the use of stamps on the receipts *taken* by them," has been received.

In reply, I have to say, that the amendatory act of March 3, 1865, exempts from stamp duty the receipts *given* by express companies, upon the delivery of goods (to them) for transportation. The receipts taken by them upon the delivery of property are still subject to stamp duty the same as heretofore; but this office has no power to decide that the express company shall pay the duty in preference to the party executing the instrument. If an instrument requiring a stamp is issued without the appropriate stamp being affixed and cancelled, the *maker* is liable to the penalty for a violation of the law, and the other party loses the benefit of the instrument.

Very respectfully,
(Signed) E. A. Rollins,
Deputy Commissioner.

To S. F. Denton,
Collector 27th District, Elmira, N.Y.

IRR v.I, April 22, 1865, p.124

Duplicate Receipts Require Stamps.

U.S. Collector's Office,
Pottsville, Schuylkill Co., Pa.
May 27, 1865.

To Hon. Joseph J. Lewis,
Commissioner of Internal Revenue.

Sir: Many coal firms doing business in this district, having their main office in Philadelphia and a branch office at the colliery, require their agents to obtain duplicate receipts for money paid by them in the course of business; the original to be sent to the main office at Philadelphia, and the duplicate to be retained at the branch office as a voucher in the settlement of accounts between their agents and themselves. Should stamps be placed on both original and duplicate at the time they are made, if the receipt comes within the amount prescribed by law?

Very respectfully,
James A. Inness,
Collector 10th District, Pa.

[Answer.]

Treasury Department,
Office of Internal Revenue,
Washington, May 29, 1865.

Sir: I reply to your letter of the 27th inst. in relation to stamp duty on duplicate receipts, that when receipts are made and issued in duplicate, both require to be stamped as originals.

Very respectfully,
E. A. Rollins,
Deputy Commissioner.

James A. Inness,
Collector 10th District, Pottsville, Pa.

IRR v.I, June 10, 1865, p.180

Stamping Of Receipts For Payment By Check.

Internal Revenue Bureau.
Washington, May 30, 1865.

Sir: In reply to your letter of the 27th inst., that a check is not money, neither is it property in the ordinary acceptance of that term, but the evidence only of a sum of money due and payable; therefore a receipt for a check is not subject to a stamp duty, unless the check is actually received as the payment of a debt due, and that fact is expressed in the receipt. In the case stated by you, a bill receipted as "paid by check," which clearly expresses that the check was received in payment, and such receipt is undoubtedly subject to stamp duty.

When a receipt merely acknowledges that a check has been received, without expressing that it was received in payment of a bill or other indebtedness, it is exempt from stamp duty.

Very respectfully,
E. A. Rollins,
Dep. Commissioner.

IRR v.I, June 24, 1865, p.196

Stamping Of Dray Receipts.

Treasury Department,
Washington, July 14, 1865.

Gentlemen: Your letter of the 8th inst., inquiring whether it is necessary for shippers of goods to foreign and domestic ports to place stamps upon the dray receipts, in addition to the one placed upon the original bills of lading, is received.

I reply, that stamps should be affixed to such receipts by *some person,* and that the person who signs and issues an *unstamped* receipt of that character thereby makes himself liable to penalty. This Bureau does not undertake to decide who shall pay for a stamp annexed to a receipt in any particular case. That question may be decided by some local law or private contract.

The dray receipts mentioned by you are not covered by the stamps affixed to the bills of lading, but should themselves be stamped like any other receipt for goods delivered.

Very respectfully,
E. A. Rollins,
Deputy Commissioner.

IRR v.II, July 29, 1865, p.28

Railroad Freight Receipts Subject To Stamp.

The clause of schedule B, in the law, section 170, which exempts from stamp duties receipts for the delivery of property when issued by persons, firms or companies doing an express business, is held not to apply to receipts given by railroad companies for property to be transported by them in the course of their business.

IRR v.II, September 2, 1865, p.68

Stamps On Bills Of Lading.

Treasury Department,
Office of Internal Revenue,
Washington, Oct. 15, 1865.

Gentlemen: Your letter of the 14th instant has been received. You state the following case:

A merchant ships a load of goods and takes a receipt for the same property stamped. Upon this receipt he obtains three bills of lading, two of which the shipper takes, and one the shipowner retains with the receipt.

You inquire how many, if any, of these bills of lading should be stamped.

I reply that a domestic bill of lading is subject to the same stamp duty as a receipt. If it is issued in triplicate the duplicate and the triplicate should each be stamped the same as the original.

The fact that a stamp is affixed to the shipping receipt in no way changes the liability of the bills of lading.

Very respectfully,
E. A. Rollins,
Deputy Commissioner.

IRR v.II, October 28, 1865, p.132

Stamping Of Bills Of Lading.

Office of Internal Revenue.
Washington, November 28, 1865.

Sir: Your letter of the 24th inst., enclosing a letter from Messrs. Glidden & Williams, has been received.

Messrs. Glidden & Williams state that on all goods sent down to their ships loading for San Francisco they sign stamped receipts; also parties holding these receipts call at their office and give them up, and Messrs. Glidden & Williams give them in exchange bills of lading; and they inquire, "Are said bills of lading subject to stamp duty?"

I reply that the stamp duty upon the bills of lading in no wise depends upon the stamp duty on the receipts: the instruments are given for two distinct transactions, and each must bear the appropriate stamp. If more than one bill of lading is issued, each must be stamped as an original.

Very respectfully,
D. C. Whitman,
Deputy Commissioner.

Otis Clapp, Esq., *U. S. Assessor,*
4th District, Boston, Mass.

IRR v.II, December 16, 1865, p.186

Receipts To Be Stamped When Given For Checks.

Office of Internal Revenue,
Washington, Dec. 8, 1865.

Sir: I reply to your letter of the 5th instant, that it was formerly held by this office that the receipt given for a stamped check was exempt from stamp duty.

It is now held, however, that the receipts for a check, note, draft, or order, when received as the *payment* of a sum of money, or of a debt due exceeding twenty dollars, is subject to a stamp duty, the same as a receipt for money paid.

Very respectfully,
D. C. Whitman,
Acting Commissioner.

IRR v.II, December 23, 1865, p.196

Stamping Of Domestic Bills Of Lading As Receipt And Agreements.

Office of Internal Revenue,
Washington, Jan. 24, 1866.

Sir: The letter of Mr. Henry Lincoln, addressed to you, and by you referred to me, has been received. Mr. Lincoln asks if domestic bills of lading are subject to stamp duty, and if so, how much; also if each and every bill of lading, should bear a stamp?

He encloses a copy of a ruling from this Office, by which inland and domestic bills of lading are held subject to stamp duties as receipts or agreements, according to their form, and says, "as we understand the law, bills of lading of vessels for ports of the United States or British North America are exempt." [Ed. note: No other record of this ruling has been found.]

An examination of Schedule B, following Section 170 of the Act of June 30, 1864, will show that a stamp duty is specifically imposed upon one class of bills of lading only, viz: upon bills of lading for any goods, merchandise, or effects to be exported from a port or place of the United States to any foreign port or place. To this even, there is an exception. In the last part of said schedule, it is provided that the stamp duties therein imposed upon bills of lading, "shall not apply to steamboats, or other vessels, plying between ports in the United States and ports in British North America."

The Act of Congress then, imposes a stamp duty of ten cents upon each foreign bill of lading, except those for goods, &c., transported upon steamboats, or other vessels, plying between the ports of the United States and ports in British North America—but it is silent respecting inland and domestic bills of lading, *as such*.

A stamp duty of two cents, however, is imposed upon each receipt for the delivery of property; a duty of five cents is imposed upon each sheet or piece of paper upon which an agreement or contract is written.

It is admitted by Mr. Lincoln that all bills of lading contain an agreement or contract. Domestic and inland bills of lading, being neither otherwise charged, nor expressly exempted from all stamp duty, fall under the general provisions of the law, and are to be taxed not "as bills of lading," with ten cents each, but with two cents or five cents, according to whether they are receipts simply or agreements.

If they are executed in sets of two or three or more, each one should be stamped. Each has the same legal effect as the other, and the holder of either of them *may* find it necessary to use his copy in evidence.

I see no good reason for making any change in the ruling in question.

Very respectfully,
(Signed) E. A. Rollins,
Commissioner.

Hon. A. H. Rice,
House of Representatives,
Washington, D. C.

IRR v.III, February 3, 1866, pp.36-7

Stamping Of Receipts And Coastwise Bills Of Lading.

New York, April 2d, 1866.

Hon. E. A. Rollins,
Commissioner Internal Revenue:

Sir: We, the undersigned agents for ships sailing from the Port of New York to the Port of San Francisco, Cal., beg to enclose a blank receipt and a blank bill of lading, asking if we are correct in using the former with a two cent stamp, and the latter as a coastwise bill of lading without stamp.

All ships to San Francisco are cleared at the Custom House as coastwise, and therefore supposed to be at liberty to use free bills of lading. Your early reply will much oblige

Your obedient servants,

Sutton & Co.,
Geo. D. Sutton,
J. R. Robinson & Co.,
Corn Comstock & Co.

Rand. M. Cooley & Co.,
W. T. Coleman & Co., per
J. W. W.

(Answer.)

Office of Internal Revenue,
Washington, April 13, 1866.

Gentlemen: Your letter of the 2d instant, with the receipt for the delivery of property and the inland or coastwise bill of lading therewith inclosed, has been received.

I reply to the inquiries made, that the receipt in question is liable to a stamp duty of two cents, and the bill of lading to a duty of five cents, as an agreement or contract; and when such bills are issued in sets of two or more, each bill of lading composing the set should be stamped as an original instrument.

Very respectfully,
D. C. Whitman,
Deputy Commissioner.

Messrs. Sutton & Co.
58 South Street, Cor. Wall, New York.

IRR v.III, April 28, 1866, pp. 132-3

Stamping Of Railroad And Freight Receipts—Conditional Receipts.

[In answer to inquiry of Assessor Neher, of the 15th district, the Department of Internal Revenue at Washington has forwarded a copy of its ruling relative to the stamp duty, applicable to *conditional receipts*. The "instruments" referred to were the ordinary receipts, in use by the New York Central Railroad Company, Troy and Boston Railroad Company, Hudson River Railroad Company, and Philadelphia, Albany and Troy line. As the ruling applies to all receipts embracing stipulations, the business public should be on their guard in issuing or receiving this class of instruments without being sufficiently stamped:]

Treasury Department,
Office of Internal Revenue,
Washington, April 25th, 1866.

Sir: Your letter of the 17th instant, and the two letters of Mr. Mann to you, and the several bills of lading therewith enclosed, have been received. The holding of this office is, that such inland or domestic bills of lading as those endorsed by you, are each liable to a stamp duty of five cents, as agreements or contracts, and if any parties, companies, or corporations, are in the habit of issuing or using them, or similar instruments with only a two cent stamp affixed, they do so without the knowledge or sanction of the Commissioner, and at the risk of being prosecuted for the recovery of the penalty which may have incurred. With only a two cent stamp affixed, such bills of lading are void and of no account until the deficiency is supplied in the manner prescribed by law. The Collector and yourself will take such steps as may be necessary to enforce a compliance with the law in this, as well as all other respects.

Very respectfully,
D. C. Whitman,
Deputy Commissioner.

IRR v.III, May 12, 1866, p.151

Stamping Of Insurance Receipts.

Assessor's Office, 10th Dist., Indiana,
Goshen, April 26th, 1866.

Hon. E. A. Rollins, Com. of Internal Revenue:

Sir: Ought the enclosed receipt or memorandum to be stamped as a receipt or a contract?

Respectfully yours,
(Signed), Geo. D. Copland,
Assessor.

(Receipt.)

Received of ____ ____, an application for Insurance by the Protection Insurance Company, of Goshen, Ind., on property to the amount of $____, for the term of   years; also, a Note or Notes for the payment of Premium as represented on the back of this Receipt; also, $____ Policy and Survey Fee, and $____ Lightning Premium, all of which are to be returned if Policy be not issued.

Date at ____, this ____ day of ____, 186__.

______ ______, *Agent.*

(Endorsement.)

You have given Note amounting to $____ for first installment upon your Premium, and for payment of Policy and Survey Fee and Lightning Premium, which will fall due on the first day of ______ ______ 1866; also a note for four installments, due as follows:

$______ due on the first day of ________ 1867.
$______ " " " ________ 1868.
$______ " " " ________ 1869.
$______ " " " ________ 1870.

You will receive a printed Notice before each installment falls due, and will be furnished with a blank Envelope, duly directed in which you can remit the amount at the risk of the Company. Do not fail to be prompt in remitting each installment.

[Answer.]
Treasury Department,
Office of Internal Revenue,
Washington, May 2, 1866.

Sir: I reply to your letter of the 26th ultimo, that the instrument therewith enclosed should, before being issued or used, be stamped with a five cent revenue stamp, as an agreement or contract.

Very respectfully,
(Signed,) D. C. Whitman,
Deputy Commissioner.

Geo. D. Copland.
Assessor, Goshen, Indiana.

IRR v.III, May 19, 1866, pp.156-7

Stamping Of Receipts.

The law requiring receipts given for the payment of money or delivery of goods to be stamped has been in force for nearly two years, and it may be asserted with little fear of contradiction, that there are few provisions of the Internal Revenue Statutes that are more uniformly and persistently violated. As for New York, whole books of receipts,—inches thick, may be found in the hands of almost any cartman, or under-clerk of many of our enterprising mercantile firms, but void of stamps, except here and there one or two scattered among the business autographs.

Is it possible that those who, in the hurry of business, sign a dray receipt for the delivery of goods, and give the same without stamp, know that they are uttering written evidence that they have violated the law for which they are liable for a penalty of fifty dollars, and that this unstamped receipt may be produced against them at any moment to convict them of the offence! What a mine of wealth to the informer would be an old receipt book of any of our large firms or active cartmen for the year 1865. Estimating them at the usual size, each book would contain twenty four hundred unstamped receipts. The penalty of fifty dollars for each offence would make the aggregate of penalties $120,000. The informer would be entitled to half of this large penalty.

And yet these violations of the law are daily, nay almost momentarily made. Even large corporations, like the Erie Rail Road Company, it is stated, under some pretext or other, wilfully and knowingly omit to stamp bills of lading and receipts given in the transaction of its [their] business.

The law in the case is plain. Section 151 of the existing statute provides that "there shall be collected and paid for, and in respect of the several instruments, matters and things mentioned and decribed in the schedule (marked B), hereunto annexed, or for or in respect of the vellum, parchment, or paper upon which such instrument, matters or things, or any of them, shall be written or printed, by any person or persons, or party who shall make, sign, or issue the same, or for whose use or benefit the same shall be made, signed or issued, the several duties or sums of money set down in figures against the same, respectively, or otherwise specified or set forth in the said Schedule."

In Schedule B—referred to—is found this paragraph:

"Receipts for the payment of any sum of money, or for the payment of any debt due, exceeding twenty dollars, not being for the satisfaction of any mortgage or judgment, or decree of any court, *and a receipt for the delivery of any property,* except receipts issued by any persons, firms, or companies doing business as an express or express company, on the delivery of any property for transportation, two (2) cents."

Every receipt given for the delivery of a package or load of merchandise requires to be stamped with a two cent stamp—to be duly cancelled with the initials of the party signing it. The law does not prescribe who shall pay for the stamp, whether the person giving or the one accepting a receipt, nor does it require that receipts shall in any case be given; it simply provides that when receipts are given they shall be properly stamped. It will be observed that the employees of a corporation, masters of a vessel, or merchants possess the physical power to refuse to give any receipt, or to sign a receipt, unless a stamp be previously affixed by the person desiring the same; but, if the receipt is signed or delivered, it must be stamped and properly cancelled with the date and initials of the person signing the same, under a penalty of fifty dollars for every omission.

This matter calls for the prompt intervention of revenue officers, especially in the city of New York, to enforce a due compliance with the law.

IRR v.III, June 2, 1866 p.169

Stamping of Promissory Notes on Renewal Thereof by Endorsement, and when Protest is Waived.

Office, St. Louis Insurance Company,
St. Louis, June 7, 1866.

To the Commissioner of Internal Revenue, Washington City:

Sir: I desire to know whether the usual stamp be necessary under the law upon the renewal of an endorsed note when protest has been waived, and the receipt of interest on the extended time acknowledged on the note.

Very respectfully, your obedient servant,
George K. McGunnefle,
President.

[Answer.]

Office of Internal Revenue,
Washington, July 6, 1866.

Sir: Your letters of the 7th and 22d ultimo, relative to the extension of the time of payment for promissory notes, have been received.

The endorsement of a partial payment on the back of a note is regarded as a new memorandum, not subject to stamp duty, and the fact that by an implication of law it operates as an extension of the time of payment, does not effect the case.

The agreement to waive protest and notice of protest, signed by the party making it, is subject to stamp duty as a contract or agreement.

Very respectfully,
E. A. Rollins,
Commissioner.

IRR v.IV, August 18, 1866, p. 55

Receipt of Attorney for Note or Claim for Collection.

No stamp is required upon the receipt of an attorney for a note or other claim left with him for collection.

IRR v.V, February 23, 1867, p.60

Receipts taken as Administrators, Executors, and Guardians.

Receipts taken by administrators, executors, guardians, trustees, &c., to be used as vouchers upon the settlement of their accounts, are subject to the same stamp as other receipts.

IRR v.V, February 23, 1867, p.60

Receipts on Pay-Rolls.

When several persons, such as the employees of a manufacturing company, sign a pay-roll, a two cent stamp should be affixed for the signature of each and every one who receipts for a sum exceeding twenty dollars, one or more stamps should be affixed thereto, "representing the whole amount of the stamp required for such signatures."

IRR v.V, March 7, 1867, p.74

Promissory Notes and their Substitutes.

It has been the practice with certain banks to take instruments in the form of a receipt instead of promissory notes. A. B. applies for a loan of $10,000, which he procures upon lodging United States bonds, &c., as collateral security. Instead of giving the bank his promissory note, he gives an instrument in substance as follows:

Received of _______ Bank ten thousand dollars advance on $10,000 United States bonds.

To this he affixes a two cent stamp only. The Commissioner of Internal Revenue has decided that such an instrument is evidence of an amount of money to be paid, and as such, is liable to stamp tax at the same rate as a promissory note, and the Comptroller of the currency has directed all bank examiners not to recognize such an instrument with a two cent stamp only affixed, as valid and legal. [Editor's "Review"]

IRR v.V, May 18, 1867, p.153

Receipts, Checks, Memorandums, &c., Money to be Paid.

Every "memorandum, check, receipt or other written or printed evidence of an amount of money to be paid upon demand or at a time designated," is subject to stamp tax at the same rate as a promissory note. When a loan is obtained from collateral security, and an instrument substantially as follows is given: ________ Received of ________ Bank, Ten Thousand Dollars advance on $10,000 U. S. Bonds, it should be stamped at the rate of five cents for each one hundred dollars or fractional part thereof.

IRR v.V, May 18, 1867, p.163

Receipts by Endorsement on Leases, or Stamped Instruments.

A receipt by endorsement upon a stamped obligation in acknowledgement of its fulfilment, is exempt from stamp tax. Fulfilment as used in this connection in Schedule B, is understood to mean completion, accomplishment, *entire* fulfilment. No receipt is subject to a stamp tax *unless it is issued*. When a receipt for an *installment* of rent is written upon that part of a lease held by the tenant and issued to him, a two cent stamp should be affixed to it, if the amount received exceeds twenty dollars.

IRR v.V, June 15, 1867, p.188

Stamp Duty on Receipts.

The following letter was addressed to the Editor of the *New York Tribune* by the Honorable Commissioner of Internal Revenue in order to correct certain mis-statements made by that widely circulated Journal, respecting the stamp tax on receipts, and therein of the obligations of tax-payers.

The communication simply confirms rulings which have formerly been published in the RECORD, and as we regularly furnish the *Tribune* each week with a copy of the same, *gratis,* there is really no excuse on this occasion for the ignorance of the Philosophers. Nor are the Ancients of the *Journal of Commerce* less blamable for misleading its readers in regard to the dealers tax on sales at auction—for we as faithfully forward the RECORD every Saturday to them, and to the *Herald,* the *World,* and the *Times*.

The snub that these grandiose pretenders to special and technical knowledge have received from Commissioner Rollins in the following corrective, has been richly deserved.

We reprint the letter because it covers the subject of the tax in question, in concise terms, and because, further, there seems to be an ever present necessity for hammering away at the noddles of some assistant assessors and tax-payers in order to make them remember and perform the commonest and plainest duties. With stupidity on the one hand, and knavery on the other, the authorities at Washington find it indeed a difficult task to secure the just dues of the revenue.

Mr. Rollins says his attention has been called to this item in the *Tribune:—*

"What constitutes a receipt?" A correspondent proposes the following questions:

"1. Is the man who acknowledges the receipt of a check in the shape of a letter, according to law, required to put a stamp on the receipt? 2. Is the party who pays the money required to furnish the stamp for the receipt he gets?"

"To answer the last question first, we believe there is no law compelling a person to give a receipt. It is an accommodation and a safeguard for the payer of money. The receiver of money can decline to give a receipt until it is stamped, and as a receipt is for the protection of the payer, he is expected to furnish the stamp. The following extract of a letter from the Commissioner of Revenue at the time it was written, contains the answer to the first of the above queries:"

Treasury Department,
Office of Internal Revenue,
Washington, January 20, 1865.

The law requires all receipts for the payment of any sum of money, or for the payment of any debt due exceeding $20, or for the delivery of any property to be stamped, excepting receipts for the satisfaction of any mortgage or judgment, or decree of any Court, which are exempt.

* * *

A credit on an account or pass-book, or on a bill without a signature is not a receipt and is not subject to stamp duty. A letter acknowledging the payment of a debt due is, to all intents and purposes, a receipt, and subject to stamp duty as such; but the acknowledgement of a note, check, or draft is not a receipt for money, nor yet of property in the ordinary acceptation of the term, and is not subject to stamp duty, unless specified to have been received in payment of a debt due exceeding $20.

Joseph J. Lewis.''

He thinks it proper to call attention to certain material changes in the law since the letter from which the above extracts were made was written. By the act of July 13, [1866], which so far as stamp taxes are concerned took effect August 1, 1866, the tax [w]as removed from receipts for the delivery of property; the words ''the payment of'' were stricken out of that part of Schedule B which related to ''receipts for the payment of money,'' and it was provided that ''the term money,'' as used in schedule B, in relation to receipts, ''shall be held to include drafts and other instruments given for the payment of money.'' Under the law, as it now stands, the written or printed acknowledgment of the receipt of a note, check, or draft, exceeding $20 in amount, requires a two cent stamp, when signed and issued. The Internal Revenue law does not designate which of the parties to an instrument shall furnish the necessary stamp, nor does this Office assume to determine that it shall be supplied by one party rather than by another; but if an instrument subject to stamp duty is issued without having the necessary stamps affixed thereto, it cannot be recorded or admitted or used as evidence in any Court until a legal stamp or stamps denoting the amount of tax, shall have been affixed as prescribed by law, and the person who thus issues it is liable to a penalty if he omits the stamps with an intent to evade the provisions of the Internal Revenue act.

IRR v.V, June 22, 1867, p.195

Executors, Administrators Receipts, Inventories and Appraisements.

Receipts taken by executors and administrators should be stamped as in other cases. Inventories of the property of deceased persons, returned for record, or otherwise, should be stamped as ''Appraisements of value,'' at the same rate as agreements.

IRR v.VI, September 28, 1867, p.105

Endorsement of Payments on Bonds.

A mere unsigned memorandum of the amount of money paid upon a bond, or contract, made upon the bond itself, in the usual way of endorsing partial payments, need not be stamped, whatever the sum paid.

IRR v.VI, November 9, 1867, p.162

Endorsement of Receipts on Contract.

When a person who has entered into a contract to convey certain lands upon payment of a certain sum, makes a written endorsement of a partial payment upon the copy of the contract *held by the party making the payment, and signs it,* he should affix a two cent stamp, if the amount received exceeds twenty dollars.

IRR v.VI, November 9, 1867, p.162

Receipts for Money or Bank Checks.

A receipt for a bank check is a receipt for money within the terms of the Internal Revenue Act (Schedule B Receipts), and if for a sum exceeding twenty dollars, requires a two cent stamp. It is not relieved by the stamp on the check.

IRR v.VI, November 23, 1867, p.179

Receipts given to State, County or Municipal Officers.

A receipt given *to* a State, County or Municipal Officer, for a sum exceeding $20, by a person in his private capacity is subject to stamp duty.

IRR v.VI, December 7, 1867, p.195

Receipts and Letters—Acknowledging Receipt of Money.

Inspector—There have been several rulings on the subject, and the practice under them has varied, but the settled opinion of the Department is stated as follows, and the practice everywhere should conform to the rule:

Letters acknowledging the receipt of money are undoubtedly "Receipts" within the meaning of the Stamp Act, and should have a two cent stamp when for an amount exceeding $20. It makes no difference whether remittances thus acknowledged are made in money or by checks, drafts or orders. In the receipt stamp law the term "money" is held to include drafts and other instruments given for the payment of money. See Schedule B, proviso under the head of "Receipts."—Ed.

IRR v.VII, March 28, 1868, p.98

U.S. Circuit Court—West Virginia.

By an Act of Congress of 1864, receipts for goods delivered to a common carrier for transportation, being in effect inland bills of lading, were not subject to stamp duty.

A corporation is liable to indictment for the act of its officer or employee, in issuing papers which the law requires to be stamped, without the proper stamps, with intent to evade the provisions of the Act of Congress.

The United States v. Baltimore and Ohio Railroad.

These were indictments numbered from 1 to 54, inclusive, for breaches of the Revenue Laws of the United States.

Fifty of these indictments were for issuing receipts for goods delivered to the defendant at their depot in Parkersburg, to be transported by them as a common carrier, to different points upon their road; and the remaining four for issuing receipts for moneys paid for tolls and transportation upon the road, without having United States revenue stamps affixed and cancelled.

To all of the indictments the defendant demurred.

George H. Lee, in support of the demurrer.—1. As to the receipts for freight, in question, at the times they were issued, in 1865 and 1866, upon the true construction of the Revenue Laws of the United States then in force, such receipts being in legal effect inland bills of lading, were not subject to stamp duty. 2. As to both classes of receipts, to constitute the offence under the Act of Congress of unlawfully issuing papers required to be stamped without having the proper stamps affixed, the party issuing must have done so with the unlawful intent to evade the provisions of the Act and to defraud the revenue, and such intent on the part of the platform-clerk or agent issuing the receipts for the company, if it existed, could not be imputed to a corporation having no sentiment or visible tangible being, and existing only in contemplation of law; but the clerk, or agent himself only, and not the corporation as such, could be held criminally responsible for the unlawful act.

Smith, District Attorney, *contra*.—By direction of the court the argument was confined, at this stage of the case, to the first point.

Chase, C. J. of the United States, after consultation, stated his opinion to be, that at the time the freight receipts in question were issued, they were not subject to stamp duty under the Acts of Congress then in force, and that the demurrers to the indictments upon them would have to be sustained.

Jackson, D. J., stated that his first impression was that the terms of the Act of 1864 were sufficiently comprehensive to embrace receipts for goods delivered to a common carrier for transportation, and to subject them to stamp duty; but that since he had heard the argument of the counsel, and had come to construe the Act of 1864, in connection with the several other Acts of Congress *in pari materia,* his views had undergone a change, and if the question were now to be decided he should not dissent from the opinion of the Chief Justice to sustain the demurrers. He added, however, that if the counsel so desired, division of opinion between the Judges might be entered *pro forma* upon the record, so that the cases might be taken to the Supreme Court of the United States.

Chase, C. J., said that upon the second point made by Lee for the demurrer, both the district judge and himself were inclined to think the demurrer could not be sustained, but that they were willing to hear argument upon it if necessary, or desired.

Upon this intimation of opinion, however, the cases were settled by counsel.—*Am. Law Reg.*, Oct., 1868.

IRR v.VIII, November 7, 1868, p.148

Stamps on Receipts for payments by Bank Checks.

Editor of Record:—

Will you please answer through your paper the followng question: If A. owes B. twenty-five dollars and pays it with his check, does the receipt from B. require a stamp? By answering the above you will oblige,

G. J. B.

The receipt from B. must be stamped with a two cent stamp under exsting laws. The receipt for the check is held to be a receipt for money within the meaning of the revenue law, see 6 RECORD, 179.—Ed.

IRR v.IX, February 20, 1869, p.62

Receipts for money given by R. R. Companies for Freight Charges must be Stamped.

Editor of Record:

Are rail road companies obliged to stamp the receipts given by them to parties, on payment of charges and freight on goods where the amount of such charges exceed twenty dollars? An early answer will greatly oblige,

Assistant Assessor.

Most assuredly. Every firm, person, or corporation, (except municipal corporations,) must stamp receipts for money in excess of twenty dollars.—Ed.

IRR v.X, November 27, 1869, p.173

Receipts Used instead of Bank Checks Exempt from Tax.

Office of Internal Revenue,
Washington, February 25, 1871.

Thomas E. Grisell, Esq., Collector of Internal Revenue, Fifth District, Upper Sandusky, Ohio.

Sir: I reply to your letter relative to stamp duty on receipts used instead of bank checks, that these seem to come under the general exemption of receipts by section 4 of the act of July 14, 1870.

If banks and their depositors choose to substitute receipts for checks, they must of course incur any legal risk which may arise from the use of such vouchers.

A. Pleasonton,
Commissioner.

IRR v.XIII, March 4, 1871, p.66

A Paper Purporting to be a Receipt, but Containing Additions from which it Appears upon its Face to be in the Nature of a Check, should be Stamped as a Check.

Office of Internal Revenue,
Washington, November 17, 1871.

Francis Springer, Esq., Collector Internal Revenue, Burlington, First District, Iowa.

Sir: Your letter of the 9th instant, relative to stamp duty on a receipt used as a substitute for a bank check, has been received.

With regard to more receipts thus substituted, see INTERNAL REVENUE RECORD, Vol. XIII., page 66. But when, as in the form enclosed by you, a paper which purports to be a receipt, contains the name of a third party as payee, negotiable words, or other additions, from which it appears upon its face to be of the nature of a check, it should be stamped as such.

Very respectfully,
J. W. Douglass,
Commissioner.

IRR v.XIV, November 25, 1871, p.170

TELEGRAPH

†Messages transmitted by telegraph and railroad companies over their own wires, on their own business, for which they receive no pay, are not taxable.

†Telegraphic despatches must be stamped, and the stamp cancelled, before the same are received for transmission.

Boutwell (1863), Decisions (from No. 30)

In reference to telegraphic messages.

January, 1863.

Telegraphic despatches or messages sent from an office without the United States to an office within the United States are not subject to stamp tax; provided, the message be transmitted direct to its final destination.

If received at an office within the United States, and repeated to another office within or without the United States, the stamp must be affixed and cancelled where the message is repeated.

NOTE—It is illegal for telegraphic operators to receive unstamped messages from the writers. It is the duty of the writer to affix and cancel the stamp; and the company or its agent receiving and transmitting an unstamped message is liable to a penalty of ten dollars.—(Statute of 1862, section 104.)

Boutwell (1863), Decisions (No. 44)

Telegraphic messages forwarded free of charge, by railroad or express companies, or which are paid for in kind, must have stamps attached to them.

Messages forwarded in the same manner for corporations or individuals, treated as free messages in their transmission, but paid for quarterly or yearly, must have stamps attached.

Messages of a railroad company require to be stamped when going over a line which they do not own and work exclusively for railroad purposes, although the stock of the telegraph line over which their messages pass may be partly or chiefly owned by the railroad company.

Only such messages as are covered by the following are entitled to exemption as "free messages":

"Messages transmitted by telegraph and railroad companies over their own wires, on their own business, for which they receive no pay, do not require stamps."

Boutwell (1863), Rulings (No. 269)

WAREHOUSE RECEIPT

All receipts for grain or other property of any kind, held on storage in any public or private warehouse or yard, are "warehouse receipts" within the meaning of the excise law, and are each subject to stamp duty of twenty-five cents, without regard to the quantity specified, or the time for which the property is stored.

Boutwell (1863), Rulings (No. 241)

Warehouse receipts for property, goods, wares, &c., where the value can be ascertained, and does not exceed $500, are chargeable with a stamp-duty of ten cents; if more than $500 and less than $1,000, a twenty-cent stamp is required. If not ascertainable, and when the value exceeds $1,000, but less than $10,000, a stamp-duty of twenty-five cents is required.

Boutwell (1865), Rulings (No. 208)

Where a party executes a note to a bank for a sum of money, and assigns a warehouse receipt for property in store, as collateral security for the payment of the money when it shall become due, both the note and the assignment of the warehouse receipt are subject to stamp duty—the latter as an agreement.

Boutwell (1865), Rulings (No. 291)

New York, November 22d, 1865.

Editor of Record:

Will you *venture,* through your paper, to call the attention of the proper Committee of Congress to the fact that "Storage Warehouse Proprietors," though frequently doing a business far more lucrative than many of their neighbors, have not the slightest business tax of any kind imposed upon them by the present law? This is justly, I think, complained of.

Equity.

We not only *venture,* but would strenuously urge upon Congress the justice of subjecting warehouse proprietors to a license tax proportionate to those imposed by existing laws upon other occupations. As a rule, the business of proprietors of warehouses is very lucrative. There are many of them, and they pay no license tax whatever. Warehouse receipts are subject to stamp tax, but the law in relation thereto is conflicting, and great diversity of practice results.

We hope that Congress will not fail to equalize the tax in this particular, by providing for a business or license tax upon warehouse proprietors, and to amend the law respecting warehouse receipt stamps.

IRR v.II, December 9, 1865, p.182

GENERAL DOCUMENTARY

In regard to stamping instruments.

October, 1862.

In affixing stamps to promissory notes or other instruments those of a smaller denomination may be used in numbers sufficient to amount in the aggregate to the sum of the stamp required: [*Provided, that they are of the kind denominated for the instrument to which the stamps are applied.*]—(See act of Dec. 25, 1862, sec. 3.)

A stamp will be required upon every certificate which has, or may have, a legal value in any court of law or equity.

Certificates, warrants, orders, and drafts, by one State officer upon another, for the purpose of carrying on the internal business of the State government, are not subject to a stamp tax.

The same rule applies to the certificates, orders, and warrants of county, city, and town officers.

†Messages transmitted by telegraph and railroad companies over their own wires, on their own business, for which they receive no pay, are not taxable.

NOTE.—Orders, drafts, and warrants, by officers of a county, city, or town, upon which other officers of the same county, city, or town, can be used only by such officers and the person or persons to whom the order, draft, or warrant is issued.

If such drafts, orders, and warrants are negotiated and put in circulation, they become thereby subject to duty.

†Telegraphic despatches must be stamped, and the stamp cancelled, before the same are received for transmission.

Boutwell (1863), Decisions (No. 30)

Concerning the affixing and cancelling of excise stamps on documents, &c.

November, 1862.

Section 94 of the excise law requires, "That on and after the first day of October [1862] certain stamp duties shall be collected on all instruments, matters, and things, as described in schedule marked B."

Section 95 provides, "That if any person or persons shall make, sign, or issue, or cause to be made, signed, or issued, any instrument, document, or paper of any kind or description whatsoever, without the same being duly stamped for denoting the duty imposed thereon, or without having thereupon an adhesive stamp to denote said duty, such person or persons shall incur a penalty of fifty dollars; and such instrument, document, or paper shall be deemed invalid and of no effect."

It seems perfectly clear that, by the provisions of section 95, the person who makes, signs, and issues the instrument, is the only person who is authorized to affix the stamp required by the law; and the person who makes, signs, and issues, &c., without affixing the stamp, incurs the penalty as aforesaid, and is liable to prosecution therefor, and the instrument or document is invalid in consequence of such neglect.

Section 99 provides, "That the person using or affixing the stamp shall write thereupon the initials of his name, date," &c.

Other portions of the law impose penalties upon persons who receive documents or articles subject to stamp duty from the person who makes, signs, and issues them, without being duly stamped.

A faithful compliance with the requirements of the provisions of the excise law demands:

First. That all papers subject to stamp tax must have the stamp affixed before the same are issued.

Second. That the stamp so affixed must be cancelled, in the manner prescribed, by the party making, signing, or issuing (in other words, executing) the instrument, document, or paper.

Hence it is a violation of the law to receive an unstamped paper. The attaching and cancelling of a stamp on a document so received is also unlawful, and the cancellation of a stamp on a paper (otherwise lawfully issued) by other than the party executing the paper to which the stamp is affixed is equally improper.

The only exception that exists in the law to the above ruling is in the case of a bill of exchange, or order for the payment of any sum of money drawn, or purporting to be drawn, in any foreign country, but payable in the United States, in which case the acceptor or acceptors shall, before paying or accepting the same, place thereupon a stamp, indicating the duty upon the same, as provided by section 101 of the excise law.

Boutwell (1863), Decisions (No. 34)

In regard to stamps upon instruments.

The fourth section of the act passed 25th December, 1862, is construed to exempt from duty only those official instruments, documents, and papers issued or used by the officers of the United States government, the duties on which, if paid, would be a charge upon the treasury of the United States.

This decision will apply also to official instruments, documents, and papers issued or used by the officers of a State.

• • •

When two or more persons join in the execution of an instrument, the stamp to which the instrument is liable under the law may be affixed and cancelled by any one of the parties.

• • •

Boutwell (1863), Decisions (from No. 75)

[Ed. note: Decisions Nos. 30 & 34 were reprinted as part of No. 75; they are not repeated here.]

The date of execution and not the date of record determines the question of liability to stamp duties, of deeds or other instruments of writing, subject to the payment of stamp duty under the provisions of the internal revenue laws.

Boutwell (1863), Rulings (No. 234)

Letters of guardianship are exempt from stamp.

Boutwell (1863), Rulings (from No. 239)

Clearing-house receipts, *if used exclusively in the business of the clearing-house, and if they are not allowed to pass into the hands of third parties,* will be regarded as ordinary receipts, which do not come within the provisions of the stamp act, and which are therefore exempt from tax.

Boutwell (1863), Rulings (No. 252)

Any power of attorney, conveyance, or document of any kind, made and issued in foreign countries, which is to have effect in the United States, and which, if made and issued within the United States, would require a stamp, may be stamped, and the stamp cancelled by the maker, at the time and place of issue, as provided in sections 94-99, excise law, or by the party to whom the same is issued or by whom it is to be used.

Boutwell (1863), Rulings (No. 254)

Bonds issued by the State, and executive warrants on the treasurer of the State, are exempt from stamp duty.

It follows also, from the same decision, that the check of the State treasurer, for moneys belonging to the State, is exempt from stamp duty.

The orders of a town treasurer upon the State treasurer for money due to or belonging to the town are not exempt.

Boutwell (1863), Rulings (No. 272)

By the first proviso of the sixteenth section of the excise law, passed March 3, it is declared that no instrument, document, or paper, made, signed, or issued prior to the 1st day of June, 1863, without being duly stamped, or having thereon an adhesive stamp to denote the duty imposed thereon, shall, for that cause, be deemed invalid and of no effect, and by the second proviso the stamp may be affixed whenever it is necessary to use the instrument or document as evidence in any court.

A deed executed and delivered prior to June 1, 1863, is not void, nor even voidable, for the reason that the same has not been stamped.

Boutwell (1863), Rulings (No. 273)

I have duly considered the several forms of papers issued and used by you as superintendent of common schools of Pennsylvania, together with your several queries in regard to their respective liability to stamp duty under the provisions of the excise law, and now beg to enclose you my decision thereon.

	Stamp duty.
1. Diplomas and certificates issued by the State Normal School to teachers	5 cents.
2. Certificates to teachers, issued by county superintendents	5 cents.
3. Certificates or returns of unpaid tax on unseated lands, to county commissioners, by district tax collectors	5 cents.
4. Certificates or returns of unpaid balance of school tax against district tax collector to prothonotary, by secretary of the board of directors	5 cents.
5. Certificates by president and secretary of the board of directors to county superintendent, that schools have been open and in operation according to law	5 cents.
6. Certificates of election of county superintendents, by president and secretary of county convention of directors	5 cents.
7. Warrants or authorities to collectors to collect school tax	Exempt.
8. Bonds of collectors of school tax	50 cents.
9. Bonds of treasurers of school districts	50 cents.
10. Deeds of ground for school-houses must bear a conveyance stamp, according to the consideration expressed in the deed or the value of the property conveyed, if over one hundred dollars.	
11. Leases of houses and lots for schools, for any term not exceeding three years	50 cents.
The same, for any term exceeding three years	$1.00
12. Agreements or contracts with contractors to build school-houses and repair them, when there is a written agreement for this purpose—on every sheet	5 cents.
13. Warrants or drafts by the State superintendent of common schools on the State treasury, for the annual State appropriation to the common school districts are	Exempt.
14. Warrants or drafts by the State superintendent on the State treasury, quarterly, for the salaries of county superintendents are	Exempt.
15. Orders or drafts by board of school directors on the district treasurer, for the payment of teachers' salaries and the other debts of the district, are	Exempt.
16. Checks by the district treasurer on banks to pay orders on the district treasury by the board of directors	2 cents.
17. Agreements or contracts between teachers and board of directors to teach	5 cents.
18. Monthly reports by teachers to board of directors, of the condition of their schools are	Exempt.
19. Petition to court for the formation of a new school district or change in a district	Exempt.
20. Petition to court for the removal of school directors	Exempt.

Boutwell (1863), Rulings (No. 304)

The *employees* of a State government, are not "*officers*" within the meaning of section 4 of the act approved December 25, 1862. Nor can their affidavit to the correctness of personal accounts be considered as "official papers," under the same section and act.

Boutwell (1863), Rulings (No. 305)

The act of March 3, 1863, and decision No. 106, cannot be construed to exempt from stamp duty applications or claims for prize-money or papers relating to such applications or claims.

Boutwell (1863), Rulings (No. 310)

When several persons are the parties of the first part, executing an instrument which is subject to stamp duty, either of said parties may affix and cancel the revenue stamp or stamps required thereon.

Boutwell (1863), Rulings (No. 314)

July 11, 1863.

Your letter of June 11 has been received. In reply thereto I have the honor to state that any instrument which is subject to stamp duty should be stamped by the party executing the same *at the time it is executed*. *Each* of the stamps used should be cancelled by the party of the first part, or one of the parties of the first part, writing or printing his or her initials *and the date* thereon.

This affixing and cancellation of stamps may be done by an attorney or agent of the party of the first part, duly authorized so to do, said party of the first part being absent; but, in this case, his or her initials, and not the initials of the attorney or agent, must be used.

The party of the first part incurs a penalty of fifty dollars by failing to affix *or* cancel the required revenue stamps to an instrument subject to stamp duty, as thus set forth. If the party of the first part has failed to *cancel* the stamp or stamps, the party of the second part may, *before the instrument is used,* correct the error by affixing and cancelling new stamps of the required value.

The party of the second part may also *affix* as well as cancel the required revenue stamp or stamps to an instrument subject to stamp duty, if the party of the first part fails to do so, *providing* he, she, or they do so before the instrument *is used;* but the party of the first part has incurred a penalty of fifty dollars by failing to affix the stamp or stamps, and also a penalty of fifty dollars if he fraudulently fails to cancel the same, and he, she, or they (the party or parties of the first part) are liable for the amount of the value of the revenue stamps which he, she, or they have failed to affix in *addition* to the penalties as above set forth.

Any instrument which is subject to stamp duty, which is executed on or after June 1, 1863, and which is *used* before the required stamp duty has been paid and the stamps cancelled, thereby becomes invalid and of no effect.

Very respectfully,
Joseph J. Lewis
Commissioner.

J. F. Morris, *Esq., Cashier, Charter Oak Bank, Hartford, Connecticut.*

NOTE.—As the foregoing letter may affect the validity of business transactions, including titles of estates, I feel bound to say, respectfully, that I dissent entirely from the opinion that a stamp can be affixed and cancelled, legally, by any person other than the signer or maker of the instrument.

When the promisor upon an unstamped note issues it to the payee, or for the purpose of negotiation, I regard it as invalid, under the law, from the moment of its issue; and I am of opinion that neither the payee nor any holder of the note can give validity to it by affixing and cancelling a stamp.

If a deed has been executed in other respects, and delivered, without the required stamp, I am of opinion that the grantee can not remedy the defect. It is no doubt true, that the promisor upon a note or the grantor of an estate might, upon general principles, affix the required stamps, subsequently to the making and delivery of the instrument, if without injury to the rights of other parties acquired subsequently to the issue or delivery. It seems to me that a note is *used* when it is delivered by the maker, or by his authority to the payee, or negotiated by a person not named therein; and a deed is *used* when it is delivered to the grantee or to any person in his behalf.

G. S. B.

Boutwell (1863), Correspondence (No. 43)

Bonds or other official papers, issued by public municipal corporations, are held to be exempt from stamp-duty.

Boutwell (1865), Rulings (No. 217)

Any instrument requiring a stamp may be stamped by either party to the same before its execution, the party affixing the stamp cancelling the same.

Boutwell (1865), Rulings (No. 219)

An acknowledgment by letter, of reception of a note at three months, having no legal value, requires no stamp.

Boutwell (1865), Rulings (No. 220)

An acknowledgment of a mortgage or other written instrument is exempt from stamp-duty.

Boutwell (1865), Rulings (No. 235)

Leases and other indentures, executed by the United States through its authorized officers on the one part, are not subject to stamp-duty from either party.

Boutwell (1865), Rulings (No. 238)

Drafts or bills of exchange drawn in, but payable out of the United States, are subject to stamp-duty, without regard to the object for which they are drawn;—therefore, a draft drawn by a foreigner (consul-general) for any public purpose, would stand in the same condition as a draft drawn by him for his own salary.

Sec. 154 exempts drafts drawn by officers of the government; and drafts drawn by them in foreign countries and payable here, are exempt.

It is intended that such practices between our own and foreign countries shall be reciprocal, and to exempt officers of any country where the same privilege is conferred on our own.

Boutwell (1865), Rulings (No. 241)

Leases, indentures, and like papers, where the government is one of the parties, are exempt from stamp-duty.

Boutwell (1865), Rulings (No. 247)

Instruments, to be valid, must be stamped before they are used. But if a party sends a note or other paper to a bank, with a request that it shall be stamped, the party affixing it acts as the agent of the person, and must cancel it by using his initials.

Boutwell (1865), Rulings (No. 250)

The stamping of letters of administration covers all orders, notices, certificates, and affidavits issued in the settlement of the estate. The bond of administrator requires an additional stamp of one dollar. Guardian's bond requires a stamp of one dollar.

Boutwell (1865), Rulings (No. 252)

In answer to a letter inquiring if a stamp can be affixed upon an instrument and entered upon the record subsequently to the time when the instrument is recorded, &c., the deputy commissioner says:—"An instrument must be stamped before *used*. The time when used might be a question for the courts. Probably the acceptance of an instrument by the second party and procuring it to be recorded would be held to be a use thereof. Affixing stamp after use, would not answer. An instrument might be surrendered and redelivered after the proper stamps are affixed. In such case it would become a new instrument, taking effect from such delivery, and if required to be recorded must be recorded anew."

Boutwell (1865), Rulings (No. 263)

Where a paper contains but one instrument, and is insufficiently stamped, the invalidity affects the whole instrument. If there are two instruments, as for instance a mortgage, which also contains a power of attorney to sell the land, the mortgage, if properly stamped as such, may be valid, while the power of attorney may be invalid for want of the proper stamp. Ordinarily the obligee in an instrument insufficiently stamped, would not have the right to say that the stamp-duty should be applied to one covenant any more than another.

Boutwell (1865), Rulings (No. 267)

In the case of an application for money due from the United States for stores or other articles used by the army, the affidavit of the applicant requires a five-cent stamp; the power of attorney, a stamp of fifty cents; and the certificate of the identity and loyalty of the claimant by the government officer, are each subject to stamp-duty as certificates.

Boutwell (1865), Rulings (No. 292)

Proposed Amendments to the Revenue Laws.

[Mr. Morrill, from the Committee of Ways and Means, reported the following Bill:]

A BILL

To amend an act entitled "An act to provide internal revenue to support the government, to pay interest on the public debt, and for other purposes," approved June thirtieth, eighteen hundred and sixty-four.

• • •

That section one hundred and fifty-eight be amended by striking out all after the enacting clause, and inserting in lieu thereof the following, to wit: "That any person who shall make, sign, or issue, or who shall cause to be made, signed, or issued, any instrument, document, or paper of any kind, or description whatsoever, or shall accept, negotiate, or pay, or cause to be accepted, negotiated, or paid, any bill of exchange, draft, or order or promissory note, for the payment of money, without the same being duly stamped, or having thereupon an adhesive stamp for denoting the duty chargeable thereon, with intent to evade the provisions of this act, shall, for every such offence, forfeit the sum of two hundred dollars, and such instrument, document, or paper, bill, draft, order, or note shall be deemed invalid and of no effect: Provided, That the title of a purchaser of land, by deed duly stamped, shall not be defeated or affected by the want of a proper stamp on any deed conveying said land by any person from, through, or under whom his grantor claims or holds title: Provided, further, That no deed, instrument, document, writing, or paper, required by law to be stamped, which was made, signed, or issued prior to the first day of August, eighteen hundred and sixty-four, without being duly stamped, or with a deficient stamp, nor any copy thereof, shall be recorded or admitted or used as evidence in any court until a legal stamp or stamps, denoting the amount of duty, shall have been affixed thereto, and the date when the same is so used or affixed, with his initials, shall have been placed thereon by the person using the same; and the person desiring to use or record any such deed, instrument, document, writing, or paper, as evidence, his agent or attorney, is authorized, in the presence of the court, register, or recorder, respectively, to affix the stamp or stamps thereon required: "And provided, further, That no instrument, document, or paper, made, signed, or issued prior to the first day of August, eighteen hundred and sixty-four, without being duly stamped, or having thereon an adhesive stamp or stamps to denote the duty imposed thereon, shall, for that cause, if the stamp or stamps required shall be subsequently affixed, be deemed invalid and of no effect; and the holder thereof, or any person desiring to use the same, his agent or attorney, is authorized to affix thereon the stamp or stamps required."

That section one hundred and sixty be amended by striking out the words " 'nor on certificates' " "the word 'or' " and inserting in lieu thereof the word "of;" and by striking out the words "other articles," and inserting in lieu thereof the word "hay."

That section one hundred and sixty-five be amended by striking out in the proviso the words "act contained," and inserting in lieu thereof the word "section."

That section one hundred and sixty-seven be amended by striking out the word "or," where it occurs the second time, and inserting after the word "sell" the words "expose for sale."

That section one hundred and sixty-eight be amended by striking out the words "lucifer or friction matches and cigar lights or wax tapers."

That section one hundred and sixty-nine be amended by inserting after the words, "who shall offer," the words "or expose;" and by inserting after the words "so offered" the words "or exposed."

That "Schedule B," preceding section one hundred and seventy-one, in the paragraphs relating to "Bill of Exchange, (inland)," be amended by striking out all of said paragraphs, and inserting in lieu thereof the following:

"Bill of exchange, (inland), draft, or order for the payment of any sum of money, otherwise than at sight or on demand, for every hundred dollars, or fractional part thereof, five (5) cents.

"Loan of money.—Any loan of money, or any advance of money on security, whether represented by note, certificate, check, receipt, or other evidence, not otherwise provided for, and not including mortgages, if on demand, for every hundred dollars, or fractional part thereof, two (2) cents.

"If to be paid at a time designated, for every hundred dollars, or fractional part thereof, five (5) cents: Provided, That any note or other evidence of debt, payable on demand, shall be void after thirty days from date unless it has been protested within that time, or shall have been stamped with duty, within that time, at the rate of five cents for every hundred dollars or fractional part thereof;

and any pawnbroker's certificate for an amount of loan less than five dollars shall not require to be stamped;'' and in the paragraph marked ''receipts,'' by inserting, after the word ''property,'' the words ''except receipts issued by any persons, firm, or companies doing business as an express or express company on the delivery of any property for transportation;'' and that ''schedule C.'' proceeding section one hundred and seventy-one, be amended in all the paragraphs concerning ''playing cards'' by striking out, wherever it occurs, the word ''retail.''

[Ed. note: Note differences between proposed amendment and that adopted March 3, 1865.]

IRR v.I, February 11, 1865, pp.41,45

State and City Securities.

State and city securities are exempt from stamp duty.

IRR v.I, March 11, 1865, p.75

Cancellation of Stamped Paper.

Treasury Department,
Office of Internal Revenue,
Washington, June 23, 1865.

Sir: Yours of the 21st inst., containing inquiries as to the cancellation of stamped paper, is received.

All stamped paper is cancelled whenever used, and the use of the paper by filling the blanks or attaching a signature, is equivalent to the ordinary form of cancelling an adhesive stamp by writing initials and date upon it.

The entire paper is regarded as the stamp, and of course no part of it can be ''cut out'' or separated from the remainder, and retain any value as a stamp. Any portion cut out and attached to another paper is worthless, and such use of it is *prima facie* fraudulent.

Very respectfully,
Joseph J. Lewis,
Commissioner.

IRR v.II, July 8, 1865, p.4

Receipts of Public Officials Exempt from Stamp.

Treasury Department,
Office of Internal Revenue,
Washington, June 27, 1865.

Sir: In reply to your letter of the 24th inst., in relation to the stamp duty on receipts issued by the State and county tax collector, I have to say that all instruments issued or used by a State, county, city or town, are exempt from stamp duty, because the use of stamps in such cases would be a charge on the public Treasury.

It was not the intention of the law to tax the exercise of municipal powers and functions, and, therefore, whenever the use of stamps would be a charge upon the State, county, city, or town treasury, none will be required.

Very respectfully,
Joseph J. Lewis,
Commissioner.

W. H. Fahnestock,
Deputy Collector.

IRR v.II, July 15, 1865, p.11

Stamp Duties in the Southern States.

Treasury Department,
Office of Internal Revenue,
Washington, September 15, 1865.

Sir: Your letter of the 23d ult. has been received. In reply I have to say, that section 163, Act of June 30, 1864, provides that if any person wishes to use or record any instrument signed or issued before that time, but *not stamped,* such person, his agent, or attorney may affix the stamp ''thereon required,'' in the presence of ''the court register or recorder.''

In relation to the remission of penalties by collectors, I can only say, that inasmuch as the amendment of March 3, 1865, to section 158, Act of 1864, grants powers to collectors to remit penalties in the cases of the instruments therein referred to, only when such instruments (being unstamped) shall be brought to them "within twelve calendar months after the making or issuing" thereof, it must be held that such grant of power should be confined to the limits of the *time therein mentioned*. It may be proper to add, however, considering the anomalous state of affairs which has existed at the South for more than four years, it is not unreasonable to suppose that Congress will adopt measures looking to the relief of those who are entitled to it, in this matter of penalties to which you refer.

Very respectfully,
William Orton,
Commissioner.

F. A. Sayer, Esq.
Collector at Charleston, S. C.

IRR v.II, October 28, 1865, p.132

Official Stamped Paper and Instruments.

Office of Internal Revenue,
Washington, January 19, 1866.

Gentlemen: I have delayed answering your communication of December last in relation to the printing of stamped instruments until now, because of my inability to write to you definitely upon the subject.

A contract was yesterday concluded between myself and Messrs. Butler & Carpenter of Philadelphia for printing not only the Adhesive Stamps, but for imprinting Revenue Stamps upon various instruments, such as are usually furnished by stationers.

I have caused notice to be given today to the American Phototype Company rescinding the contract with them for stamping printed instruments. Designs will be prepared by Messrs. Butler & Carpenter for stamps upon checks and other instruments furnished by stationers, and all parties desiring such blanks stamped will be treated with equality.

Messrs. Butler and Carpenter themselves will not sell stamped instruments. Orders for stamping them must be made upon this office, accompanied by the money in payment of the same.

It is not deemed advisable by the Secretary of the Treasury to have Revenue Stamps printed at more than a single place.

Very respectfully,
E. A. Rollins,
Commissioner.

Messrs. B. Maverick and John Kennard,
Committee, P. O. Box No. 1,170, New York City.

IRR v.III, January 27, 1866, p.28

In the Court of Common Pleas of Erie County, Pennsylvania.
Corry National Bank v. A. L. Rouse.

1. No instrument is rendered void by the omission of the requisite Revenue stamp, unless it is done "with intent to evade the provisions of the act."
2. The 158th section of the revenue act makes the collector of revenue of the proper district the judge whether the omission was with or without "any willful design to defraud the United States of the stamp duty," and from his judgment, if favorable, there is no appeal.
3. When the collector has put on and cancelled the requisite stamps the instrument is valid to all intents and purposes ab initio.
4. Promissory notes and bonds are not the instruments referred to in the 152d sec. Revenue Law.
5. The want of proper cancellation of the stamp subjects the offending party to a penalty of $50, but does not render the instrument void.

These judgments were entered on ordinary notes under seal with warrant of Attorney to confess judgment with waivers of exemptions, inquisition, &c., and agreement that real estate might be sold on a *fi.fa*. The notes were stamped as promissory notes. A motion was made to strike off the judgments on the ground that they should be stamped as bonds, with five cents additional for the agreement contained in the warranty of attorney. After the motions to strike off and rules to show cause, the notes were taken to the collector of the district, and at the request of the plaintiff he stamped them as bonds, and put on the five cent stamp to cover the agreement, and remitted the penalty of $50, supposed to have been incurred.

S. A. Davenport, for the rules, referred to stamp act, sects. 152, 156, 158, and contended that the notes were absolutely void at the time the judgments were entered, and that the subsequent stamping did not relate back to make the judgments good.

Benjamin Grant, Contra, referred to Edwards on the stamp act, pages 34, 235, 237, 241; *Brown v. Savage* 5 Jurist, 1020; *Warren v. Paul,* 13 Law Reg., 157; Stamp Act, sec. 97, 160; and contended that the collector's award, that the non-stamping was not fraudulent, was final and the judgment valid.

Dec. 13, 1865. The Opinion of the Court was delivered by

Johnson, J. A careful examination of the 158th Sec. of the U. S. Revenue Law, as amended by the Act of March 3d, 1865, leaves doubtful no question raised by the motions to srike off the judgments in these cases.

In the first place, no instrument is rendered void by the omission of the requisite stamp unless it is done *''with intent to evade the provisions of the act.''*

Secondly. The same section makes ''the Collector of revenue,'' of the proper district the judge whether the omission was with or without ''any willful design to defraud the United States of the stamp duty,'' and from his judgment if favorable there is no appeal, at least so far as the avoidance of the instrument is concerned.

Thirdly. The Collector has adjudged the omission, if any, not to have been with such design and has remitted the penalty.

Fourthly. We cannot reserve the judgment of the Collector on sight without evidence of intent.

Fifthly. The Collector having put on the requisite stamps, if they were before insufficient, the act then provides that ''the instrument shall thereupon be deemed and held to be as valid to all intents and purposes as if stamped when made or issued,'' which we hold makes it good *ab initio*.

This is not the kind of instrument meant by sec. 152.

The want of proper cancellation does not render the instrument void, but merely subjects the party offending to a penalty of $50.

The rules in each of the cases are therefore discharged.

IRR v.III, January 27, 1866, p.31

Stamping by Collectors of Instruments Made and Uttered Without Stamps.—Powers and Duties of Collectors.

Treasury Department,
Office of Internal Revenue
Washington, September 5th, 1866.

Sir: Your letter of the 16th ultimo has been received. You state that an instrument, of which the following is a copy, has been presented to you to be stamped under the provisions of Section 159 of the act now in force.

''Snow Hill, September 1, 1865.

''Received of Richardson, Moore & Co., one copy of judgment against Henry Bratton, superseded by Wm. A. Rowly and Wm. H. Bratton, assigned from Thos. S. Turpin am't thirty-five dollars and four cents, with interest from 3rd day of March, 1860, for collection according to law.

''L. T. Briddel, *Const.*''

Under the laws of Maryland, a constable's receipt, like the foregoing is *prima facie* evidence in a suit upon his official bond. Richardson, Moore & Co., are desirous of putting Briddell's bond in suit, and to that end they present that instrument to you to be stamped. R.P. Moore, a member of the firm of Richardson, Moore & Co., makes an affidavit that the receipt in question ''was not stamped at the time of making the same, by mistake of the parties, supposing that no stamp was required, and that there was no willful design to defraud the United States of the stamp duty or to evade or delay the payment thereof," and ask that the penalty of fifty dollars be remitted. The sureties upon the bond have filed a remonstrance against the affixing of the stamp; and Briddell himself certifies ''that at the time he gave this receipt with others which are also unstamped, he (Briddell) was aware of the law; but did not stamp the receipts because the parties to whom they were given were unconcerned about having them stamped, and that it was not done through ignorance.''

You ask:

1st. Is the instrument a receipt, or is it an agreement?

2d. Can the stamp be affixed and the penalty remitted upon the application of any party except the one who made, signed, and issued the instrument?

3d. Should the stamp be affixed by you against the protest of the party who made, signed, and issued the instrument, and in view of the conflicting evidence respecting the *intent* in the omission of the stamp?

I reply, That the instrument is simply a receipt, and if liable at all, is liable to a stamp duty of two cents only.

Under the 2d proviso to Section 158, it is made the duty of a Collector, upon payment of the stamp duty, a penalty of fifty dollars, and in certain cases, interest upon the amount of stamp duty from the day on which the stamp ought to have been been affixed, to affix a stamp to an instrument issued unstamped, when it is presented to him for that purpose by the party who signed and issued it, *or by any party having an interest therein*. Under the 3d proviso, the Collector is authorized to remit the penalty whenever it appears to *his satisfaction,* upon oath or otherwise, that the instrument presented to him was not duly stamped at the time it was made or issued by reason of accident, mistake, inadvertence, or urgent necessity, and that there was no willful design to defraud the United Sates of the stamp, or to evade or delay the payment thereof. It is not particularly stated in the act what parties may claim the benefit of the 3d proviso; but I think, there can be no doubt whatever that Congress designed to extend its benefits to any and all parties having an interest in an unstamped instrument.

When Richardson, Moore & Co. comply with the requirements of the statute, it is your duty to affix a stamp to the receipt, if they desire it, even though, in your opinion, it may not be chargeable with stamp duty; and if at any time the party presenting an instrument to be stamped under Section 158 insists upon having a certain amount of stamps only affixed, you should affix them, even though you may think the amount insufficient; the party in such case takes all risk of the validity of the instrument. You should not affix your stamp to an instrument as provided in Section 162 without the payment of the stamp duty which *you* deem necessary.

You are authorized to remit a penalty when it is proved to your satisfaction that the stamp was omitted by reason of accident, mistake, &c., and without intent to defraud the United States. This question of intent is one for you, and for you only; and your decision upon that point is final, so far as the affixing of the stamp is concerned. When, as in this case, the party who signed and issued the instrument, and who must be supposed to have the best knowledge of his own intentions, admits that he knowingly and intentionally violated the law, as he understood it, the evidence it would seem should be extremely full and conclusive to convince a collector that there was no fraudulent intent.

The act of July 13th, 1866, relieved receipts for the delivery of property from stamp duties, on and after August 1st, 1866. Under the present law a receipt like the one in question requires no stamp. This receipt, however, was given prior to the passage of the act of July 13th, and, if liable at all, is liable under the law in force at the time it was issued.

It is the practice of this office to withhold its opinion respecting the liability of any particular instrument, when the question has been raised, or is about to be raised, in the courts—a practice which will not be departed from in the present instance.

If you are convinced there was no fraudulent intent, you should affix a stamp to the receipt presented to you by Richardson, Moore & Co., and remit the penalty; if you are not convinced, you will, of course, decline to affix it until the penalty is paid. If the instrument should be carried into court unstamped, and be held subject to stamp duty, you should forthwith report the case to the United States District Attorney, who will undoubtedly cause Mr. Briddell to be indicted for a fraudulent omission of the stamp, and can hardly fail to convict him upon his own admissions alone.

Very respectfully,
Thomas Harland,
Deputy Commissioner

James T. McCullough, Esq.,
Collector of Internal Revenue, Elkton, Md.

IRR v.IV, September 15, 1866, pp.85-6

Distribution and Sale of Internal Revenue Stamps.—The Secretary of the Treasury has issued instructions to the Assistant Treasurers at New York, Philadelphia, Boston, St. Louis, and San Francisco, and to the Collectors of Customs, designated as depositories, at Baltimore, Buffalo, Chicago, Detroit, Cincinnati, and Charleston, under which they are required to keep on hand unbroken packages of internal revenue stamps for sale at the same rates of commission as are allowed by the Commissioner of Internal Revenue.

All national banks designated as depositories of public moneys are also required, by instructions from the Secretary of the Treasury, to keep internal revenue stamps for sale in such amounts as the public shall require, and which they may purchase from the Assistant Treasurers, or the depositories first named, or the commissioner.

The rates allowed are as follows:

Two per cent in sums of $50 and upwards.

Three per cent in sums of $200 and upwards.

Four per cent in sums of $500 and upwards.

Five per cent in sums of $1,000 and upwards.

These instructions do away with the system of advancing stamps to officers on bonds which has hitherto been the practice. It will secure a more thorough distribution, and with less risk of loss to the government. The national banks designated as depositories it is understood will be required to furnish stamps at the same rates of discount, payable in stamps, as above specified.

IRR v.IV, September 22, 1866, p.90

Supreme Court—Circuit—Part III—Oct. 22.
Before Justice Davis and a Jury.
Thomas J. Pope vs. *Oscar F. Burns and the Bank of Albion.*

A draft post-dated and stamped with a two cent stamp, held not to be properly stamped.—Plaintiff non-suited.

This action was brought to recover the sum of $3,000, the amount of a draft drawn by the defendant Burns, dated March 1, 1866, and addressed to the Bank of Albion, in this state. It was made payable to the order of the drawer. From the evidence given at the trial it appears the draft was post-dated, more than sixty days, having been drawn and put into circulation in this city, sometime in January previous. The plaintiff in the action received it for a valuable consideration at about the time it bears date, the Bank having accepted it; it was afterward presented for payment, and payment thereof refused. The counsel for the plaintiff, Mr. E. F. Brown, in opening the case to the Jury, said that so far as he could ascertain, there were two defences on the part of the Bank: First, that the drawer had no funds in the Bank, and secondly, that the draft when presented for acceptance, was accepted by the assistant cashier, who had no authority to certify checks or accept drafts. But before the close of the plaintiff's case, it became evident that there were other objections which defendants had heretofore declined to make known to their opponent or his counsel. One of the defences brought out before the Court was that the draft had not a sufficient stamp upon it. It had a two-cent stamp, but it was claimed that this is not a proper one to put on a draft of this nature, which was said to be an inland bill of exchange within the meaning of the Internal Revenue Act. This act declares that a five-cent stamp, for every $100, or fractional part thereof, represented by an inland bill of exchange, draft or order for the payment of any sum of money other than those drawn at sight or on demand, shall be paid by way of stamp duty. This having a two-cent stamp only was not regular. It was not a draft or bill of exchange payable at sight or on demand. The draft was drawn and put into circulation long before the day of its date. Counsel for the defence also read sections of the same act, for the purpose of showing that a draft of this kind, with a two-cent stamp, could not be offered in evidence. The bill, or note, or whatever it was, is void. Moreover, the bank, or any person negotiating, or attempting to negotiate such an instrument, was liable to a heavy fine.

In answer to this, the counsel for the plaintiff contended that as a matter of law, as well as for all commercial purposes, the draft in question was a sight draft, or one payable on demand. It also contended the Court had the power, and should, in its discretion, in order to further the ends of justice, direct that a proper stamp be placed upon the draft. This could be done then and there. There was no doubt, in fact there was no dispute but what the plaintiff was an innocent *bona fide* holder for a valuable consideration. It was in evidence that he had paid the full amount of its face, less the difference of exchange between New York and Albion. A man named Galladet was the holder. He had transferred it to the plaintiff in the usual course of business on the day, or the day after it bears date. The plaintiff could not possibly have known from anything that appears on the face of the draft that it had been post-dated. Counsel asks the Court if it did not seem as though the defendants were attempting to defraud an innocent holder out of that to which he is justly entitled by means of a very technical objection.

The presiding Justice said he did not know yet whether the defendants had any defence on the merits. He thought, however, that the questions presented by the defendants' counsel were grave ones. He did not think it was a question of intent in any view that could be taken of it. There was the Internal Revenue Act. He was not there to pronounce upon the necessity or the wisdom of it in all its details. But it was the law of the land, and Courts of Justice were bound to sustain it. The act says an instrument of this character shall not be admitted in evidence, unless properly stamped, and it describes what denomination of stamps shall be put upon certain kinds of commercial paper. He could not agree with the counsel that this is a sight draft or one payable on demand. It had been postdated more than sixty days. It had circulated around New York as commercial paper prior to the day of its date, which is the 1st of March.

Mr. Brown for plaintiff, was, he said, very confident that the Court could direct the suspension of its business for an hour, so that they could send to the Collector of Internal Revenue and have the appropriate stamp affixed. They could do that in an hour, and it would save the rights of his client, and avoid the necessity of commencing the suit *de novo*.

Mr. Barrows for the defendants, contended that that even would not extricate the plaintiff from the difficulty in which he was placed. They would insist most strenuously on their part that even if the Court or the Collector of the Revenue should now authorize the affixing of the proper stamp, this action cannot be maintained. The Bank of Albion, which is the substantial defendant, has never been presented with, and hence has never accepted, the draft in question when properly stamped. By the Internal Revenue Act they would be liable to a heavy penalty for accepting, certifying or paying a check or draft not stamped in pursuance of the provisions of the law.

The Judge took this view of it, and determined that the only thing he could do, under all the circumstances, was to nonsuit the plaintiff. Thirty days were granted to plaintiff in which to make a case on appeal, with a view of testing the important questions of law in a higher court.

For plaintiff, Messrs. Brown & Estes; for defendants, Mr. Roswell L. Burrows.—*N.Y.Times*

IRR v.IV, October 27, 1866, pp.133-4

Stamp Tax.

A meets his neighbor B, and asks him what he thinks of that part of our Internal Revenue Tax, the Stamp Tax? B says he does not like it. A inquires why. B says the time and trouble it takes cost more than the value of the stamp, and that if any reduction of taxes is compatible with the interest of the Department, let this, which so interferes with business, and contracts between man and man, go.

IRR v.V, January 12, 1867, p.10

Stamp Tax in the Late Insurrectionary States in Force From October 1, 1862.

The first Act imposing a stamp tax upon certain specified instruments took effect, so far as said tax is concerned, October 1, 1862. The impression which seems to prevail to some extent, that no stamps are required upon any instruments issued in the United States lately in insurrection, prior to the surrender, or prior to the establishment of collection districts there, is erroneous.

Instruments issued in those States since October 1st, 1862, are subject to the same taxes as similar ones issued at the same time in the other States.

IRR v.V, February 23, 1867, p.59

Payment For and Affixing of Stamps—Penalties.

The law does not designate which of the parties to an instrument shall furnish the necessary stamp, nor does the Commissioner of Internal Revenue assume to determine that it shall be supplied by one party rather than by another; but if an instrument subject to stamp duty is issued without having the necessary stamps affixed thereto, it cannot be recorded, or admitted, or used as evidence, in any court, until a legal stamp or stamps, denoting the amount of tax shall have been affixed as prescribed by law, and the person who thus issues it is liable to a penalty, if he omits the stamp with an intent to evade the provisions of the internal revenue act.

IRR v.V, February 23, 1867, p.59

Instruments to Which the U.S. Is a Party.

No stamp is required upon an instrument to which the United States is a party, if it is signed and executed by a person representing the government; if not signed by such a person stamps should be affixed.

IRR v.V, February 23, 1867, p.60

Cancellation of Stamps.

Each stamp when used should be separately cancelled.

IRR v.V, February 23, 1867, p.60

Instruments Executed Prior to October 1st, 1862.

No stamp is necessary upon an instrument executed prior to October 1st, 1862, to make it admissible in evidence, or to entitle it to record.

IRR v.V, March 7, 1867, p.74

Use of Stamped Paper—Instruments Imprinted by American Photograph Co.

Treasury Department,
Office of Internal Revenue,
Washington, April 15, 1867.

Sir: Instances having been brought to the notice of this office, in which instruments upon which stamps have been imprinted by your Company, have been used for purposes which subjected them to a higher rate of duty than that represented by the printed stamp, it becomes necessary to take such action as will prevent the public from being misled by this course.

It has been determined, therefore, that duplicate copies of each instrument, upon which persons may wish a stamp imprinted, shall be presented to this office, in order that the sufficiency of the stamp for the instrument may be considered. If the printing is approved, one copy will be forwarded to you, together with the customary order for printing.

The instruments which shall be hereafter stamped under this order, may be successively numbered, and such records will be kept as will enable persons desirous of procuring a second supply of instruments of the same form to avoid submitting the form a second time.

Very respectfully,
E. A. Rollins,
Commissioner.

C. Eidlitz, Esq.,
Manager of the Am. Photograph Co., N.Y. City.

IRR v.V, April 27, 1867, p.130

Revenue Stamps.

It is a subject of frequent remark, that in a country where the law requires the payment of a stamp duty in so many forms, the number of stamps used must be immense, and the revenue derived from this source be very large; and a natural curiosity has found expression in the matter among the legal fraternity and others, who are required to use stamps extensively.

Large as the number used may be supposed to be, we are induced to believe that supposition falls far short of the actual quantity. There are many persons who would feel incredulous, were they informed that the Government sell two hundred millions of revenue stamps per annum. But what will be thought when we state that *four hundred million* were sold to the people of this country within a single year? Such is the fact, as shown by the official revenue records for the year 1866. This is an immense number, but it is a correct one. The aggregate revenue yielded by these stamps, amounted to more than fifteen millions of dollars.

It may not be generally known that there are two kinds of these stamps, one being the regular public stamps, and the other the private or proprietary stamps. The former are printed with a uniform design from plates belonging to the Government, deposited in the hands of the printer. The latter are of such design as may be selected by the respective parties requiring them. The Government desiring, as far as practicable, to accommodate the peculiar requirements of general business, with its multiform specific branches, concedes the privilege to individuals in business to place upon their respective manufactures, if preferred, a stamp bearing a design of their own choice.

The plates are executed at their expense, and are deposited with the Government agents who furnish the stamps. When the parties want a supply of their own stamps, they forward an order for the desired number to the Commissioner of Internal Revenue, who gives the proper directions in the case, and the parties are promptly and correctly furnished.

The whole range of denomination of stamps now used is as follows: 1c, 2, 3, 4, 5, 6, 10, 15, 20, 25, 30, 40, 50, 60, 70c, $1, 1.30, 1.50, 1.60, 1.90, 2.00, 2.50, 3.00, 3.50, 5.00, 10.00, 15.00, 20.00, 25.00, 50.00, 200.00.

It will be seen that the smallest denomination is one cent in value, and the largest two hundred dollars, with a general division that will allow of any combination requisite to meet the rates of duty prescribed by law. The denominational range of the private stamps, however, is confined to 1, 2, 3, 4, 5, 6, 8 and 10 cents, face value.

It may surprise some persons to learn that the private stamps used considerably outnumber the Government ones, yet such is the fact; the former numbering about two hundred and thirty-seven millions in 1866, while the latter numbered about one hundred and sixty-three millions.

But while the number of stamps is in favor of the proprietary class, the revenue yielded is on the side of the public class. The private ones yielded about three and a half million dollars, and the public ones about eleven and a half millions. There are some curious facts noticeable in connection with the subject. For instance, the number of *one* cent stamps of private design, sold in 1866, was nearly one hundred and seventy millions, against only three hundred and twelve thousand of the Government class. But during the same period, the number sold of the latter class, of *two* cent denomination, was one hundred and twenty-eight and a half millions against thirty-two millions of the former class. The private *three* cent stamps sold during the same time, was eighteen millions, against only about two hundred thousand of the public class; thirteen and a half millions of *four* cent ones, private class, against one hundred and thirty-eight thousand of the public class; one and a sixth million *five* cent ones, private class, against seventeen and a half millions, public class; four hundred and sixteen thousand *ten* cent ones, private class, against four and a half million public class. The revenue accruing to the Government from this one source has steadily and largely increased each year. For the fiscal year 1863, it amounted to four and a seventh millions of dollars; for 1864, it was five and nine tenths millions; for 1865, it ran suddenly up to over eleven millions; and in 1866 still further advanced to over fifteen millions.

The use of stamps upon various instruments in writing has given rise to many interesting incidents, and for every sheet of writing it has not been unfrequent that there has been one sheet of revenue stamps. Indeed, in the case of a very large mortgage given by a Western rail road, it is stated that the stamps affixed to the instrument covered a surface of the depth of the document measuring seven feet in length. The statements we have given, present the number of stamps only that are sold and used. If to the figure given was added the number of stamps that *ought* to be used, and of which the Government is annually defrauded, the grand total reached would exhibit a sum that might well be a matter of much astonishment.

IRR v.VI, August 17, 1867, p.49

Accounts for Collecting Stamp Duty Interest, and Penalties by Collectors.

Any person who has made, signed, or issued an instrument subject to stamp duty unstamped, or insufficiently stamped, or any person having an interest therein, may present it to the collector of the proper district, who, upon payment of the price of the proper stamp required by law, a penalty of fifty dollars, and, where the whole amount of the tax donated by the stamp required exceeds fifty dollars, on payment also of interest at the rate of six per centum from the date on which such stamp ought to have been affixed, is required by law to affix the stamp and to note upon the margin of the instrument the date of his so doing, and the fact that such penalty has been paid.

When an instrument is presented to a collector to be stamped, under the provisions of Section 158, he is authorized to remit the penalty if it shall be proven to his satisfaction that such instrument was issued without the necessary stamp by reason of accident, mistake, inadvertence, or urgent necessity, and without any willful design to defraud the United States of the duty, or to evade or delay the payment thereof, *provided* such instrument is presented to him for that purpose, and the stamp tax chargeable thereon is paid within twelve calendar months after the first day of August, 1866, or within twelve calendar months after the making or issuing thereof.

By the use of the word "*after,*" the first day of August, 1866, in the one case, and the day of issuing in the other, are excluded.

The interest upon the amount of tax donated by the stamp is distinct from the penalty, forms no part of it, and cannot be remitted. It should in all cases be collected when said amount exceeds fifty dollars, even when the penalty is remitted. The amount thus collected should be entered upon Form 58, and returned to the assessor, and should also be entered under the head of Interest (252), upon the Monthly Abstract of Collections (Form 22).

IRR v.VI, August 24, 1867, p.58-9

Revenue Stamps on Bankrupt Documents.

The attention of Registers in Bankruptcy is directed to the ruling of the office of Internal Revenue respecting the revenue stamps to which certain papers in bankruptcy are held to be liable. The communication was addressed to Register Finnell, of Covington, Kentucky, under date of the 6th inst., and states:

A register's deed to the assignee should be stamped as a general contract or agreement, and if it contains powers these should have their appropriate stamps.

The bond of the assignee for the faithful discharge of duty requires a $1 stamp.

A letter of attorney to represent creditors, requires a fifty-cent stamp, as a power for a purpose not particularly specified in Schedule B.

The deed of assignee to purchasers should be stamped at the usual rate of deeds.

It is understood that the professions are not united in their opinion as to the correctness of the ruling which requires Register's deed to assignee to be stamped, inasmuch as the deed is regarded as issued by an officer of the United States, and therefore exempt. The question will probably soon be presented for judicial opinion. The expense of stamps would curtail the Register's fees.

IRR v.VI, August 31, 1867, p.68

[Ed. note: Repeated, without the final paragraph, in v.X, August 21, 1869, p.62.]

Steamboat Marine Papers, Bonds, Certificates and Returns.

Steamboat Inspectors' Certificates are exempt from stamp tax, under the amendment to Section 154, which exempts all official papers issued by officers of the United States Government. The Masters' and Owners' Oaths are exempt under the Act of March 2d, 1867, which relieves all affidavits from stamp tax. The Masters' Marine Hospital Return, is also exempt. The two Forms of Bonds, given by Masters of Steamboats, require a 25 cent stamp each, as Bonds not otherwise charged in the Stamp Schedule.

IRR v.VI, September 28, 1867, p.105

Internal Revenue Law Decisions—Stamp.

We are indebted for the following notes to the "American Law Review," a periodical that has taken a foremost rank among American law publications. This quarterly is edited with judgment and dignity, and richly merits the favor with which it has been received by the profession.

. . .

Plaintiff, in an appeal from a justice of the peace, omitted to affix to any paper connected therewith the stamp required by the Revenue Act of June 30, 1864; and, pending a motion by the defendant to dismiss said appeal on account of such omission, plaintiff offered to affix the proper stamp. *Held,* that, while the intent to defraud the government is essential to a liability for a penalty for omitting to place a stamp on any instrument, required by said act, yet, when the stamp is omitted the instrument is invalid, whether such omission is from accident or design. The courts have no power to supply such a defect when it exists: it can be done only in the manner provided by the statute.—*Hugus* v. *Strickler,* 19 Iowa, 413.

Suit upon a promissory note, dated November 7, 1862. The note was admitted in evidence, although the defendant objected on the ground that it was not stamped with an appropriate stamp. *Held,* that under the Act of July 1, 1862, the note should have been stamped, and was not admissible in evidence without a stamp; and that as the party offering the note had not removed the objection by affixing the proper stamp under Section 5 of the Act, of December 25, 1862, it was improperly admitted.—*Plessinger* v. *Depuy,* 25 Ind. 419.

. . .

A demurrer to a declaration upon a promissory note, for the reason that the copy of the note annexed to the declaration does not show that the note bore an internal revenue stamp, will not lie.—*Trull* v. *Moulton,* 12 Allen, 396.

The provisions made by the law of the United States of June 30, 1864, Section 163, for stamping, in the presence of the Court where it is used, any instrument *before* that law, signed or issued without being stamped are not repealed or affected by the law of March 3, 1865, which applies to instruments requiring stamps *under* the law of June 30, 1864.—*Garland* v. *Lane,* 4 N. H. 245.

. . .

Under the act of Congress passed June 30, 1864, "to provide internal revenue to support the Government," &c., which enacts, that any person who shall make, sign, or issue any instrument, document, or paper without the same being duly stamped, or having thereon an adhesive stamp to denote the duty chargeable thereon, *with intent to evade the provisions of this act,* shall forfeit the sum of two hundred dollars, and such instrument, &c., shall be deemed invalid and of no effect, the penalty is not incurred unless the neglect to stamp duly be willful and fraudulent; nor is the instrument invalidated unless the omission to affix a stamp be "with intent to evade the provisions" of the act; in other words, to defraud the Government of the stamp duty, in whole or in part. It is "such" an instrument, namely, one that has been attempted to be put in circulation by a fraudulent non-compliance with the terms of the act, which is to be deemed invalid and of no effect, and not one which, through haste or inadvertence or ignorance, has been mistakenly, though honestly, issued without a compliance with the law.—*Beebe* v. *Hutton,* 47 Barb. 187.

Where a chattel mortgage, upon being offered in evidence, is objected to on the ground of its having a defective stamp, it is competent for the party offering the instrument to show that the insufficiency of the stamp arose from inadvertence or mistake, and without any intent to evade the provisions of the revenue law, and thereupon to read the mortgage in evidence.—*Ib.*

IRR v.VI, November 23, 1867, p.181

Abstracts of Law Decisions.

Stamps.

On Writs—Accidental Omission of Stamp.—Under the act of Congress, approved June 30th, 1864, entitled "An Act to provide internal revenue," &c., the instrument is not forfeited, nor is the penalty incurred by an *accidental* omission to affix a United States Internal Revenue Stamp thereon. The forfeiture of the penalty and the forfeiture of the instrument are both embraced in one entire, connected proposition, and both rest on the same facts, the omission of the stamp, *with intent to evade the provisions of the act: Hitchcock* v. *Sawyer,* 39 Vt.

Therefore a motion to dismiss a suit for the reason that no stamp was affixed to the writ, without alleging that the omission was with intent to evade the provisions of the statute, was held insufficient: *Id.*

Omission to Stamp Promissory Note.—An innocent omission to stamp a promissory note made after the passage of the U.S. St. of 1864, c.173, though antedated to November 1862, will not render it inadmissible in evidence, if it is subsequently stamped in the presence of the court: *Tobey* v. *Chipman,* 13 Allen.

So an innocent omission to stamp an order for the payment of money, drawn after the passage of the U.S. St. of 1865, c. 78, will not render it invalid or inadmissible in evidence: *Id.*

Insolvent Bond—Omission of Stamp.—An insolvent's bond is a bond made necessary by legal proceedings, and does not require a stamp: *McGovern v. Hosback,* 53 Penna.

A voluntary bond unstamped is not void unless the stamp be omitted to evade the Act of Congress: *Id.*

IRR v.VI, December 21, 1867, p.211-2

Attention is called to the ruling published this week respecting the authority of the commissioner of Internal Revenue to remit penalties for failure to affix stamps to instruments. The law gives him no such authority. Appeal to him to authorize a collector to remit the penalty upon an instrument which has remained unstamped more than twelve calendar months is fruitless, and collectors should not encourage parties to make such application.

IRR v.VI, December 28, 1867, p.217

Penalty to Have Collector Stamp Instrument.

The payment of a penalty for the purpose of having an instrument properly stamped by a Collector, relieves no one from his liability to indictment, or other legal proceedings for issuing it without the necessary stamp with intent to defraud the revenue; neither does the payment of a penalty imposed by the Court for willful neglect to stamp an instrument, make the instrument valid. The two penalties are entirely distinct; the payment of the one is voluntary; that of the other is compulsory: and the payment of one does not relieve from the necessity or liability of the payment of the other.

IRR v.VI, December 28, 1867, p.218

Stamping of Unstamped Instruments Penalties—Powers of Commissioner.

The Commissioner of Internal Revenue has no authority to remit a penalty for failure to stamp an instrument; this power is vested only in the Collector (or in the Deputy, acting as Collector under Sections 39 or 40). The Collector's authority to make the remission ceases at the expiration of twelve calendar months from the issue of the instrument, and the payment of the penalty then becomes an absolute condition precedent to the affixing of the stamp, and is as essential to the validity of the instrument as is the stamp itself.

IRR v.VI, December 28, 1867, p.218

Stamping of Unstamped Instruments by Collector of Internal Revenue, on Payment of Penalty.

That the penalty paid to make valid an instrument invalid, for being issued without a stamp, renders the same as valid to all intents and purposes as if stamped when made or issued.

The penalty paid in such case is in the nature of a consideration, on the receipt of which, the Collector is authorized to do what no one else can do, to give validity to the instrument.

IRR v.VII, February 29, 1868, p.68

Revenue Stamp—Original Consideration.—In an action of general *assumpsit,* the payee of a promissory note, having no revenue stamp affixed thereto, and if, for that reason, invalid, can recover of the maker upon the original consideration for which such note was given: *Wilson* v. *Carey,* 40 Vt.—(*Am. L. R., Aug.* 1868.)

IRR v.VIII, October 10, 1868, p.118

Use Unstamped Instruments as Evidence in State Courts.

The provision of the U.S. Statute 1866, c. 184, sec. 9, that no document not duly stamped shall be used in evidence in any Court until the requisite stamps shall have been affixed thereto, applies only to Courts of the United States.—*Carpenter* v. *Snelling,* 9 Mass, 472—*Lynch* v. *Morse, ib.* 458.

IRR v.IX, January 16, 1869, p.21

When Failure to Affix Stamp Will Not Invalidate Instrument.

The omission to fix a revenue stamp to an instrument requiring one, will not invalidate the instrument unless such omission be with intent to defraud the Goverment of the stamp duty.—*Holyoke Machine Co.* v. *Franklin Paper Co.,* 97 Mass. 150. *Vorebeck* v. *Roe,* 50 Barb. 302. *Blunt* v. *Bates,* 40 Ala. 470, 475.

IRR v.IX, January 16, 1869, p.21

Affixing of Stamp to Promissory Note by Attorney.

An attorney, to whom a note, executed at a place within the United States, at which no collection district was at that time established, was intrusted for collection, had such an "interest" in the same as authorized him to affix a stamp to it, to protect his claim before January 1, 1867—The neglect to cancel it till afterwards does not matter.—*Blunt* v. *Bates,* 40 Ala. 470.

IRR v.IX, January 16, 1869, p.21

Penalty Paid on Stamping an Unstamped Instrument Not Subject to Remission.

The penalty of fifty dollars provided for by Section 158 of the Int. Rev. Law, is paid for a valuable consideration, the privilege of stamping the instrument unstamped, and it cannot be remitted by the Secretary.—*To J. A. Hall, New Jefferson, Iowa, Feb. 9, 1869.*

IRR v.IX, April 3, 1869, p.107

Supreme Court of Illinois—Jan. Term, 1868.

A chattel mortgage filed for record on the 14th day of June, without internal revenue stamp inadvertently omitted with no intent to evade the tax, and upon which proper stamp was placed by the mortgagee on the 21st, before actual record, and another stamp affixed by the Collector of Internal Revenue on the 24th of June, *Held,* to have been properly admitted in evidence in an action of replevin by the mortgagee to recover the mortgaged goods from the Sheriff who had levied upon the same under an execution issued on the 21st, upon a judgment against the mortgagor obtained on the 20th of June, the Act of Congress to the contrary notwithstanding.

The filing of the unstamped mortgage was notice to the judgment creditor.

Semble—That the power of Congress to tax does not extend to make void or invalid instruments of evidence, otherwise good and admissible by the laws of one of the States, whatever may be its power as respects evidence exclusively in the Federal Courts.—(Ed.Rec.)

Craig v. *Dimock, et al.*

Breese, C. J.—This was an action of replevin brought to the Circuit Court of Adams County, at the October term, 1867, by Gershom B. Dimock and Cyrus W. Hilborn, against Henry C. Craig, for a wagon and two horses, and tried by the Court without the intervention of a jury, and a verdict for the plaintiff. Judgment was rendered on the verdict, and the defendant appeals to this Court.

The plaintiffs claimed the property under a chattel mortgage executed on the 19th of March, 1867, by one Holden to them, to secure a note of that date for one hundred and fifty-three 25-100 dollars, payable in two years from date, with the usual clause in the mortgage, that the property should remain with the mortgagor until the maturity of the note. The mortgage, by inadvertence, had no stamp upon it, and it was in that condition when placed in the recorder's office for record, which was on the fourteenth day of June, 1867, but was not actually recorded, it not being reached in order, until the 21st day of June, on which day one of the plaintiffs, Hilborn, at the recorder's office, put the proper stamp upon it, and canceled it, and the recorder spread it on his records. Samuel R. Chittenden, on the 20th day of June, 1867, recovered a judgment in the Circuit Court of Adams County, against the same Holden, for five hundred and sixty-three 58-100 dollars, on which an execution was duly issued on the following day and placed in the hands of the defendant, then sheriff of Adams County, who levied the same on the property in question, and embraced in the chattel mortgage. It was in proof, the execution was delivered to the sheriff upon the record. The certificate of the clerk of the Circuit Court states that the mortgage was filed for record on the 14th day of June, 1867, and recorded on that day in book 7 of chattel mortgages, at page 141. On the 24th day of June, 1867, the collector of internal revenue for the Quincy District came to the recorder's office with one of the plaintiffs, Hilborn, and then and there put another fifty-cent stamp upon the mortgage and cancelled it, and advised Hilborn to have the mortgage refiled and recorded again, which Hilborn declined doing. It is admitted that Chittenden, the judgment creditor of the mortgagor. [Ed. note: Some words are evidently missing here.] Holden saw and read the mortgage in the recorder's office the day before he caused his execution to be issued and levied. The discrepancy between the certificate of the recorder, that the mortgage was recorded on the 14th day of June, and the proof that the stamp was not placed upon it until the 21st, and on that day recorded, is reconciled on the supposition that the recorder considered, and no doubt correctly, that the record should refer to the time when the deed was actually deposited in the office and filed for record, which was on the 14th of June, 1867. There is no pretense in this case that the omission of the proper stamp was with the intent to evade the provisions of the "Stamp Act" of June 30, 1864, or of any other Act of Congress, but was solely the result of neglect and inadvertence.

The facts stated raise the question argued by appellant, as to the validity of this mortgage as an instrument of evidence. He contends that it, and the record of it, are inoperative as against him, and were improperly admitted in evidence.

This question involves the consideration of the act of Congress of June 30, 1864, entitled "An act to provide internal revenue to support the government, to pay interest on the public debt, and for other purposes."

By schedule B, accompanying that act, a mortgage of real or personal property, made for the security of any certain sum of money due and owing, exceeding one hundred dollars, and not exceeding five hundred dollars, is subject to a duty of fifty cents.

Section 152 declares that it shall not be lawful to record any instrument, document or paper required by law to be stamped, unless a stamp or stamps of the proper amount shall have been affixed and cancelled in the manner required by law; and the record of any such instrument upon which the proper stamp or stamps shall not have been affixed and cancelled, shall be utterly void, and shall not be read in evidence. By Section 158, it is provided that any person who shall make, sign, or issue any instrument, document or paper of any kind or description whatsoever, without the same being duly stamped, or having thereupon an adhesive stamp for denoting the tax chargeable thereon, and cancelled in the manner required by law, *with intent to evade the provisions of this act,* shall, for every such offence, forfeit the sum of fifty dollars, and such instrument, document or paper, not being stamped according to law, shall be deemed invalid, and of no effect. Section 163 declares that hereafter no deed, instrument, document, writing, or paper required by law to be stamped, which has been signed or issued without being duly stamped, or with a deficient stamp nor any copy thereof, shall be recorded, or admitted, or used as evidence in any court, until a legal stamp or stamps, denoting the amount of tax, shall have been affixed thereto as prescribed by law. This is all the legislation of Congress necessary to be noticed now, the curative portion of Section 158 being to be hereafter considered.

The object of this act and of all other acts of Congress of like nature, is to raise money to support the government and pay its debts, and for this purpose vast powers were granted by the States in forming the Constitution of the United States, to the Congress established by it, but the powers not delegated to the United States by the constitution, nor prohibited by it to the States, were reserved to the States, respectively, or to the people. Whilst, then, the power to levy taxes for the purposes indicated in the constitution may be admitted, it cannot be admitted it can be so exercised as to take from the domain of State legislation all such subjects as are properly confided to it, and the care of which has not been surrendered to the Congress by the States. Of this nature are the process of the State courts in judicial proceedings. By the act of Congress approved July 1, 1862, which is amended by the act now under consideration, legal documents, such as writs, warrants, cognovits, etc., were made subject to a duty, and were required to be stamped, and if not stamped were to be deemed invalid and of no effect. At a very early period after the passage of that act, the question arose in the courts of several of the States as to the validity of the requirement, and although the plenary power of Congress to raise a revenue to meet the wants of the government by the imposition and collection of taxes, duties, imposts and excises was admitted, no reasoning urged in support of the general power was regarded as sufficient to establish the power of Congress to impose a tax upon the writs and processes of State courts. It could not be shown, and was not shown, that Congress had not only an unlimited power to tax the property of the country, and other subjects to which this power is applicable, but that it could directly tax the means employed by the States in exercising their powers of government. Such was the opposition of the State courts, and of the sentiments of the country to this provision of the act, that the law before us, and other subsequent acts of the same character, omitted the provision, and such documents are no longer declared to be taxable.

Ours is a complex system of government, ordained by wise men, and wholly unlike that of any other country. Its character is expressed in the motto on the seal of the United States, *E pluribus unum,* one government, or one republic, or many States confederated. This was the established and almost universally recognized view of the structure of our government for more than seventy years; to allow, then, the construction contended for by appellant, would change the system from the federative to a centralized and consolidated system. Under the first, the States which established the constitution were in the free exercise of all of the rights and powers they had not surrendered to the general government, and upon all subjects and questions within their respective spheres were regarded as sovereign and independent, to the same extent as was the general government within its sphere of action—neither having the constitutional right to interfere with the other in the exercise of its proper functions. It has never, until recently, been denied that the sovereignty of a State extended to everything which existed by its own authority, or introduced by its permission. Whilst, then, it is readily accorded to the general government, the unlimited sovereignty over everything which exists by its own authority, or is introduced by its permission, and to tax it for all constitutional purposes, it cannot be conceded this power extends to things and subjects which exist in the States, by permission of the States, and not in violation of any act of Congress or requirement of the federal constitution.

It was upon this principle the case of *McCulloch* v. *The State of Maryland* was decided, reported in 4 Wheaton, 316. It was urged in that case, with great force, by the eminent Chief Justice of that court, that the State of Maryland had no right to tax any of the constitutional means employed by the general government wherewith to execute its constitutional powers, nor to regard, impede, burden, or in any manner control the operations of a constitutional law enacted by Congress to carry into effect the powers vested in the general government. It was urged that the power to tax involved the power to destroy; that the power to destroy might defeat and render useless the power to create, and that there was a plain repugnance in conferring on one government a power to control the constitutional measures of another, which other, with respect to those very measures, is declared to be supreme over that which exerts the control.

These principles applied to the power to tax the process of State courts by the operation of an act of Congress, settles the question of power against the act of Congress, because judicial process being wholly under the control of the respective States when issuing from, or used in their courts, and being indispensable in the execution of the powers of the States, is as far removed from interference by the taxing power of Congress, as any of the instrumentalities of the general government, created to carry into execution the powers with which it is vested, and removed beyond the interference of the State authorities. If State process could be taxed by the United States, it could be absolutely prohibited and destroyed by such a power brought to bear upon it, and as the States are sovereign in respect to the matters committed to them, the Congress cannot, by taxation, or in any other manner, retard, burden, or control their operation within the field of their duty, nor impose a specific tax of any kind upon any of the indispensable governmental functions of the States.

A tax upon a writ is a tax upon a necessary means which the judicial department of every State government must use in order that justice may be administered within its borders. These means cannot be exposed to the action of any other power, or be claimed to exist only by the sufferance of Congress.

Intimately connected with this is, in our judgment, the question raised on this record. Can Congress declare what instrument shall be, or shall not be, evidence in a State court in a case therein pending, growing entirely out of a domestic transaction, and which the laws of the State declare shall be evidence?

We do not think it requires any argument to prove that Congress, under the constitution, has no such power, and under the pretence of levying taxes, cannot so direct that power as to enter into our State courts, and take from them the power with which the State laws have vested them.

It is eloquently remarked by Chancellor Kent, that "the vast field of the law of property, the very extensive head of equity jurisdiction, and the principal rights and duties which flow from our civil and domestic relations, fall within the control, and we might almost say the exclusive cognizance of the State governments. We look essentially to the State courts for protection to all these momentous interests." 1 *Comstock's Kent,* 483.

To hold that Congress, in the exercise of the taxing power, can enter into these courts and prescribe what shall be evidence therein, is so revolting to all our notions of federal and State power, as to compel us to refuse to yield any acquiescence in such a doctrine. By admitting it, the power and sovereignty of the State over legitimate subjects of State power and sovereignty, is at once annihilated.

We will not deny the power of Congress to require such instruments to be stamped, nor the consequent power to punish by fine intentional evasion of the law. By conceding this, we yield all that is necessary to enable the government to carry into full effect the taxing power, and at the same time sustain and uphold in its utmost limit the exclusive power of the state to say what shall be evidence in her own courts of justice, in a domestic transaction, wholly unconnected in every respect with the general government.

It is not questioned that the Congress has power to prescribe rules of evidence, and specify what shall be instruments of evidence in the federal courts, but is powerless to prescribe them for the State tribunals, as we think. Since the act, then, does not, in terms, prescribe such rules to State courts, we must conclude that the provisions of the act were only intended to apply to the federal tribunals. We will not, by implication, hold that the intention of the Congress was to invade the jurisdiction of the States in the administration of justice between their citizens. Similar views seem to have been entertained by the Supreme Court of Massachusetts, in *Carpenter* v. *Snelling,* 1 Brown (97 Mass.) 452, and is, doubtless, the true construction of the act.

But, perhaps the case before us does not require us to go to the extent we have gone in sustaining the circuit court in admitting this mortgage as evidence.

The question may be viewed in this light: is an instrument unstamped by reason of negligence alone, and with no design to evade the revenue laws, if thereafter stamped, void and of no effect and not to be received in evidence.

The original act of 1862 did not contain the qualification in regard to the omission to stamp the paper, that it be, "with intent to evade the provisions of the act." This qualification must apply to all the sections of the act of 1864, which we have quoted, as they are upon the same subject, and it seems clear to our minds, that the penalty is not only not incurred, unless the neglect to stamp be willful and fraudulent, but the instrument is not designed to be made invalid, unless the omission to stamp is "*with the intent to evade the provisions of this Act;*" in other words, to defraud the government of the duty. This mortgage, negligently omitted to be stamped, has, in fact, paid double duty to the government—once by the stamp placed on it by Hilborn on the 21st of June, and again by the collector of the district, on the 24th of the same month.

Under such circumstances, to declare a forfeiture of the instrument and of the property secured by it, would be monstrous. It is a forced and unnatural construction of the act to contend, that while the penalty was only incurred for a willful and fraudulent evasion of the duty, the forefeiture of the instrument, a much more serious loss, and falling upon an innocent party, was to apply to a careless and thoughtless omission to fix the proper stamp, as well as to an intentional and fraudulent omission. The law reads "such" instrument, namely: one that has been attempted to be put in circulation by a fraudulent non-compliance with the terms of the act which is "to be deemed invalid and of no effect," and not one which, through inadvertence or ignorance, or haste, has been mistakenly, though honestly, issued without a compliance with the law.

No court would convict the party failing to affix the stamp on this mortgage under the proof here exhibited, as it is clearly shown it was omitted with no fraudulent intent. Is it not then absurd to say the mortgagee shall lose the benefit of the mortgage when no willful *delictum* is established against either party? Such a judgment would outrage the sense of justice of every man.

Appellant claims, that although the appellees did all the law required of them to cure the defect in the mortgage by the intervention of the collector, still before he acted, rights had been acquired by the judgment creditor, which are protected by the last clause of Section 158, which is to the effect "that no right acquired in good faith before the stamping of such instrument or copy thereof, and the recording thereof as herein provided if such record be acquired by law, shall in any manner be affected by such stamping as aforesaid."

The first inquiry here is, what is the effect of a restamping by the collector? Clearly, it seems to us, to make the mortgage valid from its inception—it is made valid by this section "to be used in all courts and places in the same manner and with like effect as if the instrument had been originally stamped."

On the very day Hilborn placed the first stamp upon the mortgage, it having been in the office for record one week, appellant levied the execution upon the property described in it, and the day before, the mortgage had been seen in the office and read by the plaintiff in the execution. He therefore knew before he levied his execution, there was a mortgage filed for record, which the laws of this State regarded as valid, and if defective for the want of a stamp, he also knew that defect could be remedied, and his observation and knowledge of such transactions might have told him the omission of a stamp was accidental, and not with a design to defraud the government.

A purchase of an article in good faith, or a right acquired in good faith, is understood to be a right acquired without any notice of an adverse claim. Here the party had actual notice of the existence of a mortgage prior in time to his lien, and valid by the laws of this State, and we do not perceive how he can be helped by this clause in the section.

Another point is made by appellant, that under our chattel mortgage act, the deed must be actually spread upon the record before it can operate as notice and the case of *Porter* v. *Dement,* 35 Ill., 478, and *Forest* v. *Tinkham,* 20 id. 141, referred to in support of the position.

The first case turned entirely upon the effect to be given to a record of a copy of a chattel mortgage, nor can we see that the last has any bearing on the point made. In the last case it was simply decided, that an unrecorded mortgage and unacknowledged, though obligatory upon the parties, was void to third persons, whether filing such a paper for record is not equivalent to recording is not decided.

Section 2 of the chattel mortgage act provides, that any mortgage of personal property so certified, shall be admitted to record by the recorder of the county in which the mortgagor shall reside at the time when the same is made, acknowledged and recorded. So with deeds or mortgages of real property; the recorder is required to keep a book in which he shall enter every deed or writing brought to his office to be recorded, mentioning the date, the parties, and the place where the lands are situated, dating the entry on the day on which the deed or writing was brought to his office; and he must record them in regular succession, according to the priority of time of their being brought into the office.

Under this requirement, this Court held, in *Merrick* v. *Wallace,* 19 Ill. 486, that a party performs his duty by leaving his deed for record with the proper officer, and we see no reason why the same rule should not apply to chattel mortgages. In this case the mortgage was filed in the recorder's office, on the 14th of June, but not reached in the order of time to be recorded until the 21st of June. From the 14th of June, it was to all intents and purposes a record, and notice to subsequent purchasers and incumbrancers. Believing the merits of this case to be wholly with the appellees, and that the mortgage was a valid instrument under the laws of this State, and of which the plaintiff in the execution, whom appellant represents, had legal and actual notice, it would be unjust to give him preference over the mortgagees, under the circumstances of this case, and we must affirm the judgment.

Judgment affirmed.

Mr. Justice Lawrence, dissenting. I do not understand either counsel or the majority of the Court to deny that Congress has the power to impose what is known as a stamp tax. Conceding this, it follows, in my judgment, that that body has also the incidental power of declaring the penalty for failure to affix a stamp, which penalty may be a fine or the avoidance of the unstamped instrument, or both. Only by recognizing this incidental power, can the power to tax by means of stamps be made effective. I, therefore, dissent from the opinion of the majority of the Court upon this important question.—*Chicago Legal News.*

IRR v.IX, April 24, 1869, pp.129-31

Circular No. 73.

Concerning Affixing and Cancelling of Stamps.

Treasury Department.
Office of Internal Revenue.
Washington, April 23, 1869.

In all cases where an adhesive stamp shall hereafter be used, except as may be otherwise provided, the person using or affixing the same to the instrument, matter, or thing to be taxed, shall so affix the stamp or stamps denoting the tax that the entire surface of *each* stamp so affixed shall be exposed to view, and shall cancel the same by writing or imprinting in a legible manner, *with ink* upon *each* stamp so used, the initials of his name and the date upon which the same shall be affixed, or by such mechanical means as the Commissioner may hereafter prescribe and require, in order that such cancelled stamp or stamps cannot again be used.

So much of the above order as applies to the *exposure of the entire surface of each stamp* used will apply to all of the stamps prescribed by or under the internal revenue laws, but the *cancellation* of stamps for spirits and tobacco and proprietary stamps from private dies will remain as heretofore prescribed by law or regulations.

The attention of all internal revenue officers, and the public generally, is called to the provisions of section 2 of the act of April 10, 1869, which provides, "That section one hundred and fifty-five of the act entitled 'An act to provide internal revenue to support the government, to pay interest on the public debt, and for other purposes,' approved June thirtieth, eighteen hundred and sixty-four, as amended by the ninth section of the act of July thirteenth, eighteen hundred and sixty-six, be further amended by adding thereto the following: And the fact that any adhesive stamp so bought, sold, offered for sale, used, or had in possession as aforesaid, has been washed or restored by removing or altering the canceling or defacing marks thereon, shall be *prima facie* proof that such stamp has been once used and removed by the possessor thereof from some vellum, parchment, paper, instrument, or writing charged with taxes imposed by law, in violation of the provisions of this section."

The punishment imposed by the above amended section is a "fine not exceeding one thousand dollars, or imprisonment and confinement to hard labor not exceeding five years, or both, at the discretion of the court."

C. Delano,
Commissioner.

IRR v.IX, May 8, 1869, p.14

Stamp Tax on Shipping Articles.

A question under the stamp act was recently raised before Commissioner Wilkins. Three seamen libelled the steamer *Susan Ward* for wages. In defence the captain of the steamer claimed that the men were acting under shipping articles, and that the time for which they were hired not having expired the men were not legally entitled to their wages. The articles were produced in court, and showed the signatures of the men. Assistant District Attorney Finney, for the seamen, claimed that the articles were invalid, for the reason that they were not properly stamped. They showed a single five cent stamp, but it was claimed by the Assistant District Attorney that the agreement being between the captain and each man individually, was to be regarded as so many separate specific contracts, and that therefore a stamp was required for each seaman bound by it. The case was very fully argued, *pro* and *con,* and after mature deliberation the commissioner decided in favor of the ground taken by the Assistant District Attorney, that a stamp was required for each signature. The instrument in court was, therefore, held invalid, and a decision was rendered in favor of the libellants. The case is different with stevedores, who work under a foreman, who makes the contract himself for the gang. The contract is with the foreman, and hence but a single stamp is required. But in the case of seamen each man is regarded as making the contract for himself.—*Detroit Post.*

IRR v.X, October 9, 1869, p.116

Bond of State Officers Not Void for Want of U.S. Revenue Stamp.

An opinion was rendered in the Supreme Court of Indiana on the 24th ultimo, on a case from Wells County, where suit was brought upon the bond of a county officer. One of the grounds of defence was that the bond was not stamped as required by law, and was therefore void.

The Court, in an opinion pronounced by Judge Ray, after arguing the question at great length, decided that the General Government has no power to impose such a tax upon officers of a State Government, and that the bond of a county officer cannot be rendered void and of no effect by a failure to stamp it. The case of *Dobbins* v. *The Commissioner of Erie County* (16 Peters, 435) is cited, in which the argument against the right of a State to tax the salary of an officer of the United States, is that under the Constitution the General Government has the right to employ its officers and agents to execute its laws and fix its compensation for the discharge of those services, and that this being a sovereign power, it can not be controlled by the State. So the State has, under the same Constitution, the right to perpetuate itself, to employ its officers to execute its laws and fix their compensation. Again, it is said the taxation of the office or its salary is in effect a tax upon the United States Government. If so, a tax upon the State officers is to that extent a tax upon the State, and Congress can only impose such a tax by apportionment directly. True, the amount exacted is small. So it was in the case of the Government officer whose office was appraised for taxation. But the power to exact one dollar involves the power to levy one thousand. The power to tax involves the power to destroy.

IRR v.X, December 18, 1869, p.198

The Commissioner of Internal Revenue, in view of the large probable loss to the revenue by the second use of stamps on the various kinds of documents and articles requiring the same, after washing off the ink cancellation, has determined, upon a full investigation and report by a committee of gentlemen from his office, to try the efficiency of other mechanical means of cancellation in the place of the present ribbon-printing stamp machine. The two machines reported favorably upon by the committee are those of Mr. Wheeler, of New York City, and Mr. Thompson, of Buffalo, New York. After the Commissioner is informed by these parties about when they can begin to furnish the public with the machines, a time will be set for the discontinuance of the use of the "ribbon machine," and the substitution of either of the above two, at the option of the purchasers, until further orders.

IRR v.XI, January 1, 1870, p.2

Recent Decisions in State Courts.

The *American Law Review* for January, Little, Brown & Co., contains articles on Proximate and Remote Cause, Warranty of Seaworthiness in Time Policies, The Law of Insanity, Campbell's Lives of Lyndhurst and Brougham, and its usual digests and reviews. From these last we extract the following:

Sime v. *Howard,* 4 Nev. 473.—A conveyed land to B under a verbal agreement that on demand B should reconvey one-half. B mortgaged it to plaintiffs, who brought suit to foreclose. After the commencement of the suit B executed a declaration in writing of the trust which was not stamped. Held, that the writing did not require any stamp under the provisions of the United States statute of 1867, and was good evidence of the trust.

In the case of *Wigham* v. *Pickett,* S. C. Ala., quoted in the *Law Times,* it was held that a promissory note, made since the 30th day of June, 1864, is not provided for in the act of Congress of that date, and cannot be stamped in open court, and, thus stamped, read as evidence to the jury. But such note is not void, unless it was left unstamped at the time it was made with the intent to defraud the Government of its revenue. Such fraudulent intent will not be presumed, but must be proved, as any other fraud is proved. Such note may be made available, as evidence, by having it stamped by the Collector of the Revenue of the proper district, under section 158 of said act.

Howe v. *Carpenter,* 53 Barb. 382.—Under the Stamp Act of June 30, 1864, an unstamped contract is void unless the person producing it disproves intent to evade the provisions of the act.

Wayman v. *Torreyson,* 4 Nev. 124.—The defendant, in March, 1866, executed his promissory note to the plaintiff's intestate, unstamped. After the death of the promisee, the defendant, on request, affixed the proper stamps, but not in the manner prescribed in the act of Congress of March 3, 1865. Held, that the note was void.

IRR v.XI, January 15, 1870, pp.22-3

Complaints are being made of a scarcity of revenue stamps in country districts. A letter from Maine to the *Independent* attributes the scarcity to the fact that no commission is allowed to the purchasers of stamps to any less amount than fifty dollars. Country traders do not care to purchase so large a quantity of revenue stamps at a time, and as there are no authorized agents for their sale, as in the case of postage stamps, the result is a supply entirely inadequate to the demand, and a consequent disregard of their use. The writer asserts that fifty per cent of the business documents which require stamps are given and made without them. He proposes as a remedy for this state of affairs either that a supply of stamps be kept at the assessors' offices, post offices, or at the national banks and that traders be notified of this fact and allowed five per cent commission on all amounts purchased to sell again, or that a special agent be appointed for their sale in every village where there is a postmaster. Either or both of these recommendations thoroughly executed would, the writer thinks, double or triple the sale of revenue stamps in three months, greatly to the profit of the Government.

IRR v.XI, January 29, 1870, p.33

We have received a letter from an Assistant Assessor in Massachusetts complaining of the scarcity of revenue stamps in his district, and endorsing the letter from Maine on that subject which we referred to in our last number [Ed. note: *IRR* v.XI, January 29, 1870, p.33]. It seems by this that the scarcity is not confined to the backwoods.

IRR v.XI, February 5, 1870, p.44

46.—A Power of Attorney Issued by a Government Officer Requires No Stamp.

The Commissioner of Internal Revenue states that, under the 9th section of the act of July 13, 1866, "a power of attorney issued by one Government officer, in his official capacity, whether to another Government officer or to a private individual, requires no stamp." (Letter to Assistant Treasurer U.S., New Orleans, La., December 7, 1869.)

IRR v.XI, February 12, 1870, p.53

Distribution of Internal Revenue Stamps.

To the Editor of the Internal Revenue Record.

Sir: Being an Assistant Assessor of Internal Revenue, assessing legacies and successions of the Fourth District of North Carolina, I have a fine opportunity of knowing the wants of the people of this district, especially the wants in anywise pertaining to matters of revenue.

I heartily agree with the Maine correspondent of the *Independent* [Ed. note: *IRR* v.XI, January 29, 1870, p.33] in the importance of distributing revenue stamps by some means, amply satisfying the demands of the people for them. I believe, by a proper distribution of stamps, the revenue would be considerably enhanced. Every convenience must be offered the people, and there must also be a rigid enforcement of the laws, in order that the Government may receive its just dues; for in all ages and in all governments, there has been a disposition to evade revenue laws upon the slightest pretext. This disposition is equally applicable to and prevalent in our Government. It is no uncommon thing to hear one say, "I have no stamp to put on it." "Well," says the other, "it makes no difference, for I don't expect to sue you." This is no infrequent saying. I may justly say, it is all the saying among private individuals about their own individual matters. This arises in most cases, not from a disinclination to pay the value of a revenue stamp, but the trouble and inconvenience attached to obtaining it. There is, no doubt, a sufficient amount of revenue stamps issued by the Department to supply demand; but they are improperly distributed; and to remedy this evil some system should be adopted, giving a uniform and liberal distribution of stamps in every part of the country. To do this, the plans suggested by the writer are very considerate. I should however suggest (as every branch of the Government should run in and through their legitimate and proper channels) that revenue stamps be placed in the hands of revenue officers, namely, Assessors and their assistants, Collectors and their deputies, for distribution, and none others, allowing purchasers of revenue stamps ten per centum discount for any amount purchased over and above ten dollars worth. By this means the country would be at once supplied with revenue stamps, and many dollars saved to the Government.

James B. Mason,
Chapel Hill,
February 3, 1870.

IRR v.XI, February 12, 1870, p.55

Traffic In and Possession Of Internal Revenue Stamps.

Office of Internal Revenue,
Washington, February 10, 1870.

Geo. F. Heath, Esq., Poultney, Vt.

Sir: In answer to the inquiries in your letter of the 11th ult., I have to say that neither the possession, use, nor traffic in internal revenue stamps, cancelled or uncancelled, otherwise than for legitimate revenue purposes, is provided for or contemplated by the law under which the stamps are issued, but is, in all cases, contrary to the spirit of those laws, and in some cases is expressly forbidden by them. . . . [Ed. note: There follows a long section on stamps for distilled spirits, cigars, tobacco, snuff and beer] . . . As to proprietary revenue stamps from private dies, Section 156 of the act of June 30, 1864, prescribes that they "shall be so affixed on the box, bottle, or package, that in opening the same, or using the contents thereof, the said stamp shall be effectually destroyed," and a penalty is prescribed for failure to do so.

The same section further provides that any person who shall fraudulently obtain or use any such stamps or the designs therefor, "or any engraver who shall sell or give away said stamps," "shall be deemed guilty of a felony," and shall be subject to prescribed penalties, fines and forfeitures.

As to other stamps on articles named in schedule C (of the Compilation, in 1867, of Internal Revenue Laws, p.129), and as to the stamps for documents (schedule B, Ibid., p.126), while I do not find any penalty expressly prescribed by law for having such stamps in possession, cancelled, it is nevertheless evident from all the provisions of the laws relating to these stamps that they are not intended to be made articles of traffic, or of use, otherwise than for the prescribed revenue purposes.

In the case of document stamps, the Government has been largely defrauded by the repeated use of such stamps, through failure to cancel them, and also by their being washed and restored after cancelment; in view of which fact Congress passed the act of April 10, 1869, providing that the possession of a stamp which has been washed or restored shall be *prima facie* proof that such stamp has been once used and removed, *by the possessor thereof,* from some instrument or writing charged with stamp taxes.

While I have no disposition to unnecessarily interfere with the gratification of that taste which prompts the making of collections of stamps, I cannot, consistently with my views of official duty, encourage the indulgence of this taste in the collection of stamps which represent internal revenue.

Of course nothing in this letter is intended to discourage the possession of new unused document stamps by taxpayers for their own use, or by dealers who have purchased such stamps for retail sale as authorized by law. Such possession is for revenue purposes, and is not only unobjectionable, but to be encouraged.

Respectfully yours,
C. Delano,
Commissioner.

IRR v.XI, February 19, 1870, pp.57-8

Circular No. 82.—Prescribing the Method of Cancelling Adhesive Stamps Used Upon Instruments, Documents, Writings, and Papers Mentioned and Described in Schedule B.

Office of Internal Revenue,
Washington, February 10, 1870.

Section 157 of the act of June 30, 1864, is as follows: "*And be it further enacted,* That the Commissioner of Internal Revenue be, and he is hereby, authorized to prescribe such method for the cancellation of stamps, as substitute for or in addition to the method now prescribed by law, as he may deem expedient and effectual. And he is further authorized, in his discretion, to make the application of such method imperative upon the manufacturers of proprietary articles, or articles included in Schedule C, and upon stamps of a nominal value exceeding twenty-five cents."

Owing to the extensive frauds committed upon the revenues by the washing, restoration, and re-use of such internal revenue adhesive stamps as have been used and cancelled by the machine known as the ribbon stamp, it is hereby ordered and prescribed, that on and after May 1, 1870, all adhesive stamps used upon the instruments, documents, writings, and papers, mentioned and described in Schedule B of the Internal Revenue Laws, shall be cancelled by the person affixing the same, either by writing upon each and every stamp, *in ink,* the initials of his name, and the date (year, month, and day) upon which the same is attached or used, or by cutting and cancelling the same with the machine called "Wheeler's Patent Canceller," or such other machine or instrument as may hereafter be designated and prescribed by said Commissioner; and that no other method of cancelling such stamps, employed on or after that date, shall be recognized as legal and sufficient, until otherwise prescribed and ordered.

C. Delano,
Commissioner.

IRR v.XI, February 19, 1870, p.58

Cancelling Stamp.—*We shall be prepared to fill orders for Wheeler's Patent Cancelling Stamp (adopted by the Government) after April 15. Price* $10.

In accordance with the terms of Circular No. 82, issued from the office of Internal Revenue, February 10, 1870, Commissioner Delano has prescribed the following as the machines which may be used on and after May 1, 1870, for the purpose of cancelling adhesive stamps used upon instruments, documents, writings, and papers mentioned and described in Schedule B, Internal Revenue Laws, viz.:

Wheeler's Patent Canceller.
E. D. Chamberlain's Cutting and Dating Stamp.
Holt's Self-Inking Canceller.
Hill's Patent Revenue Cancelling Machine.

IRR v.XI, April 16, 1870, p.121

U.S. District Court—E. D. of Michigan.

United States v. *C. G. Learned and F. S. Ayres, impleaded with W. Wisnall.*

(Before Judge Longyear.)

On a motion by the defendant's counsel (Mr. G. V. N. Lothrop) to set aside a verdict of guilty rendered by a jury in this court in March, and for a new trial on account of errors and omissions in the charge to the jury. The facts in the matter are as follows: The defendants did business at Port Austin, and from a time anterior to the passage of the first internal revenue law were in the habit of issuing due bills to the men, of which the one upon which this case is founded read as follows:

Port Austin, Mich. No. 1,550.
October 28, 1868.
Due the bearer, or J. L. Coy, Seven Dollars, in merchandise out of our store.
(Signed) Ayers, Learned & Winsall,
Van Wart.

These due bills were not stamped, and the firm were, therefore, prosecuted for a violation of the revenue law, the Government taking the ground that they were contracts and should be stamped accordingly. In the testimony, it was shown that large numbers of these were issued by the firm, of which about one-fourth were used merely as vouchers in the store, while three-fourths went into actual circulation and were frequently traded off by the men to third parties. The defendants admitted that they were intentionally issued unstamped, and while counsel in the course of the argument stated that the firm did not believe that they came within the scope of the law, yet in the evidence no explanation of the omission of the stamps was given. The opinion of Judge Longyear was elaborate and lengthy. The following is the portion in which the legal points bearing upon the case are summed up:

Is the instrument mentioned in the indictment such an one as was required by the internal revenue law to be stamped.

If covered by the law at all, it is covered by the first clause of schedule B, under the head of "Agreement or Contract" (3 Stat., 208). The question then resolves itself simply into this: Is it an agreement or contract? The answer to this question seems too apparent to admit of argument. But as the question is presented, I shall proceed to consider it:

First. Upon the face of the instrument, the word "due" imports a consideration, an indebtedness; it is between parties capable of contracting named in the instrument; the amount of the indebtedness or consideration is fixed and definite; the manner and place of payment is clearly defined; a promise to pay is clearly implied; and it was signed by the defendants and delivered. Here are all the elements of a contract, and is pronounced to be such by the laws of the land. An action could be maintained upon it without any other proof than that of demand and refusal.

Second. Upon matters outside of the instrument: The defendants owed Coy the amount in money, for work and labor; the due bill was charged to Coy as so much money and thereby cancelled the indebtedness in that form; there was an actual consideration. It was due on open account, in money; it became due on written contract, in merchandise. Here was a new undertaking on both sides, as to the manner of payment. It is true, it was testified by one of the bookkeepers, that if any of these due bills should have been brought back and delivered up by the man to whom it was payable, he would, if requested, cancel it and credit it back to the man in his account, and so change the obligation back to a cash obligation; but there was no pretence that there was any such agreement or understanding with the men, and even if there had been it could not change the character of the instrument so long as it was out, as it was not expressed upon its face. Neither could any such verbal understanding be relied on to change the written agreement.

Therefore, by the law relating to contracts the instrument was an agreement, and by the internal revenue law it was required to be stamped.

Again, that every man is presumed to know the law; and ignorance of the law is no excuse, as general propositions are too well established to admit of dispute, and their correctness is virtually conceded by defendant's counsel. Now, apply these maxims to this case. It was clearly proven, in fact, it is conceded, that defendants authorized the instrument to be made and delivered in the form and manner in which it was made and delivered, and of course they knew it was so issued. As we have already seen, by the law relating to contracts, the instrument, by having been so made and delivered, became and was an agreement or contract. The defendants are presumed to have known this law. Therefore, knowing, as they did, all the facts constituting the instrument an agreement, they are presumed to have known it was such. Again, the instrument being an agreement, the internal revenue law made it the duty of the defendants to stamp it. Therefore, knowing, as we have seen, that it was an agreement, the defendants are presumed to have known that such was their duty.

Next, as to the intent: It is a maxim of the law that every man must be presumed to intend the necessary, legal, or legitimate consequences of his acts. In this case, the omission of a stamp was a violation or evasion of the internal revenue law. Therefore, the defendants knowing the law, their omission to obey it must be presumed, in the absence of explanation, to have been with intent to evade its provisions. It has been so held in two recent cases in the State of New York, in each of which this precise question was under consideration. (See Beebe v. Hutton, 27 Barb., S. C., Rep. 187 and 193; and Howe v. Carpenter, 53 *ib.*, 382, 4, 5.) In the case of U.S. v. Conner, 3, McLean's Rep. 574, the same question was under consideration. Conner was prosecuted under the Bankrupt Act of 1841, for perjury, in swearing to a false schedule of property with intent to defraud his creditors. In deciding the case, Judge McLean makes use of this language: "The maxim is admitted that ignorance of the law constitutes no excuse for the commission of a crime." * * * "To constitute perjury under the law" (the bankruptcy law above noticed) "the false schedule must have been made corruptly by the bankrupt and with intent to defraud his creditors. The falsity of the schedule being established, the mitigating circumstances must be shown by the defendant; and if no excuse be proved, the fraudulent intent will be inferred from the act, it being *prima facie* in violation of the law."

So too, in Cone v. Bradford, 9 Met., 272, cited by defendant's counsel, the knowledge of defendant that he had not the right to vote was treated as a presumption to be rebutted by him, the fact that he had no such right having been first established. The distinction between the two classes of cases, viz.; that in which the intent will not be presumed, and that in which it will be, is clearly drawn in 3 Gr. Ev., sec. 13, quoting Ld. Mansfield in Rex v. Woodfall, 5 Burr, 2,667, in the following language: "When an act in itself indifferent becomes criminal if done with a particular intent, then the intent must be proved and found; but when the act is in itself unlawful, the proof of justification or excuse lies on the defendant, and in failure thereof the law implies a criminal intent."

In this case the omission of the stamp was an unlawful act—an evasion of the provisions of the internal revenue law—and it must be deemed presumptively so intended. It comes clearly within that class of cases in which proof of justfication or excuse lies on the party transgressing.

A request of defendants, which was refused by the court, was in the following words:

"3. That if the defendants did not understand or believe that the paper in this case was a contract, but supposed it was only a voucher, then the defendants are not liable."

It might suffice to sustain the refusal to charge as above requested, to simply state the fact that there was no evidence in the case as to what the understanding or belief of the defendants was in relation to the character of the particular paper in question, or even as to the class of paper to which it belonged, and therefore it might have misled the jury to have submitted such a question to them. It may be said, however, that evidence of their understanding and belief as to the character of the paper is to be found in presumptions arising from their course of business in relating to this class of paper, as proven on the trial. Relying upon such presumptions alone for proof of what defendant's understanding and belief in this respect was, the case would stand as follows: So far as this class of paper was actually used as vouchers merely between the bookkeeper and clerks in the store, the defendants would be presumed to have understood and believed them to be vouchers merely, and not contracts; but so far as such paper was delivered to the parties and thereby became outstanding evidence of indebtedness and agreements to pay as therein specified, the defendants must be presumed to have understood and believed them to be what they actually were, contracts, and this latter presumption gives great force from two other facts in the case: 1st. The fact that a large proportion of these papers—the head clerk in the store says three-fourths of them—were delivered to the parties, and that only a small proportion of them were used as vouchers merely from the bookkeeper to the clerks in the store. 2d. The use of the word "bearer" in the instrument. Although that word has no effect to make the paper negotiable, yet it may be resorted to arrive at the intent, belief, or understanding of the parties as to the use to be made of the paper. That word can be of no possible use in a paper to be used as a voucher merely, but it is just the word the parties would use if they intended the paper for circulation, however mistaken they may have been as to its legal effect. It is in proof, also, that these papers did circulate, and were bought and sold to a considerable extent, to the knowledge of defendants. Presumptions, conclusions, and inferences must always be consistent, and in harmony with the facts upon which they are founded and from which they are drawn.

It might not have been error to have charged as requested, but if the Court had so charged he would have felt compelled at the same time to charge further as above stated, which would have rendered the charge requested worse than nugatory.

Therefore, whether the refusal to give this charge was right or wrong, it has worked the defendants no injury, and could not in any event constitute ground for new trial.

But it is claimed on behalf of the defendants that such understanding and belief on their part as to the character of the paper in question was induced by or was the result of their construction of the law in its application to said paper, and that therefore the charge should have been given as requested, or in other words, that notwithstanding that the defendants knew all the facts in the case, and notwithstanding that the law does make the paper a contract and liable to be stamped, yet if the defendants so construct the law for themselves as to lead them to understand and believe that said paper was not a contract, and therefore not required to be stamped, then the intent to evade the provisions of the law did not exist, and they are not liable.

In the first place, this proposition has no standing in the proofs. There was no evidence whatever as to what construction the defendants put upon the law, or that they in fact put any construction whatever upon it.

The argument seems to be, 1. That such construction of the law is a reasonable construction. 2. The action of the defendants in omitting the stamp is consistent with such construction. 3. Therefore, they must be presumed to have adopted it. A moment's reflection will show the entire fallacy of this argument. It has already been shown that such construction of the law is not correct, and therefore it is not reasonable, and the first proposition falls to the ground, and with it of course the second and third.

But aside from this, the proposition is not a sound one in law. No man has a right to set up a construction of the law for himself, and then plead it in justification of his violation of the law (see Judge Blatchford's opinion in U.S. v. A quantity of distilled spirits, etc., Internal Revenue Record, 4). The distinction between what will and what will not excuse, is very clearly drawn in McGuire v. The State, 7 Hump., 56. Applying the principles here and elsewhere laid down to this case, if the defendants knew, as they did know, of the existence of the state of facts which made the instrument liable to a stamp, and yet believed that the instrument was not so liable in point of law, such ignorance of the law will not excuse them. With a full knowledge of all the facts before them, and of the consequences of a violation of the law, they assumed to construe the law for themselves, and having misconstrued it they must abide the consequences.

In the case of U.S. v. Comer, 3 McLean, 574 (above cited), cited also by defendant's counsel, the facts relied on to rebut the intent to defraud etc., were: 1. That defendant stated the facts fully to counsel for advice in the premises; 2. That he was advised by said counsel on such statement as matter of law, that the omission complained of was not contrary to the law claimed to have been violated; and, 3. That the defendant acted upon the advice so obtained, in making out and swearing to his schedule; and this was allowed as tending to rebut the presumption of intent to violate the law for the reason as stated by the judge in his opinion, that "the defendant thereby showed a desire to conform to the law." That is very different from a case like the present, in which the defendants are claimed to have simply set up a construction of the law for themselves, without the aid of counsel or legal advice, or showing in any manner a desire to conform to the law. If parties may do this and thus shield themselves from violations of law, then it is far safer for them never to take advice.

In view of the importance of these questions to the Government and to the defendants, as well in their application to the case now under consideration as to other like cases that may hereafter arise, I have given them a careful consideration, with an earnest desire and determination to arrive at correct conclusions, and have settled down upon the conclusions above given with a feeling of confidence that they are correct.

IRR v.XI, May 7, 1870, pp.149-50

No Cancelling Machines Required for Document Stamps.

Office of Internal Revenue,
Washington, May 9, 1870.

George Q. Erskine, Esq., Collector First District, Milwaukee, Wisconsin.

Sir: Messrs. Terry & Cleaver, stationers and bookbinders at 358 Water Street, Milwaukee, have written inquiring "whether the new patent canceller is required on the two-cent revenue stamps," and stating that you have given it as your opinion that it is not.

They have been referred to you, and you are informed that no cancelling machine or instrument is *required* upon any document stamp of any denomination.

The statute (Section 157) *authorizes* the Commissioner of Internal Revenue to make the application of such method of cancellation as he may prescribe *imperative* "upon stamps of a nominal value exceeding twenty-five cents each."

This authority to make some method imperative he has not yet exercised. No person is required to use a machine of any kind for cancelling stamps used on documents, instruments, and papers under Schedule B. One may use *pen and ink* for any and all denominations of them if he chooses. What has been prescribed is simply this: that if *any* machine at all is used it must be one of those prescribed by the Commissioner. No other machine of any kind can be used for cancellation of such stamps of any denomination, whether twenty-five cents in nominal value or less; but this deprives no one of the right to discard all machines and use pen and ink if he chooses.

You will therefore see that neither the ribbon stamp, nor any other machine not prescribed by the Commissioner, is used in your district, upon such stamps *of any denomination*. You should also instruct persons that the use of the prescribed machines is entirely optional with them, but that the choice lies between the machines prescribed and pen and ink.

J. W. Douglass,
Acting Commissioner.

IRR v.XI, May 14, 1870, p.153

Supplement No. 4, to Circular No. 82, Prescribing the Method of Cancelling Adhesive Stamps Used Upon Instruments, Documents, Writings, and Papers Mentioned and Described in Schedule B.

Office of Internal Revenue,
Washington, July 15, 1870.

In accordance with the terms of Circular No. 82, reference to which is hereby made, and by virtue of the authority conferred upon me by section 157 of the act of June 30, 1864, I hereby prescribe the following method of cancelling adhesive stamps used upon the instruments, documents, writings, and papers mentioned and described in Schedule B of the Internal Revenue laws, to wit: The cutting and cancelling the same by a machine which shall affix the date, and so cut and deface the stamp as to render it manifestly unfit for reuse, and at the same time shall not so deface the stamp as to prevent its denomination and genuineness from being readily determined.

All instruments used in making cancellations according to this method, must be so constructed that an ordinary blow of the hand or pressure by lever will, at one operation, produce the required cancellation.

Any machine producing a perfect cancellation, according to the method herein prescribed, may be used.

The Commissioner reserves to himself the right to prohibit the use of any machine which, in his opinion, does not conform to the above requirement, and collectors and assessors are hereby instructed to forward a specimen of the cancellation performed by each and every machine, which shall from time to time be used in their districts, for examination at this office.

The use of any cancelling machines which simply imprint the initials and date, without cutting the stamp as herein required, has been and is hereby prohibited. Officers of this Bureau should report all cases in which this regulation is violated.

Cancellations by pen and ink are authorized as heretofore.

C. Delano,
Commissioner.

IRR v.XII, July 23, 1870, p.30

Recent Revenue Decisions.

There are two or three recent decisions relative to the admissibility in evidence of unstamped instruments that are worthy of notice. In Schermerhorn v. Burgess (55 Barb., 422), the question in point was whether the collector of the district in which the plaintiff—the holder of a promissory note—lived, or the collector of the district in which the defendant, the maker of the note, lived, was the proper person to affix the stamp to an unstamped instrument. The court held that the collector of the plaintiff's district was the one. The court remarked that it did not see that any stamp was necessary upon the note, either for the purpose of its being used as evidence upon the trial, or otherwise, in view of the express finding of the referee that the stamp was omitted by mistake and without intent to evade the law. But this was clearly *obiter*. The other cases are Bunker v. Green (48 Illinois, 243), and The United States Express Co. v. Haines (*Id.* 248), in both of which the question was directly in point, and the court held that the acts of Congress rendering invalid as evidence instruments not stamped are applicable only when such instruments are offered as evidence in the courts of the United States, and that the Legislature of the State is the only legitimate authority to declare what shall be evidence in the State courts. The same court has twice before made the same decision in Latham v. Smith (45 Ill., 29), and Craig v. Dimock (47 Ill., 308); and the Supreme Judicial Court of Massachusetts has also twice given a similar construction to the act—Carpenter v. Snelling (97 Mass., 452), Lynch v. Morse (*Id.* 458).—*Albany Law Journal.*

IRR v.XII, October 1, 1870, p.111

Where an agreement never had any revenue stamp affixed to it, and when it was offered in evidence and objected to on that ground, there was no offer to show that the proper stamp was omitted by mistake, inadvertence, or ignorance, or any other excuse given for the omission, and no offer was made to then affix the stamp; it was held that agreement was invalid, and was therefore properly excluded. (Davy v. Morgan, 56 Barbour. See Broker; Common Carrier, 5.)

IRR v.XII, October 1, 1870, p.111

Instructions As To the Proper Action To Be Taken in Regard to Instruments Which Have Been Issued Unstamped or Insufficiently Stamped.

Office of Internal Revenue,
Washington, October 25, 1870.

Otis F. Presbrey, Esq., Supervisor Internal Revenue, Washington, D.C.

Sir: In your letter of the 20th instant you state that you have caused an investigation to be made of the various records in the county clerk's offices within the district of which you are supervisor, and have obtained lists of the deeds, bonds, mortgages, etc., therein recorded without having been properly stamped. You inquire what action shall be taken in regard to these and all other instruments which have been issued unstamped or insufficiently stamped.

I reply: 1st. Under the provisions of section 158 of the act of June 30, 1864, as amended by section 9 of the act of July 13, 1866, and section 5 of the act of July 14, 1870, an instrument issued unstamped at a time when and in a place where no collection district was established, may be stamped by the party who issued it, or by any party having an interest therein, at any time prior to January 1, 1872, and the legal effect of the stamp thus affixed will be the same as though affixed by the proper collector.

2d. Collectors are authorized by said section, so amended, to affix stamps to all instruments issued unstamped or insufficiently stamped, upon payment of the price of the stamp required by law, a penalty of "double the amount remaining unpaid, but in no case less than five dollars," and, "where the whole amount of the tax denoted by the stamp required shall exceed the sum of fifty dollars, upon payment also of interest at the rate of six per centum on said tax from the day on which such stamp ought to have been affixed." They are also authorized by the same amended section, as construed by this office, to remit the penalty at any time, from July 14, 1870, to August 1, 1872, in all cases where it shall be shown to their satisfaction that the instrument or instruments presented to them were issued without the necessary stamp by reason of accident, mistake, inadvertence, or urgent necessity, and without any willful design to defraud the United States of the duty, or to evade or delay the payment thereof. I am aware that this ruling is not in strict accordance with the letter of the statute, but it agrees with what is positively known to have been the intention of Congress. You will please call the attention of the various collectors and assessors throughout your district, and through them the attention of all deputy collectors and assistant assessors, to the provisions of the law upon this point, and will direct them to take special care to bring said provisions to the knowledge of the people, and to urge the stamping of all instruments issued without the necessary stamps. As already stated, instruments issued at a time when and in a place where no collection district was established, may now be stamped by any person having an interest therein. For the date of the first establishment of such districts in the States lately in insurrection, you are referred to Series 2, No. 10, page 10.

In all cases where an instrument thus stamped has been recorded, it should either be recorded anew, or the fact that the error has been corrected should be noted upon the margin of the record, as provided in section 158.

The amendment of July 14, 1870, was made for the purpose of enabling parties to make their deeds, bonds, mortgages, notes, etc., valid, without the payment of severe penalties. It is believed that with due care upon the part of officers of this bureau in calling attention to this matter, much inconvenience and loss may be saved to persons holding such instruments, and no inconsiderable revenue be secured to the Government.

In order the more effectually to call attention to this subject, I shall cause this letter to be published in the Internal Revenue Record.

C. Delano,
Commissioner.

IRR v.XII, October 29, 1870, pp.141-2

Unstamped Instruments.
From the American Law Register, August, 1871.

With reference to this subject of great and growing importance it is purposed in the present article briefly to notice, in one or two aspects, two leading features, viz.: First, the validity of an unstamped instrument as dependent upon the intent with which the stamp was omitted; and Second, the presumption as to this intent when the fact of the omission simply appears.

First. Section 158 of the Stamp Act provides: That any person or persons who shall make, sign, or issue, or who shall cause to be made, signed, or issued, any instrument, document, or paper of any kind or description whatsoever, or shall accept, negotiate, or pay, or cause to be accepted, negotiated, or paid, any bill of exchange, draft, or order, or promissory note for the payment of money, without the same being duly stamped, or having thereupon an adhesive stamp for denoting the tax chargeable thereon, and cancelled in the manner required by law, with intent to evade the provisions of this act, shall, for every such offence, forfeit the sum of fifty dollars, and such instrument, document or paper, bill, draft, order, or note, not being stamped according to law, shall be deemed invalid and of no effect.

That in some cases unstamped instruments are void under this section is clear but in just what instances depends upon the phrase "such instrument," etc. If these words be construed to have relation to the intent of the party making the omission, then whenever any document appears unstamped, its validity depends upon the question whether or not in that particular case there had been any intention to defraud the government. If, on the other hand, the term applies to every instrument which has not been stamped, then it is the *unstamped* instrument simply which is void. And both these constructions have been adopted by different courts.

Looking at the question outside of the authority of the various decisions, considering the section within itself, a close following of the grammatical rules for the construction of sentences seems to favor the former construction. Yet the true construction of course hinges on the intention of the makers of the act; and this intention should be followed though such construction seem contrary to the strict letter. (Minor v. Mechanics' Bank of Alexandria, 1 Pet. 64; Wilkinson v. Leland, 2 Id. 622.) And statutes of this nature are not penal in the sense that they must be strictly construed, but they are to receive a liberal interpretation to advance the intention. (United States v. Twenty-five Cases of Cloth, Crabbe 356; Taylor v. United States, 3 How. 197; Jortin v. Southeastern Railway, 6 De G. M. & G. 270.)

We may derive much light on the intended meaning of the section from the way in which it was made up. It is composed of sections 95 and 100 of the original act of 1862, revised by act of 1864, and amended by acts of 1865 and 1866.

Section 95 of act of 1862 provided: That if any person or persons shall make, sign, or issue, or cause to be made, signed, or issued, any instrument, document, or paper of any kind or description whatsoever, without the same being duly stamped for denoting the duty hereby imposed thereon, or without having thereupon an adhesive stamp to denote said duty, such person or persons shall incur a penalty of fifty dollars, and such instrument, document, or paper as aforesaid shall be deemed invalid and of no effect.

Section 100 of the same act provided: That if any person or persons shall make, sign, or issue, or cause to be made, signed, or issued, or shall accept or pay, or cause to be accepted or paid, with design to evade the payment of any stamp duty,* any bill of exchange, draft or order, or promissory

*The bill as originally drawn did not contain this clause, but it was inserted in the Senate and House on motion. Mr. Sheffeld, when making the motion in the House, remarked "that it would be very unjust to impose this heavy penalty on a person who might never have read the statute or known of its provisions." See Congressional Globe 1861-2, Part 2, page 1509.

note for the payment of money, liable to any of the duties imposed by this act, without the same being duly stamped, or having thereupon an adhesive stamp for denoting the duty hereby charged thereon, he, she, or they shall, for every bill, draft, order, or note, forfeit the sum of two hundred dollars.

In the thorough revision of 1864 these two sections were brought together; doing away with the distinction between the two classes of instruments in the amount of penalty imposed, and making it in all cases the larger sum of two hundred dollars. By the amendment of 1865 the penalty was again placed at fifty dollars; and by that of 1866 there was added after the terms "such instrument," etc., the phrase "not being stamped according to law."

It is to be observed with reference to the union of the two sections 95 and 100 in the new section 158, that it is but a reenactment of the old sections, and should, therefore, carry with it the construction which belonged to them. "It is common learning," says Metcalf, J., in Commonwealth v. Hartnett, 3 Gray, 451, "that the adjudged construction of the terms of a statute is enacted as well as the terms themselves, when an act, which has been passed by the legislature of one state or country, is afterwards passed by the legislature of another. So when the same legislature, in a later statute, use the terms of an earlier one which has received a judicial construction, that construction is to be given to the later statute." In changes of this nature the intention to alter the known construction of the old law must plainly appear, the presumption being in favor of the old construction. (McKenzie v. The State, 6 Eng. 594; Burnham v. Stevens, 33 N. H., 247; Hughes v. Farrar, 45 Me., 72; Conger v. Barker, 11 Ohio N.S., 1.) And even though alterations may have been made, if terms or phrases are employed which were used in old acts, the same meaning will be given them as in former legislation. (State v. Southwaite, 3 Zabr., 143; McKee v. McKee, 17 Md., 352; Myrick v. Hasey, 27 Me., 19; Whitmore v. Rood, 20 Vt., 49.)

The phraseology of the revised section 158 was substantially the same as that in the older sections 95 and 100. The outline of section 95 was retained, incorporating within it section 100, retaining the heavier penalty and with it its accompanying clause with reference to intent. Otherwise there was no material change. And can there be any doubt as to the meaning given to the phrase "such instrument," etc., in the earlier legislation? There is no room for any other than this: that *every unstamped* instrument is to be the invalid instrument. "It seems perfectly clear," say the Revenue Department (Dec. No. 34), "that by the provisions of section 95 the person who makes, etc., without affixing the stamp, incurs the penalty as aforesaid, and the instrument or document is invalid in consequence of such neglect" (Boutwell's Tax System 234); and again in Ruling No. 302, "On and after June 1, 1863, any instrument executed without the requisite stamp will for that cause be invalid." (Boutwell's Tax System, 351.)

The legislators plainly had in mind two very distinct ideas; first, that the stamp was to be an essential, legal part of the instrument, and that without it there would be no valid instrument; and second, that the person whose duty it was to affix the proper stamp should render himself liable to a penalty for omitting to discharge this duty, the penalty where heaviest depending upon the intent of the person. In other words, the *intent* was applicable to the *person* and the *penalty* for which he was to be liable, while the *validity* of the instrument was dependent simply upon the question whether it was *stamped or unstamped;* and "such instrument" having reference solely to the unstamped instrument.

Applying, then, the rules of law as above stated to this revision, as it appears in the light of the sections from which it was drawn, and the argument seems strong that the instrument which is unstamped from any cause is invalid. At least if the phraseology be ambiguous, as would appear to be the case from the fact of the conflict between the decisions, the presumption is in favor of such a construction. And, as if to add the legislative sanction to this presumption, the amendment of 1866 makes "such instrument" the one "not being stamped according to law."

And this construction seems to advance the policy of the section in question. Having a stamp act, it should in some way be made effectual. To say that every instrument must be stamped, and then allow that the document is just as good without putting the stamp on, verges on advice more than law. Section 158 is to meet this difficulty, and its purpose is to effectually require the affixing of stamps in accordance with the provisions of the stamp act. Prescribing a penalty, as is here done, it is true, meets this in a measure, and yet it does not seem to cover the broad design which Congress had in view, that is, to make the stamp a necessary part of the instrument. This done, every person having any connection with the paper has an interest in seeing that it is properly made out in this respect as with other requirements, as, for example, that a seal should be put on a deed. Making the validity of the instrument depend upon the affixing the stamp required completely covers the object of the Legislature. It was well expressed by Mr. Fessenden, in reply to a question put to him by a member of the Senate: "The Senate will notice with respect to all these instruments which it is provided shall be stamped, that they are of no validity unless the stamp is put on, and therefore the individual who wants his business properly done must see that the stamp is on. . . . It is all provided for by the simple fact that the instrument is of no validity unless the stamp is put on." (Congress. Globe, 1861-2, Part 3, page 2,347.)

Stamp acts, however, are not the most popular in this country; and it must be admitted that the weight of authority is against this view. On the one hand, that the unstamped instrument is invalid, without reference to the intent, is held in Iowa (Hugus v. Strikler, 19 Iowa, 413) and Nevada (Maynard v. Johnson, 2 Nev., 25; 2 Id., 16). While on the other hand, that the invalidity depends upon the intention with which the stamp was omitted is held in Vermont (Hitchcock v. Sawyer, 39 Vt., 412); Massachusetts (Tobey v. Chipman, Govern. v. Littlefield, Wiley v. Robinson, 13 Allen 123-8; Crocker v. Foley, 13 Id. 376; Holyoke Co. v. Franklin Co., 97 Mass., 150); New York (Beebe v. Hutton, 47 Barb., 187; Vorebeck v. Roe, 50 Id., 302); Pennsylvania (McGovern v. Hosbeck, 53 Penn., 176); Alabama (Blunt v. Bates, 40 Ala., 470); Arkansas (Dorris v. Grace, 25 Ark., 326); California (Hallock v. Jaudin, 34 Cal., 167).

Second. Assuming that the validity of an unstamped instrument depends upon the intent with which the stamp was omitted, the practical question then often arises: if it appears that an instrument is unstamped, and there is no other evidence with respect to it, what is the presumption as to its validity?

The Supreme Court of Massachusetts in a number of cases have seemed to take the ground that in all such instances it must be presumed that the stamp was innocently left off, and that the party questioning the validity must show affirmatively, by other evidence, the fraudulent intent. See Desmond v. Norris, 10 Allen 250; Snell v. Moulton, 12 Id., 396; Govern. v. Littlefield, 13 Id., 127; Wiley v. Robinson, 13 Id., 128; Croker v. Foley, 13 Id. 376.

With great deference to the intimation from such high authority, to us there seems to be a difficulty in this view, in that by it the act itself is not taken into account. Every man is unquestionably to be presumed innocent till proved guilty; yet if it appears that he has done an unlawful act, we presume him to have intended the natural consequence of that act. In other words, the act throws the burden on the defendant to disprove the intent. Thus, in cases of murder, "the fact of killing being first proved, all the circumstances of accident, necessity, or infirmity are to be satisfactorily proved by the prisoner, unless they arise out of the evidence proved against him; for the law presumeth the fact to have been founded in malice until the contrary appeareth." (Foster's Crown Law, 255; see Commonwealth v. York, 9 Met., 93.) In cases of malicious prosecution, the want of probable cause depends not upon the actual fact but the belief of the party; yet the *fact* being shown, the belief and malicious intent may be inferred, and "the burden put upon the defendants to rebut this presumption. (Willis v. Noyes, 12 Pick., 327; 1 Phillips on Ev., 632.) And these cases are not favored in law. (Stone v. Crocker, 24 Pick., 83.) To constitute the crime of larceny, there must be a taking of property with an intent to appropriate it. (Commonwealth v. Adams, 7 Gray, 44); but the possession is *prima facie* evidence of the intent. (Commonwealth v. Willard, 1 Mass., 6); (1 Phillips on Ev., 634). In cases of false representations, the intention to deceive and defraud must be alleged and proved; but the falsehood uttered is sufficient proof of the intention. (1 Phillips on Ev., 633); and where a prosecutor, on an indictment for forging a receipt with intent to defraud him, swore that he believed the prisoner had no such intent, the judge directed the jury that the defrauding, being the necessary effect and consequence of the forgery, was sufficient evidence of the intent of the prisoner to warrant them in convicting; and the judges held the conviction to be right." (Id., 632.) In the case of Seymour T. Smith, bankrupt, Judge Hall of the United States District Court, Northern District of New York, decided that the making of a general assignment, without preference, by an insolvent debtor, was an act of bankruptcy; that an express denial under oath of intent to defeat or delay the operations of the Bankruptcy Act by making such assignment was of no avail as against the conclusive legal presumption of such intent arising out of the admission of the execution of such assignment. (3 Bankrupt Reg., 98.)

Professor Greenleaf thus lays down the general principle applicable to all cases. "The law presumes every act, in itself unlawful, to have been criminally intended, until the contrary appears:" (1 Greenleaf on Ev. section 34); and this same presumption arises in civil cases. (Ibid.)

In the case in question, the person who issues an instrument unstamped, in violation of the revenue laws, does an unlawful act of which the natural and necessary consequences are that the provisions of the stamp act are evaded and Government defrauded; and why should not this same general principle apply? Granted that the *intent* must be alleged and proved, yet proof of the unlawful act it would seem should make a *prima facie* case on the question of intent. And such appears to be the view sanctioned by some of the decisions. See Beebe v. Hutton (47 Barb. 187).

H. H. Bond.

IRR v.XIV, August 26, 1871, pp.69-70

An impression has for several years been abroad that the Government would pay the sum of $300 to any person who should collect one million cancelled postage and revenue stamps. The origin of the statement it is hard to find; it must have been started by some cruel practical joker. That it has received credence is proved by the fact that many persons are known to have attempted the task of accumulating the necessary number of defaced stamps. An instance of the kind which has lately been brought to the notice of the Post Office Department has afforded another opportunity for an official denial of the truth of the absurd statement which has misled so many simple aspirants for the reward, and benevolent people who have assisted them in their efforts. The Post Office Department this week received from the Secretary of the Treasury a box containing 19,500 cancelled postage and revenue stamps. These stamps were forwarded to the Treasury by a lady residing at Bridgeport, Conn., who said she was one of a Bible-class; that she was told by the superintendent of her Sunday school that if she would collect one million stamps the Government would give her $300. She therefore forwarded a part of the required number, and requested pay for them pro rata. The Third Assistant Postmaster-General replied to her letter, saying that cancelled stamps possess no value whatever, and that the newspaper rumor that the Government will pay for such stamps is doubtless intended as a "sell."

IRR v.XIV, November 18, 1871, p.161

By the act of June 6, 1872, all stamp taxes on instruments in writing are repealed from October 1, 1872, except the two cent stamp on checks. It is provided further, that in the meantime the holder of any instrument of writing of whatever kind and description, which has been made or issued without being duly stamped, may make application to any collector of Internal Revenue, who shall thereupon affix the stamp provided by such holder upon such instrument of writing as is required by law, subject to the provisions of section 158 of the Internal Revenue laws. It is important that collectors should call the attention of the holders of such instruments in their respective districts to the matter, that they may avail themselves of this opportunity to render them legal and valid.

IRR v.XVI, July 20, 1872, p.17

1873.—Department No. 58, Internal Revenue.—Circular No. 108—Concerning the Keeping By Collectors of a Supply of Check and Proprietary Stamps.

Treasury Department,
Office of Internal Revenue,
Washington, April 17, 1873.

Information having been received at this office from different sections of the country to the effect that great difficulty is experienced by the public in procuring check and proprietary stamps, collectors are hereby informed that they will be expected to keep, at all times, in their offices, for sale to the public a sufficient supply of such stamps to meet any reasonable demand.

A supply of such stamps should also be placed in the hands of deputy collectors for sale in their respective divisions.

Collectors will be permitted to purchase stamps for cash from this office in amounts not less than fifty dollars, or they will be furnished them without prepayment therefor on filing in this office a bond (the penal sum of which should not be less than $500), executed by the collector and three good and sufficient sureties.

In case the collector desires to file a bond, he will receive the necessary blanks from this office on application therefor, and the stamps will be furnished him subject to the following regulations, which have been approved by the Secretary of the Treasury:

"1st. Each agent shall be allowed a commission, in stamps, of five per cent on all amounts paid to the Government by him.

"2d. If the agent is a collector, he shall deposit stamps, in suitable quantities, with his deputies, and allow to them the commission provided in the regulations of this office.

"3d. Each agent, on the first day of each month, shall make return to this office of the amount of stamps sold during the preceding month, and at the time of rendering such return shall make payment therefor."

Each collector will acknowledge the receipt of this circular and advise this office of the course he intends to pursue under these instructions, and at the same time if he has not now an adequate supply of stamps on hand he will transmit an order to this office therefor, accompanied by a certificate of deposit made on account of stamps for the amount, or he will request to be furnished with a blank bond.

J. W. Douglass,
Commissioner.

IRR v.XVII, May 3, 1873, p.138

Unstamped Deeds, Mortgages, etc.

Treasury Department.
Office of Internal Revenue,
Washington, June 27, 1873.

Otis Clapp, Esq., Collector Internal Revenue, Boston, Mass.:

Sir: Please give notice, as far as practicable without expense to the Government, to parties in your district who have deeds, mortgages, etc., not duly stamped, of the importance of having such instruments stamped by a collector in order to secure their validity and thus prevent objections to titles, lawsuits, loss of property, etc.

With regard to instruments not duly stamped, see Internal Revenue Record, Vol. XII, pages 141 and 142.

Cases where there is evidence of an intent to evade the law should be reported to the United States District Attorney for prosecution.

Where parties, on being notified, refuse to have stamped deeds, etc., issued without the requisite stamps previous to October 1, 1872, it might be considered prima facie evidence tending to prove an intent to evade the law.

Any party who, with intent to evade the law, issues, accepts, negotiates, or pays any check, draft, or order not duly stamped, incurs a penalty of fifty dollars in each case.

Very respectfully,
J. W. Douglass,
Commissioner.

IRR v.XVIII, July 5, 1873, p.1

PROCEEDINGS IN U.S. COURTS.

U.S. Supreme Court—Washington, D.C., October 23.

A Stamp Act Prosecution–Drafts By a Corporation on Its Own Treasury.–No. 45–United States v. Isham–Certificate of Division Between Judges of the Circuit Court for the Eastern District of Michigan.

This is a criminal information for issuing without a stamp, and with intent to evade the provisions of the internal revenue laws, a paper in the form of a draft drawn on Charles J. Canda, treasurer of the Iron Cliffs Company, by the defendant as superintendent. The paper was as follows:

[5] Iron Cliffs Company [Five.]

[1,190] Negannee, Mich., January 3, 1870.

To Charles J. Canda, Esq., New York.

Pay to the order of E. B. Isham, Superintendent, or bearer, five dollars, value received, and charge to the account of E. B. Isham.

(Countersigned) E. S. Green, Clerk.

On the trial the court were divided on the questions—first, whether this paper, on its face, required a stamp; second, whether evidence to show that Isham was superintendent of the company and drew the paper in that capacity, or that Canda was treasurer of the company and the instrument was drawn on him in that capacity, or was drawn in the course of the company's business, was admissible; third, whether, if the paper was made and issued with the design that it should be used as a local circulating medium, and was actually used by the holders as such, it thereby became subject to be stamped, and whether evidence given by the Government tending to show these facts was admissible; fourth, whether assuming all the facts which the evidence offered tended to prove, the defendant was guilty of the offence charged; and fifth, whether the information sufficiently charges any offence under the laws of the United States. These questions were certified to this court for answer, and were now argued.

The U.S. Supreme Court at its last term made the following amendment to the 8th rule:

That hereafter, in all cases brought into this court by writ of error or appeal, to review any judgment or decree, the clerk of the court by which such judgment or decree was rendered shall annex to and transmit with the record a copy of the opinion or opinions filed in the case.

IRR v.XVIII, October 25, 1873, pp.134-5

Ed. note: [Synopsis of case only; a full exposition is given in the following listing.]

The United States v. E. B. Isham.—A Synopsis of This Case Was Published in the RECORD of October 25, 1873, Vol. XVIII, No. 17.

On a criminal information for issuing without a stamp and with intent to evade the provisions of the internal revenue act of 1866, the following instrument:

[5] Iron Cliffs Company [Five.]

Negannee, Mich., January 3, 1870.

To Charles J. Canda, Esq., New York.

Pay to the order of E. B. Isham, Superintendent, or bearer, five dollars, value received, and charge to the account of E. B. Isham.

(Countersigned) E. S. Green, Clerk.

Held, that the instrument was, in form, a draft or order for the payment of money drawn upon another than a banker or trust company, and not subject to the stamp duties imposed upon a promissory note.

Appeal on a certificate of division of opinion between the judges of the Circuit Court of the United States for the Eastern District of Michigan.

Mr. Justice Hunt delivered the opinion of the court.

This is a criminal information for issuing, without a stamp and with intent to evade the provisions of the act relating to internal revenue, a paper in the form of a draft drawn upon one Canda, who was the treasurer of the Iron Cliffs Company, by the defendant, who was its superintendent. The paper is attached to and made part of the information, and is as follows:

[5] Iron Cliffs Company [Five.]

[1,190] Negannee, Mich., January 3, 1870.

To Charles J. Canda, Esq., New York.

Pay to the order of E. B. Isham, Superintendent, or bearer, five dollars, value received, and charge to the account of E. B. Isham.

(Countersigned) E. S. Green, Clerk.

Upon the trial the following questions arose, concerning which the defendant requested the court to instruct the jury in his favor, and for a verdict of acquittal:

First. Whether the instrument annexed to the information in this case, and made a part of each count thereof, and introduced in evidence, is, on its face, subject to be stamped.

Second. Whether the evidence offered by the prosecution, tending to prove that Edwin B. Isham was superintendent of the Iron Cliffs Company, and drew the instrument in question in that capacity, or that Charles J. Canda was the treasurer of the said company, and the instrument was drawn upon him in that capacity, or that said paper was drawn in the course of said company's business, was relevant and admissible.

Third. Whether, if the paper in question was made and issued with the design that it should be used as a local circulating medium, and was actually used by the holders as such, it thereby became subject to be stamped, and whether the evidence given by the prosecution tending to prove these facts, was relevant and admissible.

Fourth. Whether, assuming every fact which the evidence in support of the prosecution tends to prove, the defendant is guilty of the offence charged.

Fifth. Whether the information in this case sufficiently charges any offence under the laws of the United States.

And the following further question, upon which the district attorney requests the court to charge in favor of the prosecution:

Sixth. Whether, if the instrument set forth in the information and adduced in evidence was issued with the design and intent to secure time for the payment of the debt it represents, it was therefore subject to stamp duty.

Upon which said question the judges were divided in opinion.

Whereupon said questions were certified to the Supreme Court for its opinion thereon.

Many questions are discussed in the briefs which will not be considered in the present opinion. If we are correct in the views we take of the one principal question presented, the others become unimportant. That question may be thus stated: The instrument referred to in the information is in the form of a draft for the sum of five dollars, drawn by Isham individually, to his own order, as superintendent, upon Charles J. Canda, individually, and is countersigned by E. S. Green, Clerk. It is proved that Isham was the superintendent of the Iron Cliffs Manufacturing Company, and that Canda was its treasurer, and that the draft was drawn and issued in the business of the company. The counsel for the United States insist that the instrument, invested with these characteristics, is in law a promissory note, and subject to the stamp duty imposed upon a promissory note. The counsel of the defendant insist that this instrument is, in form, a draft or order for the payment of money, drawn upon another than a banker or trust company; that the stamp duty is regulated by the form of the paper, and that this instrument is not subject to the duty imposed by the statute upon a promissory note. We are of the opinion that the construction of the defendant is correct—that the paper issued required no stamp, and that the prosecution must fail.

The schedule of instruments as required by the statute of 1866, to be stamped (14 Stat. at Large, 142, sec. 158) is as follows:

"Bank check, draft or order for the payment of any sum of money whatever, drawn upon any bank, banker or trust company, or for any sum exceeding ten dollars drawn upon any other person or persons, companies or corporations, at sight or on demand, two cents.

"Bill of exchange (inland), draft or order for the payment of any sum of money not exceeding one hundred dollars, otherwise than at sight or on demand, or any promissory note (except bank notes issued for circulation, and checks made and intended to be forthwith presented, and which shall be presented to a bank or banker for payment), or any memorandum, check, receipt or other written or printed evidence of an amount of money to be paid on demand or at a time designated, for a sum not exceeding one hundred dollars, five cents.

"And for every additional one hundred dollars or fractional part thereof in excess of one hundred dollars, five cents."

The schedule designates the various instruments and writing to be taxed by the well-known names and descriptions of the paper, and specifies the amounts of duty in substance as follows:

1. Every bank check . . . . 2 cts.
2. Every draft or order for the payment of any sum of money at sight or on demand (except where the draft or order is so drawn on a person, company or corporation other than a bank, banker or trust company, and for a sum not exceeding ten dollars) . . . . 2 cts.
3. Every bill of exchange, draft or order for the payment of any sum of money otherwise than at sight or on demand, for every one hundred dollars . . . . 5 cts.
4. Every promissory note for each one hundred dollars . . . . 5 cts.
5. Every memorandum, check, receipt or other written or printed evidence of an amount of money to be paid on demand or at a time designated, for a sum not exceeding one hundred dollars 5 cts.
6. If the draft or order is drawn on a person not a banker, or a bank or a trust company, and does not exceed ten dollars, then no stamp is required.

There is probably an error in the punctuation of the statute in regard to the item which reads, "memorandum, check, receipt or other written or printed evidence of an amount of money to be paid.'' It should read, ''memorandum-check (with a hyphen between the words) receipt, or other written or printed evidence.'' A ''check'' was specifically provided for already in the schedule, and it is not to be assumed that Congress would, in the same schedule, make two provisions, differing from each other, for the same subject. A memorandum-check, however, is an instrument well known in the commercial law, which, it might be claimed, did not come under the general term of a check, and which, therefore, had not been specifically provided for. A memorandum-check is in the ordinary form of a bank-check, with the word ''memorandum'' written across its face, and is not intended for immediate presentation, but simply as evidence of an indebtedness by the drawer to the holder.

Mr. Parsons, in his work on Notes and Bills (p. 66), says: ''It has been said that the word 'memorandum,' or 'mem,' '' written on the check, would not affect the right of the holder. We think this might have been doubted, because there is a well-known custom in all our commercial cities of drawing and using checks in this form merely as due-bills, or as what they are, and are called ''memorandum-checks.''

In Dykers v. The Leather Manufacturers' Bk., 11 Paige, 615, it was said: ''The weight of the testimony is, that this memorandum amounts to nothing more than an indication of an understanding that the check is not to be presented immediately for payment, so as to destroy the drawer's credit with the bank, where he has not provided funds to meet the draft.''

It is stated further in Parsons, *supra,* that the holder may present the same for payment, if the name of the bank is not cancelled on the check.

In Franklin Bank v. Freeman, 16 Pick, 535, the court speak of memorandum-checks as well known in Boston, and say that the rules of business with regard to them are well understood.

In Glover v. Graesar, 10 Rich. Eq. 446 (So. Car. Rep.), it is said that memorandum-checks, being regular bank checks, with the word ''memorandum'' written on their face, are constantly used in settlement of accounts between merchants, as admissions of amounts of money due.

This reading makes the statute harmonious and sensible, providing for bank-checks, drafts, inland bills, promissory notes, memorandum-checks, receipts, and assigning to each its proper position.

It is said that in many instances the statute refers to the same subject more than once, under different names, and with different rates of duty, and that embarrassment in the construction of the statute may arise from this cause. Thus a check, whether drawn upon a bank or an individual, is in the nature and form of an inland bill of exchange, having a drawer, a drawee and usually a payee. The statute describes checks, drafts and promissory notes, and subsequently speaks of a memorandum-check; also of a receipt or other written or printed evidence of an amount of money to be paid. These general terms plainly include the specifications already made. A bank-check, a memorandum-check, a draft, or a bill of exchange, each furnishes written or printed evidence of an amount of money to be paid. So does a promissory note. A note is indeed, the regular and usual evidence in dealings between men, that money is to be paid, whether in cities or in the country, and whether the transactions be limited or extensive; and yet, bank-checks and drafts, or orders at sight or on demand, require different stamps from memorandum checks, bills of exchange and promissory notes.

A few simple rules will dispose most of the difficulties that may arise:

1. Instruments described in technical language, or in terms especially descriptive of their own character, are classed under that head, and are not to be included in the general words of the statute.

2. The words of the statute are to be taken in the sense in which they will be understood by that public in which they are to take effect. Science and skill are not required in their interpretation, except where scientific or technical terms are used.

3. The liability of an instrument to a stamp duty, as well as the amount of such duty, is determined by the form and face of the instrument, and cannot be affected by proof of facts outside of the instrument itself.

4. If there is a doubt as to the liability of an instrument to taxation, the construction is in favor of the exemption because, in the language of Pollock, C. B., in Garr v. Scudds, 11 Exch. R. 191, ''a tax cannot be imposed without clear and express words for that purpose.'' See also Conroy v. Warren, 3 Johns. Cas., 259, to the same effect.

These principles are based in good sense, and are sustained by the authorities.

In Williams v. Jarrett, 5 Bar. and Ad. 32, where the question was, whether a bill was liable to the stamp duty imposed upon bills ''exceeding two months after date,'' it was held that the date meant the time expressed on the face of the bill, and that it did not depend upon the fact that the bill actually had more than two months to run. Denman, Ch. J., says: ''If a bill bears no date, we must ascertain by evidence the day when it issued, but where there is a date, that must be considered as the time to which the schedule refers.''

In Whistler v. Foster, 14 Com. B., N. S., 257, the same language is used by Erie, C. J., and by Miller J. The latter says: ''Drafts payable to order, not being affected by either of those enactments, fall within the law as to bills of exchange, which have been repeatedly held not to be void by post-dating, though that should have the effect of making the instrument require a less stamp than if it had been dated correctly and payable at the same time.''

In Bull v. O'Sullivan, Law Rep. 6 Q. B. 209, decided in 1871, the cases of Whistler v. Foster and Williams v. Jarrett are approved, and the rule is thus announced: ''There is nothing in the statutes to invalidate a post-dated check on a banker payable to order on demand, and in determining what is the requisite stamp to make such an instrument admissible in evidence, the instrument alone is to be looked at. Such a check is available in the hands of a person who took it with knowledge that it was post-dated, and is admissible in evidence with only a penny stamp.'' Hennen, J., further states: ''We are of the opinion that the stamp acts above referred to, so far as they relate to bills of exchange and orders for the payment of money, deal with those documents only as they appear on their face, without reference to any collateral agreement or condition by which their apparent operation may be effected.''

It is not necessary, in this view of the case, to decide whether an order drawn by one officer of a corporation upon another officer of the same corporation is in law a promissory note, nor whether it may simply be treated as such in pleading; nor is it necessary to decide whether the fact that the order is drawn upon Mr. Canda individually, and not as treasurer of the corporation, will affect the result. Whatever may be the law on this subject, it will not affect the case before us. The instrument we are considering is, in form, a draft or check upon an individual. It is not in form a promissory note. It must, therefore, pay the stamp duty of a draft or order, and not that of a promissory note. It is not permissible to the courts, nor is it required of individuals who use the instrument in their business, to inquire beyond the face of the paper. Whatever upon its face it purports to be, that it is for the purpose of ascertaining the stamp duty. The paper has the distinctive form of a promissory note. [Ed. note: This sentence appears to be in error, since it contradicts those immediately preceding it.] It falls under that specific description, and is to be taxed according to that description, not varied by proof, and not ranked under any general terms contained in the statute.

It is said that the transaction proved upon the trial in this case is a device to avoid the payment of a stamp duty, and that its operation is that of a fraud upon the revenue. This may be true, and if not true in fact in this case, it may well be true in other instances. To this objection there are two answers:

1. That if the device is carried out by the means of legal forms, it is subject to no legal censure. To illustrate. The stamp act of 1862 imposed a duty of two cents upon a bank check, when drawn for an amount not less than twenty dollars. A careful individual, having the amount of twenty dollars to pay, pays the same by handing to his creditors two checks of ten dollars each. He thus draws checks in payment of his debt to the amount of twenty dollars, and yet pays no stamp duty. This practice and this system he pursues habitually and persistently. While his operations deprive the Government of the duties it might reasonably expect to receive, it is not perceived that the practice is open to the charge of fraud. He resorts to devices to avoid the payment of duties, they are not illegal. He has the legal right to split up his evidences of payment, and thus to avoid the tax. The device we are considering is of the same nature.

Another answer may be given to the objection, more comprehensive in its character. It is this: that the adoption of a rule that the form of the instrument can be disregarded, and its real character investigated for the purpose of determining the stamp duty, would produce difficulties and inconveniences vastly more injurious than that complained of. Such a rule would destroy the circulating capacity of bills, or drafts, or orders. The present act imposes the same stamp duty upon inland bills of exchange and promissory notes, but this is an accidental circumstances only. Suppose that the draft is made subject to a tax of five cents on the hundred dollars, and the note to a tax of ten cents on the hundred dollars. The defendant contends that a draft or bill drawn by one officer of a company upon another officer of the same company is, in legal effect, a promissory note. Upon the supposition thus made, its real character would require a tax of twice the amount of that indicated upon its face, and if the stamp be too small, the instrument is absolutely void from its inception. (Stat. sec. 158.) In the language of the statute, it shall be "deemed invalid and of no effect."

Is every man to whom a paper in the form of a bill of exchange is presented, bound to inquire whether there are not outside circumstances that may affect its nature? Having ascertained this, is he bound to delay all proceedings until he can take legal advice upon its nature and character? This he must do upon the theory contended for, and he must be certain, also, that his advice is correct; otherwise he will lose the money he advances upon the bill. The same rule, it is contended, will apply where the drawee does not appear upon the face of the bill to be an officer of the company. Such is the case before us, where Mr. Canda, the drawee, does not appear upon the bill itself to be connected with the company, and yet the prosecution contends that it may be proved that he is its treasurer, and that thereupon the instrument ceases to be a draft or order for the payment of money, and becomes a promissory note.

That the rule contended for is impracticable in a commercial country is too obvious to require farther illustration. We are satisfied that the principles heretofore laid down must govern the case before us.

These views require than an answer in the negative should be given to each of the questions certified to this court. They are accordingly so answered, and the record must be returned to the court below with directions to dismiss the information.

NOTE.—In United States v. Buzzo the same court decided that, on an information for an omission of a stamp from commercial paper, the intent is the essence of the crime, and when the special verdict found by the jury does not state that the omission was with intent to evade the revenue act, no judgment can be rendered against the prisoner.

IRR v.XIX, March 14, 1874, pp.84-6

Decision as to Effect of Act of June 23, 1874, Relating to Stamping Unstamped Instruments.

Treasury Department,
Office of Internal Revenue,
Washington, August 4, 1874.

H. W. Fick, Esq., Collector Internal Revenue, 3rd District, Fayetteville, Ark.

Sir: Your attention is particularly called to the Act of June 23, 1874, providing for the stamping of [unstamped] instruments, documents, or papers, theretofore made, signed, or issued, before a judge or a clerk of a Court of Record (INTERNAL REVENUE RECORD, Vol. xx, p. 9). [Ed. note: The cited reference merely states the text of the aforementioned Act.] It is held that no penalty is required on stamping instruments in this manner.

It is considered, however, that this is an additional privilege allowed for the convenience of parties, and that it does not take away the authority of a Collector to stamp instruments under former laws still in force, if that is desired.

Very respectfully,
J. W. Douglass,
Commissioner.

IRR v.XX, August 10, 1874, p.37

Hall v. Jordan.

1. Where the consideration in a deed is expressed to be so many dollars, the stamp required is the same whether in point of fact the sum named be paid in gold or in notes of the United States, made by law a legal tender.
2. A party alleging that the stamp on a deed was too small (he being by the law of the State where the deed was made obliged to put on the stamps), who brought such a question here, delaying the judgment below for two years and a half, punished under the twenty-third rule, by a judgment of ten per cent, damages in addition to interest and cost.

Error to the Supreme Court of Tennessee; the case being thus:

Jordan on the 1st of November, 1866, sold a tract of land to Hall and Conley, the consideration as expressed in the deed being $13,000; the deed not stating, however, whether this $13,000 was gold and silver coin, or notes of the United States; a kind of notes, always up to this time, from the time of their issue, less valuable than such coin; but which in February, 1862, and afterwards had been made by act of Congress a legal tender in the payment of debts, and which in point of fact at the time of the sale were the universal currency, to the exclusion of gold and silver as currency of all parts of the United States except parts on the Pacific coast.

In point of fact the consideration of this deed was one of gold coin, or based on the value of coin; that is to say, $6,500 were paid in gold coin when the deed was made, and an agreement given to pay "on the 25th of December, 1867, an amount of legal currency of the United States sufficient to purchase $6,890 of the present gold coin of the United States;" this $6,890 being the balance ($6,500) of the $13,000 consideration money, with interest added to the day of payment.

An act of Congress in force at the date of the deed, act of June 30, 1864, 15 Stat. at Large, 295, enacted that on deeds of land there should be a stamp of "$1 for each $1,000 of consideration money," and fifty cents for every fraction of the sum last named; and that no deed not properly stamped should be received in evidence. The act makes a provision, however, for the correction of unintentional error by application to the collector, and purchase of the proper stamp. This deed was stamped with a stamp for $13, the stamp confessedly proper for one when the consideration was $13,000 in notes of the United States.

On a question in the court below whether the deed was properly stamped, or whether the stamp ought not to be such as the amount of notes which the $13,000 of gold coin, the actual consideration of the deed, would have brought if the amount represented by them had been sent forth in the deed—required, that court held the stamp sufficient, and on the 29th of June, 1871, the present writ of error was taken to its judgment. The case came on to be heard here December 16, 1873.

Messrs. R. Johnson and J. H. Imbree, for the plaintiff in error:

It is a matter of universal knowledge, that there has always been a difference between the value of what are called "legal tender notes" and of coin. At times, as in the summer of 1864, one day in which it required $285 of notes to buy $100 of gold, see Legal Tender Cases, 12 Wallace, 512, note, this difference has been immense; and it has been frequently great. Now, the question is, may parties at a time when gold and silver have in fact no currency—when the notes of the Government are the sole currency of the country, or certainly of all that part of it where the parties to this transaction lived—may parties put in their deeds the value, in gold, of the property sold, and then pay stamps on that value? The real thing which passes between them being, all the while, not gold, but paper; not $13,000 in coin, but a greater amount in notes; more or less greater according as the discount on paper in the market may be higher or lower. We submit that they cannot, because a contrary rule will tend directly to frauds upon the revenue. In cases of large deeds or of larger mortgages the temptation will be prevailing.

Mr. F. P. Stanton, contra:

No man could tell on the 1st of November, 1866, how much currency would be required to purchase gold on the 25th of December, 1867, or even that legal tenders would not be equivalent to gold at that time.

But there has never been any law requiring the stamps on deeds or other instruments to be regulated by the currency values, when the transactions were for gold coin. The stamp affixed to the deed was then exactly what the law required. Supposing the plaintiffs in error honestly doubted this, they had it in their power to correct the supposed error by applying to the collector; and as it is evident no fraud was intended, the correction would have cost them fifty cents. It is apparent, then, that the writ of error in this case, which has delayed the proceedings in the court below for two years and a half, was sued out "merely for delay," and comes strictly within the letter and spirit of the twenty-third rule of this court, which declares that "in all cases where a writ of error . . . shall appear to have been sued out merely for delay, damages shall be awarded at the rate of ten per cent per annum on the amount of the judgment."

In addition, by the practice in Tennessee, a vendee must furnish deeds and stamps. In this proceeding, therefore, the plaintiffs in error are endeavoring to take advantage of their own wrong, as it was their duty to affix the proper stamp to the deed. For this reason, as well as for those already stated, the defendant in error asks for damages at the rate of ten per cent, in addition to interest, in accordance with the rule aforesaid.

Mr. Justice Clifford announced the judgment of this court, affirming the judgment of the court below with costs, interest, and ten per cent damages.

IRR v.XX, October 26, 1874, pp.128-9

Stamping Instruments by Collectors Prior to January 1, 1876.

Treasury Department,
Office of Internal Revenue,
Washington, March 3, 1875.

Henry Fassett, Esq., Collector Internal Revenue, 19th District, Ashtabula, O.

Sir: In your letter of February 16, 1875, you inquire, "if Collectors of Internal Revenue can stamp instruments presented to them at any time, prior to January 1, 1876, as provided in the Act of June 23, 1874, without requiring the payment of penalties, as prescribed in laws in force at the time of the passage of said act."

I reply that the above act does not limit the time in which *Collectors* may stamp instruments. It allows parties to stamp their own deeds, etc., before a Judge, etc., until the period mentioned, without a penalty. But in some cases parties may still prefer having instruments stamped by a Collector, as a matter of convenience, for greater certainty as to the value of the stamps required, to avoid extra charges, or for other reasons. In such cases, the Collector is required to attach the stamps according to the provisions of Section 158, Act of June 30, 1864, amended (Section 3422, Revised Statutes), and he has no authority to remit the penalty therein prescribed even in the absence of fraudulent intent, after twelve months from the issue of an instrument.

Very respectfully,
J. W. Douglass,
Commissioner.

IRR v.XXI, March 29, 1875, p.98

1875.—Department No. 44.—Internal Revenue.—Decision No. 177.—Concerning the Stamp Tax Upon Bank Checks, Drafts, Orders, or Vouchers, and As To Stamping Instruments Issued Unstamped.

Treasury Department,
Office of Internal Revenue,
Washington, April 12, 1875.

• • •

As to the Stamping of Instruments Issued Unstamped.

The act of June 3, 1874, allows parties having an interest in instruments, documents, and papers, *theretofore made, signed, or issued* liable to stamp duty, and remaining unstamped, to stamp such papers before a judge or clerk of a court of record, in the manner prescribed by the act, at any time prior to January 1, 1876, without a penalty. But in some cases parties may still prefer to have such instruments stamped by a collector. The collector is authorized to stamp them when presented, according to the provisions of section 3422 Revised Statutes, as amended by act of February 18, 1875, but cannot remit the penalty in any case after twelve months from the issue of the instrument.

J. W. Douglass,
Commissioner.

IRR v.XXI, April 26, 1875, pp.129-30

[Ed. note: The rest of the text of this Decision is listed in the Bank Check Section.]

(From the Legal Intelligencer.)

U.S. Supreme Court of Pennsylvania.

Long, Administrator of Cottrell, Deceased, v. Spencer and Co.

1. The absence of a U.S. Revenue Stamp upon a promissory note at the time of negotiation of it is not admissible as evidence proving want of consideration.
2. Evidence of parties to a note is inadmissible in a suit by the administrator of the holder.

Error to the District Court of Philadelphia.

Opinion by Gordon, J., May 10, 1875.

The note upon which this suit is brought, bears date January 4, 1871, and was drawn by W. G. Spencer and Co., to their own order, payable four months after date, and by them endorsed to G. B. Newton, one of the members of said firm, and by him endorsed to John F. Cottrell. Cottrell died on the third of February, 1871, and this note was found among his papers.

The defence exhibited nothing which under ordinary circumstances, would put the holder of the note to proof of consideration. There was some evidence, however, that when the note came into Cottrell's possession it was unstamped, though a stamp was duly fixed thereto by the collector of the proper district at the instances of the administrator, before suit brought. This fact was submitted to the jury as evidence of the imperfection of the note as negotiable paper, and to rebut the *prima facie* presumption that it had passed to the endorsee for a valuable consideration. Upon this evidence alone, a verdict was rendered for the defendants. Now how the want of a stamp could avail, of itself, to prove want of consideration, we cannot conceive. The provisions of the act of Congress import no such effect as this. As is said by Mr. Justice Agnew, in the case of the Turnpike Co. v. McNamara, 22 P. F. S. 281, the act of Congress did but "stamp the instrument of evidence, with a disqualification, which prevented its use as evidence, until the delinquent had paid his tax." To the same effect are the cases of Tripp v. Bishop, 6 P. F. Smith, 431; and Jones' Appeal, 12 P.F. Smith, 328. Now as upon the trial of this case, the note appeared to have been duly stamped by the officer qualified so to do, the ban upon it as evidence was removed, and it occupied the same position, so far as the act of Congress was concerned, as though it had been stamped where made. Why then, shall we go beyond that act, and add a penalty not found therein? But the ruling of the court below makes the want of a stamp, at the time of endorsement to the holder, not merely a curable irregularity, but also evidences to rebut the presumption of consideration. What is this but an additional penalty? And of what avail is the curative provision of the statute, if the paper is so marred by the original default, that it, no longer of itself, imports consideration? We cannot subscribe to such an interpretation of the statute. Had there been evidence of fraud or unfair dealing in the transfer paper or a want of consideration moving from Cottrell, this irregularity might have been adduced as a link in the chain of testimony, to prove *mala fides,* but standing alone, it amounted to nothing.

Under no circumstances was the testimony of Spencer and Newton, two of the defendants, admissible. This testimony went to prove that the note was unstamped, or the stamp uncancelled when passed to Cottrell; as, however, this evidence was of matter occurring before his death, and which, if alive, he might have rebutted by his own testimony, it comes within the proviso of the act of 1869, and should have been excluded. So that part of the declaration of Hemphill, the former administrator, which contains the allegation, "that so far as he had seen or knew, there was nothing in Cottrell's books or papers to show that any consideration had been given for the note," and should also have been excluded as irrelevant.

We find nothing improper in the drawing of the jury from the struck list. The method pursued is one that, we believe, has never heretofore been doubted or called in question, and if it has arisen from an erroneous interpretation of the statute, as is contended, it is an error too long established for us now to correct. *Communis error facit jus.*

The judgment is reversed, and a *venire facias de novo* awarded.

IRR v.XXI, July 6, 1875, p.286

1875.—Department No. 135.—Internal Revenue.—Circular No. 137.—Concerning a Discontinuance of the Redemption of, or Allowance for, Internal Revenue Documentary Stamps, Except Those of the Denomination of Two Cents.

Treasury Department,
Office of Internal Revenue,
Washington, October 4, 1875.

Section 14 of the Act entitled "An Act to amend existing customs and internal revenue laws, and for other purposes," approved February 8, 1875, is as follows: "That the existing provisions of law for the redemption of, or allowance for, internal revenue documentary stamps, the use of which has been rendered unnecessary by the repeal of the taxes for the payment of which such stamps were provided, shall apply only to such of said stamps as shall be presented to the Commissioner of Internal Revenue for allowances or redemption before the first day of October, eighteen hundred and seventy-five; and no allowance, redemption, or refunding on account of such of the aforesaid stamps as shall not be so presented to the said Commissioner prior to the date last mentioned shall be thereafter made."

The above provision of law is hereby promulgated for the information of Officers and Internal Revenue and the public, and notice is hereby given that no allowance for, or redemption of, documentary stamps, except those of the denomination of two cents, can be made in any case where the same were not presented at this Office on or before the 30th ultimo.

Documentary stamps of the denomination of two cents, and all proprietary stamps, may be redeemed or exchanged as heretofore, in accordance with the provisions of Section 3426 Revised Statutes of the United States, and the regulations of this Office made under the provisions of said Section, which are set forth in the Supplement to Special No. 121, revised, issued January 8, 1873.

D. D. Pratt,
Commissioner.

IRR v.XXI, October 11, 1875, p.321

815.—Department No. 150.—Internal Revenue.—Special No. 167.—Concerning the Imprinting of Stamps Upon Bank Checks, Drafts, Orders, or Vouchers for the Payment of Any Sum of Money Whatsoever, Drawn Upon any Bank, Banker, or Trust Company, or Upon Blank Paper That May Be Furnished for That Purpose by a Person, Firm, or Corporation Desiring Stamps So Imprinted.

Treasury Department,
Office of Internal Revenue,
Washington, November 5, 1875.

Officers of Internal Revenue and the public are informed that a contract has been entered into with the Graphic Company, of Nos. 39 and 41 Park Place, New York City, for the imprinting of stamps upon all bank checks, drafts, orders, or vouchers for the payment of any sum of money whatsoever drawn upon any bank, banker, or trust company, or upon blank paper that may be furnished for that purpose by a person, firm, or corporation desiring stamps so imprinted.

The contract takes effect on the 15th inst., and on and after that date the above stamps will be imprinted only at the establishment of the above Company, and until otherwise directed the stamps will be imprinted under the regulations heretofore prescribed.

D. D. Pratt,
Commissioner.

IRR v.XXI, November 15, 1875, p.361

Collectors to Stamp Instruments Subject to Stamp Tax Under Former Laws.

Treasury Department,
Office of Internal Revenue,
Washington, January 14, 1876.

F. D. Sewall, Esq., Supervisor Int. Rev., New York, N. Y.

Sir: Your attention is particularly called to the fact that the Act of June 23, 1874, which provided for the stamping of unstamped instruments, documents, and papers subject to stamp tax under former laws, before a judge or clerk of a Court of Record, expired by limitation, December 31, 1875.

The only persons who can now render valid such instruments by attaching the requisite stamps, are Collectors of Internal Revenue, who may attach such stamps according to the provisions of Section 3422, Revised Statutes of the United States.

It is often a matter of great importance to parties, to make valid instruments now invalid for want of the proper stamps, with a view to quieting or passing the title of estates, preventing law suits, etc. Collectors should keep on hand a reasonable quantity of adhesive stamps for this object, as well as for stamping bank checks, etc. They should also continue their Quarterly returns on "Form 8," whether any instruments have been stamped or not.

Very respectfully,
D. D. Pratt,
Commissioner.

IRR v.XXII, January 24, 1876, p.21

An Act to Extend the Time for Stamping Unstamped Instruments.

Be it enacted by the Senate and House of Representatives of the United States of America in Congress assembled, That the provisions of the act, entitled "An act to provide for the stamping of unstamped instruments, documents, or papers," approved the twenty-third day of June, in the year eighteen hundred and seventy-four, be, and the same are hereby, extended to the first day of January, in the year eighteen hundred and seventy-seven.

Approved February 25, 1876.

Department of State, Washington, February 25, 1876.

A true copy.

Sevellon A. Brown,
Chief Clerk.

The act of June 23d, 1874, referred to, was published in the RECORD of July 13, 1874, vol. xx, page 9. [Ed. note: for text of this Act, see Statutes section.] It authorizes the stamping of documents subject to stamp tax and left unstamped, or of a copy thereof when the original has been lost; the stamps to be affixed, by any person having an interest in such document, in the presence of some judge, or clerk of a court of record, who shall endorse on such writing or copy a certificate under his hand, or if the clerk, under his hand and seal, setting forth the date at which and the place where such stamp was affixed, the name of the person presenting the writing or copy, and the fact that the stamp was affixed and cancelled in his presence. In a letter published in the RECORD of August 10, 1874, vol. xx, p. 37, the Department decided that the law conferred an additional privilege for the convenience of parties, and did not take away the authority of the Collector to stamp instruments under former laws still in force. The privilege expired by limitation, January 1, 1876; it is here extended another year.

IRR v.XXII, March 6, 1876, p.69

1876.—Department No. 57.—Internal Revenue.—Circular No. 147.—Concerning the Transmission of Internal Revenue Stamps by Mail.

Treasury Department,
Office of Internal Revenue,
Washington, April 25, 1876.

It having come to the knowledge of this Office that it is the practice of many Collectors to forward Internal Revenue Stamps, ordered by taxpayers located at a distance from their offices, by mail, paying the postage thereon with official postage stamps, it is hereby ordered that this practice be at once discontinued, and in future such stamps will be transmitted by mail only on receipt from the person or firm ordering the same of specific directions so to do, together with the necessary postage stamps or the amount required to purchase the same.

In the latter case, the amount should be expended in the purchase of ordinary postage stamps to be affixed to the package.

Taxpayers should be notified by Collectors that stamps will be transmitted by mail only on receipt of specific directions to that effect, and when so transmitted, they will be at the risk of the person or firm ordering the same, as the Government will in no case assume any responsibility for their safe transmission, nor can any allowance be made under existing laws on account of stamps lost.

D. D. Pratt,
Commissioner.

IRR v.XXII, May 8, 1876, p.141

1876.—Department No. 85.—Internal Revenue.—Circular No. 148.—Concerning the Redemption and Exchange of Internal Revenue Documentary and Proprietary Stamps.

Treasury Department,
Office of Commissioner of Internal Rev.,
Washington, D.C., July 12, 1876.

The act approved July 12, entitled "An act relative to the redemption of unused stamps," provides "that the fourteenth section of the act passed February eighth, eighteen hundred and seventy-five, entitled 'An act to amend existing customs and internal revenue laws, and for other purposes,' be, and the same is hereby, repealed; and all unused stamps shall be redeemed when properly presented, as was done prior to the passage of the aforesaid act: *Provided,* that from and after the passage of this act no allowance shall be made for documentary stamps, except those of the denomination of two cents, which, when presented to the Commissioner of Internal Revenue, are found to be in the same condition as when issued by the Internal Revenue Department, or, if so required by the said Commissioner, when the person presenting the same cannot satisfactorily trace the history thereof from their issue to their presentation as aforesaid."

In accordance with the above provision of law, the public is hereby notified that the redemption of documentary stamps will be resumed, subject to all the limitations imposed by the Act.

Stamps which are in the same condition as when issued by this Department may be forwarded to this Office for redemption or exchange. If for redemption, they must in every case be accompanied by a claim, made out upon the form prescribed for that purpose, which will be furnished upon application.

If the evidence is satisfactory, the amount or value, after deducting the sum of five percent, as required by Section 3426, Revised Statutes of the United States, will be refunded.

Stamps which the owner desires exchanged need not be accompanied by a claim, but a letter stating such desire should invariably accompany the stamps.

The stamps will be transmitted at the risk and expense of the owner.

It should be distinctly understood that the limitations imposed by the Act above quoted will, under no circumstances be departed from, and it will be useless to forward stamps which have been cancelled, or which are not, in every respect, in the same condition as when issued by this Office. The abrasion of the gum upon the backs of stamps will be deemed such a change from the original condition as to necessitate their rejection by this Office, as required by the terms of the Act.

In all cases where stamps of larger denominations than twenty dollars are presented, their history from their issue by the Government to their presentation should be traced by means of sworn statements from each owner through whose hands they have passed.

Claims should invariably be sworn to, and the blanks therein should be carefully filled out, so far as the affiant is able to do so, but the date of purchase and name of person from whom purchased will not be insisted upon.

Claims will be acted upon by this Office in the order in which they are received, and, in all cases, as early after their receipt as the condition of the public business will permit.

H. C. Rogers,
Acting Commissioner.

IRR v.XXII, July 17, 1876, p.221

1876.—Department No. 125.—Internal Revenue.—Circular No. 157.—Concerning the Transmission of Internal Revenue Documentary and Proprietary Stamps to Purchasers thereof.

Treasury Department,
Office of Internal Revenue,
Washington, D.C., October 4, 1876.

The Act of Congress entitled "An act making appropriations for the legislative, executive, and judicial expenses of the Government for the year ending June 30, 1877, and for other purposes," approved August 15, 1876, provides that "hereafter the transmission of internal revenue stamps to the Officers of the Internal Revenue Service shall be made through the mails of the United States in registered packages."

A contract having been entered into with Adams Express Company by the Secretary of the Treasury, May 12, 1866, for the transportation from one point to another in the United States, of all moneys and securities, including internal revenue stamps, belonging to the United States, this Office has, since that date, delivered to that Company, under such contract, all documentary and proprietary stamps purchased by manufacturers of proprietary articles and dealers in stamps; and contract rates only—which are much lower than the ordinary commercial rates—were collected from consignees. The Adams Express Company does not appear to have made any objection to the receipt of such stamps for transportation under the contract, although it is believed that it was not obligated so to do by that contract, inasmuch as the United States was not the absolute owner of the stamps delivered for transportation.

Since the passage of the Act of August 15, 1876, above quoted, this Office has been compelled thereby to forward all stamps to Officers of the Internal Revenue Service by mail, in registered packages, and as these shipments constituted the greater part of the service performed for this Office by the Adams Express Company, that Company now declines to receive, for transmission to purchasers, under the contract, packages of documentary and proprietary stamps, claiming that for this transportation it has never received the actual cost of the service.

Inasmuch, therefore, as there seems to be no authority in the contract by which this Company can be required to continue the service at the rates heretofore charged, purchasers of stamps are advised to make their own arrangements for the transportation of stamps from New York to their places of business.

Stamps will be transmitted by registered mail, if so desired by purchasers, provided the amount required to pay the postage and registry fee is advanced for that purpose, or stamps will be transmitted in such other manner as the purchaser may direct, it being distinctly understood that this Office will under no circumstances be responsible for stamps after they leave the hands of the Stamp Agent, under whose direction they are packed for shipment, nor will this Office be responsible for any shortage which may be found on opening a package, unless it can be conclusively shown by the evidence of disinterested persons that every seal upon the package was unbroken when it was received. As a proper measure of precaution, it is suggested that all the seals be carefully cut from a package when it is opened, and if the package is found short, the seals intact may then be transmitted to this Office with the evidence of shortage.

Purchasers who desire to receive their stamps by registered mail may remit to this Office, from time to time, an amount sufficient to prepay the postage and registry fee on any number of packages of stamps to be subsequently ordered.

The postage on such packages will be one cent for each ounce or fractional part thereof, with an addition of ten cents for registry fee upon each package.

Where no specific instructions as to the mode of transmission are received, stamps will be forwarded by express as heretofore.

H. C. Rogers,
Acting Commissioner.

IRR v.XXII, October 16, 1876, p.325

1877.—Department No. 97.—Internal Revenue.—Circular No. 167.—Concerning the Transportation of Internal Revenue Stamps, Coupons, Stubs, Books, Blanks, Locks, and All Other Supplies and Records Between Officers of the Internal Revenue Service, and the Mailing of Internal Revenue Stamps to Taxpayers.

Treasury Department,
Office of Internal Revenue,
Washington, D.C., July 13, 1877.

Until otherwise directed, officers of the Internal Revenue Service forwarding to another officer, or to this Office, packages containing internal revenue stamps, or coupons, stubs of stamps, books, records, blanks, locks, hydrometers, or any other official matter—excepting only legal tender or national bank notes—will transmit the same by registered mail, and the employment of express companies for this service will be entirely discontinued.

The instructions contained in Circular No. 152, issued from this Office August 17, 1876, will be carefully followed in every case.

Care should be taken that written matter, such as stubs of stamps or records, is not placed in the same package with stamps, blanks, locks, etc., thereby subjecting the whole to letter rates of postage.

When a package does not contain written matter, it may, under the regulations of the Post Office Department, be enclosed and sealed, and transmitted through the mails at the rate of postage prescribed for third-class matter (one cent for each ounce or fraction thereof), provided it has attached thereto the certificate of the officer sending the same to the effect that it contains no written matter.

Under a recent decision of the Post Office Department, officers of the Internal Revenue Service will also be permitted to forward internal revenue stamps to taxpayers in sealed packages at rates of postage for third-class matter, provided the above-mentioned certificate is attached. The requirements of Circular No. 147, dated April 25, 1876, should be observed whenever stamps are ordered by a taxpayer to be forwarded by mail.

All packages containing written matter of any kind are, of course, liable to postage at the rate of three cents for each half ounce or fractional part thereof.

All regulations or instructions heretofore issued inconsistent herewith are hereby revoked.

Green B. Raum,
Commissioner.

Approved: R. C. McCormick,
Acting Secretary of the Treasury.

IRR v.XXIII, July 23, 1877

U.S. Supreme Court, October Term, 1877.

The United States, Plaintiff in Error, v. Walter Mann.–Error to the Circuit Court of the United States for the District of Minnesota.

Section 3177, Revised Statutes, does not authorize a revenue officer to enter a place of business to examine bank checks, unless it is alleged and proved that such bank checks were not duly and sufficiently stamped at the time they were made, signed and issued.—Ed. Internal Rev. Record.

Mr. Justice Clifford delivered the opinion of the court.

Authority is given to any collector, deputy collector, or inspector of internal revenue to enter, in the day time, any building or place within his district, where any articles or objects subject to such taxation are made, produced, or kept, so far as it may be necessary for the purpose of examining such objects or articles, and the provision is that any owner of such building or place, or any person having the agency or superintendence of the same, who refuses to admit such officer or suffer him to examine such articles or objects shall for every such refusal forfeit five hundred dollars. (Rev. Stat., sec. 3177.)

Founded upon that provision in the act of Congress the complaint filed in the Circuit Court alleges and charges that the defendant, having at the time mentioned the care and superintendence of the described bank and its place of business, in which certain paid bank checks were then and there kept, refused then and there to suffer the collector of the district, who then and there entered the bank for the purpose, to examine the said paid bank checks so kept then and there in said place of business, though thereto requested by the collector, which said refusal was then and there contrary to the form of the statute in such case made and provided.

Service was made and the defendant appeared and demurred to the complaint. Hearing was had and the court sustained the demurrer, the reasons for the conclusion not being exhibited in the transcript, but the record contains a statement to the effect that the plaintiffs standing on their complaint, the court rendered judgment for the defendant. Error was assigned by the plaintiffs, and they used out the present writ of error. It is now contended by the United States that the judgment was for the wrong party, that it should have been rendered for the plaintiffs and not for the defendant, which is the only error assigned for the consideration of this court.

Bank checks, drafts, or notes for the payment of money, drawn upon any bank, broker, or trust company, at sight or on demand, are subject to a tax of two cents, to be paid by the person who makes, signs, or issues the same or for whose use or benefit the same are made, signed, or issued. (Rev. Stat., sec. 3418, 18 Stat. at Large, 310.) Exceptions exist to that requirement in behalf of Federal and State officers and in behalf of county, town, and other municipal corporations, when in the strict exercise of functions belonging exclusively to their ordinary governmental or municipal capacity. (Id., sec. 3420.)

Cases arise where such an instrument is issued without being duly stamped, and in such a case the provision is that neither the instrument nor any copy thereof shall be admitted or used in evidence in any court until a legal stamp denoting the amount of the tax is affixed thereto, as prescribed by law. Instruments of the kind are required to be stamped at the time of their issue, and the provision is that unless a stamp or stamps of the proper amount shall be affixed to the same and cancelled it shall not be lawful to record the instrument, and that the record if so made shall be utterly void. Provision is also made that parties violating those regulations by making, signing, or issuing any such instrument, document, or paper, without being duly stamped, shall for every such offence forfeit the sum of fifty dollars, and that the unstamped instrument shall be deemed invalid and of no effect. (Id., sec. 3422.)

Such officer may enter in the day time any building or place within his district where any articles or objects subject to taxation are made, produced, or kept, so far as it may be necessary for the purpose of examining said articles or objects. Unless articles or objects of taxation are made, produced, or kept in any building belonging to another, the collector derives no authority under that act to enter the building at all, and even then his right to enter the same is strictly limited by the words so far as it may be necessary for the purpose of examining such articles or objects.

Where articles or objects subject to taxation are made, produced, or kept in any building, by whomsoever owned, the provision is that the collector or other officer named may enter the same, so far as it may be necessary for the purpose of examining said articles or objects, but the act of Congress gives the officer no authority whatever, to enter the building of another, for any other purpose than that which the act specifically described.

Strictly limited as the right conferred is, it is a privilege easily defined, and it is equally clear that the prohibition addressed to the owner or person in charge of the place of business is explicitly confined to the refusal to suffer the officer to enter the building where the articles or objects subject to taxation are made, produced, or kept, for the special purpose particularly set forth in the section. Owners of such a building or persons having the agency or superintendence of the same are forbidden to refuse to admit the collector, deputy collector, or inspector to enter such building for the described special purpose, and the provision is that if they do so refuse and do not suffer the office to examine such articles or objects, they shall for every such refusal forfeit five hundred dollars.

Persons other than the owner of the building or place of business cannot be held liable to the penalty prescribed in the section unless it be alleged and proved that he or they had at the time the agency or superintendence of the same, and that it was a building or place where articles or objects subject to taxation were made, produced, or kept, and that the person or persons accused of having violated the prohibition of the section then and there refused to allow the officer to enter the building or place of business for the described purpose, or to suffer him to examine the articles or objects subject to taxation then and there kept in said building or place of business.

Informations for offences or penalties created and defined by statute, like indictments, must follow the words of the statute, and where there is no substantial departure from that requirement the information, like the indictment, is in general sufficient, except in cases where the statute is elliptical or where by necessary implication other constituents are component parts of the offence. Offences created by statute as well as offences at common law consist, with rare exceptions, of more than one ingredient, and the rule is universal that every ingredient of which the offense is composed must be accurately and clearly expressed in the indictment or information or the pleading will be held bad on demurrer. (U.S. v. Cook, 17 Wall., 74. 1 Bishop Cr. Pro., (2nd ed.,) sec. 81. Arch. Cr. Pl. and Ev., (18th ed.,) 54.)

Orders for the payment of money, including checks and drafts drawn upon any bank, banker, or trust company, are subject to a tax of two cents, and it is understood to be the opinion of the department that the exaction specified is a tax upon the instrument to be paid by the person who makes, signs, or issues the same, or the person for whose use or benefit the order or check was made, signed, or issued. (Rev. Stat., sec. 3418, 18 Stat. at Large, 310.)

Suppose that is so, then it may perhaps be suggested that a bank check, though paid, if it was made, signed, and issued without being duly stamped with a stamp denoting the amount of the tax, is still an article or object subject to taxation within the meaning of the provision under consideration, unless it can be held that the tax emerged in the penalty prescribed for the violation of the requirement that the instrument shall be stamped at the time it is made, signed, and issued. (Id., sec. 3421.)

Such a question may arise in a subsequent case but it is wholly necessary to discuss it in the case before the court, as it is not alleged in the information that the paid bank checks therein described were not duly stamped at the time the same were made, signed, and issued, as required by the act of Congress. Instead of that the charge in the information is to the effect that the paid bank checks were then and there kept in the bank or place of business then and there under the charge and superintendence of the defendant; that the collector of the district then and there entered the said bank or place of business for the purpose of examining the said paid bank checks, and that he, the collector, then and there requested the defendant to suffer him to examine the said paid bank checks so kept by the said bank then and there in their said place of business, and that the defendant then and there refused the said request of the said collector. Matters not alleged in the information cannot be regarded as confessed by the defendant, as the demurrer only admits what is well pleaded.

Certain bank checks which had theretofore been drawn upon and paid by the bank, it is alleged in the information, were then and there kept in the rooms and vaults of the bank, and it is proper to say that the said checks are described in the preliminary part of the information as "articles subject to tax," but it is no where alleged in the information that the said paid bank checks were not duly stamped with stamps denoting the tax to which the same were subject at the time the checks were made, signed, and issued.

Ingredients or elements not set forth in the information or other criminal accusation cannot be incorporated into the charge against the defendant after he is served with process, and it is equally clear that paid bank checks which were duly and sufficiently stamped at the time they were made, signed, and issued are not articles or objects subject to taxation within the meaning of the act of Congress on which the information in this case is founded, and if so, then it follows as a necessary conclusion that the defendant might lawfully refuse to suffer the collector to examine the paid bank checks described in the information.

Penal offences created by statute, whether to be prosecuted by indictment or information, must be accurately and clearly described in the pleading for the recovery of the penalty, and if the offence cannot be so described without expanding the allegations beyond the mere words of the statutes then it is clear that the allegations of the accusation must be expanded to that extent, as it is universally true that no pleading in such a case can be sufficient which does not accurately and clearly allege all the ingredients of which the charge is composed, so as to bring the accused within the true intent and meaning of the statute defining the accusation.

In general, says Marshall, Ch. J., it is sufficient in a libel of information to charge the offence in the very words which direct the forfeiture, but the proposition we think is not universally true. If the words which describe the subject matter of the prohibition are general, including a whole class, . . . we think the charge in the libel ought to conform to the true sense and meaning of the words as used by the Legislature, (The Mary Ann, 8 Wheat., 389. The Hoppet, 7 Cr., 393. 2 Pars. on Ship. and Adm., 386.)

Examples of the kind where it has been held that it is not sufficient to follow the words of the statute are quite numerous, and they show that many of the exceptions are as extensively recognized and as firmly settled as any other rule of pleading in such cases. Views of a corresponding character are expressed by this court in another case where the opinion was delivered by Mr. Justice Story. Having stated the rule that it is in general sufficient to allege the offence in the very terms of the statute, he proceeds to remark: We say in general, for there are doubtless cases where more particularity is required either from the obvious intention of the Legislature or from the known principles of law, both of which exceptional requirements are applicable in this case.

Known principles of law require greater particularity to be observed in order that all the ingredients which constitute a violation of the statutory offence may be accurately and clearly alleged, and it is equally clear that the intention of Congress requires the same thing, as it is obvious that Congress never could have intended that paid bank checks duly and sufficiently stamped at the time they were made, signed, and issued should be regarded as articles or objects subject to taxation within the meaning of the provision in the act of Congress under consideration. (The Caroline, 7 Cr., 500. The Anne, 7 Id., 571. Conkl. Treat., (5th ed.,) 546.)

Authorities other than those already referred to, are not necessary to show that an information to recover a penalty created by statute must state all the material facts and circumstances which constitute the offence: so as to bring the party impleaded precisely within the provisions of the statute defining the offence; but should it be desired to consult other authorities, it will be found that the following fully support the propositions. (2 Colby Cr. Law, 114. People v. Wilbur, 4 Park. C. C., 21. Com. v. Cook, 18 B. Monr., 149. Steel v. Smith, 1 Barn. and Ald., 99. Conkl. Treat., (5th ed.,) 548.)

Viewed in the light of these suggestions it is clear that the right conferred upon the officer to enter the building or place of business of another in such a case is strictly limited to a building or place of business in which articles or objects subject to taxation are, at the time of the proposed entry and examination, made, produced, or kept, and that paid bank checks, unless it is alleged and proved that they were not duly and sufficiently stamped at the time they were made, signed and issued, are not articles or objects subject to taxation within the meaning of the act of Congress on which the information is founded. Nothing is admitted by the demurrer except what is well pleaded in the information, and inasmuch as the only charge of the information in that regard is that paid bank checks were then and there kept in the said building or place of business described, the court is of the opinion that the information does not set forth any legal offence against the defendant, as defined by the said act of Congress.

Judgment affirmed.

IRR v.XXIV, January 21, 1878, pp.20-1

1878.—Department No. 17.—Internal Revenue.—Circular No. 178.—Concerning the Redemption and Exchange of Internal Revenue Documentary and Proprietary Stamps.

Treasury Department,
Office of Internal Revenue,
Washington, D.C., March 1, 1878.

1. Section 3426, Revised Statutes of the United States, provides that—

"The Commissioner of Internal Revenue may, from time to time, make regulations, upon proper evidence of the facts, for the allowance of such of the stamps issued under the provisions of this Chapter, or any internal revenue act, as may have been spoiled, destroyed, or rendered useless or unfit for the purpose intended, or for which the owner may have no use, or which through mistake may have been improperly or unnecessarily used, or where the rates or duties represented thereby have been paid in error, or remitted; and such allowance shall be made either by giving other stamps in lieu of the stamps so allowed for, or by repaying the amount or value, after deducting therefrom, in case of repayment, the sum of five per centum, to the owner thereof; but no allowance shall be made in any case until the stamps so spoiled or rendered useless shall have been returned to the Commissioner of Internal Revenue, or until satisfactory proof has been made showing the reason why said stamps cannot be so returned."

The Act of July 12, 1876, amends the Section quoted above, in so far as it relates to documentary stamps—other than those of the denomination of two cents—by providing:

"That from and after the passage of this act now allowance shall be made for documentary stamps, except those of the denomination of two cents, which when presented to the Commissioner of Internal Revenue are not found to be in the same condition as when issued by the Internal Revenue Department, or, if so required by the said Commissioner when the person presenting the same cannot satisfactorily trace the history thereof from their issue to their presentation as aforesaid."

2. In pursuance of the authority conferred by the statute quoted, the following regulations, for the redemption and exchange of documentary and proprietary samps, are hereby prescribed in lieu of all regulations or instructions on the subject heretofore issued:

3. Documentary and proprietary stamps, which have been spoiled, or rendered useless or unfit for the purpose intended, or for which the owner may have no use, and documentary stamps which have been improperly or unnecessarily affixed to instruments, can be presented to this Office for *redemption* or *exchange*.

4. The stamps must be transmitted at the risk and expense of the owner.

5. Stamps presented for *redemption* must be accompanied by a claim made out on Form 81, copies of which will be furnished upon application to his Office. The claim must be sworn to, and the blanks filled up as far as the affiant is able to do so.

6. Stamps presented for *exchange* should be accompanied by a letter requesting the *exchange* in lieu of the *claim* prescribed in cases of redemption.

7. The redemption of stamps will be effected by "repaying the amount or value, after deducting therefrom . . . the sum of five per centum, to the owner thereof;" the exchange, by the issue of check or proprietary stamps, of equal value, in lieu of those returned.

8. When check or proprietary stamps are presented which are not "in the same condition as when issued," their condition must be satisfactorily accounted for, and conclusive evidence that they were never used must be furnished, before they can be redeemed or exchanged.

9. When documentary stamps, other than two cent stamps, are presented, which are not in their original condition, their history must be satisfactorily traced from the time of their purchase from the Government until their presentation, by sworn statements from all parties who have owned the stamps. Each statement should set forth the name of the person or firm from whom the stamps were purchased, the date of purchase (as nearly as possible), that the stamps were never used while in the possession of the affiant, and if sold, the date of sale and the name of the person or firm to whom sold. In order to facilitate the preparation of this evidence, several blank affidavits have been printed on Form 81.

10. Stamps which have been cancelled, or which have the appearance of having been washed, or from which the mucilage has been removed, either in whole or in part, or which have been *regummed,* are not considered to be "in the same condition as when issued."

11. When stamps of larger denominations than twenty dollars are presented, their history must be traced, as herein provided, whether they are in their original condition or not.

12. Persons making application for the redemption or exchange of stamps improperly or unnecessarily affixed to instruments, should forward the instruments, *with the stamps attached,* to this Office, accompanied by the affidavit of the owner, setting forth all facts in the case. There should also be an accompanying certificate from the Collector of Internal Revenue of the proper district, that he has made a personal examination of the case, and finds the facts to be as stated. The history of the stamps must also be traced from their original issue to their presentation.

13. In cases where an allowance is asked for stamps destroyed, the evidence must be of such a character that the destruction of the stamps must necessarily be inferred therefrom.

14. Stamps will only be redeemed or exchanged when presented by a *bona fide* owner or an agent or representative of such owner. When a claim is made by a person acting as agent, executor, receiver, or in any other representative capacity, the authority of the representative to so act must be shown.

15. Stationers and others forwarding large numbers of stamped checks and drafts are requested to enclose in the package a schedule, showing the number of each description of checks and the aggregate value of stamps contained in the package. This will enable this Office to locate any error which may have been made in the count of the stamps, and the schedule can be returned to the consignee of the stamps for his information.

16. In all cases where stamped checks or drafts have been filled up and signed, satisfactory evidence must be furnished that they have never been issued or used in any manner whatsoever. If they have been passed to the payee, or endorsed, the stamps have no redeemable value.

17. Stamps will not be redeemed where the amount is less than fifty cents, but may be exchanged for check or proprietary stamps.

18. Claims will be acted upon, as nearly as possible, in the order of their receipt, and in all cases as soon after their receipt as the condition of the public business will permit.

Green B. Raum,
Commissioner.

IRR v.XXIV, March 11, 1878, pp.73-4

Supreme Court of the United States, October Term, 1880.

Charles J. Folger, Appellant, v. The United States. Distribution of Revenue Stamps.—Appeal from the Court of Claims.

Mr. Justice Harlan delivered the opinion of the court.

In the month of June, 1866, some correspondence passed between Mr. Van Dyck, then Assistant Treasurer of the United States at the city of New York, and the Commissioner of Internal Revenue, as to whether the former should be required, in addition to his ordinary duties, to assist in the distribution of adhesive stamps among those desiring to purchase them for their own use. An official communication from the Secretary of the Treasury to the Assistant Treasurer, under the date of July 2, 1866, shows upon its face that the latter officer objected to being required to perform any such services. In that communication the Secretary says: "The Commissioner of Internal Revenue has referred to me your recent letter to him in relation to the distribution of revenue stamps in the city of New York. I am aware that the cares and responsibilities of your position are burdensome, and I should not think of increasing them were it not for the seeming necessity of so doing. The adhesive revenue stamps are all printed in Philadelphia, and it is deemed imprudent to multiply the places of their production. It is indispensable, however, that every facility shall be given by the Government for their purchase and distribution. The consumption of stamps in New York alone is very large, while the amount which is naturally distributed from that city is no small part of the supply for the whole country. It seems to be very advisable, therefore, because of their great value, that they should be kept, as other property of the Government is kept, in the possession of the Government itself until actual sale. I am aware that the distribution will require a room set apart, perhaps, exclusively for that purpose, and some additional clerical force, but reasonable prudence and a proper regard for the public convenience, as I have suggested, constrain me to ask your critical consideration of the subject. It may not be improper for me to add that the Assistant Treasurer at San

Francisco is employed in the distribution of stamps, and that I am disposed to ask the same service of the several other assistant treasurers in different parts of the country."

In a subsequent communication, of date Sept. 11th, 1866, the Secretary said: "It has been deemed proper, as an additional means of facilitating the distribution of internal revenue stamps, that packages containing such denominations of stamps as are in most general demand should be placed in the hands of the assistant treasurers of the United States and some of the designated depositaries. Printed circulars will be furnished to you, specifying the contents and the cash value of each package, and the packages are to be sold, with seals unbroken, at such value, which will be stated upon each package. The amounts received from the sale of these packages should be transmitted to the Commissioner of Internal Revenue, in the form of certificates of deposit, daily or weekly, as may be most convenient."

At a later period the present appellant became Assistant Treasurer of the United States at the city of New York. Between Nov. 16, 1869, and the 22d day of July, 1870, inclusive, in obedience to the instructions and requirements contained in the foregoing communications, and without any application upon his part, he was furnished by the Commissioner of Internal Revenue with sealed packages of adhesive stamps for sale and distribution. He was not required to give, and did not give, any bond with reference to such stamps. Upon each package, as it came to him, was marked, as well the aggregate face value of the stamps placed therein for delivery to purchasers, as the amount of stamps, of like kind, to be paid out to purchasers, as their commissions under the regulations established by the Commissioner. The packages were directed to be sold and delivered without disturbing their seals.

The commissions, at the time allowed by such regulations, to purchasers of *common* stamps were: 2 per cent in purchases of fifty dollars or more, 3 per cent on $100 or more, 4 per cent on $500 or more, and 5 per cent on $1,000 or more; while as to *proprietary* stamps, the commissions allowed, by statute, were as hereinafter stated.

The sales of stamps by appellant from Nov. 16th, 1869, to July 22d, 1870, inclusive, amounted, of common stamps, to $3,642,754.60, and of proprietary stamps, to $31,589.54. These sums, respectively, included the amount, in stamps, which appellant passed over to purchasers as their commissions. Upon retirement from office his accounts were settled and adjusted at the Treasury Department, without any assertion of a right to commissions for himself. In that settlement he was allowed, or credited with, all payments made by him, in stamps, of commissions to purchasers. The appellant derived no personal advantage from the sales. He brought this action on the first day of May, 1875, to recover from the United States the sum of $184,934.95, to which he claims to be entitled as commissions upon such sales. His claim was denied, and judgment was entered for the Government.

By section 161 of the act of June 30, 1864, providing internal revenue to support the Government, to pay the interest on the public debt, and for other purposes, it is provided, among other things, that "the Commissioner of Internal Revenue be, and he is hereby, authorized to *sell to* and supply collectors, deputy collectors, postmasters, stationers, or any other persons, at his discretion, with adhesive stamps, or stamped paper, vellum, or parchment, as herein provided for, in amounts of not less than $50, *upon payment, at the time of delivery,* of the amount of duties said stamps, stamped paper, vellum, or parchment, so sold or supplied, represent; and may allow, upon the aggregate amount of such stamps, as aforesaid, the sum of *not exceeding five* per centum as commission to the collectors, postmasters, stationers, or other *purchasers;* but the cost of any paper, vellum, or parchment, shall be paid by the purchaser of such stamped paper, vellum, or parchment as aforesaid; *Provided,* That any proprietor or proprietors of articles named in Schedule C, who shall furnish his or her own die or design for stamps, to be used especially for his or their own proprietary articles, shall be allowed the following commission, namely: on amounts purchased at one time, of not less than $50 nor more than $500, five per centum; on amounts over $500, ten per centum." (13 Stat., 294.)

Section 170 of the same act declares "that in any collection district where in the judgment of the Commissioner the facilities for the procurement and distribution of stamped vellum, parchment, or paper and adhesive stamps are or shall be insufficient, the Commissioner is authorized to *furnish, supply, and deliver* to the collector and to the assessor of any such district and to any assistant treasurer of the United States, or designated depositary thereof, or any postmaster a suitable amount of stamped vellum, parchment, or paper, and adhesive stamps, *without prepayment therefor,* and shall allow the highest rate of commissions allowed by law to any other parties purchasing the same;

and may in advance require of any such collector, assessor, assistant treasurer of the United States, or postmaster, a bond with sufficient sureties to an amount equal to the value of any stamped vellum, parchment, or paper, and adhesive stamps, which may be placed in his hands and remain unaccounted for, conditioned for the faithful return, whenever so required, of all quantities or amounts undisposed of, and for the payment monthly of all quantities or amounts sold or not remaining on hand.

"And it shall be the duty of such collector to supply his deputy with, or sell to other parties within his district who may make application therefor, stamped vellum, parchment, or paper, and adhesive stamps, upon the same terms allowed by law or under the regulations of the Commissioner, who is hereby authorized to make such other regulations not inconsistent herewith, for the security of the United States and the better accommodation of the public, in relation to the matters hereinbefore mentioned, as he may judge necessary and expedient.

"And the Secretary of the Treasury may from time to time make such regulations as he may find necessary to insure the safe keeping or prevent the illegal use of all such stamped vellum, parchment, paper, and adhesive stamps." (13 Stat., 297.)

Section 161 plainly provides for sales by the Commissioner, while section 170 authorizes him to furnish and supply certain officers with stamps for sale to others. Whether stamps were purchased directly from the Commissioner of Internal Revenue, for cash, under section 161, or from one of the officers to whom they were furnished for sale and distribution under section 170, in either case, the purchaser, it is conceded, was allowed commissions according to the rate or scale established by the regulations of the Commissioner. Touching the particular sales made by appellant, the purchasers of common or general stamps were entitled, respectively, to five per cent in commissions, and the purchasers of proprietary stamps, to ten per cent. There can be no doubt of this, since the petition of appellant distinctly alleges that his sales of common stamps were in amounts of not less than $1,000, and of proprietary stamps in amounts exceeding $500. If, therefore, it be suggested that appellant was entitled to the difference between the highest rate or per cent allowed by the Government (five per cent in purchases of common stamps, and ten per cent in purchases of proprietary stamps), and the amount paid over to him, in stamps, to purchasers, the obvious answer is, that there was in this case no such difference. This interpretation of the statute, we may observe, could, therefore, be of no practical value to appellant. His contention—and upon no other ground could appellant's claim be sustained—is, that, without reference to the commissions which the purchaser of stamps received—although he may have received the highest rate allowed—appellant was, nevertheless given by the statute, to his own use, and as his personal allowance or compensation for distributing stamps, under section 170, the *highest rate* of commissions, which was allowed to any one buying from the Commissioner of Internal Revenue.

For instance, upon the theory advanced by appellant's counsel, a purchaser, from the Commissioner of Internal Revenue, of common stamps to the amount, at one time, of $1,000 or more, would be allowed five per cent, as commissions, payable in stamps (which, in some cases, would be the full extent of the Government's loss), while upon a sale, through an assistant treasurer of the United States, to the same purchaser of the same stamps, in sealed packages, the Government would lose altogether ten per cent, in commissions—five per cent to the Assistant Treasurer, and five per cent to the purchaser, that is, double commissions. In other words, according to that construction of the statute, the Government held out an inducement to officers, named in sections 161 and 170, not to become themselves purchasers, for cash, of stamps for sale and distribution in their respective localities (as they might under section 161), but to receive them, under section 170, and thereby, without advancing any money, secure for themselves (outside of what the purchasers from them would be allowed), the highest rate of which the law allowed in purchases directly from the Commissioner.

We cannot give our assent to any such construction of the statute. The officers named in section 170, were charged, at the outset, with the value of each sealed package of stamps delivered to them for distribution. In the settlement of their accounts, they were entitled to be credited with the amount of stamps unsold and returned; with the sums received upon sales, and paid over to the Government; and also, with the value of the stamps, placed in the sealed packages, for delivery to purchasers as commissions allowed *to them*. In this way they were relieved from the responsibility assumed when they were supplied with stamps for distribution under section 170. The statutory direction that the commissioner, in such cases, "shall allow the highest rate of commissions allowed by law to any other parties purchasing the same," was an awkward mode of expressing the idea that the same commissions, up to the highest rate, should be allowed, in purchases under section 170, as under section 161—that is, that those wishing stamps might purchase from the officers named in section 170 at the like rate, even the highest, accorded to "any *other* parties *purchasing* the same" stamps, for cash, directly from the commissioner.

As to assistant treasurers, distributing stamps under section 170, we are of opinion that Congress did not intend that they should receive any compensation whatever for services of that character—certainly not, in any case, where the commissions, paid to those who purchased from such officers, were as large as the highest rate prescribed in sales, by the commissioner, for cash, under section 161. It was for the better accommodation of the public that the Secretary of the Treasury required assistant treasurers to aid in the distribution of adhesive stamps. The communications addressed to the assistant treasurer of New York, announcing his purpose to adopt that course, show upon their face, that the Secretary had no expectation thereby of increasing the loss, in the way of commissions, which the Government would sustain upon sales of stamps. He believed that he had the power to impose that duty upon assistant treasurers as an additional means of facilitating the distribution of internal revenue stamps.

The conclusion we have indicated is in line with the settled policy which has existed upon the subject of extra compensation to officers, having fixed salaries or pay, especially in regard to assistant treasurers of the United States.

By an act approved March 3, 1839, making appropriations for the civil and diplomatic service, it was declared, that "no officer in any branch of the public service, or any other person whose salaries or whose pay or emoluments is or are fixed by law or regulations, shall receive any extra allowance or compensation, in any form, whatever, for the disbursement of public money, or for the performance of any other service, unless the said extra allowance or compensation be authorized by law." (5 Stat., 349.) In a subsequent act of August 23, 1842, this prohibition against extra compensation to officers, with fixed salaries, was somewhat enlarged, and this provision was inserted: "No officer in any branch of the public service, or any other person whose salary, pay, or emoluments is, or are, fixed by law or regulations, shall receive any *additional pay,* extra allowance, or compensation, in any form whatever, for the disbursement of public money, or *for any other service or duty whatsoever,* unless the same shall be authorized by law, and *the appropriation therefor explicitly set forth* that it is for such additional pay, extra allowance, or compensation." (5 Stat., 570.) And, at the same session of Congress, by an act approved August 26, 1842, it was declared that "no allowance or compensation shall be made to any clerk or other officer, by reason of the discharge of duties which belong to any other clerk or officer, in the same or any other department; and no allowance or compensation shall be made for any extra services whatever, which any clerk or other officer may be required to perform." (5 Stat., 525.)

We come, then, to the act of August 6, 1846, under which appellant was appointed to office, providing for the better organization of the treasury, and the collection, safe-keeping, transfer, and disbursement of the public revenue. Among the duties imposed by that act, upon assistant treasurers, was that of doing and performing all duties, as fiscal agents of the Government, which might be imposed by that or any other act of Congress, or by any regulation of the Treasury Department made in conformity to law; and, "also to do and perform all acts and duties required by law, or by direction of any of the executive departments of the Government, as agents for paying pensions, or for making any other disbursements which either of the heads of these departments may be required by law to make, and which are of a character to be made by the depositaries hereby constituted, consistently with the other official duties imposed upon them." (9 Stat., 60.) The same act fixed the salaries of the assistant treasurers, and declared: "And these salaries, respectively, shall be in full for the services of the respective officers; nor shall either of them be permitted to *charge* or *receive any commission,* pay, or perquisite, for *any official service, of any character or description whatsoever.*" (9 Stat., 65.) The foregoing provisions in the acts of 1839, 1842, and 1846 have been preserved in sections 1763, 1764, 1765, and 3597 of the Revised Statutes. They were all in force when the general revenue statute of 1864 was passed. Commenting upon the act of August 23, 1842, this court in Stansbury v. United States, 8 Wall., 37, said: "The law was passed to remedy an evil which had existed of detailing officers with fixed pay to perform duties outside of their regular employment, and paying them for it, when the Government was entitled, without this double pay, to all their services. The law prohibited, and was intended to do so, the allowance of such claims as these, made by public officers, for extra compensation, on the ground of extra services."

It will be observed that, while the act of August 23, 1842, allows an officer, having a fixed salary, to receive additional pay, extra allowance, or compensation, if "the appropriation therefor explicitly states that it is for such additional pay, extra allowance, or compensation," the act of 1846 contains no such reservation in favor of assistant treasurers of the United States. As to those officers, the statute expressly forbids *them* from receiving "any commission, pay, or perquisite, for any official service of any character or description whatsoever." And so the law is to this day. (R. S. sec. 3597.)

Of course these provisions would not avail the Government, should Congress, by subsequent enactment, allow assistant treasurers to receive, outside of their fixed salaries, commissions, pay, or perquisites for extra services. But, in view of the established policy of the Government, as shown in the statutes to which we have referred, the act of 1864 should not be construed as a departure from that policy. Its language does not clearly indicate an intention to allow assistant treasurers additional pay or compensation for such services as those which appellant peformed. We are not satisfied that Congress had any purpose to alter the existing statutes in reference to the allowance of extra compensation to assistant treasurers, with fixed salaries. The services of appellant, in connection with the distribution of adhesive stamps, were of a character which he might, consistently with his other official duties, be required to perform. But, if they were not, he was not entitled to compensation, because the statute does not explicitly state that he was to receive additional pay therefor.

The views we have expressed are further fortified by the 25th section of the act of 1864, which declares that "there shall be allowed to collectors, *in full compensation for their services, and that of their deputies,* a salary of $1,500 to be paid quarterly, and in addition thereto a commission of 3 per cent upon the first hundred thousand dollars, and a commission of one per cent upon sums above $100,000 and not exceeding $400,000, and a commission of one-half of one per cent, on all sums above $400,000, such commissions to be computed upon the amounts by them respectively collected and paid over and accounted for under the instructions of the Treasury Department." According to the argument advanced by counsel for appellant, collectors, notwithstanding the foregoing provision, would be entitled to receive, for their services in distributing stamps, under section 170, compensation other and beyond that which section 25 of the same act declares shall be "in full compensation for their services." Such was not, as we think the intention of Congress.

If an assistant treasurer wished to derive personal advantage or profit from the distribution of adhesive stamps, he was at liberty to do so by becoming himself a purchaser for cash, directly from the commissioner, under section 161. The stamps, in that case, would become his property; whereas, if received under section 170, they remained the property of the Government until actual sale. By *purchasing* stamps for cash in amounts of $1,000 and over, he would be allowed, as any other purchaser would be, five per cent as commissions, and, upon sales in small amounts by him to others, he could realize to his own use, the difference between five per cent and the rate (whatever it was) at which the purchaser from him could have obtained stamps directly from the commissioner. But when he received stamps, under section 170, for distribution, he could derive no advantage from their sale, certainly not, in cases where the commissions, allowed to the purchasers, amounted, in sales of common stamps, to five per cent, and in sales of proprietary stamps to ten per cent. Congress never intended that the Government should, in any contingency, lose on sales of adhesive stamps, by whomsoever and in whatever quantities made, more than five per cent of the face value of common stamps, and more than ten per cent of the face value of proprietary stamps.

Mr. Justice Swayne, who heard the argument, and participated in the decision of this case in conference, concurs in this opinion.

The judgment of the Court of Claims is affirmed.

Field, J.—I dissent from the judgment of the court. I think that Mr. Folger was entitled to the difference between the five per cent given by the Government, and the amount he allowed to the [purchasers]. Mr. Justice Bradley concurs in this dissent.

IRR v.XXVII, April 4, 1881, pp.103-4

1883.—Department No. 46.—Internal Revenue.—Circular No. 259.—Redemption of Internal Revenue Check and Proprietary Stamps.

Treasury Department,
Office of Internal Revenue,
Washington, D.C., April 19, 1883.

In view of the repeal, on and after July 1, 1883, of all taxes payable by check and proprietary stamps, the following statutory provisions governing the redemption of such stamps, and the regulations made in pursuance thereof, are published for the benefit of all concerned.

Section 3426, Revised Statutes of the United States, as amended March 1, 1879, provides that—

"The Commissioner of Internal Revenue may, upon receipt of satisfactory evidence of the facts, make allowance for or redeem such of the stamps issued under the provisions of this title, or of any internal revenue act, as may have been spoiled, destroyed, or rendered useless or unfit for the purpose intended, or for which the owner may have no use, or which, through mistake, may have been improperly or unnecessarily used, or where the rates or duties represented thereby have been excessive in amount, paid in error, or in any manner wrongfully collected; and such allowance or redemption shall be made either by giving other stamps in lieu of the stamps so allowed for or redeemed, or by refunding the amount or value to the owner thereof, deducting therefrom, in case of repayment, the percentage, if any, allowed to the purchaser thereof; but no allowance or redemption shall be made in any case until the stamps so spoiled or rendered useless shall have been returned to the Commissioner of Internal Revenue, or until satisfactory proof has been made showing the reason why the same cannot be so returned."

Section 17 of the Act of March 1, 1879, provides—

"That claims for allowance on account of stamps arising under Section 3426 of the Revised Statutes * * * may be allowed, if presented within three years after the purchase of said stamps from the Government, or a Government agent for the sale of stamps, and not otherwise."

Regulations.

1. Check or proprietary stamps presented for redemption should be addressed to "The Commissioner of Internal Revenue, Washington, D.C." and must be forwarded at the risk and expense of the consignor.

2. The stamps should be accompanied by a claim, on Form 81, copies of which form will be furnished upon application to this Office.

3. Claims may be sworn to or affidavits made before any internal revenue officer authorized to administer oaths, without fee. Any other person administering an oath or affirmation must show, by seal or certificate from the proper authority, that he is qualified to do so. An officer in signing a jurat should give the title of his office.

4. Check and general proprietary stamps will be redeemed at their face value, less 5 per centum; private-die proprietary stamps at their face value, less 5 or 10 per centum, according to the rate of commission allowed on their purchase. Stamps may be exchanged for other check or proprietary stamps of equal value until July 1, 1883.

5. In cases where stamped checks or drafts are presented which have been filled up and signed, satisfactory evidence must be furnished that they have never been issued or used in any manner whatsoever. If they have been passed to the payee, or indorsed, the stamps have no redeemable value.

6. In cases where claims for redemption of *imprinted* stamps are allowed prior to July 1, 1883, the blanks upon which the stamps are printed will, in accordance with a long-established rule of this Office, be destroyed. In the case of such claims allowed on or after July 1, 1883, the blanks will be destroyed, unless the claimant shall specially request their return. Upon receipt of such a request, the word "Redeemed" will be impressed on the check or draft in letters 3-16 of an inch in size, and the blanks, which the stamps so cancelled, will be returned to the claimant by registered mail, free of expense, unless he shall otherwise direct, in which latter case they will be returned at his expense. In cases of rejected claims, stamps are always returned to claimants.

7. In cases where an allowance is asked for stamps destroyed, the facts in the case should be submitted to this Office, and special instructions as to the evidence required will be given.

8. Stamps will only be redeemed when presented by a *bona fide* owner, or a duly authorized agent or representative of such owner. When a claim is made by a person acting as an agent, executor, receiver, or in any other representative capacity, the authority of the representative to so act must be shown.

9. In view of the limitation imposed by statute upon the presentation of claims for redemption of stamps, it will be necessary to submit evidence with each claim as to the date on which the stamps for which redemption is asked were purchased from the Commissioner of Internal Revenue or a "stamp agent." Stamps imprinted on checks are not sold by stamp agents, and it is often

impracticable to ascertain when they were purchased from the Commissioner. In such cases, evidence may be furnished as to the date on which the stamps were imprinted on the blanks. Information as to the date of imprinting can usually be obtained from the stationer who printed the checks. Full instructions concerning the form of affidavit required are printed on Form 81.

10. Claims will be acted on, as nearly as possible, in the order of their receipt, and in all cases as soon after their receipt as the condition of the public business will permit.

Green B. Raum,
Commissioner.

IRR v.XXIX, April 30, 1883, pp.137-8

1883.—Department No. 71.—Internal Revenue.—Circular No. 265.—Supplemental to Circular No. 259.—Redemption and Cancellation of Stamps Imprinted on Checks, Drafts, Etc.

Treasury Department,
Office of Internal Revenue,
Washington, D.C., June 1, 1883.

Since the issue of Circular No. 259, dated April 19, 1883, many inquiries have been received concerning the instructions in paragraph 6, which provide, in the case of claims for redemption of stamps imprinted on checks, drafts, etc., allowed on or after July 1, 1883, that the stamps may be cancelled and the blanks returned to the consignors upon receipt of a special request for such cancellation and return.

In answer to these inquiries, and in order to facilitate the work of cancellation, the following amended instructions are issued:

Imprinted stamps may be presented for redemption and cancellation at once, instead of waiting until July first. Such of the stamps received as are redeemed in June will be cancelled and the blanks returned, if possible, in time to reach the owners July first.

Stamped blanks may be presented in sheets or bound in books, and will be returned in the same condition. Blanks which have been compressed into blocks or pads must be separated before presentation.

The cancellation of stamps will be as follows, (the words "Stamp Redeemed" being in red ink:)

[The stamp consists of a diamond with the words "Stamp Redeemed" in the centre.—Ed.]

Requests for cancellation in any form other than that indicated above, or in any place other than this Office, cannot be considered.

Claims for redemption of imprinted stamps should be made on Form 81—"Revised April, 1883" copies of which will be furnished upon application. Care should be exercised in the preparation of claims, as stamps will in no case be cancelled until the claim for their redemption has been examined and found to be satisfactory.

Cases will be taken up for examination in the order of their receipt. If the claim in any case is complete, the stamps accompanying it will be ordered cancelled at once. If the claim is incomplete, and it becomes necessary to call for additional evidence, the case will be laid aside and no further action will be taken until the additional evidence is received.

Walter Evans,
Commissioner.

IRR v.XXIX, June 11, 1883, p.185

PROPRIETARY MEDICINES

Concerning proprietary medicines or preparations.

June, 1863.

Under Schedule C of the excise law, medicines or preparations made and sold, or removed and sold, wherever the person making or preparing the same has or claims to have any private formula or occult secret or art for making or preparing the same, or has or claims to have any exclusive right or title to making or preparing them, or which are recommended or held out to the public by the makers, vendors, or proprietors, as proprietary medicines, or as remedies or specifics for disease, are subject to stamp duties.

By the 107th section it is provided that the act shall not apply to any uncompounded medicinal drug or chemical, nor to any medicine compounded according to the United States or other national pharmacopoeia, nor of which the full and proper formula is published in either of the dispensatories, formularies, or text books in common use among physicians and apothecaries, nor in any pharmaceutical journal now used by any incorporated college of pharmacy, and not sold or offered for sale or advertised under any other name, form, or guise than that under which they may be severally denominated and laid down in said pharmacopoeias, dispensatories, text books, or journals.

The intention of the act of Congress is plain. It is to subject to stamp duty every kind of preparation made and sold as medicinal, and claimed by the maker or vendor to be proprietary, or recommended as possessing peculiar virtues imparted in the manufacture by the secret art or occult formula of the manufacturer; and it is to exempt from duty all medicines known in trade, or compounded according to some published formula, or any medical treatise recognized by the professors of medical science, and not offered for sale under any guise or pretence of proprietorship.

It matters not, therefore, what the commodity may be, substance or essence, that is prepared and removed for sale, if it is claimed or pretended to be a compound of which the formula is secret, or which the right of making is the exclusive property of one or more persons. Though it be only bread rolled into pills, or rainwater imprisoned in little phials, and to be taken in drops, the claim or pretence of the vendor determines its character. It cannot be treated as medicine for the customer, and bread and water only for the tax collector. The dealer must be taken for what he professes himself to be, and if he seeks profit by deluding the public, he must pay for his privilege like an honest man. The assumption must be taken for the fact, and when that of a proprietary right or secret art or knowledge clearly appears, no inquiry as to the composition of the drug will be pertinent or proper. If the packet, box, pot, phial, or other enclosure is not stamped, the penalties of the act are incurred, and ought to be enforced.

Boutwell (1863), Decisions (No. 114)

Decision concerning Stamp Duties on Proprietary Articles.

Treasury Department,
Office of Internal Revenue,
Washington, October, 1863.

The stamp duties imposed in the first paragraph of Schedule C, in the act of July 1, 1862, having been deemed by many persons to apply only to proprietary medicines, it becomes necessary to call the attention of manufacturers and dealers to the true interpretation of said schedule.

In section 99, the subjects of the duty imposed in said schedule are spoken of as ''proprietary articles;'' in section 107 they are described by the words "drugs, medicines, preparations, compositions, articles, or things;'' in the proviso to section 109 they are described as ''medicines, preparations, and compositions;" in section 110 they are spoken of as "articles or commodities." In the first paragraph under Schedule C the articles or commodities made subject to stamp duty are distributed in four classes, as follows:

1st. Any preparation or composition whatsoever wherein the person making or preparing the same has, or claims to have, any private formula or occult secret or art for the making or preparing the same.

2d. Any preparation or composition whatsoever wherein the person making or preparing the same has, or claims to have, any exclusive right or title to the making or preparing the same.

3d. Any preparation or composition whatsoever which is prepared, uttered, vended, or exposed for sale under any letters patent.

4th. Any preparation or composition whatsoever which is held out or recommended to the public by the makers, vendors, or proprietors thereof, as a proprietary medicine, or as a remedy or specific for any disease, diseases, or affections whatever affecting the human or animal body.

The descriptions contained in these four clauses embrace four distinct classes of commodities, and the first three are by no means to be treated as a mere limitation upon the fourth. The fourth class is limited and qualified by the proviso in section 107, which must be construed as heretofore explained in Decision No. 114. The mere fact of the publication of a formula in one of the text-books or journals specified in that section will not exempt a preparation, compounded according to such formula, from stamp duty, when the fact of such publication is ignored, and the claim to a private formula, or occult secret or art, is distinctly set forth upon the labels and wrappers accompanying the preparation, as is usually the case with such preparations as Godfrey's Cordial, Betton's British Oil, Turlington's Balsam of Life, Lee's Billious Pills, &c.

All articles belonging to either of the first three classes, such as inks, blackings, cements, sauces, flavoring extracts, polishes, culinary preparations, or compositions of any nature whatsoever, which purport to have been prepared under any private formula, or occult secret or art, or in the making of which the maker claims any exclusive right or title, or which are prepared under any letters patent, are as fully subject to the stamp duty as those in the fourth class.

From and after October 1, 1863, none of the articles named in Schedule C, including perfumery, cosmetics, and playing cards, as well as articles in the above-described classes, whether they are of foreign or domestic manufacture, can be lawfully offered for sale without having the requisite stamp affixed. By the 27th section of the act of March 3, 1863, any person who shall offer for sale any of the articles named without the same being duly stamped, whether he is a manufacturer or a dealer, is subject to all the duties, liabilities, and penalties imposed by the act of July 1, 1862, for a sale.

All persons, whether dealers or manufacturers, are required to affix and duly cancel the stamps at once upon all such articles as are offered for sale by them. Unstamped articles in the hands of persons other than the manufacturers, which are merely stored in the original packages, and not offered for sale, will not be liable to confiscation; but all goods which are found exposed for sale upon their shelves or counters, or which have been removed from the original package, are subject to forfeiture, under the provisions of section 109, unless the requisite stamps are affixed and cancelled.

It is not proposed by this office to require that the penalties of the law shall be enforced on account of the sale of unstamped articles in the original package prior to the first day of February, 1864, where such sales are made to dealers who purchase to sell again: *Provided,* That in all such cases the purchaser shall be furnished by the seller with the requisite amount of stamps, which must then be affixed and cancelled as soon as the package is opened. The penalties of the law will be strictly enforced for any sales of unstamped articles, whether the same are of foreign or domestic manufacture, when such sales are made on or after the first day of February, 1864.

Every person who offers any such articles for sale will be required by the Assessor of his district to take and subscribe, monthly, the oath No. 34, which, together with the affidavits of manufacturers of proprietary articles, should be filed in the office of the Collector, instead of being transmitted to this office as heretofore.

If the manufacturer of proprietary articles, or the wholesale dealer in the same, acting in good faith, and upon such information as he can obtain, affixes a stamp answering to the retail price in the market where he deals, or in the vicinity thereof, he will be exempt from proceedings for a penalty, even though in other parts of the country such articles may be sold at enhanced prices; but if such articles are subsequently sold at an enhanced price, it will be the duty of the seller to affix the additional stamps required.

When any of the above-described articles are sold in bulk, as by the gallon or barrel, they will be subject to excise tax as a manufacture, either specific or *ad valorem,* as the case may be, in lieu of the stamp duty; but if they are subsequently offered for sale in a box, bottle, or other similar enclosure, the stamps will require to be affixed. For instance, ink which is claimed as proprietary, will be subject, when sold in bulk, to three per cent. tax, as a manufacture not otherwise provided for. Glue which is claimed as proprietary, but sold in bulk in the liquid state, will be subject to the specific tax of twenty-five cents per gallon, &c.

When any manufacturer of proprietary articles, who has paid to this office a sum of money in lieu of the stamp duties, upon articles manufactured and sold since September 1, 1862, without having the requisite stamps affixed, shall furnish satisfactory proof to this office that he has actually affixed stamps to any of the identical articles upon which the duty has been thus paid heretofore, the amount thus affixed will be refunded in stamps: *Provided,* They are thus affixed on or before the first day of January, 1864.

Boutwell (1863), Decisions (No. 126)

The manufacturer of a medicine who has or claims to have any private formula or occult secret or art of making or preparing the same, must cause the appropriate stamp to be affixed to each bottle or package, although he may intend to administer, and shall actually administer the same to patients who are under his personal charge.

Boutwell (1863), Rulings (No. 231)

"Plantation Bitters" are a proprietary medicine, and subject to a proprietary stamp. "Bourbonia Whiskey," "Wolfe's Schiedam Schnapps," and "Bininger's Gin," if not claimed as proprietary, and stamped as such, must be regarded the same as other liquors, subjecting the person who sells them to the liability of a liquor-dealer's license.

Boutwell (1863), Rulings (No. 242)

Proprietary medicines, given to the poor, are exempt from taxation.

Boutwell (1863), Rulings (No. 247)

If the manufacturer of proprietary articles, acting in good faith, and upon such information as he can obtain, affixes a stamp answering to the retail price in the market where he deals, or in the vicinity thereof, he will be exempt from proceedings for penalty, even though in other parts of the country the articles so manufactured and stamped may be sold at enhanced prices.

Articles enumerated in Schedule C, when sold in bulk or in quantities greater than specified or contemplated in the part of the excise law relating to said schedule, will be taxed as manufactures. If such articles are afterwards prepared and sold in such packages as are mentioned or described in Schedule C, the appropriate stamps must be affixed to the packages.

Boutwell (1863), Rulings (No. 244)

It appears from the evidence submitted that the article sold as "Husbands's Calcined Magnesia" is an uncompounded medicinal chemical; but inasmuch as it is offered for sale under a name not laid down in the pharmacopoeias, dispensatories, text-books, or journals mentioned in section 107 of the excise law, and inasmuch as it is advertised and offered for sale under a form or guise not described or denominated in said text-books, it is subject to stamp duty under Schedule C. The maker claims upon the label that the article is prepared by no other person than said "Husbands," which is, in substance, a claim to an exclusive right for making or preparing the article advertised and sold by him.

Boutwell (1863), Rulings (No. 263)

If parties making articles known as essences, such as cinnamon, peppermint, lemon, cloves, &c., do not claim a private formula or occult secret or art for the manufacture, nor an exclusive right or title by letters patent, and if they are not used or applied as perfumes or applications to the hair, mouth or skin, the articles are exempt from stamp duty.

Boutwell (1863), Rulings (from No. 289)

The design of the stamp offered by Mr. ____ cannot be approved. He has proceeded under a misconstruction of the law.

Stamps are not issued to be used upon articles which are exempt from duty; it however appears from Mr. ____ letter that the article prepared by him is subject to stamp duty. He should use either the general proprietary stamp, or furnish a suitable design for a stamp, for which, when engraved and printed, he will be required to pay to the government the customary stamp duties.

The letter of Mr. ____, the assistant assessor, sets forth that the eye salve prepared by Mr. ____ is fully described in the American Eclectic Dispensatory, printed in 1851, at Cincinnati; but it also appears from the letter of Mr. ____ that the eye salve is advertised and sold as "Petitt's eye salve," and that Mr. ____ claims to have a private formula for the making or preparing the same. It is also apparent that this article is offered for sale under a name, form, or guise different from that in which it is laid down or described in the dispensatory mentioned.

Either of these circumstances, if true, will deprive Mr. ____ of the right to sell the article without affixing upon each package the stamp, as required in Schedule C.

It does not appear that the dispensatory referred to is in common use among physicians and apothecaries. If it be not in such use, then the fact of the publication of the formula would not exempt the manufacturer of the medicine from liability to duty.

Upon the evidence presented, I am obliged to rule that the article prepared by Mr. ____ is subject to a stamp duty, and that the sale of such article, without the use of stamps, renders him liable to the penalty prescribed in the 109th section of the excise law.

Boutwell (1863), Rulings (No. 290)

"Bininger's Old London Dock Gin" is represented as being a pure article of liquor, and not a preparation, and so is exempt from stamp-duty.

Boutwell (1865), Rulings (No. 288)

Medical Compounds.

All medical compounds, following the formula of the U.S. or National Pharmacopoeia, Dispensatories, formularies or text-books, in common use among Physicians and Apothecaries, are not liable to stamp or ad valorem duties, and no special license is required to use them.

IRR v.I, January 21, 1865, p.19

Medical Compounds by Druggists.

Treasury Department,
Washington, July 20, 1865.

Sir: Under section one hundred and sixty-five of the act of June 30, 1864, druggists are exempt from stamp duty upon any uncompounded medicinal drug or chemical, or any medicine compounded according to the United States or other national pharmacopoeia, or according to the formula of either of the dispensatories, formularies, or text-books in common use among physicians and apothecaries, including homoeopathic and eclectic, or any pharmaceutical journal now used by any incorporated college of pharmacy, and not sold or offered for sale, or advertised under any other name, form, or guise than that under which they may be severally denominated and laid down in said pharmacopoeias, dispensatories, text-books, or journals. But under section 94 of said act druggists may be liable to an ad valorem duty of six per cent. upon any drugs, medicines, medicinal preparations or compositions, made, prepared, and sold, or removed for consumption or sale, by them, as manufactures not otherwise provided for, though the same are exempt from stamp duty under schedule C.

Very respectfully,
E. A. Rollins,
Deputy Commissioner.

IRR v.II, July 29, 1865, p.28

R. B. L.—Patent medicines must be stamped by the manufacturer according to the *retail* price in the market at the place of production. If articles thus stamped are sold for greater prices than for which stamped, the deficiency of stamps must be supplied by the dealer, in conformity to the provisions of section 169, making dealers in such articles liable to all the duties, liabilities, and penalties of manufacturers.

IRR v.II, November 18, 1865, p.155

Proposed Revenue Amendments.–The Secretary of the Treasury has received the report of the United States Revenue Commission, on proprietary and other medicines, perfumery, playing cards, etc., as sources of revenue. . . .

The commission recommend that schedule C, under the head of "Medicinal Preparations," be changed and amended by inserting near the end of the first paragraph, after the words "retail price or value," the words "as fixed by the maker of the article, the sum of ten cents, one cent; and for every additional ten cents, or fractional parts thereof the sum of one cent additional," and by omitting all under this head after the words "retail price or value" in the first paragraph.

This recommendation would increase the general stamp duty upon this head of schedule C to ten per cent., and upon articles which retail at twenty-five and seventy-five cents to twelve and eleven per cent.

IRR v.III, March 24, 1866, p.89

Proprietary and other Articles, and Medicines liable to Stamp Tax.

Office of Internal Revenue,
Sept. 18th, 1867.

Sir: I have received your letter of the 14th inst., in which you inquire if patent medicines, manufactured prior to the passage of the Internal Revenue Law, are liable to stamp duty.

In reply I have to say that if such medicines are sold or removed for consumption and sale, they are liable to stamp duty. The language of schedule C, is that "For and upon every packet, box, bottle, pot, phial, or other enclosure, containing any pills, powders, tinctures, &c. &c., made and sold, or removed for consumption and sale, &c.'' The statute does not declare that *hereafter* every person making or perparing such articles shall be liable to the stamp duty; but the liability is upon the articles *already made,* when the same are sold, or removed for consumption and sale.

The language of the enacting clause is different from that used in section 94 with regard to specific and ad valorem duties. Section 94 declares expressly that the tax shall be paid by the *manufacturer,* or *producer,* and upon articles which shall be produced and sold or be manufactured, or made, and sold, &c.

The reason for this difference is obvious. Section 94 imposes taxes only on domestic manufactures. But the stamp duties imposed by schedule C apply equally to imported articles, on which impost duties have been paid, as to domestic manufactures, and the time of manufacture, and the date of importation are immaterial. If the imported articles are offered or exposed for sale, except in original and unbroken packages, they are required to be stamped. The law does not require the manufacturer of articles liable to stamp duty under Schedule C, to make monthly returns of products and sales. The stamp is the evidence of the payment of the tax. The absence of a stamp is *prima facie* evidence of fraud.

Section 169 of the Act of June 30th, 1864, still in force, declares that *any person who shall offer or expose for sale,* any of the articles named in Schedule C, or in any amendments thereto, whether the articles so offered or exposed are imported, or are of foreign or domestic manufacture, shall be deemed the manufacturer thereof, and subject to all duties, liabilities and penalties imposed by law in regard to the sale of domestic articles without the use of the proper stamp, or stamps, denoting the tax paid thereon.

By this section, whoever *offers* or *exposes* for sale articles enumerated in Schedule C, is to be regarded as the *manufacturer,* and whether the articles are of *foreign* or *domestic* manufacture, he incurs the manufacturer's liabilities; the first of which is the affixing of proper stamps; and second, if he fails to affix such stamps, denoting the proper tax, he incurs a penalty of fifty dollars for every omission. This penalty is imposed under Section 165, first, if he *makes, prepares* and sells; and second, if he *removes* for *consumption* or *sale*. Either of these conditions imposes the liability; the latter ''removed for *consumption* or *sale,*'' equally with the former. This must be so, inasmuch as the liability attaches to *foreign articles,* made in a foreign country, by *persons unknown to our Revenue laws*. It is clear, therefore, that the time of manufacture has not, and cannot have anything to do with the question of liability to stamp tax. The only questions to be asked with regard to such articles are, first, do they come under either of the specifications named in the schedule of articles liable to stamps; and second, are they, or have they been sold, removed, offered, or exposed for sale. If so, the person selling, exposing or offering for sale, whether the actual maker of the articles, or only a dealer in them, and whether made before or subsequent to the passage of the Internal Revenue law, must affix the proper stamps denoting the payment of the tax, or incur the penalty of the law.

Respectfully,
Thomas Harland,
Acting Commissioner.

IRR v.VI, October 5, 1867, p.123

Liabilities of Manufacturers of Bitters, for Medicinal use Exclusively and for Beverage–with Respect to Special Tax–Manufacturers', Rectifiers' and Proprietary Stamp Tax.

Office of Internal Revenue,
Washington, August 23, 1869.

Sir: I have received a letter from Edmund Dexter & Sons, in which they state that demand has been made upon their firm by Assistant Assessor Autenheimer for the payment of the special tax of fifty cents per barrel on spirits used by them in the composition of Bitters.

They further state, that under a rectifier's license (special tax) they manufacture ''Bitters'' put up for medical use; that they purchase all the spirits they use from another rectifier, who pays all taxes thereon to which he is liable; that after the necessary compounding, their whole manufacture is limited to packing in bottles, which are enclosed in cases, with a four cent internal revenue stamp affixed to each bottle.

Under this statement of facts, they enquire (1) Whether they are liable to pay the special tax of fifty cents per barrel on their products.

(2) Whether they are not entitled to have refunded to them the amounts paid by them as rectifiers, not having as yet acted under this special tax receipt, and (3) If a manufacturer's license (special tax) together with the stamps required to be affixed to each bottle, does not cover the full amount of their liability.

I am not prepared, upon an *ex parte* statement of this case, to answer the enquiries thus submitted. I have therefore referred Dexter & Sons to you, and will endeavor to give you such general instructions in relation to the matter as will enable you, with full knowledge of the facts before you, to decide correctly with regard to their liability under the law.

You are aware that there are two classes of bitters known to the trade, taxed at different rates and under different provisions of law.

The first comprises all those bitters known as medicinal preparations or compositions, sold almost exclusively by druggists and apothecaries, and *always* used as a medicine —*never* as a beverage.

The second class, which comprises by far the greater portion of all the articles put up or sold under the name of "bitters," although almost always claimed to be medicinal, are in fact nothing more than an "imitation or compound liquor," sold at almost every bar and by almost every liquor dealer in the country, more or less, and drunk as a beverage.

The first of these two classes, viz.: bitters that are *medicines,* and only medicines, if falling under either of the five conditions enumerated in Schedule C, are liable to the stamp tax, and must in all cases be stamped according to their retail value, before they are sold or removed for consumption and sale. Bitters of this class are to be regarded and treated as manufactures, or manufactured articles, the same as any other medicines or medicinal preparations, and may be made or manufactured under a manufacturer's special tax receipt.

A manufacturer of *medicinal* bitters, such as are liable to stamp tax, is not to be regarded as a rectifier, unless at the same time he purchases raw or unrectified spirits and rectifies them before using the same in the manufacture of bitters. In case he rectifies the spirits he uses, he becomes both rectifier and manufacturer and is liable for both taxes.

The second class of bitters referred to, viz.: bitters sold or used, or capable of use as beverages—made by mixing spirits, wine or other liquor with any materials to be sold under the name of "Wine Bitters," or any other name, can properly be manufactured, made or mixed only under a special tax receipt as rectifier.

Every person producing this second class of bitters, becomes liable to the special tax of fifty cents per barrel, as provided in the 59th section of the act of July 20, 1868, as amended by the act of April 10th, 1869.

Dealers in such bitters are to be treated the same as dealers in any other liquors.

If, upon a careful examination, you shall find that Messrs. Dexter & Sons are manufacturers or compounders of the second class of bitters herein described, they are properly held liable as rectifiers, and for the tax of fifty cents per barrel for each barrel produced in excess of 200 barrels.

But if you shall find that their bitters are already of the first class described, and that they do not rectify the spirits they use in the production of their bitters, then a special tax as manufacturers, with the stamps attached to each bottle or other enclosure, according to its retail value, covers their liability, and they will be entitled to have the tax paid as rectifiers refunded.

Very respectfully,
C. Delano,
Commissioner.

Horace G. Stoms, Assessor,
Cincinnati, O.

IRR v.X, August 28, 1869, p.65

Brown's Essence of Jamaica Ginger.

Editor of Record:

Is the "Essence of Jamaica Ginger" liable to stamp duty as a proprietary medicine?

Yours, etc.,
Assistant-Assessor.

It is clearly so in our judgment, though we do not remember that any ruling of the Department has been published; perhaps, because no one questioned the liability.—Ed.

IRR v.X, November 20, 1869, p.164

Bitters Drawn off in Bottles and Sold as Proprietary Medicines by Purchasers thereof in Bulk under Rectifier's Brand.

Montgomery, Ala.,
Oct. 25th, 1869.

Hon. C. Delano, *Commissioner of Internal Revenue, Washington, D.C.*

Sir: I have the honor to request information as to whether "Bitters," 2nd class, as referred to in your letter to Assessor Horace G. Stoms, Cincinnati, Ohio, of date August 23d, 1869, (RECORD, August 28th, 1869,) if drawn from original package as rectified, and put up in bottles, is liable to stamp duty under Schedule C.

If such bitters are put up in bottles and not liable to stamp duty, it will be almost impossible to determine to which class bitters in bottles belong.

I have the honor to remain, Sir,

Very respectfully, your obedient servant,
Francis Widmer,
Collector, 2nd District, Ala.

[Answer.]

Office of Internal Revenue,
Washington, November 9th, 1869.

Sir: I have received your letter of the 25th ultimo, in which you inquire if bitters of the 2nd class as described in my letter of August 23d, 1869, to Assessor Stoms of Cincinnati, when drawn from original packages as rectified, and put up in bottles are liable to stamp duty under Schedule C.

In reply I have to say that it has not been in contemplation by this office to hold the same article liable to the rectifier's tax as a beverage, and also to the manufacturer's tax as a medicine.

The manufacturer of bitters is entirely to be classed under one head or the other, and having been so classed, and complied with the requirements of law either as a rectifier of imitation or compound liquors, or as a manufacturer of medicines, he should be regarded as having discharged the full measure of his liability. Should the purchaser of such bitters as are sold in barrels under the rectifier's brands, marks and stamps, afterwards draw off into bottles such bitters, I do not conceive that he would, by so doing, incur any liability which a dealer in other kinds of liquors would not incur by drawing from barrels and putting up in bottles for the convenience of trade.

If, however, he should attach to such bottles labels giving them the appearance of patent or proprietary medicines, he might thereby expose these liquors to the liability of seizure.

Very respectfully,
J. W. Douglass,
Acting Commissioner.

Francis Widmer, Esq., *Collector,*
2nd District, Montgomery, Ala.

IRR v.X, November 27, 1869, p.172

Liabilities of Manufacturers of Medicinal Bitters in Respect of Stamping Packages thereof sold in Bulk and otherwise, with Proprietary Revenue Stamp.

Office of Internal Revenue,
Washington, Dec. 13, 1869.

Gentlemen:—In reply to your letter of the 10th inst., in which you propound several questions with regard to the privileges and liability of manufacturers of medicinal bitters, in case they are required to affix revenue stamps as per Schedule C on said bitters when sold in bulk, as for instance in packages containing ten, twenty, or forty gallons each, I have to say that the manufacturer must determine the denomination and value of the stamp or stamps to be affixed to each such package by the price at which he sells a single original package. If he sells a single package containing forty gallons of bitters including the barrel for $100, he would be required to affix a stamp or stamps of the value of $4, and in like manner for a package containing any other quantity. The price of a single original package or enclosure is the measure by which to determine the amount or value of stamps to be affixed.

2. This office does not so construe the law, and will not so endeavor to enforce it, as to prohibit a manufacturer from selling his medicinal bitters in original packages, whatever may be the capacity of such original packages, or to prohibit purchasers from breaking original packages and putting the contents into phials or bottles for sale if they wish to do so.

3. This office holds that the purchaser of an original package containing ten, twenty, forty or any other number of gallons of medicinal bitters or other patent or proprietary medicine, who should break such original package, and repack into phials, bottles or other small enclosures, and affix the manufacturer's labels showing that the article was a patent or proprietary article, or should affix a label bearing his own name and trade-mark, and then expose or offer such packages for sale, he would be liable to affix revenue stamps according to his retail price of such packages with their contents.

The reasons for this ruling you will find in the provisions of the 169th section of the Act of June 30th, 1864, as amended, and in the definition of a manufacturer, as given in the 31st paragraph of the 79th section of the same act, as amended by the Act of March 2, 1867.

Yours respectfully,
C. Delano,
Commissioner.

Messrs. Chipman, Hosmer & Co.,
Attorneys for Fletcher, Hoag & Steel,
Washington, D.C.

IRR v.X, December 18, 1869, p.193

Cough Candies Require Stamps.

Office of Internal Revenue,
Washington, April 6, 1870.

D. H. Stanton, *Assessor Seventeenth District, Malone, N. Y.*

Sir: I am in receipt of samples of cough candy (Greenfield's and P. D. Ballou's) said to be sold extensively in your district, and without stamps.

The cough candies are both liable to stamp duty, and you will therefore require all persons in your district selling or offering the same for sale to stamp them immediately.

These cough candies when sold or offered for sale without stamping are liable to seizure, and the parties so selling or offering for sale are liable to prosecution under the internal revenue law.

J. W. Douglass,
Acting Commissioner.

IRR v.XI, April 16, 1870, p.123

Manufacturers of Bitters Put Up, Advertised, and Sold in Good faith as Medicine, not held to be Rectifiers.

Office of Internal Revenue,
Washington, March 28, 1870.

Eben F. Stone, *Assessor, Newburyport, Mass.*

Sir: I reply to yours of the 23d instant, that persons who manufacture any medicinal compound containing alcoholic spirits, advertise, put up, stamp, and sell the same, in good faith, *only as a medicine,* even though the same may subsequently be sold and used to some extent as a beverage, should not be held subject to special tax as rectifiers, but should be treated as manufacturers, and required to stamp their products under "Schedule C."

IRR v.XI, April 30, 1870, p.137

Manufacturers of Bitters may be Taxed Either as Rectifiers or as Manufacturers.

Office of Internal Revenue,
Washington, May 18, 1870.

John S. Nixon, *Esq., U. S. Collector, Covington, Ky.*

Sir: Your letter of the 28th ult. with four enclosures in the matter of "tonic bitters" manufactured by W. M. Ward & Co. and W. B. Wood in your city, has been received and contents carefully noted.

You complain, and perhaps rightly, of your inability to reconcile the different rulings of this office on the subject of bitters.

To exactly survey the boundary line between "spurious, imitation or compound liquors," sold under the name of wine bitters, or other name, as provided for under section 59 of the act of July 20, 1868, as subsequently amended, and medicinal preparations or compositions sold under the name of "tonics" or "bitters" as described and provided for in Schedule C, and to lay down a rule so clear and distinct that every man's product can immediately be classified and placed in the correct category, is not an easy task.

The fact is that the two provisions of law conflict, and in many cases the same article is embraced within the terms of both of these provisions.

Again, in the division of labor rendered necessary by the varied and multiplied subjects presented to this office, all subjects relating to distilled and rectified spirits are assigned to one division, while another division has sole charge of medicines and all medicinal preparations and compositions liable to tax under Schedule C.

The persons in charge of these different divisions, writing on the subject of bitters—looking at the subject from different standpoints, and each referring the facts in a given case to different provisions of law, would not be very likely to exactly harmonize in all their rulings and decisions.

This explanation, I trust, will account to you sufficiently for any seeming or real contradictions in rulings.

Another trouble has been, that among the manufacturers themselves of bitters of the same general character—while one has stoutly contended that he was only a rectifier and was not liable to the stamp tax under Schedule C, another has just as strenuously contended for the right to stamp his bitters as medicines, contending that their sale almost entirely depended upon the medicinal qualities and properties stamped upon them, and alleging that to be placed in the category of a rectifier—compounding merely "spurious, imitation or compound liquors" would result in the ruin of his business.

Still another difficulty arises from the fact that bitters put up in the style of proprietary medicines and claimed to be proprietary, labelled as "medicinal," advertised in newspapers and by public handbills for popular sale and use as having special proprietary claim to merit, and as remedies or specifics for various diseases, cannot pass current upon the market without proprietary stamps—either the general ones, or those from private dies.

Every officer of the revenue who finds such articles on the market will question the propriety of their sale, and very properly, too, inasmuch as the makers and venders put them upon the market, not as imitation or compound liquors, but as *medicines*.

In view of these facts, this office has somewhat modified its first rulings on this subject, at least to this extent, that every man who prepares or compounds bitters, using in their preparation rectified spirits on which the tax has been paid, and who prefers to be placed in the class of manufacturers of medicines rather than that of rectifiers of distilled spirits, and to stamp the bitters which he manufactures or compounds according to the provisions of Schedule C before selling the same or removing them from the place of manufacture, shall be allowed to pay special tax as manufacturer, and shall not be required to pay special tax as rectifier. And in the case of Messrs. Ward & Co. and of Mr. Wood, who manufacture "tonic bitters," the sale of which depends, as I understand, largely upon their medicinal characters, I would suggest that hereafter they be taxed as manufacturers of medicines.

If, however, they prefer to be taxed as rectifiers for compounding these tonic bitters, they must not put them up in the style of proprietary medicines, nor vend them as medicines.

J. W. Douglass,
Acting Commissioner.

IRR v.XI, May 28, 1870, p.169

Directions for Determining what Preparations Containing Distilled Spirits are to be Taxed under Schedule C.

Office of Internal Revenue,
Washington, Dec. 27, 1870.

B. R. Cowen, Esq., Supervisor, Cincinnati, Ohio.

Sir: You ask, "How am I to determine what preparations containing distilled spirits are to be taxed under schedule C?"

In reply I have to say that none but medicinal preparations or compositions are taxed under said schedule, and only such medicinal preparations or compositions wherein the person preparing or making the same has or claims to have any private formula or occult secret or art for the preparing or making the same, or claims to have the exclusive right or title to the making or preparing the same, or such as are prepared, uttered, vended, or exposed for sale under any letters patent, or held out or recommended to the public by the makers, vendors, or proprietors thereof as proprietary medicines, or as remedies or specifics for any disease or affection whatever affecting the human or animal body. Whether the preparation or composition is really a medicinal one or not may generally be determined from the manner in which it is put up, or from the character of the labels or advertisements thereof, or from all of these; and in the same way it may be determined whether the preparation is put up under any claim of private formula or occult secret, or by virtue of any exclusive right under letters patent or otherwise; or whether it is held out or recommended as a proprietary medicine, or as a remedy or specific for any disease. When by any of these evidences either of these characters are given to the preparation or composition it should be regarded as medicinal and as coming under schedule C, and each enclosure should have the proper stamp.

If, however, the preparation is an imitation wine, not made from grapes grown in the United States, or contains distilled spirits, and does not come under schedule C, it is to be taxed under section 48 or 59 of the act of July 20, 1868, as will be seen by reference to letter of November 23 to Supervisor S. B. Dutcher, and published to the Internal Revenue Record of December 23, 1870.

J. W. Douglass,
Acting Commissioner.

IRR v.XII, December 31, 1870, p.213

Packing and Stamping of Bay–Use of Schedule B stamps on Medicines, etc., Taxed under Schedule C, Discouraged, but not Forbidden.

Office of Internal Revenue,
Washington, Jan. 4, 1871.

W. Raymond Lee, Esq., Assessor, Boston, Mass.

Sir: I have received your letter of the 24th ultimo, relative to the packing and stamping of bay rum.

In reply I have to inform you that where manufacturers put up this article for sale in ten-gallon packages, they should affix to each such package stamps corresponding in value to the price received for a single package with its contents.

A dealer may sell at retail from such stamped package, and where his customers furnish vessels in which to take it away no additional stamps are required.

A dealer who breaks the original package, and repacks in smaller vessels and puts his own name or trade-mark on the bay rum so repacked, would be liable to stamp all such packages.

If the original package is broken and the contents drawn off into pint and quart bottles and exposed or offered for sale without proper stamps affixed, the goods would be liable to seizure, even though the dealer did not attach his own name or trade-mark. Any person who offers or exposes for sale any of the articles named in Schedule C is deemed to be the manufacturer thereof, and subject to all the duties, liabilities, and penalties imposed by law in regard to the sale of domestic articles, without the use of the proper stamp or stamps denoting the tax paid thereon. (See section 169, act of June 30, 1864, as subsequently amended.)

Bay rum is simply and purely a cosmetic, and in all cases liable to stamp tax under Schedule C. It is properly manufactured only under a special tax receipt as manufacturer. Every package put up for sale should be stamped, and when stamped it may be sold like any other stamped cosmetic, perfumery, medicine, or medicinal preparation.

The regulations issued by this office do not forbid the use of Schedule B stamps on medicines, medicinal compounds, cosmetics, etc., taxed under Schedule C. The law is not entirely clear on the subject. While, therefore, I would not encourage the use of such stamps on articles liable to stamp tax under Schedule C, I would not advise interference with articles thus stamped, provided the stamps represent an amount equal to the tax to which the package with its contents is liable, inasmuch as it is apparent that in all that class of cases there can be no fraudulent intent in the use of the stamps.

J. W. Douglass,
Acting Commissioner.

IRR v.XIII, January 7, 1871, p.1

How to Determine whether a Preparation containing Distilled Spirits should be Taxed under Section 59, and put up and Stamped under Section 25, or not.

Office of Internal Revenue,
Washington, April 24, 1871.

Joseph D. Webster, Esq., Assessor, First District, Chicago, Ill.

Sir: From numerous communications received at this office, it appears that a misunderstanding exists as to the liability of ''Warner's Proprietary Medicine Company'' of your city to pay tax on account of the manufacture of ''Warner's Vinum Vitae, or Wine of Life.''

As the preparation contains distilled spirits, there seems to be no question but that the manufacturers are liable to some one of the taxes imposed under the revenue laws, but the difficulty is to determine which of these taxes.

If the preparation when completed may be properly classifed as distilled spirits, then it should be taxed under section 59, and put up and stamped under section 25, act July 20, 1868. If, however, it is not classified as distilled spirits, but "produced by being rectified or mixed with distilled spirits or by the infusion of any matter in spirits,'' it should be taxed under section 48 of said act, unless it is found to be a medicinal preparation, such as is described in Schedule C.

When other materials are compounded with distilled spirits to such an extent as that the predominance of the other material reduces the proof of the spirits, as shown by the United States standard hydrometer, to 50 per cent. proof spirits or less, it is held not to be distilled spirits within the meaning of that term as used in said section 59.

This distinction between distilled spirits and liquors compounded therefrom is based upon the alcoholic strength of wine, and the recognized fact that when distilled spirits are reduced to 50 per cent proof spirits by the addition of any material, it ceases to be recognized and sold as distilled spirits.

Applying this rule, you will be able at once to determine whether the liquor should be taxed under section 59, and put up and stamped under section 25, or not.

A liquor, though produced by being rectified or mixed with distilled spirits or by the infusion of any matter in spirits, will not come under the provisions of section 48 if it be a medicinal preparation. This can generally be determined from the manner in which the preparation is put up, the character of the labels and advertisements, and the manner in which it is offered for sale.

If the manner of putting up, labelling, advertising, and selling is such as to show that the preparation is held out to the public as a medicinal preparation only, this may be taken as satisfactory evidence of its medicinal character. A medicinal preparation is only subject to tax under Schedule C when the person making or preparing the same has or claims to have any private formula or occult secret or art for making or preparing the same, or has or claims to have any exclusive right or title to the making or preparing the same, or when the preparation is uttered, offered, or vended or exposed for sale under any letters patent, or held out or recommended to the public by the makers, venders, or proprietors thereof as a proprietary medicine or as a remedy or specific for disease. Whether the preparation is so made, uttered, vended, or held out can also generally be determined from the manner in which it is put up and the character of the labels and advertisements.

By these rules you will be enabled to determine under which of said sections all such products are to be taxed. It was by these rules that ''Warner's Vinum Vitae'' was held in letter to you of January 24, 1870, to be a medicinal preparation, and subject to tax as such.

A. Pleasonton, Commissioner.

IRR v.XIII April 29, 1871, p.129

Corn Plasters and Gelatine Capsules of Pure Balsam Copaiva Liable to Stamp Duty under Schedule C.

Office of Internal Revenue,
Washington, January 30, 1872.

Messrs. Fuller & Fuller, 22 Market St., Chicago, Ill.

Gentlemen: Your letter of January 25, enclosing a sample of imported ''Corn Plasters,'' and a sample of imported ''Gelatine Capsules of Pure Balsam Copaiva,'' has been received.

You wish to know whether these articles are liable to stamp duty under ''Schedule C.''

In answer, I have to say that in regard to medicinal articles taxation is the rule, and exemption the exception. This office is of opinion that both the articles above named are liable to stamp duty under ''Schedule C.''

Very respectfully,
(Signed) B. J. Sweet,
Acting Commissioner.

IRR v.XV, February 15, 1872, p.45

Soaps Advertised and Recommended as Having Special Virtues as Medicinal Preparations or Cosmetics, are Liable to Stamp Tax under Schedule C.

Treasury Department,
Office of Internal Revenue,
Washington, May 27, 1873.

Alex. P. Tutton, Esq., Supervisor, Philadelphia, Pa.

Sir: I have received your letter of the 23d inst., enclosing eight labels and wrappers used upon soaps which you say are largely sold throughout your district, and asking for my decision as to whether these labels render the soap to which they are attached, and by which they are held out and recommended for sale to the public by the makers and vendors, liable to stamp tax under Schedule C.

In reply I have to inform you that soaps of all descriptions, including fancy, scented, honey, cream, transparent, toilet, and shaving soaps, are exempt from taxation when they are not placed in the category of medicinal preparations, nor held out as remedies or specifics for diseases, or affections of the body, nor placed in the category of cosmetics and as such recommended for popular use and sale.

But on the contrary, when such soaps are held out and recommended to the public as medicinal preparations and cosmetics, and special merit is claimed for them, and patronage solicited on account of their healing, improving, and beautifying qualities and properties, and when these claims are clearly and prominently set forth on the wrappers, labels, and circulars accompanying each packet, or box, or pot, or other enclosure, they become liable to stamp tax under Schedule C. I have examined these labels and marked such of them as, in my opinion, set up claims which render the soaps covered by them liable to stamp tax, and those that are not liable.

When it is claimed for any soap that ''it removes unhealthy emanations from the skin,'' ''cures cutaneous eruptions," "renovates and freshens the complexion," "alike good in the sickroom, nursery, or on the toilet stand,'' I hold that it is liable to the stamp tax. When a particular soap is claimed ''to be beneficial in removing tan, sunburn, moth, and freckles,'' when it is advertised ''to cleanse and invigorate the skin, and to improve the complexion,'' as it is claimed of the oat-meal and glycerine soap, such soap is placed in the category of cosmetics, and as such must be stamped.

When a soap is especially recommended for ''the healthy action'' which it produces ''upon the skin,'' for its power to remove ''eruptive humors from the face,'' its tendency ''to ward off infectious diseases," and its tendency to "improve the complexion generally"—recommendations and claims set up for the ''Camphor Ice Soap''—such soap is placed in the category of cosmetics, and must be so regarded by revenue officers.

The ''Tar Soap,'' according to the label, has been well tested as to ''its efficacy in curing salt rheum and other obstinate cutaneous diseases.'' While the ''Tar and Glycerine Soap,'' aromatic and extra fine in quality, ''renovates the complexion and removes pimples, tan, and sunburn,'' improving, healing, and beautifying properties which give the special value to cosmetics.

These soaps, with such claims, and accompanied with such labels and wrappers, are clearly covered by the language of the statute defining what medicinal and cosmetic articles shall be stamped. And so long as the makers and vendors of such soaps elect to place them in this category, it will be the duty of revenue to see that they are properly stamped.

Enclosed I return the labels.

Yours respectfully,
J. W. Douglass,
Commissioner.

IRR v.XVIII, July 19, 1873, p.17

Description of Medicines and Medicinal Preparations liable to Stamp Tax under Schedule C.

Treasury Department,
Office of Internal Revenue,
Washington, September 9, 1873.

Alexander P. Tutton, Esq., Supervisor, Philadelphia, Pa.

Sir: I have received your letter of the 28th ult., enclosing samples of labels ''used upon medicinal preparations and compositions largely manufactured and sold by all druggists and apothecaries,'' and which you state have hitherto been considered by you as not liable to stamp duty under Schedule C. These labels you have separated, characterizing them as ''officinal'' and ''non-officinal,'' the first being ''all published in the United States Dispensatory;'' the second, prepared or compounded according to the full and proper formulae "published in the different books or journals of pharmacy in general use among physicians and apothecaries."

You state in your letter that there seems to be considerable difficulty in determining which of these regular medicines are liable to stamp tax, and which not–that this matter is more or less perplexing to the trade as well as to the revenue officers themselves, and that therefore you ask for a decision from this office with regard to the liability or non-liability of the medicinal preparations covered by these different labels, and which may apply, in general, to all medicinal preparations with similar labels attached.

In reply I have to say that the opinion has been very generally entertained heretofore by manufacturers, compounders, and vendors of medicines and medicinal articles that only such medicines and medicinal preparations and compositions as were patent, or proprietary, or made or prepared by some private formula, or occult secret, or art, were liable to stamp tax; and that all medicines, etc., compounded according to the United States, or other national pharmacopoeia, or where the full and proper formula is published in any standard medical authority, are exempt from such tax; and many revenue officers have, without a careful examination of the precise terms of the law, too generally acquiesced in the same opinion.

But the law in fact gives only a conditional exemption to any medicine or class of medicines. The class of medicines exempted, and the conditions of such exemption, are to be found in the 13th section of the act of July 13, 1866. Having carefully described what classes of medicines, and under what conditions said medicines, etc., are exempt, it is declared peremptorily that ''nothing in this section (viz., in section 13 of the act of July 13, 1866, and this is the only section in the law that authorizes any exemption) shall be construed to exempt from stamp tax any medicinal articles, whether simple or compounded by any rule, authority, or formula, published or unpublished, which are put up in a *style or manner similar* to that of patent or proprietary medicines in general, or advertised in newspapers, or by public hand-bills for popular sale and use, as having any special proprietary claim to merit, or to any peculiar advantage in mode of preparation, quality, use, or effect, whether such claim be real or pretended.''

It is held therefore by this office that all medicines and medicinal preparations put up in a style or manner *similar* to that of patent or proprietary medicines in general are liable to stamp tax.

The style or manner of putting up need not be exactly like the style adopted in putting up patent or proprietary articles. There need be only a similarity of style, a likeness in the general points.

What, then, is the general style or manner adopted by the makers and vendors of patent or proprietary medicines? This is a matter required to be known in order to determine whether in a particular or given case the style or manner of putting up a medicine, not claimed to be patent or proprietary, is ''similar,'' and whether, on account of such style or manner, it ought to be stamped.

I reply that it is not alone or mainly in the shape or kind of bottle or enclosure containing the article, though liquid medicines are frequently put into peculiar shaped bottles, having the name of the proprietor or patentee blown into the glass, but the leading characteristics of this style are (1) that such medicines are almost always put up in *retail packages,* packages which are sold *with their contents* directly to the consumer, and (2) each package is accompanied with a label, a hand-bill, or a wrapper containing an enumeration of the diseases or affections for which the medicine is a specific or remedy, containing also directions as to where and how it is to be taken, what constitutes a proper dose, either for an adult or a child, how frequently such doses are to be taken, etc., and generally such directions with regard to the mode of administering the medicine as physicians give when called to prescribe for a patient.

These are the distinguishing characteristics in the mode or style adopted in putting up patent and proprietary medicines. It is a style adapted to popular sale and use–to enable the sick to supply themselves with the most popular remedies, and to use the same without the aid or assistance, or even of the advice, oftentimes, of a physician or medical practitioner.

Medicines and medicinal preparations, whether ''officinal'' or ''non-officinal,'' by whatever rule or authority or formula compounded, put up in such a style, *in retail packages,* and accompanied with a label, a circular, or a wrapper giving the disease, diseases, or affections for which such medicines have been and are to be used, and also specific directions as to the dose to be taken, or how the medicine is to be used, are in the opinion of this office liable to stamp tax under Schedule C.

Again, the same class of medicines become liable to the stamp tax, if the maker or compounder, or the person offering them for sale, advertises them in newspapers or by public hand-bills as having any special proprietary claim to merit.

Such proprietary claim may be implied by the use of the possessive case in describing the article, as for instance, ''A's'' pills, or ''B's'' tincture, or ''C's'' powders, etc., implying special merit because such pills, tinctures, powders, etc., were made or compounded by A, B, or C, as the case may be. Or again such medicines become liable when the maker, compounder, or vendor advertises them, as above, as having any peculiar advantage in mode of preparation, quality, use, or effect, whether such claim be real or pretended.

In fine, medicines and medicinal preparations, to be exempt from the stamp tax, must *not be patent or proprietary*. They must *not be put up in a style* or manner *similar* to that of patent or proprietary medicines. They must *not be advertised* as having any *special proprietary claim to merit,* etc. They must not be sold or offered for sale, or advertised under any other *name, form,* or *guise,* than that denominated and laid down in the *authorized* published medical works or journals.

Whoever departs from these plain and simple rules in making, preparing, recommending to the public, and vending, or offering or exposing his medicines, etc., for sale, has no claim under the law to exemption from the stamp tax.

I return, as per your request, the sample labels you sent with your letter, and have only to remark that in my opinion medicines put up in retail packages with such labels affixed are put up in a style similar to patent or proprietary medicines, and are not entitled to the exemption from stamp tax provided in the 13th section of the act of July 13, 1866. If there are any exceptions, I think you will be able without difficulty to determine them with the aid of this letter.

Yours respectfully,
J. W. Douglass,
Commissioner.

IRR v.XVIII, September 13, 1873, pp.82-3

1873.–Department No. 121.–Internal Revenue.–(Special No. 145.)–Instructions, Regulations, Decisions, etc. Including the Most Important Sections of the Law Relating to the Stamping, Manufacture, Removal and Sale of Medicines, and Medicinal Preparations, and Compositions, Perfumeries, and Cosmetic Articles, under Schedule C.

Treasury Department,
Internal Revenue Bureau,
Washington, Oct. 1, 1873.

By the act of June 30, 1864, and under what is known as Schedule C, a stamp tax was imposed on medicines and medicinal preparations or compositions, and also on perfumeries and cosmetics, with certain conditional exemptions, provided for in section 165 of the same act, which exemptions were further limited by additional conditions under the act of July 13, 1866.

The text of the statute imposing this tax is in the following words:

SCHEDULE C.

MEDICINES OR PREPARATIONS.

For and upon every packet, box, bottle, pot, phial, or other enclosure, containing any pills, powders, tinctures, troches, lozenges, syrups, cordials, bitters, anodines, tonics, plasters, liniments, salves, ointments, pastes, drops, waters, essences, spirits, oils, or other medicinal preparations or compositions whatsoever, made and sold, or removed for consumption and sale, by any person or persons whatsoever, wherein the person making or preparing the same has, or claims to have, any private formula or occult secret or art for the making or preparing the same, or has or claims to have, any exclusive right or title to the making or preparing the same, or which are prepared, uttered, vended, or exposed for sale under any letters patent, or held out or recommended to the public by the makers, venders, or proprietors thereof as proprietary medicines, or as remedies or specifics for any disease, diseases, or affections whatever affecting the human or animal body, as follows: Where such packet, box, bottle, pot, phial, or other enclosure, with its contents, shall not exceed, at retail price, or value, the sum of twenty-five cents, one cent.

Where such packet, box, bottle, pot, phial, or other enclosure, with its contents, shall exceed the retail price or value of twenty-five cents, and not exceed the retail price or value of fifty cents, two cents.

Where such packet, box, bottle, pot, phial, or other enclosure, with its contents, shall exceed the retail price or value of fifty cents, and shall not exceed the retail price or value of seventy-five cents, three cents.

Where such packet, box, bottle, pot, phial, or other enclosure, with its contents, shall exceed the retail price or value of seventy-five cents, and shall not exceed the retail price or value of one dollar, four cents.

Where such packet, box, bottle, pot, phial, or other enclosure, with its contents, shall exceed the retail price or value of one dollar, for each and every fifty cents or fractional part thereof over and above the one dollar, as before mentioned, an additional two cents.

PERFUMERY AND COSMETICS.

For and upon every packet, box, bottle, pot, phial, or other enclosure, containing any essence, extract, toilet water, cosmetic, hair oil, pomade, hair dressing, hair restorative, hair dye, tooth-wash, dentifrice, tooth-paste, aromatic cachous, or any similar articles, by whatsoever name the same heretofore have been, now are, or may hereafter be called, known, or distinguished, used or applied, or to be used or applied as perfumes or applications to the hair, mouth, or skin, made, prepared, and sold or removed for consumption and sale in the United States, where such packet, box, bottle, pot phial, or other enclosure, with its contents, shall not exceed, at the retail price or value, the sum of twenty-five cents, one cent.

Where such packet, box, bottle, pot, phial, or other enclosure, with its contents, shall exceed the retail price or value of twenty five cents, and shall not exceed the retail price or value of fifty cents, two cents.

Where such packet, box, pot, phial, or other enclosure, with its contents, shall exceed the retail price or value of fifty cents, and shall not exceed the retail price or value of seventy-five cents, three cents.

Where such packet, box, bottle, pot, phial, or other enclosure, with its contents, shall exceed the retail price or value of seventy-five cents, and shall not exceed the retail price or value of one dollar, four cents.

Where such packet, box, bottle, pot, phial, or other enclosure, with its contents, shall exceed the retail price or value of one dollar, for each and every fifty cents or fractional part thereof over and above one dollar, as before mentioned, an additional two cents.

The entire text of the statute providing for conditional exemptions is in these words, to wit:

Sec. 13. *And be it further enacted,* That no stamp tax shall be imposed upon any uncompounded medicinal drug or chemical, nor upon any medicine compounded according to the United States or other national pharmacopoeia, or of which the full and proper formula is published in any of the dispensatories now or hitherto in common use among physicians or apothecaries, or in any pharmaceutical journal now issued by any incorporated college of pharmacy, when not sold or offered for sale, or advertised under any other name, form, or guise than that under which they may be severally denominated and laid down in said pharmacopoeias, dispensatories, or journals as aforesaid; nor upon medicines sold to or for the use of any person, which may be mixed and compounded for said person according to the written receipt or prescription of any physician or surgeon. But nothing in this section shall be construed to exempt from stamp tax any medicinal articles, whether simple or compounded by any rule, authority, or formula, published or unpublished, which are put up in a style or manner similar to that of patent or proprietary medicines in general, or advertised in newspapers or by public handbills for popular sale and use, as having any special proprietary claim to merit, or to any peculiar advantage in mode of preparation, quality, use, or effect, whether such claim be real or pretended.

The following sections of the same act, as subsequently amended, are still in full force and operation, and clearly define the persons liable for these taxes, and the fines and penalties incurred by any person, firm, company, or corporation who shall make, prepare, and sell, or remove for consumption or sale, or who shall offer or expose for sale any of the articles named in Schedule C, as above, without the proper stamps having been previously affixed thereto, or who shall, with fraudulent intent, remove, or take off, any such stamp, or permit it to be done, or who shall use any stamp, or stamped wrapper, or cover, to stamp or protect any other article than that originally covered by such stamp, wrapper, or cover:

Sec. 165. *And be it further enacted,* That if any person, firm, company, or corporation shall make, prepare, and sell, or remove for consumption or sale, drugs, medicines, preparations, compositions, articles, or things, including perfumery, cosmetics, lucifer or friction matches, cigar lights, or wax tapers, and playing-cards, . . . whether of domestic manufacture or imported, upon which a duty or tax is imposed by law, as enumerated and mentioned in Schedule C, without affixing thereto an adhesive stamp or label denoting the tax before mentioned, he or they shall incur a penalty of fifty dollars for every omission to affix such stamp.

Sec. 166. *And be it further enacted,* That every manufacturer or maker of any of the articles for sale mentioned in Schedule C, after the same shall have been so made, and the particulars hereinbefore required as to stamps have been complied with, who shall take off, remove, or detach, or cause, or permit, or suffer to be taken off, or removed, or detached, any stamp, or who shall use any stamp, or any wrapper or cover to which any stamp is affixed, to cover any other article or commodity than that originally contained in such wrapper or cover, with such stamp when first used, with the attempt to evade the stamp duties, shall for every such article, respectively, in respect of which any such offence shall be committed, be subject to a penalty of fifty dollars, to be recovered together with the costs thereupon accruing; and every such article or commodity as aforesaid shall also be forfeited.

Sec. 167. *And be it further enacted,* That on and after the passage of this act every maker and manufacturer of any of the articles or commodities mentioned in Schedule C, as aforesaid, who shall sell, expose for sale, send out, remove, or deliver any article or commodity, manufactured as aforesaid, before the duty thereon shall have been fully paid by affixing thereon the proper stamp as provided by law, or who shall hide or conceal, or cause to be hidden or concealed, or who shall remove or convey away, or deposit, or caused to be removed or conveyed away from or deposited in any place, any such article or commodity, to evade the duty chargeable thereon, or any part thereof, shall be subject to a penalty of one hundred dollars, together with the forfeiture of any such article or commodity.

Sec. 169. *And be it further enacted,* That any person who shall offer or expose for sale any of the articles named in Schedule C, or in any amendments thereto, whether the articles so offered or exposed are imported or are of foreign or domestic manufacture, shall be deemed the manufacturer thereof, and subject to all the duties, liabilities, and penalties imposed by law in regard to the sale of domestic articles without the use of the proper stamp or stamps denoting the tax paid thereon, and all such articles imported, or of foreign manufacture, shall, in addition to the import duties imposed on the same, be subject to the stamp tax, respectively, prescribed in Schedule C, as aforesaid.

As there has always been more or less misunderstanding, not only among manufacturers and importers of medicines and medical preparations and compositions, and the dealers in these articles, but also among revenue officials, with regard to the precise requirements of the various provisions of law herein quoted, and also in determining practically what medicines require to be stamped, and what are exempt from stamp tax, it is deemed proper to publish in this connection abstracts from some of the more important of the rulings and decisions of this office which have from time to time been rendered, with such directions as seem necessary to be given for a correct understanding of the law, and to insure uniform practice in the trade throughout the country:

1. All medicines, medicinal and cosmetic articles and perfumeries which are imported from foreign countries are liable to the same stamp tax as similar articles of domestic manufacture, and the stamps must be affixed by the importers or owners before the same are sold or offered for sale, and affixed in the same manner upon every packet, box, bottle, pot, phial or *other enclosure* containing the same. No exception is made in this respect for articles sold in original and unbroken packages in which the bottles or other enclosures were packed by the manufacturers before the importation.

2. It is the duty of the manufacturer of such articles, if they are of domestic manufacture, or of the importer or owner, if they are imported from a foreign country, to properly stamp each and every packet, box, bottle, pot, phial, or other enclosure containing the same, before it is removed from the place of manufacture, or before it is sold or offered or exposed for sale. But if such articles have been removed from the manufactory, or have been sold by the importer, and are in the hands of a dealer, then it becomes the duty of the dealer to stamp the same before he sells them or offers or exposes them for sale. (See section 169.)

3. Perfumeries and cosmetic articles are liable to the stamp tax without conditions or exemptions–those that are compounded or prepared according to published authorities, no less than those which are or are claimed to be patent or proprietary.

4. The first and absolutely prerequisite condition for holding any article subject to a stamp tax under the head of "medicines or preparations" is, that the article, the preparation or composition, shall be, or shall be claimed to be by the maker or vender, a *medicated* or *medicinal* article or compound, an article of *materia medica*. No other patent or proprietary article can be held subject to stamp tax under this head.

5. Articles used exclusively in *materia medica,* or whose general use is for the cure of human or animal diseases, *may* be liable to stamp tax though the labels, wrappers, etc., attached to or accompanying the retail package, do not particularly specify in what diseases they are to be used.

6. Articles which are not necessarily or generally medicinal in their character or uses, but which have or are claimed to have medicinal properties and virtues, in order to be subject to the stamp tax, must be held out or recommended by the makers or venders by labels, wrappers, handbills, circulars, or otherwise, as remedies or specifics for some disease, diseases, or affections of the human or animal body.

7. All patent or proprietary medicines, medicinal preparations and compositions, which are really such, or claimed to be such, and all such medicinal articles which are made, prepared, or compounded by any private formula, occult secret or art, or of which the full and proper formula is not published in some standard medical authority, are subject to the stamp tax.

8. The opinion has been too generally entertained heretofore by manufacturers, compounders, and venders of medicines and medicinal articles, that only such preparations and compositions as were patent, or proprietary, or made and compounded in the manner described in paragraph 7, as above, were subject to stamp tax, and that all medicines, etc., compounded according to the United States or other national pharmacopoeia, or where the full and proper formula is published in any standard medical authority, are exempt from such tax. But the law, in fact, gives only a *conditional* exemption to any medicine or class of medicines. The class of medicines exempted and the conditions of such exemption are found in section 13 of the act of July 13, 1866, heretofore quoted. Said section having carefully described what classes of medicines and under what conditions said medicines, etc., are exempt, declares peremptorily that nothing contained therein "shall be construed to exempt from stamp tax any medicinal articles, whether simple or compounded by any rule, authority, or formula, published or unpublished, which are put up in a *style or manner similar* to that of patent or proprietary medicines in general, or advertised in newspapers or by public handbills for popular sale and use, as having any special proprietary claim to merit, or to any peculiar advantage in mode of preparation, quality, use, or effect, whether such claim be real or pretended."

9. All medicines and medicinal preparations, put up in a style or manner *similar* to that of patent or proprietary medicines in general, are liable to stamp tax.

10. The style or manner of putting up need not be exactly like the style adopted in putting up patent or proprietary articles. There need be only a *similarity* of style, a likeness in the general points. The leading points or characteristics of this style are *(a)* that such medicines are almost always put up in *retail packages,* packages which are sold *with their contents* directly to the consumer; and *(b),* each package is accompanied with a label, a handbill, or a wrapper, containing an enumeration of the diseases or affections for which the medicine is a remedy or a specific; containing, also, directions as to when and how it is to be taken, what constitutes a proper dose, how frequently such doses are to be taken, etc., with such general directions with regard to the mode of administering the medicine as physicians give when called to prescribe for a patient. It is a style adapted to popular sale and use, to enable the sick to supply themselves with remedies, and to use the same without the aid or advice of a physician or medical practitioner. Medicines and medicinal preparations, whether officinal or non-officinal, by whatever rule or authority, or formula compounded, put up in such a style, *in retail packages,* and accompanied with a label, a circular, or a wrapper, giving the disease, diseases, or affections for which such medicines are to be or have been applied or used, directions how to use, etc., are liable to stamp tax under Schedule C. The law makes no provision for exempting such medicines, but expressly declares that the statute *shall not be construed* so as to give exemption.

11. Medicines and medicinal articles, though made or compounded strictly according to the United States or other national pharmacopoeia, or according to formulas generally known and fully published in standard medical journals, are made liable to the stamp tax, if the maker or compounder, or person offering them for sale, advertises them in newspapers, or by public handbills, as having any special proprietary claim to merit. Such an advertising deprives the article of a claim to

exemption, which it might otherwise clearly be entitled to have. Under this head, it is to be observed, further, that a proprietary claim to merit would be implied by the use of the possessive case in describing the article: as, for instance, "A's pills," or "B's tincture," or "C's powders," etc.–implying that such pills, tinctures, or powders possessed some special merit, or were better than others because they were made by A, B, or C, as the case might be.

12. The claim to exemption is lost for any medicines where the maker, compounder, or vender advertises them as having any peculiar advantage in mode of preparation, quality, use, or effect, whether such claim be real or pretended.

13. To recapitulate: medicines and medicinal preparations, to be exempt from the stamp tax, *must not be (a) patent or proprietary; (b)* they must not be *put up in a style* or manner *similar* to that of patent or proprietary medicines; *(c)* they must not be advertised as having any *special proprietary claim to merit, etc.; (d)* they must not be sold, or offered for sale, or advertised under any other *name, form,* or *guise* than that denominated and laid down in the authorized published medical works or journals.

14. In the preparation of labels for use on packages or enclosures, no objection is or can properly be made to the printing upon such labels the name of the article, the formula according to which it is made or compounded, the ingredients of which the article, if a compound, is composed, with the relative strength of such ingredients, and with the name of the manufacturer, maker, or compounder. Labels containing so much information only may properly be attached to any-sized bottle or enclosure containing officinal or standard medicines, compounded according to well known and acknowledged standard medical authorities, without rendering the article with such label attached liable to stamp tax.

15. While some articles and substances are used exclusively, or nearly so, in *materia medica,* others are only partially used, employed, or recommended as medicines or medicinal articles. In the latter case, in order to become subject to stamp tax, there must be upon the enclosure containing them, or upon the labels and wrappers accompanying them, or in the circulars, handbills, or other mode used for advertising them, a clear and express claim to patronage, on the score that the article so held out, recommended, or advertised to the public, is a medicine, or a medicated or medicinal article, or a cosmetic article.

Attention is called to the fact, in illustration of what is said above, that cod-liver oil is not necessarily and always a medicinal oil. It is only within a few years comparatively that the use of this oil in consumption and lung diseases has been recommended by physicians. Previous to that time, and even now, cod-liver oil is largely used for like purposes as fish oils in general. Bitters and plasters are among the articles enumerated in Schedule C as liable to stamp tax; but bitters are not necessarily and always a medicinal article. The term "bitters" may be only another name for a spirituous liquor, and a plaster may be only a mechanical contrivance or device, or means by which surgeons and physicians protect wounds from gaping, or sores from any or all extraneous matter or influences. These articles, and such as these, are not subject to the stamp tax in the absence of any claim made upon the label, wrapper, handbill, circular, or in other mode adopted for advertising the article, that said article is a medicated or a medicinal article, when it is not held out or recommended to the public as a remedy or a specific for any disease, diseases, or affections of the human or animal body.

Soaps are ordinarily laundry or toilet articles. They may, however, and do become medicinal or cosmetic articles, whenever the maker, manufacturer, or vender holds them out and recommends them to the public for their curative or healing virtues or properties, or for the softening and beautifying effects produced by their use upon the hair, mouth, or skin, or their general improvement of the complexion. In other words, whenever the manufacturer or vender takes them out of the category of ordinary laundry or toilet soaps and places them in the category of medicinal or cosmetic articles, he must stamp them.

16. Articles that are patent or proprietary, and therefore subject to the stamp tax, and all perfumeries and cosmetic articles, are equally liable to the stamp tax when sold in what are termed bulk packages as when sold in retail packages, and the value of the stamp or stamps to be affixed must correspond with the price charged for a single package with its contents. This decision specially applies to imported bay rum and cologne waters, which are held to be cosmetic articles, and to bitters claimed to be medicinal, when sold in kegs, half-barrels, barrels, etc.

17. Dealers may retail directly from such bulk packages, which have been properly stamped by

the manufacturer or importer, drawing from the same in quantities to suit their customers, without any additional stamping, but the stamps attached to such bulk packages will only protect the original article contained therein, and only protect that so long as it is kept within such stamped package. If bulk packages are broken and their contents drawn off into smaller vessels, thereby ceasing to be identified with the stamped package in which they were put up by the manufacturer or sold by the importer, such contents become liable to seizure if stamps are not affixed to the articles thus sold, or offered, or exposed for sale.

18. A manufacturer of any article liable to stamp tax under Schedule C must stamp every package, large or small, in which *he delivers* such article to the purchaser, whether he furnishes the vessel or package himself or fills a vessel or package furnished by the purchaser.

19. The fact that any article has not been heretofore stamped will not be accepted as a good and sufficient reason for longer omitting to stamp such article, if it comes within either of the rules or decisions herein contained, whatever may have been the reason heretofore given or held for not stamping; and all letters, rules, or decisions containing any views contrary to or conflicting with those herein embodied are hereby revoked, annulled, and declared to be of no binding force or effect.

J. W. Douglass,
Commissioner.
IRR v.XVIII, October 11, 1873, pp.113-5

Concerning Liability to Stamp Tax on "Thomsonian Composition Powders."

Treasury Department,
Office of Internal Revenue,
Washington, Oct. 16, 1873.

Lucian Hawley, Esq., Supervisor, 83 Cedar Street, New York.

Sir: I have received your letter of the 11th instant, with a label enclosed, or a paper wrapper, intended to accompany "Thomsonian Composition Powders."

This wrapper gives directions for administering said powders, the dose, and specifies certain diseases, such as relax, pain in the stomach and bowels, etc., for which it is recommended as a valuable medicine or cure.

These directions, etc., are alleged to have been copied *verbatim* from "Thomson's Materia Medica and Anatomy," claimed to be a dispensatory now and hitherto in common use among physicians and apothecaries. You ask if this medicine put up in such a wrapper, and not sold or offered for sale, or advertised under any other name, form, or guise, is liable to tax under Schedule C.

I reply that, if this medicine is put up in retail packages–packages that are intended to be, and are, sold directly to consumers, accompanied each package with this wrapper; that the style of putting up is similar to the style of putting up patent or proprietary medicines in general, and therefore they are liable to the stamp tax.

It is held by this office that where the medicine is accompanied with all the directions as to the time when, and the manner in which the article is to be taken, and the article is put up by the maker, manufacturer, or compounder, with the view of giving such specific directions directly to the patient, no matter from what source such directions and such information is obtained, from the experience and observation of a physician, from medical books, or otherwise, the style is the same, and it is similar to the style which the makers and venders of patent medicines adopt, as witness the thousands of such articles on the market, and the labels, handbills, and wrappers which accompany them.

Yours respectfully,
J. W. Douglass,
Commissioner.
IRR v.XVIII, October 18, 1873, p.121

Concerning Articles liable to Stamp Tax under Schedule C.

Treasury Department,
Office of Internal Revenue,
Washington, Oct. 20, 1873.

Alex. P. Fulton, Esq., Supervisor, Philadelphia, Pa.

Sir: I wish to call your attention to the fact that in my letter to you under date of September 9, and in Special No. 145, issued from this office on the 1st instant, no new doctrine, or new construction of law relating to the liability of articles to stamp tax under Schedule C is enunciated. Since the passage of the act of June 13, 1866, this office has held that not only patent and proprietary medicines were liable to stamp tax, but all medicines put up in a style or manner similar to patent and proprietary medicines were in like manner liable. The object of the letter to you, but more particularly of Circular No. 145, was to so define what is the said style, and to point out such leading characteristics of style as should be deemed and taken to establish a similarity, such as the law makes a rule and a reason for imposing the stamp tax.

I presume that there may have been numerous articles placed upon the market heretofore unstamped, under the impression that they were not liable, which are now found to be so under the construction and ruling lately more definitely and generally promulgated in the letter and circular referred to. In regard to such articles whenever they shall be found unstamped, until a reasonable time shall have been given for all persons holding such articles to stamp them, I would not recommend any seizures or detentions, but that the persons holding such articles for sale be required to stamp them. This direction, you will understand applies only in cases where the style of putting up officinal or standard medicines has rendered them liable to stamp tax, and not to medicines, medicinal articles, perfumeries, or cosmetics about which no question as to the style of their putting up can enter, and about which no question has ever been made– articles clearly liable.

Yours respectfully,
J. W. Douglass,
Commissioner.

IRR v.XVIII, October 25, 1873, p.129

Liability of Druggists as Liquor Dealers.

Treasury Department,
Office of Commissioner of Int. Rev.,
Washington, May 4, 1874.

John M. Sullivan, Esq., Collector, 23d District, Allegheny City, Pa.

Sir: I reply to your letter of the 27th ult., respecting the liability of Druggists to special tax as liquor dealers: That the law imposing a special tax upon Apothecaries as such, and making a limited exemption in their favor with regard to the sale of wines and distilled spirits, in quantities not exceeding half a pint at one time, etc., was repealed by the act of June 14, 1870, section 1, taking effect May 1, 1871. Apothecaries and Druggists are now, and they have been since that date, precisely on the same footing as other parties, with regard to the sale of wines and distilled spirits. The law imposes a special tax upon every person who sells, or offers for sale, distilled spirits or wines in any quantity for any purpose. (Act of April 10, 1869, section 1, amended by act of June 6, 1872, section 13). Every such person, even if he sells only on the prescriptions of physicians, is technically a liquor dealer. (Series 6, No. 4, page 28, par. 13).

It is held, however, that the sale of articles containing wines or distilled spirits, which cannot be used as a beverage, or of mixtures put up as medicines, and bearing the proper U. S. proprietary stamps, according to the provisions of Schedule C, does not involve a liability to special tax. (Int. Rev. Rec., Vol. X, p. 172, and Vol. XI, p. 169).

Very respectfully,
J. W. Douglass,
Commissioner.

IRR v.XIX, May 11, 1874, p.145

Liquor Claimed as a Medicinal Article and Put up in the Style of a Proprietary Medicine Subject to Stamp Duty.

Treasury Department,
Office of Internal Revenue,
Washington, August 4, 1874.

M. Bullard, Esq., Deputy Collector, 18th District, Wellsboro, Pa.

Sir: Your letter of July 28 inclosing a label for "Pure Old Bourbon Whiskey put up expressly for Medicinal use," by Larmore Bros. and Co., at Elmira, N. Y., has been received.

The label names the various diseases for which this article claimed to be medicinal, is a remedy, and gives directions for its use.

You wish to know whether whiskey put up in bottles for retail and covered by such a label is liable to stamp under "Schedule C."

In answer I have to say that the claims usually made for patent or proprietary medicines are made for the whiskey covered by this label, and similar directions are given for its use. The whiskey in question being claimed as a medicinal article, and put up in a style similar to that of patent or proprietary medicines in general is, in the opinion of this Office, liable to stamp duty under "Schedule C."

Very respectfully,
J. W. Douglass,
Commissioner.

IRR v.XX, August 10, 1874, p.37

Medicines heretofore held to be liable to Stamp Tax and conditionally Exempt therefrom by Section 22 of Act of February 8, 1875.

Treasury Department,
Office of Internal Revenue,
Washington, March 4, 1875.

A. P. Tutton, Esq., U. S. Supervisor, Philadelphia, Pa.:

Sir: Your letter of February 27th, inclosing a lot of labels for various kinds of medicine has been received. You wish to know whether the medicines covered by these labels as changed by the written matter inserted will be relieved from stamp by Section 22, Act of February 8, 1875. In answer, I have to say that two classes of medicines heretofore held to be liable to stamp tax are conditionally exempt therefrom by Section 22, Act of February 8, 1875.

1st. Officinal medicines, or medicines made and compounded according to formulas published in authorized standard medical authorities, but which have been heretofore put up in a style or manner similar to that of patent or proprietary medicines in general as defined and held in Special No. 145.

2d. Medicines unofficinal, or made and compounded, according to unpublished formulas.

In the first of these cases, the condition on which the exemption is made to depend is that *the formula shall be published on the label,* and the dispensatory or pharmacopaeia or pharmaceutical journal or other standard medical authority where such formula is published shall be *distinctly referred* to on the label.

In the second case no proprietorship must be claimed, and to remove all semblance of any claim to proprietorship, or claim to have any private formula, or occult secret or art for making or preparing the same, the maker or compounder must publish on his labels the *exact formula* which he uses, so that the medicinal article may be free and open to the trade, if they see fit to make or compound the same article.

The formulas in all cases must be published in form and in manner, and indicated by such weights and measures as are generally adopted in standard medical authorities.

The labels are herewith returned.

Very respectfully,
J. W. Douglass,
Commissioner.

IRR v.XXI, March 15, 1875, p.82

Requirements of the Law in Regard to Officinal Medicines.

Treasury Department,
Office of Internal Revenue,
Washington, March 30, 1875.

F. D. Sewall, Supervisor, Boston, Mass.

Sir: Yours of the 23d inst. is received, and contents noted. You state that some of the druggists of Boston claim that under the first clause of section 22, act of February 8, 1875, officinal medicines prepared in accordance with a formula published in any standard medical authority, are not liable to any stamp tax if the formula and where found are distinctly referred to on the printed label— in other words, without the formula itself being printed on the label as held by this office, they claiming that the condition of said section is sufficiently complied with if there is published on the label the dispensatory, or pharmacopoeia, or pharmaceutical journal, with the page, etc., where such formula is published.

In reply I have to inform you that such a reference as you have indicated does not, in the opinion of this office, answer the requirements of the law.

It will be noticed that the statute does not simply provide for a reference to the medical authority where the formula is published.

Two things are required to be distinctly referred to– the formula and where found. This office is of opinion that the shortest, easiest, and most definite manner of referring *distinctly* both to the ''formula and where found,'' is the manner prescribed in office letter of March 4, but does not insist upon the publication, in full, of the formula. If in addition to the other matter printed on the label, the name of the medicine, dose, direction, etc., the maker or compounder distinctly sets forth that the article is made, prepared or compounded by him according to a published formula, and gives the medical authority– the book, edition, page, etc., or the medical journal, the volume and page, or the number and page– and if two or more different formulas are given by the same authority on the same page, designating the particular formula by its number on the page, as ''No. 1,'' or ''No. 2,'' or in some other manner equally definite and *distinct,* this office will regard the condition of exemption complied with.

Modifying the rulings and decisions of the office as heretofore published in Special 145, to correspond with the changes required by the 22d section of the act of February 8, 1875, the following summary is given for your direction and that of revenue officers generally, with regard to the present liability of medicines and medicinal preparations, to stamp tax under the law in force.

(1.) That all patent and proprietary medicines and medicinal preparations, and all such medicines, etc., for which any proprietary claim is made, real or pretended, must be stamped when sold, offered or exposed for sale.

(2.) That officinal and standard medicines, etc., prepared according to formulas published in authorized medical books or journals, put up and labelled simply with the name of the article and the name of the maker or compounder, are exempt from stamp tax, without the ''formula and where found'' being printed or referred to in any manner upon such label.

(3.) That officinal medicines, etc., put up in a style or manner similar to patent or proprietary medicines in general– the same being in retail packages with labels attached stating diseases for which they are remedies, stating the dose, and giving directions for use– are liable to stamp tax, unless in addition to such matter as indicated above, there shall be also printed, on the label, the formula and the reference to the standard medical book or journal where such formula is found, or a distinct announcement that the article in question is made or compounded according to a published formula with a distinct reference to the standard authority where found in the manner hereintofore described. In this latter case such medicines, etc., so put up are not liable to stamp tax.

(4.) Unofficinal medicines, or medicines, etc., made, prepared, or compounded, but not in accordance with formulas published in any standard dispensatory, or pharmacopoeia, pharmaceutical journal, etc., are liable to stamp tax, unless the exact formula is printed upon the labels attached to such articles, and unless there is an absence of all claim to any proprietorship in the making or preparing of the same.

Very respectfully,
J. W. Douglass,
Commissioner.

IRR v.XXI, April 12, 1875, p.113

Articles Purporting to be Bitters, Medicated Brandies, Medicated Whiskies and Medicated Wines, etc.

Treasury Department,
Office of Internal Revenue,
Washington, April 16, 1878.

William A. Gavett, Esq., Revenue Agent, St. Louis, Mo.:

Sir: This Office is in receipt of your letter of the 8th instant, enclosing a variety of labels used by certain parties in Springfield, 5th Collection District, Missouri, in putting upon the market articles purporting to be bitters, medicated brandies, medicated whiskies, medicated gins, and medicated wines, etc. You also refer to a letter lately addressed to collector J. H. Sturgeon, March 23, 1878, relative to the liability of a manufacturer of herb bitters; also to letters published in the INTERNAL REVENUE RECORD of May 28, 1870, volume 11, and May 11, 1874, volume 19. These several letters contain the views of this Office relative to the liability of articles which are manufactured, compounded, made, or prepared, and put up and sold as medicinal bitters. It has been and is still the opinion of this Office that when these articles are so advertised, held out, and recommended for their medicinal virtues and properties as to be fairly taken out of the category of ordinary beverages, such as whiskey, brandy, wine, etc., and are placed unequivocally in the category of medicinal articles, they are liable to the stamp tax, and the vender may sell them, properly put up and stamped, as he sells any other medicinal article, without becoming liable as a liquor dealer under the U.S. Internal Revenue Law.

I do not, however, think that the articles covered by such labels as the following are so taken from the category of beverages or liquors and placed in the category of medicinal articles, even when stamped, as to relieve the vender from liability to pay special tax as a liquor dealer or the person who prepares them from special tax as a rectifier. These labels are as follows: ''Stearn's medicated Bourbon whiskey. Dose, one wine glassful three times a day.'' ''Medicated Apple Brandy. Dose, wine glassful three times a day.'' ''Pure medicated Bourbon whiskey. Dose, wine glassful three times a day.'' ''Port wine, medicated. Dose, wine glassful three times a day.'' ''Cognac Brandy, medicated. Dose, wine glassful three times a day.''

Liquors bearing these labels and labels such as these are not entitled to be sold, even by druggists and apothecaries, unless they have paid a special tax as liquor dealers to qualify them to sell such liquors.

Labels like the following: ''Peach Brandy Bitters;'' ''Old Crow Bitters;'' ''Old Kentucky Bitters;'' and ''Bourbon Bitters,'' with nothing else upon the label except the words, ''Dose, a wine glassful three times a day,'' are hardly sufficient, in the opinion of this Office, to take the articles out of the category of beverages, alcoholic liquors, and to place them in the category of medicines.

Persons selling these articles should, in the opinion of this Office, pay special tax as liquor dealers.

I have further to say that an exemption from the payment of special tax as a liquor dealer under the Internal Revenue Law for selling even medicinal bitters would not, in itself, exempt a person from any special tax imposed under State law on the sale of articles made subject to a local tax as alcoholic liquors.

Very respectfully,
Green B. Raum,
Commissioner.

IRR v.XXIV, April 29, 1878, pp.129-30

Liability to Special Tax of Dealers in Alcoholic Beverages for which Medicinal Virtues are Claimed.

Treasury Department,
Office of Internal Revenue,
Washington,
September 2, 1878.

Isaac H. Sturgeon, Esq., Collector First District, St. Louis, Mo.:

Sir: Your letter of the 16th ultimo has been received, transmitting a letter from Messrs. Stern and Albert, of your city, making inquiries about the goods which they put up and sell as proprietary articles, also sundry formulas according to which those articles are compounded. I have also received from that firm, by express, samples of their goods with the labels they use attached.

In their letter Messrs. Stern and Albert claim that these articles are really medicines, put up as such, intended for use as tonics and alteratives in the West, where fevers and other malarial diseases so much prevail, and they ask to be informed as to whether these goods are, 1st, Proprietary medicines or medicinal preparations subject to stamp tax? and 2d, Whether parties selling such articles, properly stamped, are liable to special tax as liquor dealers?

The law, see section eighteen of the act of Feb. 8, 1875, defines a dealer in liquors as a person who sells or offers for sale, foreign or domestic distilled spirits, wines, or malt liquors, and imposes a special tax of twenty five, or one hundred dollars, according as he sells at retail or at wholesale.

The fact that a rectifier, manufacturer, or dealer, attaches labels to the bottles, flasks, phials or other enclosures containing distilled spirits or wines, and holds such spirits and wines out, and recommends them for popular sale and use as tonics, diuretics, appetisers or as specifics and remedies for the cure of various diseases, does not relieve the dealer in such spirits and wines from the special tax if they are sold under the name of brandy, wine, gin, or whiskey, or are substantially and essentially in use and effect, distilled spirits or wines.

A large class of wines and distilled spirits is being put upon the market under the several names of "Medicated French Brandy," "Medicated Holland Gin," "Medicated Port Wine," etc., for the reason, it may be, that there is a popular demand for such spirits. The character, quality, use and effect of these liquors are substantially those of ordinary wines and distilled spirits, slightly modified in flavor by decoctions of barks, bitter herbs, etc.

But the law imposes a special tax for selling distilled spirits or wines, and liability to this tax cannot be cancelled or evaded by any process of medication, nor by any holding out, or recommendations of the medicinal virtues and qualities of such spirits, whether real or pretended, if they are sold under the name of wine, gin, brandy, or whiskey, or if they are substantially wines or distilled spirits, or are used or sold as alcoholic beverages.

Labels, such as have been referred to, attached to such liquors, may subject them to a stamp tax under Schedule A, as similar imported liquors are subjected to it though classed as liquors at the Custom Houses, and taxed there as such.

The liability to the special tax as liquor dealer, attaches for the sale of spirits as those above described, and attaches whether they are sold by the drink or in the unbroken packages. All rulings in conflict with this are hereby revoked.

You will please communicate to Messrs. Stern and Albert the decision herein made, of the questions submitted by them.

Yours respectfully,
Green B. Raum,
Commissioner.

IRR v.XXIV, September 9, 1878, p.281

Taxes on Medicated Liquors.

Treasury Department,
Office of Internal Revenue,
Washington,
September 20, 1878.

Collector A. B. Carroll, Cape Girardeau, Mo.:

Sir: I am in receipt of a letter from Dameron and Thurber, of Marquand, in your District, dated the 3d instant, in which they enclose a label they propose to use upon a medicated whiskey which they wish to manufacture and sell, and inquire whether they will be required to pay any Government tax except the stamp tax, under Schedule A, Revised Statutes of the United States; and they also inquire whether parties who buy this medicated whiskey from them and retail the same by the single bottle, can do so without paying the special tax as retail liquor dealers.

I have referred this firm to you for specific answers to their several inquiries; and for your information, and for the decision of this Office in regard to the liability of persons selling such medicated liquors, I have to refer you to a letter addressed, from this Office on the 2d instant, to Collector Isaac H. Sturgeon, of St. Louis, and published generally in the newspapers of the country, a copy of which you will find in the INTERNAL REVENUE RECORD of the 9th instant.

The label Messrs. Dameron and Thurber have enclosed, holds out an article under the title of "HEGEMONY Medicated Whiskey. A pleasant and safe remedy for indigestion, heartburn, and all forms of dyspepsia, whether chronic or acute."

They recommend the article on the label as a "tonic and stimulant, adapted to impart untold benefit to persons recovering from fevers or protracted illness," and claim to be "sole proprietors and manufacturers."

Articles which are labelled and sold as medicated liquors, wine, gin, brandy, whiskey, cordials, and bitters, and which are substantially wines or distilled spirits, or are used or sold as alcoholic beverages, even though having stamps attached to the packages such as the law requires to be attached to patent and proprietary medicines, cannot be legally sold except under a special tax stamp of a liquor dealer, and the maker, compounder, or manufacturer of such liquors and beverages is liable to pay special tax as a rectifier. See Section 3244, Revised Statutes of the United States.

Such, in the opinion of this Office, is the character of the article in question, and such the liability of the manufacturers of it to pay special taxes.

Bitters, tonics, stimulants, etc., which do not come within the class of liquors above described, and which are really medicinal and proprietary articles, must be stamped in all cases. But neither the makers nor vendors are liable to pay special tax for the manufacture or sale.

Yours respectfully,
H. C. Rogers,
Acting Commissioner.

IRR v.XXIV, September 30, 1878, p.305

Hostetter's Bitters and Plantation Bitters Subject to Special Tax–Previous Rulings Revoked.

Treasury Department,
Office of Internal Revenue,
Washington, Oct. 2, 1878.

Mr. A. B. Carroll, Collector 2d District, Cape Girardeau, Mo.:

Sir: Mr. Caspar H. Reipe, of Drake, Gasconade Co., Missouri, in a letter to this Office, dated the 16th ult., asks whether special tax is required to be paid for the sale of Hostetter's Stomach Bitters.

After a careful inquiry into the nature and use of "Hostetter's Stomach Bitters," and "Drake's Plantation Bitters," I am of the opinion that, for special tax purposes, they should be treated as distilled spirits or wines, and that the person who sells them or offers them for sale, either by the drink or by the unbroken package or bottle should be required to pay special tax as a liquor dealer; and that persons who manufacture them are rectifiers, and subject to special tax as such.

This ruling being a revocation of previous rulings of this Office with regard to these particular bitters, it is deemed advisable that it should take effect, and be enforced only on and after Nov. 1, 1878. Persons, therefore, engaged in selling such bitters, or offering them for sale on or after that date should be required to pay special tax as liquor dealers for the remaining portion of the special tax year ending April 30, 1879.

Mr. Reipe has been referred to you. Please advise him in accordance herewith.

Respectfully,
Green B. Raum,
Commissioner.

IRR v.XXIV, October 7, 1878, p.313

Tax on Bitters and Alcoholic Liquors and Beverages Stamped as Medicines.

Treasury Department,
Office of Internal Revenue,
Washington, October 17, 1878.

A. B. Carroll, Esq., Collector 2d District, Cape Girardeau, Mo.:

Sir: By the Commissioner's letter, addressed to you under date of the 2d instant, and published in the INTERNAL REVENUE RECORD, October 7, you were instructed that on and after November 1, 1878, persons selling Hostetter's Bitters, Drake's Plantation Bitters, and similar stamped Bitters and Alcoholic liquors and beverages—though stamped as medicines—should be required to pay special tax as liquor dealers for the remaining portion of the special tax year ending April 30, 1879.

Not from any doubt respecting the correctness of the general principles of the law as laid down in that letter, and in certain other letters recently published on the same subject, but for certain reasons of a practical nature, the taking effect of the ruling is hereby still further postponed until January 1, 1879.

Yours respectfully,
H. C. Rogers,
Acting Commissioner.

IRR v.XXIV, October 21, 1878, p.329

List of Bitters that May be Classed for Taxation as Medicines.

Treasury Department,
Office of Internal Revenue,
Washington, December 14, 1878.

Since the publications of the late rulings and decisions of the Commissioner of Internal Revenue on the subject of spurious, imitation, and compound liquors, or medicated liquors and beverages, and medicinal articles and preparations sold under the name of bitters, cordials, etc., the manufacturers and compounders of various bitters, cordials, etc., have submitted samples of their preparations with the formulas certified to, according to which the several articles are compounded, and certificates of physicians, chemists, druggists, and apothecaries giving their opinions as to the medicinal character, properties, and qualities of the articles in question, together with the circulars, hand-bills, and labels, showing the manner of holding out and recommending these articles for popular sale and use. And they have asked from this Office decisions as to the proper classifications of each particular article.

Upon a careful examination of the several articles, and of the testimony submitted, this Office has decided that the following articles and preparations shall be classed, for purposes of taxation, under internal revenue law, as medicines, subject to stamp tax under Schedule A, Revised Statutes of the United States, and when properly stamped, they may be sold without subjecting the vendor to liability to pay special tax as liquor dealer.

Allen's Tonic Bitters, made in St. Paul, Minn.
Bull's Superior Stomach Bitters, St. Louis, Mo.
Callender's Celebrated Liver Bitters, Peoria, Ill.
Diamond Tonic Bitters, St. Louis, Mo.
Empire Tonic Bitters, St. Louis, Mo.
Elixir of Wild Cherry, St. Louis, Mo.
Globe Tonic Bitters, Portland, Maine.
Herbine, St. Louis, Mo.
Home Stomach Bitters, St. Louis, Mo.
Hop Bitters, Rochester, N. Y.
Hop Tonic, Detroit, Michigan.
Hostetter's Stomach Bitters, Pittsburgh, Penn.
McLean's Strengthening Cordial, St. Louis, Mo.
Sulphur Mountain Bitters, Elmwood, Ark.
Wakefield's Strengthening Wine Bitters, Bloomington, Ill.
Webb's Improved Stomach Bitters, Jackson, Mich.

Additions may hereafter be made to the above list, and when made will be published.

Green B. Raum,
Commissioner.

IRR v.XXIV, December 16, 1878, p.393

List of Bitters that May be Classed for Taxation as Medicines.

Treasury Department,
Office of Internal Revenue,
Washington, March 7, 1879.

Official notice was given in the INTERNAL REVENUE RECORD published December 16, 1878, that upon a careful examination of the several articles, and of the testimony submitted, this Office had decided that sixteen articles and preparations therein named shall be classed for purposes of taxation under internal revenue law, as medicines, subject to Stamp tax under Schedule A, Revised Statutes of the United States, and when properly stamped they may be sold without subjecting the vendor to liability to pay special tax as liquor dealer. Since the date of that notice the above list has been largely increased, and, therefore, a new list, including the articles enumerated in that notice, has been prepared and is hereby officially promulgated. It comprises:

Allen's Tonic Bitters, made in ....St. Paul, Minn.
American Regenerative Bitters ....Baltimore, Md.
Angostura Bitters ....New York City.
Apple Brandy Bitters ....Knoxville, Tenn.

Aromatic Elixir of Ginger .... Austin, Tex.
Aromatic Stomach Bitters .... New Albany, Ind.
Aromatic Stomach Bitters (Fine) .... Nashville, Tenn.
Baker's Premium Bitters .... Richmond, Va.
Baxter's Mandrake Bitters .... Burlington, Vt.
Bazemare's Kiwassee Bitters .... Charleston, Tenn.
Bell's English Bitters .... Burlington, Vt.
Benson's Superior Health Bitters .... Rochester, Minn.
Bissell's Tonic Bitters .... Peoria, Ill.
Boker's Bitters .... New York City.
Botanic Aromatic Bitters .... New York City.
Bull's Superior Stomach Bitters .... St. Louis, Mo.
Burwell's Virginia Bitters .... Richmond, Va.
Calisaya Tonic Bitters .... St. Louis, Mo.
Callender's Celebrated Liver Bitters .... Peoria, Ill.
Cameron's (Prof.) Blackberry Cordial .... St. Louis, Mo.
Chill Cure (Home Bitters Co.) .... St. Louis, Mo.
Coca Bitters .... New York City.
Compound Tonic Bitters .... New York City.
Constitution Bitters .... Richmond, Va.
Diamond Tonic Bitters .... St. Louis, Mo.
Drake's Plantation Bitters .... New York City.
Eagle Tonic Bitters .... St. Louis, Mo.
Edward Wilder's Stomach Bitters .... Louisville, Ky.
Elixir of Wild Cherry (Harter's) .... St. Louis, Mo.
Empire Tonic Bitters .... St. Louis, Mo.
Eureka Aromatic Schnapps .... Monroe, N. C.
Flinn's Peruvian Bitters .... Danville, Va.
Gilmore's Aromatic Wine .... Pavilion, N. Y.
Globe Tonic Bitters .... Portland, Maine.
Gray and Cloud's Liver Invigorating and Blood Purifying Bitters .... St. Louis, Mo.
Gregory's Scotch Bitters .... Minneapolis, Minn.
Haller's (Surgeon) Canteen Bitters .... Lancaster, Pa.
Hart's Stomach Bitters .... Knoxville, Tenn.
Home Stomach Bitters .... St. Louis, Mo.
Hop Bitters .... Rochester, N. Y.
Hop Tonic .... Detroit, Mich.
Hopkins' Celebrated Union Stomach Bitters .... Hartford, Conn.
Hostetter's Stomach Bitters .... Pittsburgh, Pa.
Huntington's Celebrated Dandelion and Wild Cherry Bitters .... Dubuque, Iowa.
Hutchinson's Bitters .... Mobile, Ala.
Indian Botanic Bitters .... Sherburne, Ky.
Jackson's Celebrated Root and Herb Cordial .... St. Louis, Mo.
Jaundice Bitters .... Boston, Mass.
Jepson's Golden Bitters .... Hartford, Conn.
Jones' Celebrated Stomach Bitters .... Memphis, Tenn.
Kampfer's Stomach Bitters .... Philadelphia, Pa.
Kentucky Tonic Bitters .... Louisville, Ky.
Keystone Tonic Bitters (Livingstone's) .... St. Louis, Mo.
Knickerbocker Bitters .... New York.
Kreitzer's German Stomach Bitters .... Philadelphia, Pa.
Livingstone's African Elixir of Wild Cherry .... St. Louis, Mo.
London Juniper Cordial .... St. Louis, Mo.
Loveridge's Capital Bitters .... Buffalo, N. Y.
Loveridge's Wahoo Bitters .... Buffalo, N. Y.
McLean's Strengthening Cordial and Blood Purifier .... St. Louis, Mo.

Magnolia Gin . . . . Chicago, Ill.
Mansfield's Highland Stomach Bitters . . . . Memphis, Tenn.
Maryland Tonic Bitters . . . . Baltimore, Md.
Miller's (Dr.) Bitters . . . . Minneapolis, Minn.
Mishler's Green Label Bitters . . . . Lancaster, Pa.
Mishler's Herb Bitters . . . . Lancaster, Pa.
Mishler's Red Label Bitters . . . . Lancaster, Pa.
Morley's Texas Tonic Cordial . . . . Austin, Tex.
Morning Star Bitters . . . . Baltimore, Md.
Orolo Bitters . . . . New Albany, Ind.
Payne's Indian Vegetable Bitters . . . . Scottsboro, Ala.
Phosphated Cereal Tonic . . . . New York City.
Pike's Plantation Bitters or Log Cabin Tonic . . . . Louisville, Ky.
Prairie Tonic Bitters . . . . Rochester, Minn.
Reed's Gilt Edge Tonic . . . . New Haven, Conn.
Rejuvenating Bitters . . . . Bainbridge, Pa.
Richard's Bitters . . . . Minneapolis, Minn.
Richardson's Renowned Medicinal Bitters . . . . Chicago, Ill.
Rodgers' Tonic Bitters . . . . Knoxville, Tenn.
Sarracenia Life Bitters . . . . Brooklyn, N. Y.
Sherman's Compound Prickly Ash Bitters . . . . Kansas City, Mo.
Sherry Wine Bitters . . . . Boston, Mass.
Smith and Shakman's Stomach Bitters . . . . Baltimore, Md.
Sulphur Mountain Bitters . . . . Elmwood, Ark.
Van Damm's Tonic Elixir . . . . Dubuque, Iowa.
Von Hopf's Curaco Tonic Bitters . . . . Marion, Iowa.
Wakefield's Strengthening Wine Bitters . . . . Bloomington, Ill.
Wampoo Bitters . . . . New York City.
Webb's Improved Stomach Bitters . . . . Jackson, Mich.

Green B. Raum,
Commissioner.

IRR v.XXV, March 10, 1879, pp.69-70

List of Bitters that May be Classed for Taxation as Medicines.

Treasury Department,
Office of Internal Revenue,
Washington, July 29, 1879.

Since the date of the Official notice given in the INTERNAL REVENUE RECORD, published March 10th, 1879, this Office has decided that the following additional articles and preparations shall be classed, for purposes of taxation under the internal revenue law, as medicines, subject to stamp tax under Schedule A, Revised Statutes of the United States, and, when properly stamped, they may be sold without subjecting the vendor to liability to pay special tax as liquor dealer:

Aromatic Blackberry Brandy . . . . Lawrence, Kas.
Adkins Golden Stomach Bitters . . . . Kansas, City, Mo.
Amazon Aromatic Tonic Bitters . . . . New York City.
Aromatic Tonic . . . . Washington, D.C.
Capitol Bitters . . . . Buffalo, N. Y.
Columbia Stomach Bitters . . . . St. Louis, Mo.
Centennial Bitters . . . . Wheeling, W. Va.
Campbell's (Dr. Alexander) Scotch Bitters . . . . Lynchburg, Va.
Dunlap's Anchor Bitters . . . . Grand Rapids, Mich.
Dr. Hardy's Western Stomach Bitters . . . . St. Joseph, Mo.
Foley's (Dr. James) Bitters . . . . Louisville, Ky.
Fitzpatrick's Fifty-cent Stomach Bitters . . . . Helena, Ark.
Griffith's Medicinal Blackberry Cordial . . . . St. Louis, Mo.
Great Western India Bitters . . . . Dallas, Texas.

Greenback Bitters, or Gentian Tonic ..... Little Rock, Ark.
Granger Tonic ..... Little Rock, Ark.
Gordon and Dilworth's Blackberry Brandy ..... New York City.
Home Strengthening Cordial ..... St. Louis, Mo.
Hunter's Stomach Bitters ..... Knoxville, Tenn.
Hayes' Superior Stomach Bitters ..... St. Joseph, Mo.
Henri's French Border Splenetic Compound ..... Galveston, Tex.
Imperial Tonic Bitters ..... St. Louis, Mo.
Jenkins' Stomach Bitters ..... Oxford, Miss.
Mars Stomach Bitters ..... St. Louis, Mo.
Mandrake Bitters ..... Topeka, Kas.
Old Uncle Joe's Stomach Bitters ..... Ashton, Mo.
Our Own Louisiana Aromatic Bitters ..... New Orleans, La.
Peruvian Strengthening Elixir ..... Atchison, Kas.
Peruvian Tonic ..... Lawrence, Kas.
Reed's Aromatic Stomach Bitters ..... New Haven, Conn.
Rattinger's Root and Herb Bitters ..... St. Louis, Mo.
Rocky Mountain Bitters ..... Kirksville, Mo.
Sawen's Life Invigorating Bitters ..... Utica, N. Y.
Smith's Iron and Gentian Bitters ..... Minneapolis, Minn.
Sandberg's Indian Bitters ..... Cannon Falls, Minn.
St. Gotherd Herb Bitters ..... St. Louis, Mo.
Sarsaparilla Bitters ..... Chicago, Ill.
Tonic Bitters "Graves" ..... Louisville, Ky.
Tonic Bitters ..... Girard, Kas.
Van Cise's California Port Wine Tonic ..... Mt. Pleasant, Ia.
Winfree's Tonic Anti-Spasmodic and Alternative Bitters ..... Richmond, Va.
Winfree's Aromatic Stomach Bitters ..... Richmond, Va.
White's Celebrated Granger Bitters ..... Newport, Ark.
West India Stomach Bitters ..... St. Louis, Mo.
West India Strengthening Cordial ..... Oxford, Miss.
Wine of Wild Cherry Bark ..... Lawrence, Kas.

Green B. Raum,
Commissioner.

IRR v.XXV, August 4, 1879, p.237

Medicinal Character of Home Sanative Cordial.

Treasury Department,
Office of Internal Revenue,
Washington, September 27, 1879.

George S. Shyrock, Esq., Secretary and Treasurer, Home Bitters Company, St. Louis, Missouri:

Sir: Agreeably to the request contained in our letter of the 24th instant, this Office re-affirms its former decision with regard to the medicinal character of a compound made and sold, or to be sold, by your company under the name of "Home Sanative Cordial," provided the same is compounded accordingly to the certified formula heretofore submitted to this Office. When properly stamped under the provisions of Schedule A, Revised Statutes of the United States, the sale of this "Cordial" will be permitted without requiring the vendors thereof to pay special tax as liquor dealers.

Very respectfully,
H. C. Rogers,
Acting Commissioner.

IRR v.XXV, November 10, 1879, p.349

Supplementary List of Compounds Classed as Medicinal Bitters.

Treasury Department,
Office of Internal Revenue,
Washington, April 10, 1880.

Messrs. W. C. and F. P. Church, 240 Broadway, New York City:

Messrs. Editors: Please publish the following supplementary list, to the lists which you have heretofore published, giving the names of compounds which this Office has decided, may, for purposes of taxation under the internal revenue law, be classed as medicinal bitters, and when properly stamped may be sold by persons who have not paid special tax as liquor dealers.

Yours respectfully,
Green B. Raum,
Commissioner.

Anti-Malarial Bitters made in Rocky Hill, S.C.
Aromatic Iron Tonic made in Paris, Texas.
Angelica Bitters made in Paris, Texas.
Brown's Cordial made in Home, Tenn.
Bolivian Indian Cocaine Bitters made in Plattsburgh, N. Y.
Betterton's Evening Star Bitters made in Knoxville, Tenn.
Baer's Liver Bitters made in Charleston, S. C.
Bodeza Bitters made in Staunton, Va.
Black Cohosh Bitters made in Pana, Ill.
Betterton's Celebrated Corn Bitters made in Knoxville, Tenn.
Betterton's Celebrated Apple Brandy Bitters made in Knoxville, Tenn.
Bardenwerper's Blood Purifier made in St. Louis, Mo.
Bonekamp Maag Bitters made in Pittsburgh, Pa.
Caldwell's Herb Bitters made in Harrisburg, Pa.
Chill's Boneset Bitters made in Ninety-Six, S. C.
Creale Bitters made in Selma, Ala.
California Stomach Bitters made in Terre Haute, Ind.
Combined Extract of Rye Refined, Rock Candy, and Extract of Red Root made in Philadelphia, Pa.
Combined Extract of Rye Refined, Rock Candy, and Extract of Seneka made in Philadelphia, Pa.
Clayton and Russell's Cel. Stomach Bitters made in New York City.
Celery Bitters made in Halifax, C. H., Va.
Chamomile Bitters made in Harrisonburg, Va.
Dandelion Bitters made in Terre Haute, Ind.
Electric Bitters made in Lancaster, Mo.
Fritsch's Prussian Stomach Bitters made in St. Louis, Mo.
Family Bitters made in Lynchburg, Va.
Forest Bitters made in St. Louis, Mo.
Garnet's Compound Vegetable Bitters made in Richmond, Va.
Halland Strengthening Bitters made in Ottumwa, Iowa.
Husband's Rock, Rye, and Hoarhound made in New York City.
Harwiz Karotowicz Stomach Bitters made in New York City.
Henry Clay's Old Kentucky Bitters made in Lexington, Ky.
Heineman's Improved Extract of Rye, Rock Candy, Fluid Extract of Virginia Prunes, and Balsam of Tolu, made in Jamestown, N. Y.
Indian Valley Bitters made in St. Louis, Mo.
Jepson and Rathburn's Tonic Bitters made in Utica, N. Y.
Keystone Bitters made in Philadelphia, Pa.
Lynch's Euttericon Tonic made in St. Louis, Mo.
Minnesota Tonic Bitters made in Mankato, Minn.
Medicated Bourbon Whiskey made in Terre Haute, Ind.
Old North State Bitters made in Hickory, N. C.
Old Carolina Bitters made in Charleston, S. C.
Otto's German Bitters made in Pana, Ill.
O. K. Bitters made in Rocky Hill, Ky.
Plant Bitters made in Terry, Miss.
Peruvian Bitters made in Wheeling, W. Va.
Rector's Stomach Bitters made in Lincoln, Neb.

Rosenheim's Celebrated Stomach Bitters made in Baltimore, Md.
Stone's Celebrated Stomach Bitters made in Home, Tenn.
Swiss Imported Bitters (Alspenkrueter Magenbetter) made in New York City.
Sumpter Bitters made in Charleston, S. C.
Smoke's Tonic Bitters made in Winchester, Va.
Schuable's Rock and Rye Cordial made in New York City.
Strasberg Herb Bitters made in Fond du Lac, Wis.
Staunton Bitters made in Staunton, Va.
Sunny South Bitters made in East Saginaw, Mich.
Steketee's Blood Purifying Bitters made in Grand Rapids, Mich.
Tolu Rock and Rye made in Chicago, Ill.
Voigt's Cherry Tonic made in Louisville, Ky.
Warner's Safe Bitters made in Rochester, N. Y.
Warner's Safe Tonic made in Rochester, N. Y.
White Ash Bitters made in Little Rock, Ark.
Young's Extract of Malt made in St. Louis, Mo.
Zu Zu Bitters made in Baltimore, Md.

IRR v.XXVI, April 19, 1880, p.121

Correction in the List of Medicinal Bitters Published.

Treasury Department,
Office of Internal Revenue,
Washington, April 30, 1880.

J. M. Melton, Esq., Collector 2d District, Knoxville, Tennessee:

Sir: In reply to your letter of the 28th instant I have to say that, in the list of *medicinal* bitters published in the INTERNAL REVENUE RECORD of the 9th [Ed. note: Should be 19th] of April, 1880, by a clerical mistake in making up said list the liquors compounded and sold by Messrs. Betterton and Co., under the different names of "Betterton and Co.'s Celebrated Corn Bitters" and "Betterton and Co.'s Celebrated Apple Brandy Bitters," were included.

This Office has no reason for changing the classification made after a careful examination of the formula and sample of these compounds and communicated to you in Office letter dated March 2d, 1880.

Yours respectfully,
Green B. Raum,
Commissioner.

IRR v.XXVI, May 3, 1880, p.137

Liability of Alcohol Bitters to Tax.

Treasury Department,
Office of Internal Revenue,
Washington, June 1, 1883.

Messrs. C. Chamberlin & Co., 905 West Market Street, Louisville, Kentucky.

Gentlemen: In reply to your letter of the 2d ultimo, I have to inform you that the necessity for such a special classification of Alcoholic Bitters by this Office as has heretofore been made for purposes of taxation under the Internal Revenue law will not exist on and after July 1st, 1883, when the repeal of the stamp taxes imposed on articles enumerated in Schedule A, following Section 3437, U.S. Revised Statutes, will take effect under the provisions of the Act of March 3rd, 1883.

On and after July 1st, 1883, as now, distilled spirits can be mixed with other materials and thereby manufactured into imitation or compound liquors for sale only by persons who have paid special tax as Rectifiers, and such liquors can be sold only by persons who have paid special tax as liquor dealers.

It will be immaterial as to what name, or under what form or guise, or with what recommendations such compounds are held out to the public, if they are known to be in composition, quality, use, and effect compound liquors or alcoholic beverages.

Primarily: Collectors in their several Districts will be called upon to decide the liability of persons to pay special tax who manufacture and sell compounds containing distilled spirits, wine or other spirituous liquor. In general, only such cases as involve appeals from the decisions of Collectors to the Commissioner of Internal Revenue will be considered by this Office.

The sale of alcoholic beverages in different States and Cities is regulated and controlled by State and Municipal laws. See Section 3243, U. S. Revised Statutes.

For purposes of taxation under these local laws the State Courts will determine questions relating to the classification of compounds containing distilled spirits which are made and sold within their jurisdiction. Collectors of Internal Revenue will be materially aided by such decisions, in determining the questions of liability to special tax as Rectifiers or liquor dealers under the Internal Revenue law. But these decisions will not be accepted as final and conclusive in disputed cases either by the Collectors or by this Office.

Wherever in considering these questions of liability, any serious difficulty is experienced, this Office as at present advised, prefers that the decision of the question shall be left to the Federal Courts.

Respectfully,
Walter Evans,
Commissioner.

IRR v.XXIX, June 11, 1883, p.185

Status of Hostetter's Bitters as to Taxation.

Treasury Department,
Office of Internal Revenue,
Washington, August 22, 1883.

Messrs. Hostetter and Smith, Pittsburgh, Pa.:

Gentlemen: Your letter of the 1st instant addressed to this office, and in which you state that, having many inquiries put to you by your customers as to whether it is necessary to take out a special license to sell your bitters, you desire to be able intelligently to inform them what they should do in the premises, and in which you also submit a statement of certain grounds upon which you think your customers should not be required to take out licenses, has been received and very carefully considered.

Your firm is understood to prepare, according to a formula the nature of which you will not disclose, the article called "Hostetter's Bitters," in very large quantities, and to sell it to dealers in all parts of the United States.

Clifford Richardson, Esq., assistant chemist of the Agricultural Department, has done me the favor to make a careful analysis of a bottle of the "bitters," and finds it to contain as follows:

Absolute alcohol .... 32 per cent.
Water .... 64 per cent.
Extracts, only .... 4 per cent.

He says it is made from a strong alcoholic liquor flavored with various essential oils, as oil of anise, coriander, etc., and contains some vegetable bitters, such as gentian, cinchona, etc. It will be seen that the bitters contain at least 65 per cent of proof spirits, which will be equal to about 82 per cent of ordinary whiskey at 80 per cent proof, obviously much more spirits than is absolutely necessary to hold the other ingredients in solution.

Containing, as it does, no deleterious drugs, and only four per cent of anything like a drug, I should probably be entirely justified in deciding outright that one who sells it for any purpose is a retail liquor dealer within the meaning of clause four of Section 3244, Revised Statutes, which reads as follows:

"Retail dealers in liquors shall pay twenty five dollars. Every person who sells or offers for sale, foreign or domestic distilled spirits or wines in less quantities than five wine gallons at the same time, shall be regarded as a retail dealer in liquors."

Such a ruling would seem to be supported by a letter of the honorable Assistant Secretary of the Treasury, dated January 8, 1883, as follows:

Treasury Department,
Office of the Secretary,
Washington, D.C., January 8, 1883.

Collector of Customs, Sitka, Alaska:

Sir: This Department duly received your letter dated August 26th last, relating to a seizure in your district of two cases of Hostetter's Bitters imported there from Portland, Oregon.

It appears from your letter that on being requested by an officer of this Department to seize the bitters, you "peremptorily refused," and thereupon that he made the seizure and delivered the merchandise into your custody, in which it now remains.

The importers claim that the bitters are a patent medicine, not a distilled spirit, nor wine, and that they, therefore, may be admitted into Alaska under the present regulations.

A letter from the Commissioner of Internal Revenue, dated December 6, 1878, states that such bitters contain a sufficient quantity of alcohol to hold the other ingredients in solution, and that they are sometimes sold by the glass by retail liquor dealers; and that it is stated that the merchandise is sold "by the drink" in saloons at Sitka.

The Department is of opinion that, notwithstanding they may be classified under the internal revenue laws as medicinal bitters, they should be excluded from Alaska under the Executive order of February 4, 1870, forbidding the importation of distilled spirits into that Territory.

The courts have decided that certain bitters, substantially similar in character, imported into the United States are dutiable as distilled spirits.

You will take action accordingly, and in future seize importations of such bitters into Alaska, and dispose of them in the usual manner.

The bitters already imported and in your custody, as aforesaid, may be released, provided they shall be sent out of the Territory at the expense of the claimant.

Very respectfully,
H. F. French,
Assistant Secretary.

The last clause of Section 3246, Revised Statutes, is the only other provision of positive law bearing upon the subject. That clause is as follows:

"Nor shall any special tax be imposed upon *apothecaries* as to wines or spirituous liquors which they use exclusively in the preparation or making up of medicines."

It is, to say the very least, doubtful whether that provision in any way applies to your bitters; but inasmuch as this bureau has for many years classified the preparation as a proprietary medicine and collected stamp taxes upon it as such, I cannot avoid treating the subject raised by the questions you propound in a manner somewhat different from what I probably should if the point were one of first impression.

In view of the premises, the question of whether dealers in your bitters should be required to pay special tax as liquor dealers seems to me should depend upon the use made of the article sold, If in good faith it is, in fact, sold as a medicine only by a dealer, and especially if sold to fill a *bona fide* prescription given by a reputable physician precisely as other prescriptions are given and filled, such dealer will not be required to pay the special tax, and he will, it is presumed, feel no uneasiness upon the subject as long as he is conscious that he is certainly selling it only as a medicine. On the other hand, if a dealer sells it as an alcoholic beverage, stimulant, or intoxicant, and especially if he does so habitually, there is no reason why he should not be compelled to pay the special tax imposed by law upon all liquor dealers, for in such a case he is really selling it for the whiskey it contains, and the other ingredients are sold only incidentally. Whether a dealer falls within one category or the other will depend upon the facts, and the revenue officers, while claiming no tax from dealers in genuine medicines, will endeavor not to be deceived by any device which may be resorted to by any dealer who may have an intent to sell it merely as an intoxicating beverage, and who may wish to cover up that intent and evade the law.

As all compounders and rectifiers of spirits and all wholesale and retail liquor dealers *are* required by law to pay special taxes to the United States, it is the manifest duty of this office to see that they do so.

No mere medicine is any longer taxable in any form, but to draw the line nicely, and to fix definitely where the medicine may end, and the alcoholic beverage begin, is a task which has often perplexed and still greatly perplexes revenue officers, and especially where a preparation contains so large a proportion of alcoholic spirits as yours does. This difficulty is not relieved in this case by the showing made by the analysis.

The medicinal or vegetable ingredients used do not appear to so predominate as certainly to give an absolute medicinal character to the preparation. Indeed, it might be concluded, without doing much violence to the probabilities of the case that the distilled spirits are, proportionately, so large as to not be materially affected by the other mild ingredients, and that, therefore, while the preparation may, in some cases, be useful as a medicine, it may also be used very well as a mere "drink." The bitters do not present the case of a preparation like laudanum or camphor, in which, although the greater proportion is distilled spirits, yet the other ingredients are of such a powerful and predominating quality as to give character to the compound and unfit it for use as a beverage.

It is well known that various compounds, composed for the most part of alcohol or distilled spirits, are upon the markets of the country, and that they are especially adapted and probably designed for sale to the minority in those communities where so-called local option laws prevail, or where the sale of distilled spirits is otherwise forbidden by statute. Such compounds also find purchasers among a small class who prefer to drink stimulating or intoxicating beverages under some name less unpopular than that of whiskey.

These preparations usually sail into market under a medicinal flag, and while the law was such as to enable them to be taxed by stamps under a classification as proprietary medicines, the tendency of policy in this office was toward a liberal judgment in the direction of so classifying them, and especially where a formula, by which they were claimed to be made, was presented, accompanied by an affidavit that they were made according to it, and that they were designed, in good faith, only to be used as medicines. The result of such a tendency, it is true, was to get the largest amount of revenue for the Government; at the same time it gave a greatly increased salable and mercantile value to the preparation so classified. Though an inquiry was made in each case, probably it was not so strict as it should be now, since the law is changed, and since this office has information that such preparations are being extensively used in a manner different from what was stated by their makers to be designed at the outset.

It may well be that a compound can be used both as a medicine and as a beverage. When used in good faith as a medicine only, though it may contain distilled spirits, dealers in it, under such circumstances, will not be held liable to pay the special tax; but suppose it is not only capable of being used as an intoxicating beverage, but also that it is in fact sold and used as such by individual or by a large class of a community, surely the law, as well as justice to the regular liquor dealer who pays his tax, requires that the special tax shall also be collected from those who make and from those who thus sell such compounds for such a purpose.

If Hostetter's Bitters is in any locality sold and used as an alcoholic beverage, stimulant, or intoxicant, those who thus sell it will be liable to pay the special tax. The circumstance that it is used only as a medicine in one community will not exempt from liability to tax those dealers in it in any other locality who may, in fact, sell it as an alcoholic beverage. Each case must depend upon its own facts, and hence this office cannot now lay down any other general rules than such as are stated in this letter, and in a circular recently issued from this office, No. 268, dated July 16, 1883.

A copy of the circular is enclosed, and your attention is directed to it. It was called out by numerous letters addressed to this office, and in view of the law, as I construe it to be, since the repeal of Schedule A, following Section 3437 of the Revised Statutes. That circular will be adhered to, and you will observe that while a compound is not regarded as a medicine simply because it is called so, nor unless the name and use of it as a medicine agree, still the circular advises collectors to regard as presumptively medicines those preparations heretofore paying stamp taxes as such, but that if in fact, they are now sold and used as alcoholic beverages, the presumption that they are medicines is destroyed in such instances. It may also be added that so studious was this office to avoid a duplication of the special taxation, that it also instructed collectors that where parcels of a proprietary preparation had in fact been made and, under the policy then prevailing, stamped prior to July 1, 1883, Circular No. 268 would not apply to such goods as were actually made and stamped before that date. This clause of the circular was perfectly plain, though some designing persons have attempted to misrepresent its intent and meaning.

District attorneys and collectors will, no doubt, carefully investigate the facts in each particular case, and will be able to discriminate between a case where a preparation is used only as a medicine in good faith and a case where a preparation is called a medicine because of some mercantile advantage in doing so, but which is in fact used as an intoxicating beverage.

I have been at pains to state quite at length the position of this office, and you will observe that I do not decide whether, in the abstract, your preparation is a medicine or not.

Should I hold it to be a medicine, I should probably do violence to an almost irresistible tendency of the mind to conclude that no genuine medicine needs so much whiskey and so few drugs in it, unless under very unusual circumstances. On the other hand, should I decide that it is not a medicine at all, I would be confronted by a ten years' *quasi* recognition by this office to the contrary, as well as by the practice of many people who use it as such.

Since Circular No. 268 was issued I have been careful not to decide directly whether a preparation was a medicine or not, unless I had before me a report from the collector stating all the facts. Such a report I have not in this case.

My efforts will be directed to the ascertainment of the facts as to the use to which your preparation is put, for upon the character of its use in a given case will depend the question of the liability of the dealer to pay special tax.

The courts have decided one case since Circular No. 268 was issued, viz.; that of the United States v. Frederick Cota, which was tried before Judge Withey of the western district of Michigan.

The views of the learned judge in that case were identical with those entertained by this office as to the law in the premises. A full report of the case as found in the INTERNAL REVENUE RECORD is as follows:

UNITED STATES DISTRICT COURT, WESTERN DISTRICT OF MICHIGAN, NORTHERN DIVISION.

United States vs. Frederick Cota.

Before Hon. S. L. Withey, District Judge.

Information for carrying on the business of a retail liquor dealer without the payment of the special tax.

Trial, July 24, 1883.

The evidence in this case showed that the defendant kept a boarding-house and had a bar where he sold cider and an article known as "Reed's gilt edge tonic," by the glass or drink, to all persons who called for the same; that the tonic was sold in considerable quantities, by the glass or drink, to persons who drank it as a beverage as other liquors are drank, and that persons became intoxicated thereby; that said tonic was generally sold at saloons and drinking places in that vicinity, and contained a large percentage of distilled spirits.

It was claimed on the part of the Government that the evidence showed that this tonic was "compound liquors," within the meaning of the *third* subdivision of Sec. 3244, U. S. R. S., and that the manufacturer of such compounds was liable to pay a rectifier's special tax, and that the defendant was guilty under the information for selling the same in the manner shown by the evidence.

The court charged the jury in substance, that if the article sold was a medicine and contained spirits simply to preserve its medicinal qualities, and was sold and taken as a medicine in good faith, that the defendant should be acquitted. But if the jury found from the evidence that the article was a compound containing such a quantity of spirits as to be intoxicating, and was sold by the defendant as a beverage, he knowing its intoxicating quality, and was drank by persons *not* as a medicine but as a *beverage, because* of its intoxicating and stimulating qualities, then, no matter by what name it was known or called, the defendant was guilty as charged.

The jury returned a verdict of guilty, and the defendant was fined $300 and sentenced to imprisonment in the custody of the marshal for thirty days.

It is not desired to exact a dollar in taxes not fairly due, nor to claim any tax from dealers in any preparation which is fairly a medicine and in good faith used as such; but we do not doubt that all the Federal courts will hold views similar to those announced by Judge Withey, and, unless the special taxes are paid without question, I desire the courts speedily appealed to, wherever there are fair and reasonable grounds to believe that a preparation containing a large proportion of distilled spirits is sold and used as an intoxicating beverage, and not *bona fide* as a medicine.

The law is my only guide in such matters, and in such cases I regard it as requiring the payment of the tax, and I have no option but to collect it.

As to the suggestion that you should be repaid the amount you have heretofore paid the United States upon your bitters as a proprietary medicine, only a few lines need be added. There has never been any disposition on my part to inquire whether your preparation was used or sold otherwise than as a medicine previous to July 1, 1883. I have your sworn statement that it was before that date a proprietary medicine only, and you voluntarily, and from choice, had it classed as a medicine, and paid the stamp tax upon it as such, without question, up to that date. The Government took you at your word, and still does so as to everything done before July 1, 1883.

The whole question was carefully considered when Circular No. 268 was framed, and it was not doubted, either by this office or by the honorable Secretary of the Treasury, whose advice was asked upon it, that all claims for a refund of such taxes would be wholly unfounded, nor was it doubted that the makers of such compounds would be estopped from claiming such refund by their own assertions that their preparations were medicines and by their voluntary payment of the stamp tax as such.

Since July 1, 1883, if the preparations have also, in fact, been sold and used as alcoholic beverages, special taxes as liquor-dealers will have to be paid by those who sell them as such, and who by doing so pervert the original purpose of their preparation, as stated under oath by the makers of them. Whatever may have been done prior to July 1, 1883, when the article was taxed as a proprietary medicine, and was, as I assume, in good faith so used, *now,* in cases where the original purpose of the preparation is perverted, and instead of being used as a medicine it is used as an alcoholic beverage or intoxicant merely, the seller of it in this manner must be treated as a liquor-dealer, and taxed accordingly.

It is argued that Congress by repealing Schedule A, whereby stamp taxes were removed, meant to relieve such articles altogether from taxation. It is certainly true that Congress did repeal the law laying a tax upon *medicines, but it is equally true that Congress did not remove the tax from retail liquor-dealers,* and our efforts must be directed to ascertaining whether, as a matter of fact, a dealer *bona fide* sells medicine and is exempt from tax, or sells alcoholic beverages and is liable to it, our whole difficulty arising from the fact that such preparations are susceptible of use both as a medicine and as a "drink." You can therefore see how, acting in good faith, your customers can determine, each for himself, whether there is a liability to pay special tax as liquor-dealers—in other words, to "take out licenses."

When a preparation, considered with reference to its ingredients, may be one thing or another, according to its use, I will let the use give character to it. If used or administered *bona fide* as a medicine, as a medicine it will be treated, but if persons ignore its medicinal properties and sell it to be drank as an intoxicating beverage, the act should be regarded as a retailing of spirituous liquors, and the seller made to pay the tax accordingly. This seems to me to be the true rule, and an article containing so little that is even nominally medicinal as yours does ought and will be subject to very close scrutiny as to its use.

Very respectfully,
Walter Evans,
Commissioner.

IRR v.XXIX, August 27, 1883, pp.273-5

Relative to Certain Preparations Made by the St. Louis Wine Company.

Treasury Department,
Office of Internal Revenue,
Washington, September 13, 1883.

Gen. Green B. Raum, Washington, D. C.:

Sir: Your letter of the 27th ultimo, in which you request a decision by this Office as to whether certain preparations made by the St. Louis Wine Company (formerly the Home Bitters Company) are medicines, has been received, and, together with the papers which accompanied it, has been carefully considered.

In the view I have of the case you present, no action should be taken by this Office in respect to the matters about which you write.

Since the repeal of Schedule A, following Section 3437, Revised Statutes, I have very maturely considered the subject in all its bearings, and have reached the conclusion that where a preparation has been heretofore classed by this Office as a medicine, but which, by reason of the large proportion of distilled spirits it contains, is susceptible of being used either as a medicine or as an alcoholic beverage, the *manner of its sale and use,* will be the test of whether a seller of it will be treated as a liquor dealer or not.

I am aware that in your letter you argue against this position, but in doing so you probably overlook the only judicial opinions delivered upon the subject since the repeal of Schedule A. I allude to that of Judge Withey in the case of the United States versus Frederick Cota.

There is entire harmony between the views of that learned judge and those announced by this Office, as you will see from our circular No. 268, dated July 16, 1883, and my letter to Messrs. Hostetter and Smith of August 22, 1883, copies of which I enclose for your perusal.

If the preparations of the St. Louis Wine Company are certainly medicines, and are, in good faith, only sold and used as such, no special tax will be required of the seller of them, but, in case they are used as alcoholic beverages, the seller of them as such, will be made to pay tax as a liquor dealer.

I say this in view of the large proportion of alcohol which they seem to contain.

Primarily, the question of fact, as to the manner in which a preparation is sold and used is to be determined by the Collectors of Internal Revenue. As no collector has found that your client's preparations have been used as alcoholic beverages since July 1, 1883, there is nothing for me to decide, and certainly no action of which the St. Louis Wine Company can justly complain, or from which it can properly appeal to this Office.

Your clients have already, heretofore, obtained the decision of this Office, that their preparations are medicines. Collector Sturgeon has so found upon a reinvestigation, and until I hear, or until some officer of the Government ascertains, that the preparations are being, in fact, sold and used as alcoholic beverages (in which event the actual facts will justify a contrary course), nothing further will be done.

Having fixed the *manner of sale and use* as the test in such cases, I must decline, *where preparations have been already classed as medicines, but which contain a large proportion of alcohol,* to *further* decide the abstract question of medicine or no medicine in any case.

Very respectfully,
Walter Evans,
Commissioner.

Approved:
Chas. J. Folger, Secretary, etc.

IRR v.XXIX, September 24, 1883, p.305

Relative to Hostetter's Bitters.

Treasury Department,
Office of Internal Revenue,
Washington, August 25, 1883.

A. H. Clark, Esq., Revenue Agent, New York City, N. Y.:

Sir: Your attention is very specially called to a letter addressed to Messrs. Hostetter and Smith on the 22d instant, in regard to a preparation known as Hostetter's Bitters, printed copies of which letter you will find enclosed.

The analysis of the compound shows it to be made of a very strong alcoholic liquor and very little else, so little of anything else, that information received at this Office leads to the belief that it is now being sold very extensively as an alcoholic beverage, and that efforts are being made to evade the law requiring payment of the tax due the United States from retail liquor dealers.

These facts, and especially the analysis of the Bitters, which itself justifies very great suspicion, lead me to enjoin the utmost vigilence upon all revenue officers, so that no one liable for the tax shall escape its payment by any evasion or false pretence whatever.

It may also be added that the terms of the letter to Messrs. Hostetter and Smith are applicable to the case of every other preparation of a like alcoholic character, and especially where there are grounds for strong suspicion that the distilled spirits are sold under the guise of a medicine. All such articles should receive attention at your hands.

Respectfully,
Walter Evans,
Commissioner.

IRR v.XXIX, September 24, 1883, p.306

PERFUMERY AND COSMETICS

As prepared chalk is used almost exclusively as a cosmetic, each packet, bottle, pot, phial, or other enclosure or envelope, in which it is contained, is subject to stamp duty, as provided in Schedule C.

If not sold as a cosmetic, it will be subject to a duty of three per cent. *ad valorem,* under section 75, as a manufacture not otherwise provided for.

Boutwell (1863), Rulings (No. 260)

Cologne water is subject to stamp tax under Schedule C.

Boutwell (1863), Rulings (No. 267)

All articles enumerated in Schedule C, under head of "perfumery and cosmetics," must be stamped, whether "proprietary" or not.

Boutwell (1863), Rulings (No. 287)

If parties making articles known as essences, such as cinnamon, peppermint, lemon, cloves, &c., do not claim a private formula or occult secret or art for the manufacture, nor an exclusive right or title by letters patent, and if they are not used or applied as perfumes or applications to the hair, mouth or skin, the articles are exempt from stamp duty.

Boutwell (1863), Rulings (from No. 289)

All perfumery and cosmetics enumerated in Schedule C of the excise law are subject to stamp duty, whether manufactured with or without a private formula. They are also equally subject to stamp duty when sold in irregular packages and quantities, or when sold in regular packages. Perfumery and cosmetics put into and sold in bottles or packages, furnished by the purchasers, are also subject to stamp duty.

Boutwell (1863), Rulings (No. 296)

Playing-cards and perfumery, purchased prior to the act of June 30, 1864, and appropriately stamped under the laws in force at the time of purchase, may be exported without payment of more stamp-duty, but if sold in the United States at this time, must be stamped according to rates of act of June 30.

Boutwell (1865), Rulings (No. 264)

Toilet and Domestic and Imported Soaps not Liable to Stamp Duty as Cosmetics.

February 26th, 1866.

Sir:—Enclosed herewith please find samples of highly scented toilet soaps. A question has arisen as to whether they can be considered "Cosmetics," or "similar articles," and therefore be liable to stamps tax, although having paid impost duty; and secondly, whether they can be considered proprietary from the claim put forth on the labels. Specimen marked A, "Spermaceti Tablet made only by Baylay & Co. of London," strikes me as setting up secret manufacture or exclusive right. Specimen B, "Lowe's highly perfumed Brown Windsor Soap," I have not regarded as requiring stamps, but as some inspectors have insisted that it should be stamped by dealers I submit it for your decision.

Bazin's Tonquin Mask Soap, a domestic manufacture, imparting a pleasant and lasting perfume, is also submitted as to its liability to stamp and specific duty of five cents per lb. under the 94th section. Imported specimen of Glycerine and Honey Soaps also inclosed, I take it, are not liable to any further tax than impost inasmuch as each cake is not inclosed. An inclosure of the article when sold at retail being indispensable, as I understand it, to determine liability and the price thereof, to establish the amount of tax due, I have regarded that a proprietary claim when set upon the label of an enclosed cake of soap, or the recommendation of the same for the cure of affection of the skin, &c., subjects the article to stamp duty rather than to the requirements of the 94th section of the Internal Revenue laws. Your early answer is requested.

Respectfully,
Pierre C. Van Wyck.
Assessor 4th District,
New York.

To Hon. E. A. Rollins,
Commissioner Internal Revenue.
Washington, D.C.

[Answer.]

Treasury Department,
Office of Internal Revenue,
Washington, March 6, 1866.

Sir:—Your letter of the 26th ultimo, with the accompanying specimens of Toilet Soap has been received.

You state that a question has arisen as to whether they can be considered "cosmetics" or "similar articles," and therefore liable to stamp duty, although having paid impost duty; and secondly, whether they can be considered proprietary.

In answer, I have to say that these specimens, the imported as well as the domestic, are Toilet Soap, clearly and accurately described in section 94, under the head of soaps, and specifically taxed. Were they all of domestic manufacture, we should not think of taxing them otherwise than is provided in section 94. even though the manufacturer should claim some secret or exclusive right in the manufacture.

The impost duty is supposed to have been adjusted, or at least should be, with reference to the excise duty, and *imported articles* are not held liable to stamp duties under Schedule C, when the same kind or class of articles are not liable when they are of domestic manufacture.

Fancy, scented, honey, cream, transparent, and shaving soaps are to be regarded as Toilet Soap, and not as perfumery or cosmetics for purposes of taxation.

Very respectfully,
D. C. Whitman,
Deputy Commissioner.

Pierre C. Van Wyck, Esq.,
U. S. Assessor, N.Y.

IRR v.III, March 17, 1866, p.85

Tax on Cologne Sold in Bottles and by the Gallon.

Assessor's Office,
8th District, Illinois,
Springfield, Oct. 9th, 1866.

Hon. E. A. Rollins,
Commissioner of Internal Revenue.

Sir: Is cologne, manufactured by druggists by a formula published in the United States Dispensatory, and sold by the manufacturer at retail, said manufacturer claiming no secret or art whatever in making the cologne, subject to a stamp duty?

Very respectfully,
D. Wickersham,
Assessor.

[Answer]

Office of Internal Revenue,
Washington, Oct. 15, 1866.

Sir: In reply to your letter of Oct. 9th, in relation to cologne water, I have to say that cologne water is regarded as perfumery, and when manufactured and put up in bottles, phials, &c., as provided in Schedule C, it should be properly stamped before being sold or offered for sale; but when it is not so put up but is manufactured and sold by the gallon, &c., it is liable to an ad valorem tax of 5 per cent. under the general provisions of section 94.

Very respectfully,
Thomas Harland,
Deputy Commissioner.

D. Wickersham, Esq.,
Assessor 8th Dist., Springfield, Illinois.

IRR v.IV, October 27, 1866, p.133

Stamp on Manufactured and Imported Articles—Original Packages—Exposure for Sale.

The law imposes a stamp duty upon essences, extracts, toilet water, cosmetics, hair oils, &c. &c., whether the same are imported or of domestic manufacture. (See Record, Vol. VI, p. 123.) It further provides that where such imported articles are sold in the original and unbroken packages in which the bottles or other enclosures were packed by the manufacturer, the person so selling said articles shall not be subject to any penalty for want of the proper stamp. By the term "original packages," as here used, is meant the cases or packing boxes in which the bottles, &c., are packed by the manufacturer, and not the bottles themselves. This provision was intended to apply in cases where the imported articles are sold at wholesale to be sold again, and was intended to relieve the importer from the trouble, expense and damage of opening his boxes, unpacking his articles, stamping and repacking for sale.

When the original packages are opened, and the contents offered, or exposed for sale, each bottle, pot, can, phial, or other single package must be stamped according to the requirements of Schedule C, Internal Revenue Laws.

IRR v.VI, November 2, 1867, p.154

Editor of Internal Revenue Record.

In doing the rounds of my district for the purpose of instructing grocers, druggists and others in regard to stamping certain articles as required under Schedule C, I found it difficult at times to answer the questions asked, and the objections which were sometimes raised to stamping some articles, which, in my opinion, required a stamp; and I did not feel perfectly sure afterwards, that I decided right in every instance. I have no doubt that other assistant assessors have experienced the same difficulty. As you are good authority in such matters, will you be so good as to give your opinion in the next number of the Record in regard to the necessity of stamping the following articles, viz.: ground mustard and spices in cans and bottles; pickles, such as cucumbers, and olives, and capers, in bottles; olive oil, in bottles; castor oil, in bottles; cologne water, in bottles. By answering the above I have no doubt you will oblige more than one Asst. Assessor.

Dry ground mustard and spices are held to be exempt from stamp duty, but *prepared* or French mustard is liable. Cucumbers, olives, and capers, pickles, in bottles, are exempt from stamp duty. Castor oil is not held liable to stamp duty. Cologne, in bottles, is liable to stamp duty as a cosmetic. Ed.

IRR v.VI, November 23, 1867, p.178

Stamp—Bay Rum.

"Bay rum" is covered by the provisions of Schedule C. concerning toilet-water; and every packet, box, bottle, pot, phial, *or other enclosure,* containing it, then sold, offered for sale, or removed for consumption or sale, by any person or persons whatsoever, should be stamped.

IRR v.VII, January 11, 1868, p.11

Vegetable Tooth Soap—Soaps Sold for Dentifrices—Liability to Stamp.

Office of Internal Revenue,
Washington, June 28th, 1869.

Sir: Your letter of June 24th, in relation to "C. S. Bates' Vegetable Tooth Soap," has been received.

In reply I have to say that I have just received from C. S. Bates, the manufacturer, a cake of the soap in question, neatly done up in a printed enclosure, and have informed him that the soap is liable as a dentifrice, to stamp, under Schedule C.

All persons having on hand any of the soap in question should see that the proper Internal Revenue stamp is affixed to each package before selling or exposing it for sale, if they would not incur the penalty imposed in section 165 of the act of June 30, 1864, as amended by the act of July 13, 1866.

Very respectfully,
J. W. Douglass,
Deputy Commissioner.

J. P. Murphy, *Esq., Assessor 29th District,*
Lockport, N. Y.

IRR v.X, July 3, 1869, p.5

Stamps are Required for Bottles of Imported Perfumery when the Original Package is Broken and the Bottles Taken therefrom.

Treasury Department,
Office of Internal Revenue,
Washington, July 29, 1871.

Wm. T. Mercer & Son, Newark, N. J.

Sirs: In reply to your letter of July 12, in relation to stamping imported perfumery, I have to say that imported perfumery may be sold in the original and unbroken package, as entered at the custom-house, without being stamped; but when the original package is broken and the smaller packages are taken therefrom, the bottles contained in the smaller packages must be stamped before they are sold or offered for sale.

In regard to stamping a barrel or gallon bottle of cologne water to retail from, I would say that the law does not authorize such a practice. The law requires the stamp to be affixed to the bottle or other enclosure in which the article is sold and delivered, even though the bottle or enclosure may be furnished by the purchaser.

Very respectfully,
A. Pleasonton,
Commissioner.

IRR v.XIV, August 12, 1871, p.41

Articles coming under Head of ''Perfumery and Cosmetics'' in Schedule C are not Exempt from Tax because manufactured according to a Published Formula, and the Vessels in which they are delivered must be Stamped even though furnished by the Purchaser.

U. S. Internal Revenue Collector's Office,
1st District, N. Y. 44 Court St.,
Brooklyn, January 26, 1872.

Hon. J. W. Douglass, Commissioner of Internal Revenue.

Sir: I have a case now pending for penalties for not stamping cologne, hair oil, and extracts . . . and submit the facts to obtain the ruling of the Department:

Cologne.–The party is a druggist, who makes the cologne after the recipe found in the Pharmacopoeia, published for use in making prescriptions. He puts it up in bottles of various fancy designs, with a label on the bottle "Cologne;" no name or address.

Hair Oil.–This is made after the formula in the Pharmacopoeia, put in bottles with the label ''Hair Oil,'' or is sold to parties by the few cents' worth–purchasers sometimes bringing their own bottles, and sometimes teacups.

Extracts.–These are imported in tin packages holding about one pint (called pound packages). These packages are stamped, after importation, with the internal revenue stamps. The contents are then poured into small vials for toilet sets and sold.

Are all the bottles of cologne liable to be stamped? If a customer brings a bottle or other vessel for receiving it, must a stamp be placed on the bottle or vessel at the time of sale?

Are all the bottles of hair oil liable to a stamp? If a customer brings a bottle or other vessel for receiving a small quantity purchased, must the vessel be stamped?

When the pint package of extract has been imported and stamped according to law, or when a case containing several such packages has been imported and each pint package stamped according to law, and the contents emptied into small vials for toilet sets, must each of the small fancy vials be again stamped. You will oblige me by replying early.

Respectfully,
James Freeland,
Collector 1st District, N.Y.

Office of Internal Revenue,
Washington, January 29, 1872.

James Freeland, Esq., Collector 1st District, Brooklyn, N.Y.

Sir: In reply to your letter of January 26, in relation to cologne water, hair oil, and extracts, I have to say that all articles which come under the head of ''Perfumery and Cosmetics'' in ''Schedule C,'' are liable to stamp duty thereunder, though manufactured according to a published formula. The fact that they are manufactured according to a published formula does not in the least affect their liability to tax. Every bottle or vessel in which the manufacturer sells or delivers the article must have the proper stamp affixed, whether the bottle or vessel is furnished by the purchaser or the party selling the article.

Perfumery extracts imported in tin cans after being stamped, may be sold in the stamped can, but if they are drawn therefrom into smaller bottles and thus exposed and offered for sale, the bottles must be stamped.

Very respectfully,
B. J. Sweet,
Deputy Commissioner.

IRR v.XV, February 24, 1872, p.54

Soaps Advertised and Recommended as Having Special Virtues as Medicinal Preparations or Cosmetics, are Liable to Stamp Tax under Schedule C.

Treasury Department,
Office of Internal Revenue,
Washington, May 27, 1873.

Alex. P. Tutton, Esq., Supervisor, Philadelphia, Pa.

Sir: I have received your letter of the 23d inst., enclosing eight labels and wrappers used upon soaps which you say are largely sold throughout your district, and asking for my decision as to whether these labels render the soap to which they are attached, and by which they are held out and recommended for sale to the public by the makers and vendors, liable to stamp tax under Schedule C.

In reply I have to inform you that soaps of all descriptions, including fancy, scented, honey, cream, transparent, toilet, and shaving soaps, are exempt from taxation when they are not placed in the category of medicinal preparations, nor held out as remedies or specifics for diseases, or affections of the body, nor placed in the category of cosmetics and as such recommended for popular use and sale.

But on the contrary, when such soaps are held out and recommended to the public as medicinal preparations and cosmetics, and special merit is claimed for them, and patronage solicited on account of their healing, improving, and beautifying qualities and properties, and when these claims are clearly and prominently set forth on the wrappers, labels, and circulars accompanying each packet, or box, or pot, or other enclosure, they become liable to stamp tax under Schedule C. I have examined these labels and marked such of them as, in my opinion, set up claims which render the soaps covered by them liable to stamp tax, and those that are not liable.

When it is claimed for any soap that "it removes unhealthy emanations from the skin," "cures cutaneous eruptions," "renovates and freshens the complexion," "alike good in the sickroom, nursery, or on the toilet stand," I hold that it is liable to the stamp tax. When a particular soap is claimed "to be beneficial in removing tan, sunburn, moth, and freckles," when it is advertised "to cleanse and invigorate the skin, and to improve the complexion," as it is claimed of the oat-meal and glycerine soap, such soap is placed in the category of cosmetics, and as such must be stamped.

When a soap is especially recommended for "the healthy action" which it produces "upon the skin," for its power to remove "eruptive humors from the face," its tendency "to ward off infectious diseases," and its tendency to "improve the complexion generally"—recommendations and claims set up for the "Camphor Ice Soap"—such soap is placed in the category of cosmetics, and must be so regarded by revenue officers.

The "Tar Soap," according to the label, has been well tested as "its efficacy in curing salt rheum and other obstinate cutaneous diseases." While the "Tar and Glycerine Soap," aromatic and extra fine in quality, "renovates the complexion and removes pimples, tan, and sunburn," improving, healing, and beautifying properties which give the special value to cosmetics.

These soaps, with such claims, and accompanied with such labels and wrappers, are clearly covered by the language of the statute defining what medicinal and cosmetic articles shall be stamped. And so long as the makers and vendors of such soaps elect to place them in this category, it will be the duty of revenue to see that they are properly stamped.

Enclosed I return the labels.

Yours respectfully,
J. W. Douglass,
Commissioner.

IRR v.XVIII, July 19, 1873, p. 17

MATCHES

Imported Friction Matches.

Treasury Department,
Office of Internal Revenue,
Washington, March 18, 1865.

Sir: The following is a copy of section second of the late act of Congress approved on the 3d inst. Section 2: And be it further enacted, "That from and after the passage of this act the proviso to Section one hundred and sixty-nine of the act to which this act is an amendment, shall not be held to apply to lucifer matches, friction matches, or other articles made in part of wood, and used for like purposes, nor to cigar lights and wax tapers."

You will observe that in consequence of this provision of the law, all lucifer and friction matches exposed to sale without being stamped are liable to seizure notwithstanding their importation from Canada, or other foreign countries, and their sale in original packages. Whenever you find packages of matches, large or small, offered for sale without being stamped, you should therefore immediately seize the same, and proceed to enforce the penalties of the law.

Yours respectfully,
Joseph J. Lewis,
Commissioner.

IRR v.I, March 25, 1865, p.90

Review.

Many ingenious contrivances are conceived by designing individuals to avoid tax. One of the latest to escape the payment of stamp tax on matches, receives its quietus in the decision we publish to-day. The matches in question, are sawed out in blocks containing about one hundred matches each, and dipped in brimstone. They are accompanied by a small bottle of liquid match composition, into which the brimstone ends are to be dipped by the purchaser, and when dry are ready for use. These matches have hitherto been sold without stamp tax, as not being friction matches, within the meaning of the law, as sold by the manufacturer. The decision discusses their character and composition, and holds them to be clearly liable to stamp tax, and orders proceedings to be instituted to enforce compliance with the law by all parties enagaged in their manufacture.

• • •

New Kind of Matches, Stamp Tax, Penalties, Etc.

Office of Internal Revenue,
Washington, February 15, 1866.

Sir: My attention has been called to a new article of matches being made in your District, and sold extensively throughout the country without any stamps affixed, and in fraud of the Internal Revenue law.

These matches are sawed out in blocks containing, I judge, one hundred matches each, and dipped in brimstone. These matches are accompanied with a bottle of phosphoric composition, or liquid match composition. The directions for using are as follows: "Touch the sulphured end of your splints to the compound. As soon as dry, they are ready for use. If the composition should not adhere readily to the splint, warm it slightly. Prepared by the Liquid Match Composition Company. Patented by N. B. & D. Shaw, Sanbornton, N. H., Aug. 29, 1865. Post Office address, Box 17, Hill, N. H."

I have specimens of those matches before me, and find that, by following the above directions, the result indicated is immediately obtained.

The law provides (Section 170, Schedule C) that friction matches, or lucifer matches, or other articles made in part of wood and used for like purposes, in parcels or packages containing one hundred matches or less, for each parcel or package, a one cent Revenue stamp shall be affixed.

Are the matches described above, friction or lucifer matches, or other articles made of wood and used for like purposes? If so, they are liable to stamp duty; and any person, firm, company, or corporations who shall make, prepare, and sell, or remove for consumption or sale, such matches without affixing thereto an adhesive stamp or label denoting the duty, incurs a penalty of ten dollars for every omission to affix such stamp (see Section 165), and further, Section 167 declares that every maker or manufacturer of such matches who shall sell, expose for sale, send out, remove, or deliver any such article before the duty thereon shall be fully paid by affixing thereon the proper stamps, &c., shall be subject to a penalty of $100, together with the forfeiture of the article. And Section 169 provides, that any person who shall offer or expose for sale any articles named in Schedule C, shall be deemed the manufacturer thereof, and subject to all the duties, liabilities, and penalties imposed by law in regard to the sale of domestic articles without the use of the proper stamp, or stamps, denoting the duties paid thereon.

Webster defines a match as a splint of wood dipped at one end in a preparation of sulphur, phosphorus, or the like, and ignited by rubbing. A lucifer, loco foco, or friction match, is a sliver of wood tipped with a combustible substance, and ignited by friction.

These definitions accurately describe the matches in question. They are splints or slivers of wood, sawed in the usual mode of preparing match wood, and dipped in sulphur. It is true, the phosphoric composition is liquid, is not applied by the manufacturer, but is sold by him as an accompaniment, which the purchaser or consumer applies, as he has occasion to use the matches.

No doubt the inventors of these matches intended by this process to evade the stamp duty imposed upon friction matches, under the plea that, as sold by them, they are not friction or lucifer matches, inasmuch as they cannot be lighted by friction till after being dipped in the accompanying liquid. This plea, however, cannot avail them. The law exempts "match wood." But the article in question is *not* match wood. They are strictly *matches,* by the definition already quoted from Webster. They are also friction or lucifer matches, or articles used for like purposes. They are *made* for friction matches–they are *used* for friction matches. They are made with no other design, intent or purpose; they are so used, and have no other use. By their design and use they are friction matches. By the definition of matches quoted from Webster, they are friction matches, and by the express language of the statute, they are friction matches, and as such, liable to the stamp duty. And the makers and venders of these matches are liable to all the duties, forfeitures, and penalties provided in the excise law which I have before quoted.

Numerous attempts have been made by slight variations from the usual mode of manufacturing matches to evade the duty imposed by law. Thus far these attempts have all proven failures. And so long as the law remains as it now is, I shall endeavor to enforce its provisions upon all manufacturers of the article equally and impartially.

You are, therefore, instructed immediately to institute proceedings to enforce the law upon all parties engaged in the manufacture and sale of these matches, that the government may not be defrauded of its revenue, and that honest tax-paying manufacturers may be protected in their business.

Yours respectfully,
D. C. Whitman
Deputy Commissioner.

IRR v.III, February 24, 1866, pp.57, 60

Stamp on Matches—Action to recover Penalties.
U.S. District Court, Oregon.
[July term, 1867, before Judge Deady.]

United States vs. *J. F. Walsh, action to recover penalties.*

Deady, J.—This action was commenced by filing complaint on May 23d, 1867. On the same day an order for the arrest of the defendant was allowed at chambers. On May 27th, 1867, the defendant was arrested and gave bail to the action in the sum of $800. On the tenth of July following the defendant's counsel filed a motion to vacate the order allowing the arrest.

This motion was made and argued as the cause was called for trial. The trial proceeded, while the decision of the motion was reserved for further consideration. On the trial a verdict was given for the plaintiff for the sum of $800.

The grounds of the motion are;

1st. Because the order was improperly made.

2d. Because the affidavit was insufficient.

3d. Because there is no undertaking for the writ.

The complaint is verified by the oath of the informer, S. P. Reed, and charges that the defendant, on April 22, 1867, did manufacture and sell eight packages of friction matches, without stamping the same or either of them as required by the statutes of the United States; and also, that on May 1st,

1867, did in like manner manufacture and sell eight other packages of friction matches.

At the time of allowing the order of arrest there was also filed the separate affidavit of the informer, containing substantially the same facts as the complaint, except that the articles therein alleged to have been manufactured and sold, were described simply as *matches,* without being designated as either *lucifer* or *friction* matches.

Section 9, of the Internal Revenue Act, of July 13, 1866, requires that *lucifer* or *friction* matches shall be stamped as prescribed in schedule C, and imposes "a penalty of fifty dollars for every omission to affix such stamp." Counsel for the defendant maintains that this affidavit is insufficient to authorize the order of arrest, because it does not specifically allege that the matches manufactured and sold by the defendant without stamps, were either *lucifer* or *friction* matches.

The only kind of matches subject to stamp duty under the Internal Revenue Act, are by that act designated or called *lucifer* or *friction* matches. Whether there are any other kinds of matches known to the arts or commerce, which are not subject to such duty, is a question of fact, of which I cannot take judicial knowledge. Ought I, in the absence of proof pro or con, to presume that there are other kinds of matches, not subject to duty, and that therefore the act stated in the affidavit, may or may not be a cause of arrest? I incline to think not. But admitting for the purpose of the argument that the affidavit is insufficient for want of certainty in this particular, it cannot affect this motion. Where the cause is sufficiently set forth in the complaint, and the cause of action and arrest are identical, there is no necessity for an additional or separate affidavit to authorize the order for an arrest. In this case, the cause of action and arrest are identical, and the statement of the facts in the complaint is sufficient for either purpose. The order allowing the arrest of the defendant may be made when it appears by affidavit that a sufficient cause of action and arrest exists (Gen. Laws, 165). Upon the same principle, an execution is allowed against the body, without affidavit or other proof than the record, when it appears from the record that the cause of action, on account of which the judgment was given, was also a cause of arrest (Gen. Laws 210).

The statute only requires that the facts necessary to authorize the order of arrest shall appear by *affidavit.* If the complaint shows a cause of action and no more as that the defendant is indebted to the plaintiff for, money loaned, then it would be necessary to show by affidavit in addition to the complaint, that a cause of arrest exists also—as that the defendant obtained the loan by fraud.

The statute should not be so construed as to require the plaintiff to do a useless act to obtain the order. A verified complaint is in this respect an affidavit. It is a statement of facts, verified by the oath of the party making it. If it appears from such a complaint that there exists against the defendant both a cause of action and arrest, enough is shown to justify the order of arrest.

The objection, that no undertaking was given for the writ, to indemnify the defendant, will be next considered. The subject of arrest and imprisonment in civil actions in the courts of the United States is regulated by the acts of Congress of February 28, 1839, and January 14, 1841, the latter being declaratory of the former. The first of these acts substantially provides that no person shall be imprisoned for debt on process issuing out of the courts of the United States, in any State where by the laws of such State imprisonment for debt has been abolished, and that where imprisonment for debt was allowed upon conditions and restrictions, it should be allowed in like manner in the United States courts. This act was not prospective and therefore did not adopt the future legislation of the States. It was also held not to apply to actions in which the United States were plaintiff. On this latter account the act of January 14, 1841, was passed, which declared, that the act of February 28, 1839, should be construed to abolish imprisonment for debt in the United States courts, in all cases where by the laws of the State, imprisonment for debt has been or *shall hereafter be abolished.*

This act is prospective in its terms, so far as future laws of the States abolishing imprisonment for debt, are concerned. Whether Congress has the power to adopt prospectively State legislation on any given subject, I do not propose to discuss. The power has been seriously questioned, and upon apparently good grounds. (2 Curtis C. C. and the authorities there cited.) But the act of 1841 is silent concerning the future laws of the States imposing restrictions and conditions upon the allowance of imprisonment for debt. It does not purport to adopt them. The law of this State regulating arrest in civil actions, requires as a condition precedent to an arrest, that the plaintiff shall give an undertaking to pay the defendant "all costs that may be adjudged to him and all damages which he may sustain by reason of the arrest, if the same be wrongful or without sufficient cause exceeding the sum specified in the undertaking." (Gen. Laws 165-6.) This is a condition or restriction imposed upon the allowance of an order of arrest, and is not adopted by act of Congress. The adoption of this law by a rule of court, might make it of force as a rule of court between private suitors, and even this is questionable. But the United States as plaintiff in an action could not be bound by such a law unless enacted or adopted by Congress. This court could not by rule require the United States to give security for costs, nor damages. The United States never pays costs to the adverse party, and it would not be bound by any undertaking entered into on its behalf to pay any one, unless authorized by act of Congress.

The objection that the order was improperly allowed raises the question, whether the United States is entitled to arrest a defendant in an action for a penalty, in this State. The Constitution of this State (Bill of Rights, clause 19), enacts: "There shall be no imprisonment for debt except in case of fraud or absconding debtors." (Gen. Laws 99.)

The law of this State provides, among other causes, that the defendant may be arrested on a civil "action for a fine or penalty." (Gen. Laws 164.)

Counsel for the defendant maintains that this act of the Legislative Assembly, is in this particular repugnant to the Constitution of the State, and therefore void. No decision of the Supreme Court is cited in support of this position, and none is known to have been made.

The word *debt* is of very general use, and has many shades of meaning. Looking to the origin and progress of the change in public opinion, which finally led to the abolition of imprisonment for debt, it is reasonable to presume that this provision in the State Constitution was intended to prevent the useless and often cruel imprisonment of persons, who having *honestly* become indebted to another, are unable to pay as they undertook and promised. In this view of the matter the clause in question should be construed as if it read; "There shall be no imprisonment for debt *arising upon contract express or implied,* except, etc." Such is substantially the language employed in the Legislative acts of most of the States, abolishing imprisonment for debt; and there can be but little doubt that this was the end which the framers of the Constitution had in view, as well as the popular understanding of the clause, when the instrument was adopted at the polls.

General or abstract declarations in Bills of Rights are necessarily brief and comprehensive in their terms. When applied to the details of the varied affairs of life, they must be construed with reference to the causes which produced them and the end sought to be obtained. A person who wilfully injures another in person, property or character, is liable therefor in damages. In some sense he may be called the debtor of the party injured, and the sum due for the injury a debt. But he is in fact a wrong doer, a trespasser, and does not come within the reason of the rule which exempts an honest man from imprisonment because he is pecuniarily unable to pay what he promised to. For instance, a person who wrongfully beats his neighbor, kills his ox or girdles his fruit trees, ought not to be considered in the same category as an unfortunate debtor. He ought to be liable to arrest in action for damages by the party injured. Deny him this remedy, and in the majority of such cases it would amount to a denial of justice, and a deliberate repudiation and disregard of the injunction contained in clause 10 of the Bill of Rights—"every man shall have remedy by due course of law for injury done him in person, property or reputation." It may be admitted that a penalty given by statute is technically a debt. It does not, however, arise upon contract but by operation of law. It is imposed as a quasi punishment for the violation of law or the neglect or refusal to perform some duty to the public or individuals enjoined by law. Penalties are imposed in furtherance of some public policy and as a means of securing obedience to law. Persons who incur them are either in morals or law wrong doers, and not simply unfortunate debtors unable to perform their pecuniary obligations. I do not think the constitutional provision prohibiting imprisonment for debt was intended to apply to or include such cases. From these premises it follows of course that the act of the Assembly allowing the arrest of the defendant in an action for a penalty, is not in conflict with the constitution, and therefore valid and binding.

But admitting, for the sake of the argument, that these penalties are a debt within the meaning of the clause prohibiting imprisonment for debt, do they not come within the exception—*"except in case of fraud."* The International [sic] Revenue Act, required the defendant to affix a certain amount of stamps upon all the matches manufactured by him before selling the same or removing them for consumption or sale. As a means of enforcing or securing the payment of this tax, the act also imposed a penalty of fifty dollars upon the defendant for every omission to affix such stamp. The payment of this tax was *a duty* imposed upon the defendant by law. When he sold these sixteen packages of matches without affixing the stamps to them, he acted fraudulently. Thereby he cheated and defrauded the United States, the plaintiff in this action.

These penalties were incurred by this fraudulent act, and if they can be considered a debt within the meaning of clause 19 of the bill of rights, it is such a debt as falls exactly within the exception—being to all intents and purpose, *"a case of fraud,"* both in morals and law. Of course, in this respect there can be no distinction between cheating or defrauding the government of the United States, and an individual.

The order for the arrest was properly allowed, and the motion of defendant must be denied.

IRR v.VI, December 21, 1867, p.212-3

All Matches, Imported or Domestic, Liable to Stamp Duty.

Treasury Department,
Office of Internal Revenue,
Washington, May 17, 1873.

Geo. L. Clark, Esq., Assessor Sixteenth District, Plattsburgh, N.Y.

Sir: In reply to your letter of May 12 in relation to stamping imported matches, I have to say that all matches, whether imported or of domestic manufacture, are liable to stamp duty under "Schedule C."

Very respectfully,
J. W. Douglass,
Commissioner.

IRR v.XVII, May 24, 1873, p.161

To Collectors of Customs.

Treasury Department,
Washington, D.C., June 3, 1875.

The following Decisions of the Department for the month of May, 1875, upon the construction to be given to Acts of Congress relating to the Tariff, Navigation, and other subjects, are published herewith for the information and guidance of Officers of the Customs.

B. H. Bristow,
Secretary.

• • •

2218—Internal-Revenue Stamps cannot be Affixed prior to Importation.

This Department is in receipt of a communication from the United States consul at Quebec, Canada, dated the 16th ult., inquiring whether the internal-revenue stamps required to be affixed to imported matches can be so affixed prior to their importation into this country. With reference thereto I beg leave to state that section 3423 of the Revised Statutes requires that where an internal-revenue stamp is affixed to a box, bottle, or package, it must be so done "that in opening the same, or using the contents thereof, the said stamp will be effectually destroyed." If such stamps are affixed in the manner prescribed to boxes containing matches, prior to their importation, the examination required to be made of such merchandise, on its being imported, for the purpose of determining the duty, cannot be made without destroying the stamps and thereby defeating the intent of the internal revenue law, that such stamps are not to be destroyed until the goods enter into consumption. In view of the premises this Department is of opinion that the privilege requested cannot be allowed under existing laws, and I will thank you to inform said consul to that effect. (Hon. Hamilton Fish, Secretary of State, Washington, D.C., May 4.)

IRR v.XXI, June 21, 1875, pp.194-5

2841.—Internal Revenue Stamps can be Affixed before Importation.

Respectfully referring to this Department's communication of the 4th of May last, requesting you to instruct the United States Consul at Quebec, Canada, to the effect that internal revenue stamps, required to be affixed to boxes containing imported matches, cannot be so affixed prior to their importation, I have to state that such instructions should have been limited to *proprietary* stamps [Ed. note: i.e., private-die stamps], which under the law, are required to be affixed to the box or package containing the article subject to tax in such manner that it cannot be opened without destroying the stamps. If the ordinary adhesive stamps are used and are affixed to the match boxes in such manner that the latter can be opened without injuring the stamps, I can see no objection to allowing such stamps to be so affixed prior to the importation of the matches, provided they are

also, at the same time, properly cancelled. I will thank you to communicate these views to the United States Consul at Quebec.
(Hon. Hamilton Fish, Secretary of State, Washington, D.C., July 14.)

IRR v.XXI, August 16, 1875, p. 260

1876.–Department No. 3.–Internal Revenue.–Circular Letter No. 26.–Concerning the Detachment and Transmission to Commissioner of Specimens of Stamps Found Upon Packages of Matches in the Hands of Dealers.

Treasury Department,
Office of Internal Revenue,
Washington, Jan. 4, 1876.

With a view to the detection of counterfeit match stamps, if any are in use, Collectors will, on receipt of this circular, visit the establishments of the principal dealers in matches in their respective districts, and, with their consent, detach from packages of matches found in stock, one or more of the private-die stamps found upon the matches of different manufacturers, selecting the most suspicious-looking stamps and forwarding the same to this office for inspection.

Enclosed herewith will be found twenty proprietary stamps of the denomination of one cent, to be attached in place of those removed by the Collector. It is believed that dealers will not object to this request, and will permit stamps to be removed for the purpose named in this circular.

Collectors will number each stamp forwarded, and keep a register, so that in case any are found to be counterfeit, they can be referred to by numbers, and traced to the dealers from whom they were obtained.

D. D. Pratt,
Commissioner.

IRR v.XXII, January 10, 1876, p.5

United States District Court, D. of Mich.

Schmitt and Schmittdiel v. Luther S. Trowbridge, Coll.
Charge of Brown, J.

Gentlemen of the Jury: This is an action against the collector of internal revenue of this district, and in fact against the Government through him as defendant, to recover certain taxes said to have been illegally assessed and collected upon 243 boxes of matches made by the plaintiffs. The law provides that in all cases where the assessment is disputed, the amount of the tax shall be paid, and upon protest being made and an appeal taken to the commissioner of internal revenue, in case his decision sustains the validity of the tax, a suit may be brought against the collector and the case submitted to a jury. That is the only way which the law provides for the rehearing of assessments, so that in the end the validity of these assessments may always be submitted to a jury. And I charge you as requested by plaintiff in his first request, that the payment of the assessment in this case and under the circumstances approved, is not to be considered a voluntary one. All that his request means is that where the assessment is illegally exacted under protest and the appeal properly taken, the plaintiff may sue to recover it back.

The law provides that an appeal shall be taken from these assessments to the commissioner of internal revenue. An appeal was taken in this case from the assessment, and I charge you upon that point, that it is sufficient to enable the party to bring this action without the necessity of a further appeal from the collection of the tax.

I may say one word here with regard to the relative position of the parties. It is the plaintiff upon the one hand, a manufacturer of matches, and the Government upon the other. In cases of this kind, where the Government sues or is sued with relation to the validity of a tax, it is almost a matter of course for the Government to be represented in an unfavorable light. Now, gentlemen, it is hardly necessary for me to say that that is an erroneous view to take of the relations between a Government like this and its citizens. In former times when taxes were imposed by arbitrary power, and tax collectors were sent from the seat of the Government to extort them from the people, complaints of that kind were very frequently and justly made; but in this case you must bear in mind that these taxes are laid by you, through your representatives in Washington, and are collected by your fellow citizens, and it is a matter as much between you and the tax payers as between the Government and the tax payers. You are here representing the Government as much as I am, and you are also representing the people of this Government. The people having imposed these taxes, they have also delegated certain agents to collect them, and you, as a portion of the people, are to decide whether the action of these officers was correct or not. It is as much a matter of interest for you, as it is for these gentlemen, that a tax honestly due the Government should be honestly collected and honestly paid. It is a matter in which these officers of the Government have not the slightest personal interest, no more so than any two of you gentlemen, sitting on the jury, and they are entitled as much to your protection as are the two plaintiffs in this case. It is a mere question of fact, were these taxes illegally collected or not?

It appears that the Government officers were informed in Louisville, by certain rivals in business of the plaintiffs, that the plaintiffs' boxes containing matches were overrunning—that the boxes contained more than three hundred matches. The law provides that if the box shall contain one hundred or less there shall be a stamp put upon it of one cent; if it contains two hundred or less a stamp of two cents shall be put upon the box, and for each hundred in excess of two hundred, or for each fraction of one hundred an additional stamp of one cent shall be imposed; so that it was the business of these plaintiffs to see that none of their boxes contained over three hundred matches, as the stamp they put upon them were stamps appropriate to that amount.

I feel compelled, gentlemen, in the discharge of my duty in this case, to disagree with plaintiffs' counsel in their construction of the law. It was urged that if some of the boxes fell short and some overran, that the jury might strike an average, and say that if the boxes in the different cases did not average over three hundred in the box, there had been no offence committed, and this tax had been illegally laid. I charge you otherwise. It was the duty of the plaintiffs to see that none of these boxes contained over three hundred matches, and for every box that contained over three hundred, the commissioner of internal revenue was authorized to impose the extra cent, notwithstanding there were other boxes that fell short of three hundred. The plaintiffs were at liberty to lump them, to fill each box, we will say, without counting them. The Government does not require they shall be counted, but it does require there shall not be over three hundred in a box, so the safer way in that case was to do as Mr. Richardson did—see that the boxes did not contain *over* three hundred. If they chose to lump them they should have made sure that the contents of the boxes ran from say 290 to 300 or 295; that is, if there were any chances to be taken, the chances should not be taken against the Government.

In determining these tax cases the Government is entitled to certain presumptions. It is a matter of necessity that it should be so. For instance, I charge you that where the commissioner of Internal Revenue makes an assessment of this kind, the presumption is that the assessment is correctly made. You may say that where a Government officer imposes a tax upon one hundred thousand boxes of matches, for instance, that it is his duty to see that the tax is properly imposed upon each of these hundred thousand boxes. As between man and man that would seem to be so, but the necessities of the case require a different rule. It would never do to say that, in order to sustain this assessment, it was necessary for the Government to prove that each one of these hundred thousand boxes contained more than three hundred matches, because that would necessitate the counting of the entire number of matches in each one of these boxes, which would be entirely impossible. So then it is a fundamental principle of the law in this connection, that the commissioner shall lay the tax as he believes it to be just, and that the assessment when made by him shall be regarded as prima facie legal, and the burden is thrown upon the plaintiff to show that it is illegal. There is another reason for it. The Government cannot know the contents of each one of these boxes because the most of them have been sold, and are scattered all over the country. The proofs are lost. The Government would not be able, in the nature of things, to prove that each one of these boxes contained over three hundred matches, even if the law required that a count should be made; whereas, on the other hand, the proof is in the hands of the plaintiffs to show through his workmen the course of business, and the care he took in packing those boxes and in counting the matches. The facts in relation to these things are all in the hands of the plaintiffs, and for that reason among others, the law imposes upon them the duty of showing that the assessment was illegally made. It is the duty of the plaintiffs to show that in fact there were not over three hundred matches in these boxes, and it is for the plaintiffs to show how many of these boxes did not overrun. The Government has shown that some of the boxes did overrun. They have not shown that all of them did. Now then, how far does their proof go in that regard? As I said before, it is impossible for the Government to count the matches in these boxes, but where we find one or two or a few boxes in a case overrunning, it is a fair presumption that all the boxes in the case overrun; and where you find boxes in one case overrunning, it is fair to be presumed that all the boxes in that class overrun; but it would not follow that if other matches were made of a different class, or if they were boxed differently, as if the boxes were differently shaped, or of different sizes, they would all overrun; but here there were one hundred thousand boxes of a certain size, the matches being all of a size, and of a certain quality of timber. And you find in that number of boxes, that twenty of fifty boxes indifferently chosen overran, and none of them underran. It would be a fair presumption that the entire one hundred thousand would overrun, and the commissioner would fairly exercise his discretion in imposing the tax on the whole one hundred thousand. But that evidence may be contradicted by showing that an equal number did not overrun; so after all it is a fact for you to say, how much of the tax was illegally collected, and for that amount the plaintiffs are entitled to judgment.

It is claimed here that there were one hundred smaller boxes made first that did not overrun, and that there is no evidence here one way or the other upon that point; that the count related only to the larger class of boxes.

With regard to that I have this to say, that there is no evidence one way or the other with regard to these overrunning, and in that connection you are entitled to consider on whom lies the burden of proof. The Government has assessed these boxes as overrunning. The assessment is prima facie evidence of its own legality, that is, it is prima facie correct, and it imposes upon the plaintiffs the burden of showing that the matches in these one hundred boxes did not overrun. There is no evidence on that point one way or the other, except that some of these were not assessed, and I think it is a question proper to be submitted to the jury, whether these hundred smaller boxes did overrun or not.

The course of business of the factory seems to have been about this: they did not count each box, but that once a day each packer was required to count one or two boxes, and that the superintendent went through and examined, every day, the boxes, to see whether they overran or not. It seems that the plaintiffs became aware in the fall of 1876 that they did overrun, but whether they overran in the smaller boxes or not the testimony leaves us in a very painful state of uncertainty. The Government can only rely in that case upon the prima facie validity of the assessment. It is upon the plaintiffs to show that it was illegal. If you shall find here, under all the circumstances of the case, that the boxes contained in these hundred packages did not overrun, then for that amount the plaintiffs would be entitled to a judgment. The same is the fact with regard to the one hundred and twenty-six cases of round matches. It is insisted here by the plaintiff that they did not overrun; that the round matches were not of the same size as the square matches, and that there is no evidence here that they overran. To that the Government replies again that this assessment is prima facie legal, and that the burden is upon the plaintiffs to show it.

Mr. McGrath—I would remind your honor that five out of the seven boxes at Toledo were round matches, and that the five counted there did not overrun; and there is further evidence that the collector examined these eighteen cases at Buffalo, and informed the dealer there to go on and sell them; that they were all right; those were round matches.

The Court—Those facts are proper for you to consider, gentlemen, in this connection bearing in mind, however—and that may become material in your deliberations—that the burden of proof in all these matters rests upon the plaintiff.

It seems that on the attention of the Government officers in Detroit being called to the fact that these matches overran they visited the factory; that a visit was made by Gen. Trowbridge and Capt. Gavett, the internal revenue agent, and that they there requested Mr. Schmittdiel to make a statement. The manner in which this was done has been criticised by the plaintiffs' counsel, and it is proper for me to comment upon it here. On the one hand, Mr. Schmittdiel says that the statements he made were dictated by Capt. Gavett, although he admits himself that Gen. Trowbridge, the collector, told him to be cautious and not make the statements if they were not true, and he says that in reply to that caution he said, "I do know," or "we do know they overrun." On the other hand, both Capt. Gavett and Gen. Trowbridge deny that any dictation was used, and assert that the statements made were entirely voluntary on the part of Mr. Schmittdiel. The statements are here, in the handwriting of and signed and sworn to by Mr. Schmittdiel, and they are certainly presumed to be voluntary, the burden being upon the plaintiffs to show that they were involuntary. Now, if you believe Gen. Trowbridge and Capt. Gavett's testimony in this regard I think that you will find their conduct was entirely correct. I see no opportunity to criticise the way this business was done. On their attention being called to this alleged overrunning it was entirely proper for them to go to these parties and ask them to make a statement. There seems to have been no compulsion exercised, their establishment was not seized, and there has been no attempt to impose a penalty upon these parties—simply an attempt to collect the tax honestly due. Now if you believe their version of this affair, I charge you their conduct was entirely justifiable and correct, and I see nothing whatever to criticise in that regard. If there was an attempt made at using the power of the Government to dictate to this party what he should write down, that would be unjustifiable; but Mr. Schmittdiel says in that connection that Gen. Trowbridge urged him to be cautious in making this statement, and both Gen. Trowbridge and Capt. Gavett deny that any dictation was used whatever, but that the statements were entirely voluntary on the part of Mr. Schmittdiel. As I said before, the burden of proof is upon the plaintiff to convince you of this fact.

On the 29th day of June Mr. Schmittdiel made this statement: "Sir: We have manufactured of the kind of matches which we denominate No. 7 and being the same as the 13 cases we shipped to H. Wedekind and Co., Louisville, Ky., in all only 279 cases containing 144 boxes in each case, and each box containing 300 matches; and that we never represented the said boxes to contain more than 300 matches each, and that we never received or demanded pay for them as containing more than 300 matches each; that we were aware that some of the boxes overran, but that we expected some would fall short. We sold this class of matches, No. 7, to the following parties: H. Wedekind, Louisville, Ky.; Granger and Co., Buffalo, N. Y.; W. J. Benedict, Milwaukee, Wis.; Jacob Wellaur, Milwaukee, Wis.; and Matthews, Schaunsenbach and Co., Toledo, O., and we have only nine cases of said matches left.

"We commenced the manufacture of matches about the year 1871, and in 1872 our establishment was destroyed by fire, and in 1873 we resumed operations. Thee is no other brand of our matches except No. 7 which we are aware of that the boxes contain or have contained more matches than was represented by our stencil and by the amount of revenue stamps thereon."

It seems that on the same day, thinking that his statement was not exactly correct, he made another statement in which he says: "Sir: We have manufactured matches as follows: Since March 12, 1877, that being the date on which we resumed manufacturing, 3,325 cases No. 9 matches, 3 gross each," etc. And he adds, Detroit, June 30, the following day: "We were aware that some of these boxes overran. We were also aware that many fell short of the number represented by the stamps on the boxes, and we felt confident that there were no more matches in the entire cases than the stamps indicated." In other words, they seek to justify themselves by saying that the average was no greater than 300 in the box. On consulting counsel they made another statement on the 2d day of July in which they say: "These matches were manufactured during the year 1876, some of them early in the year and others in the fall. It was our custom at times to ourselves count a box of a particular lot, to ascertain how they are running, and in the fall of last year we made the discovery that a particular batch of these matches did overrun, and we immediately gave instructions to our packers to put a less number in the boxes. It is impossible to count each box of matches, for if we did so, the counting would cost several times more than the total price received for the matches." That is entirely true, gentlemen, that the counting of each one of these boxes would undoubtedly make them cost more than they would realize upon each box; at the same time it is their duty if they do not count each box, to see that the boxes do not overrun, and if there is any loss it should be a loss to them, not a loss to the Government in their overrunning. I believe I have covered all the material points in this case and all the requests to charge, except as I have given the plaintiff's requests. I decline to give them.

IRR v.XXIV, December 2, 1878, pp.381-2

The Committee of Ways and Means have given a hearing to Mr. William H. Swift and other match manufacturers in opposition to the repeal of the stamp tax on matches. The principal argument urged against the repeal was that the whole business, even to the sizes and shapes of the boxes and packages, is, and has been for years, adjusted to the existence of the tax as an element in the cost of production, and that the proposed change would wipe out a large amount of capital invested in special machinery and make necessary a troublesome and costly readjustment to the new order of things, while the Government would lose annually about $3,500,000 of revenue, which is now collected in the least burdensome manner.

The Ways and Means Committee will report a bill abolishing the tax on matches, bank deposits, including those of saving banks, bank checks, patent medicines, and perfumery.

IRR v.XXVII, February 7, 1881, p.37

1883.—Department No. 45.—Internal Revenue.—Circular No. 258.—Regulations for the Removal of Matches from the Place of Manufacture to Warehouses within the United States without the payment of the Tax thereon, and for other Purposes.

Treasury Department,
Office of Internal Revenue,
Washington, April 18, 1883.

Section 1 of the act approved March 3, 1883, entitled "An act to reduce internal-revenue taxation and for other purposes," provides for the repeal of the tax on matches imposed by Schedule A, following section 3437 of the Revised Statutes, on and after the 1st day of July, 1883. Said section also provides that on and after May 15, 1883, "matches may be removed by manufacturers thereof from the place of manufacture to warehouses within the United States without attaching thereto the stamps required by law, under such regulations as may be prescribed by the Commissioner of Internal Revenue."

To enable manufacturers to avail themselves of the provision of law last aforesaid, the following regulations are prescribed:

It shall be lawful for any manufacturer of matches in the United States to establish a warehouse for the storage of matches under said act at any of the following-named places, where the offices of collectors of internal revenue are located, to wit:

Alabama—1st district . . . . . Mobile
2d district . . . . . Montgomery
Arizona . . . . . Tucson
Arkansas . . . . . Little Rock
California—1st district . . . . . San Francisco
4th district . . . . . Sacramento
Colorado . . . . . Denver
Connecticut—1st district . . . . . Norwich
2d district . . . . . Bridgeport
Dakota . . . . . Yankton
Delaware . . . . . Wilmington
Florida . . . . . Jacksonville
Georgia—2d district . . . . . Atlanta
3d district . . . . . Savannah
Idaho . . . . . Boise City
Illinois—1st district . . . . . Chicago
2d district . . . . . Aurora
3d district . . . . . Sterling
4th district . . . . . Quincy
5th district . . . . . Peoria
7th district . . . . . Champaign
8th district . . . . . Springfield
13th district . . . . . Cairo
Indiana—1st district . . . . . Evansville
4th district . . . . . Lawrenceburg
6th district . . . . . Indianapolis
7th district . . . . . Terre Haute
10th district . . . . . Warsaw
11th district . . . . . Anderson
Iowa—2d district . . . . . Davenport
3d district . . . . . Dubuque
4th district . . . . . Burlington
5th district . . . . . Des Moines
Kansas . . . . . Leavenworth
Kentucky—2d district . . . . . Owensboro
5th district . . . . . Louisville
6th district . . . . . Covington
7th district . . . . . Lexington
8th district . . . . . Lancaster

9th district . . . . Maysville
Louisiana . . . . New Orleans
Maine . . . . Portland
Maryland—3d district . . . . Baltimore
4th district . . . . Cumberland
Massachusetts—3d district . . . . Boston
5th district . . . . Newburyport
10th district . . . . North Adams
Michigan—1st district . . . . Detroit
3d district . . . . Hillsdale
4th district . . . . Grand Rapids
6th district . . . . East Saginaw
Minnesota—1st district . . . . Albert Lea
2d district . . . . St. Paul
Mississippi . . . . Jackson
Missouri—1st district . . . . St. Louis
2d district . . . . Cape Girardeau
4th district . . . . Louisiana
5th district . . . . Springfield
6th district . . . . Kansas City
Montana . . . . Helena
Nebraska . . . . Omaha
Nevada . . . . Virginia City
New Hampshire . . . . Portsmouth
New Jersey—1st district . . . . Camden
3d district . . . . Somerville
5th district . . . . Newark
New Mexico . . . . Santa Fe
New York—1st district . . . . Brooklyn
2d district . . . . New York
3d district . . . . New York
11th district . . . . Middletown
12th district . . . . Hudson
14th district . . . . Albany
15th district . . . . Troy
21st district . . . . Utica
24th district . . . . Auburn
26th district . . . . Binghamton
28th district . . . . Rochester
30th district . . . . Buffalo
North Carolina—2d district . . . . New Berne
4th district . . . . Raleigh
5th district . . . . Winston
6th district . . . . Statesville
Ohio—1st district . . . . Cincinnati
3d district . . . . Dayton
4th district . . . . Bellefontaine
6th district . . . . Wilmington
7th district . . . . Columbus
10th district . . . . Toledo
11th district . . . . Chillicothe
15th district . . . . Marietta
18th district . . . . Cleveland
Oregon . . . . Portland
Pennsylvania—1st district . . . . Philadelphia
8th district . . . . Reading
9th district . . . . Lancaster

12th district	Wilkes Barre
14th district	Sunbury
16th district	Somerset
19th district	Erie
20th district	Greenville
22d district	Pittsburgh
23d district	Allegheny
Rhode Island	Providence
South Carolina	Columbia
Tennessee—2d district	Knoxville
5th district	Nashville
8th district	Memphis
Texas—1st district	Galveston
3d district	Austin
4th district	Marshall
Vermont	Montpelier
Virginia—2d district	Petersburgh
3d district	Richmond
4th district	Danville
5th district	Lynchburg
6th district	Harrisonburg
Washington Ter	Olympia
West Virginia—1st district	Wheeling
2d district	Fairmont
Wisconsin—1st district	Milwaukee
2d district	Madison
3d district	Fond du Lac
6th district	Sparta
Wyoming	Cheyenne

And all shipments under said act shall be made to the proper collector of internal revenue, for the benefit of the manufacturer.

Any manufacturer of matches who has established a warehouse at any of the places above named, desiring to remove any matches unstamped from his manufactory to such warehouse after the 15th day of May, for storage until the 1st day of July, 1883, must make application in the following form to the collector of the district in which the manufactory is situated for a permit to make such removal. The application must give the name of the manufacturer, firm, or company; the location of the manufactory, giving State and collection district; the quantity or number of matches which are to be removed; the location of the warehouse, and the name of the collector of the district to whom the shipment is to be made:

Form of Application for Permit to Remove Matches from Manufactory to Warehouse without Payment of Tax.

A permit is requested for removal from the manufactory owned by ____________, situated in the county of ________, State of ________, being in the _____ collection district of said State, of the following described merchandise, namely:

Number of cases.

Marks and numbers.

Article.

Number of taxable packages.

Rate of tax—cents.

Amount of tax.

The above described merchandise to be consigned to ____________, collector of internal revenue for the _____ collection district of the State of ________, located at ________, in said State.

____________, Manufacturer.

To ____________,

Collector of Internal Revenue, District of ________

Before the permit is issued by the collector of the district where the manufactory is located, the manufacturer will file with said collector a good and sufficient bond to the United States, with two or more sureties, to be approved by said collector; said bond to be in a penal sum equal to the amount of tax to which the matches removed are liable, and shall be in the following form:

Form of Bond.

Know all men by these presents, That we, ________, as principal, and ________ and ________, as sureties are held and firmly bound unto the United States of America in the full and just sum of _______ dollars; for the payment of which sum we do bind ourselves, our heirs, executors, and administrators, jointly and severally, firmly by these presents.

Sealed with our seals, and dated at ________, this _____ day of ________, 1883.

Whereas, on the _____ day of ________, 1883, the above-bounden _________ has made application, under the provisions of section 1 of the act of March 3, 1883, to remove from his manufactory to a warehouse, situated at ________, in the _____ internal revenue collection district of the State of ________, the following described merchandise, namely:

Number of cases.
Marks and numbers.
Article.
Number of taxable packages.
Rate of tax—cents.
Amount of tax.

The conditions of this obligation are such that, if the above-bounden ___________ shall, after the 15th day of May, 1883, obtain a permit and remove the said merchandise to the warehouse aforesaid for storage, consigned to the collector for the internal revenue district located at that place, for the benefit of the consignor, in accordance with the law and the regulations of the Commissioner of Internal Revenue governing such removal, and shall not remove, or cause to be removed, from said warehouse prior to the 1st day of July, A. D. 1883, any of said goods, and shall perform, all and singular, the requirements of law and regulations relative thereto, then this obligation is to be void; otherwise, to be and remain in full force and virtue.

___________ [L. S.]
___________ [L. S.]
___________ [L. S.]

Sealed and delivered in the presence of—

____
____

Or, if the manufacturer should desire to remove his matches from the place of manufacture by the car-load to some distant point within the United States, having them arrive at their destination about the 1st day of July, he may make application to the collector of the district where his manufactory is located for a permit to do so upon a transportation bond, the penal sum thereof to be equal to the tax upon the matches so shipped; the conditions of the bond to provide that the matches shall not be taken from the car in which shipment is made prior to the 1st day of July, 1883:

Form of Application for Permit to Remove Matches from Manufactory, by the Car-Load, in Bond, to any point within the United States, without the Payment of Tax.

A permit is requested for removal from the manufactory owned by ________, situated in the county of ________, State of ________, being in the _____ collection district of said State, of the following-described merchandise, by the car-load, in bond, namely:

Number of cases.
Marks and numbers.
Article.
Number of packages.
Rate of tax—cents.
Amount of tax.

The above-described merchandise to be consigned to ________, collector of internal revenue for the _____ collection district of the State of ________, located at ________, in said State, and not to be removed from said car until after the 1st day of July, 1883.

___________, *Manufacturer.*

To ———,

Collector of Internal Revenue, District of ———

Form of Transportation Bond where Matches are Removed by the Car-Load without the Payment of Tax.

Know all men by these presents, That we, ———, as principal, and ——— and ———, as sureties, are held and firmly bound unto the United States of America in the full and just sum of ——— dollars; for the payment of which sum we do bind ourselves, our heirs, executors, and administrators, jointly and severally, firmly by these presents.

Sealed with our seals, and dated at ———, this day of ———, 1883.

Whereas, on the ——— day of ———, 1883, the above-bounden ——— has made application, under the provisions of section 1 of the act of March 3, 1883, to remove from his manufactory, by the car-load, in bond, to the ——— internal revenue collection district of the State of ———, the following-described merchandise, namely:

Number of cases.

Marks and numbers.

Article.

Number of packages.

Rate of tax—cents.

Amount of tax.

The conditions of this obligation are such that, if the above-bounded ——— shall, after the 15th day of May, 1883, obtain a permit and remove the said merchandise, by the car-load, consigned to the collector for the internal revenue collection district located at ———, for the benefit of the consignor, in accordance with law and the regulations of the Commissioner of Internal Revenue governing such removal, and shall not remove, or cause to be removed, from said car, prior to the 1st day of July, A. D., 1883, any of said goods, and shall perform, all and singular, the requirements of law and regulations relative thereto, then this obligation is to be void; otherwise, to be and remain in full force and virtue.

——— [L. S.]
——— [L. S.]
——— [L. S.]

Sealed and delivered in presence of—

———
———

Blanks for said permits and bonds will be furnished to collectors by this office.

When shipment is made to warehouses, as hereinbefore provided, said warehouses may be any room or building that will be satisfactory to and approved by the collector of the district in which the same is located, and that will afford the necessary protection against the unlawful removal of the matches to be stored therein, and can only be used for the storage of matches of one manufacturer or firm of manufacturers, and for no other purposes.

When matches are removed to a warehouse in any other collection district than that in which the manufactory is located, the collector of the district from which the removal is to be made shall immediately notify the collector of the district in which the warehouse is situated of the removal or intended removal, and furnish him with a descriptive memorandum of the merchandise shipped.

The collector of the district in which the warehouse is situated shall, at the close of business on the 30th day of June, 1883, make, or cause to be made, an examination of the boxes or cases received into said warehouse, and if he finds the packages unbroken, and the contents thereof intact, and all goods in the warehouse that had been stored therein, he shall furnish the manufacturer thereof with a certificate to that effect, and may notify the collector to whom the bond was given by the manufacturer to cancel the same.

As soon after the 1st day of July, 1883, as may be practicable, the several collectors in whose districts the match manufactories or warehouses herein referred to are located will transmit to the Commissioner of Internal Revenue a statement showing the quantity of matches removed from, or warehoused in, their respective collection districts under the provisions of these regulations.

Green B. Raum,
Commissioner.

Instructions to Match Manufacturers.

The following instructions are hereby given to manufacturers of matches relative to the redemption of stamps upon packages of matches which have been stamped, and which have never been sold or removed from the manufactories for consumption or sale:

An inventory shall be taken of all matches in manufactories which have been stamped, and which have never been removed from said manufactories for consumption or sale; and, on the 1st day of July, these inventories shall be verified by two disinterested witnesses, and the manufacturer and witnesses shall make affidavits as to their correctness; and the collector of internal revenue in whose district the match manufactory is situated shall detail one of his deputies to be present at said manufactory on the date aforesaid, who shall verify the inventories and assist the claimant to prepare a claim on Form 38, attaching the inventory and affidavits thereto, and see that the same is forwarded to the proper collector of internal revenue for certification and transmission to this Office.

Green B. Raum,
Commissioner.

IRR v.XXIX, May 7, 1883, pp.145-7

PRESERVED FOODS

Stamping of Canned Meats, &c.—Exposure for Sale.

Assessor's Office,
Fourth District New York,
New York, Oct. 2, 1866.

Sir: Are canned meats, &c., as enumerated in Schedule C, liable to stamp duty when removed or sold at wholesale, after October 1, 1866, by the owner who was not the manufacturer.

Judging from the context, I have thought the exposure for sale, and sale spoken of in the 210th paragraph of the Department edition of the Internal Revenue act, rendering the seller liable as a manufacturer to be the exposure and sale of the retailer, not subjecting the goods sold at wholesale to stamp tax.

Wholesale dealers, willing to pay the additional stamp duty on goods that they have purchased already having paid an ad valorem tax, nevertheless complain that the law should require them to destroy their packages (as it would do) in order to stamp them, the retailers having the opportunity to attach the stamps to the cans, &c., without detriment. Other wholesale dealers have also asked me, if it is required that they shall pay the additional stamp duty, that they may be allowed to put the amount due in stamps in the cases ready to be attached to the cans when sold.

Large shipments of goods await your decision on these questions.

Respectfully,
Pierre C. Van Wyck,
Assessor.

Hon. E. A. Rollins,
Commissioner of Internal Revenue.

[Answer.]

Office of Internal Revenue,
Washington, Oct. 3, 1866.

Sir: In answer to your enquiries in your letter dated 2d instant, I have to say that, all canned goods, either in the hands of the manufacturer or purchaser, sold or offered for sale on or after the 1st inst., are required to be stamped as specified in Schedule C, of the act of July 13, 1866.

When canned goods have been packed in cases, and it would be difficult and expensive to unpack them and affix the requisite stamps, the parties will have complied substantially with the law, if, when sold, the manufacturer encloses in an envelope to the purchaser a sufficient number of cancelled stamps to be affixed when goods are unpacked.

Yours respectfully,
Thomas Harland,
Deputy Commissioner.

Pierre C. Van Wyck,
U.S. Assessor, New York City.

IRR v.IV, October 13, 1866, p.117

(No. 171)

Decision Relative to the Taxes upon Canned Meats, Vegetables, &c.

Office of Internal Revenue,
Washington, Oct. 27, 1866.

By the amendatory act of July 13, 1866, a stamp duty is imposed upon "every can, bottle, or other single package containing meats, fish, shell fish, fruits, vegetables, sauces, sirups, prepared mustard, jams, or jellies contained therein, and packed or sealed, made, prepared, and sold, or offered for sale, or removed for consumption, in the United States, on or after the 1st day of October, 1866."

While it is believed that it was the purpose and intent of Congress to impose a stamp tax upon the above named articles, if sold or offered for sale or removed for consumption in the United States, on or after October 1, 1866, regardless of the time of their manufacture or production, that intent is so imperfectly expressed as to render it doubtful whether, under a proper construction of the language of the statute, such a tax can be collected.

Internal revenue officers are therefore instructed not to interfere with the possession or sale of such articles of domestic manufacture or production, when satisfactory evidence is furnished that they were prepared and passed out of the possession of the producer prior to the first day of October.

Oysters and other shell fish are often removed from the shell, and without undergoing any process for their preservation, are placed, in a raw state, in tin or other vessel for the sole purpose of transportation in ice. When put up in this manner, and for this purpose only they are not regarded as *canned* within the meaning and intent of the law, and no stamps will be required upon them.

Articles named in schedule C, when imported or of foreign manufacture, are liable to the stamp tax *in addition* to the import duties thereon. When, however, such imported articles, except playing cards, lucifer or friction matches, cigar lights and wax tapers, are sold in the original and unbroken packages in which the bottles or other enclosures were packed by the manufacturer, the person so selling them is not subject to any penalty on account of the want of a proper stamp; but when such packages are opened, the articles should not under any circumstances, be offered or exposed for sale until they have been appropriately stamped.

E. A. Rollins,
Commissioner.

IRR v.IV, November 3, 1866, p.140

Stamp Tax on Syrups in Bottles, and Ad Valorem Tax on Syrups sold in Bulk.

New York,
September 29, 1866.

Dear Sir: We are engaged in the manufacture of fruit syrups such as are used for soda water, &c. The syrup is prepared from the juice of the fruit and sugar. We put up our goods in bottles, kegs, demijohns, barrels and jugs, and have been subjected to a tax of six (6) per cent. heretofore.

We are now advised by our assistant assessor that our goods are subject to *stamps*. If this is correct, we beg to be advised in what manner we shall stamp demijohns, barrels, kegs, &c., our goods mostly being in such packages.

Very respectfully,
S.

Hon. E. A. Rollins,
Commissioner of Internal Revenue.

[Answer.]

Office of Internal Revenue,
Washington, Oct. 11, 1866.

Gentlemen: Your letter of the 29th ult., enquiring relative to the liability of stamp duty on syrups which you manufacture has been received.

In answer, I have to say that syrups, when put up in cans, bottles, or other similar packages, are liable to a stamp tax of one cent, when such cans, bottles, or other similar packages, with their contents, do not exceed two pounds in weight, respectively.

When they exceed two pounds in weight, they are liable to stamp tax of one cent for every additional pound or fractional part thereof.

When syrups are not put up in cans, bottle, or other similar packages, they are liable to an ad valorem tax of 5 per cent.

Very respectfully,
Thomas Harland,
Deputy Commissioner.

IRR v.IV, November 17, 1866, p.156

Canned Meats, Shell Fish, Fruits, Vegetables, &c.—Sardines, Fish, Sauces, Syrups, prepared Mustard, Jams and Jellies.

Under the Act of March 2nd, 1867, canned meats, shell fish, fruits, and vegetables, including pickles and preserves in glass packages, are exempt from tax. This exemption does not include fish, sauces, syrups, prepared mustard, jams or jellies. All sardines put up in packages are liable to stamp tax.

IRR v.V, May 11, 1867, p.148

Stamp Duty on Canned Fish, Sauces, &c.

A party interested states that a large number of persons putting up *fruits, meats,* and *vegetables* in tin cans, are compelled by some revenue officers to attach revenue stamps to said cans, while others are allowed to bring their productions into the market without such stamps.

It is indispensable to justice that all revenue officers act alike in the premises. Dissatisfaction exists among manufacturers of this class at such diversity of practice. Prior to July 13, 1866, these goods paid an ad valorem tax of 5 per cent. The amendment of said date changed this to a stamp tax of 1 cent and over in proportion to weight of cans; the same amendment (page 88) exempts tin cans used for fruits, meats, &c., from an *internal tax,* while the amendment of March 2, 1867, exempts the fruits, meats and vegetables put up in cans from *internal* tax. Under *Internal* tax is to be understood, stamp tax as well as Ad valorem, income, special, or any other tax, levied under internal revenue acts.

Therefore, as tin cans used for fruits, &c., as well as for canned fruits, &c., themselves were exempt, and as all acts or parts of acts inconsistent with the amended act of March 2, 1867, are expressly repealed, (Sec. 34), no stamp tax accrues on canned fruits, meats and vegetables. Yet in some instances such stamp tax is stated to be still enforced, officers basing their action on Series 3, No. 10, which being issued May 10, 1867, has a paragraph in Schedule C, which they construe as directing such goods to be stamped.

On a careful perusal of Schedule C, no authority will be found for imposing stamps on canned "meats," fruits or vegetables, but canned *fish, sardines, sauces, sirups, prepared mustard, jams and jellies* are liable, and should be appropriately stamped.

IRR v.VI, November 9, 1867, p.161

Correspondence.

Asst. Assessor—A ruling was published at least three months since, holding sardines to be liable to stamp duty, but there is an unaccountable ignorance which appears still to prevail on the subject. Your attention is therefore directed to the following decision, confirmatory of previous rulings:

''Parties claim that jellies are preserved fruits; that they undergo the same process in their manufacture, the same articles are used, and the jellies and preserved fruits are the same, except in one particular, viz.: that one is the *juice* of the fruit, while the other is the *fruit itself.*'' To this the Department replies, that ''the Act of July 13, 1866, imposed on canned meats, fish, shellfish, fruits, vegetables, sauces, sirups, prepared mustard, jams or jellies, a stamp duty, varying in amount according to the weight of the package and its contents.

''The Act of March 2nd, 1867, exempts canned and preserved meats, shell-fish, fruits, and vegetables. No mention is made in the exemption, of fish, sauces, sirups, prepared mustard or jams or jellies.

"If jams and jellies are preserved fruits, why was it necessary to insert both terms in the provisions imposing the tax, and why was 'jams or jellies' omitted in the exemption.

''The section of the law providing for the exemption of certain articles, also provides 'that the exemptions aforesaid shall in all cases be confined exclusively to said articles, in the state and condition specified in the foregoing enumeration, and shall not extend to articles in any other form, nor to manufactures from said articles. '*Therefore,* while the law specially exempts canned and preserved meats, shell-fish, fruits and vegetables,' 'fish, sauces, sirups, prepared mustard, and jams or jellies,' are held liable to stamp duty.''

IRR v.VI, November 23, 1867, p.178

Editor of Internal Revenue Record.

In your issue of November 9, I find the following in an editorial on the first page: ''On a careful perusal of Schedule C, no authority will be found for imposing stamps on canned *meats, fruits, or vegetables,* &c., &c." Is not that statement an error, a mistake? Schedule C, page 130, Act March, 1867, reads that canned meats, fruits and vegetables, *are* liable to *stamp* duty, *or* I cannot understand plain English. In our District we have notified dealers in the above articles to *stamp all of them.*

Mem. I have never seen that decision under the ''Official'' heading of your paper. Has it been or will it be there? Asst. Assessor.

Section 11 of the Act March, 2, 1867, (p. 89 of Compilation—Record, Vol. V., p. 76) expressly exempts from ''internal tax,'' construed to include stamp duty, *''canned and preserved meats and shell fish,* and *canned and preserved vegetables, and fruits.''* The reference in our article was intended for Schedule C, ''as promulgated in Series 3, No. 10,'' (Record, Vol. V., p. 174,) which is *law* for Revenue officers. Ed.

IRR v.VI, November 23, 1867, p.178

Editor of Internal Revenue Record.

In going the rounds of my district for the purpose of instructing grocers, druggists and others in regard to stamping certain articles as required under Schedule C, I found it difficult at times to answer the questions asked, and the objections which were sometimes raised to stamping some articles, which, in my opinion, required a stamp; and I did not feel perfectly sure afterwards, that I decided right in every instance. I have no doubt that other assistant assessors have experienced the same difficulty. As you are good authority in such matters, will you be so good as to give your opinion in the next number of the Record in regard to the necessity of stamping the following articles, viz.: ground mustard and spices in cans and bottles; pickles, such as cucumbers, and olives, and capers, in bottles; olive oil, in bottles; castor oil, in bottles; cologne water, in bottles. By answering the above I have no doubt you will oblige more than one Asst. Assessor.

Dry ground mustard and spices are held to be exempt from stamp duty, but *prepared* or French mustard is liable. Cucumbers, olives, and capers, pickles, in bottles, are exempt from stamp duty. Castor oil is not held liable to stamp duty. Cologne, in bottles, is liable to stamp duty as a cosmetic. Ed.

IRR v.VI, November 23, 1867, p.178

Sardines.

Grocer, Boston—There is not, in our judgment, the shadow of a legal doubt that *Sardines* are liable to stamp duty under existing laws. If Congress *''intended''* to exempt them, they certainly did not say so. There has been too much weight placed on the belief of what Congress *meant* to do in construing provisions of the revenue laws. A legislation must be held to *intend* precisely what the statutes say. The *intention* must be gathered from the words of the law, and not from opinions of Congressmen. A recent ruling on the point is as follows, from which you will be satisfied that the question is not an open one:

''Sardines are liable to a stamp duty as a canned fish, under the act of July 13, 1866. When sold in the original and unbroken package, in which the smaller boxes are packed before importation, no penalty is incurred on account of the want of the proper stamp, but when such package is opened and the contents offered or exposed for sale, each box must be stamped according to its weight as provided in schedule C.''

IRR v.VII, January 11, 1868, p.10

Stamp Duty on Canned Articles and Cosmetics.

We hear from various sources that manufacturers, grocers, druggists and others who vend sardines, prepared mustard, sirups in bottles, jams, jellies, sauces, colognes, cosmetics, articles enumerated in Schedule C, as subject to stamp duty, have ceased to stamp such articles since the passage of the Act of March 31, 1868, repealing the tax on manufactures, formerly imposed by sections 94 and 95 of the statute. They are said to act under the belief that the stamp tax on the manufactures, preparations and articles above referred to, was also removed by the act in question. This idea is erroneous. The stamp tax is not affected in any manner by the recent act, but the law respecting the same continues in full force and effect. Each of the articles above described are still subject to stamp tax on being exposed or offered for sale. Sardines, sauces, sirups, prepared mustard, jams, and jellies are subject to stamp tax according to the weight; one cent stamp, if a package does not exceed two pounds in weight, and stamp of one additional cent for every pound or fraction of a pound in excess of two pounds in weight.

Imported articles of the kind are subject to stamp duty at the same rate, and vendors thereof must affix proper stamps when the same are offered or exposed for sale, except in original or unbroken packages, which are understood to be those in which the *manufacturer* furnishes them to the trade, and not the single bottle or box which the retailer dispenses to the consumer. The vendor of such articles of domestic or foreign manufacture incurs a penalty of $50 for each offence by failure to affix stamp denoting the proper tax.

Assistant Assessors should look into this matter and advise dealers of the law, and prevent further loss to the revenue, and if dealers would protect themselves from informers and penalties, they should acquaint themselves with the law, and comply with it.

IRR v.VII, April 25, 1868, p.129

Law Relating to Stamps on Articles.

The act of July 13, 1866, amended Schedule "C" of the act of 1864, requiring every can, bottle, or other single package containing meats, fish, shell-fish, fruits, vegetables, sauces, sirups, prepared mustard, jams or jellies on and after the 1st day of October, 1866, made, prepared and sold or offered for sale or removed for consumption in the United States to be stamped.

Prior to this time these articles were subject to an *ad valorem* tax.

Section 165 of the act of June 30, 1864, as amended by the act of July 13, 1866, declares that any person, firm, company or corporation, who shall make, prepare and sell or remove for consumption, * * * prepared mustard, preserved meats, fish, shell-fish, fruits, vegetables, sirups, jams and jellies, &c., without affixing stamps denoting the tax, shall incur a penalty of $50 for every omission.

Section 169 of the same act as amended, declares that any person who shall sell or offer for sale any of the articles named in Schedule C, whether the articles were imported or of domestic manufacture, shall be deemed the manufacturer thereof, and subject to all the duties, liabilities and penalties imposed by law in regard to the sale of domestic articles without the use of the proper stamps, &c., and imported articles are made subject to the stamps in addition to the import duties imposed on the same, Provided that when such imported articles, (with exceptions named,) are sold in the original and unbroken packages in which the bottles or other inclosures were packed by the manufacturer, the person so selling said articles shall not be subject to any penalty on account of the want of the proper stamps.

The act of July 13, 1866, changed the tax on meats, fish, shell-fish, fruits, vegetables, sauces, sirups, prepared mustard, jams and jellies from the *ad valorem* tax to a stamp tax, and allowed from the 13th of July, the date of the passage of the act, till the first of October following for all persons having stocks of these articles on hand to dispose of them prior to the time when the stamps were required to be affixed. From and after that date, all such articles, whether in the hands of producers, or in the hands of dealers, were required to be stamped, without regard to the time when they were manufactured, prepared or produced, or whether they had or had not previously paid an *ad valorem* tax. The person selling, or offering for sale, was held and deemed to be the manufacturer, and required to affix the stamps.

The act of March 2, 1867, exempted from tax canned and preserved *meats,* and *shell-fish,* and also canned and preserved *vegetables* and *fruits,* leaving fish other than shell-fish, sauces, sirups, prepared mustard, jams and jellies, still liable to tax, and no subsequent law has removed the tax upon the articles last named. (See Series 3, No. 10, 5 Record, 174, and 6 Record, 123 and 154, also 9 Record, 45-46.)

IRR v.IX, February 13, 1869, p.51

Desiccated Cod Fish.

There has been doubt, and consequent diversity of practice, among assistant-assessors, arising from the question whether this article, which is prepared by reducing the dried salt fish to a fibrous condition, and then put up in paper boxes, is liable to a stamp duty as "canned fish."

Mr. C. B. Huntington, of Philadelphia, Treasurer of the Boston and Philadelphia Salt Fish Company, manufacturers of the article, submitted the matter for the decision of the Commissioner. His ruling, which is herewith given, will settle the practice. It will be seen that the fish is not liable to stamp duty, but the sales thereof are taxable as sales of manufactures.

The Commissioner's letter, under date of the 3d instant, in reply to one from Mr. Huntington, reads as follows:

"Your letter of the 1st instant, together with a box of desiccated cod fish, has been received. You inquire whether this fish is liable to stamp duty?

"I reply that the desiccated cod fish is not regarded as 'canned fish' within the meaning of the law, not being put up in the manner therein contemplated; it is not, therefore, liable to stamp duty.

"Under the fourth section of the act of March 31, 1868, the sales of this article in excess of $1,250 per quarter, are liable to a tax of $25 per thousand."

IRR v.IX, March 6, 1869, p.78

U.S. Circuit Court—Massachusetts.

A party sold a box of sardines without affixing thereto an appropriate Revenue stamp, and was indicted to recover the penalty thereby incurred. Defendant demurred.

Held, That the indictment would lie as a proper proceeding under the provisions of the act July 13, 1866, sec. 9—14 Stat., at large, 145. (Dept. Compilation Sec. 165 p.121 and Sec. 169 p.124.)

(Clifford & Lowell J. J.)

United States by indictment v. *James E. Abbott.*

The opinion of the Court was delivered by

Clifford J.—Divested of all mere formal allegations, the indictment in this case charges against the defendant that he, at Boston, in his district, on the third day of September, 1868, did unlawfully and knowingly sell to the person therein named, a certain box containing sardines, not exceeding two pounds in weight, without affixing to the same an adhesive stamp or label denoting the tax or duty imposed thereon by law. 13 *Stat. at Large,* 296. 14 *Stat. at Large,* 145.

When set at the bar to be arraigned, the defendant demurred to the indictment, and the District Attorney joined in the demurrer. Views of the defendant are that the penalty prescribed for the omission to affix a stamp to the package sold as alleged, cannot be recovered by indictment, and the demurrer was filed to raise that question. Single packages of that character which do not exceed two pounds in weight are by law subject to a tax or duty of one cent and the requirement of the act of Congress is that a stamp or label denoting the tax or duty shall be affixed to the package before the same is sold or removed, either for consumption or sale. 14 *Stat. at Large,* 145. Packages, such as the one described in the indictment, are included in that requirement, and the provision is that if any person, &c., shall make, prepare and sell or remove for consumption or sale, any such package as is therein enumerated and mentioned, without affixing thereto an adhesive stamp or label denoting the tax or duty imposed upon the same by law, he shall incur a penalty of fifty dollars for every omission to affix such stamp. 14 *Stat. at Large,* 144 & 145.

Federal Courts have no jurisdiction of any crime or offence, except that of treason, which is defined in the Constitution, and such as are defined in some Act of Congress, as the United States have no unwritten criminal code to which resort can be had as a source of jurisdiction in such cases. *U.S.* v. *Hudson et al.,* 7 *Cran.* 32; *U.S.* v. *Coolidge* 1 *Wheat.* 415; *U.S.* v. *Beavans,* 3 *Whea.* 336; *U.S.* v. *Wiltberger,* 5 *Whea.* 76 *Conk, Trea.* 165.

Power to try and punish an offender does not exist in a Federal Court, unless the defence is defined as before explained, nor unless the punishment is prescribed by an act of Congress. No such difficulty, however, arises in this case, as the provision already referred to shows that the offence as charged, is clearly defined in the act of Congress, and that the punishment annexed to it is a penalty of fifty dollars. Exclusive original cognizance of seizures under laws of impost, navigation or trade, whether made on water or on land, was conferred upon the District Courts by the ninth section of the judiciary act, and also of all suits for penalties and forfeitures incurred under the laws of the United States. 1 *Stat. at Large,* 77. But the provision applicable to this case is that all fines, penalties and forfeitures, which may be imposed or incurred (under that act), shall, and may be sued for and recovered, where not otherwise provided, in the name of the United States, in any proper form of action or by any appropriate form of proceeding, before any Circuit or District Court of the United States for the district within which said fine, penalty or forfeiture may have been incurred, &c. 14 *Stat. at Large,* 145; 13 *Stat. at Large,* 305. Evidently the phrase *by any appropriate form of proceeding,* was intended to be more comprehensive than the phrase in any proper form of action, which precedes it, and it is difficult to see what other procedure than indictment could be meant, as informations in Revenue cases are exclusively cognizable in the District Courts, except on appeal of writ of error.

Examined in any point of view it is quite clear that the decision as to the construction of the eighty-ninth section of the act of the second of March, 1799, does not control the case before the Court. 1 *Stat. at Large,* 695; 3 *Stat. at Large,* 782; *U.S.* v. *Andrews,* Circuit Court, Main Dis. Sept. T., 1868. Material provision of that section is, that all penalties accruing by any breach of the act, shall be sued for and recovered with costs of suit, in the name of the United States, in any Court competent to try the same, and that the trial of any fact which may be put in issue, shall be within the judicial district in which any such penalty shall have occurred. Penalties and forfeitures incurred by force of the act of the third of March, 1823, are required to be sued for, recovered, distributed and accounted for in the manner prescribed in the act next before referred to, and this Court held that such penalties and forfeitures could not be recovered by indictment; but it is obvious that that decision has no just application to this case. Different remedies are often given to recover the same penalty, but the general rule is that when a statute prohibits a matter of public grievance, or commands a matter of public convenience, and no special mode is expressly or impliedly directed, it may be prosecuted by indictment. *Colburn v. Swett;* 1 *Met.,* 235. When a statute, says Bacon, commands or prohibits a matter of public concern, the person guilty of disobedience to the statute, besides being answerable to the party injured, is likewise liable to be indicted for the disobedience. 9 *Bac.,* 259, *per. Bouv.* 5 *Ibid,* 56. Where a statute, says Chitty, prohibits an act to be done under a certain penalty, though no mention is made of indictment, the party offending may be indicted and fined for the amount of the penalty, which is the precise case under consideration. 1 *Chitt, Cr. L.* 163. Authorities to the same effect are numerous, but they all agree that where a statute creates an offence, and points out a particular remedy, that the mode pointed out in the statute must be observed. 1 *Chitt. Cr. L.* 163; *U.S.* v. *Mann,* 1 *Gall., p.* 2; *U.S.* v. *Simms,* 1 *Cran.* 252.

The rule at common law was that if a statute prohibited a matter of public grievance or commanded a matter of public convenience, all violations of the prohibition or commands of the statute were at least misdemeanors, and as such were punishable by indictment, unless the statute specified some other mode of proceeding. 1 *Am. Cr. S. sec.* 10; 2 *Hawk P.C. Chap.* 25 Section 4; *Rex.* v. *Davis, Law,* 133; *Rex.* v. *Sainsbury,* 4 *Term* 477; *State* v. *Fletcher,* 5 *N.H.* 257; *Rex.* v. *Harris,* 4 *Term* 202; *Keller* v. *State,* 11 *Md.* 525, *People* v. *Bogart,* 3 *Park Cr. C.* 143; *Watson* v. *Com.,* 10 *Serg. & R.* 375. Application of that rule was not defeated at common law, because the statute did not in terms annex a penalty to the offence, but the rule can only be applied in the jurisprudence of the United States in cases where the offence is defined, and the punishment is prescribed, in the acts of Congress containing the prohibition or command, or in some other applicable to the same subject matter. Additional explanations to show that the offence is defined in the act of Congress, and that the punishment is also prescribed, are unnecessary, and in our opinion there are no words in the provision to exclude a remedy by indictment. On the contrary it is our opinion that the phrase "by any appropriate form of proceeding" was intended to authorize a public prosecution by indictment. Demurrer overruled.

IRR v.IX, June 12, 1869, p.186

All Packages, Large or Small, in Bulk or otherwise, containing Prepared Mustard, must be appropriately Stamped.

Office of Internal Revenue,
Washington, Oct 14th, 1869.

Sir: I have received your letter of the 7th inst. in reply to mine of the 25th ultimo, regarding the practice of manufacturers of prepared mustard in your district sending out casks of prepared mustard without stamping the same.

I have also received a letter from the assessor of the 5th District, N.Y., to whom I wrote on the same subject in regard to manufacturers in *his* district, and also a letter from the manufacturers themselves.

These letters all confirm the information I had received from other parties, that manufacturers of prepared mustard in the City of New York, were selling the same in large casks without stamps. For the future and until the law is repealed imposing the tax on prepared mustard, I am compelled to require that all packages or enclosures containing prepared mustard shall be stamped according to their retail price or value.

If barrels, casks, jugs, &c., are inconvenient packages to stamp, it is the duty of the manufacturer to use such packages as are *convenient*.

It is no reason why the Government should be deprived of its lawful revenue, because manufacturers find it inconvenient to stamp certain kinds of packages.

I know it is alleged that this mustard shipped in bulk when packed for retailing is stamped by the dealer, but I have more reason to believe, that if not stamped by the manufacturer it is not stamped at all, the dealer arguing that if the article was liable to stamp, it would not have been permitted to be sold, or removed from the district where prepared without such stamp affixed. All such packages put upon the market unstamped are liable to seizure, and are constantly being seized; and the only way to avoid this, is to have the goods stamped according to law when sold or removed from he place of manufacture.

Hereafter you will require all these goods to be stamped, no matter what the size of the package may be.

Very respectfully,
J. W. Douglass,
Deputy Commissioner.

IRR v.X, October 23, 1869, p.124

Cases in which Manufacturers of Prepared Mustard may pay Tax otherwise than by Affixing Appropriate Stamp to Cumbersome Packages.

Office of Internal Revenue,
Washington, October 21, 1869.

Sir: Charles Gulden, Esq., of the firm of Charles Gulden & Co., Excelsior Mustard Mills, on behalf of their own firm, and other manufacturers of prepared mustard, has represented to this office the difficulties in the way of a strict compliance on their part with the ruling requiring all prepared mustard sold, to be stamped before being removed from the place of manufacture irrespective of the kind of package or inclosure used for putting up the same.

I have informed Mr. Gulden that the manufacturers, as above, may make sale of their goods in bulk, until the first of January, 1870, without affixing stamps, provided they make a full and accurate return of the quantities sold in bulk for each and every month on or before the tenth day of the following month; and upon such returns the assessor will assess the amount of the tax which has been omitted to be paid by stamps, and certify the same to his Collector as provided in the 5th section of the act of March 2, 1867.

You are authorized and instructed to assess this tax in the mode herein described of any and all manufacturers of prepared mustard in your district, who prefer to make such returns instead of stamping their packages, when they pack in bulk.

Very respectfully,
C. Delano,
Commissioner.

James M. McCartin, Esq., *Assessor*,
5th District, New York City.

IRR v.X, November 6, 1869, p.146

Collection of Taxes on Entire List of Articles in Schedule C, under the head of Canned Meats, etc., Suspended.

Office of Internal Revenue,
Washington, July 15, 1870.

M. Friedsam, Esq., U. S. Assessor, New York City.

Sir: I have received your letter of the 14th inst., in which you ask for instructions in regard to sales of prepared mustard in bulk, the time having expired during which you were authorized to collect the taxes on such goods by an assessment under the provisions of section 5, act of March 2, 1867.

In reply, I have to inform you that this mode of collecting this tax, as authorized by the letter to you from this office, was limited to the first of July, under the impression that in the meanwhile Congress would, according to the recommendation of the Commissioner, repeal the stamp tax imposed upon canned fish, prepared mustard, sauces, syrups, jams, and jellies, under schedule C, by the act of July 13, 1866. The act of Congress approved July 14, 1870, exempts canned and preserved fish, but does not exempt the other articles named.

I cannot but think that this was the result of an oversight on the part of the Senate and the Conference Committee which finally agreed upon the disputed points in the tax bill, as the House, as it originally passed that body, made provision for exempting the entire list of articles in schedule C, under the head of "Canned meats, etc.," which had not been previously exempted.

The amount of taxes collected upon prepared mustard, sauces, syrups, jams, and jellies, is comparatively very small, and the collection of it attended with no inconsiderable amount of trouble and vexation. I cannot, therefore, think that it was deliberate purpose of Congress to continue this tax, while exempting more fruitful sources of revenue, and those which were vastly easier of collection and less vexatious and troublesome to the taxpayer.

Acting under this belief, this office upon due deliberation has decided to suspend the collection of any further taxes upon the list of articles herein named until the next meeting of Congress, and the intention of that body in relation thereto is clearly understood.

C. Delano,
Commissioner.

IRR v.XII, August 6, 1870, p.45

Collection of Tax on Sauces, Syrups, Prepared Mustard, Jams, or Jellies, not to be Suspended. The Commissioner's Reasons for Declining to Suspend the Collection.

Office of Internal Revenue,
Washington, April 11, 1871.

Hon. C. B. Farwell, House of Representatives, Washington, D.C.

Sir: I have before me the petition of R. W. Tansill and other merchants of Chicago, presented by you, in which they ask to have the law imposing taxes on sauces, syrups, prepared mustard, jams, and jellies repealed; or if time is not afforded to do so at the present sitting of Congress, that the collection of the tax be suspended until the next session, so as to afford them opportunity to petition Congress to repeal said law.

On examination I find that this tax was imposed in the act of July 13, 1866, on "every can, bottle, or other single package containing meats, fish, shell-fish, fruits, vegetables, sauces, syrups, prepared mustard, jams, or jellies." The act of March 2, 1867, exempted "canned and preserved meats and shell-fish," and "canned and preserved vegetables and fruits."

In section 4 of the act "to reduce internal tax, and for other purposes," approved July 14, 1870, "canned and preserved fish" are enumerated among the exemptions to take effect on and after the 1st day of October, 1870. In the act "to amend existing laws relating to internal revenue," approved on the same day, it is provided "that on and after the passage of this act, in addition to the articles now exempt by law, the articles hereinafter enumerated shall be exempt from internal tax, namely: canned and preserved fish, shell-fish, meats, fruits, and vegetables."

You will observe that none of these provisions exempt sauces, syrups, prepared mustard, jams, or jellies. On the day following the passage of these two last named acts, my predecessor, in a letter to Assessor Friedsam, Fifth District, New York, suspended the collection of the tax on the articles not exempted, giving as a reason therefor the opinion that their omission from these acts was an oversight. The collection was suspended until the next meeting of Congress. In his annual report for 1870, page 14, the late Commissioner recommended the exemption of these articles for reasons stated, and I may here say that I fully concur in the recommendation.

The Forty-first Congress having adjourned with this recommendation of my predecessor before it, and without having taken any action upon this subject, I felt called upon to infer therefrom that it was not the purpose of Congress to exempt these articles, and therefore, in letter of March 11, 1871, to Otis Clapp, Assessor Fourth District of Massachusetts, ordered that prepared mustard, sauces, syrups, jams, and jellies thereafter sold or offered for sale, or removed for consumption, must be stamped according to the provisions of Schedule C.

While I would earnestly recommend that these articles should be exempted from taxation, yet I do not feel authorized under these circumstances to further suspend the collection of the tax, and must refer the petitioners and all others interested to Congress for the relief which they desire.

A. Pleasonton,
Commissioner.

IRR v.XIII, April 22, 1871, p.121

Stamps Required for Raspberry and other Syrups under Schedule C.

Treasury Department,
Office of Internal Revenue
Washington, July 29, 1871.

G. H. Laughlin, Esq., Baltimore, Md.

Sir: In reply to your letter of July 17, in relation to raspberry and other syrups, I have to say that syrups are liable to stamp duty under Schedule C, and the amount of tax upon a single package depends upon the weight of the package with its contents.

A package with its contents weighing two pounds or less requires a one cent stamp, and an additional cent for each additional pound or fractional part thereof in excess of two pounds, whether the package is large or small, and whether the vessel is furnished by the purchaser or not. Very respectfully,

A. Pleasonton,
Commissioner.

IRR v.XIV, August 12, 1871, p.41

GENERAL PROPRIETARY

Proprietary stamp regulations.

Treasury Department,
Office of Internal Revenue,
January, 1863.

1. Every proprietor can furnish a design for a stamp, which if approved, will be engraved by the government engravers, Messrs. Butler & Carpenter, of Philadelphia, at the cost of the proprietor.

2. In such case, the proprietor of the article will be entitled to the commission specified in the 102d section of the excise law.

3. If the designs do not exceed in superficial area 13/16 of an inch for the denomination of one and two cent stamps, or 63/64 of an inch for the denomination of three and four cent stamps, these being the sizes established by the office for the above specified denominations, there will be no additional charge to purchasers. If, however, proprietors desire to increase the size of the stamps for the denominations above mentioned, then an additional charge will be made for the cost additional of paper and printing. This additional charge will be ten cents per thousand for stamps of 3⅛ inches superficial area, and a proportionate sum for intermediate sizes.

4. Every stamp must be rectangular in form.

5. All dies and plates will be retained by, and be under the exclusive control of the government.

6. The general stamp must be cancelled by writing or stamping thereon the initials of the proprietor of the stamped article, and the date of cancelling; while the private stamp must be so affixed on the package, that in opening the same the stamp shall be effectually destroyed.

7. Where printing in more than one color is desired, the additional expense must be borne by the proprietor.

8. Each stamp must bear the words, or a proper abbreviation of them–United States Internal Revenue. Also, in words and figures, the denomination of the stamp.

The manufacturers of proprietary articles will be required to use the general stamp, until they severally furnish designs for individual use, and engravings have been prepared therefrom.

Orders for the general stamp may be sent to this office. The stamps will be forwarded upon receipt of funds in treasury notes, or an original certificate of a United States assistant treasurer, or a designated depositary, of a deposit made for the purchase of stamps.

The following commission will be allowed upon the purchase of the general proprietary stamp, and will be payable in stamps: On purchases of $50 or more, 2 per cent.; of $100 or more, 3 per cent.; $500 or more, 4 per cent.; and on $1,000 or more, 5 per cent. If not otherwise instructed, stamps thus ordered will be sent by mail.

Boutwell (1863), Stamp Duties (No. 2)

Concerning unstamped proprietary articles.*

April, 1863.

There is reason to believe that many manufacturers of proprietary articles, such as patent medicines, perfumery, cosmetics, playing cards, and all other articles mentioned in Schedule C of the excise law, who issued such articles after September 1, 1862, without placing stamps upon them, in accordance with the 107th section of the excise law, have failed to make returns of such issues, and to make payment to this office of amounts equal to those they would have paid for stamps, had stamps been obtainable when said articles were issued; or, if they have issued no unstamped proprietary articles, that they have failed to subscribe and file with you the oath (Form No. 34) as required by section 110 of the excise law.

With a view, therefore, to correct this state of things, I have to request that you will, as soon as possible, make two lists of the names and residences of all manufacturers of proprietary articles doing business in your district, and that you will annex to their names the names of the various proprietary articles they manufacture, and that you will retain one list for your own use and forward the other to this office. Your own list should be inscribed in a book kept for that purpose, and the list to be forwarded to this office should be upon foolscap paper.

You will then notify each such manufacturer that he is required to make sworn returns through you to this office of all unstamped articles he has issued since the first of September, 1862, together with the retail price of each such article, the value of the stamp required to be placed thereon, and the sum total of their united value, specifying the amount of such issue since September 1, 1862, up to the date on which he discontinued the issue of unstamped proprietary articles, after the manner of the enclosed form.

When any such manufacturer claims to have made his return to this office, under previous instructions, and to have paid the stamp tax thereon, you will require that he exhibit to you, or to one of your assistants, the receipt of this office for the amount; and you will note the amount of such receipt opposite the name of the holder upon your list of manufacturers of proprietary articles, and make return of the fact to this office.

When you have received the returns, you will immediately satisfy yourself, as far as possible, of their correctness, not only as to fact, but as to form, and then transmit them to this office; and you will note upon your list of manufacturers of proprietary articles, opposite to each manufacturer's name, the fact that you have received and sent forward his return. You will also notify manufacturers of proprietary articles in your district, who claim to have stamped all proprietary articles they have issued, that they must subscribe and file in your office an oath (Form No. 34) that they have not issued any unstamped articles since September 1, 1862, or since the date of their last return of unstamped articles, up to April 1, 1863, and, after noting the reception of such oath opposite the name of its subscriber, upon your list of manufacturers of proprietary articles, you will transmit the oath itself to this office.

And you will further require of said manufacturers that they subscribe and file in your office, on the first day of each month, after April 1, 1863, an oath, in conformity to Form No. 34, covering the issues of the preceding month, until October 1, 1863; and you will, after noting its receipt opposite the name of its subscriber, forward such oath at once to this office.

You will, from time to time, review this list, and make note of such manufacturers of proprietary articles as have failed to make returns, or file oaths as above, and you will give them notice at once of their duty in the premises; and if they shall, for five days after such notice, neglect to make returns or file oaths, you will report their names, with the facts, to this office.

Yours, very respectfully,
Joseph J. Lewis,
Commissioner of Internal Revenue.

To ___ ___, Esq.,
Assessor ___ District of ___.

(* Addressed to assessors.)

Boutwell (1863), Decisions (No. 97)

If the manufacturer of proprietary articles, acting in good faith, and upon such information as he can obtain, affixes a stamp answering to the retail price in the market where he deals, or in the vicinity thereof, he will be exempt from proceedings for penalty, even though in other parts of the country the articles so manufactured and stamped may be sold at enhanced prices.

Articles enumerated in Schedule C, when sold in bulk or in quantities greater than specified or contemplated in the part of the excise law relating to said schedule, will be taxed as manufactures. If such articles are afterwards prepared and sold in such packages as are mentioned or described in Schedule C, the appropriate stamps must be affixed to the packages.

Boutwell (1863), Rulings (No. 244)

The retail price of articles subject to proprietary stamp duty is in all cases the measure of that duty. The stamp duty upon this class of articles, as well as medicines, &c., is one cent for every twenty-five cents or any fractional part thereof of the retail price; two or more stamps of a smaller denomination may be used in numbers, sufficient to make a required stamp duty.

Boutwell (1863), Rulings (from No. 287)

Inks are not subject to stamp-duty, but to an ad valorem duty. Foreign inks to import duty only.

Boutwell (1865), Rulings (No. 227)

Stamp on Manufactured and Imported Articles—Original Packages—Exposure for Sale.

The law imposes a stamp duty upon essences, extracts, toilet water, cosmetics, hair oils, &c.&c., whether the same are imported or of domestic manufacture. (See Record, Vol. VI, p. 123.) It further provides that where such imported articles are sold in the original and unbroken packages in which the bottles or other enclosures were packed by the manufacturer, the person so selling said articles shall not be subject to any penalty for want of the proper stamp. By the term "original packages," as here used, is meant the cases or packing boxes in which the bottles, &c., are packed by the manufacturer, and not the bottles themselves. This provision was intended to apply in cases where the imported articles are sold at wholesale to be sold again, and was intended to relieve the importer from the trouble, expense and damage of opening his boxes, unpacking his articles, stamping and repacking for sale.

When the original packages are opened, and the contents offered, or exposed for sale, each bottle, pot, can, phial, or other single package must be stamped according to the requirements of Schedule C, Internal Revenue Laws.

IRR v.VI, November 2, 1867, p.154

Special Instructions Relative Stamp Duty on Articles.

Office of Internal Revenue,
Washington, Oct. 25, 1867.

Sir: From information received at this office it appears that the requirements of the law in regard to the stamp duty on perfumery and other articles enumerated in schedule C, are not generally complied with, through ignorance of the law or from other causes.

You are, therefore, instructed to order your Assistant Assessors and also Revenue Inspectors to visit all druggists, grocers, dry and fancy goods dealers and all others in their respective divisions and districts who may sell articles liable to stamp duty under Schedule C, and inform them with regard to their liabilities and see that the law is, in future, strictly complied with by all such parties.

E. A. Rollins,
Commissioner.

IRR v.VI, November 2, 1867, p.155

Ink Exempt.

Articles liable to stamp duty under Schedule C. are arranged under three heads, as follows: (1) ''Medicines or preparations, embracing medicinal articles only;'' (2) ''Perfumery, cosmetics, matches and cards," and (3) "Canned meats, &c." Ink, belonging to neither of these classes, cannot be held liable to stamp duty, though the manufacturer may claim an occult secret, or art, in its preparation.

IRR v.VI, November 9, 1867, p.162

Stamp Duties on Articles.

A number of grocers in different parts of the country have got into trouble through inattention to or ignorance of their obligations under the revenue laws with respect to articles liable to stamp. We will state explicitly for the information of such, that Sardines, Anchovies, Prepared Mustard, Sirups in Bottles, Jams, Jellies, Meat and Fish Sauces of different kinds, Colognes, Cosmetics, and all the articles enumerated in Schedule C, as printed below, are liable to stamp duty, whether made in the United States or imported. The stamp must be affixed on each package offered or exposed for sale. An article is offered or exposed for sale when placed on the shelves, or in the show cases of the merchant. Sardines, Anchovies, Sauces, Sirups, Prepared Mustard, Jams and Jellies, are subject to tax according to the weight of each package; a one-cent stamp if the package does not exceed two pounds in weight, and stamp of additional cent for every pound or fraction of a pound in excess of two pounds in weight.

Parties selling imported articles of the kind mentioned, must affix and cancel appropriate stamp, such articles being subject to the like stamp tax with domestic manufactures. Where the importer sells in the *original packages*, i. e., those in which the original *manufacturer* or producer furnishes them to the trade, and not the single package which the retailer sells to a customer, he need not break open such original package and stamp each separate article, but may sell the same without stamp in the original package, case or box, and the dealer who breaks the package to sell a single article, must affix and cancel stamps on each. The absence of stamp from an article offered or exposed for sale is *prima facie* evidence of fraud.

Canned Fruits, Canned Vegetables and Canned Oysters, are exempt. Dry Mustard is exempt; also Olives, Capers, and Pickles. *Cooking* Essences, and Extracts are also exempt. But all Essences, Extracts, Toilet Waters, cosmetics, including Bay Rum and Florida Water, Hair Oils, Pomades, Tooth Washes, Powders, Dentifrices of all kinds, are subject to stamp. Boxes of Aromatic Cachous, Pastiles or Troches, must be stamped, and Matches, Wax Lights and Tapers and playing cards. Every dealer is regarded as a manufacturer, and is subject to all the liabilities of such for selling, removing, offering or exposing for sale such articles without proper stamp. The penalty is $50 for each offence, one-half to the informer. We refer Assistant Assessors to Series 3, No. 10, 5 Record, p. 174, and decisions in the Record, especially 6 Record, 123, and 154, in connection with this subject.

Schedule of Stamp Duties upon Articles in Schedule C, and in the Amendments thereto.

	Stamp Duty.
Proprietary Medicines and Preparations.–	
For and upon every packet, box, bottle, pot, phial or other enclosure, containing any pills, powders, tinctures, troches, lozenges, sirups, cordials, bitters, anodynes, tonics, plasters, liniments, salves, ointments, pastes, drops, waters, essences, spirits, oils, or other medicinal preparations or compositions whatsoever, sold, offered for sale, or removed for consumption and sale, by any person or persons whatever, where such packet, box, &c., with its contents, does not exceed, at retail price or value, the sum of twenty-five cents	1 cent.
Exceeding twenty-five and not exceeding fifty cents	2 cents.
Exceeding fifty and not exceeding seventy-five cents	3 cents.
Exceeding seventy-five cents and not exceeding one dollar	4 cents.
Exceeding one dollar, for every additional fifty cents, or fractional part thereof in excess of one dollar	2 cents.
Officinal preparations, and medicines mixed or compounded specially for any person according to the written recipe or prescription of any physician or surgeon	exempt.
Perfumery and Cosmetics.–For and upon every packet, box, bottle, pot, phial, or other enclosure containing any essence, extract, toilet-water, cosmetic, hair-oil, pomade, hair dressing, hair restorative, hair dye, tooth-wash, dentifrice, tooth-paste, aromatic cachous, or any similar articles, by whatsoever name the same heretofore have been, now are, or may hereafter be called, known, or distinguished, used or applied, or to be used or applied as perfumes or applications to the hair, mouth, or skin, sold, offered for sale, or removed for consumption and sale, the same rates per package, &c., as for medicines and preparations.	
Friction Matches.–For and upon every parcel or package of 100 or less	1 cent.

More than 100 and not more than 200 .... 2 cents.
For every additional 100, or fractional part thereof .... 1 cent.
Wax tapers.—Double the rates for friction matches.
Cigar Lights, made in part of wood, wax, glass, paper, or other materials, in parcels or packages containing twenty-five lights or less in each parcel pr package .... 1 cent.
When in parcels or packages containing more than twenty-five and not more than fifty lights .... 2 cents.
For every additional twenty-five lights, or fractional part of that number, one cent additional.
Playing-Cards.—For and upon every pack not exceeding fifty-two cards in number, irrespective of price or value .... 5 cents.
Articles, &c.—For and upon every can, bottle, or other single package containing fish, sauces, sirups, prepared mustard, jams, or jellies, contained therein, and packed or sealed, made, prepared and sold, or offered for sale, or removed for consumption in the United States, on and after the first day of October, 1866, when such can, bottle, or other single package, with its contents, shall not exceed two pounds in weight .. 1 cent.
For every additional pound or fractional part thereof .... 1 cent.

IRR v.IX, February 6, 1869, pp.45-6

Liability of Importers of Perfumeries and Cosmetics, etc., to Stamp their Articles—Definition of the Terms "Original Package" and "Manufacturer."

Office of Internal Revenue,
Washington, April 21, 1871.

Howard Sanger & Co., and ten other persons and firms, New York City.

Gentlemen: In reply to your communication of the 12th instant, relative to the liability of importers of perfumeries, cosmetics, etc., to stamp such articles before offering them for sale, and also with regard to the proper interpretation of the expression ''original and unbroken packages,'' as used in the 169th section of the act of June 30, 1864, as subsequently amended, I have to say that prior to the 1st of October, 1863, no internal tax was collected on imported medicines, perfumeries, cosmetics, etc., while the act of July, 1862, did impose a stamp tax, under Schedule C, on all domestic articles of this character. The consequence was that imitation goods in large quantities were put upon the market, and by the simulating of foreign labels, brands, styles of package, trade marks, etc., these goods were sold in fraud of the revenue.

This condition of things, however, was remedied by subsequent legislation, and more particularly by the Act of June 30, 1864, section 169, as afterward amended. Said section 169 declares ''that any person who shall offer or expose for sale any of the articles named in Schedule C, or in any amendments thereto, whether the articles so offered or exposed are imported or are of foreign or domestic manufacture, *shall be deemed the manufacturer thereof,* and subject to all the duties, liabilities, and penalties imposed by law in regard to the sale of domestic articles without the use of the proper stamp or stamps denoting the tax paid thereon; and all such articles, imported or of foreign manufacture, shall, in addition to the import duties imposed on the same, be subject to the stamp tax respectively prescribed in Schedule C aforesaid.''

When Congress, by the act of July 20, 1868, changed the mode of collecting the tax on manufactured tobacco, snuff, and cigars, from an assessment and collection of the same from the manufacturer to a stamp tax, they provided, and for the same reason, that all tobacco, snuff, and cigars imported from foreign countries, in addition to the import duties, should pay the same internal taxes respectively, and that all such goods, before leaving the custody of custom-house officers, should be packed by the owner or importer in the same manner as prescribed in the act for like articles manufactured in the United States. (See sections 77 and 93, act of July 20, 1868.)

When a tax or duty is paid by stamps, it is only by requiring a uniform tax upon all articles subject to such stamp tax, whether of foreign or domestic manufacture, that such a tax could be collected, owing to the facility and success with which foreign styles of packages, labels, trade marks, etc., may be simulated and counterfeited.

In the case of imported medicines, perfumeries, cosmetics, etc., the law does not require, as it does in the case of imported tobacco, snuff, and cigars, that the stamp shall be affixed and cancelled while in the custody of the custom-house officers, and before they are permitted to pass out of the custody of said officers. But the law declares that the importer of such articles, if he offers or exposes them for sale, *shall be deemed the manufacturer thereof,* and makes him subject to all the duties, liabilities, and penalties imposed by law in regard to the sale of domestic articles without the use of the proper stamp or stamps denoting the tax paid thereon.

From the penalty imposed by the 165th section of the act of June 30, 1864, for selling articles in Schedule C without proper stamps, persons selling imported articles, except playing cards, lucifer or friction matches, cigar lights, and wax tapers, are exempted, provided such articles are sold in the original and unbroken packages in which the bottles or other enclosures were packed by the manufacturer.

This leads to the inquiry as to the proper import of the term "original and unbroken packages." Clearly by this expression is not meant the primary enclosure, the packet, box, bottle, pot, vial, or other enclosure in which the actual manufacturer or maker of any medicine, perfumery, or cosmetic puts up the same into a convenient form for sale; but the original package here referred to is unquestionably a *packing box* or *case,* in which the actual manufacturer's original packet, box, bottle, pot, vial, etc., is enclosed for safe transportation or for exportation. It is a package within which are enclosed other packages. It is a packing box or a packing case; for such is the express language of the statute. The expression does not necessarily imply a packing box such as the actual manufacturer of the article employs to ship from the place of manufacture to the merchant, jobber, or dealer; for these are often broken by the agent of the importer or his commissionnaire, and the goods are repacked for exportation.

The "original package," as the term is understood by this office, refers to the packing box or case in which bottles or other enclosures are packed for shipment from a foreign country to this country; the package in which the goods are entered at the custom-house; the importer's package, who ordered the goods from his agent abroad and offers or exposes them for sale in the home market.

The term *manufacturer,* in the body of the section (section 169), is declared to mean the person who offers or exposes for sale any of the articles named in Schedule C. The term manufacturer, in the proviso to section 169, must, according to every principle of correct interpretation of law, apply in like manner to the person who offers or exposes the articles for sale, and not, as is claimed by the importers of these articles, to the actual maker of the goods in the countries from which they are imported, unless the articles are exported in the same enclosures in which they were packed by the actual manufacturer.

If every box or enclosure containing a dozen, half or quarter dozen perfumery, as the case may be, duly wrapped and tied and labelled by the manufacturer, is to be regarded and held to be the original package, as is claimed, why may not a less number so wrapped and tied and labelled with equal propriety be held to be the original package, till every single packet, box, bottle, etc., becomes an original package when imported, and thus the importer relieved from all liability to stamp his articles?

While the law relieves the importer selling in original and unbroken packages from any penalty on account of the want of the proper stamps, it at the same time contemplates the collection of a tax by means of stamps on all such articles as are named in Schedule C, and it contemplates the collection of the tax from the first person who breaks the original package. It may put the importer, offering or exposing for sale a broken package of perfumery or cosmetics to some trouble and inconvenience to stamp each packet, box, pot, vial, or other enclosure, before he sells, but not to more inconvenience than he will put Government to collect the tax after he has sent the goods broadcast over the land without previously affixing the proper stamps for the payment of the tax as the law provides.

If the jobber or importer sells broken packages unstamped, the retail dealer is encouraged to believe that no stamps are required, and he affixes no stamps unless perchance some revenue detective shall overhaul his stock and find him offering or exposing for sale unstamped goods.

The ruling of this office given in a letter addressed to M. F. Dickenson, U.S. Assistant District Attorney, December 17, 1869, and according to which Supervisor Tutton and other revenue officers have been instructed to act, is that the largest package containing the same kind of articles only is to be regarded as the original within the meaning of the law. If this package is unbroken by the importer, he incurs no liability to any penalty on account of the want of the proper stamps; but if he breaks such packages and offers for sale anything less than an original export package, he must affix stamps.

Since writing the foregoing, I am informed by the Commissioner of Customs that the ruling of this office exactly coincides in this matter of original packages with the rulings of the Secretary of the Treasury, given by him for the direction of custom-house officers.

A. Pleasonton, Commissioner.

IRR v.XIII, April 29, 1871 pp.129-30

Regulations concerning the Stamping of Packages Taxed under Schedule C.

Office of Internal Revenue,
Washington, September 6, 1871.

Alexander Fulton, Esq., Supervisor, Baltimore, MD.

Sir: I have received your letter of the 4th inst. in which you state that a great deal of annoyance is created in your district by the lack of a proper understanding, both on the part of officials and of the public generally, of the law and regulations in reference to the stamping of packages of syrups, etc., under Schedule C, and asking for specific instructions on several points which you present.

In reply I have to inform you that every person, firm, company, or corporation making, manufacturing or preparing fruit syrups, or other syrups, or articles enumerated under the head of canned meats, etc., in Schedule C, and which have not been specially exempted, or manufacturing or preparing any medicinal article or preparation not specially exempted, or manufacturing, mixing, preparing, or compounding any perfumery, cosmetic, essence, extract, toilet water, hair oil, hair restorative, hair dye, etc., or any similar articles by whatsoever name the same heretofore have been, now are, or may hereafter be called, known, or distinguished, used or applied, or to be used or applied as perfumes or applications to the hair, mouth, or skin, must be stamped before being sold or removed for consumption for sale.

The liability to affix proper and suitable revenue stamps is placed upon the manufacturer or person making, preparing, mixing, or compounding the articles subject to the tax, and imposes a penalty of fifty dollars for every omission, if he sells or removes for consumption or sale without affixing the proper adhesive stamps.

2. The language of the statute is that "for and upon every packet, box, bottle, pot, phial, or *other enclosure,*" "for and upon every can, bottle, or *other single package,*" the stamp or stamps shall be placed. The terms "other enclosure" and "other single package" are held to be sufficiently broad and comprehensive to embrace, and were intended to embrace every kind of package or enclosure that the manufacturer or maker of such articles might employ for packing, or enclosing for delivery to the purchasers, or for removal from the place of manufacture for consumption or sale.

It therefore follows (3) that *every person,* be he rectifier, dealer, manufacturer, druggist, or apothecary, who makes or prepares syrups, or any other article liable to stamp tax under Schedule C, and puts up the same in barrels, kegs, demijohns, or other vessel or package, or puts up "in bulk," as this mode of packing is frequently characterized, must affix the proper stamp according to the price received for each single package, or according to the weight of each single package with its contents, before the articles can legally be removed from the premises of the maker or manufacturer.

4. Dealers who purchase syrups or other articles liable to stamp tax under Schedule C in bulk, that is to say, in barrels, kegs, or other large vessels or packages, and retail directly from these packages in quantities to suit their customers, are not held to be liable to affix stamps to the sales thus made, provided the original packages, the barrels, kegs, or other vessels or enclosures, *with their contents,* were properly stamped by the manufacturer or maker before being removed from his premises; and there would be no difference in this respect whether the dealer provides the vessel, or the purchaser furnishes his own vessel for the reception of the article purchased.

5. Inasmuch as the law, section 169, holds every person who sells or offers or exposes for sale any of the articles named in Schedule C to be the manufacturer thereof and subject to all the duties, liabilities, and penalties imposed by law in regard to the sale of domestic articles without the use of the proper stamp or stamps denoting the tax paid thereon, this office holds that the dealer, or the druggist, or the apothecary, who purchases any of these articles in bulk or in large-sized vessels, though properly stamped by the manufacturer or maker according to the price for which he sold each single package, and repacks the same in small packets, boxes, pots, phials, bottles, or other enclosures, and marks or labels the same, and sells, or offers or exposes the same for sale, is liable to affix stamps to his packages of a value corresponding to his retail price or to the weight.

6. Every person purchasing any article liable to stamp tax under Schedule C directly of the

manufacturer, maker, or compounder, is entitled to receive the same duly and properly stamped; and therefore it is held by this office that such manufacturer, etc., cannot legally stamp his articles in bulk and retail from large stamped packages, but that every package put up by the manufacturer, whether he furnishes the vessel or package or the same is furnished by the purchaser, must have a suitable stamp affixed.

Any ruling or decision which may have been heretofore issued from this office conflicting with the rulings herein contained, is hereby revoked.

Yours respectfully,
J. W. Douglass,
Commissioner.

IRR v.XIV, September 16, 1871, pp.89-90

1875.–Department No. 134.–Internal Revenue.–Circular No. 136.–Containing Regulations under which Private Dies for Proprietary Stamps will be Engraved and Transferred from one Person, Firm, or Corporation to another Person, Firm, or Corporation, and Stamps therefrom Printed and Issued.

Treasury Department,
Office of Internal Revenue,
Washington, September 30, 1875.

Section 3423 Revised Statutes of the United States provides that, "in all cases where an adhesive stamp is used for denoting any tax imposed under this chapter, except as hereinafter provided, the person using or affixing the same shall write thereon the initials of his name and the date on which such stamp is attached or used, so that it may not again be used. And every person who fraudulently makes use of an adhesive stamp to denote any tax imposed by this chapter without so effectually cancelling and obliterating such stamp, except as before mentioned, shall forfeit the sum of fifty dollars: *Provided,* That any proprietor of proprietary articles, or articles subject to stamp tax under Schedule A, shall have the privilege of furnishing, without expense to the United States, in suitable form, to be approved by the Commissioner of Internal Revenue, his own dies or designs for stamps to be used thereon, which shall be made under the direction and retained in the possession of the said Commissioner, for the separate use of such proprietor, and shall not be duplicated to any other person; and that in all cases where such stamp is used, instead of said proprietor writing the date thereon, the said stamp shall be so affixed on the box, bottle or package, that in opening the same or using the contents thereof, the said stamp will be effectually destroyed; and, in default thereof, such proprietor shall be liable to a penalty of fifty dollars. And every person who fraudulently obtains or uses any of the aforesaid stamps, or designs therefor, or who forges or counterfeits, or causes or procures to be forged or counterfeited, any representation or similitude, or colorable imitation of the said last-mentioned stamp, or any engraver or printer who sells or gives away said stamps, or selling the same, or, being a merchant, broker, peddler, or person dealing, in whole or in part, in similar goods, wares, merchandise, manufactures, preparations, or articles, or those designed for similar objects or purposes, has knowingly or fraudulently in his possession any such forged, counterfeited likeness, similitude, or colorable imitation of the said last-mentioned stamp, shall forfeit the said stamps and the articles upon which they are placed, shall be deemed guilty of felony, and be punished by a fine not exceeding one thousand dollars, or by imprisonment and confinement to hard labor not exceeding five years, or both, at the discretion of the court."

Under the above provisions of law, the following Regulations are hereby prescribed for the presentation of dies or designs for stamps, the engraving of the same, the printing and issue of the stamps, and the transfer of the right to receive stamps printed from such dies from one person, firm, or corporation, to another person, firm, or corporation.

Any proprietor of an article named in Schedule A may furnish a design for a stamp, which, if approved, will be engraved under the direction of the Commissioner of Internal Revenue, at the cost of the proprietor.

The design should be forwarded to this Office for its approval, and, if approved, the same will be transmitted to the person, firm, or corporation, with whom there may exist at the time a contract for the engraving and printing of such stamps.

The contractor will then make an estimate of the cost of engraving the die, and preparing the necessary plate, which he will transmit to the person, firm, or corporation presenting the design, and on receipt from such person, firm, or corporation of directions that the work be proceeded with, accompanied by a satisfactory assurance of the prompt payment of the estimated cost, the contractor will proceed to engrave the die and prepare the necessary plate.

If the person, firm, or corporation desire stamps printed in anticipation of the receipt of orders therefor, he or they will then file in this Office the bond, estimate, and request hereinafter referred to.

All private dies hereafter engraved must bear the words "United States Internal Revenue," or a proper abbreviation of them, the denomination of the stamp in words and figures, and the name of the person, firm, or corporation presenting the design; and the stamps will be printed in such colors as the Commissioner may at any time prescribe.

If the design does not exceed in superficial area thirteen-sixteenths of an inch no additional charge to purchasers for stamps furnished will be made, but where the superficial area exceeds thirteen-sixteenths of an inch, the contractor will be permitted to charge for the additional labor and expense of printing, rendered necessary by the increased size, such rate as may be agreed upon between the contractor and the person, firm, or corporation ordering the same, or, in case of disagreement, such rate as may be decided by the Commissioner to be fair and reasonable.

The dies and plates will be retained by, and be under the exclusive control of, the Government.

It appears that it has heretofore been the practice of this Office to print supplies of private-die proprietary stamps in anticipation of orders therefor from the person, firm, or corporation furnishing the design, and in the event of the failure or retirement from business from any cause of such person, firm, or corporation, the Government has been subjected to a loss of the amount expended for paper and the printing and preparation for issue of the stamps left on hand.

It is believed that this Office is not warranted in subjecting the Government to losses of this character, and that the printing of private-die stamps before the receipt of orders therefor should be discontinued, or that proper measures should be taken to secure the Government against losses arising from such printing.

In future, therefore, such persons, firms, or corporations, as order stamps printed from private dies and desire to avoid the delays consequent upon the printing and preparation of the stamps, subsequent to the receipt of an order therefor, will be required to execute and file in this office a bond conditioned for the payment to the Treasurer of the United States for the use of the United States, whenever so required by the Commissioner of Internal Revenue, of such sum or sums as may have been paid by the Treasury Department for the paper upon which the stamps are printed, together with the printing, perforating, gumming, and preparing for issue of such private-die proprietary stamps, not exceeding an estimated three months' supply, as may be prepared under the directions of the Commissioner of Internal Revenue, in accordance with the estimate and request of the person, firm, or corporation ordering the same.

After the approval of the bond, or simultaneously with the filing thereof, an estimate of a three months' average consumption of stamps should be made by the person, firm, or corporation desiring stamps printed in anticipation of orders, and the same should be accompanied by a request that such number be printed and kept continuously on hand awaiting orders therefor.

Orders for private-die proprietary stamps should be addressed to the "Commissioner of Internal Revenue, Washington, D.C.," and, except in the case of manufacturers of matches, purchasing stamps without prepayment therefor, must be accompanied by a certificate of a deposit made on account of stamps with an Assistant Treasurer or Designated Depositary of the United States.

Commissions payable in stamps will be allowed on private-die proprietary stamps, as prescribed in Section 3425 of the Revised Statutes of the United States, as follows, viz.:

"On amounts purchased at one time of not less than fifty nor more than five hundred dollars, five per centum, and on amounts over five hundred dollars, ten per centum on the whole amount purchased."

Transfers of dies will be permitted only in cases where the transferree succeeds to the business of the transferrer, and to the manufacture of the particular article or articles upon which stamps printed therefrom have been used.

In such cases a formal assignment from the assignor to the assignee of the entire interest in the die of such assignor must be executed, duly acknowledged, and filed in this Office.

If the transfer is approved, the assignee, at his own expense, will then be required to have the name of his predecessor cut from the die and his own name inserted in lieu thereof.

In all cases where stamps bearing the name of a proprietor have heretofore been transferred to another person, firm, or corporation, a change, in accordance with the above regulation, should be at once made at the expense of the transferree.

The stamps printed from the original die prior to its transfer, which have been prepared in accordance with the aforementioned estimate and request of the person, firm, or corporation ordering the same, will be destroyed, and such person, firm, or corporation will be required to reimburse the United States for the amount expended in the preparation thereof.

Whenever a plate becomes so worn as to fail to produce a perfect impression the same will be re-entered by the contractor at the expense of the person, firm, or corporation to whom stamps printed therefrom are issued.

D. D. Pratt,
Commissioner.

IRR v.XXI, October 21, 1875, pp.321-2

1882.—Department No. 46.—Internal Revenue.—Circular No. 243.—The Owners of Private Dies from Which Stamps are Printed for Proprietary Articles.

Treasury Department,
Office of Internal Revenue,
Washington, D.C., April 28, 1882.

You are hereby authorized and requested, in making remittances accompanied by order for stamps, to remit but ninety-five per centum of the face value of the stamps ordered, when the amount ordered exceeds fifty dollars, and does not exceed five hundred dollars, and to remit but ninety per centum of the face value of the stamps ordered when the amount ordered exceeds five hundred dollars—for example:

For orders of $500, remit $475.

For orders of $1,000, remit $900.

For the convenience of this Office it is requested that orders for stamps be in multiples of twenty-five dollars.

This change of practice is made in conformity with the recent decision of the Supreme Court of the United States in the case of the Swift & Courtney & Beecher Company v. United States, on appeal from the United States Court of Claims.

Respectfully,
Green B. Raum,
Commissioner.

IRR v.XXVIII, May 8, 1882, p.141

Supreme Court of the United States, October Term, 1881.

The Swift and Courtney and Beecher Company, Appellant, v. The United States.-Appeal from the Court of Claims.

The statute allows a commission of ten per cent on all sales of stamps exceeding five hundred dollars in amount, to dealers in proprietary articles purchasing stamps made from their own dies.

Held, That this commission is payable in money and cannot lawfully be diminished by being paid in stamps at their face value. The contrary practice has not acquired the force of law, and has not been acquiesced in by the appellant. The judgment of the Court of Claims to the contrary is reversed.—Ed. Int. Rev. Record.

Mr. Justice Matthews delivered the opinion of the court.

The appellant filed its petition in the Court of Claims for the recovery of certain commissions alleged to be due to it on purchases of proprietary stamps under the internal revenue laws.

It alleged that it was, during the period covered by the transactions set out, the proprietor, manufacturer, and vendor of friction matches; that, as such, at the beginning of its business, it furnished to the Commissioner of Internal Revenue its own die for stamps, to be used especially for its own proprietary articles; that, during said period, from time to time, and continuously on different days of each and every month, it sent to the Commissioner of Internal Revenue sums of money from one thousand to ten thousand dollars as suited its convenience, and that said commissioner transmitted to it stamps, as it needed and ordered; so that in the account between it and the commissioner as to said stamps the creditor side showed moneys received by the latter in certain sums and at certain dates, but showed the receipt of no sum less than one thousand dollars, and the debtor side of said account showed that stamps were sent by the commissioner to the appellant in different sums and at different dates, but never in amounts less than one thousand dollars.

It is further averred that upon the whole amount of stamps purchased, during the period referred to, it was entitled to a commission of ten per centum in money, amounting to $389,720.40, which the commissioner has refused to allow; and has allowed in lieu thereof $354,291.27 in stamps at their face value; insisting such to be the long-established practice of the office, to which he must adhere, till changed by legislation or judicial decision. The appellant, in the petition, in reference to this practice, avers "that the allowances made to it from time to time between May 6, 1870, and December 24, 1878, have been in accordance with the uniform practice of said internal revenue office from its organization, but petitioner avers that at different times prior to 1866 protests were made to the commissioner of internal revenue by and on behalf of the manufacturers of friction matches against such a construction of the statute by him, by which only ten per cent commissions in stamps at their face value were allowed by him upon the amount of money paid by the purchasers, instead of ten per cent upon the whole amount of stamps purchased, and that such facts are and have always been known to petitioner."

It is also averred that the appellant gave the required security for a credit of sixty days upon its purchase of stamps, as provided for in the internal revenue act of June 30, 1864 (13 Stat. at Large, 294), which enacted, "That the commissioner of internal revenue may from time to time furnish, supply, and deliver to any manufacturer of friction or other matches, cigar lights or wax tapers, a suitable quantity of adhesive or other stamps, such as may be prescribed for use in such cases, without prepayment therefor, on a credit not exceeding sixty days, requiring in advance such security as may be judged necessary to secure payment (*payment* in statute) therefor to the treasurer of the United States within the time prescribed for such payment."

The defendant filed a general demurrer, which was sustained, and judgment rendered dismissing the petition. To review this judgment the present appeal has been prosecuted.

The act of July 1, 1862, sec. 102, to provide internal revenue, etc. (12 Stat. at Large, 477), authorized the commissioner of internal revenue to sell to and supply collectors, deputy collectors, postmasters, stationers, or any other persons, at his discretion, with adhesive stamps, upon the payment at the time of delivery of the amount of duties said stamps represent, and thereupon to allow and deduct from the aggregate amount of such stamps the sum not exceeding five per centum as commission, with the proviso, "that any proprietor or proprietors of articles named in schedule C, who shall furnish his or their own die or design for stamps, to be used especially for his or their own proprietary articles, shall be allowed the following discount, namely: on amounts purchased at one time of not less than fifty nor more than five hundred dollars, five per centum; on amounts over five hundred dollars, ten per centum."

By the amendatory act of March 3, 1863 (12 Stat. at Large, 714), the word "commission" was substituted for "discount" in this proviso.

This section as thus amended was re-enacted as sec. 161 of the act of June 30, 1864 (13 Stat. at Large, 294), and schedule C enlarged as so to include friction matches—(p. 302).

The act of July 14, 1870, sec. 4 (16 Stat. at Large, 257), continued in force the same provision, directing that proprietors of articles named in Schedule C, who shall furnish their own dies, shall be allowed commissions, on amounts over five hundred dollars, "ten per centum on the whole amount purchased."

It will be perceived, on examining this legislation, that while, in respect to adhesive stamps sold, other than those to proprietors of articles named in Schedule C from their own dies for their own use, the rate of the commission to be allowed to the purchaser shall not exceed five per centum, but within that limit, is subject to the discretion of the commissioner of internal revenue; while, in respect to those of the latter class, including stamps on friction matches, the rate is fixed by the statute itself, and in the form as expressed in the act of 1870, where the amounts of purchases are over five hundred dollars, the commissions are established at ten per centum on the whole amount purchased. So that, while in the sale of adhesive stamps of the former description, in the excercise of his discretion as to the rate, the commissioner might lawfully provide that the commissions should be paid only in stamps at their face value; yet, in the sale of stamps to proprietors of friction matches, he was not authorized to diminish the commission by any such regulation, but was required to allow and pay in money, ten per centum calculated on the amount of stamps purchased, on all sales exceeding five hundred dollars in amount.

In the present case the appellant was allowed commissions, not on the whole amount of stamps furnished him nor in money, but in stamps at their face value, calculated on the amount of money paid by him. The difference between the amounts, resulting from these two modes of calculating and allowing commissions, is the amount sought to be recovered by the appellant.

There is no serious question raised as to the proper construction of the internal revenue acts upon the point, it being virtually admitted that the contention on the part of the appellant upon the provisions of the statutes is correct.

It is met, however, in the opinion of the Court of Claims, and in argument on behalf of the Government here, that the contrary construction, to pay these commissions in stamps, at their face value, has been acted upon by the Commissioner of Internal Revenue from the beginning; has been acquiesced in by purchasers and dealers; and has never been changed by Congress; and as an official practice has thus acquired the force of law; or if not, then, at least, it was a course of dealing, well known to the appellant, and acquiesced in, by which it accepted stamps at their face value in payment of its commissions, which it is not at liberty now to open, question, and reverse.

The right construction of the internal revenue acts, upon the point of the allowance of commissions to dealers in proprietary articles, purchasing stamps made from their own dies, and for their own use, is too clear to bring the case within the first alternative. The rule which gives determining weight to contemporaneous construction, put upon a statute, by those charged with its execution, applies only in cases of ambiguity and doubt. (Edwards' lessee v. Darby, 12 Wheat., 210; Smythe v. Fisk, 23 Wall., 382; U.S. v. Moore, 95 U.S., 763; U.S. v. Pugh, 99 U.S., 269.)

And we are of the opinion that the averments of the petition, admitted by the demurrer, do not bring it within the operation of the principle invoked in the second alternative. The case made by the petition is not that of successive and independent purchases of stamps, settled for, at the time, when the commissions given by the law were paid by the commissioner, the purchaser voluntarily accepting payment, not in money, but in other stamps; and new dealings, of the same character, but separate as to each instance, had, afterwards, upon the same footing and by mutual understanding. On the contrary, the business was conducted upon the footing of a running account. Money was paid on account of stamps furnished, in sums, differing in amount, but not less in any case than five hundred dollars; and stamps were supplied in varying quantities, as ordered, without reference to corresponding and equivalent payments of cash; a bond with satisfactory security, in pursuance of law, having been given and accepted, to secure the Government against loss, in consequence of purchases on credit. The dealing is, undoubtedly, evidence that the appellant was willing to purchase stamps, to be paid for by a credit in account, in lieu of cash for commissions; but it does not prove that he was willing to waive his right to a commission upon the stamps so purchased. And it would be incumbent on the Government, in order to deprive him of his statutory right, not only to show facts from which an agreement to do so might be inferred, but an actual settlement based upon such an understanding. The allegations in the petition, in our opinion, do not constitute such a bar to the recovery sought, and the demurrer interposed should not, therefore, have been sustained.

For this error, the judgment of the Court of Claims is reversed, and the cause remanded for further proceedings in accordance with law; and it is so ordered.

IRR v. XXVIII, May 15, 1882, pp.149-50

PLAYING CARDS

Manufacturers of "playing cards" must affix stamps upon each pack of cards corresponding in price to that at which they are sold by the manufacturer.

Boutwell (1863), Rulings (No. 301)

Playing-cards and perfumery, purchased prior to the act of June 30, 1864, and appropriately stamped under the laws in force at the time of purchase, may be exported without payment of more stamp-duty, but if sold in the United States at this time, must be stamped according to rates of act of June 30.

Boutwell (1865), Rulings (No. 264)

[Special No. 11.]
Relating to the Sale of Playing Cards in the Original Package.
Treasury Department,
Office of Internal Revenue,
Washington, April 5, 1865.

Assessors and Collectors are hereby informed, that, where the manufacturer of Playing Cards shall indicate by a mark upon the outside of the original package in which such cards are sold, that stamps of a certain denomination are affixed to the respective packs enclosed in such package, in the view of this office it will not be consistent with the late act of Congress to require that any penalty shall be imposed upon jobbers, who may sell such cards in the original and unbroken package thus marked by the manufacturer: *Provided,* That the price at which the cards are sold by the jobber is such as is covered by the stamps said to be affixed.

Whenever any such package is broken, and the several packs exposed for sale, it will be the duty of the holder to affix any additional stamps that may be required by the price at which he offers them for sale.

Joseph J. Lewis,
Commissioner.

IRR v.I, April 22, 1865, pp.124-5

Relating to the Sale of Playing Cards in the Original Package.
[Amendatory of Special No. 11 of April 5, 1865. (RECORDER, Vol. I., No. 14.)]
Treasury Department,
Office of Internal Revenue,
Washington, May 29, 1865.

Assessors and Collectors are hereby informed that, where the manufacturer of playing cards shall indicate by a mark upon the outside of the original package in which such cards are sold, that stamps of a certain denomination are affixed to the respective packs enclosed in such package, in the view of this office it will not be consistent with the late act of Congress to require that any penalty shall be imposed upon jobbers who may sell such cards in the original and unbroken package thus marked by the manufacturer.

Whenever such package is broken and the several packs exposed for sale, it will be the duty of the holder to affix any additional stamps that may be required by the price at which he offers them for sale.

Joseph J. Lewis,
Commissioner.

IRR v.I, July 1, 1865, p.203

Concerning Stamp Duties on Playing Cards.
Treasury Department,
Office of Internal Revenue,
Washington, October 3, 1865.

Under schedule C, preceding section 171 of the act of June 30, 1864, as amended by the act of March 3, 1865, the amount of stamp duty required upon each pack of playing cards is made to depend upon the "price per pack" and the question which arises is, *whose* price is the one intended by Congress? Is it sufficient if each pack is stamped according to the price at which it is sold by the manufacturer, or does the law require each subsequent vendor to affix additional stamps whenever the "price per pack" at which *he* sells is advanced beyond eighteen cents, twenty-five cents, fifty cents, &c., as the case may be?

By the act of July 1, 1862, certain stamp duties were imposed upon playing cards. The amount of said duties was based upon the "price per pack." This tax was made payable by the person, persons, firms, companies, or corporations which should *make, prepare, and sell,* the cards, or remove them for consumption or sale, (section 107) and under the provisions of section 109 of said act, every *maker* or *manufacturer* of them who shall sell, send out, remove, or deliver them before the stamp duty thereon had been *fully* paid, to avoid said duty, was made subject to a penalty of one hundred dollars, together with the forfeiture of the cards. The *full* stamp duty thereon was required of the manufacturer or maker.

This tax was imposed upon the *actual maker* or *manufacturer,* and, until section 27 of the act of March 3, 1863, took effect, *upon him only*. The fact that cards and other proprietary articles manufactured after the act imposing stamp duties thereon took effect might be offered for sale *unstamped,* under a pretence that they were manufactured prior to that time, or that they were imported, made further legislation necessary to prevent frauds which might otherwise be practised; and to this end it was enacted in section 27 aforesaid, that any persons who should offer cards or other proprietary articles for sale, whether imported or of foreign or domestic manufacture, should be deemed the manufacturer thereof, and subject to all the duties, liabilities, and penalties imposed by the act of July 1, 1862, in regard to the sale thereof, without the use of the proper stamp or stamps.

But said taxes, liabilities, and penalties under the act of July 1, 1862, were imposed upon the *actual* manufacturer *only*. The tax, therefore, which should have been paid by *him,* was the only one which could lawfully be required of the subsequent vendor of unstamped cards of domestic manufacture.

The act of March 3 made *other persons* subject to *the same* taxes and penalties as the actual manufacturer; but it did not subject them to *other taxes* or *other penalties*.

Congress evidently foresaw that cards and other articles mentioned in schedule C, which were manufactured and sold prior to the passage of the act of July 1, 1862, might be found in the hands of dealers, and inasmuch as the tax upon them was designed to be not a tax upon *sales,* but upon *manufacturers,* to enable the dealer to dispose of that portion of his stock upon which the law had imposed no duty, it was provided that said section 27, making the *dealer* the *manufacturer,* should not take effect until seven months after its passage, to wit, until after the thirtieth day of September, 1863.

No good reason can be assigned why Congress should have made such a provision, if it was the design, under any circumstance, to impose an additional tax upon proprietary articles in the hands of the *dealer* upon which the full amount of tax required of the manufacturer had once been paid.

The stamp duty upon playing cards under the act of July 1, 1862, was, as already stated, based upon the "price per pack." In the act of June 30, 1864, the word "retail" was inserted, and the stamp duty based upon "the *retail* price per pack;" and, under what seems to me to have been the proper construction of said act, the stamp duty upon playing cards was to be determined by "the retail price per pack" in the immediate vicinity of the place of manufacture.

By the act of March 3, 1865, the word "retail" was struck out and the phraseology of the act of 1862 was restored. It must be conceded that Congress had some *purpose* in making a change so palpable, and it seems too evident to admit of any doubt, that the sole object was to change the basis of stamp duty from the "retail" to the *wholesale* price per pack. To require now that cards be restamped as they pass by sale from one dealer to another, and from the retailer to the consumer, whenever and wherever the price charged by the dealer exceeds the price of the manufacturer, would be, in effect, to nullify said amendment; and I am of the opinion, that when the manufacturer of playing cards has affixed stamps appropriate to "the price per pack" at which *he* sold them, the subsequent vendor should not be required to affix any additional stamps thereto, whatever may be the price at which he offers them.

William Orton,
Commissioner.

[Ed. note: This is Decision No. 161.]
IRR v.II, October 28, 1865, p.132

Proposed Revenue Amendments.—The Secretary of the Treasury has received the report of the United States Revenue Commission, on proprietary and other medicines, perfumery, playing cards, etc., as sources of revenue.

• • •

They also recommend that for and upon every pack of cards not exceeding fifty-two in number, irrespective of price or value, a tax of five cents should be enforced.

IRR v.III, March 24, 1866, p.89

PHOTOGRAPHS

All photographs, whether sold at retail or wholesale, require to be stamped at the retail price.

Boutwell (1865), Rulings (No. 204)

Copies of engravings or works of art are not subject to stamp, but to ad valorem duty. Copies of photographs from negatives are subject to stamp duty.

Boutwell (1865), Rulings (No. 243)

Photographs taken from a negative are liable to stamp-duty when the negative was taken from the person himself who is represented. But where a negative is taken from a picture, photographs taken from *that* negative are regarded as copies (sec. 94, act of June 30), subject to six per cent ad valorem (p.61).

Boutwell (1865), Rulings (No. 262)

Treasury Department,
Office of Internal Revenue,
Washington, February 23, 1865.

In reply to yours of the 22nd inst. I have to say that all photographs printed from the original negative as taken from the person or object represented (except paintings and drawings) are properly subject to stamp duty.

Under this ruling photographic views of battle scenes, &c., should properly be stamped, and I know of no reason for exempting stereoscopic pictures, taken as above indicated.

In some cases photographers have been allowed to omit the use of stamps upon pictures, which, if stamped, would thereby be injured or materially lessened in value, *provided* that at the close of each and every month they shall furnish to the Assessor a sworn statement of the number and value of the pictures sold without stamps accompanied by a sufficient number of proprietary stamps, properly cancelled, to cover the amount of duty chargeable upon the pictures.

This course is not strictly that laid down in the law, but if honestly complied with will satisfy the requirements of this office.

Very respectfully,
E. A. Rollins,
Dep. Commissioner.

Messrs. E. & H. T. Anthony & Co.,
501 Broadway, New York.

IRR v.I, March 4, 1865, p.67

Photographs Required Hereafter to Have Stamps Affixed.

Treasury Department,
Office of Internal Revenue,
Washington, May 8, 1865.

Sir: In reply to yours of the 17th ult., in relation to stamping photographs, I have to say, that in October last the Commissioner authorized Fredricks & Co., of New York, to omit the stamps from such pictures as would be materially injured and sale prevented by reason of the affixing of stamp: provided they would make a monthly return to the Assessor, affixing thereto such number of stamps as would have been required, had the pictures been properly stamped. This permission was granted in the expectation that Congress would, in accordance with the recommendation of the Commissioner, take action in the matter; no such action having been taken by that body, the aforesaid permission has been revoked, and photographers will in future be expected to stamp their pictures in accordance with the law.

Very respectfully,
E. A. Rollins,
Deputy Commissioner.

Theophile Papin, Esq.,
U.S. Assessor, St. Louis, Mo.

IRR v.I, May 13, 1865, p.149

Photographs Liable to Stamps.

Treasury Department,
Office of Internal Revenue,
Washington, April 27, 1865.

Sir: In reply to yours of the 6th inst., I have to say: that a number of letters were received by this office from the leading photographers, stating that the pictures known as *"Cartes de Visite"* adhered to each other so closely after being stamped, that it was impossible to separate them without defacing the pictures to an extent which rendered them unsalable.

In view of these circumstances, they were authorized, by this office, to omit the stamp where the affixing would materially injure the picture and prevent its sale; provided that at the end of each month they would make a return under oath to the Assessor of their district of the number and value of the pictures sold without stamps, and affix to such return the number of stamps which would have been required had the pictures been stamped according to law, cancelling the stamps in the presence of the Assessor.

Although the proceeding was not in strict accordance with the law, it was tolerated by this office in view of the alleged hardships of the requirements of the law, until those interested could have an opportunity to apply to Congress for relief.

As Congress failed to make any change in the law in this respect, at its late session, although such action was recommended by this office, I do not feel authorized to give countenance to any continued departure from the literal requirements of the statute.

Very respectfully,
Joseph J. Lewis,
Commissioner.

IRR v.I, May 20, 1865, p.155

Assessor's Office,
U.S. Internal Revenue
Fifteenth District, State of New York,
Troy, May 1, 1865.

Hon. Joseph J. Lewis, *Commissioner:*

Photographers through the country generally, I am credibly informed and believe, have discontinued the use of stamps, claiming that all photographs are "*seriously injured* or defaced thereby," consequently, under the ruling of the department, they omit the stamp. Was the intent of the Commissioner to give the broad construction to said ruling that has been claimed by the artists?

Very respectfully,
P. H. Neher,
Assessor.

[Answer.]

Treasury Department,
Office of Internal Revenue,
Washington, May 3, 1865.

Sir: In reply to yours of the 1st inst., I have to say that the permission given to photographers to omit the use of stamps upon certain pictures has been revoked and hereafter all photographs not otherwise provided for in section 94, must be stamped.

Very respectfully,
E. A. Rollins,
Deputy Commissioner.

To P. H. Neher, *Assessor, Troy, N. Y.*

IRR v.I, May 20, 1865, p.155

Stamping of Photographs.

Much diversity of practice in stamping photographs has hitherto prevailed throughout the country, which it is highly desirable, both for the interests of the revenue, and the satisfaction of photographers, should, if possible, be made uniform.

Section 94 of the Act of June 30, 1864, imposed an *ad valorem* duty on "photographs or any other sun picture, being copies of engravings or works of art, or used for the illustration of books, and on photographs so small in size that stamps cannot be affixed.''

In Schedule C, Section 170, of the same act, a stamp duty of two cents upon each picture of retail price not over twenty-five cents, was imposed on photographs, ambrotypes, daguerreotypes, and other sun pictures, except as above indicated.

It is apparent that the intention of Congress was to subject to a stamp duty all ''life'' pictures, such as cartes de visite, views from nature, &c., except when used for illustrating books, or where the picture was too small for a stamp to be affixed.

The terms of the law are plain and not to be mistaken. For sufficient reasons, however, the Commissioner of Internal Revenue, in the fall of 1864 authorized certain photographers to sell *cartes de visite* without stamp, provided they returned to the Assessor a verified statement each month, of the sales thereof, accompanied by the proper amount of stamps duly cancelled. This proceeding was contrary to law, and revenue officers not being generally apprised of it, great confusion arose. Some photographers affixed stamps as the law required, others sold their pictures without stamps, under permission given as above, and thereby secured undue advantage in the business. The trade was fast drifting under this state of affairs into a systematic disregard of the provisions of law, and the revenue from this source became seriously imperilled.

Recently the Commissioner has revoked an authority to sell such photographs without stamps, (RECORDER, vol. I, p. 155), and directs that the same be hereafter in all cases properly stamped. Section 94, as above cited, having been amended by the act of March, 1865, the clause relating to photographs now reads as follows, the amended words being italicized:

''On photographs or any other sun pictures, being copies of engravings or works of art, *when the same are sold by the producer at wholesale at a price not exceeding ten cents each, or are* used for the illustration of books, and on photographs so small in size that stamps cannot be affixed, a duty of five per centum ad valorem.''

From the law as it now stands, and the rulings of the Commissioner in force, all photographs of ''life'' pictures, including those from the original negative as taken from the person or object represented (except paintings and drawings), are subject to a stamp duty. Photographic views of battle scenes, and stereoscopic pictures thereof, taken from the original negative, it is decided are liable to stamp duty. (RECORDER, vol. I, p. 67.) Photographic copies of paintings and drawings, engravings and works of art, are also liable to stamp duty, unless sold at wholesale by the producer, at prices not over ten cents each, or are used for illustrating books, or are so small that stamps cannot be affixed. In these exceptional cases an ad valorem duty of six per centum accrues on the sales thereof; the additional one per centum to the rate specified in section 94, being imposed by section 5 of the amendatory act.

The use of a life picture for illustrating books does not, it would appear by the amendment, relieve it from stamp duty. Only copies of engravings or works of art so used, can, irrespective of the price at which sold by the producer, be subjected on account of such use to an ad valorem instead of a stamp duty.

It is to be hoped that officers of the revenue will now be enabled to correct the diversity of practice in the premises. Uniformity in the administration of the Internal Revenue Laws is most difficult to attain, it is true, yet it is grossly unjust to conscientious tax payers, nay, a premium is offered for dishonest evasions of the law, if the least effort to obtain it is spared on the part of the Government and its officers.

IRR v.I, June 17, 1865, p.185

Photographs and Other Sun Pictures.

Treasury Department,
Office of Internal Revenue,
Washington, July 26, 1865.

The act of June 30, 1864, as amended by the act of March 3, 1865, imposes a tax on all photographs or other sun pictures, either ad valorem, under the 94th section, or a stamp duty, under schedule C, section 170.

Copies of engravings or works of art, and photographs so small in size that stamps cannot be affixed, are liable to the ad valorem duty. All other sun pictures, including photographs, ambrotypes and daguerreotypes, are liable to stamp duties, varying in value according to the retail price of the pictures.

Copies of engravings or works of art cannot be construed to include *copies of original life pictures*. All such pictures are liable to stamp duty, at whatever price they may be sold, and all copies of engravings or works of art, when the wholesale price exceeds ten cents each, unless used for the illustration of books, are subject to a stamp duty.

From the above principles we deduce the following general rules:

1. Copies of engravings, &c., sold at a price not exceeding ten cents wholesale, 6 per cent ad valorem.
2. Copies of engravings, &c., used for the illustration of books, 6 per cent ad valorem.
3. Pictures so small that stamps cannot be affixed, 6 per cent ad valorem.
4. Copies of engravings, &c., sold at a price exceeding ten cents wholesale, must be stamped when the size will admit.
5. Copies of original life pictures, at whatever price sold, must be stamped when the size will admit.
6. All original life pictures must be stamped when the size will admit.

By the 16th section of the excise law it is enacted that any person who shall offer or *expose* for sale any of the articles named in schedule C, whether the articles so offered or exposed are imported, or are of foreign or domestic manufacture, shall be deemed the manufacturer thereof, and subject to all the duties, liabilities, and penalties imposed by law in regard to the sale of domestic articles without the use of the proper stamp or stamps denoting the duty paid thereon.

It is not believed to have been the intention of the law under the above provision to impose any additional duty, by way of stamps, upon pictures subject to an ad valorem duty, as hereinbefore mentioned. But when pictures are sold without stamps affixed, and it cannot be readily discovered from an inspection of the pictures themselves that they *are* copies of engravings, or works or art, this will be regarded *prima facie* evidence of liability to stamp duty. In all such cases positive evidence of the payment of an ad valorem duty must be given, or the stamps must be affixed.

The coloring or painting of sun pictures on which no duty has been paid, or stamps affixed, will be regarded as a part of the process of manufacture, and the liability to duty will be determined by the price at which such painted or colored pictures are sold.

The painting or coloring of pictures on which an ad valorem duty has been paid, or stamps have been affixed, will subject the same to an ad valorem duty of 5 per cent on the increased value.

By the 167th section of the excise law, in addition to the forfeiture of the picture or pictures, there is imposed a penalty of one hundred dollars on any maker or manufacturer of photographs, &c., who shall sell, *expose for sale,* send out, remove, or *deliver* any of the same, before the duty to which they were liable shall have been fully paid by affixing thereon the proper stamps.

William Orton,
Commissioner

[Ed. note: This is Decision No. 157.]
IRR v.II, August 12, 1865, p.44

Photographic Copies of Works of Art.

Photographic pictures which are merely copies of works of art are exempt from stamp duty whenever they are sold by the producers, at wholesale, at a price not exceeding ten cents each. But if sold at retail, at any price, or sold at wholesale at a price exceeding ten cents each, they are subject to the same stamp duty as originals.

IRR v.II, August 12, 1865, p.45

Stamping of Photographs Sold by the Dozen.

Where a party pays, say three dollars and seventy-five cents for a dozen photographs or sun pictures, the person who sells or delivers the pictures must affix a 3 cent stamp on each. The pretence that the first picture is worth a dollar, and hence requires a five cent stamp, while each of the remaining eleven is worth but twenty-five cents, and consequently requires a two cent stamp, is an evasion of the law, and cannot be tolerated.

August 22, 1865.

IRR v.II, September 2, 1865, p.68

Stereoscopic Views From Nature.

"Stereoscopic views taken as original pictures of mountain scenery, buildings, &c., must be stamped under Schedule 'C' of the law."
To Assessor Lovell, June 30, 1865.

IRR v.II, September 30, 1865

Photographs and Other Sun Pictures.

Copies of engravings or works of art, when the same are sold by the producer at wholesale at a price not exceeding fifteen cents each, or are used for the illustration of books, are exempt. All other photographs and sun pictures are subject to an ad valorem tax of 5 per cent upon the price at which the photographer sells his pictures. The law recognizes no other basis of taxation where the tax does not accrue till after a sale.

A photographer who colors a picture or otherwise ornaments it, thereby increasing its value or increasing the price received for it, will not satisfy the law by returning the price which he would have received for the picture without such coloring or ornamentation. Nothing short of the actual price received by the photographer or artist satisfies the requirements of the law. [Ed. note: from Official Series 2, No. 8, September 8, 1866]

IRR v.IV, September 29, 1866, p.100

APPENDIX.

Official Regulations and Schedules of Stamp Duties.

The Office of Internal Revenue printed a series of official Schedules of Stamp Duties. These were presumably intended primarily for the use of its own employees, but evidently reached a larger audience, since as pointed out by the editor of the *Internal Revenue Record,* "It [specifically, the schedule for 1869] contains much information of great value to all businessmen." It is understood that Collectors and Assessors have been, or are to be, furnished with copies of it for judicious distribution among Notaries Public, Justices of the Peace, Clerks of Courts, Registers, Conveyancers and others who have frequent occasion to use stamps, and especially to Editors, who it is thought will be found willing to publish extracts from it for the good of their readers as well as the public revenue. (*IRR,* v.IX, May 15, 1869, p.153)

We have noted these schedules first in Boutwell (1863; Stamp Duties, No. 3), and as follows in the *Internal Revenue Record:* v.I, January 14, 1865, pp.9-10; v.I, April 29, 1865, pp.132-3; v.IV, August 25, 1866, pp.60-1 (referred to as Series 2, No. 10); v.IV, November 24, 1866, pp.162-6 (Series 2, No. 10); v.V, June 1, 1867, pp.171-5 (Series 3, No. 10); v.IX, May 22, 1869, pp.161-7 (Series 5, No. 10); v.XIV, August 12, 1871, pp.49-55 (Series 6, No. 10); v.XVI, November 2, 1872, p.137 (Supplement to Series 6, No. 10); and v.XIX, January 3, 1874, p.8. We have chosen to reprint here just one official schedule, that of Series 2, No. 10, from the November 24, 1866 *IRR*. Two aspects of this decision deserve comment. As to why the other schedules are not included, they are largely repetitive, and more to the point, with few exceptions the material in all the schedules appears elsewhere in this volume, albeit in slightly different form or format, since the information in the selected Decisions, Rulings, or Correspondence of the Office. This raises the question of why even one official schedule is included here. We chose to do so because we felt it was important to illustrate the primary contemporary means by which specialized information on the documentary and proprietary taxes was disseminated. Equally important, the official schedules contain at least three pieces of information that we found nowhere else, and two appear in the 1866 schedule printed below: one is the sentence prohibiting the use of postage stamps on documents [This appears first in the 1864 schedule (*IRR,* January 14, 1865, p.10), and in all thereafter.]; the other is the passage giving the dates on which collection districts were first established in the South during or after the Civil War, with related instructions regarding the stamping of unstamped instruments. The third such item is an important interpretation of the Act of June 6, 1872, which we found only in the Supplement to Series 6, No. 10, which is reprinted here for that reason. Finally, we include significant regulations which give the earliest statement of the official commission on stamp purchases, and the composition of packages of stamps furnished to Assistant Treasurers and Designated Depositaries.

Regulations in regard to revenue stamps.
Office of Internal Revenue,
January 12, 1863.

Revenue stamps may be ordered from this office in quantities to suit purchasers. Orders should cover remittance of treasury notes, or an original certificate of a United States assistant treasurer, or designated depositary, of a deposit made for the purchase of stamps.

The following commission, *payable in stamps,* will be allowed:

On purchases of $50 or more, 2 per centum.
On purchases of $100 or more, 3 per centum.
On purchases of $500 or more, 4 per centum.
On purchases of $1,000 or more, 5 per centum.

As each stamp expresses upon its face its kind as well as its denomination, it is desirable that every order should refer to kinds as well as denominations. By the third section of the act passed December 25, 1862, every instrument is valid, provided a legal stamp, or stamps, denoting a duty of the amount required, shall have been duly affixed and used thereon. Proprietary stamps, however, cannot be used upon any instrument specified in schedule B.

Stamps of every kind and denomination can be furnished in sufficient quantities; and collectors are hereby required and directed to commence proceedings, under the law, against all persons who shall willfully neglect to use stamps as required.

Special attention is called to the ninety-fifth section of the excise law:

"*And be it further enacted,* That if any person or persons shall make, sign, or issue, or cause to be made, signed, or issued, any instrument, document, or paper of any kind or description whatsoever, without the same being duly stamped for denoting the duty hereby imposed thereon, or without having thereupon an adhesive stamp to denote said duty, such person or persons shall incur a penalty of fifty dollars; and such instrument, document, or paper as aforesaid, shall be deemed valid and of no effect."

Every correspondent is requested to give the State as well as town and county of his residence.

If not otherwise ordered, stamps will be transmitted by mail.

George S. Boutwell,
Commissioner.

Boutwell (1863), Stamp Duties (No. 1)

[Special No. 44]
Revenue Stamps for Sale in Assorted Packages.
Office of Internal Revenue,
Washington, September 11, 1866.

For the better accommodation of the public, Revenue Stamps will be kept by the United States Assistant Treasurers and Designated Depositaries, other than National Banks, and will be delivered in packages of the following denominations and quantities, and at the full commissions allowed by law:

CONTENTS OF PACKAGES.

A.

3 sheets, or		630 stamps,	@	2 cents	$12 60
1	"	170	"	5 cents	8 50
	"	19	"	10 cents	1 90
	"	72	"	25 cents	18 00
	"	20	"	50 cents	10 00
					$51 00

Cash Value, $50.

B.

5 sheets, or		1,050 stamps,	@	2 cents	$21 00
3	"	510	"	5 cents	25 00
1	"	170	"	10 cents	17 00
1	"	102	"	25 cents	25 50
	"	20	"	50 cents	10 00
	"	4	"	$1 00	4 00
					$103 00

Cash Value, $100.

C.

20 sheets, or	4,200	stamps, @	2 cents......	$84 00
10 "	1,700	"	5 cents......	85 00
3 "	510	"	10 cents......	51 00
4 "	408	"	25 cents......	102 00
2 "	170	"	50 cents......	85 00
1 "	90	"	$1 00........	90 00
"	9	"	2 00........	18 00
"	1	"	5 00	5 00
				$520 00

Cash Value, $500.

D.

50 sheets, or	10,500	stamps, @	2 cents.....	$210 00
20 "	3,400	"	5 cents.....	170 00
4 "	680	"	10 cents.....	68 00
8 "	816	"	25 cents.....	204 00
4 "	340	"	50 cents.....	170 00
2 "	180	"	$1 00	180 00
"	14	"	2 00.......	28 00
"	4	"	5 00.......	20 00
				$1,050 00

Cash Value, $1,000.

E.

150 sheets, or	31,500	stamps, @	2 cents....	$630 00
40 "	6,800	"	5 cents....	340 00
"	320	"	25 cents....	80 00
				$1,050 00

Cash Value, $1,000.

IRR v.V, January 12, 1867, p.2

(Series 2, No. 10)

United States Internal Revenue.—Stamp Duties, Schedules B and C.—Law and Regulations Concerning the Purchase and Use of Internal Revenue Stamps.—October 24, 1866.

Schedule of stamp duties on and after August 1, 1866.

	Stamp duty.
Accidental Injuries to persons, tickets or contracts for insurance against	exempt.
Affidavits in suits or legal proceedings	exempt.
Agreement or Contract, other than domestic or inland bills of lading: For every sheet or piece of paper upon which either of the same shall be written	5 cts.
Agreement, renewal of, same stamp as original instrument.	
Appraisement of value or damage, or for any other purpose: For each sheet of paper on which it is written	5 cts.
Assignment of a Lease, same stamp as original and additional stamp upon the value or consideration of transfer, according to the rates of stamps on deeds. (*See Conveyance.*)	
Assignment of Policy of Insurance, same stamp as original instrument. (*See Insurance.*)	
Assignment of Mortgage, same stamp as that required upon a mortgage for the amount remaining unpaid. (*See Mortgage.*)	
Bank Check, draft, or order for any sum of money drawn upon any bank, banker, or trust company, at sight or on demand	2 cts.
When drawn upon any other person or persons, companies or corporations, for any sum exceeding $10, at sight or on demand	2 cts.
Bill of Exchange, (Inland) draft, or order for the payment of any sum of money not exceeding $100, otherwise than at sight or on demand, or any promissory note, or any memorandum, check, receipt, or other written or printed evidence of an amount of money to be paid on demand or at a time designated: For a sum not exceeding $100	5 cts.
And for every additional $100, or fractional part thereof in excess of $100	5 cts.

	Stamp duty.
Bill of Exchange (Foreign) or letter of credit, drawn in, but payable out of, the United States: If drawn singly, same rates of duty as inland bills of exchange or promissory notes.	
If drawn in sets of three or more, for every bill of each set, where the sum made payable shall not exceed $100, or the equivalent thereof in any foreign currency	2 cts.
And for every additional $100, or fractional part thereof in excess of $100	2 cts.
Bill of Lading or receipt (other than charter party) for any goods, merchandise, or effects to be exported from a port or place in the United States to any foreign port or place	10 cts.
Bill of Lading, to any port in British North America	exempt.
Bill of Lading, domestic or inland	exempt.
Bill of Sale by which any ship or vessel, or any part thereof, shall be conveyed to or vested in any other person or persons: When the consideration shall not exceed $500	50 cts.
Exceeding $500, and not exceeding $1,000	$1 00
Exceeding $1,000, for every additional amount of $500, or fractional part thereof	50 cts.
Bond for indemnifying any person for the payment of any sum of money: When the money ultimately recoverable thereupon is $1,000 or less	50 cts.
When in excess of $1,000, for each $1,000 or fraction	50 cts.
Bond for due execution or performance of duties of office	$1 00
Bond, personal, for security for the payment of money. (See *Mortgage.*)	
Bond of any description, other than such as may be required in legal proceedings, or used in connection with mortgage deeds, and not otherwise charged in this Schedule	25 cts.
Broker's Notes. (See *Contract.*)	
Certificates of Measurement or weight of animals, wood, coal, or hay	exempt.
Certificates of Measurement of other articles	5 cts.
Certificates of Stock in any incorporated company	25 cts.
Certificates of Profits, or any certificate or memorandum showing an interest in the property or accumulations of any incorporated company: If for a sum not less than $10 and not exceeding $50	10 cts.
Exceeding $50 and not exceeding $1,000	25 cts.
Exceeding $1,000, for every additional $1,000, or fractional part thereof	25 cts.
Certificate. Any certificate of damage or otherwise, and all other certificates or documents issued by any port warden, marine surveyor, or other person acting as such	25 cts.
Certificate of Deposit of any sum of money in any bank or trust company, or with any banker or person acting as such: If for a sum not exceeding $100	2 cts.
For a sum exceeding $100	5 cts.
Certificate of any other description than those specified	5 cts.
Charter, renewal of, same stamp as on original instrument.	
Charter Party for the charter of any ship or vessel, or steamer, or any letter, memorandum, or other writing relating to the charter, or any renewal or transfer thereof: If the registered tonnage of such ship, or vessel, or steamer, does not exceed 150 tons	$1 00
Exceeding 150 tons, and not exceeding 300 tons	$3 00
Exceeding 300 tons, and not exceeding 600 tons	$5 00
Exceeding 600 tons	$10 00
Check. Bank check	2 cts.
Contract. Broker's note, or memorandum of sale of any goods or merchandise, exchange, real estate, or property of any kind or description issued by brokers or persons acting as such: For each note or memorandum of sale	10 cts.
Bill or memorandum of the sale or contract for the sale of stocks, bonds, gold or silver bullion, coin, promissory notes, or other securities made by brokers, banks, or bankers, either for the benefit of others or in their own account: For each hundred dollars, or fractional part thereof, of the amount of such sale or contract	1 ct.
Bill or memorandum of the sale or contract for the sale of stocks, bonds, gold or silver bullion, coin, promissory notes, or other securities, not his or their own property, made by any person, firm, or company not paying a special tax as broker, bank, or	

Stamp duty.

banker: For each hundred dollars, or fractional part thereof, of the amount of such sale or contract .... 5 cts.

Contract. (See *Agreement*.)

Contract, renewal of, same stamp as original instrument.

Conveyance, deed, instrument, or writing, whereby any lands, tenements, or other realty sold shall be granted, assigned, transferred, or otherwise conveyed to or vested in the purchaser or purchasers, or any other person or persons, by his, her, or their direction, when the consideration or value does not exceed $500 .... 50 cts.

When the consideration exceeds $500, and does not exceed $1,000 .... $1 00

And for every additional $500, or fractional part thereof, in excess of $1,000 .... 50 cts.

Conveyance. The acknowledgement of a deed, or proof by a witness .... exempt.

Conveyance. Certificate of record of a deed .... exempt.

Credit, Letter of. Same as Foreign Bill of Exchange.

Custom-house Entry. (See *Entry*.)

Custom-house Withdrawals. (See *Entry*.)

Deed. (See *Conveyance–Trust Deed*.)

Draft. Same as Inland Bill of Exchange.

Endorsement of any negotiable instrument .... exempt.

Entry of any goods, wares, or merchandise at any custom house, either for consumption or warehousing: Not exceeding $100 in value .... 25 cts.

Exceeding $100, and not exceeding $500 in value .... 25 cts.

Exceeding $500 in value .... 50 cts.

Entry for the withdrawal of any goods or merchandise from bonded warehouse .... 50 cts.

Gauger's Returns .... exempt.

Indorsements upon a stamped obligation in acknowledgement of its fulfillment .... exempt.

Insurance (Life) policy: When the amount insured shall not exceed $1,000 .... 25 cts.

Exceeding $1,000, and not exceeding $5,000 .... 50 cts.

Exceeding $5,000 .... $1 00

Insurance (Marine, Inland, and Fire) policies, or renewals of the same: If the premium does not exceed $10 .... 10 cts.

Exceeding $10, and not exceeding $50 .... 25 cts.

Exceeding $50 .... 50 cts.

Insurance contracts or tickets against accidental injuries to persons .... exempt.

Lease, agreement, memorandum or contract for the hire, use, or rent of any land, tenement, or portion thereof: Where the rent or rental value is $300 per annum or less 50 cts.

Where the rent or rental value exceeds the sum of $300 per annum, for each additional $200, or fractional part thereof in excess of $300 .... 50 cts.

Legal Documents:

Writ, or other original process by which any suit is commenced in any court of record, either of law or equity .... 50 cts.

Where the amount claimed in a writ, issued by a court not of record, is $100 or over 50 cts.

Upon every confession of judgment, or cognovit, for $100 or over (except in those cases where the tax for the writ of a commencement of suit has been paid) .... 50 cts.

Writs or other process on appeals from justice courts or other courts of inferior jurisdiction to a court of record .... 50 cts.

Warrant of distress, when the amount of rent claimed does not exceed $100 .... 25 cts.

When the amount claimed exceeds $100 .... 50 cts.

Letters of Administration. (See *Probate of Will*.)

Letters of Credit. Same as Bill of Exchange, (Foreign).

Manifest for custom-house entry or clearance of the cargo of any ship, vessel, or steamer, for a foreign port:

If the registered tonnage of such ship, vessel, or steamer does not exceed 300 tons . $1 00

Exceeding 300 tons, and not exceeding 600 tons $3 00

Exceeding 600 tons $5 00

[These provisions do not apply to vessels or steamboats plying between ports of the United States and British North America.]

	Stamp duty.
Measurer's Returns	exempt.
Memorandum of Sale, or Broker's Note. (See *Contract.*)	
Mortgage of Lands, estate, or property, real or personal, heritable, or moveable whatsoever, a trust deed in the nature of a mortgage, or any personal bond given as security for the payment of any definite or certain sum of money: Exceeding $100, and not exceeding $500	50 cts.
Exceeding $500, and not exceeding $1,000	$1 00
And for every additional $500, or fractional part thereof in excess of $1,000	50 cts.
Order for payment of money, if the amount if $10 or over	2 cts.
Passage Ticket on any vessel from a port in the United States to a foreign port, not exceeding $35	50 cts.
Exceeding $35, and not exceeding $50	$1 00
And for every additional $50, or fractional part thereof in excess of $50	$1 00
Passage tickets to ports in British North America	exempt.
Pawner's Checks	5 cts.
Power of Attorney, for the sale or transfer of any stock, bonds, or scrip, or for the collection of any dividends or interest thereon	25 cts.
Power of Attorney or proxy for voting at any election for officers of any incorporated company or society, except religious, charitable, or literary societies, or public cemeteries	10 cts.
Power of Attorney to receive and collect rent	25 cts.
Power of Attorney to sell and convey real estate, or to rent or lease the same	$1 00
Power of Attorney for any other purpose	50 cts.
Probate of Will, or letters of administration: Where the estate and effects for or in respect of which such probate or letters of administration applied for shall be sworn or declared not to exceed the value of $2,000	$1 00
Exceeding $2,000, for every additional $1,000, or fractional part thereof, in excess of $2,000	50 cts.
Promissory Note. (See *Bill of Exchange,* Inland).	
Deposit note to mutual insurance companies, when policy is subject to duty	exempt.
Renewal of a note, subject to same duty as an original note.	
Protest of note, bill of exchange, acceptance, check, or draft, or any marine protest	25 cts.
Quit Claim Deed to be stamped as a conveyance, except when given as a release of a mortgage by the mortgagee to the mortgagor, in which case it is exempt; but if it contains covenants may be subject as an agreement or contract.	
Receipt for satisfaction of any mortgage or judgment or decree of any court	exempt.
Receipts for any sum of money or debt due, or for a draft or other instrument given for the payment of money: Exceeding $20, not being for satisfaction of any mortgage or judgment or decree of court	2 cts.
(See *Indorsement.*)	
Receipts for the delivery of property	exempt.
Renewal of Agreement, contract or charter, by letter or otherwise, same stamp as original instrument.	
Sheriff's Return on writ, or other process	exempt.
Trust Deed made to secure a debt, to be stamped as a mortgage.	
Warehouse Receipts	exempt.
Warrant of Attorney accompanying a bond or note, if the bond or note is stamped	exempt.
Weigher's Returns	exempt.
Writs or other process in any criminal or other suits commenced by the United States or any State	exempt.
Official documents, instruments, and papers issued by officers of the United States Government	exempt.
Official instruments, documents, and papers issued by the officers of any State, county, town, or other municipal corporation, in the exercise of functions strictly belonging to them in their ordinary governmental or municipal capacity	exempt.

CANCELLATION.

In all cases where an *adhesive* stamp is used for denoting the stamp duty upon an instrument, the person using or affixing the same must write or imprint thereupon *in ink* the initials of his name, and the date on which the same is attached or used. When stamps are printed upon checks, &c., so that in filling up the instrument, the face of the stamp is and must necessarily be written across, no other cancellation will be required.

All cancellation must be distinct and legible, and except in the case of proprietary stamps from private dies, no method of cancellation which differs from that above described will be recognized by this office as legal and sufficient.

STAMPING OF INSTRUMENTS BY COLLECTORS PRIOR TO THE ISSUING OF THE SAME, AND BY COLLECTORS AND PARTIES INTERESTED AFTER THEY HAVE BEEN ISSUED.

Any person having an instrument about to be issued, may present it to the collector, who, under the authority conferred upon him by section 162, will so stamp it as to place the sufficiency of that particular instrument beyond all question so far as stamp duties are concerned. The provisions of the section can in no case be applied to an instrument *after* it has been issued or used. The collector should decline to stamp or impress an instrument, under this section, until the stamp duty with which *he* thinks it chargeable has been paid. In cases of reasonable doubt he is recommended to obtain the opinion of this office before affixing his stamp, unless immediate action is essential to the interests of the parties concerned.

Any person who has made, signed, or issued an instrument subject to stamp duty unstamped or insufficiently stamped, or any person having an interest therein, may present to it the collector of the revenue of the proper district, who, upon payment of the price of the proper stamp required by law, a penalty of fifty dollars, and, where the whole amount of the tax denoted by stamp required exceeds fifty dollars, on payment also of interest at the rate of six per centum from the day on which such stamp ought to have been affixed, is required by law to affix the stamp and to note upon the margin of the instrument the date of his so doing, and the fact that such penalty has been paid. This duty is obligatory upon the collector and he has no legal right to refuse to perform it.

When there is a difference of opinion respecting the stamp proper to be affixed, the collector should affix such a one as the applicant prefers: the applicant takes the risk of the validity of his instrument. In such cases, however, it is advisable to refer the question to this office.

When an instrument is presented to a collector to be stamped, under the provisions of section 158, he is authorized to remit the penalty if it shall be proven to his satisfaction that such instrument was issued without the necessary stamp by reason of accident, mistake, inadvertence, or urgent necessity, and without any willful design to defraud the United States of the duty, or to evade or delay the payment thereof; *provided* such instrument is presented to him for that purpose, and the stamp tax chargeable thereon is paid, within twelve calendar months after the first day of August, 1866, or within twelve calendar months after the making or issuing thereof.

An instrument stamped by the collector in conformity with the foregoing instructions is as valid to all intents and purposes (except as against rights acquired in good faith before such stamping and the recording of the instrument, if a record be required) as if properly stamped when made and issued.

An instrument issued unstamped at a time when, and in a place where, no collection district was established, may be stamped by the party who issued it, or by any party having an interest therein, at any time *prior to January 1st,* 1867, and the legal effect of the stamp thus affixed will be the same as though affixed by the collector.

When the originals are lost the necessary stamps may be affixed to copies in all cases which fall under section 158 or 162.

The following table is designed to show the date of the first establishment of collection districts in those portions of the country where the foregoing provision is principally applicable.

West Virginia—October 10, 1862—Counties of Brooke, Hancock, Ohio, Marshall, Witzell, Lewis, Pleasants, Tyler, Doddridge, Harrison, Ritchie, Wirt, Gilmer, Calhoun, Roane, Wood, Monongalia, Preston, Taylor, Tucker, Barbour, Marion, Upshur, Randolph, Webster, Jackson, Mason, Putnam, Braxton, Clay, Kanawha, Cabell.

October 16, 1862—Counties of Hampshire, Hardy, Morgan, Berkeley, Jefferson.

April 27, 1865—Counties of Pocahontas, Pendleton, Nicholas, Greenbrier, Monroe, Mercer, McDowell, Wyoming, Raleigh, Fayette, Boone, Wayne, Logan.

Virginia—October 16, 1862—Counties of Frederick, Shenandoah, Clark, Warren, Loudon, Fauquier, Fairfax, Prince William, Alexandria, Westmoreland, Richmond, Northumberland, Lancaster, Middlesex, Essex, Matthews, King and Queen, Gloucester, New Kent, York, James City, Warwick, Elizabeth City, Accomac, Northampton, Norfolk, Princess Anne, Nansemond, and Isle of Wight, and the cities of Norfolk and Williamsburg.

May 3, 1865—Remainder of the State.

North Carolina—May 10, 1865.

South Carolina—May 30, 1865.

Georgia—May 30, 1865.

Florida—May 4, 1865.

Alabama—May 16, 1865.

Mississippi—June 2, 1865.

Louisiana—February 16, 1863.

Tennessee—February 7, 1863.

Arkansas—March 1, 1865.

Texas—June 5, 1865.

Each collector will keep a record of all instruments stamped or impressed by him under the provisions of sections 158 and 162, in which must be given the names of the parties to each instrument, the date of its execution, and a sufficient description of its nature to show the reasons for impressing or affixing the particular stamp. A certified copy of this record will be transmitted to this office at the close of each month during which any entry is made. If, however, during any month the only instruments stamped or impressed have first been submitted to this office for instructions, the transmission of such copy may be deferred until a subsequent month.

The following is a suitable form for such record, and for the sake of uniformity should be adopted by all collectors:

No.	Names of parties.	Date of instrument.	Description of instrument.	When stamped.	How stamped.	Penalty remitted or amount collected

The whole amount of penalties paid to collectors for validating unstamped instruments should be returned on Form 58, with other unassessed penalties, and the money should be deposited to the credit of the Treasury of the United States with other collections.

That part of the act of July 1, 1862, which relates to stamp duties upon certain instruments therein specified, took effect October 1, 1862. The stamp laws have been amended and changed from time to time since that date, viz: by the amendatory act of March 3, 1863, which took effect upon its passage; by the act of June 30, 1864, which, so far as pertains to stamp duties upon instruments took effect [August] 1, 1864; by the amendatory act of March 3, 1865, which took effect upon its passage, and by the amendatory act of July 13, 1866, which, so far as regards such duties, took effect August 1, 1866. Instruments should be stamped according to requirements of the law in force at the time they were made, signed, or issued, and collectors and others, when affixing stamps to instruments which were issued unstamped, should bear this fact strictly in mind.

A person who holds an unstamped conveyance founded upon a "confederate currency" consideration will be allowed to affix such stamps thereto as he may think sufficient, and no prosecution will be instituted by direction of this office for the recovery of a penalty for failure to stamp it according to the nominal *amount* of such consideration. If the parties interested elect to stamp it according to the actual *value* of the consideration in United States currency at the date of delivery, they will be allowed to do so, taking their own risk of the sufficiency of the stamp.

The validity of a deed is a question for the courts. It is one of importance to the parties, but not to this office, any farther than the insufficiency of the stamp may affect the revenue.

The foregoing is applicable to other instruments as well as to deeds.

PENALTIES.

A penalty of fifty dollars is imposed upon every person who makes, signs, or issues, or who causes to be made, signed, or issued, any paper of any kind or description whatever, or who accepts, negotiates, or pays, or causes to be accepted, negotiated, or paid, any bill of exchange, draft, or order, or promissory note, for the payment of money, without the same being duly stamped, or having thereupon an adhesive stamp for denoting the tax chargeable thereon, cancelled in the manner required by law, with intent to evade the provisions of the revenue act.

A penalty of two hundred dollars is imposed upon every person who pays, negotiates, or offers in payment, or receives or takes in payment, any bill of exchange or order for the payment of any sum of money, drawn or purporting to be drawn in a foreign country, but payable in the United States, until the proper stamp has been affixed thereto.

A penalty of fifty dollars is imposed upon every person who fraudulently makes use of an adhesive stamp to denote the duty required by the revenue act, without effectually cancelling and obliterating the same in the manner required by law.

It is not lawful to record any instrument, document, or paper required by law to be stamped, or any copy thereof, unless a stamp or stamps of the proper amount have been affixed and cancelled in the manner provided by law; and such instrument or copy and the record thereof are utterly null and void, and cannot be used or admitted as evidence in any court until the defect has been cured as provided in section 158.

All willful violations of the law should be reported to the United States district attorney within and for the district where they are committed.

GENERAL REMARKS.

Revenue stamps may be used indiscriminately upon any of the matters or things enumerated in Schedule B, except proprietary and playing card stamps, for which a special use has been provided.

Postage stamps cannot be used in payment of the duty chargeable on instruments.

It is the duty of the maker of an instrument to affix the stamp thereto and to cancel the same in the manner required by law. Proper cancellation is essential.

Suits are commenced in many States by other process than writ, viz: summons, warrant, publication, petition, &c., in which cases these, as the original processes, severally require stamps.

The jurat of an affidavit, taken before a justice of the peace, notary public, or other officer duly authorized to take affidavits, is held to be a certificate, and subject to a stamp duty of five cents, except when taken in suits or legal proceedings.

Certificates of Loan in which there shall appear any written or printed evidence of an amount of money to be paid on demand, or at a time designated, are subject to stamp duty as "Promissory Notes."

When two or more persons join in the execution of an instrument, the stamp to which the instrument is liable under the law may be affixed and cancelled by either of them; and "when more than one signature is affixed to the same paper, one or more stamps may be affixed thereto, representing the whole amount of the stamp required for such signatures."

No stamp is required on any warrant of attorney accompanying a bond or note, when such bond or note has affixed thereto the stamp or stamps denoting the duty required; and, whenever any bond or note is secured by mortgage, but one stamp duty is required on such papers—such stamp duty being the highest rate required for such instruments, or either of them. In such case a note or memorandum of the value or denomination of the stamp affixed should be made upon the margin or in the acknowledgement of the instrument which is not stamped.

Particular attention is called to the change in section 154, by striking out the words "or used;" the exemption thereunder is thus restricted to documents, &c., *issued* by the officers therein named. Also to the changes in sections 152 and 158, by inserting the words "and cancelled in the manner required by law."

The acceptor or acceptors of any bill of exchange, or order for the payment of any sum of money drawn or purporting to be drawn in any foreign country but payable in the United States, must, before paying or accepting the same, place thereupon a stamp indicating the duty.

It is only upon conveyances of realty *sold* that conveyance stamps are necessary. A deed of real estate made without valuable consideration need not be stamped as a conveyance, but if it contains covenants, such, for instance, as a covenant to warrant and defend the title, it should be stamped as an agreement or contract.

When a deed purporting to be a conveyance of realty sold, and stamped accordingly, is inoperative, a deed of confirmation, made simply to cure the defect, requires no stamp. In such case, the second deed should contain a recital of the facts, and should show the reasons for its execution.

A conveyance of realty sold subject to a mortgage should be stamped according to the consideration, or the value of the property *unencumbered*. The consideration in such case is to be found by adding the amount paid for the equity of redemption to the mortgage debt. The fact that one part of the consideration is paid to the mortgagor and the other part to the mortgagee does not change the liability of the conveyance.

A receipt for a sum of money exceeding twenty dollars and not being for satisfaction of any mortgage, or judgment or decree of court, is subject to a stamp duty of two cents; but no stamp is necessary upon a receipt for a *package* of money as distinguished from a receipt for a specified sum. If, however the amount contained in the package is named in the receipt and exceeds the sum of twenty dollars, a stamp should be used.

A mere *copy* of an instrument is not subject to stamp duty unless it is a certified one, in which case a five-cent stamp should be affixed to the certificate of the person attesting it; but when an instrument is executed and issued in duplicate, triplicate, &c., as in the case of a lease of two or more parts, each part has the same legal effect as the other, and each should be stamped as an original.

Written or printed assignments of agreements, bonds, notes not negotiable, and of all other instruments the assignments of which are not particularly specified in the foregoing schedule, should be stamped as agreements.

When, as is generally the case, the caption to a deposition contains other certificates in addition to the jurat to the affidavit of the deponent, such as a certificate that the parties were or were not notified, that they did or did not object, &c., it is subject to a stamp duty of five cents.

When an attested copy of a writ or other process is used by a sheriff or other person in making personal service, or in attaching property, a five-cent stamp should be affixed to the certificate of attestation.

The stamp duty upon the probate of a will, or upon letters or administration, is based upon the sworn or declared value of all the estate and effects, real, personal, and mixed, undiminished by the debts of the estate for or in respect of which such probate of letters are applied for.

When the property belonging to the estate of a person deceased lies under different jurisdictions and it becomes necessary to take out letters in two or more places, the letters should be stamped according to the value of all the property, real, personal, and mixed, for or in respect of which the particular letters in each case are issued.

SCHEDULE OF STAMP DUTIES UPON ARTICLES IN SCHEDULE C, AND IN THE AMENDMENTS THERETO.

	Stamp duty.
Proprietary Medicines and Preparations.—For and upon every packet, box, bottle, pot, phial, or other enclosure, containing any pills, powders, tinctures, troches, lozenges, sirups, cordials, bitters, anodynes, tonics, plasters, liniments, salves, ointments, pastes, drops, waters, essences, spirits, oils, or other medicinal preparations or compositions whatsoever, sold, offered for sale, or removed for consumption and sale, by any person or persons whatever, where such packet, box, &c., with its contents, does not exceed, at retail price or value, the sum of twenty-five cents	1 cent.
Exceeding twenty-five and not exceeding fifty cents	2 cts.
Exceeding fifty and not exceeding seventy-five cents	3 cts.
Exceeding seventy-five cents and not exceeding one dollar	4 cts.
Exceeding one dollar, for every additional fifty cents, or fractional part thereof in excess of one dollar	2 cts.
Officinal preparations, and medicines mixed or compounded specially for any person according to the written recipe or prescription of any physician or surgeon	exempt.

	Stamp duty.
Perfumery and Cosmetics.—For and upon every packet, box, bottle, pot, phial, or other enclosure, containing any essence, extract, toilet water, cosmetic, hair oil, pomade, hair dressing, hair restorative, hair dye, tooth-wash, dentifrice, tooth-paste, aromatic cachous, or any similar articles, by whatsoever name the same heretofore have been, now are, or may hereafter be called, known, or distinguished, used or applied, or to be used or applied as perfumes or applications to the hair, mouth, or skin, sold, offered for sale, or removed for consumption and sale, the same rates per package, &c., as for medicines and preparations.	
Friction Matches.—For and upon every parcel or package of 100 or less	1 cent.
More than 100 and not more than 200	2 cts.
For every additional 100, or fractional part thereof	1 cent.
Wax Tapers, double the rates for friction matches.	
Cigar Lights, made in part of wood, wax, glass, paper or other materials, in parcels or packages containing twenty-five lights or less in each parcel or package	1 cent.
When in parcels or packages containing more than twenty-five and not more than fifty lights	2 cts.
For every additional twenty-five lights or fractional part of that number, one cent additional.	
Playing Cards.—For and upon every pack not exceeding fifty-two cards in number, irrespective of price or value	5 cts.
Canned Meats, &c.—For and upon every can, bottle, or other single package containing meats, fish, shell-fish, fruits, vegetables, sauces, sirups, prepared mustard, jams, or jellies, contained therein and packed or sealed, made, prepared, and sold, or offered for sale, or removed for consumption in the United States, on or after the first day of October, 1866, when such can, bottle, or other single package with its contents shall not exceed two pounds in weight	1 cent.
For every additional pound or fractional part thereof	1 cent.

Cigar lights and playing cards in the hands of manufacturers and dealers should be stamped according to the rates fixed by the law now in force. The fact that they were manufactured prior to August 1, 1866, and are stamped in accordance with the law in force at the time of manufacture, does not relieve them from payment of the increased rates by affixing additional stamps.

No stamp tax is imposed upon any uncompounded medicinal drug or chemical, nor upon any medicine compounded according to the United States or other national Pharmacopoeia, or of which the full and proper formula is published in any of the dispensatories now or hitherto in common use among physicians or apothecaries, or in any pharmaceutical journal now issued by any incorporated college of pharmacy, *unless* sold or offered for sale or advertised under some other name, form, or guise than that under which they are severally denominated and laid down in such pharmacopoeias, dispensatories, or journals.

No stamp tax is imposed upon medicines sold to or for the use of any person, which may be mixed and compounded for said person according to the written recipe or prescription of a physician or surgeon. But all medicinal articles whether simple or compounded by any rule, authority, or formula, published or unpublished, which are put up in a style or manner similar to that of patent or proprietary medicines in general, or advertised in newspapers or by public hand-bills, for popular sale and use, as having any special proprietary claim to merit, or to any peculiar advantage in mode of preparation, quality, use, or effect, whether such claim be real or pretended, are liable to the tax.

Stamps appropriated to denote the duty charged upon articles named in Schedule C, and in the amendments thereto, cannot be used for any other purpose; nor can stamps appropriated to denote the duty upon instruments be used in payment of the duties upon articles enumerated in this Schedule.

When proprietary stamps from a private die are used, if they are so affixed to the boxes, bottles, or packages, that, in opening the same, or in using the contents thereof, they shall and must be unavoidably and effectually destroyed, no cancellation is necessary; but if they cannot be so affixed, they should be cancelled in the ordinary manner by writing or imprinting thereon the initials and date. When general proprietary stamps are used, they must be cancelled by writing or imprinting thereon the date and the initials of the part using or affixing them.

When proprietary medicines and preparations, perfumery, and cosmetics are stamped according to their retail price or value in the immediate vicinity of the place of manufacture, no additional stamps are necessary upon them, whatever may be the price at which they are offered.

Any person who offers or exposes for sale any of the articles named in Schedule C, or in any of the amendments thereto, whether they are imported or of foreign or domestic manufacture, is to be deemed the manufacturer thereof, and subject to all the duties, liabilities, and penalties imposed by law in regard to the sale of domestic articles without the use of the proper stamp or stamps for denoting the tax paid thereon. The stamp tax upon such articles imported or of foreign manufacture, is in addition to the import duties, but when such imported articles, except playing cards, lucifer or friction matches, cigar lights, and wax tapers, are sold in the original or unbroken packages in which the bottles or enclosures were packed by the manufacturer, no penalty is incurred for want of the proper stamps. When the packages are opened stamps should be affixed.

REGULATIONS FOR THE PURCHASE OF STAMPS.

Revenue stamps may be ordered from this office in amounts of not less than fifty dollars. Purchasers desiring smaller amounts should make application to a collector of internal revenue, or deputy collector, assessor, assistant treasurer of the United States, postmaster, or other dealer in stamps. Payments to this office should be made in the form of a *duplicate* certificate of a United States assistant treasurer or designated depositary of a deposit made on account of stamps. Revenue stamps may likewise be obtained of any national bank which is a designated depositary at the rates of commission at which they are furnished from this office. They will also be deposited with the assistant treasurers and designated depositaries other than national banks.

GENERAL STAMPS.

The following commission, *payable in stamps,* will be allowed in purchases of general stamps, Schedule B:

On purchases of $50 or more, 2 per centum.

On purchases of $100 or more, 3 per centum.

On purchases of $500 or more, 4 per centum.

On purchases of $1,000 or more, 5 per centum.

By the 153d section of the excise law, all stamps denoting duties under Schedule B may be used indiscriminately.

If any revenue stamps for which the owner may have no use are returned to this office in good order and free of expense, others will be given in exchange, at a discount of one per cent. Stamps that have been improperly or unnecessarily used and cancelled, when returned to this office for exchange must be attached to the instruments on which they were used, and accompanied by an affidavit setting forth the facts, when other stamps will be given for them, at a discount of one per cent. The papers to which the stamps are affixed will be retained by the office. Stamps spoiled in transportation, or rendered useless by any modifications of the law, will be exchanged free of charge. When the affidavit is made before a person who has no official seal, his authority to administer oaths generally should be certified to by the clerk of a court of record under the seal of the court.

Where the facilities for procuring and distributing stamps are deemed insufficient in the Southern States, the Commissioner of Internal Revenue will, on application, furnish to a collector or assessor, assistant treasurer, designated depositary, or postmaster of the United States, a suitable quantity for the supply of the proper district, and will allow the highest rate of commissions allowed by law to any purchaser of common stamps for cash. Such stamps will be furnished under section 170 of the excise law; and the officer applying to be furnished with such stamps will give bond with three sufficient sureties, conditioned for the faithful return, whenever so required, of all quantities or amounts undisposed of, and for the payment, monthly or otherwise, according to instructions, for all quantities and amounts sold or not reported as remaining on hand. No bond will be accepted for a less sum than five hundred dollars and no more agencies will be established in the northern States.

Persons to whom stamps shall be furnished under this section will be expected to conform to the following rules:

Agents for the sale of stamps will make return under oath to this office on Form 55, on the first day of each month, of the amount of stamps sold during the preceding month, and of the amount actually on hand and unsold.

Each collector shall supply his deputies with adhesive stamps, and sell them to other parties within his district who make application therefor, allowing the same commission as specified above.

The collector may require such security from his deputies as he sees fit for the stamps placed in their hands, as he alone is responsible, and is to make returns and payment for them to this office.

Orders may be made from time to time for such stamps as are desired, in no case to exceed three-fourths of the penal sum designated in the bond.

Every agent will be charged upon the books of this office with the stamps furnished him, and credited with the amount of each remittance for the sale of stamps, and five per cent commission on the same.

STAMPED PAPER.

An arrangement has been made with the American Phototype Company, of New York, to print Internal Revenue stamps upon bank checks and other instruments which may be furnished them by various parties for that purpose. Persons ordering will send to this office, as heretofore, the duplicate certificate of deposit in some designated depositary, stating what kind of stamps they desire; an order then will be sent to the phototype company for the amount, adding the same commission as upon general stamps. The price which the company shall charge to the public for printing such stamps is to be such as may be agreed upon between themselves and the parties ordering the same; but is not to exceed one cent for each impression containing not more than six stamps, excepting clearing house receipts and other documents which ordinarily contain more than six stamps.

A contract has also been made with Messrs. Butler & Carpenter, of Philadelphia, to furnish similar stamps, to be printed on bank checks and other instruments, from steel plates. The extra expense in the latter case is to be arranged between Butler & Carpenter and the purchasers, subject to the decision of the Commissioner of Internal Revenue in case of dissatisfaction with the rates charged. The documents to be stamped should be furnished in *sheets,* as the stamps could not be conveniently printed in a bound book.

All stamps will hereafter be forwarded by express, unless ordered by mail, at the expense of the person ordering the same, under a contract with the Adams Express Company, at the following rates, viz.: Between any two points in the territory of the Adams Express Company, and reached by it, twenty-five (25) cents per one thousand dollars; between any two points in the territory of the Southern Express Company, except to points within the States of Arkansas and Texas accessible as aforesaid, thirty-five (35) cents per one thousand dollars, (it being understood that the territory of the Southern Express Company includes the States of North and South Carolina, Georgia, Alabama, Mississippi, Louisiana, Texas, Arkansas, Tennessee, and that part of the State of Virginia lying south of Richmond and west of Lynchburg); between any two points in the State of Texas or in the State of Arkansas, or between any two points severally in those two States respectively, reached by the lines of the Southern Express company in manner aforesaid, fifty (50) cents per one thousand dollars; between any two points in the territory of another Express company than the Adams and the Southern Express Companies, reached as aforesaid, thirty-five (35) cents per one thousand dollars; between any two points, one of which is in the territory of one express company and the other within the territory of another express company, reached as aforesaid, excluding herefrom the States of Texas and Arkansas, sixty (60) cents per one thousand dollars; between any two points, one of which is in the State of Texas or Arkansas and the other in any of the other States, eight-five (85) cents per one thousand dollars. The above amounts in all cases to be computed on the *face value* of the stamps; and any fractional part of one thousand dollars shall be paid for as one thousand dollars.

PROPRIETARY STAMPS—SCHEDULE C.

Any proprietor of any article named in Schedule C may furnish a design for a stamp, which, if approved, will be engraved by the government engravers at the cost of the proprietor.

In such case, the proprietor will be entitled to the commission specified in the 161st section of the excise law, viz: On amounts purchased at one time of not less than fifty nor more than five hundred dollars, five per centum; on amounts over five hundred dollars, ten per centum.

If the designs do not exceed in superficial area 13-16 of an inch for the denomination of one and two cent stamps, or 63-64 of an inch for the denomination of three and four-cent stamps, these being the sizes established by the office for the above specified denominations, there will be no additional charge to purchasers. If, however, proprietors desire to increase the size of the stamps for the denominations above mentioned, then an additional charge will be made for the additional cost of paper and printing. This additional charge will be ten cents per thousand for stamps of $3^{1}/_{8}$ inches superficial area, and in the same proportion for other sizes.

All dies and plates will be retained by, and be under the exclusive control of the government.

The general stamp must be cancelled by writing, stamping, or printing thereon the initials of the proprietor of the stamped article, and the date of cancelling; *while the private stamp must be so affixed on the package that in opening the same the stamp shall be effectually destroyed.*

Where printing in more than one color is desired, the additional expense must be borne by the proprietor.

Each stamp must bear the words, or a proper abbreviation of them "United States Internal Revenue;" also, in words and figures, the denomination of the stamp.

Manufacturers of friction or other matches, cigar lights, or wax tapers, who desire to avail themselves of the provisions of the 161st section of the law, and receive stamps on a credit of not exceeding sixty days, will be furnished, on application to this office, with a blank bond in proper form, to be filled up and executed by them.

The manufacturers of proprietary articles will be required to use the general proprietary stamps until stamps are furnished from their own designs. The same commission will be allowed on the general proprietary stamps as on stamps under Schedule B.

All stamps denoting duties under Section C, excepting those from private designs, may be used indiscriminately.

Every correspondent is requested to give the State, as well as town and county, of his residence.

E. A. Rollins,
Commissioner.

IRR v.IV, November 24, 1866, pp.162-6

United States Internal Revenue.—(Supplement to Series 6, No. 10.)

Treasury Department,
Office of Internal Revenue,
Washington, October 30, 1872.
Schedule B.

Section 36 of the act of June 6, 1872, provides as follows:

"That on and after the first day of October, eighteen hundred and seventy-two, all the taxes imposed by stamps under and by virtue of Schedule B of section one hundred and seventy of the act approved June thirtieth, eighteen hundred and sixty-four, and the several acts amendatory thereof, be, and the same are hereby repealed, excepting only the tax of two cents on bank checks, drafts, or orders: *Provided,* That where any mortgage has been executed and recorded, or may be executed and recorded before the first day of October, anno Domini eighteen hundred and seventy-two, to secure the payment of bonds or obligations that may be made and issued from time to time, and such mortgage not being stamped, all such bonds or obligations so made and issued on or after the said first day of October, anno Domini eighteen hundred and seventy-two, shall not be subjected to any stamp duty, but only such of their bonds or obligations as may have been made and issued before the day last aforesaid: *And provided further,* That in the meantime the holder of any instrument of writing of whatever kind and description which has been made or issued without being duly stamped, or with a defunct [deficient] stamp, may make application to any collector of internal revenue, and that upon such application such collector shall thereupon affix the stamp provided by such holder upon such instrument of writing as required by law to be put upon the same, and subject to the provisions of section 158 of the internal revenue laws."

By virtue of this section it is announced that on and after October 1, 1872, all the stamp taxes mentioned and described in Schedule B of the internal revenue laws (and detailed in Series 6, No. 10, from pages 5 to 12, inclusive) are repealed, excepting only the stamp tax of two cents each upon such inland checks, drafts, or orders as shall be drawn at sight or on demand upon a bank, banker, or trust company.

As to a large number of instruments dated previous to the 1st day of October, 1872, but not actually issued or delivered until that date or afterwards, the question has been presented to this office whether internal revenue stamps were in such cases required. The ruling upon these inquiries is that such instruments do not require to be stamped, but in view of the *prima facie* presumption of the delivery of an instrument on the day of its date, it is suggested that upon instruments of the description in question, some memorandum should be made showing that they were not issued until on or after October 1, 1872, so as to explain the absence of the stamps which the date would indicate were required.

Schedule C.

The stamp taxes under Schedule C remain the same as detailed in Series 6, No. 10, except the tax *on any can, bottle, or other single package containing sauces, sirups, prepared mustard, jams, or jellies,* which was repealed by the act of March 5, 1872.

J. W. Douglass,
Commissioner

IRR v.XVI, November 2, 1872, p. 137

SECTION III.

Tables summarizing all documentary and proprietary tax rates specified by statute, and all penalties for fraudulent use of documentary and proprietary stamps.

Table 1. Summary of all documentary and proprietary tax rates specified by statute.

	October 1, 1862	March 3, 1863	August 1, 1864	1865–1870
A. Documentary				
AGREEMENT. Agreement or contract, not specified elsewhere; appraisement;	For each sheet of paper, .05		Provided, that for more than one agreement, contract, or appraisement on the same sheet of paper, each taxed at .05.	
Renewal or continuance of agreement or contract,			Taxed at same rate as original instrument.	
BANK CHECK/CHECK. Bank check, draft, or order, payable at sight,	Amount over $20, .02		Drawn on any bank, banker, or trust company, for any amount, .02 Drawn on any other person or company, amount over $10, .02	
BILL OF LADING. Bill of lading for goods exported to any foreign port except those in British North America,	.10			
Domestic or inland bill of lading,				August 1, 1866 Exempt.
BILL OF SALE OF SHIP.		Value up to $500, .25 Over $500 to $1000, .50 Each additional $1000 or fraction, .50	For each $500 or fraction, .50	

	October 1, 1862	March 3, 1863	August 1, 1864	1865–1870
BOND, SURETY.	For payment of any sum of money or for performance of the duties of any office, .50		For payment of money, for each $1000 or fraction, .50 For performance of the duties of any office, 1.00	
BOND. Bond, other than those required in legal proceedings or specified elsewhere in this schedule,	.25			
CERTIFICATE. Certificate of damage, or other document issued by port warden or marine surveyor,	.25			
Certificate of deposit,	Amount up to $100, .02 Over $100, .05			
Certificate of profits, or any certificate or memorandum concerning property or accumulations of any incorporated company,	Amount $10 to $50, .10 Over $50, .25		Amount $10 to $50, .10 Over $50 to $1000, .25 For each additional $1000 or fraction, .25	
Certificate of stock in any incorporated company,	.25			
Certificate of measurement or weight,		Exempt.	For animals, coal, or wood, exempt; all others taxed as measurer's or weigher's returns	For animals, coal, wood, or hay, exempt; all others, .05.

	October 1, 1862	March 3, 1863	August 1, 1864	1865–1870
Certificate of the record of a deed or other instrument, or of the proof thereof,		Exempt.		
Affidavit,			If used in legal proceedings, exempt.	March 1, 1867 All affidavits exempt.
Certificate, not specified elsewhere,	.10	.05		
CHARTER PARTY. Contract for the charter of any ship,	Registered tonnage up to 300 tons, 3.00 Over 300 to 600 tons, 5.00 Over 600 tons, 10.00	Registered tonnage up to 150 tons, 1.00 Over 150 to 300 tons, 3.00 Over 300 to 600 tons, 5.00 Over 600 tons, 10.00		
Renewal or continuance of any charter party,			Taxed at same rate as original instrument.	
CONTRACT. Broker's contract, note, or memo of sale of any kind, except as specified below,	.10			
Contract for purchase or sale of gold or silver coin or bullion; or contract for loan secured by gold or silver coin; period exceeding three days,		0.5% of principal, plus 6% per annum	Tax rescinded.	
Sales or contracts for sale of stocks, bonds, bullion, notes or other securities,				August 1, 1866 For each $100 or fraction: If made by broker, .01 If made by any other person, .05

	October 1, 1862	March 3, 1863	August 1, 1864	1865–1870
CONVEYANCE. Deed or other conveyance of land, tenements or other real property,	Value over $100 to $500, .50 Over $500 to $1000, 1.00 Over $1000 to $2500, 2.00 Over $2500 to $5000, 5.00 Over $5000 to $10,000 10.00 Over $10,000 to $20,000, 20.00 For each additional $10,000 or fraction, 20.00	Tax on any conveyance shall not exceed $1000.	For each $500 or fraction, .50 $1000 tax limit rescinded.	
ENTRY OF GOODS. Entry of goods at any custom-house, for consumption or warehousing,	Value to $100, .25 Over $100 to $500, .50 Over $500, 1.00 Entry for withdrawal from bonded warehouse, .50			
EXPRESS. Express company receipt,	Charge up to .25, .01 Over .25 to 1.00, .02 Over 1.00, .05	Taxes rescinded, effective May 1, 1863		
FOREIGN EXCHANGE. Bill of exchange drawn in but payable out of the U.S.,	If drawn in sets of three or more, for each bill, Amount up to the equivalent of $150 U.S., .03 Over $150 to $250, .05 Over $250 to $500, .10 Over $500 to $1000, .15 Over $1000 to $1500, .20		If drawn in sets of three or more, for each bill, for each $100 U.S. or fraction, .02 If drawn otherwise than in sets of three or more, taxed at the same rate as bills of inland exchange.	

	October 1, 1862	March 3, 1863	August 1, 1864	1865–1870
	Over $1500 to $2250, .30 Over $2250 to $3500, .50 Over $3500 to $5000, .70 Over $5000 to $7500, 1.00 Each additional $2500 or fraction, .30			
	If drawn otherwise than in sets of three or more, taxed at the same rate as bills of inland exchange.			
Bill of exchange drawn in a foreign country but payable in U.S.,	Taxed before payment at the same rate as bills of inland exchange.			
GAUGER'S RETURN.	Quantity up to 500 gallons gross, .10 Over 500 gallons, .25			<u>August 1, 1866</u> Tax rescinded.
INLAND EXCHANGE. Bill of exchange payable in U.S., draft, or order, payable other than at sight, or any promissory note,	Amount over $20 up to $100, .05 Over $100 to $200, .10 Over $200 to $350, .15 Over $350 to $500, .20 Over $500 to $750, .30 Over $750 to $1000, .40 Over $1000 to $1500, .60 Over $1500 to	Amount over $20, for each $200 or fraction: Payable within 33 days (3 days grace), .01 Payable in 33 to 63 days, .02 Payable in 63 to 93 days, .03	For each $100 or fraction, .05	<u>October 1, 1870</u> Tax rescinded for amounts less than $100.

	October 1, 1862	March 3, 1863	August 1, 1864	1865–1870
	$2500, 1.00 Over $2500 to $5000, 1.50 Each additional $2500 or fraction, 1.00	Payable in 93 days to four months, three days, .04 Payable in four months, three days to six months, three days, .06 Payable in over six months, three days, .10		
Note or bond secured by mortgage,		Only one stamp tax required, to be placed on either instrument, provided it is the higher of the two required on the separate instruments.		
Deposit note to mutual insurance company,		Exempt.		
INSURANCE. Insurance on property to any description,	Each policy, .25	Premium up to $10, 10 Over $10, .25	Premium up to .10, .10 Over $10 to $50, .25 Over $50, .50	
Assignment or transfer of policy of insurance,		Taxed at same rate as original instrument.		
LEASE. Lease of any land or tenement,	Period up to three years, .50 Over three years, 1.00		Yearly rent up to $300, .50 Each additional $200 or fraction, .50	

	October 1, 1862	March 3, 1863	August 1, 1864	1865–1870
Assignment or transfer of lease,		Taxed at same rate as original instrument.		April 1, 1865 Tax equal to that on original instrument, plus that on a conveyance of property of equal value.
LIFE INSURANCE.	Policy up to $1000, .25 Over $1000 to $5000, .50 Over $5000, 1.00			
Insurance against fatal or non-fatal injury,		Against injury while travelling, exempt.		April 1, 1865 Against any accidental injury, exempt.
LOTTERY TICKET.		(After May 1, 1863) For each $1 or fraction purchase price, .50	Tax rescinded.	
MANIFEST. Manifest for custom-house entry or clearance of cargo of any ship, for a foreign port except those in British North America,	Registered tonnage up to 300 tons, 1.00 Over 300 to 600 tons, 3.00 Over 600 tons, 5.00			
MEASURER'S RETURN.			Quantity up to 1000 bushels, .10 Over 1000 bushels, .25	August 1, 1866 Tax rescinded.
MORTGAGE. Mortgage of real or personal property, or personal bond for the payment of money,	Amount over $100 to $500, .50 Over $500 to $1000, 1.00 Over $1000 to $2500, 2.00 Over $2500 to $5000, 5.00	For each $200 or fraction, .10 Tax on any mortgage shall not exceed $1000.	Over $100, for each $500 or fraction, .50 $1000 tax limit rescinded.	

	October 1, 1862	March 3, 1863	August 1, 1864	1865–1870
	Over $5000 to $10,000, 10.00 Over $10,000 to $20,000, 15.00 Each Additional $10,000 or fraction, 10.00			
Assignment or transfer of mortgage,		Taxed at same rate as original instrument.		August 1, 1866 Taxed at same rate as a mortgage for the amount remaining unpaid. October 1, 1870 When original is stamped, assignment exempt from tax. March 1, 1867 All taxes on legal documents rescinded.
ORIGINAL PROCESS/LEGAL DOCUMENTS. Writ or other other original process whereby any suit is commenced in a court of record,	.50			
Writ, summons, or other process issued by a justice of the peace, or issued in suits commenced by the United States or any state,	Exempt.		Exemption extended to police or municipal courts.	
Writ issued by a court not of record, where amount claimed exceeds $100,			.50	

	October 1, 1862	March 3, 1863	August 1, 1864	1865–1870
Upon confession of judgement for more than $100, the tax for writ of commencment not having been paid,			.50	
Writ or other process of appeal from a court of inferior jurisdiction to a court of record,			.50	
Warrant of distress,			Amount of rent claimed up to $100, .25 Over $100, .50	
PASSAGE TICKET. Passage ticket for a voyage from the U.S. to any foreign port except those in British North America,	Price up to $30, .50 Over $30, 1.00		Price up to $35, .50 Over $35 to $50, 1.00 Each additional $50 or fraction, 1.00	
POWER OF ATTORNEY.				
Power of attorney to sell, convey, rent or lease real estate,	1.00			
Power of attorney to receive or collect rent,	.25			
Power of attorney for sale or transfer of stock, bonds, or scrip, or for the collection of interest or dividends thereon,	.25	Exception: for sale or transfer of scrip or certificate of profit for amounts up to $50, .10	Exception rescinded.	
Power of attorney or proxy for voting at any election of officers of any incorporated company or society except religious, charitable, or literary societies, or public cemeteries,	.10			

	October 1, 1862	March 3, 1863	August 1, 1864	1865–1870
Power of attorney, not specified elsewhere,	1.00		.50	
Power of attorney or other paper relating to application for bounty, arrearage of pay, or pension, etc., or receipt thereof; warrant of attorney accompanying properly stamped bond or note,		Exempt.		
PROBATE OF WILL. Probate of will, or letters of administration,	Value of estate up to $2500, .50 Over $2500 to $5000, 1.00 Over $5000 to $20,000, 2.00 Over $20,000 to $50,000, 5.00 Over $50,000 to $100,000, 10.00 Each additional $100,000 or fraction, 10.00		Value of estate up to $2000, 1.00 Each additional $1000 or fraction, .50	March 1, 1867 Value of estate up to $1000, exempt.
PROTEST. Protest on check or note, or marine protest,	.25			
RECEIPT. Receipt for the payment of any sum of money, or for the payment of any debt exceeding $20, except for satisfaction of mortgage or court decree; or receipt for delivery of property,			.02	April 1, 1865 Receipts of express companies exempt. October 1, 1870 Tax on receipts rescinded.

	October 1, 1862	March 3, 1863	August 1, 1864	1865–1870
TELEGRAPH. Telegraph dispatch,	Charge for first ten words up to .20, .01 Over .20, .03		Tax rescinded.	
WAREHOUSE RECEIPT. Warehouse receipt for any property held in storage in any warehouse or yard,	.25		Value of goods up to $500, .10 Over $500 to $1000, .20 Each additional $1000, .10 Value not ascertained, .25	August 1, 1866 Tax rescinded.
WEIGHER'S RETURN.			Weight up to 5000 pounds, .10 Over 5000 pounds, .25	August 1, 1866 Tax rescinded.
All official documents issued or used by officers of the United States Government,	December 25, 1862 Exempt.			
Any power of attorney, conveyance, or document of any kind made in a foreign country to be used in the United States,		Same tax as if made in the United States.		

	October 1, 1862	August 1, 1864	1865–1870
B. Proprietary			
MEDICINES. Medicines or preparations, where the maker has, or claims to have, a private formula for preparation, or an exclusive right to preparation, or which are otherwise held out to the public as proprietary medicines,	For each box, bottle, or other enclosure, retail value up to .25, .01 Over .25 to .50, .02 Over .50 to .75, .03 Over .75 to $1.00, .04 Each additional .50 or fraction, .02		
PERFUMERY AND COSMETICS.	For each box, bottle, or other enclosure, retail value up to .25, .01 Over .25 to .50, .02 Over .50 to .75, .03 Over .75 to $1.00 .04 Each additional .50 or fraction, .02		
PLAYING CARDS.	For each pack, price up to .18, .01 Over .18 to .25, .02 Over .25 to .30, .03 Over .30 to .36, .04 Over .36, .05	For each pack, retail price up to .18, .02 Over .18 to .25, .04 Over .25 to .50, .10 Over .50 to $1.00, .15 Each additional .50 or fraction, .05	April 1, 1865 The word "retail" stricken from rate table. August 1, 1866 For each pack not exceeding 52 cards, .05

	October 1, 1862	August 1, 1864	1865–1872
MATCHES. Friction matches,		(September 1, 1864) For each 100 or fraction, .01	
Cigar lights,		For each 100 or fraction, .02	<u>August 1, 1866</u> For each 25 or fraction, .01
Wax tapers,		For each 100 or fraction, .02	
PHOTOGRAPHS.		Retail price up to .25, .02 Over .25 to .50, .03 Over .50 to $1.00, .05 Each additional $1.00 or fraction, .05	<u>August 1, 1866</u> Tax on photographs rescinded.
Photographs, being copies of engravings or works of art, or used for the illustration of books, and photographs so small in size that stamps cannot be affixed,		Exempt from stamp duty, and subject to a 5% ad valorem duty.	<u>April 1, 1865</u> Photographs of engravings or works of art exempt from stamp duty only when wholesale price does not exceed ten cents each.
PRESERVED MEATS, FISH, ETC. Meats, fish, shell-fish, fruits, vegetables, sauces, sirups, prepared mustard, jams or jellies			<u>October 1, 1866</u> For each can, bottle, or other package, for each two pounds weight or fraction thereof, .01 <u>March 1, 1867</u> Meats, shell-fish, fruits and vegetables exempt. <u>July 14, 1870</u> Fish additionally exempted. <u>March 5, 1872</u> All remaining stamp taxes on preserved goods rescinded.

Table 2. Summary of penalties for violations of documentary and proprietary stamp tax laws.

Offense	October 1, 1862 (and later as noted)	August 1, 1864	1865–1874
A. Documentary			
Failure to duly stamp document,	$50 penalty and document invalid. Act of July 14, 1862, effective October 1 Documents executed before January 1, 1863 without being stamped not to be therefor invalid, provided that no such document shall be used in court until being duly stamped, and on payment of $5 to Collector of district where court is held. December 25, 1862 Grace period extended to March 1, 1863. $5 penalty rescinded. Any interested party may affix stamp. March 3, 1863 Grace period extended to June 1, 1863.	If done with intent to evade the law, $200 penalty and document invalid (except that title to land conveyed by a deed duly stamped not to be defeated by failure to stamp any preceding deed to the same land). No document to be recorded without being stamped.	April 1, 1865 If done with intent to evade the law, $50 penalty and document invalid. If unstamped document to be subsequently stamped and stamp tax exceeds $50, interest of 6% to be paid from date of execution. If document to be stamped within twelve months after execution, Collector empowered to remit $50 penalty when satisfied that failure to stamp was through accident, mistake, inadvertence, or urgent necessity, with no intent to evade the law. August 1, 1866 Grace period for remitting $50 penalty extended to twelve months after August 1, 1866, or within twelve months after execution. For any unstamped document executed in a place where no collection district was established, the document (or a copy thereof, if the original be lost) may be stamped before January 1, 1867.

Offense	October 1, 1862 (and later as noted)	August 1, 1864	1865–1874
			<u>August 1, 1870</u> Penalty for failure to affix stamp remains at $50; however, when it is desired to stamp an unstamped document, penalty reduced to double the amount of tax remaining unpaid, or $5, whichever is greater. Collectors may remit penalty within twelve months after August 1, 1870, or within twelve months after execution. Unstamped documents executed where no collection district was established may be stamped before January 1, 1872. <u>June 6, 1872</u> Collectors may remit penalty for stamping unstamped document, until October 1, 1872. <u>June 23, 1874</u> Any unstamped document may be stamped without penalty before a judge or clerk of court, until January 1, 1876. (This grace period extended until January 1, 1877 on February 25, 1876.)

Offense	October 1, 1862 (and later as noted)	August 1, 1864	1865–1874
Failure to stamp bill of exchange, draft or order, either by maker or acceptor, with intent to evade the law,	$200 penalty.	Subsumed under general provision regarding failure to affix stamp (see above).	
Failure of acceptor to stamp before payment foreign bill of exchange payable in U.S.,	$100 penalty.	Subsumed under general provision regarding failure to affix stamp (see above).	
Receipt or transmission of unstamped telegraph despatch by telegraph company,	$10 penalty.	[Stamp tax on telegraph despatches rescinded.]	
Failure of express company to deliver stamped receipt,	$10 penalty. March 3, 1863 [Tax on express receipts rescinded.]		
Fraudulent failure to cancel stamp,	$50 penalty.		
Failure to use stamp whose title matches the type of document stamped,	Document invalid. December 25, 1862 No document to be invalid for want of a particular type of stamp, provided that Playing Cards, Proprietary, or private-die stamps not to be used.		
Forging stamps, selling forged stamps, or knowingly using such stamps,	Felony offense. Fine to $1000, imprisonment to five years, and forfeiture of stamps and any documents on which they are placed.		

Offense	October 1, 1862 (and later as noted)	August 1, 1864	1865–1874
Failure of seller to stamp lottery ticket,	May 1, 1863 $50 penalty and ticket invalid. Purchaser may recover from seller twice the purchase price.		
Failure to properly stamp contract, loan or sale of gold or silver coin or bullion,	March 3, 1863 In addition to general penalties for failure to stamp instrument (see above), any party to contract may bring suit to recover the money paid on contract. July 2, 1864 [Contracts for gold or silver coin or bullion made illegal; penalties implicitly rescinded.]		
Removing cancellation from stamp, selling washed or restored stamps, or knowingly using such stamps,		Same penalty as for forging stamps.	April 10, 1869 Possession of washed or restored stamps to be considered *prima facie* evidence of violation of this provision.
B. Proprietary			
Failure to affix private-die stamp so that it will be effectually destroyed on opening package,	$50 penalty.		
Failure to affix stamp,	$10 penalty.		August 1, 1866 $50 penalty. March 2, 1867 Additional penalty of amount of tax omitted, to be assessed at any time within two years of offense.

Offense	October 1, 1862 (and later as noted)	August 1, 1864	1865–1874
Omission of stamp in attempt to evade tax,	$100 penalty and forfeiture of unstamped article.		
Re-using stamp or wrapper, or removing stamp for re-use, with intent to evade stamp duty,	$50 penalty for each article, plus costs, and forfeiture of article.		
Fraudulently obtaining private-die stamps, forging such stamps, or knowingly possessing forged stamps,	Misdemeanor offense. Fine to $1000, imprisonment to five years, and forfeiture of stamps and any articles on which they are placed.	Felony offense. Same penalties.	
Failure of manufacturer to make monthly declaration of compliance with law,	$100 penalty.	Penalty rescinded.	
Making false statement of compliance,	$500 penalty.	Penalty rescinded.	

INDEX